World Development Report 1986

Published for The World Bank
Oxford University Press

Oxford University Press

NEW YORK OXFORD LONDON GLASGOW
TORONTO MELBOURNE WELLINGTON HONG KONG
TOKYO KUALA LUMPUR SINGAPORE JAKARTA
DELHI BOMBAY CALCUTTA MADRAS KARACHI
NAIROBI DAR ES SALAAM CAPE TOWN

© *1986 by the International Bank*
for Reconstruction and Development / The World Bank
1818 H Street, N.W., Washington, D.C. 20433 U.S.A.

First printing July 1986

ISBN 0-19-520517-0 clothbound
ISBN 0-19-520518-9 paperback
ISSN 0163-5085

The Library of Congress has cataloged this serial publication as follows:
World development report. 1978–
[New York] Oxford University Press.
v. 27 cm. annual.
Published for The World Bank.
1. Underdeveloped areas—Periodicals. 2. Economic development—
Periodicals I. International Bank for Reconstruction and Development.

HC59.7.W659   330.9 '172 '4   78-67086

This book is printed on paper that adheres to
the American National Standard for Permanence of Paper
for Printed Library Materials, Z39.48-1984.

Foreword

This Report is the ninth in the annual series assessing development issues. Part I reviews recent trends in the world economy and the policy framework required for sustained growth. Part II is devoted to trade and pricing policies in world agriculture. As in the past, the Report includes an updated World Development Indicators annex, which provides selected social and economic data for more than a hundred countries.

The world economy is entering its fourth consecutive year of growth since the 1980–82 recession. Yet the recovery continues to be hesitant, and many developing countries are facing serious problems of adjustment. Although the recent declines in oil prices, real interest rates, and inflation will provide a useful stimulus to industrial and developing countries alike, many heavily indebted developing countries, particularly oil exporters, will find it difficult to maintain growth in the near term. In addition, the beneficial effects of the recovery have been much weaker for many low-income sub-Saharan African countries.

Part I of this year's Report explores the policies required to restore sustained growth in the world economy. It stresses the importance of maintaining the commitment of industrial countries to policies that have both reduced inflation and moderated market distortions and rigidities. A recurring concern, however, is the increase in international trade restrictions. If high and sustainable growth is to be attained, the reform of domestic institutions and incentives needs to be accompanied by a renewed effort to move toward freer international trade. The progress that developing countries have made in reforming their policies and adjusting to the rapid, and often large, changes in the world economy since 1980 is charted. Despite considerable progress, many of them enter the second half

of the decade weighed down by the cumulative effects of domestic policies, large foreign debt obligations, and, in the case of oil exporters, the recent decline in export earnings. Continued domestic policy reforms, designed to restore and maintain a stable macroeconomic environment and to improve the incentive structure, are stressed as the prerequisites for growth. Increased reliance on international trade will be a necessary component of this reform process. Policy reforms in developing countries, however, will need to be supported by reductions in trade barriers and increases in net flows of foreign capital.

Part II of this Report develops these themes in the context of agricultural policies. It examines the policies of developing and industrial countries in an integrated framework, bringing out the interdependence of domestic agricultural policies throughout the world and the potential for large gains from more liberal trade in agriculture. It suggests that liberalization of trade should be a high priority for international action in agriculture.

An examination of the policy options for developing countries suggests that economic stability and growth would be greatly enhanced if pricing and trade policies were improved. In many developing countries, both macro- and microeconomic policies have hindered agricultural development. Overvalued exchange rates, the protection provided to domestic manufacturing activities, and the taxation of agricultural exports and import-competing food crops have discouraged domestic agricultural production. In addition, programs for subsidizing consumers and farm inputs and for stabilizing consumer and producer prices have often led to significant losses in the real national incomes of developing countries. These problems, however, are being increasingly acknowledged, and some developing countries have initiated significant—in some cases sweeping—policy reforms.

Agricultural policy reforms are also under serious consideration in many industrial countries. The policies they have pursued in the past several decades have limited trade opportunities for developing countries and have been counterproductive for themselves as well. As preparations are made for the next round of GATT negotiations, it is well to recognize the opportunities that exist for bringing about a more efficient world agricultural system—a system which will benefit both industrial and developing countries. The progress that has been achieved in agricultural technology presents an opportunity for a rapid expansion of agricultural output if more open and competitive world markets are established.

Like its predecessors, this Report is a study by the staff of The World Bank, and the judgments in it do not necessarily reflect the views of our Board of Directors or of the governments they represent.

A. W. Clausen
President
The World Bank

May 19, 1986

This Report was prepared by a team led by Anandarup Ray and comprising Trent Bertrand, Ajay Chhibber, Bruce Gardner, Orsalia Kalantzopoulos, Odin Knudsen, Donald O. Mitchell, Alan Walters, John Wilton, and L. Alan Winters, assisted by Therese Belot, Zohreh Hedjazi, M. Shahbaz Khan, Donald F. Larson, Tani Maher, Yasmin Saadat, Rodney Smith, and Robert Wieland. D. Gale Johnson, Ulrich Koester, and many others in and outside the Bank provided helpful comments and contributions (see the bibliographical note). The Economic Analysis and Projections Department, under the direction of Jean Baneth, supported the work on Part I, and Enzo Grilli, Peter Miovic, and Heywood Fleisig coordinated the work of that department on projections. Ramesh Chander, assisted by David Cieslikowski, also of that department, supervised the preparation of the World Development Indicators; Elizabeth Crayford edited the Indicators, and Shaida Badiee was responsible for systems design. Special thanks also go to the production staff, especially Joyce Eisen, Pensri Kimpitak, and Victoria Lee, and to the support staff, headed by Rhoda Blade-Charest and including Banjonglak Duangrat, Jaunianne Fawkes, Carlina Jones, and Patricia Smith. The work was carried out under the general direction of Anne O. Krueger and Constantine Michalopoulos, with John Parker as the editorial adviser.

Contents

v

Text tables

Boxes

Definitions and data notes

The principal country groups used in the text of this Report and in the World Development Indicators are defined as follows:

- *Developing countries* are divided into: *low-income economies*, with 1984 gross national product (GNP) per person of less than $400; and *middle-income economies*, with 1984 GNP per person of $400 or more. Middle-income countries are also divided into *oil exporters* and *oil importers*, identified below.
- *Middle-income oil exporters* comprise Algeria, Angola, Cameroon, People's Republic of the Congo, Ecuador, Arab Republic of Egypt, Gabon, Indonesia, Islamic Republic of Iran, Iraq, Malaysia, Mexico, Nigeria, Peru, Syrian Arab Republic, Trinidad and Tobago, Tunisia, and Venezuela.
- *Middle-income oil importers* comprise all other middle-income developing countries not classified as oil exporters. A subset, *major exporters of manufactures*, comprises Argentina, Brazil, Greece, Hong Kong, Israel, Republic of Korea, Philippines, Portugal, Singapore, South Africa, Thailand, and Yugoslavia.
- *High-income oil exporters* (not included in developing countries) comprise Bahrain, Brunei, Kuwait, Libya, Oman, Qatar, Saudi Arabia, and United Arab Emirates.
- *Industrial market economies* are the members of the Organisation for Economic Co-operation and Development, apart from Greece, Portugal, and Turkey, which are included among the middle-income developing economies. This group is commonly referred to in the text as industrial economies or industrial countries.
- *East European nonmarket economies* include the following countries: Albania, Bulgaria, Czechoslovakia, German Democratic Republic, Hungary, Poland, Romania, and U.S.S.R. This group is sometimes referred to as nonmarket economies.
- *Sub-Saharan Africa* comprises all thirty-nine developing African countries south of the Sahara, excluding South Africa, as given in *Toward Sustained Development in Sub-Saharan Africa: A Joint Program of Action* (World Bank 1984).
- *Middle East and North Africa* includes Afghanistan, Algeria, Arab Republic of Egypt, Iran, Iraq, Israel, Jordan, Kuwait, Lebanon, Libya, Morocco, Oman, Saudi Arabia, Syrian Arab Republic, Tunisia, Turkey, United Arab Emirates, Yemen Arab Republic, and People's Democratic Republic of Yemen.
- *East Asia* comprises all low- and middle-income countries of East and Southeast Asia and the Pacific, east of, and including, Burma, China, and Mongolia.
- *South Asia* includes Bangladesh, Bhutan, India, Nepal, Pakistan, and Sri Lanka.
- *Latin America and the Caribbean* comprises all American and Caribbean countries south of the United States.
- *Major borrowers* are countries with disbursed and outstanding debt estimated at more than $15 billion at the end of 1984 and comprise Argentina, Brazil, Chile, Egypt, India, Indonesia, Israel, Republic of Korea, Mexico, Turkey, Venezuela, and Yugoslavia.

Economic and demographic terms are defined in the technical notes to the World Development Indicators. The Indicators use the country groupings given above but include only countries with a population of 1 million or more.

Billion is 1,000 million.

Tons are metric tons, equal to 1,000 kilograms, or 2,204.6 pounds.

Growth rates are in real terms unless otherwise stated. Growth rates for spans of years in tables cover the period from the beginning of the base year to the end of the last year given.

Dollars are current U.S. dollars unless otherwise specified.

The symbol .. in tables means "not available."

The symbol — in tables means "not applicable."

All tables and figures are based on World Bank data unless otherwise specified.

Data from secondary sources are not always available through 1984. The numbers in this *World Development Report* shown for historical data may differ from those shown in previous Reports because of continuous updating as better data become available and because of recompilation of certain data for a ninety-country sample. The recompilation was necessary to permit greater flexibility in regrouping countries for the purpose of making projections.

Acronyms and initials

CIAT International Center for Tropical Agriculture.

CIMMYT International Maize and Wheat Improvement Center.

CFF Compensatory Financing Facility.

DAC The Development Assistance Committee of the Organisation for Economic Co-operation and Development comprises Australia, Austria, Belgium, Canada, Denmark, Finland, France, Federal Republic of Germany, Ireland, Italy, Japan, Netherlands, New Zealand, Norway, Sweden, Switzerland, United Kingdom, United States, and Commission of the European Communities.

EC The European Communities comprise Belgium, Denmark, France, Federal Republic of Germany, Greece, Ireland, Italy, Luxembourg, Netherlands, Portugal, Spain, and United Kingdom. Greece joined the EC in 1981; Portugal and Spain joined in 1986.

ECU European currency unit.

FAO Food and Agriculture Organization.

GATT General Agreement on Tariffs and Trade.

GDP Gross domestic product.

GNP Gross national product.

IBRD International Bank for Reconstruction and Development.

IDA International Development Association.

IFC International Finance Corporation.

IFPRI International Food Policy Research Institute.

IRRI International Rice Research Institute.

IMF International Monetary Fund.

LIBOR London interbank offered rate.

ODA Official development assistance.

OECD The Organisation for Economic Co-operation and Development members are Australia, Austria, Belgium, Canada, Denmark, Finland, France, Federal Republic of Germany, Greece, Iceland, Ireland, Italy, Japan, Luxembourg, Netherlands, New Zealand, Norway, Portugal, Spain, Sweden, Switzerland, Turkey, United Kingdom, and United States.

SDR Special drawing right.

UNCTAD United Nations Conference on Trade and Development.

1

Introduction

Agriculture and economic growth are the subjects of this *World Development Report*. Because agriculture accounts for a large share of many developing countries' economies, success there will play a large role in determining the course of their national economies for decades to come. At the same time, policies that affect the national economy as a whole—for example, policies on exchange rates, trade regimes, or government spending—influence the performance of the agricultural sector. Within a country and throughout the interdependent economies of the world, better policies are needed to improve the allocation of resources and raise real incomes. In agriculture, using resources more efficiently would involve removing both the policy-induced biases that generally discriminate against production and trade in developing countries and the excessive subsidies that generate overproduction in industrial ones. In the wider economy, better resource allocation policies are needed to help developing countries adjust to changing external circumstances—a process which is essential for growth—and to correct certain deep-seated problems that have constrained economic growth in industrial countries.

The two parts of this Report explore these themes. Part I examines the way the world economy has performed since 1980 and looks at the prospects for the next ten years. It concludes that, although recent declines in interest rates and oil prices are likely to provide a stimulus to the world economy, further policy reforms at both the domestic and international levels are essential to take full advantage of this stimulus. At a less aggregate level, however, it is apparent that certain subgroups of developing countries—particularly the heavily indebted oil exporters and some of the low-income African countries—will continue to face a very difficult period of adjustment in the near term. For these countries, domestic policy reforms are necessary, but they are not sufficient: access to additional external resources and export markets will also be required.

Part II explores the connection between government policy and agriculture and emphasizes the interdependence of agricultural policies in different parts of the world. Public policies in both developing and industrial countries greatly influence the growth of agriculture and of rural incomes. This influence often extends far beyond national frontiers. What is perhaps most surprising is the fact that it is the developing world which, on the whole, discriminates against its farmers, even though they account for large shares of gross domestic product (GDP) and export earnings. And it is the industrial countries which provide subsidies to agricultural production, even though their farmers account for small shares of GDP and employment. The Report examines the potential gains to the world economy from removing these distortions and concludes with a discussion of the priorities for reform.

Prospects for the world economy

The world economy is entering the fourth year of its recovery from the deep recession of 1980–82. The output of the five largest industrial economies grew by 3.0 percent in real terms in 1983 and by 4.2 percent in 1984, and annual rates of inflation have fallen sharply. In developing countries the growth in output increased from 2.0 percent in 1983 to 5.4 percent in 1984. Yet growth, though sustained, has recently slowed. The five largest industrial economies saw their growth rates fall to 2.8 percent in 1985, and unemployment and real interest rates have remained high. In developing countries growth slowed to 4.4 percent in 1985. Despite the recent declines in oil prices, real interest rates, and inflation, many developing countries continue to face serious problems that will constrain growth over the medium term.

These developments are the subject of Chapter 2, which explores the policies that have shaped the character of the world economy since 1980. It argues that, although many industrial countries have been successful in moderating the rate of monetary growth and thereby inflation, they have been less successful in pursuing a consistent fiscal policy. The increased acceptance of the view that high and uneven marginal tax-benefit rates distort incentives and entail efficiency losses has made governments understandably reluctant to increase tax rates. But social and political pressures have also made it difficult to curtail benefits or reduce total public expenditure. As a result, public sector deficits have not been significantly reduced and have remained large in absolute terms in the United States. This combination of monetary and fiscal policies was in large part responsible for the interest rate and U.S. dollar movements that occurred between 1980 and early 1986. The recent falls in the U.S. dollar and in interest rates reflect three developments: a renewed commitment to reduce the U.S. federal budget deficit, the decline in oil prices, and the coordinated actions of the Group of Five countries (France, the Federal Republic of Germany, Japan, the United Kingdom, and the United States).

While the movements in interest rates and the U.S. dollar imposed significant adjustment costs on many economies earlier in the decade, there were mitigating factors, the most important of which was the large U.S. trade deficit. This increased the growth in world trade, particularly in 1984, which greatly assisted outward-oriented developing countries. But the coexistence of large trade deficits and record high levels of unemployment in some industrial countries has had an unfortunate side effect: a marked increase in the pressure for more restrictions on international trade. Ironically, this pressure comes at a time when industrial countries are beginning to reap the benefits of the moderate progress they have made in reducing rigidities and distortions in their domestic factor and goods markets.

For developing countries, the first half of the 1980s was a period of adjustment to a rapidly changing world economy. The reforms they implemented to improve resource allocation and in-

crease efficiency were necessary irrespective of developments in the world economy. But the magnitude of the changes in real interest rates, commodity prices, export markets, and net capital inflows led them to adjust quickly, which in some cases entailed high costs. Yet, those developing countries that maintained macroeconomic stability and implemented policies to make the best of the changing world economy have emerged with strong growth rates and bright prospects. Others, however, have found it difficult to restore growth. In many cases, inappropriate domestic policies that have misallocated resources and reduced efficiency over long periods of time have resulted in little, if any, increase in output. The developments in the world economy after 1980 exposed the underlying vulnerability of these economies and in some cases brought about a downturn in growth. Declining per capita incomes, which had until the early 1980s occurred mostly in sub-Saharan Africa, became more widespread, especially in Latin America. While growth did pick up in 1984, it has proved difficult to sustain.

It is clear that developing countries have, on the whole, made an effort to reform domestic policies and to adjust to the changing international environment. In addition, for most countries the recent declines in oil prices and real interest rates have created an external environment which will facilitate domestic reform efforts. For some countries, however, the slower growth in world trade (caused in part by protectionism), weak export prices, large repayment obligations on existing external debt, and the continued decline of net capital inflows threaten to overwhelm these gains. The heavily indebted oil-exporting countries will face a particularly difficult period over the next few years. Many developing countries will have difficulty in maintaining imports and domestic investment at the levels required to support growth over the medium term and service their external debt. A further reduction in per capita consumption levels will exacerbate political and social tensions in these countries and, as their imports contract, reduce the number of jobs in other countries.

Chapter 3 explores two divergent paths that the world economy might take during the next ten years. The High case illustrates what could happen with appropriate policies that build upon the stimulus given to the world economy by recent developments. The Low case presents the alternative outcome if policies dissipate the results of these developments. In the High case, industrial countries could increase their real GDPs by an annual average of 4.3 percent, whereas in the Low case the rate of growth would be only 2.5 percent. For developing countries the divergence would be greater: 5.9 percent a year in the High case and 4.0 percent in the Low. It should be emphasized that these are not forecasts; they merely illustrate what might be achieved if certain policies are pursued.

For industrial countries the domestic policies needed to achieve the growth rates of the High case involve instituting stable monetary and fiscal policies, reducing price distortions, and introducing more flexibility into labor markets. Internationally, a concerted effort to reduce trade restrictions would be needed to increase world trade. Because industrial countries account for so large a share of world output, their policies will play a principal role in determining how the world economy performs. But this does not mean that developing countries cannot reap benefits by changing their own policies. On the contrary, it is their policies that will determine the extent to which they take advantage of, or offset, changes in the international economy over the medium term. If developing countries were to adopt policies that encourage domestic savings, increase the efficiency with which they use resources, and increase their links with the world economy, they could raise their growth rates significantly regardless of what the industrial countries do.

Nonetheless, the heavily indebted middle-income countries will need extra help over and above those policies to keep growth from stagnating and thus contributing to the instability of the world's financial markets. Additional assistance will also be required to reverse the decline in low-income African countries. Chapter 3 argues that a coordinated domestic and international effort is re-quired to restore creditworthiness and growth, an effort in which the World Bank will play an important role.

Trade and pricing policies in world agriculture

The need to improve trade and pricing policies and to reform institutions is no less important in agriculture than in the economy as a whole. And success in agriculture will, in turn, largely determine economic growth in many low-income developing countries and help to alleviate poverty in rural areas, where most of the world's poorest people live.

Agriculture is the basic industry of the world's poorest countries. It employs roughly 70 to 80 percent of the labor force in low-income developing countries and about 35 to 55 percent in middle-income developing ones. It is also a main source of GDP, accounting for 35 to 45 percent of GDP in low-income developing countries (see Table 1.1). During the nineteenth century, almost all of to-day's industrial nations had roughly the same percentage of their labor forces engaged in agriculture that the low-income developing countries now have. Some countries, notably Italy and the U.S.S.R., had more than 70 percent of their labor forces engaged in agriculture well into the twentieth century. Today, the industrial countries of Western Europe and North America have less than 10 percent of their labor forces employed in agriculture, and the average for all industrial countries is now just 7 percent. Already, agriculture's share of GDP in all developing economies has fallen from 30 percent in the mid-1960s to about 20 percent in the early 1980s. Among industrial countries, agriculture accounts for a little more than 3

Table 1.1 Agriculture's share of GDP, employment, and exports, selected years, 1964–84
(percent)

| | Share of agriculture in: | | | | | |
| | GDP | | Employment | | Exports[a] | |
Country group	1964–66	1982–84	1965	1980	1964–66	1982–84
Low-income countries	42.8	36.3	76.0	72.0	58.6	32.8
Africa	46.9	41.3	84.0	78.0	70.7	68.4
Asia	42.5	35.7	74.0	71.0	54.0	25.9
Middle-income oil exporters	21.8	14.8	62.0	50.0	40.8	13.6
Middle-income oil importers, excluding						
major exporters of manufactures	25.2	18.0	63.0	53.0	54.2	44.8
Major exporters of manufactures	19.3	12.1	50.0	36.0	56.9	20.2
Developing countries	30.2	19.9	66.9	63.2	52.3	22.0
Industrial countries	5.1	3.1	13.7	7.1	21.4	14.1

Note: Data for developing countries are based on a sample of ninety countries.
a. Includes reexports.

Table 1.2 Agriculture's share of exports in developing countries, 1979–83

Country group	Countries with 30–60 percent share	Countries with 60–80 percent share	Countries with 80–100 percent share
Low-income countries	4	6	11
Africa	3	3	11
Asia	1	3	0
Middle-income countries	16	12	1
Oil exporters	1	0	0
Oil importers	11	11	1
Major exporters of manufactures	4	1	0
All developing countries	20	18	12

Note: Shares are the percentage of agricultural export earnings in total merchandise exports. Exports include reexports. Data are based on a sample of ninety developing countries.

percent of GDP and approximately 14 percent of exports.

The share of agriculture in national income generally declines as real per capita incomes rise, because as people's incomes increase, they spend a decreasing percentage on food. Also, as farmers increase the productivity of their land and labor, the share of a country's resources required to grow food for the rest of the population decreases. In low-income developing countries, a farm family provides enough food for itself and two other people; in most industrial economies, a farm family produces enough food for itself and as many as fifty other people.

For many developing countries, therefore, a healthy farm economy is connected with long-term development. It is also connected with short-term stability. Although agriculture's contribution to the export earnings of developing countries has fallen from about 52 percent in the mid-1960s, it still contributed 22 percent by the early 1980s. It was higher in low-income African countries and in those middle-income oil-importing countries that

are not yet major exporters of manufactures. The importance of agricultural exports is brought out in greater detail in Table 1.2.

Food production

Agricultural output has grown rapidly in many developing countries during the past fifteen years. The growth in food production, which was faster in developing countries than in the industrial and East European nonmarket economies, was made possible largely by the Green Revolution (see Figure 1.1 and Table 1.3). This revolution began in the mid-1960s with the development of high-yielding varieties of wheat at the International Maize and Wheat Improvement Center (CIMMYT) in Mexico and of high-yielding varieties of rice at the International Rice Research Institute (IRRI) in the Philippines and the International Center for Tropical Agriculture (CIAT). The new seeds were so productive that they made it profitable for farmers to update their farming methods by using more fertilizer and other modern inputs and for both

Table 1.3 Growth of agricultural production by major commodity group, 1961–84
(*average annual percentage change*)

Country group	Beverages 1961–70	Beverages 1971–84	Food 1961–70	Food 1971–84	Raw materials 1961–70	Raw materials 1971–84	Total agriculture 1961–70	Total agriculture 1971–84
Developing countries	−0.4	1.9	2.2	3.2	4.5	2.3	2.4	3.0
Low-income countries	1.9	1.2	1.3	3.2	5.7	3.8	1.9	3.3
Africa	2.3	−0.5	2.6	2.0	6.0	−1.8	3.0	1.2
Asia	1.2	3.6	1.2	3.4	5.7	4.3	1.8	3.6
Middle-income oil exporters	3.5	0.5	3.0	3.1	1.5	−0.9	2.7	2.2
Middle-income oil importers	−2.9	2.8	3.5	3.2	4.8	1.0	2.9	2.9
High-income oil exporters	−6.8	0.6	4.9	14.6	8.0	−0.5	5.0	14.1
Industrial market economies	0.9	0.4	2.9	2.1	−4.9	0.4	2.2	2.0
East European nonmarket economies	5.3	7.0	3.6	0.5	4.3	1.9	3.7	0.7
World	−0.3	1.9	2.7	2.4	2.2	2.0	2.5	2.3

Note: Data are weighted by the 1978–82 world export unit prices to permit cross-country comparisons. Growth rates are least-squares estimates. Beverages comprise coffee, cocoa, and tea. Food comprises cereals, sugar, meat, poultry, dairy products, roots and tubers, pulses, fruits, and vegetables. Raw materials comprise cotton, jute, rubber, and tobacco.
Source: Based on FAO data.

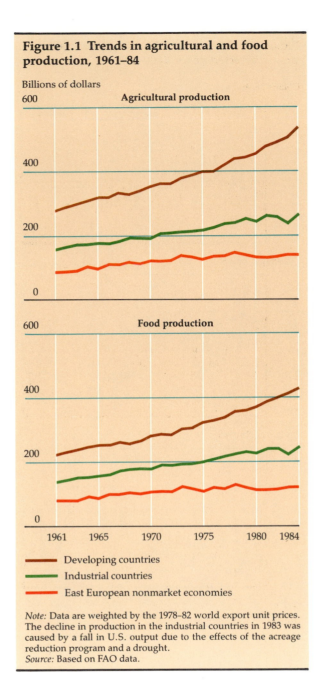

Figure 1.1 Trends in agricultural and food production, 1961–84

Billions of dollars

Agricultural production

600

400

200

0

Food production

600

400

200

0

1961   1965   1970   1975   1980   1984

— Developing countries
— Industrial countries
— East European nonmarket economies

Note: Data are weighted by the 1978–82 world export unit prices. The decline in production in the industrial countries in 1983 was caused by a fall in U.S. output due to the effects of the acreage reduction program and a drought.
Source: Based on FAO data.

Table 1.4 Growth of cereal production in selected developing countries, 1971–84

Country group	Average annual percentage change
High performers	
Indonesia	5.2
Korea	5.0
Philippines	4.5
Pakistan	4.3
Low performers	
Gambia	−0.3
Haiti	−1.1
Zambia	−2.2
Ghana	−2.4

Source: Based on FAO data.

a year, respectively, both rates exceeding population growth. Some countries achieved even higher growth rates (see Table 1.4). But the Green Revolution was, for the most part, confined to irrigated land. It left some areas untouched, especially in Africa.

The ramifications of technological progress are great. The fact that some countries still lag far behind others in yields implies that there is great scope for future production increases on existing land (see Figure 1.2). More technological breakthroughs are possible. Biogenetic research is likely to lead to the development of new crop varieties that require fewer inputs and are more tolerant of pests, drought, and disease. As more research and investment take place in agriculture, the cost of producing food should continue to decline, as it has for more than a century.

Real wholesale prices of wheat, sugar, and maize (corn) from 1800 to 1985 and rice prices for a shorter period are shown in Figure 1.3. While the prices have fluctuated widely, the trend has clearly been downward since the mid-1800s. Even the soaring prices of the early 1970s were not extraordinary by historical standards. Maize prices have been in more or less continuous decline since World War II, owing to the introduction of hybrid varieties and their subsequent improvements. Despite a boom in the early 1970s, the price of rice is at its lowest level since 1900. These trends are a reminder that, for more than a hundred years, costs of agricultural production have fallen in real terms. It is also worth noting that the numerous periods of sharp price increases were of short duration, generally three years or less. Table 1.5 presents a broader summary of the price trends since 1950.

farmers and governments to invest more on improving irrigation. In India's Punjab, for example, thousands of irrigation wells were dug between 1967 and 1972, mainly by farmers. Fertilizer consumption rose from 0.76 million tons in 1966 to 2.38 million tons in 1972.

The combination of improved seeds, more fertilizer, and improved irrigation doubled yields on irrigated land in developing countries. China and India, the two most populous countries, expanded cereal production at the rate of 3.2 and 4.1 percent

5

Robert Malthus had suggested in the early nineteenth century that the world would run short of food as population expanded faster than the capacity to produce food. The decline in real food prices

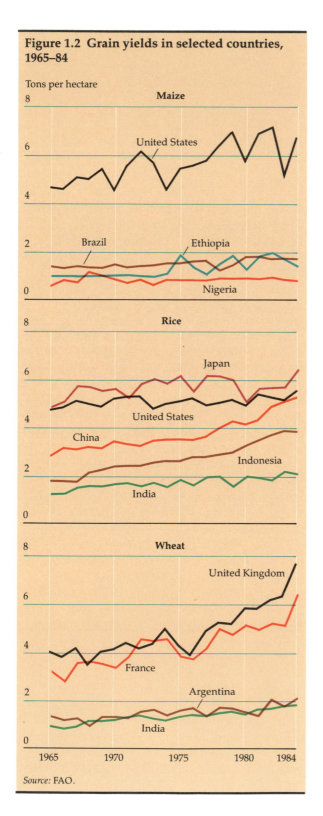

Figure 1.2 Grain yields in selected countries, 1965–84

Tons per hectare

Maize

United States

Brazil   Ethiopia

Nigeria

Rice

Japan

United States

China

Indonesia

India

Wheat

United Kingdom

France

Argentina

India

Source: FAO.

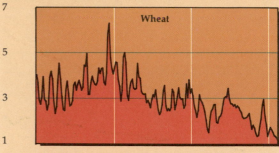

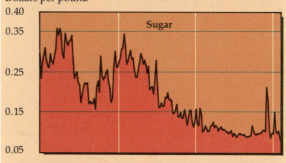

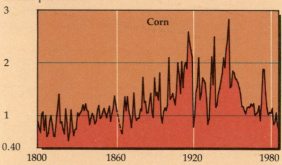

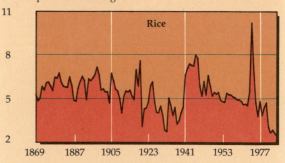

Figure 1.3 Trends in U.S. real agricultural prices, selected years, 1800–1985

Dollars per bushel

Wheat

Dollars per pound

Sugar

Dollars per bushel

Corn

Dollars per hundredweight

Rice

Note: Producer prices are deflated by the U.S. wholesale price index (1967 = 100). Corn prices before 1866 are estimates based on Virginia prices. Rice prices before 1904 are estimates based on New York prices. The broken line indicates data are not available.
Source: USDA *Agricultural Statistics,* various years; U.S. Bureau of the Census 1975, 1982, 1985; Strauss and Bean 1940; Peterson 1928.

Table 1.5 Real growth of commodity prices, 1950–84
(average annual percentage change)

Commodity	1950–59	1960–69	1970–79	1950–84
Total agriculture	−2.92	0.00	0.01	−1.03
Beverages	−2.08	−1.26	7.46	−1.13
Cereals	−3.84	2.72	−1.31	−1.30
Fats and oils	−3.73	−0.73	−0.81	−1.29
Raw materials	−2.51	0.50	−1.72	−1.08
Metals and minerals	0.08	6.12	−4.06	−0.09

Note: Data are deflated by the World Bank's manufacturing unit value (MUV) index. The MUV index is the c.i.f. index of U.S. dollar prices of industrial countries' manufactured exports to developing countries. Annual exponential growth rates were calculated using ordinary least-squares estimates.

since Malthusian times is, however, dramatic testimony to the ability of farmers to adopt new technologies for the benefit of all, especially those with the lowest incomes, as economic growth proceeds.

Malthusian pessimism still prevails about the prospects for food production in Africa. But if the prospects in that region seem poor, this is not because all possibilities of technological progress have been exhausted, but because the introduction of new technologies has barely begun. There is much need for better rural infrastructure and more research, especially on food crops. The coordination of research with extension services also needs to be improved. At the same time, farmers need better prices, easier access to inputs, and lower marketing costs. As discussed in Chapter 4, economic policies that discriminate against agriculture deter technological progress. Macroeconomic and sector-specific policies strongly influence the profitability of farming, the movement of labor and capital into, or out of, agriculture, and the pace at which new technologies are developed and adopted by farmers.

Malnutrition and famine

Although production of food has grown faster than population in developing countries, consumption of food has grown even faster because of imports. Food consumption in developing countries grew at 3.5 percent a year between 1971 and 1984, while population grew at 2.0 percent a year. In Africa, however, consumption grew at only 2.6 percent a year—which was less than the region's 2.8 percent annual growth in population. For the world's thirty-six poorest countries, twenty-six of them in Africa, the level of per capita food consumption declined by about 3.0 percent during the 1970s.

Precise estimates of the incidence of chronic malnutrition in developing countries are not possible,

but by any account the problem is vast. A recent World Bank paper, *Poverty and Hunger: Issues and Options for Food Security in Developing Countries* (1986), put the number somewhere between 340 million and 730 million people—and that excluded China. Malnutrition poses a challenge for all low-income developing countries, large or small. Governments naturally want to take special measures to alleviate it—such as by providing cheap food for the poor, by income transfers, by aid relief efforts, or by other types of food and nutrition programs. But, beyond a certain point, these types of measures will reduce economic growth and make it harder to finance the measures the government wants. That point is soon reached in low-income countries with low rates of economic growth.

Developing countries—and the world in general—are justifiably concerned about malnutrition. The causes of widespread malnutrition, however, are often not the insufficiency of food production but, rather, poverty and uneven distribution of income. Special programs, if undertaken in a cost-effective manner, can alleviate malnutrition, but there is little hope that low-income developing countries will be able to make significant and sustained progress in reducing malnutrition unless they increase their rates of economic growth (see Box 1.1). The best policies for alleviating malnutrition and poverty are those which increase growth and the competitiveness of the economy, for a growing and competitive economy facilitates a more even distribution of human capital and other assets and ensures higher incomes for the poor. Progress in the battle against malnutrition and poverty can be sustained if, and only if, there is satisfactory economic growth.

With the terrible images of the African famine still fresh in mind, it is hard to believe that the occurrence of famine is declining. Yet, it is true. Until the twentieth century a famine was recorded nearly every year somewhere in the world, often

Box 1.1 Food security

A main message of this Report is that, in the long run, people can attain food security only if they have adequate incomes. Food security and policies designed to enhance it are the subjects of a recent World Bank study, *Poverty and Hunger: Issues and Options for Food Security in Developing Countries* (1986). Among its findings are:

• Food security is access by all people at all times to enough food for an active and healthy life. There are two kinds of food insecurity: chronic and transitory. Chronic food insecurity is a continuously inadequate diet caused by the inability to acquire food. It affects households that persistently lack the ability either to buy enough food or to produce their own. Transitory food insecurity is a temporary decline in a household's access to enough food. It results from instability in food prices, food production, or household incomes—and in its worst form it produces famine.

• Food security issues are important because improved nutrition is an investment in the productivity of a nation's population. Also, the adjustment measures countries undertake to improve economic performance are more likely to succeed if food security objectives are not compromised in the process.

• Problems with food security do not necessarily result from inadequate food supplies; they arise from a lack of purchasing power on the part of nations and of households. Food security can be ensured in the long run only by raising the real incomes of households so that they can afford to acquire enough food.

Poverty and Hunger discusses a variety of cost-effective ways to increase food security in the short term. Many measures to address chronic insecurity are fully compatible with efficient economic growth because they involve raising people's productive capacity. But others involve tradeoffs of one kind or another. However, as both that study and Chapters 4 and 5 of this Report point out, some of the measures that governments take to increase food security work against both economic growth and food security in the long run. Such measures include persistently overvalued currencies, large expenditures on consumer food subsidies, and costly storage facilities to hold excessive stocks of food grain. When tradeoffs are present, targeting food assistance to the most vulnerable groups is far more effective and less costly than other measures.

---

with death tolls which, even by modern experience, were distressingly high. More than 10 million people may have died from famines in Bihar, India, in the early 1770s, in eastern India in the late 1860s, and in northern China in the 1870s.

Although the world has suffered a dozen famines since 1940, all but a few were much smaller in scale than the famines of previous centuries. Moreover, while the Sahel famine in the early 1970s conformed to the popular image of crops withering in the dry land, leading to starvation, many of the famines since 1940 resulted from war or civil strife rather than from weather conditions or shortfalls in food availability.

The example of Africa and the memory of past famines should not divert attention from the striking success that the past quarter century has seen in preventing famine—particularly in India. Four factors have contributed to the success. First, the increase in international grain trade has meant that countries in need can import food more readily. Second, governments, assisted by the Food and Agriculture Organization (FAO) and other international agencies, have become more willing to provide early warnings of impending shortages. Third, countries have become better able to distrib-

ute food to drought-stricken areas and to provide the hungry with the means to acquire available food. Fourth, and most important, many governments have come to recognize that famine is a complex phenomenon. Economic policies—such as those on internal and external trade, producer prices, and methods of financing and distributing food—affect a country's vulnerability to famine (see Box 1.2).

Trade and prices

Despite the fact that the global food outlook is favorable, one cannot be sanguine about the state of world agriculture. The outlook could be much more favorable if trade and pricing policies were improved. Most agricultural goods are traded in world markets, providing all countries with opportunities to increase their incomes by specializing in products in which they have a competitive advantage. The strides made by developing countries in agriculture during the past few decades show that developing countries as well as industrial countries benefit from an efficient system of world trade. Yet, trade barriers in industrial countries have become more restrictive, and most developing countries pursue policies that inhibit the growth of agricultural output and of rural incomes. As a result, most of the world's food exports are grown in industrial countries, where the costs of food production are high, and consumed in developing ones, where the costs are lower.

So many developing countries depend on agricultural exports that what happens in world agricultural markets is critical. Between 1965 and 1970, world agricultural exports grew more slowly than those of any other major commodity group—the growth rate was only 3.21 percent a year compared with 8.46 percent a year for manufactured exports (see Table 1.6).

Since 1970 the growth of agricultural exports has increased while that of manufactured exports has slowed. Between 1971 and 1984, agricultural ex-

ports grew at 4.64 percent a year while manufactured exports grew at 4.78 percent. The growth of trade in food has been most rapid—5.27 percent a year. The developing countries have largely accounted for the rapid growth of food imports (see Figure 1.4). The middle-income developing countries accounted for 80 percent of the growth in developing-country imports between 1962 and 1984, although they account for only about one-third of that group's population. The fastest growth of food exports came from industrial countries.

Changes in the structure of food trade have been just as important as the expansion of food exports. As shown in Figure 1.4, food imports by the developing countries have surged since 1975 and by 1984 nearly equaled the level of food imports of the

Box 1.2 Adam Smith on the causes of famine and the modern evidence

Famine can be caused by a variety of factors. Drought, flood, war, inflation, sharp losses of employment—all these and other developments can deprive large parts of a population of the means to acquire adequate amounts of food. The complexity of famine was discussed illuminatingly by Adam Smith more than 200 years ago. Smith repudiated the then commonly held view that famine often results from manipulation of markets by traders. He argued that "a dearth never has arisen from any combination among the inland dealers in corn" (Smith [1776] 1976, bk. 4, chap. 5, p. 32). No less important, Smith analyzed the relation between a general economic decline—not specifically of food output—and the development of a famine. He discussed the role of wages and employment in providing subsistence and showed how starvation can be caused by declines in employment or in real wages.

In a situation of economic decline, he wrote, "the demand for servants and labourers" could go down sharply, and "many who had been bred in the superior classes, not being able to find employment in their own business, would be glad to seek it in the lowest," so that "the competition for employment would be so great in it, as to reduce the wages of labour to the most miserable and scanty subsistence of the labourer. Many would not be able to find employment even upon these hard terms, but would either starve, or be driven to seek a subsistence either by begging, or by the perpetration perhaps of the greatest enormities. Want, famine, and mortality would immediately prevail in that class, and from thence extend themselves to all the superior classes" (ibid, bk. 1, chap. 8, p. 82).

Smith's conclusions about the general economic causes of famine have been confirmed by recent stud-

ies of contemporary famines by Amartya Sen (1981, 1986). The economic processes through which different occupation groups establish their entitlements to food have to be closely examined to explain the economic changes that lead to "want, famine, and mortality," and Smith's reference to the economic means of subsistence (such as wages and employment) is particularly helpful. For example, in the Ethiopian famine of 1973, there was a crop failure in the province of Wollo, but no serious decline in total food availability for Ethiopia as a whole. The famine victims in Wollo lacked the economic ability to command food from elsewhere in Ethiopia (indeed, some food moved out of famine-stricken Wollo to the more prosperous parts of the country, particularly Addis Ababa and Asmera). Similarly, in the Bengal famine of 1943 and in the Bangladesh famine of 1974, declines in real wages and employment in the rural sector were the proximate causes, and there was no great reduction in food availability (in fact, total food per head was at a peak during the Bangladesh famine). In the case of the Bengal famine, the interprovincial trade barriers that prevented movements of food grains from other provinces to Bengal helped to worsen the famine.

Policies on famine require a many-sided economic analysis of the factors affecting the market entitlements of the vulnerable groups. They call for an understanding of the exact roles of production and trade of non-food items, as well as of food, and of the nature of government policy, including the negative role of arbitrary internal and external trade barriers and the positive contribution of income generation through public projects.

Table 1.6 Growth of world exports, 1965–84
(annual percentage change in constant 1980 prices)

Exports	1965–70 average	1971–84 average	1981	1982	1983	1984
Agriculture	3.21	4.64	7.33	−0.63	−0.31	7.18
Food	2.66	5.27	8.68	1.58	−0.05	7.79
Nonfood	4.33	3.00	3.71	−2.02	−1.08	5.39
Metals	9.65	4.90	−13.96	−6.39	4.59	4.87
Fuel	12.70	−3.25	−12.03	−7.23	−2.02	2.01
Manufactures	8.46	4.78	4.23	−2.40	4.81	11.15
Total	9.32	2.60	0.04	−3.07	2.61	8.55

Note: Exports include reexports. East European nonmarket economies are not included in this table. Growth rates were calculated using ordinary least-squares estimates.

industrial market economies. Food imports by the East European nonmarket economies also have grown. The food trade balance has shifted sharply against developing countries at a time of growing indebtedness and foreign exchange scarcities.

The changing pattern in food trade shown in Figure 1.4 has clearly been the most striking feature of world trade in agriculture in recent decades. It also explains the evolution of export shares. As shown in Table 1.7, the developing countries as a group have had only modest losses of export market shares in beverages and raw materials since the early 1960s, but their losses in market shares in food have been large.

These changes reflect not only population growth but also changing consumption patterns and economic policies in developing countries. The best example is the growing importance of wheat in the diets of poor people. Between 1964 and 1966 the developing countries' share of world wheat consumption was 39 percent; the average in 1979–81 was 49 percent. The growth of urbaniza-

tion, the convenience of bread, and low international prices all contributed, as did overvaluations of exchange rates and urban food subsidies in many developing countries. Still another factor was the availability of food aid in some countries. In Bangladesh (then East Pakistan) in 1960, wheat consumption was less than 2 percent of total grain consumption. Because of the subsidized distribution of wheat from food aid, and also increased local production, wheat now constitutes about 20 percent of grain consumption. The increasing dependence on wheat and the inability to produce it economically in many countries means that it has to be imported in greater quantities. Between 1979 and 1981, wheat accounted for 59 percent of food grains imported into developing countries. While wheat consumption increased, consumption of coarse grains—maize, barley, and so on—mostly decreased as a portion of total cereal consumption. The exceptions were those rapidly growing developing economies where meat has become important in the diet. Hong Kong, the Republic of Korea,

Table 1.7 Export shares of major agricultural commodity groups, 1961–63, 1982–84
(percent)

Country group	Beverages		Food		Raw materials		Total agriculture	
	1961–63	1982–84	1961–63	1982–84	1961–63	1982–84	1961–63	1982–84
Developing countries	98.1	94.9	44.8	34.2	69.2	65.3	63.1	48.4
Low-income countries	27.6	23.8	9.0	3.6	15.6	13.6	15.1	8.3
Africa	19.6	15.8	1.5	0.3	6.0	4.9	6.9	3.5
Asia	8.0	8.0	7.5	3.3	9.6	8.7	8.0	4.8
Middle-income oil exporters	17.1	17.6	6.5	3.3	33.9	24.7	14.8	8.8
Middle-income oil importers	53.4	53.5	29.3	27.3	19.7	27.0	33.3	31.3
High-income oil exporters	0.0	0.0	0.1	0.1	0.0	0.0	0.0	0.1
Industrial market economies	1.7	4.7	46.2	62.7	23.5	24.0	30.5	47.9
East European nonmarket economies	0.2	0.4	8.9	3.0	7.3	10.7	6.4	3.6

Note: Data are weighted by the 1978–82 world export unit prices to permit cross-country comparisons. Beverages comprise coffee, cocoa, and tea. Food comprises cereals, sugar, meat, poultry, dairy products, roots and tubers, pulses, fruits, and vegetables. Raw materials comprise cotton, jute, rubber, and tobacco.
Source: Based on FAO data.

Malaysia, the Philippines, and Thailand increased their indirect consumption of coarse grains as feed to livestock and poultry.

These changes in the structure of consumption and trade have been heavily influenced by pricing and trade policies. Agricultural trade restrictions—at least among the industrial countries—have increased greatly. The levels of protection before World War I and during the 1920s and 1950s were modest in comparison, as discussed in Box 1.3. The unprecedented growth in exports of manufactures, first in Japan and recently in Hong Kong, Korea, and Singapore, was made possible by the creation of an open trading system. This has served the world well by stimulating economic growth in both industrial and developing countries. The opposite has occurred in agriculture. Interventions are almost universal, and much trade is managed by public sector agencies and marketing boards. Bilateral trade deals, food aid, and special preferences have further distorted trade flows in agriculture.

When domestic prices are kept below world prices at country borders, producers of import-competing products or of exports are taxed; similarly, when domestic producers get prices that are higher than border prices, they are supported. The ratio of domestic prices to border prices—or the nominal protection coefficient (NPC)—is thus a convenient indicator of policies that bear on trade.

The pattern of policies followed by industrial and developing countries is summarized in Figure 1.5, which is based on a large number of nominal protection coefficients for food and nonfood crops (including exports and imports). Developing countries clearly tend to tax agricultural commodities and thus encourage imports and discourage exports. The effect is often stronger than reflected in Figure 1.5 because of overvalued exchange rates. Industrial countries, in contrast, tend to support domestic production and thereby inhibit imports and encourage exports.

As this pattern suggests, the bias against agriculture in developing countries is exacerbated by the high levels of protection in the industrial ones. The industrial countries have erected high barriers to imports of temperate-zone products from developing countries and then have subsidized their own exports. The special trade preference schemes they have extended to many developing countries have not been a significant offset to their trade restrictions.

Policies in industrial countries affect the level, direction, and stability of world prices. A few de-

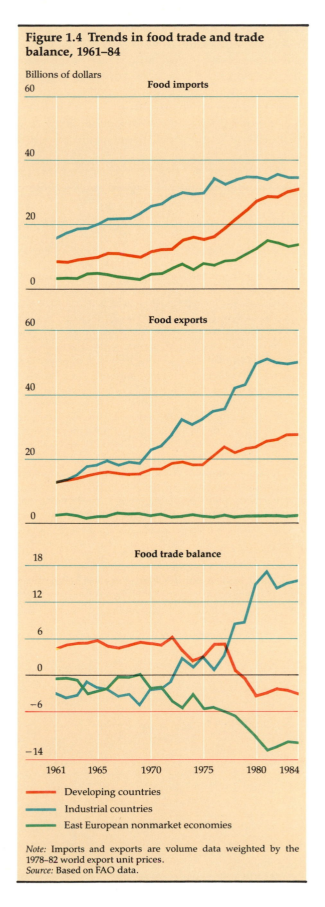

Figure 1.4 Trends in food trade and trade balance, 1961–84

Billions of dollars

Food imports

Food exports

Food trade balance

Developing countries
Industrial countries
East European nonmarket economies

Note: Imports and exports are volume data weighted by the 1978–82 world export unit prices.
Source: Based on FAO data.

veloping countries can also affect world prices of beverages, raw materials, and some foods. Collectively, the policies in developing countries can alter the world prices of temperate-zone products. The fact that both industrial and developing countries insulate domestic prices from world markets makes world prices more volatile than they would be otherwise. A principal theme of this Report is that a global perspective is necessary in examining the development and future growth of agriculture because the domestic agricultural policies and programs of various countries are interdependent.

Part II of this Report examines policies in developing and industrial countries and shows how they inhibit both economic and agricultural growth and delay the alleviation of malnutrition and pov-

Box 1.3 Agricultural protectionism in historical context

Governments have protected farmers for centuries. Since the beginning of industrialization, there has been only one brief interlude of free trade in agriculture in Europe. It began with the abolition of the Corn Laws by the United Kingdom in 1846 and by 1860 had spread throughout most of Western Europe. But free trade lasted less than two decades. During the next fifty years, only Denmark, the Netherlands, and the United Kingdom resisted the drift back to protectionism that culminated in the high tariff levels imposed during the Great Depression.

The protection of agricultural products before World War I and during the 1920s was still modest compared with that of the 1930s. Box table 1.3A shows a sample of estimated tariff levels for 1913, 1927, and 1931 for foodstuffs and manufactured goods. For Western Europe the tariff levels on foodstuffs in 1913 were roughly the same as those on manufactured goods. In 1927 they were only slightly higher. By 1931, however, tariffs on foodstuffs had soared above those on other

commodities. In the extreme case of Finland, tariffs on agriculture were five times higher than those on semimanufactured goods. Germany's agricultural tariffs were four times higher than its industrial tariffs.

Levels of protection in the 1950s in Western Europe had been reduced to those of the 1920s. A decade later, however, they had substantially increased (see Box table 1.3B). The average level for the European Communities (EC) was more than three times what it had been a decade earlier, and in France and Italy the protection had almost returned to its level in 1931.

In East Asia no less than in Western Europe, the origins of agricultural protection go back beyond the recent past. In 1904, Japan imposed a tariff on rice imports. During the 1920s and 1930s it kept domestic prices high to encourage self-sufficiency. A measure of this protection was the difference between rice prices in Japan and Thailand. In the 1920s the price in Japan was three times higher than in Thailand, too great a variation to be explained by differences in quality. The

Box table 1.3A Estimated tariff levels in Europe as a percentage of border prices, 1913, 1927, and 1931

Country	Foodstuffs			Semimanufactured goods			Industrial manufactured goods		
	1913	1927	1931	1913	1927	1931	1913	1927	1931
Austria	. .	16.5	59.5	. .	15.2	20.7	. .	21.0	27.7
Belgium	25.5	11.8	23.7	7.6	10.5	15.5	9.5	11.6	13.0
Bulgaria	24.7	79.0	133.0	24.2	49.5	65.0	19.5	75.0	90.0
Czechoslovakia	. .	36.3	84.0	. .	21.7	29.5	. .	35.8	36.5
Finland	49.0	57.5	102.0	18.8	20.2	20.0	37.6	17.8	22.7
France	29.2	19.1	53.0	25.3	24.3	31.8	16.3	25.8	29.0
Germany	21.8	27.4	82.5	15.3	14.5	23.4	10.0	19.0	18.3
Hungary	. .	31.5	60.0	. .	26.5	32.5	. .	31.8	42.6
Italy	22.0	24.5	66.0	25.0	28.6	49.5	14.6	28.3	41.8
Poland	. .	72.0	110.0	. .	33.2	40.0	. .	55.6	52.0
Romania	34.7	45.6	87.5	30.0	32.6	46.3	25.5	48.5	55.0
Spain	41.5	45.2	80.5	26.0	39.2	49.5	42.5	62.7	75.5
Sweden	24.2	21.5	39.0	25.3	18.0	18.0	24.5	20.8	23.5
Switzerland	14.7	21.5	42.2	7.3	11.5	15.2	9.3	17.6	22.0
Yugoslavia	. .	43.7	75.0	. .	24.7	30.5	. .	28.0	32.8

Note: The numbers show the percentages by which domestic producer prices exceeded border prices.
Source: Based on Liepmann 1938, p. 413.

erty in the developing world. Chapters 4 and 5 review the scope in developing countries for improving agricultural policies and performance regardless of policy changes in industrial countries. These chapters show why and how the policies in developing countries have often discriminated against agriculture. The sources of bias include inward-looking development strategies and inap-

propriate macroeconomic and exchange rate policies. These chapters also show the importance of reforms in tax policies, price stabilization measures, marketing arrangements, and consumer

Republic of Korea, which was a part of the Japanese empire from 1919 to 1945, maintained the same level of protection.

After 1945, Japan continued to protect its agriculture, but Korea, in its effort to industrialize, began to tax farmers. The level of taxation, however, was modest compared with the taxation rates in some low-income developing countries today. In the mid-1950s, domestic producer prices in Korea were about 15 percent lower than border prices. The level of protection in Japan during the late 1950s was more than 40 percent. Since then, both countries have dramatically increased agricultural protection. By 1965, Japan's level of farm protection had risen to 76 percent, while Korea, in less than two decades, had gone from taxing its farmers to substantially protecting them. On average, domestic producer prices in Korea exceeded border prices by 55 percent from 1970 to 1974 and by 166 percent from 1980 to 1982.

Box table 1.3B Estimated tariff levels as a percentage of border prices, 1956 and 1965–67

Country	1956	1965–67 average
Belgium	5	54
Denmark	3	5
EC	16[a]	52
France	18	47
Germany	22	54
Ireland	4	3
Italy	16	64
Japan	42[b]	76[c]
Netherlands	5	37
Sweden	27	54
United Kingdom	32	28
United States	2[d]	8[e]

Note: The numbers are calculated as in Box table 1.3A.
a. Excludes Denmark, Greece, Ireland, Portugal, Spain, and the United Kingdom.
b. Data are for 1955–59.
c. Data are for 1965–69.
d. Data are for 1955.
e. Data are for 1965.
Source: McCrone 1962, p. 51; Howarth 1971, p. 29; Saxon and Anderson 1982, p. 29; Honma and Hayami, forthcoming. The McCrone and Howarth estimates have been adjusted to measure protection in international prices instead of in domestic prices.

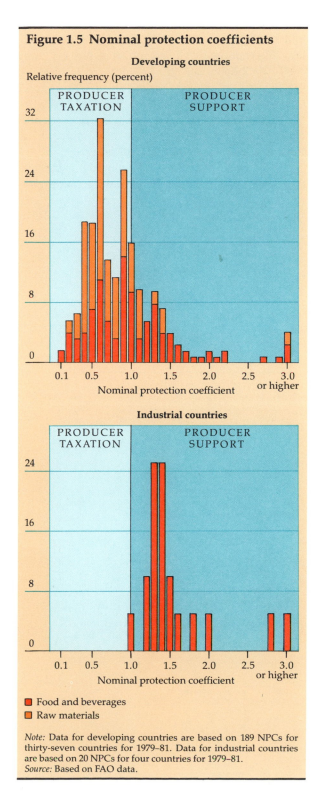

Figure 1.5 Nominal protection coefficients

Note: Data for developing countries are based on 189 NPCs for thirty-seven countries for 1979–81. Data for industrial countries are based on 20 NPCs for four countries for 1979–81.
Source: Based on FAO data.

13

and producer subsidies. Developing countries can greatly improve their prospects by changing their economic and institutional policies, as some of them have already done or are in the process of doing. The emerging trend toward policy reforms in developing countries is reviewed in Chapter 5.

Chapter 6 reviews policies in industrial countries and counts their costs and benefits domestically and internationally. Their policies are not only costly nationally, but are an important source of inefficiency in world agriculture. The chapter stresses the international consequences of the industrial countries' policies and the large potential gains to the world economy from more liberal trade and domestic policies in all countries.

The interactions between developing and industrial countries are shown to be of particular importance. In the short run, industrial countries and some developing countries are likely to gain most from free trade, but the gains should spread rapidly to other countries if they undertake appropriate economic policy reforms.

Chapter 7 looks at the major international initiatives that have been proposed or taken to increase the benefits of trade for developing countries—international commodity agreements, compensatory financing, special trade preferences, and food aid. It is argued that these types of initiatives address the symptoms rather than the problem itself, which is the inappropriateness of trade and domestic policies in both industrial and developing countries. The Report ends by summarizing in Chapter 8 the priorities for policy reforms.

2

The hesitant recovery

Industrial countries have emerged from the depths of the 1980–82 recession with growth in output being sustained for longer than in previous recoveries. In most industrial countries output started expanding after 1982, and growth has continued through to 1986 (see Table 2.1). Yet, the world economy is in an uneasy and unsettled state. Except for the United States and Japan in 1984, expansion in the industrial countries has been slower than in the early years of past recoveries.

For developing countries, growth in output has followed a similar pattern. Growth picked up after 1982, reaching its peak in 1984 (see Figure 2.1). But a downturn in commodity prices in 1985, combined with restricted capital flows and a marked slowdown in the growth of world trade, has made it difficult for developing countries to sustain this performance. As a result, many of the underlying weaknesses in developing economies began to resurface in 1985. This has refocused international attention on the policy initiatives required to attain strong and sustained growth in the medium term.

In industrial countries unemployment increased sharply during the recession of 1980–82, and it has remained at high levels in most of them during the recovery. In Europe unemployment remains at between 9 and 10 percent of the labor force. Even in the United States, where unemployment has fallen since the recession, the unemployment rate is between 6 and 7 percent. In contrast, as GDP has

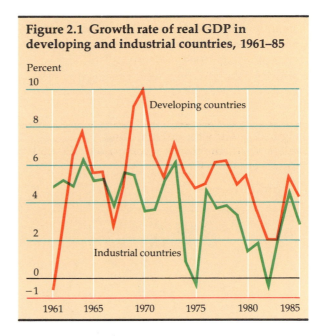

Figure 2.1 Growth rate of real GDP in developing and industrial countries, 1961–85

Table 2.1 Growth of real GNP in selected industrial countries, 1979–85
(annual percentage change)

Country	1979	1980	1981	1982	1983	1984	1985
France	3.5	1.1	0.3	1.8	0.7	0.6	1.0
Germany	4.4	2.0	−0.1	−1.2	1.3	2.7	2.3
Japan	5.2	4.8	4.1	3.3	3.4	5.8	5.0
United Kingdom	1.8	−2.6	−1.4	1.5	3.7	2.3	3.3
United States	3.2	−0.2	3.4	−2.1	3.7	5.2	2.5
Average for the five	3.6	0.9	2.2	−0.2	3.0	4.2	2.8

Note: Data for 1985 are estimates.
Source: For 1979–84: World Bank data; for 1985: OECD 1985c.

grown, there have been no obvious signs of a revival of inflation. On the contrary, inflation has gradually subsided during the recovery, falling from the double-digit rates of the depth of the recession to around 4 percent in 1985.

For most developing countries the early 1980s was a difficult period. Many attempted to implement badly needed domestic reforms, but found that wide fluctuations in the world economy made their task that much harder. Mounting debts, low commodity prices, and reduced commercial bank lending led many countries to cut imports and to try to expand exports. In the short run this was achieved mainly by curtailing consumption and investment through lower exchange rates, higher taxes, and reduced government spending. Although the exchange rate realignments often stimulated exports and helped import-competing industries, these short-term adjustments initially depressed incomes and employment. As a result, real per capita incomes dropped in both Latin America and sub-Saharan Africa between 1980 and 1983.

Beginning in 1984, renewed growth in the industrial countries and the policy reforms adopted by developing countries bore fruit. The developing countries as a group enjoyed a recovery, led by a

marked improvement in the economic performance of many middle-income economies. But growth slowed again in 1985 as a result of three main changes: slower growth in the industrial countries—particularly in the United States—starting from the middle of 1984, a slower rate of expansion in world trade relative to industrial-country growth, and a further deterioration in developing countries' terms of trade. In addition, inflows of external capital continued to decline. While many economies should grow more rapidly this year, some—oil exporters in particular—will experience very low growth.

During the process of adjustment, however, many governments saw that fundamental changes were needed in institutional arrangements to avoid the problems that had gradually overtaken them in the 1970s and that had caused such distress in the 1980s. Many have seen the need to reform the incentive framework to reduce the distortions caused by inflation, regulations, overvalued exchange rates, trade controls, and excessive public expenditure. It is difficult to change institutions and policies even at the best of times. Many countries nevertheless embarked on programs of reform during the early 1980s. These programs may, if resolutely pursued, provide a basis for sustained growth and development.

However difficult the external conditions, domestic policies that improve the incentive framework and reduce uncertainties will contribute to growth. But the more favorable the international environment, the greater will be the benefits of policy reforms to developing countries. Thus, the performance of industrial economies is an important determinant of the progress of developing economies. To understand what has happened in developing countries, therefore, the policies and performance of industrial countries must also be reviewed.

The industrial countries

Figure 2.2 illustrates the performance of the seven largest OECD economies since the mid-1960s. Behind the cycles of GDP growth, unemployment, and inflation lie some disturbing long-term trends. Each peak in GDP growth has been lower than the preceding one; peaks as well as troughs in unemployment have been rising. Progress has been made only in curbing inflation. Lower inflation, however, has been accompanied by unemployment rates roughly two to three times higher than the level in the 1960s.

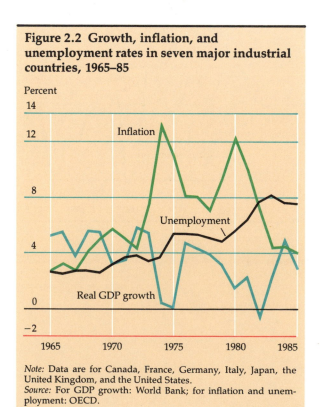

Figure 2.2 Growth, inflation, and unemployment rates in seven major industrial countries, 1965–85

Percent

Note: Data are for Canada, France, Germany, Italy, Japan, the United Kingdom, and the United States.
Source: For GDP growth: World Bank; for inflation and unemployment: OECD.

Table 2.2 Budget balance as a percentage of GNP in seven major industrial countries, 1979–85

Country	1979	1980	1981	1982	1983	1984	1985
Canada	−1.8	−2.7	−1.6	−5.0	−6.2	−6.4	−6.0
France	−0.7	0.2	−1.8	−2.7	−3.1	−2.8	−3.2
Germany	−2.7	−3.1	−3.8	−3.4	−2.8	−2.3	−1.5
Italy	−9.5	−8.0	−11.9	−12.6	−12.4	−13.5	−13.1
Japan	−4.8	−4.5	−4.0	−3.6	−3.5	−2.6	−1.4
United Kingdom	−3.2	−3.9	−3.2	−2.3	−3.5	−4.0	−3.6
United States	0.6	−1.2	−0.9	−3.8	−4.1	−3.4	−3.7

Note: Negative signs indicate deficits.
Source: OECD 1985c.

Monetary and fiscal policies

After inflation accelerated at the end of the 1970s to historically high rates, most of the industrial countries attempted to reduce the rate of growth of monetary expansion. The details of the policy measures adopted in the early 1980s differed from country to country, but in substance they were similar. First, they were medium-term strategies— that is to say, they were concerned with a period of at least four to five years. Second, they encompassed both fiscal and monetary measures. Governments sought to reduce their budget deficits as a fraction of GNP as well as the rate of growth of the money supply. For the most part, they recognized that proposed reductions in the rate of growth of the money supply would be credible only if associated with a reduction in the government's need to borrow.

Despite high levels of unemployment, anti-inflationary strategies were maintained throughout the recession of 1980–82. As a result, rates of inflation in the industrial countries subsided rapidly and in 1986 were at their lowest levels in twenty years.

But governments were more successful in reducing the rate of growth of the money supply than in cutting the public sector deficit. Some OECD countries gradually brought down the high deficits that had emerged in the late 1970s. But there were exceptions, the most important of which was the United States (see Table 2.2).

Since 1981, tax cuts and expenditure growth have increased the U.S. federal deficit to $200 billion (nearly 4 percent of GNP), in spite of the recovery after 1982. Indeed, at the peak of the business cycle, one would have expected the federal budget to have been in approximate balance. But the deficit of the United States has persisted and has been large enough to draw capital from other countries.

Budget deficits and interest rates

The domestic effects of large and persistent deficits are mainly on real interest rates and expected inflation. The manifest difficulties of cutting public spending lead people to expect that revenues will eventually have to rise to finance deficits. Boosts to public revenue may come from high growth, conventional taxes, or the seigniorage of inflation (see Box 2.1). Worries about future inflation tend to keep long-term nominal interest rates higher than they would otherwise be, and large budget deficits contribute to high real interest rates.

Real interest rates were negative during the early part of the 1970s, but they rose sharply in the early 1980s. Even though they declined moderately from 1982 on—and more sharply in 1985 and 1986—they remain high. During most recessions (particularly those not associated with sharp monetary contraction), the private sector's demand for credit falls. This usually encourages a decline in interest rates. But in the recession of 1980–82 and during the subsequent recovery, this pattern was not repeated, largely because of the fiscal-monetary imbalance. One consequence was that indebted developing countries received little relief from high real interest rates. Their reliance on cheap finance in the 1970s became a heavy burden in the 1980s as interest rates increased. Like most cumulative processes, the problem matured slowly, even after the steep rises in interest rates. But it finally became pressing at the lowest point of the business cycle in mid-1982. This led to severe debt problems, the main theme of last year's Report.

Capital flows, current account deficits, and trade flows

Governments in industrial countries have generally financed their increased deficits by borrowing from domestic and external sources. Private do-

Box 2.1   Inflation as a tax

The need for revenue may lead governments to increase the money supply. The resulting increase in inflation erodes the real value of all financial assets, except those that are fully indexed—creating what is termed the inflation tax. Debtors gain and creditors lose. In a credit market that is reasonably free, financial assets that pay interest, such as bonds, are likely to have a yield that compensates for any erosion in their real value caused by steady and foreseeable inflation. Unless bonds are indexed, however, a sudden or unexpected burst of inflation is unlikely to be compensated for by suitably high nominal interest rates, and bondholders will suffer an erosion of the real value of their assets. Since the main issuers of bonds are usually governments and the main holder is the domestic private sector (although foreigners may also hold substantial amounts), a sudden or unexpected increase in the rate of inflation will reduce the real value of the government's debt. The effect of inflation is analogous to levying a tax on bonds and using the revenue to pay off debt.

In developing countries, however, the bond market tends to be small and to have low, controlled interest rates. Most bonds are held by banks, primarily to satisfy reserve requirements; other bondholders are often involuntary lenders to government. In these circumstances bonds are rarely a principal source of financing and thus will yield little tax in response to a sudden or unexpected inflation. On the international capital mar-

kets, bank loans tend to be denominated in foreign currency, usually the dollar, so there is no real erosion of these assets as a result of domestic inflation.

In countries where the financial system is rudimentary, the main financial asset is currency. Governments usually have a monopoly on issuing notes and coin (although there are exceptions: Liberia and Panama use dollars), and the currency is held almost entirely by domestic residents. Cash pays no interest, so the erosion of its real value cannot be offset during inflation. Since notes and coin are a government liability and an asset of the private domestic sector, the reduction in their real value is similar to a tax on currency. It reduces the outstanding real liabilities of government.

There is a limit to the size of this taxation. The greater the tax rate, the more those who are being taxed try to avoid it. The higher the rate of inflation, the smaller the amount of money (in real terms) which the public will be willing to hold, and so the narrower the tax base. This can be seen in the extreme case of the last stages of hyperinflation, when people largely give up using money and switch to barter. Nonetheless, although the tax base (that is, the quantity of money in real terms) may become very small, the slow adjustment of prices to the accelerating growth of the money supply usually still guarantees some tax revenue. But when the pace of monetary expansion slows, revenues can fall sharply.

Theoretically, the maximum tax revenue from infla-

mestic residents or foreigners buy additional government paper—currency notes, Treasury bills, government bonds, or public deposits—to finance the public deficit.

When foreign capital, attracted by high real interest rates, finances the deficit, the result is a current account deficit in the balance of payments. In 1985 in the United States, for example, the federal government deficit of about $200 billion was financed to the tune of $87 billion by the financial surplus of the domestic private sector (including state and local governments), but the remaining $113 billion came from foreigners through the current account deficit.

The funds to finance fiscal deficits must of necessity come from one of three sources: increased domestic private savings, reduced private investment, or lower exports net of imports. In spite of high real interest rates, the increase in the U.S. federal budget deficit in 1982 was not accompanied by an offsetting increase in domestic private savings. Thus, the deficit had to be financed by re-

duced domestic investment or by increased foreign borrowing. During the recovery, however, private investment increased at a faster rate than domestic savings, partly in response to earlier tax cuts that favored investment. As a result, a growing proportion of the financing burden of the increased budgetary deficit was borne by imports of capital. The large current account deficit in the balance of payments reflected this (see Table 2.3).

The way the burden of financing a budget deficit is shared among savings, investment, and capital imports is determined by interest rates, expected returns on investment, and exchange rates. All of these are, in important respects, determined by monetary and fiscal policies. Since 1981, when the U.S. budget deficit began to increase, the Federal Reserve Board has pursued a tight monetary policy. As a result, interest rates have been high by industrial-country standards. Although the negative effect that high interest rates had on domestic investment was offset by the positive effects of other policy changes, higher interest rates at-tion is obtained when the proportionate increase in the price level equals the resulting reduction in real currency balances. Thus, at the margin, what the government gains from an additional notch of inflation is exactly offset by people reducing their real currency holdings.

Many governments increase the money supply at a rate far greater than that which would theoretically maximize real public revenue. Although periods of high inflation occasionally occur accidentally, the main cause is usually the government's immediate need for cash to pay its bills. To obtain the cash, the government simply prints more money.

In more sophisticated monetary systems, checking accounts are important as a means of exchange. Banks usually pay little or no interest on checking accounts, and so check balances are similar to currency. With inflation, the banks are the immediate recipients of the reduction in the real value of checking accounts, since these appear as liabilities on their balance sheets. But, by increasing reserve requirements or taxation, the government usually acquires the banks' gains and prevents them from profiting unduly from inflation.

Like any other form of revenue raising, the inflation tax must be judged on its merits. But inflation as a tax has disadvantages not shared by alternative forms of taxation. It distorts relative prices (because some prices increase faster than others), generates uncertainty, and falls heavily upon low-income holders of cash. Fur-

thermore, inflation erodes other kinds of government revenue. Lags in the collection of taxes and delays in adjusting some tax rates to rising prices mean that the real revenues of government fall as inflation increases. In practice, this more than offsets any tax increase attributable to "bracket creep," and even tends to outweigh the inflation tax itself. Except at low levels of inflation, raising revenues by inflationary finance is likely to pay off only in the short run.

The lower and more stable the inflation, the more likely it is that a government will be able to raise substantial resources by seigniorage. Seigniorage is the benefit the central bank derives from being the monopoly supplier of domestic currency. Domestic residents will hold a larger stock of cash, in real terms, if prices are known to be stable. Such stability also makes a currency attractive to foreigners whose own economies are unstable and inflationary. This is vividly illustrated by the substantial (and often illegal) foreign holdings of dollars by many Latin American countries. In Ghana, there were substantial holdings of, and transactions in, the CFA franc of neighboring Côte d'Ivoire. Because of the relative stability of their economies, the United States and Côte d'Ivoire were able to acquire real resources in exchange for their currency notes. The desire of foreigners to share in Switzerland's stability has enabled Swiss banks to import capital at very low cost. These are the significant and continuing benefits of a stable financial system.

tracted an unprecedented net inflow of foreign capital. This, in turn, was one of the factors that contributed to the appreciation of the dollar relative to other major currencies (see Table 2.3).

During 1985 and in early 1986, however, interest rates fell faster in the United States than in other industrial countries, and the dollar weakened. This partly reflects the recent strengthening of the U.S.

commitment to reduce the federal budget deficit during the next five years. The concerted efforts of the Group of Five countries have also assisted in bringing about an orderly adjustment. But a decline in the current account deficit or in the demands of the United States on the world's savings will take time. This is due in part to lags in the process of adjustment as U.S. export and import

Table 2.3 Current account balances and exchange rates in Germany, Japan, and the United States, 1981–85

Country and item	1981	1982	1983	1984	1985
Germany					
Current account balance (billions of dollars)	−5.4	3.2	4.2	6.1	13.2
Exchange rate index	100.0	100.5	102.4	109.5	111.5
Japan					
Current account balance (billions of dollars)	4.8	6.9	20.8	35.0	49.7
Exchange rate index	100.0	105.7	97.6	93.6	93.2
United States					
Current account balance (billions of dollars)	6.4	−8.0	−40.8	−101.6	−113.6
Exchange rate index	100.0	93.6	90.7	86.9	86.7

Note: The exchange rate index is calculated relative to SDR 1981 = 100. Data for 1985 are estimates. Current account balance includes official transfers.
Source: IMF.

substitution activities begin to expand in response to the weakened dollar. It is also apparent that capital has been attracted into the United States because of the country's political stability, low taxes, lack of exchange controls, and wage restraints.

The large current account deficit in the United States and high dollar interest rates have had different—and offsetting—effects on the rest of the world. Increased deficits stimulated the exports of, and thus the aggregate demand of, the United States' trading partners. Countries that do not export to the United States also gained from the indirect effects. Where there was spare capacity, this promoted an increase in exports and GDP that, for some trading partners, more than offset the cost of higher interest payments.

Part of the increase in the U.S. current account deficit since 1981 was mirrored by an improvement in the current account balances of the rest of the OECD countries. For example, Japan's surplus rose sharply, reaching the equivalent of about 30 percent of the increased deficit of the United States.

Developing countries were also successful in capturing part of the buoyant U.S. demand, particularly in manufactures. Their manufactured exports, which had close to zero growth in 1982, grew by 10 percent in 1983 and by more than 16 percent in 1984. But the smaller increase in the U.S. current account deficit in 1984–85 was not offset by an expansion in the imports of other OECD countries. The result has been a marked slowdown in developing countries' export growth. In addition, up until 1985 some of the newly industrialized countries in Asia had lost competitiveness in the U.S. market because their exchange rates did not depreciate in real terms against the dollar by as much as the exchange rates of their competitors in industrial countries.

The large increase in the U.S. current account deficit from 1981 to 1984 eased the adjustment of the trade and current accounts in many developing countries, particularly the heavily indebted ones. But this was offset, in part, by higher world interest rates. Although it is difficult to measure the net impact on developing countries, it is clear that those which adjusted most quickly and exploited the booming export market made a net gain.

However, the export opportunities that existed in 1983–84 for developing countries are unlikely to return unless other OECD countries expand import demand and thereby reduce their current account surpluses. Again, though, there is an offsetting effect: if the U.S. budget deficit declines, interest rates will fall and capital hitherto absorbed by the government will be redirected to alternative investments. This would provide increased opportunities for those developing countries that have implemented the reforms necessary to attract foreign lenders or investors. Capital could again flow voluntarily from OECD countries to more productive uses in developing countries—as it normally does. The OECD's current account surpluses and the developing countries' deficits would be as rational and sustainable as their investments would be profitable.

Public sector spending and controls

One of the main causes of budget deficits in industrial countries, particularly in Europe, has been burgeoning public expenditure. In all industrial countries, public spending expanded faster than GDP between 1964 and 1983 (see Table 2.4). Excluding defense, the fastest growing items of public spending were social benefits—health services, welfare, social security, and pensions. They are hard to cut because their size is dictated by the number of people claiming guaranteed (and usually indexed) benefits. Interest payments on public debt have also grown much faster than GDP.

Governments in industrial countries have ex-

Table 2.4 Total public expenditure as a percentage of GDP in selected industrial countries, 1964–83

Country	1964	1968	1972	1976	1980	1983
Canada	28.9	33.0	37.2	39.4	40.9	46.8
France	38.0	40.3	38.3	44.0	46.4	51.5
Germany	35.9	39.1	40.8	48.0	48.4	48.6
Italy	31.8	34.7	38.6	42.2	46.1	57.4
Japan	..	..	21.8	27.9	32.4	34.8
United Kingdom	33.6	39.2	39.8	45.6	45.1	47.2
United States	28.3	31.3	32.0	34.5	35.0	38.1
Average for all industrial countries	30.6	33.7	33.3	37.4	39.3	41.6

Source: OECD 1985c.

panded their subsidies to manufacturing (particularly the steel and shipbuilding industries) in the hope of easing the strains of structural change. But it is the unanticipated rapid growth of subsidies to agriculture that has recently drawn most attention. In the United States, agricultural production has been encouraged by a number of measures, including the setting of target prices above world prices for wheat and corn. In Western Europe, internal prices of many agricultural products are kept even further above world prices, and exports are subsidized.

The result has been to encourage domestic production and depress domestic consumption, especially in Europe. The resulting flood of surplus grain, sugar, meat, poultry, and dairy products at depressed world prices has been particularly damaging to those developing countries that are trying to stimulate the output of agricultural products in which they often have an absolute advantage. The implications of these policies are the subject of Chapter 6 in Part II of this Report.

In the 1980s, governments made numerous attempts to cut public spending but had little success. The rates of growth of public expenditure have been cut, but this has not reduced on average the level of overall spending either absolutely or relative to GDP.

Higher public spending and greater public sector involvement in the economy were indirectly responsible for other problems that hindered growth in the industrial countries:

• *Marginal tax rates.* In the 1950s and 1960s, many governments thought that high public spending would not only offset cyclical downturns but also promote long-term expansion in GDP. That view lost favor, however, after the experience of the 1970s, when growth in GDP faltered but the growth in public spending did not. The higher level of public spending meant that average rates of taxation had to increase. What mattered more than the average tax rate, however, was the extent to which tax varied with changes in income and wealth—the marginal rate of tax. To preserve a ''progressive'' tax structure (that is, one in which the better-off pay proportionately more tax), marginal tax rates had to increase by at least as much as average tax rates. In real terms, marginal tax rates on interest income often exceeded 100 percent. For example, if interest rates are 20 percent and inflation is 15 percent, the real return on a marginal investment of $100 is $5. But if tax is levied at a marginal rate of 25 percent on the nominal yield of $20, the income net of tax is only $15.

Thus, the tax payment absorbs all of the $5 of real income, and the marginal real tax rate is 100 percent. One result of the failure to reduce public spending was, therefore, the erosion of incentives for wealth creation.

• *Benefits.* Along with the increase in tax rates came an increase in benefits. Again, it was not the level of benefits that mattered, but the marginal loss of benefit as one moved into or out of employment. Other social benefits, from housing subsidies to free school meals, were also reduced or withdrawn as one earned additional income. The combined disincentive effects of the marginal tax and benefit rates reached very high levels— particularly for those workers with average (or slightly below average) wage levels and with ordinary family commitments. Combined marginal tax-benefit rates of 85 percent became common. For some income groups the combined rate exceeded 100 percent. For example, in the United Kingdom in December 1984 the combined marginal tax-benefit rate for a married man with two dependent children and an income between one-half and two-thirds of the average wage reached 180 percent. At such high rates, it pays people not to work.

• *Regulations and controls.* A proliferation of regulations and controls sharply increased business costs and introduced distortions. For example, with the aim of promoting jobs in areas of high unemployment, governments directed capital through planning controls and fiscal incentives. Unfortunately, capital investment was channeled into industries which could not survive without government subsidies. As a result, capital-intensive, rather than job-intensive, industries were attracted to these areas, which created low-productivity capital but few jobs.

Of more importance has been the increase in government intervention in the labor market, which created damaging rigidities in the wage structure. In addition to specifying minimum wage levels, governments reduced the flexibility of management to change conditions of employment. Employment protection measures often protected incumbents, but at the cost of hindering the creation of new jobs with higher productivity.

Controls and regulations were more common in Europe than in the United States and Japan. The resulting market rigidities and the erosion of incentives were widely acknowledged in the 1970s to be slowing growth in Europe. This weaker performance had important effects on developing countries too. European growth had been an important factor in the growth of world demand in the 1960s. The halving of that growth from the level of the early 1970s was a significant change in the international economy, and it made the problems of adjustment that much more difficult in both Europe and the developing countries.

By the 1980s, as Europe's unemployment rate increased to levels not seen since the 1930s, European governments began gradually loosening controls and regulations. They have also made considerable progress in financial deregulation and in reducing the scope of credit rationing.

• *Protection.* Although the 1980s have seen steps, however slow and hesitant, to dismantle domestic constraints to efficiency, the restrictions on international trade have increased. This reverses the long process of reducing trade restrictions and jeopardizes the principle of nondiscrimination that was pursued so successfully in the 1960s.

Most of the increase in protection has taken the form of nontariff barriers (NTBs). Table 2.5 shows how NTBs on the imports of industrial countries increased between 1981 and 1984. The NTBs in 1984 affected $9.4 billion more imports (based on

---

Box 2.2 Protectionism: who pays?

It is often claimed that tariff and nontariff barriers to trade are justified as a way of saving jobs in domestic industries. But protection has many direct and indirect effects that need to be considered. Nontariff barriers against imports result in higher domestic prices for the products that substitute for imports. Although the domestic industries producing these substitutes may gain, consumers or industrial users of the products lose. The net result is always a loss in real national income, a loss that is variously described by economists as an efficiency loss, a welfare loss, or a deadweight loss. If protection is proposed as a means of saving jobs, then the question arises as to how much real national income needs to be sacrificed to do so.

The efficiency losses or costs of nontariff barriers used by the United States and the EC against imports of clothing, automobiles, and steel have been estimated at well above a billion dollars in each case (see Box

Box table 2.2 Effects of selected nontariff barriers in the clothing, automobile, and steel industries
(millions of dollars, unless otherwise noted)

Effect	Clothing United States, 1980	Clothing EC, 1980	Automobiles, United States, 1984	Steel, United States, 1985
Efficiency loss in the protecting country	1,509	1,409	2,192	1,992
Increased payments on imported goods	988	1,050	1,778	1,530
Loss of consumer surplus on imports	408	289[a]	229	455
Resource cost of producing the additional quantity domestically	113	70	185	7
Jobs saved through protection (thousands)	8.9	11.3	45.0	28.0
Efficiency loss per job saved (thousands of dollars)	169.6	124.7	48.7	71.1
Average labor compensation (thousands of dollars per year)	12.6	13.5	38.1	42.4
Ratio of efficiency loss to average compensation	13.5	9.2	1.3	1.7
Lost revenues for exporters	9,328	7,460	6,050	1,508
Ratio of increased payments on imported goods to lost revenues for exporters	0.11	0.14	0.29	1.01

Note: The nontariff barriers are: for textiles, the Multifibre Arrangement; for automobiles, the voluntary export restraint (VER) agreement between the United States and Japan; and, for steel, the VERs between the United States and major suppliers.
a. Excludes tariff revenues forgone because of quotas.
Source: Kalantzopoulos, ''The Costs of Voluntary Export Restraints'' (background paper).

Table 2.5 Share of imports subject to nontariff barriers in industrial-country markets, 1981 and 1984

| | Percentage of imports from: | | | |
| | Industrial countries | | Developing countries | |
Market	1981	1984	1981	1984
EC	10.3	10.7	21.1	21.7
Japan	12.3	12.4	14.5	14.5
United States	7.2	9.2	12.9	16.1
All industrial countries	10.5	11.3	19.5	20.6

Note: Data are based on 1981 weighted averages for all world trade in all products except fuels. Nontariff barriers do not include administrative protections such as monitoring measures and antidumping and countervailing duties.
Source: World Bank estimates based on UNCTAD data.

table 2.2). However, the number of jobs saved in the protected industries was small, so that the cost per job saved exceeded the average labor compensation in each case. For each job saved in clothing, for example, the U.S. economy as a whole sacrificed about $169,600 to protect a worker earning about $12,600. Clearly, the resources wasted in the process could have been better used in other activities and in retraining and reallocating the affected workers. This example demonstrates that saving jobs is not a tenable defense of protectionism.

It is also sometimes thought that foreign producers do not necessarily lose from nontariff barriers, especially under so-called voluntary export restraints, since those who are able to sell despite the barriers receive higher prices. While the higher prices paid for imports represent a transfer to some foreign producers, non-tariff barriers reduce the volume of imports and thereby lead to losses in the total revenue received by foreign producers. In the case of clothing, for example, the transfer to foreign producers amounted to only one-tenth of their loss of revenue in 1980. Only in the case of steel in 1985 was the price increase large enough to offset the loss in export volume.

Not only is protectionism very costly, it does not assist poorly paid workers. Indeed, it penalizes them. Import restraints are equivalent to a sales tax and often apply to necessities. When they do, they weigh heaviest on those who spend proportionately more of their income on these items: the poor. The impact of such a sales tax on different income groups can be seen by treating the tax as a surcharge on income tax. Box figure 2.2 does so by weighting the price increases caused by protective measures on clothing, sugar, and automobiles in the United States in 1984 by the average amount that different income groups spent on those goods. It shows the regressive effect of the protection tax and the distortionary effect on income distribution.

Existing import restrictions in the United States may amount to as much as a 66 percent surcharge on lower-income families, but only a 5 percent surcharge on higher-income families.

Box figure 2.2 Income tax surcharge equivalent of the cost of tariff protection in the United States, 1984

Income tax surcharge equivalent (percent)[a]

Income group (thousands of dollars per year)
7.0 9.4 11.7 14.1 16.4 18.7 23.4 28.1 35.1 46.8 58.5

Note: Income groups are based on the 1972–73 consumer expenditure survey of the U.S. Department of Labor and are adjusted for consumer price inflation in 1984.
a. Cost of protection as a percentage of income divided by the applicable federal income tax rate.
Source: Hickok 1985.

1981 weighted averages) than did those in place in 1981. Moreover, this figure understates the increase because it takes into account only new restrictions, not the effects of tightening existing ones. Although the NTB coverage for the United States has declined since 1984 as a result of the lifting of voluntary export restraints on Japanese automobiles, the decline has been offset by increased protection for the U.S. steel industry.

Restrictions have been imposed on a larger number of small trade flows from developing countries and a smaller number of large trade flows from industrial countries. In 1984, 20.6 percent of industrial countries' imports from developing countries were subject to NTBs—nearly two times the corresponding figure for imports from industrial countries. This was primarily due to restrictions on the clothing, textile, and footwear exports of developing countries. The tightening of existing NTBs on these items continues to restrict developing countries' most important manufactured exports. But recent NTBs have also been imposed on such products as steel and electrical machinery—products which developing countries are beginning to export. So, while developing countries have been encouraged to open their economies to trade, their access to the markets needed to obtain the most benefit from trade liberalization has been restricted.

It is a widely recognized irony that, although the prosperity and high level of employment of the 1960s were made possible in part by the dismantling of trade restraints, protectionism is now advocated on the grounds that it will create jobs. In point of fact, it will delay recovery, inhibit the creation of jobs, and prolong the decline of uncompetitive industries (see Box 2.2).

 ## The developing countries

In the first half of the 1980s, real GDP growth slowed throughout most of the developing world, and per capita incomes declined in many countries. At the lowest point of the recession, in 1982–83, GDP growth fell to 2.0 percent (see Table 2.6). Although the growth in GDP quickened significantly in 1984, it slowed again in 1985 and during the first part of 1986.

But averages conceal wide differences in individual performances. One of the most worrisome aspects of the early 1980s has been the continued decline in low-income African countries. Inappropriate domestic policies, a weakening of their terms of trade, and reduced capital inflows have resulted in low, and even negative, growth rates. The average annual GDP growth rate for low-income Africa declined from 2.7 percent during 1973–80 to 0.7 percent in 1982 and reached a record low of 0.2 percent in 1983. Although growth picked up in 1984 and 1985, per capita incomes have continued to decline.

Two groups of middle-income countries were also hard hit. First, oil exporters—hitherto protected from external energy shocks, if not from inappropriate domestic policies—faced lower oil prices and falling export volumes. As a result, real GDP, which had grown by 5.8 percent a year in 1973–80, fell by almost 2 percent in 1983 and has grown by less than 3 percent in every year since 1981. Second, heavily indebted countries that had

Table 2.6 Real growth of GDP, 1965–85
(annual percentage change)

Country group	1965–73 average	1973–80 average	1981	1982	1983	1984	1985
Developing countries	6.6	5.4	3.5	2.0	2.0	5.4	4.4
Low-income countries	5.6	4.7	5.0	5.3	7.8	9.4	7.8
Africa	3.9	2.7	1.7	0.7	0.2	0.7	2.1
Asia	5.9	5.0	5.4	5.8	8.6	10.2	8.3
China	7.8	5.4	4.9	7.7	9.6	14.0	10.6
India	4.0	4.1	5.8	2.9	7.6	4.5	4.0
Middle-income oil exporters	7.1	5.8	4.4	1.0	−1.9	2.5	2.5
Middle-income oil importers	7.0	5.5	2.1	0.8	0.8	4.1	3.0
Major exporters of manufactures	7.6	5.9	1.6	1.2	0.8	4.4	3.1
Brazil	9.6	6.8	−1.5	1.0	−3.2	4.5	7.0
Other middle-income oil importers	5.4	4.5	3.4	−0.6	0.8	3.1	2.8
High-income oil exporters	9.2	7.7	1.6	−1.7	−7.1	1.3	−5.0
Industrial market economies	4.7	2.8	1.9	−0.6	2.3	4.6	2.8

Note: Data for developing countries are based on a sample of ninety countries.

24

Table 2.7 Change in export prices and in terms of trade, 1965–85
(annual percentage change)

Country group	1965–73 average	1973–80 average	1981	1982	1983	1984	1985
Change in export prices							
Developing countries							
Food	5.0	9.6	−8.2	−8.8	5.6	2.0	−8.1
Nonfood agriculture	4.2	10.5	−14.4	−8.6	5.7	−2.0	−10.0
Metals and minerals	2.4	4.8	−7.6	−8.5	−0.1	−1.7	−4.9
Fuels	7.9	27.2	12.5	−3.2	−12.4	−2.1	−2.5
Manufactures	7.2	8.1	0.2	−3.2	−2.5	−1.9	1.3
Industrial countries							
Manufactures	5.4	11.0	0.5	−1.4	−2.6	−1.8	1.3
Change in terms of trade							
Low-income countries							
Africa	0.1	−1.8	−11.8	−0.9	4.8	5.0	−5.6
Asia	3.2	−2.4	1.1	1.2	−1.2	1.5	−1.9
Middle-income countries							
Oil exporters	−0.4	8.5	5.4	0.2	−7.7	0.3	−2.9
Oil importers	0.0	−3.0	−4.4	−0.6	2.3	0.1	−0.1
All developing countries	0.8	1.5	−1.0	−0.1	−1.3	0.4	−1.1

Note: Data are based on a sample of ninety developing countries.

not used borrowed funds efficiently were caught by rising interest rates, falling voluntary private lending, and declining export earnings. Per capita incomes and imports fell sharply in some of the biggest debtors, particularly in Latin America.

By contrast, those more outward-oriented economies (such as Korea and Malawi) that maintained domestic macroeconomic stability and adjusted to external changes were soon able to reattain high growth rates after 1982. India and China also continued to grow vigorously, pushing up the overall growth rate for low-income countries in Asia. If India and China are excluded from the low-income Asia group, the average growth rate for the region since 1980 falls to approximately 5.0 percent.

India benefited from domestic policy changes as well as from a large, expanding domestic market and good harvests; these offset, to some degree, fluctuations in the world economy. This was also true in China, but its economy gained more from far-reaching domestic reform. While there are recent signs that the challenge of managing monetary and fiscal policy in a more open economy may have introduced a degree of macroeconomic instability, China's strong growth provides a vivid illustration of the potential gains to be made from undertaking domestic reforms that raise the productivity of existing resources. A detailed analysis of the Chinese policy changes in agriculture is provided in Chapter 5.

In 1984, oil-importing developing countries had

reason to hope for a revival in growth and a remission of the debt problem. World merchandise trade volumes increased by 9 percent. Developing countries increased their export volumes by 10.7 percent and benefited from a slight (0.4 percent) improvement in their terms of trade. For many developing countries the extra export earnings and rescheduling of existing debt permitted the first increase in per capita incomes and imports since 1980. Those countries which had already implemented significant domestic reform programs, particularly the reduction of disincentives to exports, gained most—Mauritius, Thailand, and Turkey, for example.

In 1985, however, the hopes of 1984 were moderated. Slower growth in industrial countries and in world trade reduced the rate of growth of developing-country exports, and commodity prices fell (see Tables 2.7 and 2.8). The expansion in total world merchandise trade slowed markedly to 3 percent, breaking the normal relationship in which total trade expands at a faster rate than total world production. World market prices, particularly of primary commodities, also declined. Overall, the terms of trade for developing countries declined by 1.1 percent in 1985; low-income countries and oil exporters fared the worst. As net capital flows into developing countries also declined, many governments were forced to slow the growth in imports.

Although many developing countries have

Table 2.8 Growth of exports from developing countries, 1965–85
(annual percentage change)

Item	1965–73 average	1973–80 average	1981	1982	1983	1984	1985
Change in export volume by commodity							
Manufactures	11.6	13.8	8.6	0.1	10.0	16.6	3.3
Food	3.3	3.9	9.7	−2.3	−1.1	7.6	3.9
Nonfood agriculture	3.1	1.1	2.5	−1.6	1.5	1.0	4.5
Metals and minerals	4.8	7.0	−2.6	−2.8	0.5	3.4	4.8
Fuels	4.0	−0.8	−9.2	0.6	2.3	7.1	−1.4
Change in export volume by country group							
Low-income countries							
Africa	4.6	1.3	−4.5	−9.3	−0.2	4.9	2.0
Asia	0.6	6.8	9.1	6.3	7.2	6.6	3.8
Middle-income countries							
Oil exporters	4.3	0.0	−7.2	−1.9	3.6	8.6	−0.8
Oil importers	7.1	9.0	7.4	−0.4	5.0	12.8	3.7
All developing countries	5.0	4.6	2.1	−0.5	4.7	10.7	2.3

gained from the recent decline in interest rates and oil prices, the situation for others has worsened considerably. For a group of low-income African countries, the deterioration in their terms of trade, declining private capital flows, and the increasing proportion of their debt that is ineligible for rescheduling have combined to create a serious problem. Things are no better for many middle- and high-income oil exporters, because they bear the direct costs of the rapid decline in oil prices. In addition, the slowdown in their growth rates has had negative effects on those developing countries that supply them with migrant laborers. In some developing countries, remittances from migrant workers are a significant source of foreign exchange earnings. But the reduction in remittances has been mitigated by the lower cost of oil imports and the decline in interest rates.

At the end of 1985, some countries faced considerable short-term constraints on the resources that they could earn or borrow from abroad. As discussed at the end of this chapter, this has serious implications for developing countries in the near term. But in the medium term it is how efficiently resources (whether domestic or foreign) are used which determines a country's economic performance—and this, in turn, depends upon domestic policy. It is to that issue that we now turn.

Domestic policies

Developments in the world economy during the early 1980s have obviously made it more difficult for developing countries both to adjust and to maintain growth in the near term. However,

growth inevitably slows down when adjustment is not undertaken. And, over the longer term, the divergent performance of developing countries faced with similar external trends points to the overriding importance of domestic policy. Those countries that have used external resources to facilitate adjustment to changed external circumstances have been able to resume growth after a brief slowdown. Those that continually borrowed to avoid making changes often found that debt accumulated without contributing to the increased output needed to service it.

Table 2.9 provides one measure of how closely growth is related to domestic policy, as measured by the level of investment and the efficiency with which resources are used. It lists net investment as a proportion of GDP and the capital used per unit of extra output for twenty-four developing economies. The ten economies with the lowest rates of growth had an average rate of net investment of only 10.8 percent of GDP, whereas net investment in the high-growth economies was 18.4 percent. The low-growth economies also used twice as much capital to produce each extra unit of GDP than did the high-growth ones. It was estimated that the inefficient use of resources, measured by the high incremental capital-output ratio, is a more significant determinant of performance for the group of ten low-growth economies than the level of net investment.

The fact that countries in both groups experienced similar changes in their external circumstances indicates that domestic policies are of primary importance in determining performance over the medium term. Previous *World Development Re-*

ports have argued that developing countries benefit if they adopt:

• Stable monetary and fiscal policies—that is, policies necessary to ensure that their budget and current account deficits are sustainable.

• Microeconomic policies that minimize price distortions in goods and factor markets largely by opening the economy to international trade and abandoning discrimination against agriculture.

• Appropriate and stable real exchange rates.

MONETARY AND FISCAL POLICIES. During a recession, public revenues fall and public spending often rises. This increases the budget deficit and the need for extra finance. The more severe the recession—such as that of 1980–82—the more pressing the need. Since 1980, with the exception of 1984, many developing countries have experienced a decline in tax receipts. But many governments could increase their tax receipts without impairing the efficiency of their economies. For example, trade reforms such as replacing quotas with tariffs, auctioning import licenses, and reducing high tariffs and exemptions can often increase revenue and reduce distortions.

How governments raise revenue determines the efficiency effects of the tax system. As in industrial countries, high marginal tax rates can have far-reaching negative effects. Not only do they encourage tax avoidance and the proliferation of tax exemptions, but also they are distortionary and, as a result, do not accomplish the objectives of raising revenues or improving income distribution. In early 1986, Jamaica undertook tax reforms to address these problems. By adopting a single personal income tax rate above a threshold level, the

Table 2.9 Growth, net investment, and capital-output ratio in twenty-four developing economies, 1960–84

Country or territory	Average annual percentage change in GDP per capita[a]	Net investment (as percentage of GDP)[b]	Incremental capital-output ratio[c]
Economies with low growth			
Ghana	−1.7	6.4	12.1
Somalia	−1.0	12.6	8.6
Zambia	−0.5	13.6	7.9
Jamaica	0.3	16.7	13.0
Chile	0.6	11.7	7.4
Peru	0.7	9.8	4.7
Mali	1.0	11.0	4.8
Argentina	1.3	14.0	7.0
Bolivia	1.3	8.8	4.0
Uruguay	1.7	6.0	5.3
Group average	0.4	10.8	7.2
Economies with high growth			
Philippines	2.5	16.8	4.3
Malawi	2.6	17.3	4.3
Colombia	2.7	13.6	3.9
Turkey	3.1	13.8	3.6
Dominican Republic	3.3	12.9	3.1
Mexico	3.4	15.7	3.3
Malaysia	4.3	16.4	3.3
Brazil	4.4	19.3	3.7
Thailand	4.5	17.4	3.3
Greece	4.6	18.2	4.5
Hong Kong	6.1	26.6	3.9
Korea	6.4	17.0	2.7
Botswana	7.3	28.6	3.2
Singapore	7.4	23.8	3.3
Group average	4.5	18.4	3.6

a. The exponential real growth rate per capita averaged over the period.
b. Calculated as gross domestic investment minus depreciation divided by GDP averaged over the period.
c. Calculated as the ratio of the average annual share of gross investment in GDP to the exponential real growth rate of GDP for the period. This ratio cannot be derived from the first two columns because it does not use per capita growth rates or the same definition of investment.
Source: Cavallo, Cottani, and Khan (background paper).

government eliminated high marginal tax rates as well as many complex exemptions. This reduced the distortionary effects of the income tax system and the discrimination against lower income classes. Another desirable reform that many developing countries could undertake is to broaden the tax base away from border taxes (especially on agricultural exports) and simultaneously lower marginal tax rates. This would make their economies more efficient and reduce the impact that volatile commodity prices have on tax revenue.

The main fiscal problem, though, is spending. As in industrial countries, public spending in the developing countries remained high during the early 1980s—and in many cases increased in real terms. In most developing countries increased government expenditures led to record fiscal deficits in 1982 and 1983. Although both spending and deficits have since fallen, even the reduced levels of 1985 are unsustainable in the long run. Spending cuts were often made in the areas of maintenance and investment—which will slow medium-term growth—and many heavily indebted countries are finding it difficult to reduce current expenditures further because of large interest payments on outstanding debts. The burden that this places on the budget is particularly heavy for those economies which failed to direct the previously borrowed funds into efficient activities, which would have increased output and thereby the tax base. As few developing countries have full-fledged bond markets, most governments have financed their budget deficits (after deducting overseas aid) by borrowing from the banking system—or by printing money.

Large increases in the money supply, generated by fiscal deficits, have been the main cause of the rapid increase in inflation in most Latin American and some African and Middle Eastern countries during the 1980s. Governments and central banks have sometimes tried to suppress the symptoms of inflation by overvaluing domestic currencies and controlling prices of politically sensitive goods or services. This has added to the public sector deficit and thus has exacerbated, rather than reduced, inflation. In contrast, some low-income countries in Asia (for example, India and Indonesia) have pursued prudent fiscal and monetary policies and reduced their inflation to more manageable levels.

As in industrial countries, governments in developing ones have found it easier to increase budget spending and the rate of monetary growth than to reduce them. However, as developing countries with high inflation rates have learned, macroeconomic stability is needed to achieve sustained growth. This lesson is particularly relevant to the oil-exporting countries that are struggling to bring public expenditure in line with the recent drop in oil prices and the inevitable decline in public revenues.

At least as important as the level and growth of public spending is the use to which these resources are put. Many overambitious public investment programs included large, expensive projects which yielded low returns. To some extent, the slower growth of developing countries in the 1980s reduced the actual return on some public investments, particularly in the energy field, even though they may have been attractive at the planning stage. But many projects would have had low rates of return even under normal conditions. These projects were not only unproductive in comparison with other projects, but they utilized resources that would have been more productive if directed to operation and maintenance programs. Such programs are essential in keeping the existing capital stock working efficiently. In much of sub-Saharan Africa, the basic infrastructure—highways, waterworks, railroads, and power—is in an alarming state of disrepair.

Cuts in public investment, and ever-larger proportionate decreases in maintenance expenditure, were often the results of the exigencies of stabilization programs. But, just as in industrial countries, many large items of current expenditure were not reduced. These included spending on government employees, defense, and state pensions, as well as transfers and subsidies to state enterprises. One of the main policy issues, therefore, is how to control popular government programs while at the same time ensuring that the essential role of government is performed efficiently.

DISTORTIONS AND GOVERNMENT POLICIES. Since few governments have been able or willing to broaden the tax base, higher public spending has been financed domestically partly by accelerated inflation but mainly by increasing marginal rates of taxation. In developing countries, as Part II argues, the burden of higher marginal tax rates falls heavily on agriculture, either implicitly or explicitly, and domestic manufacturing is often subsidized. This antiagriculture (and often antiexport) bias weakens incentives to invest in a sector in which developing countries are frequently competitive—agriculture. These price distortions are probably most serious in Africa because of overvalued exchange rates and the operation of compulsory marketing schemes for export crops. As China's recent experience has shown, developing countries can attain much faster rates of growth by correcting policy-induced price distortions. Some reforms, such as lower, more uniform tariffs or the abolition of maximum prices on domestically produced staple foods, can be implemented without any loss of tax revenue. Indeed, revenue can be increased.

Labor markets are no less distorted in developing countries than they are in industrial ones. Wage costs to employers in the formal sector have often been raised because of legislative interventions by governments. For example, minimum wage laws and regulations against layoffs, ostensibly designed to protect poorer workers, have benefited (when effective) better-off workers in the formal economy at the expense of output and jobs. Wage indexation has slowed the adjustment of real wages to changes in the terms of trade and has made it harder to reduce inflation.

Although some wage indexation schemes have been dismantled, the reform of labor markets has been slow. High wage costs and subsidized capital, especially in the formal economy, reduce output and encourage the substitution of capital for labor. This not only leads to lower rates of job creation, but also limits growth, because investment is used to substitute for labor rather than to expand capacity.

Nearly all developing countries control interest rates and ration credit according to various "planning priorities." Low interest rates on bank deposits (often below the rate of inflation) depress savings and encourage the holding of physical assets. This stifles the development of the financial sector. In the early 1980s, Mexico provided an example of how much financial markets can suffer. In this period about 60 to 70 percent of credit in Mexico was administratively allocated or subsidized. As a result, most of the credit was channeled to relatively inefficient public enterprises or agricultural programs, and the private sector was left to compete for the remaining smaller share of nonallocated or nonsubsidized credit. This inevitably drove up real interest rates in the "free" market to more than 30 percent, crowding out relatively profitable private sector investments. Distortions in credit markets have been increased by rapid inflation, as the experience in Latin America during the 1970s illustrates, because governments are often reluctant to allow interest rates to rise to a commensurate level.

Many developing countries have recognized the need to reform their credit markets. Reforms usually begin with extra indexation and more frequent adjustment of controlled interest rates. For example, countries such as Argentina, Brazil, and Chile have reduced controls on interest rates. As a result of continued budget deficits, tighter monetary policy, and restricted inflows of foreign savings, interest rates in these countries have risen and are often high in real terms. If supported by credible macroeconomic policies designed to restore and maintain stability, these high rates will encourage the required increase in domestic savings. Adjustment of interest rates on deposits is also necessary to stem capital flight, a significant problem in a number of heavily indebted countries. But, although tentative reforms have been started, few developing countries have capital markets which generate or allocate credit efficiently.

EXCHANGE RATE AND TRADE POLICY. Governments in developing countries intervene in the conduct of international trade and commerce by means of a host of measures such as exchange rate management, import tariffs and restrictions, export taxes, and exchange controls. These trade-affecting policies have a powerful influence on the patterns of domestic production and consumption and thus on efficiency and growth.

Many governments have tried to maintain their official domestic exchange rates—particularly in the face of changing international economic conditions—by supporting them with restrictive trade and exchange controls and foreign borrowing. An overvalued exchange rate depresses the price of tradable goods relative to that of nontraded goods and encourages expansion of the nontraded sector at the expense of the tradable sector. If the government also protects import-competing goods, the disincentive to export production is even stronger.

The case for adjusting the exchange rate to reflect changes in external factors, such as a lasting shift in the terms of trade, seems clear. If the price of a country's exports declines, the preexisting equilibrium in terms of the domestic price level and employment can be maintained only by running down reserves or by borrowing from abroad. If the change in export prices is permanent, this is not a sustainable strategy. If domestic prices and wages do not adjust downward, the exchange rate will have to be devalued. Oil-exporting countries, as they come to grips with the decline in oil prices, face this issue. It is also clear that if the domestic inflation rate is higher than those of one's trading partners, an adjustment in the nominal exchange rate will be needed to maintain competitiveness.

What is less obvious is that domestic policies which seem to be unrelated to the exchange rate may also have a significant effect on the real exchange rate (defined here as the ratio between the price of traded goods and the price of nontraded goods). By changing the relative domestic demand and supply of nontraded and traded goods, commercial policy, monetary and fiscal policy, and capital inflow all affect the real exchange rate. Unless exchange rate policy is compatible with these policies, an unsustainable current account imbalance

---

Box 2.3 Inconsistency in macroeconomic policymaking: the case of the Philippines, 1980–83

In 1980, after a decade of rapid growth, the Philippine economy confronted problems of short-term stabilization and longer-term structural adjustment. The current account deficit (which had been negligible earlier in the decade) rose to 5 percent of GNP by 1979 and was financed mostly by heavy foreign borrowing. High and variable protection diverted resources from agriculture and traditional exports, areas in which the Philippines has a comparative advantage, toward relatively inefficient activities. Growth in GDP was achieved, but at a high cost. Each additional unit of output required about 35 percent more capital than in comparable Asian countries.

These problems were exacerbated by the downturn in the world economy after 1979. The government's ability to delay further adjustment by borrowing more was limited by large existing debt obligations that weakened the country's creditworthiness. In 1980, therefore, the government began to implement a comprehensive series of reforms. One of the main components was a trade liberalization program designed to reduce the level and variance of effective protection to production activities so as to increase efficiency and improve the allocation of resources. The aim was to stimulate exports so that the economy could expand without being constantly constrained by the current account deficit.

By the end of 1982 the government had made progress in implementing the first stage of the program. By reforming import tariffs and adjusting the system of domestic sales taxes (see Box table 2.3), the government had succeeded in lowering effective protection rates (EPRs) and in making them more uniform across activities. Most quantitative restrictions had

been removed on schedule. A number of export promotion schemes had been introduced to offset, to some degree, the remaining bias against exports.

However, beginning in late 1982 the pace of liberalization slackened, and in some cases measures were reversed. Why? Undoubtedly, external factors made adjustment more difficult. By the first quarter of 1984 the Philippines' external terms of trade were 53 percent lower than in 1973 and 16 percent below their previous low in 1977. High interest rates and protectionism in potential export markets worsened the current account balance. But what turned a difficult economic situation into an unsustainable one was the government's domestic macroeconomic policy.

Until 1983, partly because they expected an early resumption of world economic growth, the Philippine authorities continued to expand public spending and to finance it through foreign borrowing. As a result, the budget deficit increased from 1.3 percent of GDP in 1980 to 4.2 percent in 1982, and the current account deficit grew from 5.8 percent in 1980 to 8.0 percent by 1982. Most of the increase in public spending was due to investments made by relatively inefficient public corporations. They accounted for 60 percent of total public investment, and since only 15 percent was financed domestically, large foreign loans were required. As a result, the public sector's share of medium- and long-term debt increased from 50 percent in 1974 to an average of 74 percent in 1979–82.

The government compounded the problems created by its expansionary fiscal policies by adopting an exchange rate which was not consistent with the opening up of the economy. Given the declining terms of trade and the liberalization program, an exchange rate deval-

Box table 2.3 Effective protection rates, 1979 and 1985

Sector	Average EPRs (percent)		Standard deviation	
	1979	1985	1979	1985
All[a]	14	8	53	35
Primary and agricultural	−2	−5	29	21
Manufacturing	27	20	53	32
Exports	−11	−10	15	12
Importables	43	29	104	51

a. EPRs include the effect of sales taxes on protecting domestic production.
Source: Philippine Institute of Development Studies.

will occur, which will have the same effect on an economy as a change in the terms of trade.

A recent study investigated the effects of real exchange rate misalignment and instability on economic performance. The study examined the impact of these two factors on growth, net investment, and exports during the period 1960–83. While it is difficult to define misalignment precisely, in this case a counterfactual example was used to define what the real exchange rate would have been had sustainable domestic policies been pursued. Real exchange rate instability was defined as the coefficient of variation (that is, the variance of the rate relative to its mean). The results are shown in Figures 2.3 and 2.4.

The study found that, on average, a 10 percent increase in the misalignment of the real exchange rate was associated with a GDP growth that was

uation would have been necessary to maintain a sustainable current account. Moreover, since the currency was overvalued before 1980, even holding the real exchange rate at that level would have been inappropriate. But between the first quarters of 1979 and 1984 the real exchange rate appreciated by 17 percent. This undermined the trade reforms. What was needed was real devaluation. A real devaluation would have partially compensated existing efficient manufacturers of import substitutes for the effect of reduced tariffs and, more important, would have provided a uniform stimulus to new exporters and new manufacturers of import substitutes.

The appreciation of the exchange rate and the widening public sector deficit discouraged domestic savings and reduced the flow of controlled credit to the private sector. As expectations of a devaluation increased and the government kept deposit interest rates low, domestic savings declined. As in many other countries, the more obvious it became that the status quo could not be maintained, the greater became the incentive to transfer savings abroad. This, in turn, exacerbated the pressure on the external account.

The inconsistency between the policy of liberalization on the one hand and the monetary, fiscal, and exchange rate policies on the other brought about a crisis in 1983. The government responded by delaying or reversing some of the liberalization measures. In December 1982 a 3 percent import surcharge was imposed as an "emergency" measure. By the end of 1985 it had been increased to 5 percent and an additional 1 percent tax had been imposed on foreign transactions. The second phase of the program to reduce quantitative restrictions on imports was also delayed. The momentum for reducing trade taxes was lost as the government attempted to raise revenue and reduce the growth in imports. Also, although some export incentives were increased, most of the benefits were captured by existing exporters, especially exporters of electronics. As Box table 2.3 shows, the same pattern of distortions remained in 1985, including the strong bias against exports, particularly agricultural and primary goods. Faced with worsening domestic and external deficits, the government attempted to regain control by increasing restrictions and taxes on trade instead of changing the public expenditure and exchange rate policies which had caused the imbalance.

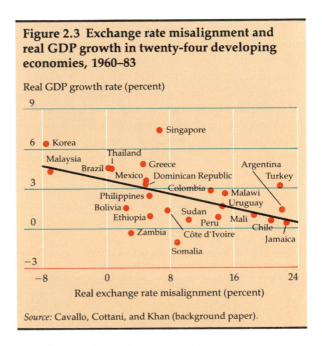

Figure 2.3 Exchange rate misalignment and real GDP growth in twenty-four developing economies, 1960–83

Source: Cavallo, Cottani, and Khan (background paper).

Figure 2.4 Exchange rate instability and net investment in twenty-four developing economies, 1960–83

Source: Cavallo, Cottani, and Khan (background paper).

0.8 percentage points lower and an export growth that was 1.8 percentage points lower than would have prevailed without the increase in misalignment (see Figure 2.3). In high-growth economies such as Korea and Thailand, the real exchange rate was far less out of line than in poor performers such as Jamaica and Ghana, where misalignment (before recent reforms were undertaken) averaged 23 and 73 percent, respectively, for the period 1960–83. For the same group of countries, a 10 percent average increase in the real exchange rate's instability was found to be associated with a reduction of 4.8 percentage points in the net investment ratio (see Figure 2.4).

When the two measures are considered together, they explain more of the variation in the indicators of economic performance. Misalignment seems to be more important than instability in explaining changes in GDP and export growth, while instability seems more important in explaining changes in investment. One would expect this. Exchange rate overvaluation discourages export and GDP growth; investment decisions are affected mainly by uncertainty about relative prices.

The underlying message is simple: a flexible exchange rate policy is critical if the economy is to adjust and resources are to be allocated and used efficiently. Those developing countries that do not allow their exchange rates to change will be forced to resort to other measures, such as trade barriers or foreign exchange controls, to avoid running down reserves. This will lead to wasted resources and efficiency losses. Indeed, a number of countries, particularly in Latin America, have recently improved their exchange rate policies significantly. Nevertheless, although permitting the exchange rate to adjust is necessary to maintain the openness of an economy, it cannot substitute for adjustment in other policies. If the cause of an unstable macroeconomic situation is monetary or fiscal policy, that is where reforms must be made (see Box 2.3).

In addition to managing their exchange rates, many developing countries impose a complex array of taxes and quantitative controls on imports and (to a lesser extent) exports. These trade policy measures are directed at such goals as protecting domestic industries, raising revenue, and shoring up international reserves. They create an unstable set of disparate incentives that cut across a broad range of domestic production activities and consumption goods. But within this variability is a ba-

Table 2.10 Change in U.S. interest rates and the export prices of developing countries, 1978–85

Item	1978	1979	1980	1981	1982	1983	1984	1985
Six-month dollar LIBOR	9.5	12.1	14.3	16.6	13.3	9.9	11.2	8.7
Export price index (percentage change)								
Oil exporters	3.2	36.6	46.3	6.3	−4.4	−9.2	−1.0	−3.6
Oil importers[a]	3.8	19.4	12.0	−2.1	−4.8	−1.0	−1.3	−1.6
U.S. GDP deflator (percentage change)	6.7	8.5	8.9	9.2	6.0	3.8	3.8	3.5
U.S. real interest rate[b]	2.6	3.3	5.0	6.8	6.9	5.9	7.4	5.2

a. Includes China.
b. Defined as six-month dollar LIBOR deflated by the U.S. GDP deflator.

Table 2.11 Debt indicators for developing countries, 1980–85
(percent)

Indicator	1980	1981	1982	1983	1984	1985
Ratio of debt to GNP	21.1	22.8	26.8	31.8	32.7	33.0
Ratio of debt to exports	90.1	97.5	116.4	134.3	130.4	135.7
Debt service ratio	16.1	17.7	20.7	19.4	19.8	21.9
Ratio of debt service to GNP	3.8	4.1	4.7	4.6	5.0	5.3
Ratio of interest service to exports	7.0	8.3	10.4	10.0	10.5	11.0
Total debt outstanding and disbursed (billions of dollars)	431.6	492.5	552.4	629.9	674.1	711.2
Private debt as a percentage of total debt	63.3	64.5	64.9	66.1	65.7	64.5

Note: Data are based on a sample of ninety developing countries.

Table 2.12 New commitments to public and publicly guaranteed borrowers in developing countries 1978–84
(billions of dollars)

Item	1978	1979	1980	1981	1982	1983	1984
All developing countries							
Total commitments	83.7	95.1	93.1	103.0	99.2	87.2	69.9
Private source	53.4	64.0	50.1	64.2	61.4	49.6	36.3
Official source	30.3	31.0	42.9	38.8	37.7	37.6	33.6
Bilateral	16.5	16.4	23.5	19.5	17.4	16.2	13.6
Multilateral	13.8	14.6	19.4	19.3	20.3	21.4	20.0
Low-income Africa							
Total commitments	3.8	4.5	5.2	3.7	3.6	3.1	3.0
Private source	1.1	1.6	1.5	0.8	0.5	0.2	0.4
Official source	2.8	2.9	3.8	2.9	3.1	2.9	2.6
Bilateral	1.6	1.4	1.9	1.2	1.4	1.4	0.9
Multilateral	1.2	1.5	1.9	1.7	1.7	1.5	1.7
Heavily indebted countries[a]							
Total commitments	50.8	62.2	54.6	79.0	61.7	41.8	29.9
Private source	42.4	54.4	44.7	65.9	49.2	28.7	20.1
Official source	8.4	7.8	9.9	13.1	12.5	13.1	9.7
Bilateral	3.6	2.5	4.5	5.9	5.0	4.7	3.5
Multilateral	4.8	5.3	5.4	7.2	7.5	8.4	6.2

a. Argentina, Bolivia, Brazil, Chile, Colombia, Costa Rica, Côte d'Ivoire, Ecuador, Jamaica, Mexico, Morocco, Nigeria, Peru, Philippines, Uruguay, Venezuela, and Yugoslavia. These countries accounted for nearly half of all developing countries' debt at the end of 1985.

sic pattern of encouraging manufacturing activities relative to agriculture and import substitution activities relative to exports.

There is a convincing body of quantitative evidence from cross-country studies that developing countries with less distorted trade policy regimes (particularly those that are less biased against exports) have fared better in terms of growth performance, coping with external shocks, and employment creation. Recognition of this has encouraged some reappraisal of trade policies and led to certain reforms to promote efficiency and growth. The basic objectives are to simplify and unify trade incentives and, most important, to reduce the biases against agriculture and exports. The reforms generally involve a commitment to follow a more appropriate exchange rate policy and to implement an import liberalization program. Components of such a program should include the removal of quantitative restrictions on imports and lower, more uniform tariffs and other charges on imports.

The international environment

At the root of the poor performance and debt problems of developing countries lies their failure to adjust to the external developments that have taken place since the early 1970s, coupled with the magnitude of the external shocks. Many develop-

ing countries tried to offset the effects of external shocks, higher inflation, and lower growth by borrowing more, mostly at short-term maturities and floating rates. The shift in favor of commercial bank lending at floating rates in the 1970s left developing countries vulnerable to an increase in interest rates and to reductions in the volume of private lending. The 1979 oil price increase and the recession of the early 1980s exposed these weaknesses.

The monetary and fiscal policy mix pursued by industrial countries after 1979 drove interest rates up at the same time that the export prices for many developing countries declined. In 1982, oil-importing developing countries were paying a nominal rate of interest of around 13 percent for commercial loans while their export prices declined by 5 percent (see Table 2.10). These external developments made the process of stabilization and adjustment that much more difficult (see Box 2.4).

As interest rates rose and developing countries continued to borrow, their creditworthiness indicators deteriorated. Between 1980 and 1982, the proportion of debt to GNP rose from 21.1 percent to 26.8 percent; that of debt to exports rose from 90.1 percent to 116.4 percent; and the debt service ratio (interest payments plus amortization as a percentage of exports) increased from 16.1 percent to 20.7 percent (see Table 2.11). Although the ratio of

Box 2.4   Reacting to a debt crisis

''The international debt crisis'' is a threadbare phrase, but it does express the fact that although many different countries have experienced debt problems, their experiences have certain features in common. At the same time, differences in the ways countries have reacted (or failed to react) to these problems suggest guidelines for policymakers in the future. A debt crisis usually has its origin in an unusually large inflow of capital. This inflow adds to total spending and pushes GDP beyond the level that would be achieved with domestic resources alone. As capital flows in, the trade account moves into deficit and the real exchange rate tends to appreciate.

The onset of a debt crisis occurs when these movements are sharply reversed. The reduced capital inflow requires a corresponding improvement in the balance of trade, which is brought about in part through a reduction in spending and in part through a real exchange rate depreciation.

Box figure 2.4A shows how in four countries the real exchange rate fell during the period of capital inflow and increasing trade deficit and then rose as the trade balance improved in response to a debt crisis. Also, as Box figure 2.4B shows, real GDP rose to a peak during the period of large capital inflows, then fell sharply as the country adjusted to the reduction in these flows. These oscillations partly reflect the direct impact of foreign capital on GDP, but the decline in GDP is also associated with the tighter monetary and fiscal policies adopted in an attempt to improve the trade balance.

The triple pressure—from reduced capital flows, tighter macroeconomic policies, and a falling real exchange rate—produced a sharp decline in the volume of imports in all four countries (see Box figure 2.4B). In the short term, imports tend to bear the brunt of the trade account's adjustment because exports respond only with a lag.

Different countries' exports responded differently in the wake of a debt crisis, the story here being complicated by other factors such as weather cycles and world price movements of principal export commodities. Thus, Argentina's export volumes rose by 10 percent in the first year of adjustment (1981), only to fall back to near their 1980 levels in the following two years. Chile's exports stayed roughly constant in volume terms, despite a substantial real devaluation, mainly because of declining world copper prices. The exports of Mexico and the Philippines grew, but only moderately, in the years following their debt crises (1982 and 1983, respectively).

One important difference among countries that faced a debt crisis is the way in which inflation impinged on their adaptation to the crisis. Box table 2.4 summarizes the experience of eleven countries. It shows the maximum real exchange rate devaluation achieved by each country as it adjusted to the crisis (column 3). It also

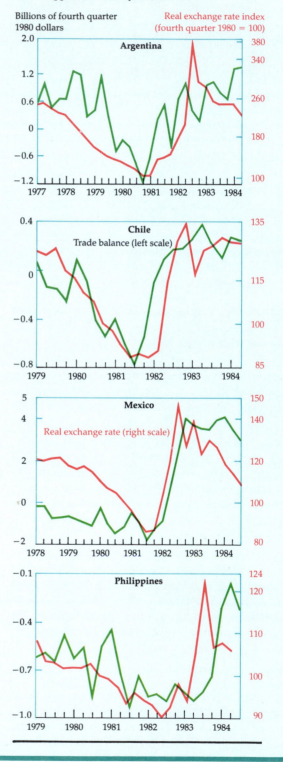

Box figure 2.4A Movements in the trade balance and real exchange rate in Argentina, Chile, Mexico, and the Philippines, selected years, 1977–84

shows the contemporaneous rise in the consumer price index (column 4). Since a devaluation of the nominal exchange rate increases the internal prices of tradable goods, it is almost inevitable that a large devaluation will entail a rise in the general price index. (Otherwise, a major fall in the prices of nontradable goods would be required.) The policy challenge is to limit this price rise. The figures in column 5 can be taken as an index of how successfully different countries met this challenge. Venezuela, the Philippines, Uruguay, and Chile were the most successful; Argentina, Bolivia, Peru, and Brazil saw inflation increase more than might be expected from the extent of their real devaluations.

Box table 2.4 Real devaluation and inflation in countries that faced a debt crisis

| Country | Time periods being compared (year and quarter) | | Ratio of real exchange rate[a] (3) | Ratio of CPI[b] (4) | Inflation relative to real devaluation[c] (5) |
	Precrisis trough (1)	Postcrisis peak (2)			
Argentina	1980 IV	1984 I	2.57	53.34	20.75
Bolivia	1982 III	1984 II	1.59	18.83	11.85
Brazil	1982 III	1984 III	1.48	7.23	4.89
Chile	1982 I	1984 III	1.45	1.61	1.11
Mexico	1981 IV	1983 III	1.50	3.13	2.08
Peru	1982 I	1984 III	1.11	5.86	5.28
Philippines	1982 III	1983 IV	1.36	1.19	0.87
Portugal	1979 III	1983 III	1.48	2.15	1.45
Turkey	1979 IV	1984 II	1.92	5.65	2.94
Uruguay	1982 III	1984 II	2.00	2.09	1.05
Venezuela	1983 II	1984 II	1.74	1.11	0.64

a. Measured from peak to trough.
b. Consumer price index at peak divided by consumer price index at trough.
c. Column (4) divided by column (5).
Source: Harberger, ''Reacting to a Debt Crisis'' (background paper).

Box figure 2.4B Changes in real GDP and real imports in Argentina, Chile, Mexico, and the Philippines, selected years, 1978–84

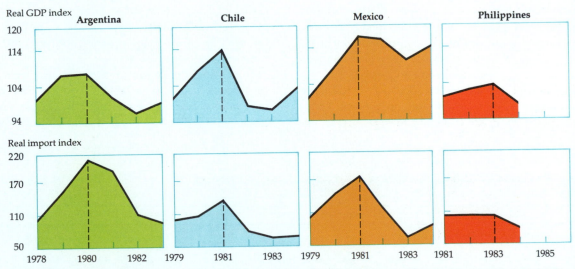

Note: The GDP index is calculated from *International Financial Statistics* data with the starting year equal to 100. The real import index is calculated by deflating nominal imports by an SDR-weighted index of wholesale prices of major industrial countries. The broken line indicates the onset of the debt crisis.
Source: IMF *International Financial Statistics,* various years.

debt to exports improved slightly in 1984, all the major creditworthiness indicators deteriorated again in 1985, primarily because the drop in export earnings exceeded the benefits derived from lower interest rates.

The deteriorating creditworthiness of developing countries did not go unobserved by creditors. By 1982 they had become reluctant to extend new loans to public borrowers. Table 2.12 provides estimates of new loan commitments to all developing countries. It also splits out two of the most vulnerable subgroups—low-income Africa and the most heavily indebted developing countries. New commitments of capital from private sources to all developing countries declined from a peak of $64.2 billion in 1981 to $36.3 billion by 1984. The onus of most of the reduction fell on the most heavily indebted developing countries. For this subgroup new private commitments fell by more than two-thirds between 1981 and 1984. Official new commitments to all developing countries also declined during this period, from $38.8 billion to $33.6 billion, principally because of reductions in bilateral commitments. It should be noted, however, that the data in Table 2.12 understate the amount of long-term lending actually made, because the table excludes new loans that are made when existing obligations are rescheduled.

The heavily indebted middle- and low-income developing countries became unable to service their debts normally. The causes and circumstances varied from country to country, as the contrast between Brazil, Mexico, and Turkey demonstrates. But attempts to restore macroeconomic stability and growth had certain policy components in common. Because an improvement in export performance in response to policy changes can take time, countries began addressing their severe external imbalances by focusing on reducing spending, particularly spending on imports. Many countries embarked on stabilization programs, of-

ten with assistance of the International Monetary Fund (IMF). Policies designed to reduce government expenditure, increase taxes, realign the exchange rate, and restrict credit were implemented to move the economy toward internal and external balance in the near term.

As a result, there was a sharp reduction in the overall current account deficit of developing countries, from the trough of $105.6 billion in 1981 to $34.1 billion in 1984 and $40.6 billion by 1985 (see Table 2.13). Initially, this was achieved mainly by a drastic reduction in imports. The adjustment of the external account followed partly from necessary adjustments in exchange rates and cuts in public spending, but also partly from a more worrisome increase in import restrictions and tighter rationing of private sector credit. Toward the end of the period, however, particularly in 1984, the increase in exports brought about by exchange rate adjustments and trade policy reforms made a significant contribution to reducing the external deficit. The buoyant world economy in 1984 supported this adjustment effort.

But during 1985 a combination of adverse developments in the world economy and, in some cases, inappropriate domestic policies hindered further progress. Even those economies that had made credible policy changes continued to face considerable problems in restoring growth. Because debtors needed to run trade surpluses to service their debts, slower growth in industrial countries and the larger relative decline in the growth of world trade volumes in 1985 made it difficult to expand exports. Because export prices also declined, many developing countries attempted to adjust by contracting imports and domestic investment further.

The overall decline in developing countries' export prices is shown in Table 2.7. Since 1980, non-oil commodity prices have fallen by 26 percent in dollar terms, or by 23 percent relative to the price

Table 2.13 Current account balance in developing countries, 1980–85
(billions of dollars)

Country group	1980	1981	1982	1983	1984	1985
Low-income countries	−15.5	−12.5	−6.7	−4.3	−7.9	−22.0
Africa	−5.8	−6.3	−5.5	−4.4	−4.6	−5.1
Asia	−9.7	−6.2	−1.2	0.1	−3.3	−16.9
Middle-income oil exporters	1.5	−27.3	−35.8	−11.0	−1.9	−5.5
Middle-income oil importers	−53.8	−65.8	−57.9	−37.1	−24.3	−13.0
All developing countries	−67.8	−105.6	−100.4	−52.4	−34.1	−40.6

Note: Data for developing countries are based on a sample of ninety countries. Data for 1984 and 1985 are provisional estimates. The current account balance excludes official transfers.

Table 2.14 Public and private long-term capital flows to developing countries, 1975 and 1980–85

(billions of dollars)

Country group and item	1975	1980	1981	1982	1983	1984	1985
All developing countries							
Disbursements	46.4	102.6	121.9	115.5	95.3	86.8	92.9
From private creditors	31.4	75.3	91.4	84.2	64.8	54.3	55.5
Principal repayments	15.8	43.8	47.3	49.3	42.8	46.8	57.4
Net flows	30.6	58.9	74.6	66.2	52.5	40.0	35.5
Low-income Africa							
Disbursements	2.0	4.2	4.0	3.3	3.0	2.5	3.4
From private creditors	0.8	1.6	1.3	0.9	0.6	0.3	1.7
Principal repayments	0.4	0.8	0.8	0.9	0.8	1.0	2.0
Net flows	1.6	3.4	3.1	2.3	2.2	1.4	1.4
Heavily indebted countries[a]							
Disbursements	21.3	53.1	69.0	57.6	38.3	32.5	31.9
From private creditors	17.3	45.9	60.5	48.3	28.8	22.6	18.5
Principal repayments	8.9	24.7	26.1	25.7	18.1	18.2	21.8
Net flows	12.4	28.4	42.9	31.8	20.2	14.3	10.1

Note: Data for 1984 and 1985 are provisional estimates of amounts paid, not amounts due. Private nonguaranteed debt has been estimated where not reported by a country. Official grants are excluded. Data are based on a sample of ninety developing countries.
a. Argentina, Bolivia, Brazil, Chile, Colombia, Costa Rica, Côte d'Ivoire, Ecuador, Jamaica, Mexico, Morocco, Nigeria, Peru, Philippines, Uruguay, Venezuela, and Yugoslavia. These countries accounted for nearly half of all developing countries' debt at the end of 1985.

of manufactures. This fall can be attributed to slower growth in demand from industrial countries, the strength of the dollar until early 1985, and high real interest rates that increased the cost of holding inventories. The fall in agricultural prices has been accentuated by large increases in the supply of agricultural raw materials, which were triggered in part by price support measures and trade protection in industrial countries. The fall in the price of metals has reflected worldwide overcapacity and, in some cases (tin, for example), the breakdown of previous agreement among producers to constrain supply and inventory levels. But the decline in the price of primary commodities relative to the price of manufactures also reflects an underlying trend toward more efficient use of materials and increased substitution of synthetics. Cyclical fluctuations do, however, play an important role; since 1980, with the exception of 1984, their effect has generally been unfavorable.

In addition, net long-term capital flows to developing countries have continued to decline since 1981 (see Table 2.14). By 1985, net long-term inflows were approximately $35.5 billion, down 52 percent from the $74.6 billion reached in 1981. For the group of heavily indebted countries, the decline has been approximately 76 percent, from $42.9 billion in 1981 to an estimated $10.1 billion in

1985. Net flows to low-income Africa have been cut to less than half their 1981 level, dropping from $3.1 billion to $1.4 billion. In the case of low-income Africa, however, official grants remain important—these increased slightly, from $3.2 billion in 1981 to $3.3 billion in 1984.

In real terms, the drop in net capital flows was even larger. In addition, total interest payments by developing countries on external public and private long-term debt amounted to $57.6 billion in 1985 (up from $41.8 billion in 1981), which represented 11 percent of their export earnings. Thus, developing countries paid out approximately $22 billion more in long-term debt service in 1985 than they received in disbursements of long-term lending. The heavily indebted countries accounted for most of this net transfer.

In response to the growing debt problems of developing countries, rescheduling agreements increased markedly in both number and value in 1983 (see Figure 2.5). The dip in the value of reschedulings recorded in 1984 reflects the slippage of several agreements that were agreed to in principle in that year but not signed until 1985. As a result, reschedulings reached a record value of $93 billion in 1985. The most prominent example was Mexico's $49 billion multiyear rescheduling agreement (MYRA). Important agreements were also

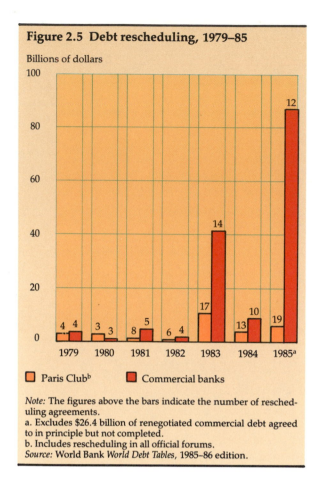

Figure 2.5 Debt rescheduling, 1979–85

Billions of dollars

□ Paris Club[b]   ■ Commercial banks

Note: The figures above the bars indicate the number of rescheduling agreements.
a. Excludes $26.4 billion of renegotiated commercial debt agreed to in principle but not completed.
b. Includes rescheduling in all official forums.
Source: World Bank *World Debt Tables,* 1985–86 edition.

concluded for Argentina, Chile, Ecuador, and the Philippines.

Yet, the underlying pace of rescheduling agreements with private creditors has slackened in comparison with 1983. Of the eleven reschedulings that had been agreed to in principle in 1984 but not completed, only three were signed in 1985. It is clear that some major debtors still have a long way to go in restoring their access to voluntary commercial lending.

The debt overhang

Monetary and fiscal reforms, the reduction of distortions to minimize efficiency losses, and appropriate exchange rate policies—all these are parts of a necessary process of long-term adjustment for developing countries. But the pressing short-run problems of some developing countries have led them to undertake major adjustments quickly. In addition, some countries have adopted policies that have produced often unnecessary conflicts between short-term stabilization and longer-term growth.

Partly as a result of unavoidable stabilization measures, real wages have declined at the same time that interest payments on public debt have increased. This has made it difficult for either individuals or governments to increase gross domestic savings. Since many countries have also had their access to foreign savings curtailed, gross domestic investment has been reduced. This will retard recovery over the medium term, even if policy changes create profitable investment opportunities. In addition, despite high interest payments, some governments have not reduced other items of public expenditure in line with declining national income. The resulting budget deficit has led to tighter credit rationing or higher real interest rates and thus has exacerbated the crowding out of profitable private investment. It has also been observed that higher import tariffs have often been applied to raise tax revenue as well as to reduce the trade deficit. But this lowers the relative incentives to export, thereby reducing the export growth required to restore creditworthiness. In some cases the distortions have been made worse by recourse to additional export taxes as a quick and easy source of government revenue.

The problems are particularly serious in low-income Africa. Export earnings have fallen at a time when private capital inflows and domestic savings have slumped. So, on top of the rapid population growth and inefficient use of investment that characterized much of low-income Africa throughout the 1970s has been added an absolute shortage of savings in the early 1980s. The resulting decline in productive investment is jeopardizing future growth. As the next chapter argues, special efforts are needed to reform institutions and incentives in many African countries, and these reforms must be supported by a coordinated international effort to increase resource flows.

The so-called debt overhang is restricting the access of many heavily indebted countries that are undertaking credible economic reforms to the resources needed to increase investment and stimulate growth. The recent fall in the price of oil, though it has helped oil importers, has worsened matters for those major debtors—Indonesia, Mexico, Nigeria, and Venezuela—that depend heavily on crude oil exports. It lowers their immediate export earnings and weakens their ability to attract more commercial capital.

Thus, many developing countries enter the second half of the 1980s confronted with the problem of how to stabilize and restore growth within, what is for some, an inhospitable world environment. The lower interest rates and declining oil prices have undoubtedly helped many developing countries in 1985 and the first half of 1986. But the slower growth in world trade, declining or stagnant export prices, increased trade barriers, and reduced net capital inflows have overwhelmed these gains for many others. Those developing countries that have not attempted to stabilize their economies, or have faltered mid-course, will have to press ahead with the types of policy reform discussed in this chapter. But, in any event, domestic reform efforts will succeed more readily in an improved international environment. Sustained growth—of the type experienced in the 1960s—can be achieved. But it will take a commitment to policy reform by both developing and industrial countries and a reduction in international trade restrictions. The policies and international initiatives needed to attain adjustment with growth are the subjects of Chapter 3.

3

Opportunities for growth

As growth slows, governments turn their attention to reviving it—and to addressing the problems that slower growth creates. Developing countries have taken many steps to improve their economic performance and to adjust to the changing international economic environment. But as they look ahead to the rest of this decade and beyond, they recognize that there is room for further improvement. Better policies are especially needed because the international environment is fraught with uncertainty. Commodity prices are depressed, real interest rates are still above historical levels, and the debt service burden imposes serious constraints on many countries' long-term prospects for growth.

As the economies of the world become increasingly interdependent, future prospects for the world economy depend upon the policies that both the industrial and developing countries adopt. This chapter describes two possible paths for the world economy during the next ten years and the policies that might bring them about. Both High and Low cases presuppose the same moderate improvements in the economic policies of developing countries. However, if the pace of reform were to quicken, or if more countries were to implement corrective policies, the average growth rates for developing countries would exceed our estimates in each case. As the recent success of countries as diverse as Turkey and China illustrates, it is the developing countries' own policies that determine how much they can take advantage of, or offset, changes in the world economy.

Developing countries cannot assume a stable or favorable external environment. It is, therefore, important to outline the kinds of policy which would improve their ability to adapt to unpredictable circumstances and to use capital flows most productively to sustain growth over the medium term.

Policies for growth in developing countries

A useful way to approach this issue is to consider the distinction between stabilization policies and structural adjustment policies. Stabilization policies include the monetary, fiscal, exchange rate, and incomes policies that governments use to maintain macroeconomic balance. Structural adjustment policies concern those things which influence production, trade, and distribution decisions: changes in incentives, government institutions, and the rules governing property rights, liability, and information. Obviously, the two sets of policies overlap and can complement each other. An exchange rate adjustment not only stabilizes the current account but also will increase the share of exports in domestic output. Similarly, restructuring a public enterprise may improve its efficiency and also reduce the public sector deficit.

Sometimes the two policies work against each other. A rapid reduction in distortionary trade taxes can, if there are no new revenue-raising measures, increase the budget deficit in the short run. Unless macroeconomic policy is consistent with longer-term structural aims, governments run the risk of having to reverse or abandon policy reforms for the wrong reasons. The Philippines is a case in point (see Box 2.3 in Chapter 2).

While the exact mix of appropriate policies varies from country to country, the overall aim is to restore and maintain economic stability while simultaneously improving the incentive and institutional structure to encourage domestic savings and the efficient allocation of resources. Whether the initial problems are caused by unsustainable domestic policies (for example, a large fiscal deficit), sudden changes in the external environment (such as a drop in the price of oil), or a combination of both, the sooner the economy can be stabilized, taking due account of adjustment costs, the greater its ability to deal with subsequent shocks. If budget deficits or external imbalances are allowed to continue unchecked, the country will be forced to run down its foreign exchange reserves and exhaust its access to foreign borrowing. Once this happens, domestic demand can no longer be maintained above income. Given such a situation, governments have only two options: to address the fundamental policy issues or to further constrain growth. And they must do something without delay. The flexibility provided by access to foreign borrowing will have been lost because of past policy errors.

An example is provided by those countries in sub-Saharan Africa and elsewhere that failed to adjust spending after the commodity price boom in the mid-1970s. They continued to maintain exchange rates and spending (especially public investment) at levels which were sustainable only if export prices quickly returned to previous peak levels. But commodity prices did not rise, and, moreover, these countries soon had to cope with the second oil shock, high real interest rates, and a worldwide recession. This would have been a burden under any circumstances, but many countries had already exhausted their access to short-term capital and depleted their foreign exchange reserves.

Other countries have demonstrated the longer-term benefits of implementing policies which quickly restore macroeconomic stability. Indonesia faced the prospect of sharply declining income in the early 1980s. Oil prices began to weaken, world growth slowed, and capital flight began to put pressure on the current account. The government quickly cut subsidies to oil consumers, canceled or postponed nearly fifty import-intensive investment projects, devalued the currency, and shifted to a managed float. Zero real GDP growth in 1982 was followed by a 3.3 percent growth rate in 1983 and growth rates of 6.6 percent in 1984 and 1985. The current account deficit as a proportion of GDP declined from 8.5 percent in 1982 to 2.5 percent in 1984.

Turkey provides an example of a country where domestic policies, as opposed to a sudden change in external circumstances, created an unsustainable macroeconomic position that slowed growth until corrective action was taken. Throughout the 1970s the government pursued expansionary monetary and fiscal policies, financed the current account deficits with heavy foreign borrowing, and protected domestic industry with high import barriers. When it could no longer borrow abroad, the government implemented a comprehensive policy package designed to both restore domestic stability and restructure the economy over the medium term. Exchange rate adjustment accompanied by tighter monetary and fiscal policies restored stability. This created the conditions needed to support the structural adjustment policies, the objectives of which were to open up the economy, increase efficiency, and stimulate growth. As a result, between 1980 and 1984, Turkey increased the dollar value of its merchandise exports by 120 percent at a time when world non-oil exports rose by only about 5 percent. The average annual real GDP growth increased to 4.6 percent during this period.

This example illustrates the point that stabilization is not an end in itself. Rather, stabilization policies should be thought of as facilitating measures in the transition toward a new framework which permits a higher, but sustainable, rate of economic growth. Once domestic stability is restored, growth needs to be stimulated by policies that encourage increased savings and investment, greater efficiency, and higher productivity.

Structural adjustment policies focus on changing institutions and incentives. The main objectives should be (a) to mobilize resources by raising the domestic savings rate, attracting foreign capital, and, if necessary, reversing capital flight; (b) to allocate resources more efficiently and raise the productivity of the existing capital stock; and (c) to create employment and income in areas where the economy has a comparative advantage.

Domestic savings

If investment is to be restored to the level required to sustain growth while debt obligations are met, many developing countries will have to increase domestic savings. Ultimately, an increase in domestic savings depends on the government's commitment to adopt the policies needed to establish a stable macroeconomic environment. Reduced budget deficits, an appropriate rate of monetary growth, and stable real exchange rates will do much to stimulate savings. Such policies would also deter and, it is hoped, reverse the transfer of domestic savings abroad. Capital flight has become endemic in many economies with inappropriate exchange and interest rates. A reversal of this process will provide a clear and important signal to foreign investors and commercial banks that the nationals within a country have had their confidence in the economy restored by credible government policies.

With respect to public savings, governments have two fundamental options: they can either reduce expenditures or raise revenues. Many developing countries could reduce public spending without slowing economic growth or adversely affecting the poor. This would entail such measures as reducing military spending, improving public sector wage and pricing policies, reducing and reallocating current expenditures, and improving the efficiency of the public sector. For example, many developing countries would benefit if they increased public utility (electricity, water, gas) and transport charges to reflect the long-term opportunity costs and rationalized their agricultural support programs. A higher level of efficiency in the public sector could be attained by management and institutional reforms designed to improve the planning and budgeting process and to strengthen the degree of public sector accountability.

An important potential source of public sector savings is reduced expenditures on loss-making and inefficient public enterprises. For example, in Argentina the 353 state-owned enterprises lose an estimated $2 billion annually and hold about $11 billion of the country's $46 billion foreign debt. Many countries in sub-Saharan Africa could also gain by eliminating the deficits associated with parastatals; they should close down the worst and introduce reforms to increase the efficiency and accountability of the remainder. There is also considerable scope for rationalizing the public sector through divestiture. This would provide a one-time increase in public savings and improve resource allocation over the medium term.

Governments can also raise public savings by increased taxation (including the inflation tax). Increased taxation, where unavoidable, needs to be formulated in such a way as to minimize the efficiency losses and tax evasion effects discussed earlier. Furthermore, the decline in per capita consumption levels in many Latin American and African countries means that the positive effect that an increase in taxation may have on the budget deficit must be weighed against the negative effect it will have on real income levels. There is, however, scope for raising revenues by reforming and improving the tax administration. This includes measures designed to simplify the tax system—with fewer exemptions or allowances and

increased penalties for evasion—and broaden the tax base.

Private savings could also be encouraged by tax reform. By limiting the taxation of interest payments to inflation-adjusted receipts and by reducing marginal tax rates, personal savings can be increased. This should be supported by the removal of distortions in credit markets, particularly through proper interest rate policies on deposits. A recent World Bank review of financial sector policies in Bangladesh, Kenya, Nigeria, Peru, Thailand, Turkey, and Uruguay suggested that in many cases the elimination of government control of interest rates and bank fees and increased competition among financial institutions would improve financial intermediation and increase private financial savings. These measures would also limit the outflow of capital. But, to return to our opening point, the restoration of private sector confidence is crucial to raising domestic savings rates.

The level and efficiency of investment

The method by which many developing countries adjusted to the changing external environment of the early 1980s led to a considerable fall in domestic investment. Policies designed to reverse this trend and, more important, to increase the efficient allocation and utilization of investment are necessary to sustain growth over the medium term.

With respect to public investment, those cuts that have scaled down or eliminated low-return projects (such as the Majes irrigation scheme in Peru or the extension of the metro systems in Chile and Colombia) have clearly been beneficial to the economies involved. Before the 1980s, the quality of public investments in many developing countries was at best mixed. Some governments, however, are unable or unwilling to make selective cuts. Public investment programs have often been reduced by damaging across-the-board cuts. There would, therefore, be considerable efficiency gains from creating the institutional capability to systematically evaluate projects at the planning stage and to allocate adequate resources toward maintenance and rehabilitation after the projects are completed.

Adjustment to a lower level of (more efficient) public investment could also be achieved by having government draw a clearer distinction between what is, and what is not, appropriate for public sector involvement. Many developing countries stand to gain from reducing and preventing further public sector investment in activities where the private sector has a comparative advantage (for example, production and marketing activities in industry, energy, and agriculture). Public investment should be directed toward activities with externalities and long payback periods (for example, human resource development and physical infrastructure).

Governments can contribute further to increasing the efficiency of investment—and to reducing unemployment and alleviating poverty—by creating a policy environment which will encourage foreign and domestic private investment. For private investment to be efficient, governments need to provide a set of clear and nondiscriminatory policies over an extended time period. This would include many of the policies discussed earlier: trade policy reform, reduced administrative controls, a less distortionary tax system, removal of distortions in labor and capital markets, changes and clarification of foreign investment codes, and so forth. Furthermore, in many heavily indebted countries, such as Argentina, Brazil, Chile, and Mexico, a major disincentive to new private investment has been the record level of real interest rates in recent years. These high rates reflect both inflationary expectations and the pressure exerted on credit markets by the need to finance large budget deficits and preferential credit programs for sectors such as agriculture. Breaking inflationary expectations and reducing government borrowing will contribute greatly to a lowering of real interest rates and will thereby stimulate private investment. The recent monetary and fiscal reforms adopted in Argentina and Brazil represent serious attempts to tackle this problem.

Policies to stimulate exports

There is a strong link between an economy's international trade and exchange rate regime and the flexibility required to maintain growth. A competitive exchange rate and a fairly neutral trade and tax system tend to limit excessive foreign borrowing and encourage exports and efficient import substitution. Countries which sell on world markets can exploit economies of specialization, size, and scale. This helps to create efficient producers who are competitive both at home and abroad. In inward-oriented economies, producers are limited to selling their goods in small, highly protected domestic markets. The level of public investment in inward-oriented economies tends to be higher to compen-

sate for a somnolent private sector—and much of that public investment is misallocated because of the distorted incentive system. Finally, the more efficient investment in outward-oriented economies encourages domestic savings, with foreign borrowing or direct investment playing a complementary role. In inward-looking economies, foreign borrowing often acts as a substitute for domestic savings.

For example, Korea, Thailand, and, more recently, Turkey have countered adverse external shocks primarily by undertaking domestic policy reforms. By allowing their exchange rates to adjust, controlling public expenditures, and adopting export promotion measures, they boosted exports, reduced the need for foreign borrowing, and dampened inflation. In contrast, countries as diverse as Argentina, Jamaica, Mexico, and Tanzania have attempted to finance their increased current account deficits with more foreign borrowing or increased aid. This enabled them to maintain existing exchange rates, which discouraged import substitution and exports, which, in turn, increased their dependence on foreign borrowing. When the accumulation of debt denied them access to new funds, they were forced to deflate in order to lower real incomes and import demand.

The adoption of policies designed to stabilize and restructure the economy will stimulate growth, even in an adverse world environment. But for the most heavily indebted developing countries, the debt overhang is so constraining that corrective domestic policies alone will not provide a viable solution to their problems. The domestic adjustment effort will have to be supported by additional capital inflows and growing export markets. For these countries, as discussed later, future trends in the external environment have the potential to undermine domestic adjustment efforts.

These trends are illustrated in our High case and Low case scenarios. The future stability and growth of the world economy depend on the economic policies adopted by both industrial and developing countries—especially policies related to international trade—and on the behavior of world capital markets which interact with these policies. The two scenarios provide illustrations of a consistent set of outcomes for a range of possible policies. They are not intended as forecasts and do not allow for any exogenous shocks to the world economy, such as major disruptions in commodity or capital markets. They show what is achievable, rather than what is likely to be achieved.

A decade of opportunity, 1985–95

Policies in developing countries are expected to improve moderately, along the lines discussed in the previous section, in both scenarios. Even with these improvements, however, the Low case scenario will pose serious problems for many countries. But without policy improvements, the situation of some developing countries is likely to be untenable under any scenario.

The recent declines in oil prices and real interest rates could provide a useful stimulus to most developing countries in the second half of the 1980s. Both our High and Low cases reflect the beneficial effects that these developments, if sustained for three to five years, would have on inflation and growth. For many oil exporters, however, the lower oil price presents severe difficulties. How successful governments are in building upon this stimulus, or in coping with their problems, will be determined by the policies they adopt.

The favorable results illustrated in the High case are based on the assumption that there would be a steady reduction in the fraction of world credit absorbed by government deficits in industrial countries. This would lead to a higher rate of growth of investment in productive assets. Increased capital stock would, in turn, lead to higher output and

employment, which would ease social tensions and help reduce barriers to trade. The end result would be accelerated growth.

Under these circumstances, growth in industrial countries would increase to an average of about 4.3 percent a year. This is more than the average for 1973–80, but is below the rapid annual growth of 4.7 percent between 1965 and 1973. Industrial countries, particularly those in Europe, would enjoy lower unemployment than has prevailed in the past five years, and inflation would remain at a moderate rate. If the United States and other industrial countries with large public deficits were to gradually eliminate the structural part of their budget deficits, the world's demand for credit would fall and nominal interest rates would decline to an average of about 5.6 percent. Real interest rates would then return to around 2.6 percent, their historic average.

Under these conditions most developing countries would find it easier to service their debts through more rapid export growth and lower rates of interest. Annual rates of real GDP growth in developing countries would increase to 5.9 percent, or 3.9 percent in per capita terms. Furthermore, the international debt burden would be lightened by increased export earnings, a revival in commercial bank lending, and higher direct invest-

Table 3.1 Average performance of industrial and developing countries, 1965–95
(average annual percentage change)

Country group	1965–73	1973–80	1980–85	1985–95 High	1985–95 Low
Industrial countries					
GDP growth	4.7	2.8	2.2	4.3	2.5
Inflation rate[a]	5.1	8.3	−0.3	4.8	7.0
Real interest rate[b,c]	2.5	0.7	6.7	2.6	4.5
Nominal lending rate[c]	5.8	8.4	12.0	5.6	10.2
Developing countries					
GDP growth	6.6	5.4	3.3	5.9	4.0
Low-income countries					
Africa	3.9	2.7	0.9	4.0	3.2
Asia	5.9	5.0	7.8	6.4	4.4
Middle-income oil exporters	7.1	5.8	1.4	4.8	3.4
Middle-income oil importers					
Major exporters of manufactures	7.6	5.9	2.1	6.4	4.0
Other oil-importing countries	5.4	4.5	1.7	5.5	3.8
Export growth	5.0	4.6	4.1	7.1	3.2
Manufactures	11.6	13.8	7.9	9.8	5.0
Primary goods	3.8	1.1	1.4	4.3	1.5
Import growth	5.8	5.9	0.9	7.7	3.4

Note: Projected growth rates are based on a sample of ninety developing countries.
a. Industrial countries' weighted GDP deflator expressed in U.S. dollars. Inflation in the United States is 3.0 percent per year in the High case and 5.7 percent in the Low case. But for the industrial countries as a whole, it is higher in dollars because of an assumed depreciation of the dollar between 1985 and 1990.
b. Average for six-month U.S. dollar Eurocurrency rates deflated by the rate of change in the GDP deflator of the United States.
c. Average annual rate.

Table 3.2 Growth of GDP per capita, 1965–95
(average annual percentage change)

Country group	1965–73	1973–80	1980–85	1985–95 High	1985–95 Low
Industrial countries	3.7	2.1	1.7	3.8	2.0
Developing countries	4.0	3.2	1.3	3.9	2.0
Low-income countries	3.0	2.7	5.2	4.4	2.5
Africa	1.2	−0.1	−2.0	0.8	0.0
Asia	3.2	3.0	5.9	4.8	2.8
Middle-income oil exporters	4.5	3.1	−1.1	2.3	0.9
Middle-income oil importers	4.5	3.2	−0.1	4.1	1.9
Major exporters of manufactures	5.2	3.7	0.2	4.6	2.2
Other oil-importing countries	2.8	2.1	−0.8	3.1	1.4

Note: Projected growth rates are based on a sample of ninety developing countries.

ment in developing countries. This favorable overall result conceals some variability, however. Even in the High case, a number of sub-Saharan African countries and some heavily indebted oil exporters would find it very difficult to adjust and grow. If they are to share in an expanding world economy, additional measures—over and above those underlying our High case—would have to be taken.

The Low case illustrates what would happen if industrial countries were to abandon the tentative policy reforms adopted in the early 1980s. It reflects unchecked budget deficits, particularly in the United States. Even if lax fiscal policy were combined initially with restrictive monetary policies, it is likely that, under the cumulative pressure of debts and deficits, monetary discipline would be relaxed. This would lead to increasing real interest rates because financial markets, expecting that the deficits would sooner or later be monetized, would demand an inflation premium. These high rates would tend to reduce commercial bank lending to developing countries. At the same time, growing trade account deficits in industrial countries would exacerbate the demands for increased protection, which would, in turn, lead to reduced demand for developing-country exports and to lower commodity prices.

The consequences for industrial countries would be growth rates similar to, or even less than, those of the uncertain 1970s. Annual GDP growth would average 2.5 percent between 1985 and 1995. Real interest rates would remain high—around 4.5 percent—and inflation would rise to around 5–7 percent.

The consequences for developing countries would range from awkward to grim. For developing countries as a whole, average annual GDP growth rates would be 4.0 percent in the years to 1995 (see Table 3.1). Per capita growth would be a

precariously low 2.0 percent a year.

Under these circumstances some of the more outward-oriented middle-income exporters of manufactures could sustain growth, albeit at comparatively low rates. But for others the Low case would mean another decade of low or negative growth. Middle-income oil exporters would be unlikely to achieve any significant increase in real income, and the low-income African countries would suffer another decade of stagnation (see Table 3.2).

In the Low case, even those countries that implement domestic reforms may find it difficult to earn or borrow the resources required for growth. The consequences of slow industrial-country growth and limited additional financing for heavily indebted middle-income countries would be severe. Following five years of stagnation and declining per capita incomes, these countries would face the hard choice of how much of their resources to channel to service existing debt and how much to allocate to current consumption and investment. It is impossible even to sketch the consequences of such choices. Here, only the tensions, not the outcomes, can be illustrated.

Policy requirements for the High case

Assuming that moderate policy reforms continue in developing countries, the High case also requires improved performance in industrial countries. That, in turn, depends upon:

• *Monetary and fiscal policy.* Continued large budget deficits in the major industrial countries would make it very difficult to sustain a higher rate of growth in the world economy. Higher real rates of interest would eventually be accompanied by an accelerating rate of inflation and increased protection. The resulting stop-go policy mix that would be adopted by governments as they attempted to control inflation, unemployment, or the trade deficit would slow world growth to the disappointing rate obtained in the 1970s. Therefore, a primary policy requirement of the High case is that those economies with persistently large deficits reduce them. As argued in Chapter 2, this should be achieved primarily by cutting public expenditures. Where tax increases are unavoidable, care needs to be taken to minimize the distortionary effects and efficiency losses created by high marginal taxes. This combination of monetary and fiscal policies

needs to be reinforced by lowering targets for monetary growth to cut inflation and reduce long-term nominal interest rates. Such an adjustment in the aggregate deficits of industrial countries could be achieved in a less disruptive manner if the largest economies coordinate their macroeconomic policies. The recent success in reducing interest rates and the value of the dollar illustrates the potential usefulness of such cooperation.

• *Labor markets.* Chapter 2 argued that rigid and high real wages contribute to increases in unemployment. To create jobs, therefore, policies to en-

---

Box 3.1   Multilateral trade negotiations and the GATT

Throughout the post-World War II era, multilateral trade negotiations under the aegis of the GATT have proved effective in stemming the tide of protectionism and in achieving broad-scale reductions in tariff barriers to trade. Partly as a consequence of the limited participation of developing countries, reductions in tariff barriers have been less substantial on their exports. Developing countries have, however, benefited from the extension to them, on a "most favored nation" basis, of tariff reductions negotiated among industrial countries.

In the past several years, protectionism in industrial countries on average has intensified, and nontariff barriers to trade (as opposed to tariffs) have proliferated in markets that are of present or potential interest to developing countries—such as textiles and clothing, steel, and agricultural products. Nontariff barriers to trade across a wide range of product categories have also continued to play a significant role in the trade regimes of developing countries.

Following extensive discussions in the past two years, the GATT is now preparing for a new round of multilateral negotiations. A preparatory committee is expected to produce a report on the substance and modalities of the new round in July 1986. To produce meaningful results, this round should focus on nontariff barriers more than it has in the past, because they are the most important impediments to trade today. The new round should also promote institutional reforms in the GATT that would strengthen the international trading system and help prevent the growth of protectionism. An important unresolved issue on which views differ is whether trade in services should be included in the negotiations—and if so, in what manner.

The developing countries have an important stake in these negotiations. Liberalization and rationalization of their own trade regimes are likely to bring them important economic gains through increased efficiency

and the reduction of the distortions that bias production against exports. The reciprocal and multilateral nature of the negotiations implies that developing countries have an opportunity to obtain greater access to markets in industrial countries in exchange for their own liberalization efforts. Strengthening of the GATT system could also serve the developing countries' own trading interests, especially if the result is a reduction of the arbitrary and discriminatory protection practices of industrial countries against their exports.

Issues of access to markets in industrial countries are critical to the success of multilateral negotiations from the standpoint of developing countries. Such issues arise with respect to both manufacturing and agricultural products. In the case of agricultural products, the key issues are nontariff barriers and the subsidization by many industrial countries of temperate-zone agricultural products.

The developing countries will not be able to reap significant benefits unless they participate actively in these multilateral negotiations. Active participation implies a willingness to offer some reciprocal concessions to industrial countries in the form of rationalization and liberalization of their own regimes. Certain import controls which developing countries often maintain create problems for export interests in the industrial countries, and the support of these export interests may well be critical to the industrial countries' ability to reduce import barriers on products of interest to the developing countries.

If the more developed of the developing countries are unwilling to provide reciprocal reductions in trade barriers as part of the negotiations, they face another danger: industrial countries interested in pursuing trade liberalization through multilateral negotiations—especially the United States—will engage in negotiations that exclude the developing countries. Such an outcome would be detrimental both to developing countries and to the international trading system:

courage flexibility and reduce marginal labor costs are needed. This means encouraging training and mobility, lowering unemployment insurance and welfare benefits, and keeping wage settlements in line with productivity increases. It also entails reducing the protection afforded certain industries, so as to encourage the movement of labor into more efficient and competitive activities.

• *Trade liberalization.* While governments in industrial countries have started to correct some of the distortions caused by fiscal and monetary policies and labor rigidities, their trade policies have often gone the other way: toward protectionism. By adopting the type of policies discussed above (in particular, lower fiscal deficits), the industrial countries could create the conditions for strong sustained growth. This would increase import demand among industrial countries and boost both exports and imports of developing countries. It would also create the conditions needed to reduce international trade restrictions. That would, in turn, increase the volume of world trade over and above that resulting directly from higher growth. A new round of trade liberalization for manufac-

trade barriers would tend to be reduced primarily on items of interest to industrial countries, and, at the same time, the multilateral nature of the trade system would be undermined by the spread of bilateral arrangements.

The degree of reciprocity in negotiations should take into account the varying stages of economic development. The enabling clause of the GATT states that there is the "expectation of the developing countries that they will be able to participate more fully in the framework of rights and obligations under the GATT with the progressive development of their economies and improvement in their trade situation." In keeping with this principle, those developing countries that have already made significant strides in economic development and that offer promise of further growth in the future may be expected to shoulder increasing obligations in a new round of multilateral negotiations.

While many institutional changes may be desirable, perhaps the most important is the establishment of an effective system of safeguards. Such a system is needed to ensure that the reductions in protection that the negotiations secure are not arbitrarily and unilaterally reversed and that temporary protection is provided for specific industries that need it. Thus, to promote longer-term adjustment, a safeguard system should be uniform, temporary, and reduced progressively over time.

The effective application of a safeguard system would also require strengthening the system for settlement of trade disputes in the framework of the GATT. Institutional strengthening of the GATT would be helpful to developing countries insofar as it is they, as the weaker trading partners, that have the most to gain from the greater adherence of nations to rules governing international trade.

The process of trade liberalization through multilateral negotiations has been, and is likely to remain, slow. Not only do the actual negotiations typically require several years to complete, but the trade liberalization agreed to is normally implemented in stages in subsequent years. As a result, significant trade liberalization from a new multilateral round cannot be expected to take place before the end of this decade. However, many developing countries, especially the heavily indebted ones, need to increase their export earnings within a much shorter time span. Increasing their exports requires the reduction of the disincentives to efficient exports created by their own highly protectionist trade regimes and improved access to markets in the industrial countries. Every encouragement should be given to both industrial and developing countries so that they undertake the needed trade rationalization and liberalization now.

The current preparations for a multilateral trade negotiation may, however, prompt many countries to consider delaying trade liberalization in order to preserve their bargaining power for the multilateral negotiations. It would be truly unfortunate if the negotiation process undermined the prospects for critical structural change as a result of the adoption of such a negotiation strategy.

One possible way to address this issue could be the provision, within the framework of the multilateral negotiations, of appropriate "credit" for the adoption of such prior reforms by developing countries. There are precedents for credit being extended in negotiations between industrial and developing countries during the earlier Kennedy Round. Industrial countries might wish to agree in principle at the beginning of the negotiations that credit would be given for liberalization or other trade reforms undertaken by developing countries after a certain date. Such an action may encourage developing countries to liberalize their trade regimes when it appears desirable to effect the structural transformation they want rather than to wait until the round has been completed.

tures and agricultural imports of industrial nations would be needed for the growth rates of the High case to be achieved. In addition, by 1995 the tariff equivalents of major nontariff barriers would have to be significantly lower than they were in 1984 (see Box 3.1).

Developing-country prospects

The 5.9 percent growth rate of GDP in the High case illustrates how fast developing countries can grow, given continued domestic reforms and a favorable external environment. It implies a healthy 3.9 percent growth rate in per capita income. In contrast, per capita income would grow at only 2.0 percent in the Low case.

As both High and Low cases presuppose similar improvements in developing-country policies, the difference between the two cases for a particular group of countries provides a rough estimate of the extent to which changes in the world economy affect the performance of that group. In low-income Asia, the growth rate in per capita income shown in the High case is a strong 4.8 percent; in the Low case the rate is 2.8 percent. For the major exporters of manufactures, the High case leads to a per capita growth rate of 4.6 percent and the Low case only 2.2 percent. But in low-income African countries, the corresponding rate is 0.8 percent in the High case, and in the Low case per capita incomes would not increase at all.

The large differences between the High and Low cases for low-income Asia and for middle-income major exporters of manufactures (2.0 and 2.4 percentage points, respectively), as compared with the narrow gap for low-income Africa (0.8 percentage point), reflect the greater integration of the

newly industrialized countries into the world economy. Changes in export markets and interest rates would cause the performance of these economies to fluctuate more than that of the more inward-looking and agriculture-based African economies. But this does not mean that the newly industrialized countries are worse off. Indeed, their Low case growth rate exceeds the High case growth rate for low-income Africa. Developing countries that attempt to insulate themselves from the world economy may reduce the impact of international cycles, but they pay the high price of lower growth rates under any world scenario.

The higher per capita growth rate in low-income Asia is also due to the lower rate of population growth as compared with the rate in Africa. This reflects the relative success, particularly in China, that low-income Asia has had with population control programs.

The High case

If OECD growth is strong, low-income Asia and major exporters of manufactures would attain the highest growth rate. Both groups would expand their exports of goods by more than 8.0 percent a year (see Table 3.3). Much of the growth in per capita income levels in low-income Asia reflects the performance of China and India. Their strong performance results from continued domestic policy reforms and an increased level of foreign borrowing. The further opening up of these two important economies to international trade would lead to increased efficiency in domestic production and a higher rate of export growth. This, coupled with a greater reliance on international capital markets (debt indicators for this country group in-

Table 3.3 Change in trade in developing countries, 1965–95
(*average annual percentage change*)

	Exports of goods					Exports of manufactures				
				1985–95					1985–95	
Country group	1965–73	1973–80	1980–85	High	Low	1965–73	1973–80	1980–85	High	Low
Developing countries	5.0	4.6	4.1	7.1	3.2	11.6	13.8	7.9	9.8	5.0
Low-income countries	1.9	5.4	5.0	8.0	4.3	2.3	8.3	7.4	11.1	6.5
Africa	4.6	1.3	−1.5	5.3	2.6	5.4	2.0	−2.1	9.3	4.6
Asia	0.6	6.8	6.6	8.4	4.6	2.0	8.7	7.8	11.1	6.5
Middle-income oil exporters	4.3	0.0	1.2	5.1	1.5	10.7	8.0	15.4	11.5	5.9
Middle-income oil importers	7.1	9.0	5.6	7.8	3.8	15.5	15.3	7.4	9.4	4.7
Major exporters of manufactures	9.2	10.6	5.9	8.1	3.9	15.6	15.9	7.0	9.3	4.6
Other oil-importing countries	2.4	3.5	4.3	6.6	3.4	14.8	9.1	13.0	10.6	6.5

Note: Historical growth rates of volume of international trade reflect revisions in the nominal trade figures, as well as revisions in the methodology of calculating trade deflators.

crease), supports the stronger growth shown in our High case.

For major exporters of manufactures, such as Korea and Brazil, stronger growth in industrial countries plus the accompanying reduction in protection would provide the growing markets they need to expand production and exports. Export growth, plus an increase in private capital inflows from abroad, would raise their capacity to import by close to 9 percent a year. As a result, these economies could sustain a faster rate of growth over the next ten-year period.

Even if our High case growth rates are achieved, the prospects for middle- and high-income oil exporters will be lower than they were last year. For middle-income oil exporters (for example, Egypt, Indonesia, and Malaysia), the recent drop in the price of oil has led commercial banks to lower their assessment of how much debt they can carry. For those oil exporters that have had debt-servicing difficulties (for example, Mexico and Nigeria), the oil price decline exacerbates an already difficult situation. As a consequence, significant steps need to be taken to moderate the decline in their real incomes. Of primary importance will be policy measures designed to increase domestic savings and to allocate and utilize resources more efficiently. A reduction of the disincentives to new export activities will be particularly important, as will the reduction of trade barriers in industrial economies. As argued later, for the heavily indebted middle-income oil-exporting countries, this domestic adjustment effort needs to be be supported by continued and increased access to external capital flows. Under these conditions, middle-income oil exporters as a group will be able to finance a sustainable expansion in imports. Furthermore, in the

longer term, the oil price can be expected to strengthen as the faster growth in the world demand for oil begins to press against existing supply capacity. As a consequence, in a stronger world economy oil exporters could regain an annual per capita growth rate of 2.3 percent over the decade 1985–95 (see Box 3.2).

Middle-income countries that are not major exporters of manufactures could also attain a significant improvement in their export growth, to 6.6 percent a year. However, as this larger group of countries depends more on commodity exports, the boost from higher world demand would be less relative to that for exporters of manufactures. Demand for primary commodities is comparatively income inelastic—that is, does not rise proportionately to people's income—and substitutes are becoming increasingly competitive. Nevertheless, strong OECD growth would provide those middle-income economies undertaking reforms (such as Côte d'Ivoire, Mauritius, Morocco, and Senegal) with the growing world markets they require to realize the largest growth gains from their reforms. Foreign exchange earnings would increase, and, given access to adequate foreign capital, these countries would be able to increase imports as well as service their debt (see "Capital flows and debt" below).

In low-income Africa, the negative per capita income growth rates of the recent past would be reversed in the High case. Low-income African countries would gain significantly from the lower oil price. But if the world economy were to grow at the rates indicated by our High case, they would also gain from the assumed reduced protection of agricultural markets, particularly in Europe. But even under these favorable conditions, per capita

Exports of primary goods					Imports of goods					
			1985–95					1985–95		
1965–73	1973–80	1980–85	High	Low	1965–73	1973–80	1980–85	High	Low	Country group
3.8	1.1	1.4	4.3	1.5	5.8	5.9	0.9	7.7	3.4	Developing countries
1.6	3.6	3.1	4.6	2.0	0.8	6.1	5.9	6.0	1.7	Low-income countries
4.5	1.2	−1.5	4.9	2.4	3.4	2.1	−3.0	3.9	1.2	Africa
−0.6	5.2	5.4	4.4	1.9	−0.5	7.7	8.2	6.4	1.8	Asia
4.2	−0.4	−0.1	4.0	0.8	3.7	9.1	−2.0	7.0	1.6	Middle-income oil exporters
3.8	3.3	2.8	4.5	2.1	8.0	4.7	0.9	8.3	4.4	Middle-income oil importers
										Major exporters of
5.5	3.8	3.6	4.7	2.2	9.6	4.8	1.1	8.9	4.9	manufacturers
1.2	2.4	1.4	4.3	1.7	3.6	4.3	0.0	5.6	2.1	Other oil-importing countries

Box 3.2 How a drop in the price of oil affects developing countries

Does the developing world gain from cheaper oil? All things considered the answer is yes. If the price of oil fell from around $20–22 a barrel to $10–12 a barrel and stayed there for the next five years, the direct loss for oil-exporting developing countries (lost oil revenue) would outweigh the direct benefits for oil importers. But for developing countries as a group, the indirect effects of a $10-a-barrel price fall would more than offset the direct impact.

The crucial indirect benefits for developing countries derive from the impact of an oil price decline on the industrial countries. Developing countries would benefit from the boost to export demand and lower interest rates that cheaper oil is likely to create in industrial countries. Under the oil price fall postulated above, GDP growth in industrial countries would increase by at least 0.4 percentage points a year from 1986 to 1990 according to our estimates.[1] This would lead to a greater demand for exports from developing countries. However, some developing countries would experience an offsetting negative indirect effect because of lower remittances from migrant workers employed in high- and middle-income oil-exporting countries.

In industrial countries, the drop in the price of oil would cause both inflation and interest rates to fall in the short term. Because oil has a greater weight in the price deflators for the United States than in those for European countries, price levels and interest rates can be expected to fall more in the United States than in Europe; as a consequence, the dollar would also tend to depreciate.

Although the total value of developing countries' exports would fall (because of lower worldwide inflation), the volume of their exports would rise. The value of exports from the non-oil-exporting regions would also fall, partly because of the drop in the rate of inflation and partly because each region exports some oil. Box tables 3.2A and 3.2B provide conservative estimates of the effect of a $10-a-barrel decline in the price of oil on developing countries. The first table shows the effect on the nominal value of exports, interest payments, and lending, and the second table shows the effect on export and import volumes.

While the data in these tables show that oil-importing developing countries would gain, they also show the magnitude of the negative impact on oil-exporting developing countries. For the middle-income oil exporters, export revenues would fall by 24 to 28 percent between 1986 and 1990 (see Box table 3.2A). As a consequence, it is likely that these countries would be less able to obtain new capital inflows and thus would have to reduce their domestic expenditures in order to lower their real imports. The magnitude of the reduction needed in real imports could be as much as $20 billion to $30 billion a year. This could

1. Other estimates tend to exceed this figure. To the extent that OECD growth is higher than postulated here, the net positive effect of the oil price decline on developing countries will also exceed the estimates shown here.

Box table 3.2A Estimated effects of a drop in the price of oil of $10 per barrel on export revenues, interest payments, and medium- and long-term private lending to developing countries, 1986, 1987, and 1990

| | Export revenues | | | | | | Interest payments on medium- and long-term debt | | | | | |
| | Difference in billions of dollars | | | Percentage difference | | | Difference in billions of dollars | | | Percentage difference | | |
Country group	1986	1987	1990	1986	1987	1990	1986	1987	1990	1986	1987	1990
Developing countries	−42.8	−49.7	−54.4	−8.3	−8.6	−6.4	−0.7	−4.7	−3.6	−1.1	−7.0	−5.1
Low-income countries	−3.2	−3.7	−3.2	−5.2	−5.4	−3.1	0.0	−0.4	−0.3	0.0	−7.3	−3.2
Africa	−0.3	−0.4	−0.5	−2.9	−3.9	−3.1	0.0	−0.1	0.0	0.0	−4.9	0.0
Asia	−2.9	−3.3	−2.8	−5.6	−5.7	−3.1	0.0	−0.3	−0.3	0.0	−8.3	−3.4
Middle-income oil exporters	−32.3	−36.1	−44.0	−27.9	−27.7	−24.0	−0.2	−1.5	−1.0	−1.1	−7.1	−5.0
Middle-income oil importers	−7.3	−9.8	−7.2	−2.2	−2.6	−1.3	−0.4	−2.7	−2.3	−1.1	−7.0	−5.5
Major exporters of manufactures	−5.8	−7.5	−4.9	−2.1	−2.4	−1.1	−0.3	−2.2	−2.0	−1.1	−7.4	−6.4
Other oil-importing countries	−1.5	−2.3	−2.3	−2.5	−3.4	−2.3	−0.1	−0.5	−0.3	−0.9	−5.6	−2.9

Note: Data are based on the difference between the base line price per barrel of oil—$20 in 1986, $22 in 1987, and $23 in 1990—and the scenario price of $10 less.
Source: Fleisig (background paper).

Box table 3.2B Estimated effects of a drop in the price of oil of $10 per barrel on developing countries' trade, 1986, 1987, and 1990

	Exports						Imports					
	Difference in billions of 1980 dollars			Percentage difference			Difference in billions of 1980 dollars			Percentage difference		
Country group	1986	1987	1990	1986	1987	1990	1986	1987	1990	1986	1987	1990
Developing countries	2.4	9.2	17.6	0.5	1.8	3.0	8.7	11.2	5.9	1.6	2.0	0.9
Low-income countries	0.2	1.0	2.2	0.4	1.7	3.1	2.8	3.8	4.8	3.1	4.2	4.8
Africa	0.0	0.1	0.2	0.3	1.0	1.8	0.6	0.8	0.8	3.7	5.7	5.1
Asia	0.2	0.9	2.0	0.5	1.8	3.4	2.2	3.0	4.0	3.0	4.0	4.7
Middle-income oil exporters	0.6	2.4	4.6	0.4	1.7	2.7	−19.0	−23.8	−31.3	−16.9	−21.7	−24.5
Middle-income oil importers	1.5	5.8	10.8	0.5	2.0	3.1	24.9	31.2	32.4	7.1	8.4	7.0
Major exporters of manufactures	1.3	5.2	9.6	0.6	2.1	3.3	19.5	24.4	24.9	7.1	8.2	6.7
Other oil-importing countries	0.2	0.6	1.2	0.3	1.2	2.1	5.4	6.8	7.5	7.2	8.9	8.6

Note: Data are based on the difference between the base line price per barrel of oil—$20 in 1986, $22 in 1987, and $23 in 1990—and the scenario price of $10 less.
Source: Fleisig (background paper).

be achieved by reducing real GDP through increased taxes, reduced government spending, and tighter monetary policy. If the oil exporters reduced imports by these measures, their GDP levels could fall by as much as 6 to 12 percent below what they would have been otherwise. That would cut their average rates of growth by roughly four percentage points annually during the period of adjustment. The same price decline would also adversely affect the growth prospects of high-income oil-exporting countries. It is estimated that a $10 decline in the price of oil would reduce their

export revenues by about $60 billion in aggregate.

Some of the pressure to reduce output could be offset if oil-exporting developing countries undertook substantial devaluations. The rise in the price of traded goods relative to nontradables could raise exports, lower imports, and thereby assist the economy to adjust. This would offset some of the loss of output that might otherwise occur. But while such adjustment would be necessary, the supply response of exports may take time, and some output loss in the short term would be unavoidable.

Medium- and long-term private lending						
Difference in billions of dollars			Percentage difference			
1986	1987	1990	1986	1987	1990	Country group
−1.4	−4.1	−15.9	−5.5	−16.6	—	Developing countries
0.0	−0.1	−0.4	−0.2	−0.7	−3.9	Low-income countries
0.0	0.0	0.0	0.0	0.0	0.0	Africa
0.0	−0.1	−0.4	0.0	−0.7	−3.4	Asia
−0.4	−1.3	−4.6	—	—	—	Middle-income oil exporters
−1.0	−2.7	−11.0	−7.7	−24.0	—	Middle-income oil importers
−0.9	−2.6	−10.5	−10.0	−29.6	—	Major exporters of manufactures
0.0	−0.1	−0.5	0.0	−5.0	20.4	Other oil-importing countries

Box 3.3   The sub-Saharan Africa debt problem

Although the absolute size of sub-Saharan Africa's debt is relatively small, the cost of servicing it is not. Total long- and short-term liabilities increased from $38.5 billion in 1978 to approximately $80.0 billion in 1984, or from 30 percent of the region's combined GNP to 50 percent. Although much of low-income Africa's loans come from bilateral and multilateral sources on concessional terms, debt service obligations as a percentage of exports of goods and nonfactor services have still risen to unsustainable levels.

Box figure 3.3 shows the latest available data on the cost of servicing long-term debt in sub-Saharan Africa as a whole and in two subgroups, low-income IDA countries and others. The data for 1979–84 are what countries actually paid out in principal and interest, those for 1985 and onward are what they were scheduled to repay based on existing debt. Clearly, scheduled debt service payments greatly exceed the payments actually made. Total debt service was $6.4 billion in 1983 and $7.9 billion in 1984, whereas scheduled payments are about $12.0 billion in 1985 and 1986. The debt service ratio, which had been 21.6 percent in 1984, is scheduled to rise to a projected 33.2 percent in 1985 for the continent as a whole. For IDA countries, the increase is even larger, rising from 18.5 percent to 39.6 percent.

Though debt payments have not been the fundamental cause of Africa's low growth, the debt problem is becoming more acute for three principal reasons: First, the proportion of debt payments that are not eligible for rescheduling (mainly repayments on loans from multilateral organizations) is rising rapidly. Second, the process by which high scheduled debt repayments are translated into lower manageable actual payments is proving very costly. It has created an atmosphere of uncertainty, which reduces confidence and discourages private investment. Third, net financial flows to sub-Saharan Africa have fallen substantially. As the data in Box table 3.3 show, the small

increase in net capital flows from multilateral sources in 1984 was outweighed by the decline in net bilateral flows. When the precipitous drop in net private flows is also taken into account (they fell from a peak of $4.3 billion in 1982 to a negative $0.3 billion in 1984), the magnitude of the problem becomes apparent.

Moreover, the debt burden is not distributed equally. In some countries, including Botswana, Cameroon, and Lesotho, the debt service ratio is less than 15 percent; in others, it is more than 50 percent. And, while some countries' debt is primarily from commercial sources (for example, Côte d'Ivoire, Nigeria, and Zimbabwe), for others it is largely official (for example, Tanzania, Zaire, and Zambia).

A total of ten countries in the region rescheduled debt at the Paris Club in 1985, matching the record of 1983 and 1984. But a potentially more serious problem emerged in 1985. Several sub-Saharan countries did not reschedule at the Paris Club primarily because they were unable to reach agreement with their creditors on adjustment programs. Most of these countries are additionally hampered by arrears to the IMF, which technically prohibits rescheduling negotiations.

Can African countries grow fast enough to meet existing debt obligations and maintain adequate domestic investment? The prospects are poor. Although it may be possible to manage the debt obligations of the non-IDA countries through domestic policy reforms and rescheduling (given strong economic growth in the world economy), this will not be enough for a group of approximately twelve IDA countries. Even in the High case, these countries could not generate the export earnings they need to finance debt obligations and the investment required to support growth. This would be true even if a large portion of the debt were rescheduled.

This year's World Bank report on sub-Saharan Africa (1986a) argues that it is possible to achieve a lasting solution to the region's debt problem. But this will

Box table 3.3 Sub-Saharan Africa's net public flows, 1978–84
(millions of dollars)

Type of flow	1978	1979	1980	1981	1982	1983	1984
Total net flows	5,861.4	6,372.3	7,158.4	7,091.3	8,185.4	7,650.3	2,753.0
Official creditors	2,512.5	3,527.5	3,788.0	3,944.7	3,846.5	4,034.9	3,062.2
Multilateral	1,347.5	1,281.0	1,799.7	1,649.8	1,890.9	1,782.5	1,834.1
Bilateral	1,164.9	2,246.5	1,988.3	2,294.9	1,955.6	2,252.4	1,228.1
Private creditors	3,348.9	2,844.8	3,370.4	3,146.7	4,338.9	3,615.4	−309.2
Suppliers	341.2	87.5	409.0	140.7	122.0	41.8	170.7
Financial markets	3,007.7	2,757.3	2,961.4	3,005.9	4,216.8	3,573.6	−479.9

Source: World Bank *World Debt Tables*, 1985–86 edition.

require a coordinated effort by official agencies, commercial banks, and the African countries.

The first step must be a commitment to the type of domestic reforms recently implemented by Ghana, Togo, and Zambia. The report argues that the key areas on which governments should focus are the incentive framework, public investment, and domestic savings. The aim should be to correct the bias against agriculture and exports, which often favors urban wage earners. A greater reliance on prices and markets is essential if the level and efficiency of investment are to rise. This would mean redefining the role of the government to free resources for the private sector and to create an environment where the profits from investment would once again become commensurate with the risks.

This is particularly important if foreign direct investment is to be encouraged so as to provide badly needed resources over and above domestic savings plus foreign lending. In the past, many sub-Saharan countries actively discouraged overseas investment. But it can play a useful role. It directs foreign capital toward investments with potential returns that exceed interest rates; it is often associated with transfers of technology; and, more important, it keeps the risks of the investment firmly with those who provide the capital. If the investment fails to yield an adequate return, the investor takes the loss, whereas if a publicly guaranteed loan is misspent, the repayment obligations continue.

A narrower definition of the activities that properly belong to government would also help to focus public resources (including the time of overstretched officials) on essential public goods and services. Many countries could achieve substantial gains in efficiency by ensuring that public investment programs are prioritized according to their rates of return and by keeping investment spending consistent with resource availability, after allowing for crucial recurrent and maintenance expenditures.

Policies to increase domestic savings are also required to ensure that domestic investment is not unduly constrained by the reduced flow of foreign savings. Increasing public savings implies a renewed effort to reduce budget deficits, particularly the operating losses of inefficient government-owned parastatals. Private savings could be raised through tax reform and by allowing domestic interest rates to reflect the inflation-adjusted market value of capital.

If these microeconomic reforms are to work, they must be supported by consistent fiscal, monetary, and exchange rate policies. As demonstrated in Part II of this Report, inappropriate exchange rates, large fiscal

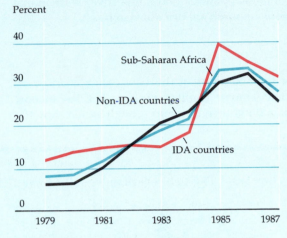

Box figure 3.3 Long-term public debt service as a percentage of exports in sub-Saharan Africa, 1979–87

Percent

Sub-Saharan Africa

Non-IDA countries

IDA countries

Note: Data for 1984 are estimated; data for 1985–87 are projected.

deficits, and inflationary monetary policies in sub-Saharan Africa have created major distortions in incentives. Neither savings nor investment will increase unless people are confident that policy-induced macroeconomic instability will not penalize those that forgo current consumption.

Since the reduced flow in nonconcessional lending is appropriate, given the weak creditworthiness of many African countries, domestic reforms will have to be supported by increased bilateral and multilateral concessional loans, at least in the immediate future. This is particularly so for IDA countries, where conventional debt rescheduling will merely postpone, and not solve, the debt problem.

But, if Africa's decline is to be reversed, such concessional lending must go hand in hand with policy reforms. This year's sub-Saharan Africa report recommends that for low-income Africa the mandate of the consultative groups of donors, which meet under the World Bank's auspices, be adapted to provide a more comprehensive assessment of resource needs and policy reform. While donors should be expected to make decisions on resource transfers with reference to the medium-term financial needs of the country, recipient governments should, for their part, clearly outline the program of adjustment that they intend to follow. Institutions such as the Bank and the IMF will have an important role in monitoring the policy reforms and in helping direct the loans and grants to the most productive purpose.

growth is a low 0.8 percent. Sub-Saharan Africa could exceed this level of performance only by pushing even more strongly ahead with the policy changes that some countries have begun to implement. This domestic adjustment effort should be assisted by a coordinated international effort to increase the level of external resources available and the efficiency with which they are used. The types of domestic policies and supportive international actions required are discussed in Box 3.3.

The Low case

The repercussions of the Low case scenario vary widely among country groups. For low-income Asia a downturn in world growth would slow the expansion in exports to below what has recently been achieved (see Table 3.3). Since China is a net oil exporter, a greater effort to stimulate alternative export activities via trade policy reform would be necessary to offset a marked decline in its export earnings. While some low-income Asian countries have the capacity to increase their current external debt obligations, lower export growth would ultimately limit their ability to increase imports and would thereby restrict growth.

Those high-growth middle-income East Asian countries which carry modest debt burdens and have flexible economies could still attain annual per capita GDP growth rates of close to 3 percent under the Low case. Other middle-income oil importers would suffer from continued low commod-

Box 3.4 The debt overhang and the heavily indebted middle-income countries

In 1985 it became widely accepted that the debt-servicing problems of some developing countries would last longer than had earlier been thought and that their solution depends critically on the restoration of sustained growth.

The scale of the problem can be gauged from the adjustments made in the early 1980s. The bulk of the adjustment has been undertaken through lower demand, which has meant, in practice, reducing imports and investment. The volume of imports for the heavily indebted middle-income countries in 1985 was 32 percent below its 1981 level. The ratio of investment to GDP fell from 25 percent in 1981 to 18 percent in 1985. GDP has stagnated since 1980, and per capita incomes have declined substantially. The reduction in demand has pushed the collective trade balance of these countries into a large surplus, which has brought their current account into rough balance. Yet, the main indicators of debt at the end of 1985 were close to their previous peaks. Despite their adjustment efforts, these countries seem to be as far as they ever were from reconciling growth and creditworthiness.

The problem is so intractable that for the biggest debtors sound policies and world growth, though essential, will not be enough to restore growth. Because debt-servicing obligations absorb 5 to 7 percent of GNP in many countries, domestic savings are not enough to service debt and maintain the level of investment needed to permit adequate growth. Thus, a significant amount of new private and official lending is required. But how much?

According to World Bank estimates, the growth rate of real GDP in seventeen heavily indebted countries needs to average at least 4 percent a year for the next ten years. This permits a per capita growth rate of consumption of 1 percent annually. Per capita consump-

tion over the next decade needs to increase by at least that much. Otherwise, it may not be politically possible to maintain the course of adjustment.

To achieve even this modest rate of growth, the heavily indebted countries must aim to reduce external debt relative to total output and export earnings. The efficiency of investment would need to increase, and domestic savings would have to rise from its present average rate of about 21 percent to about 26 percent over the next five years. Export growth, boosted not only by improved policies in developing countries but also by sustained recovery in industrial countries and trade liberalization policies, would have to average about 5 percent a year in volume terms. And interest payments need to be moderated by lower real interest rates, though the impact of this depends on the size and makeup of each country's debt.

Even with such significant adjustments, restoration of growth and creditworthiness in the heavily indebted group would require satisfactory growth in industrial countries and net flows of capital of the order of $14 billion to $21 billion a year over the next five years. This net capital inflow would have to come from loans from commercial banks, export credit agencies, and multilateral lenders, as well as equity investment and repatriated capital.

Despite the size of these projected flows, however, the debt of these countries would still be growing more slowly than their GDP, so that the debt-to-GDP ratio would decline significantly, as would the aggregate debt service ratio.

Note: All data in this box refer to seventeen countries: Argentina, Bolivia, Brazil, Chile, Colombia, Costa Rica, Côte d'Ivoire, Ecuador, Jamaica, Mexico, Morocco, Nigeria, Peru, the Philippines, Uruguay, Venezuela, and Yugoslavia.

ity prices, high interest rates, and reduced capital flows. Their imports would be unlikely to rise at much more than a slow 2.1 percent a year, and investment would be contained at present depressed levels. That would, in turn, hold per capita growth down to a low 1.4 percent a year on average. Access to foreign capital would be a critical factor in determining how much these middle-income economies are led to squeeze domestic demand because of slower growth in industrial countries (see Box 3.4).

Because of the fall in oil prices, the prospects for oil exporters have deteriorated sharply from the Low case presented in the 1985 *World Development Report*. Under the conditions prevailing in the world economy last year, the GDP per capita growth estimated for middle-income oil-exporting countries in the Low case was 2.0 percent during the period 1985–95; this year the estimate has been revised downward to less than 1.0 percent. Cheaper oil would reduce oil exporters' growth rates under any circumstances, but the Low case reflects the additional effects of significantly reduced capital inflows and lower demand. As discussed in the following section on capital flows and in Box 3.2, this combination seriously curtails the import capacity of both middle- and high-income oil exporters just as sluggish world demand makes a shift to alternative export activities more difficult.

The implications for low-income Africa are even more serious. Depressed demand for primary commodities and continued protection in industrial countries would result in a slow increase in export earnings from the current low level. Even those countries currently engaged in serious policy reform efforts (for example, Guinea, Kenya, and Malawi) would have difficulty maintaining growth. Aid would not increase enough to offset the continued decline in net private capital inflows from abroad. As a result, imports would barely increase beyond their already depressed levels. Without resources to increase investment, many low-income African countries would suffer another ten years of declining per capita incomes. Private investors would remain hesitant, and many countries would risk sliding further into a vicious cycle of economic deterioration and political instability.

Capital flows and debt

How efficiently developing countries use their resources largely determines their rate of economic growth. But the level of those resources is still important. Foreign capital flows are one such resource: they supplement domestic savings and can compensate temporarily for foreign exchange shortages. Tables 3.4 and 3.5 provide a powerful illustration of the way the availability of these resources changes between the High and Low cases. In the High case, increased demand for developing-country exports, lower interest rates, and a resumption of voluntary capital flows to a large group of countries would encourage growth. This, in turn, would gradually ease the debt burden of the developing countries. But in the Low case, a reversal of these external circumstances—particularly lower exports and restricted capital flows—would seriously test the ability of developing countries to adjust. That, in turn, might precipitate a sweeping restructuring of international financial obligations.

The High case

In the High case, lower interest rates would reduce the interest costs on medium- and long-term debt from $58.5 billion in 1985 to $47.3 billion by 1995 (in constant prices, see Table 3.4). Sustained growth in real export earnings during the same period would result in a sharp reduction in debt service as a percentage of exports, from 21.9 percent in 1985 to 13.4 percent in 1995. In the long term this would make developing countries more creditworthy. Additional borrowing would increase the debt outstanding and disbursed from $723 billion in 1985 to $864 billion in 1995 and thus provide the additional financing required to sustain increased current account deficits. More than one-half of the current account deficit by 1995 is attributable to the rapidly growing economies within two country groups, low-income Asia (particularly India and China) and major exporters of manufactures. Indeed, some of the economies in low-income Asia have the capacity to increase their debt service ratios in the High case. Oil exporters would also be able to sustain larger current account deficits as the strengthening of the oil market in the early 1990s and the growth of other export activities reestablish their capacity to carry additional debt.

In the High case, the improved creditworthiness of many developing countries would lead to a reversal of the recent decline in net financing flows (see Table 3.5). In constant prices, total net flows would increase from a low $62.3 billion in 1985 to $97.0 billion by 1995. This represents a steady

Table 3.4 Current account balance and its financing in developing countries, 1985 and 1995
(billions of constant 1980 dollars)

Item	All developing countries 1985[a]	All developing countries 1995 High	All developing countries 1995 Low	Low-income Africa 1985[a]	Low-income Africa 1995 High	Low-income Africa 1995 Low	Low-income Asia 1985[a]	Low-income Asia 1995 High	Low-income Asia 1995 Low
Net exports of goods and nonfactor services	−4.1	−87.0	−24.0	−4.2	−4.3	−3.4	−23.0	−22.4	−9.0
Interest on medium- and long-term debt	−58.5	−47.3	−49.4	−1.3	−0.8	−0.8	−2.2	−7.3	−5.6
Official	−13.1	−15.9	−16.1	−0.8	−0.8	−0.8	−1.2	−2.5	−2.3
Private	−45.4	−31.4	−33.3	−0.4	0.0	0.0	−1.0	−4.8	−3.3
Current account balance[b]	−41.3	105.4	−50.3	−5.2	−4.3	−3.7	−17.1	−22.4	−7.8
Net official transfers	15.2	19.8	17.2	2.3	2.8	2.4	2.0	2.5	2.2
Medium- and long-term loans[c]	36.1	58.1	18.6	1.4	1.7	1.5	6.8	18.7	4.9
Official	21.2	28.8	15.5	0.5	1.9	1.6	4.8	7.4	5.0
Private	15.0	29.3	3.1	0.9	−0.2	−0.2	2.0	11.4	−0.1
Debt outstanding and disbursed	722.9	864.2	560.9	28.9	28.6	23.4	60.1	167.4	92.7
As a percentage of GNP	33.0	22.3	17.2	58.6	38.5	33.9	10.2	15.5	10.3
As a percentage of exports	135.7	88.5	86.7	318.5	174.7	206.3	120.7	156.7	129.8
Debt service as a percentage of exports	21.9	13.4	16.7	35.8	13.5	17.2	11.9	18.0	18.0

Note: The table is based on a sample of ninety developing countries. The GDP deflator for industrial countries was used to deflate all items. Details may not add to totals because of rounding. Net exports in this table exclude factor services and thus differ from those in Table 3.5. Net exports plus interest does not equal the current account balance because of the omission of net workers' remittances, private transfers, and investment income. The current account balance not financed by official transfers and loans is covered by direct foreign investment, other capital (including short-term credit and errors and omissions), and changes in reserves. Ratios are calculated using current price data.

Table 3.5 Net financing flows to developing countries in selected years, 1980–95

Type of flow	Amount (billions of dollars at constant prices) 1980	1984	1985	1995 High	1995 Low	Growth rate (percent)[a] 1970–80	1985–95 High	1985–95 Low
Official development assistance[b]	23.4	21.6	22.4	29.6	25.7	5.9	2.8	1.4
Nonconcessional loans	47.1	33.4	28.9	48.3	10.1	12.6	5.3	−10.0
Official	8.7	13.9	14.0	19.0	7.0	12.6	3.1	−6.7
Private	38.4	19.5	15.0	29.3	3.1	12.6	7.0	−14.7
Direct investment	10.6	10.8	11.0	19.1	14.2	5.8	5.7	2.6
Total	81.1	65.9	62.3	97.0	49.9	9.2	4.5	−2.2
Memo items								
Net export of goods and nonfactor services[c]	−92.8	−61.9	−66.5	−135.2	−76.5	8.9	7.4	1.4
Current account balance[d]	−67.8	−35.3	−41.3	−105.4	−50.3	7.5	9.8	2.0
ODA from DAC countries as a percentage of their GNP	0.38	0.38	0.37	0.37	0.37	—	—	—

Note: All items are net of repayments. Data are for a sample of ninety countries.
a. Average annual percentage change.
b. Includes ODA grants (official transfers). DAC reporting includes, and the World Bank Debtor Reporting System excludes, ODA flows from nonmarket economies and the technical assistance component of grants. There are no differences in coverage of recipient countries in the two data sources.
c. Net exports of goods and nonfactor services plus net investment receipts minus interest on medium- and long-term debt.
d. Excludes official transfers.

Middle-income countries									
Oil-exporting countries			Major exporters of manufactures			Other oil-importing countries			
	1995			1995			1995		
1985[a]	High	Low	1985[a]	High	Low	1985[a]	High	Low	Item
									Net exports of goods and nonfactor
15.2	−12.8	6.5	19.8	−35.1	−14.0	−12.0	−12.4	−4.2	services
									Interest on medium- and long-term
−21.1	−13.0	−10.5	−25.5	−20.3	−26.5	−8.4	−5.9	−6.0	debt
−3.3	−4.4	−4.4	−4.7	−4.1	−4.3	−3.0	−4.2	−4.4	Official
−17.8	−8.6	−6.1	−20.8	−16.2	−22.2	−5.4	−1.7	−1.6	Private
5.6	−25.8	−4.9	−0.2	−43.8	−31.2	−13.1	−9.0	−2.7	Current account balance[b]
2.0	3.4	2.9	5.4	6.9	6.0	3.5	4.3	3.7	Net official transfers
1.8	12.7	−2.4	19.3	21.6	16.5	6.7	3.3	−1.8	Medium- and long-term loans[c]
4.4	7.8	3.7	5.7	4.4	1.9	5.8	7.3	3.2	Official
−2.6	4.9	−6.1	13.7	17.3	14.5	1.0	−4.0	−5.1	Private
230.2	227.5	111.4	288.9	329.6	263.6	114.8	111.1	69.8	Debt outstanding and disbursed
39.4	24.6	13.6	37.9	22.9	22.9	54.5	30.4	22.2	As a percentage of GNP
160.8	116.4	90.5	108.2	60.5	72.9	180.1	98.5	87.5	As a percentage of exports
									Debt service as a percentage
31.6	17.4	17.8	17.2	10.7	15.9	26.1	14.7	17.2	of exports

a. Estimated.
b. Excludes official transfers.
c. Net disbursements.

growth rate of 4.5 percent a year. As ODA is assumed to remain at a constant 0.37 percent of DAC countries' GNP, it moves in line with their economic performance. Thus, an expanding world economy not only would provide improved export markets for developing countries but also would lead to a real increase in the level of concessional finance. This is crucial for sub-Saharan Africa, where even the higher level of ODA assumed in our High case would be insufficient to avoid future debt repayment problems in a dozen or more countries. Appropriate domestic policies, particularly in newly industrialized countries, would attract more foreign investment. Thus, private direct investment could increase at about 5.7 percent a year, as rapid growth in industrial countries produces more investment-seeking capital and positive real rates of interest make equity finance more attractive to developing countries.

If a concerted effort is made by developing countries to adjust and support from bilateral and multilateral agencies is increased, total nonconcessional capital flows would also grow. Under the High case, they would increase at a moderate 5.3 percent a year, primarily as a result of the restora-tion of private lending. As commercial banks respond to the improved creditworthiness of developing countries, within a more stable and growing world economy, private lending would increase from the low 1985 level of $15.0 billion to $29.3 billion by 1995, a growth rate of 7.0 percent a year over the next ten years. This is, quite appropriately, much lower than the 12.6 percent rate of growth in private lending that occurred during the 1970–80 period, when economies adjusted to the two oil price increases. Official nonconcessional lending is also anticipated to increase at about 3.1 percent a year. The resulting net flow of official nonconcessional lending of $19.0 billion in real terms by 1995, up from $14.0 billion in 1985, reflects the third leg of a combined effort by bilateral, multilateral, and private financiers to assist developing countries in adjusting.

The increase in total net capital inflows and the corresponding larger current account deficit in the High case are sustainable because export earnings increase faster than debt service payments. A higher rate of growth in the world economy and freer trade create the conditions for this to occur. For developing countries as a whole, total debt would decline as a proportion of GNP from 33.0 percent in 1985 to 22.3 percent in 1995. As a proportion of exports the figures would be 135.7 percent and 88.5 percent, respectively. These broad measures indicate the improvement in creditworthiness as most of the developing countries grow out of the debt problem. Before this could happen, however, additional international initiatives would be required in the near term to address the pressing debt problems of some heavily indebted countries and a group of low-income sub-Saharan countries. The type of initiatives required are discussed in the last section of this chapter.

The Low case

In the Low case, total interest payments would decline not because of lower interest rates (as in the High case) but because of a decline in capital flows to developing countries. Total debt outstanding and disbursed would decline from $723 billion in 1985 to $561 billion in 1995 (see Table 3.4). This decline in the real level of outstanding debt would entail a much lower current account deficit than the one implied in the High case. Given slow export growth, the level of imports and investment would be constrained below the level attained in the High case, which would inevitably result in slower growth.

As developing countries become less creditworthy and growth in industrial countries slows in the Low case, total net capital flows to developing countries would fall from $62.3 billion in 1985 to $49.9 billion in 1995 (see Table 3.5). The Low case assumes, perhaps optimistically, that industrial countries would maintain development assistance at 0.37 percent of their GDP. But the slower growth of industrial countries' GNP in the Low case would mean that by 1995 ODA would be $3.9 billion less than in the High case. As commercial banks reduce their exposure in uncreditworthy countries, net private lending would also fall from the already low level of $15.0 billion in 1985 to $3.1 billion in 1995. This low figure reflects very limited rescheduling as commercial banks gradually reduce their portfolio in noncreditworthy developing countries. Under these conditions the developing countries would have to make very painful adjustments to a sluggish world economy with diminished capital inflows.

To maintain creditworthiness, developing countries would have to improve their trade balances, mainly by increasing exports and not by cutting imports further. With slow growth in world trade,

however, only the most efficient developing countries could achieve this—mainly by increasing their share of export markets. In aggregate this situation is untenable. Squeezed between higher debt servicing and reduced capital flows, many developing countries would face an unenviable choice: cut imports yet further by reducing investment and lowering consumption—which will reduce growth and exacerbate social tensions—or reschedule debt, if possible. Without growth, creditworthiness cannot be restored.

International initiatives and the role of the Bank

The duration and magnitude of the economic and financial crises which many developing countries have experienced over the past half decade have heightened recognition of the longer-term, rather than temporary, nature of the debt problem. A consensus is evolving that the restoration of economic growth in these countries is critical to achieving a lasting and effective solution. The pursuit of this adjustment with growth objective will require close collaboration among the governments of the developing countries, the governments of the industrial countries, the multilateral institutions, and, in many cases, the commercial banks.

Recently, attention has focused on the heavily indebted middle-income developing countries, primarily because of the potential impact that action or inaction in addressing their problems could have on the international economy. In the fall of 1985, U.S. Secretary of the Treasury James A. Baker III suggested a plan of action to address the problems of these countries. It emphasized the critical importance of an adjustment with growth strategy and supported the proposal for a collaborative international effort by debtors and creditors alike. Restoring growth is no less important for low-income countries in sub-Saharan Africa. The impact that these economies have on the world economy is smaller, but the costs of a further decline in their per capita incomes is very high in terms of its impact on the poor.

Increased private and official net flows

Mobilizing additional capital flows from private and official sources will be a crucial factor in establishing the conditions required for growth. On the private side, Baker's initial proposal envisioned an increase in the net exposure of commercial banks during the next three years. One estimate of the increase in net flows required to help the heavily indebted middle-income countries adjust is provided in Box 3.4. To attain this transfer it will be necessary to strengthen the link between private bank debt restructuring, the provision of additional new financing, and comprehensive growth-oriented policy reforms by recipient countries, In some cases this collaborative effort needs to include a strengthening of the links between the commercial banks and institutions such as the World Bank that are capable of assisting in the development and monitoring of policy reform programs. This effort will, over time, help mobilize private flows by reducing the private banks' perception of risk. On the official side, a comparable effort needs to be made to increase flows from export credit agencies.

The increased economic stability provided by corrective domestic reforms, coupled with renewed access to external capital flows, will also help restore foreign private investors' confidence. Aside from providing an additional source of finance, direct private foreign investment has another advantage: it keeps the risks associated with investments that require foreign finance firmly in the hands of foreign investors and does not, as is the case for guaranteed loans, increase the obligations of the government.

An adjustment with growth strategy is no less important for the low-income countries of sub-Saharan Africa. While some progress has been made in pursuing structural adjustment, much more remains to be done to correct the accumulated policy distortions of the past. As in the heavily indebted middle-income countries, the prime responsibility rests with the domestic policymakers. They must implement reforms to reduce distortions, improve the allocation of resources, and increase domestic savings. Additional external resources will ease adjustment toward growth. But unlike the middle-income countries, most of these countries have very limited creditworthiness and debt-servicing capacity—a dozen or so are facing acute debt difficulties. This means that external private nonconcessional lending is likely to remain limited for at least the remainder of the decade. This implies the need for significant increases in official concessional flows to support countries committed to reform. Bilateral increases could involve both additional aid flows and more extensive debt relief actions.

The bulk of the multilateral flows will come from the International Monetary Fund and the International Bank for Reconstruction and Development.

The IMF has recently established a structural adjustment facility which is expected to lend a total of SDR 2.7 billion on concessional terms over the next five years to low-income countries undertaking macroeconomic and structural adjustment. The other major source of additional multilateral flows is likely to be the International Development Association (IDA). The negotiation of the Eighth Replenishment of IDA (IDA-8) is now under way. The critical need of all low-income countries, especially those in sub-Saharan Africa, coupled with the role which the World Bank will have to play in the designing and financing of adjustment programs in these countries, argues strongly for a substantial replenishment. Virtually all ministers at the April 1986 Development Committee meeting expressed the strong hope that an IDA-8 replenishment of $12 billion will be achieved. This would maintain in real terms the concessionary resources now available through IDA-7 and the Special Facility for Sub-Saharan Africa.

The role of international trade

Increased export earnings for developing countries is the second linchpin in the effort to reestablish sustainable growth and creditworthiness. This requires the reduction of the disincentives to exports created by the developing countries' own policy regimes in both industry and agriculture (see Chapters 4 and 5). It is therefore important that many of these countries undertake a rationalization and liberalization of their trade regimes in order to develop the export potential of their economies.

Developing-country exports are also affected by the trade policies of the industrial countries. The 1980s have been marked by a rise in protectionist pressures in both manufacturing and agriculture. Particularly worrisome is the increasing use of nontariff measures to restrict trade. Industrial-country tariff and nontariff barriers are often more restrictive on those products of specific interest to the developing countries than on others. This is seen most dramatically in the restrictions on agricultural and textile trade. Agricultural trade policy issues have, however, been largely excluded from earlier multilateral trade negotiations. While resistance remains strong, preliminary discussions within the GATT have pointed to an increased willingness to open the agricultural trade issue to international discussion.

Experience has shown that a multilateral approach can be effective in stemming the tide of

protectionist action and achieving broad-scale reductions in trade barriers. The GATT is now preparing for a new round of multilateral negotiations. As argued in Box 3.1, it is important that
developing countries in general, and middle-
income countries in particular, participate in the
negotiations. Because of the potential benefit to industrial and developing countries alike, particularly for agricultural commodities, this trade liberalization effort deserves strong international
support.

The role of the World Bank

There are four dimensions to the World Bank's expanded role in undertaking initiatives to revive
growth in developing countries:
  • To assist in the development, implementation,
and monitoring of medium-term adjustment programs in pursuit of the objectives of member countries committed to policy reform.
  • To expand greatly its own lending in support
of such programs.
  • To extend its catalytic role and, consistent with
its role as preferred creditor, help establish a
process for coordinated mobilization of private and
official support of developing countries' efforts.
  • To strengthen coordination with the IMF.
To play this expanded role effectively, the Bank
would also need to use its own human and financial resources in an even more efficient way.

Since the introduction of its structural adjustment lending program in 1980, the World Bank has
been involved in designing and monitoring adjustment programs to maintain or restore growth. As a
result, an increased proportion of its lending has
been in the form of fast-disbursing policy-based
loans and loans in support of maintenance and
rehabilitation projects. The Bank's involvement in
this adjustment effort is needed not only to help
resolve the difficulties involved in developing and
implementing such medium-term programs, but
also to generate increased confidence of private
and public creditors. In addition to its work on
policy reform, the World Bank is supporting the
acceleration of foreign private direct investment
through an expanded role of the International Finance Corporation (IFC) and through the establishment of the Multilateral Investment Guarantee
Agency (MIGA), which is designed to promote increased investment by providing noncommercial
risk insurance to investors and a wide range of
advisory and technical assistance.

The larger role played by donors in providing
finance to low-income countries also increases the
need for coordination among donors to improve
effectiveness. Individual donors at times have pursued their own agenda, which can sharply reduce
the benefit derived from their assistance. Some recipient governments have also had difficulty managing a large number of donors and donor
projects. This, coupled with the increased need to
provide aid in quick-disbursing form to support
policy action and for rehabilitation and maintenance, has led donors and recipients to look to the
World Bank to increase its coordination efforts.

Monitoring arrangements for adjustment programs will have to be designed on a case-by-case
basis, in light of each borrower's relationship with
the Bank, the IMF, and other multilateral institutions. It is clear that increased collaboration between the World Bank and the IMF is required.
The areas of economic policy dealt with by each
institution are related and complementary, as is
the financial assistance each can provide. Furthermore, macroeconomic stabilization and structural
adjustment must be pursued simultaneously and
in a unified way: in short, as two sides of the same
coin—growth. Bank-Fund collaboration has grown
substantially in recent years as the two institutions
have sought to increase the complementarity of
their programs and their capacity to respond to the
needs of developing countries. Exploration of
ways to further improve this collaboration continues.

An integral component of this concerted international adjustment with growth effort is increased
World Bank lending to countries that implement
serious policy reform. Higher levels of lending are
needed both to support these reform programs
and to stimulate other financial flows. The timing
and level of additional World Bank lending will, of
course, depend on the adoption and implementation by these countries of medium-term adjustment programs. Since increased lending by the
Bank will naturally affect its own resource requirements, additions to its capital base will be needed
in the near future. As the ministers at the spring
1986 meeting of the Development Committee
agreed, the Bank should be provided with the capacity to increase its quality lending and should
not be constrained by lack of capital or borrowing
authority in meeting future demand. As a result,
increased attention is being given to the issue of
the potential size and timing of a general capital
increase for the Bank.

4

Agricultural policies in developing countries
Exchange rates, prices, and taxation

Increased production of food and cash crops and higher rural incomes have been important objectives for governments of developing countries. In pursuing these objectives, governments, with the support of foreign assistance, have made substantial public investments to improve the physical infrastructure in rural areas, expand irrigation and flood control, and organize research and extension in agriculture. Resources have also been directed to programs which aim to raise productivity through better farm management and improved rural health and education services. In many cases, these efforts have succeeded in raising food production, as shown in Chapter 1. The spread of the Green Revolution in rice and wheat is testimony to the effectiveness of public expenditures in research and irrigation.

The general economic policies that developing countries have pursued have, however, limited the growth of agricultural production and hampered efforts to reduce rural poverty. In many cases, sector-specific pricing and tax policies have also resulted in substantial discrimination against agriculture. In addition, government interventions at all stages of production, consumption, and marketing of agricultural products and inputs, though undertaken to improve the efficiency of markets, have frequently resulted in greater inefficiencies and lower output and incomes. As a consequence, farm incomes in many developing countries are stagnating, and little progress is being made in overcoming the problems of poverty.

Paradoxically, many countries which have been stressing the importance of agricultural development have established a complex set of policies that is strongly biased against agriculture. Thus, some developing countries impose taxes on agricultural exports while lamenting the adverse impact of declining commodity prices on the farm sector. Some pay their producers half the world price for grains (or even less), and then spend scarce foreign exchange to import food. Many have raised producer prices at various stages, but have followed macroeconomic and exchange rate policies that have left real producer prices unchanged or lower than before. Many have set up complex systems of producer taxation, and then have set up equally complex and frequently ineffective systems of subsidies for inputs to offset that taxation. Many subsidize consumers to help the poor, but end up reducing the incomes of farmers who are much poorer than many of the urban consumers who actually benefit from the subsidies. Most developing countries pronounce self-sufficiency as an important objective, but follow policies that tax farmers, subsidize consumers, and increase dependence upon imported food.

The discrimination against agriculture derives from several factors. First of all, it is very much an integral part of development strategies that promote domestic industries behind high trade barriers. Such strategies are intended to accelerate the shift of resources out of agriculture by lowering its profitability compared with that of industry: in other words, by turning the internal terms of trade between agriculture and industry so that agriculture is worse off than it would be if domestic prices were aligned with relative world prices. Agricultural exports suffer as a result; so do agricultural products that compete with imports. This is not just because their domestic prices become lower relative to the prices of protected industrial products, but also because the costs of the industrial inputs the farmers use increase. Moreover, the protectionist policies result in an appreciation of the real exchange rate. This means that traded agricultural goods become less profitable than non-traded goods, with further adverse consequences on developing countries' agricultural exports.

During the past fifteen years, this traditional bias against agriculture has often been exacerbated by the way countries have responded to changing economic circumstances. Some countries have failed to adjust exchange rates sufficiently in periods of rapid inflation, thus allowing their exchange rates to become overvalued, and have relied instead on excessive foreign borrowing and on ad hoc exchange and trade controls. Such ad hoc measures usually come on top of more permanent trade restrictions and make the discrimination against agriculture worse.

Sectoral policies that keep the domestic farm prices of agricultural products below their world prices at country borders (adjusted for internal transport and distribution margins) have also contributed significantly to the bias against agriculture. It makes little difference from this point of view whether farmers receive low prices because of taxes on their outputs or because of excessive margins charged by parastatal marketing agencies. The effects of low prices for farm output are not generally offset by the subsidies that many governments provide on credit and modern farm inputs. Typically, these subsidies lead to rationing and shortages and benefit larger and better-off farmers more than smaller and poorer farmers.

This chapter discusses the extent to which economy-wide trade and exchange rate policies, as well as sectoral tax and price policies, discriminate against agriculture in developing countries and examines the effects of this discrimination on agricultural output and incomes. It also discusses how costly agricultural taxation can be in practice and points to several alternative ways of moderating the costs.

The next chapter reviews the rationale for government programs for price stabilization, consumer subsidies, and producer input subsidies—all three of which are used to promote a variety of distributional and income objectives. It is shown that these programs are far less effective than they are thought to be in promoting either a more efficient allocation of resources or a more even distribution of income.

Economy-wide policies and agriculture

Trade, exchange rate, fiscal, and monetary policies have a significant impact on agriculture in developing countries, and their effects often overshadow those of sector-specific policies. These policies are leading determinants of the movement of capital and labor between agriculture and the rest of the economy, the growth and composition of agricultural output, and the volume and composition of trade in agricultural products. They are often the principal sources of bias against agriculture, and as such they inhibit the growth of real incomes in rural areas, where the concentration of poverty is greatest.

Sources of bias

Many developing countries have continued to promote industrialization through generous protection to industry. This strategy increases the prices of industrial import substitutes relative to the prices of agricultural import substitutes and exports. It also raises the prices of protected farm inputs. By lowering output prices relative to industry and by increasing the cost of modern inputs, inward-looking strategies implicitly tax agriculture. Table 4.1 gives some indication of how the differential protection given to industry has lowered the relative profitability of agriculture in many

Table 4.1 Protection of agriculture compared with manufacturing in selected developing countries

Country and period	Year	Relative protection ratio[a]
In the 1960s		
Mexico	1960	0.79
Chile	1961	0.40
Malaysia	1965	0.98
Philippines	1965	0.66
Brazil	1966	0.46
Korea	1968	1.18
Argentina	1969	0.46
Colombia	1969	0.40
In the 1970s and 1980s		
Philippines	1974	0.76
Colombia	1978	0.49
Brazil[b]	1980	0.65
Mexico	1980	0.88
Nigeria	1980	0.35
Egypt	1981	0.57
Peru[b]	1981	0.68
Turkey	1981	0.77
Korea[b]	1982	1.36
Ecuador	1983	0.65

a. Calculated as $(1+EPR_a)/(1+EPR_m)$, where EPR_a and EPR_m are the effective rates of protection for agriculture and the manufacturing sector, respectively. A ratio of 1.00 indicates that effective protection is equal in both sectors; a ratio greater than 1.00 means that protection is in favor of agriculture.
b. Refers to primary sector.

countries. The ratios in the table show the extent to which value added in agriculture has been protected relative to value added in industry. With the sole exception of Korea, all countries in the sample discriminated against agriculture, especially Nigeria, Colombia, and Egypt.

But this is not the only way inward-looking strategies affect agriculture. There is another effect that works through the real exchange rate (the ratio of the prices of traded goods to the prices of nontraded goods). Industrial protection makes the real exchange rate lower than it would be otherwise. Thus, the production of import substitutes and exports in agriculture suffers for two reasons: increased profitability of protected industrial outputs and increased profitability of nontraded goods. Resources move from the traded agriculture sector to these other sectors, and as they do, rural real wages may rise; this increases the cost of farming, which is typically very labor-intensive in developing countries.

Several studies have shown how policies that protect industry affect the prices of agricultural products compared with the prices of protected industrial products and of nontraded goods. In the Philippines, from 1950 to 1980, heavy protection for industrial consumer goods meant that prices of agricultural exports were between 44 and 71 percent lower (depending on the category of imports) relative to the prices of protected traded goods and were 33 to 35 percent lower relative to the prices of nontradable goods. In Peru, a 10 percent increase in tariffs on nonagricultural importables was found to decrease the prices of traded agricultural goods by 10 percent relative to the prices of those importables and by 5.6 to 6.6 percent relative to the prices of nontradables. Similar results have been obtained in countries as varied as Argentina, Chile, Colombia, Nigeria, and Zaire.

Policies on money supply and credit, public revenues and expenditures, foreign borrowing and investment, and exchange rate regimes have all been of critical importance during the 1970s and 1980s. When expansionary monetary and fiscal policies have led to higher inflation at home than abroad, governments have often failed to adjust exchange rates and have relied instead on increasing import protection by employing such devices as quotas, exchange controls, and licensing. In such circumstances, the currency becomes overvalued and the bias against agriculture becomes stronger because the increased protection usually accrues to industry. Typically, food imports are excluded from restrictive measures in order to keep

urban food prices low: consequently, food imports are implicitly subsidized. Furthermore, in trying to reduce fiscal deficits, countries usually increase sectoral taxes on agricultural exports and curtail subsidy programs for agricultural inputs. As a result of both implicit and explicit taxation, agriculture—and the low-income groups that depend on it—tends to bear the brunt of the adjustment programs that ensue from destabilizing macroeconomic policies.

The impact on agriculture can be especially pronounced when import quotas are used, since changes in the domestic price of an imported commodity are then determined not by supply, which is fixed, but by the level of demand alone. Thus, by increasing overall demand, an expansionary fiscal policy would raise the domestic prices of goods whose imports are restricted. The net effect would be to reduce relative prices for agriculture and increase discrimination against it.

Capital inflows from abroad and sharp increases in the world prices of key exports also cause the real exchange rate to appreciate. But this by itself is not distortionary, although special sectoral measures may be needed to offset the effects on agriculture if the commodity boom is temporary and if factor movements out of agriculture are difficult to reverse. Typically, however, countries react to commodity booms by initiating expansionary monetary and fiscal policies, which leads to inflation and a greater appreciation of the real exchange rate than would occur simply because of the favorable change in the external terms of trade. The effects of this reaction continue even after the boom ends, because by then commitments to large investment programs or to large recurrent costs have already been made. This is what happened in Colombia (see Box 4.1).

SECTORAL POLICIES. Policies within the agricultural sector—such as trade duties, subsidies, and parastatal margins—can, of course, mitigate or exacerbate the implicit taxation caused by general economic policies. What are the levels of trade duties and subsidies in agriculture? Is agriculture actually taxed by sectoral policies, or is it subsidized? Figure 4.1 provides an overview of sectoral trade taxes and subsidies in various developing countries. These are measured as the difference between farmgate prices and border prices at official exchange rates, after adjustments for internal transport and marketing margins. This procedure is employed because, apart from conventional trade duties and subsidies, the use of quotas and

Figure 4.1 Ratio of farmgate prices to border prices for selected commodities of developing countries in the late 1970s and early 1980s

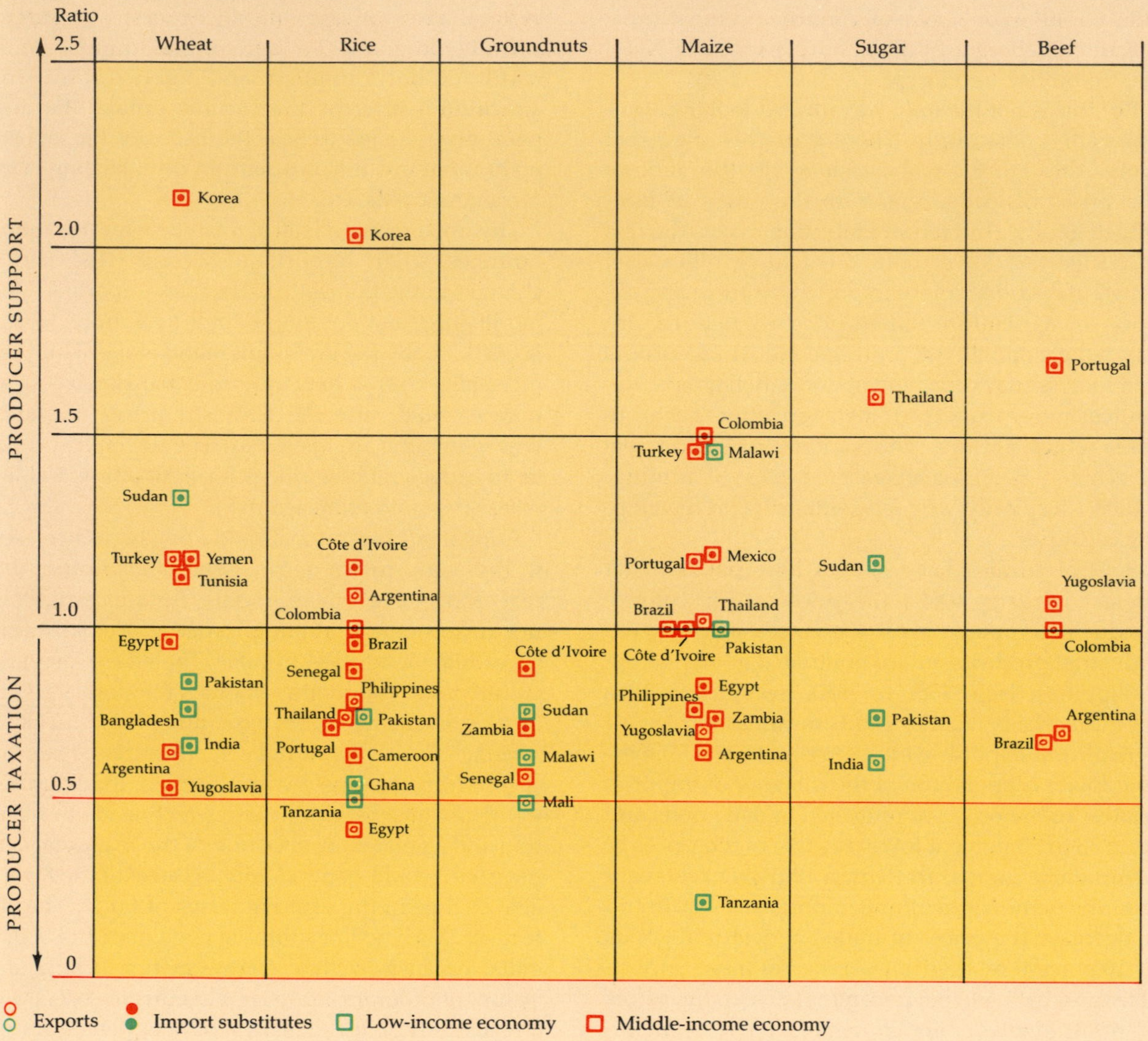

Ratio

PRODUCER SUPPORT

PRODUCER TAXATION

Columns: Wheat | Rice | Groundnuts | Maize | Sugar | Beef

Ratio axis values: 2.5, 2.0, 1.5, 1.0, 0.5, 0

Data labels by column:

Wheat: Korea (≈2.1); Sudan (≈1.2); Turkey, Yemen, Tunisia (≈1.0–1.05); Egypt (≈0.9); Pakistan (≈0.8); Bangladesh, India (≈0.65); Argentina, Yugoslavia (≈0.5)

Rice: Korea (≈2.0); Côte d'Ivoire (≈1.1); Argentina (≈1.0); Colombia (≈1.0); Brazil (≈0.9); Senegal, Philippines (≈0.8); Thailand, Pakistan (≈0.7); Portugal, Cameroon (≈0.65); Ghana (≈0.55); Tanzania, Egypt (≈0.45)

Groundnuts: Côte d'Ivoire (≈0.85); Sudan (≈0.7); Zambia (≈0.7); Malawi (≈0.6); Senegal (≈0.5); Mali (≈0.5)

Maize: Colombia (≈1.5); Turkey, Malawi (≈1.4); Portugal, Mexico (≈1.1); Brazil, Thailand (≈1.0); Côte d'Ivoire, Pakistan (≈0.9); Philippines, Egypt (≈0.8); Yugoslavia, Zambia (≈0.7); Argentina (≈0.6); Tanzania (≈0.25)

Sugar: Thailand (≈1.55); Sudan (≈1.1); Pakistan (≈0.7); India (≈0.55)

Beef: Portugal (≈1.6); Yugoslavia (≈1.05); Colombia (≈0.9); Argentina (≈0.7); Brazil (≈0.65)

Legend:
○ Exports ● Import substitutes □ Low-income economy □ Middle-income economy

Note: Border prices are converted to domestic currency at official exchange rates.
Source: Binswanger and Scandizzo 1983; FAO data.

large parastatal marketing margins can contribute to the sectoral taxes and subsidies that farmers in effect face.

• *Export crops.* Figure 4.1 indicates that many countries tax export crops, sometimes at very high rates. In Togo, the farm price for coffee was a third of the border price. In Mali, cotton and groundnut farmers received half the border prices, and in Cameroon and Ghana cocoa producers received less than half.

The costs of high agricultural taxation are discussed later in this chapter. The first questions to

ask are: How do governments tax agricultural output and exports, and why do they do it? Some taxation of export crops involves conventional border taxes or quotas, but frequently taxation is a result of the pricing policies pursued by marketing agencies in the public sector. This is especially so in Africa, where statutory monopolies, or marketing boards, have traditionally controlled export crops. Created in colonial times, marketing boards were almost always required to use the bulk of their funds for the benefit of the farming community. But most of them became de facto taxation

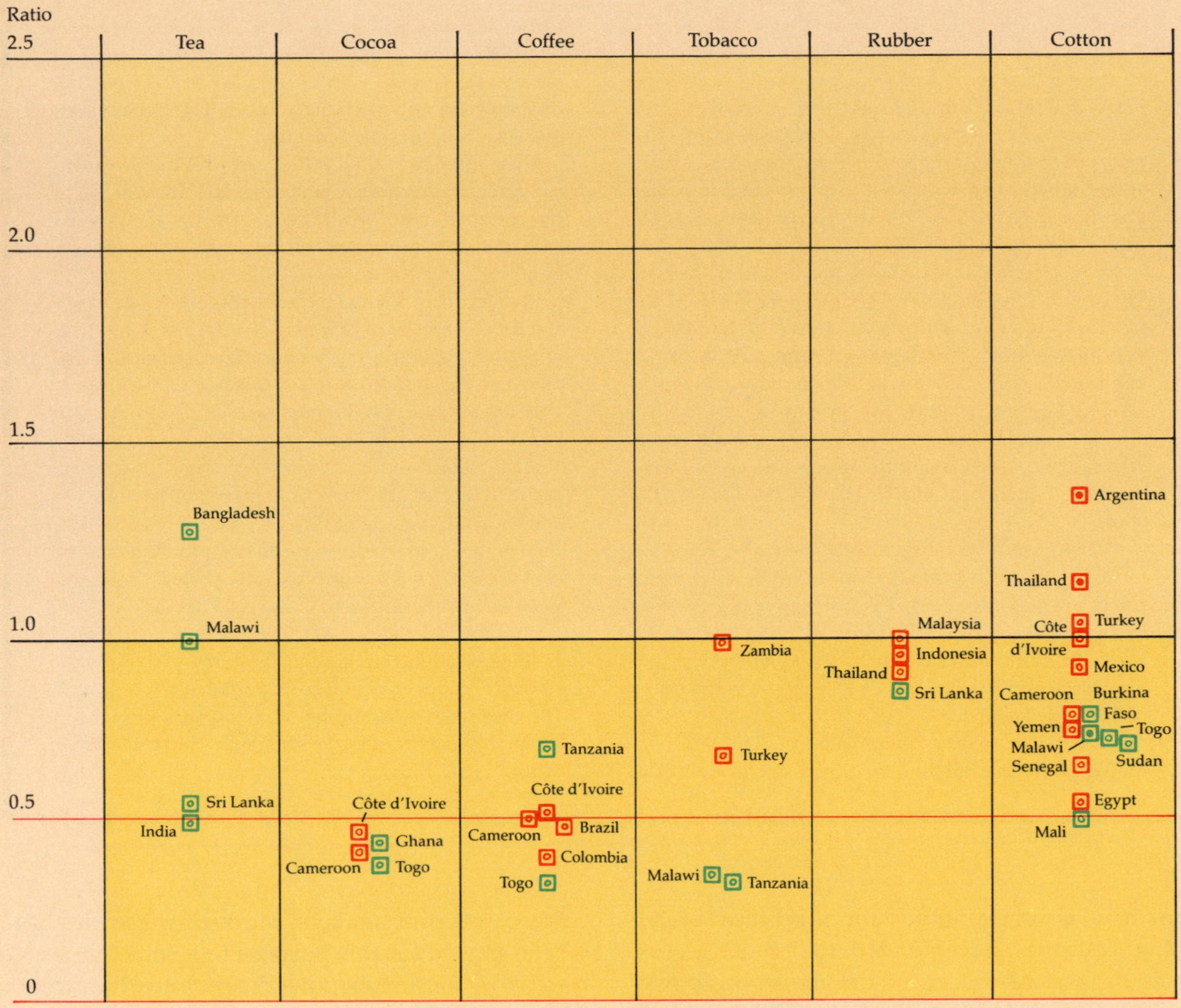

Ratio

	Tea	Cocoa	Coffee	Tobacco	Rubber	Cotton

2.5

2.0

1.5

- Argentina (Cotton, ~1.3)
- Bangladesh (Tea, ~1.2)
- Thailand (Cotton, ~1.1)

1.0

- Malawi (Tea, ~1.0)
- Malaysia / Côte d'Ivoire / Turkey
- Zambia (Tobacco, ~0.95)
- Thailand / Indonesia (Rubber)
- Mexico (Cotton)
- Sri Lanka (Rubber)
- Cameroon / Burkina Faso
- Yemen / Togo
- Malawi / Sudan
- Senegal

- Tanzania (Coffee, ~0.6)
- Turkey (Tobacco, ~0.6)
- Egypt (Cotton, ~0.55)

0.5

- Sri Lanka (Tea)
- Côte d'Ivoire (Coffee)
- India (Tea)
- Côte d'Ivoire / Brazil (Cocoa/Coffee)
- Cameroon
- Ghana (Cocoa)
- Colombia (Coffee)
- Cameroon / Togo (Cocoa)
- Togo (Coffee)
- Malawi / Tanzania (Tobacco)
- Mali (Cotton)

0

agencies—important public instruments for extracting resources from export agriculture in support of the postindependence drive to industrialize. High rates of export taxation, of the order of 50–75 percent, have not been unusual.

Marketing boards are also common in other regions. For example, commodity boards exist by statute for virtually all the major agricultural export crops in Jamaica, including sugar, bananas, citrus, coconuts, coffee, cocoa, and spices. While the boards were initially required only to assemble, package, and export these products, over the years their activities have expanded to cover many other functions, including price stabilization and, in some cases, processing. One study indicated that during the 1970s they in effect taxed producers at rates varying between 17 and 42 percent, depending on the commodity: the highest rates were on bananas and coffee. Moreover, domestic prices were usually at least as variable as export prices, and in some cases more so.

The primary reason for export taxes is, of course, to raise revenue for the use of either the marketing boards or the central government. But other reasons have also been important in practice. Developing countries have tended to impose export taxes to take advantage of the monopoly power they believe they have in world markets. Many developing countries have also sought to encourage agro-industries by taxing, or restricting by quota, the exports of the agricultural raw materials they use. Export taxes on cash crops have also been used to encourage the production of domestic food crops in order to attain self-sufficiency. As will be discussed later, export taxation for these purposes has been very costly in terms of national incomes and agricultural performance.

• *Agricultural import substitutes.* A few developing countries have protected agricultural import substitutes to promote self-sufficiency—especially in wheat and dairy and livestock products. In most cases, however, domestic producers of import substitutes are paid less than the import prices (adjusted for internal marketing costs). In an attempt to keep urban food prices low, governments often try to procure food at prices that are lower than

those on world markets. Marketing agencies have been created for this purpose too, sometimes with statutory monopoly powers to ensure that farmers do not sell their products elsewhere. However, policing is difficult with food crops, and many farmers find more lucrative markets.

In Ethiopia, for example, a parastatal marketing agency controls about 30 percent of the total marketable surplus and almost 100 percent of the interregional grain trade from two of the three main grain-surplus areas. Its farmgate procurement prices have been far below the import parity prices; in 1985, for instance, the import parity prices (at the official exchange rate) for maize, sorghum, and wheat were respectively about 80 percent, 50 percent, and 45 percent above the farmgate prices. And, as shown in Figure 4.1, the maize procurement price in Tanzania was only a quarter of the border price. In Cameroon, Ghana, and Tanzania, rice producers were paid only about half the border price. This is by no means a phenomenon that occurs in sub-Saharan Africa alone.

The tendency to discriminate against domestic production relative to imports produced by foreign producers has been observed in Egypt, Mexico, and other developing countries with large urban food subsidy programs, although the degree of discrimination against domestic producers and the mechanisms used have varied. The costs of this discrimination are discussed later in this chapter.

It is often thought that if the border prices relevant to a country are depressed by policies abroad—for example, due to export subsidies—the country concerned should take countervailing measures to keep its domestic prices higher. The issue, however, is not how border prices are formed but what they are likely to be in the future. When countries can indefinitely obtain goods more cheaply from abroad than they can produce them, the usual arguments for open trade apply. Thus, if prevailing prices are expected to continue, countervailing actions will hurt rather than help a country. However, countervailing measures may be warranted if the average level of a border price is likely to increase sharply in the short run because of policy changes abroad. The practice of paying domestic producers of import substitutes and exportables less than border prices is, of course, precisely the opposite of countervailing measures.

SECTORAL POLICIES AND REAL EXCHANGE RATES. While sectoral pricing and trade policies frequently exacerbate the general economic bias against agriculture, their effects cannot be assessed in isolation from real exchange rate movements. Efforts to improve sectoral policies can easily be outweighed by appreciations in real exchange rates resulting from inappropriate macroeconomic policies. This is most easily seen in sub-Saharan Africa, where, for a variety of reasons, real exchange rates appreciated most sharply during the 1970s and early 1980s. For the sub-Saharan African countries as a group, real exchange rates appreciated by 31 percent between 1969–71 and 1981–83, as shown in Table 4.2. Exchange rate overvaluations were particularly large in Ghana, Nigeria, and Tanzania.

Since in sub-Saharan Africa—as in many other areas of the developing world—the cost of modern farm inputs imported or produced at home is only a small fraction of total farm costs, the importance of real exchange rate appreciations with regard to sectoral policies can be seen by looking at trends in farm output prices. Insofar as real labor costs increased as a result of the out-migration of labor

Table 4.2 Index of real exchange rates in selected African countries
(1969–71 = 100)

Country	1973–75	1978–80	1981–83
Cameroon	75	58	80
Côte d'Ivoire	81	56	74
Ethiopia	93	64	67
Ghana	89	23	8
Kenya	88	69	86
Malawi	94	85	94
Mali	68	50	66
Niger	80	56	74
Nigeria	76	43	41
Senegal	71	60	85
Sierra Leone	100	90	73
Sudan	76	58	74
Tanzania	85	69	51
Zambia	90	79	86
All sub-Saharan Africa	84	62	69

Note: The real exchange rate is defined as the official exchange rate deflated by the ratio of the domestic consumer price deflator to the U.S. consumption deflator. A fall in the index indicates exchange rate appreciation. Data are three-year averages.
Source: Kerr (background paper).

from agriculture, the adverse effects of macroeconomic policies would have been greater than indicated by output price trends alone.

Suppose, for example, that in one year farmers received only half the border price at the official exchange rate—that is, the nominal protection coefficient was 0.5. Suppose also that the government eliminated this difference over a period of time, during which the exchange rate became overvalued by 50 percent because it was not adjusted in line with the excess of domestic inflation over inflation abroad. Even though farmers would seem better off nominally, in real terms they would actually be as badly off as they were originally.

The trends shown in Table 4.3 show how real farm incentives have been eroded over time despite apparent improvements in nominal terms. Using official exchange rates, one would infer that incentives for cereal production in Africa increased by 51 percent between 1969–71 and 1981–83, or, in other words, that domestic prices increased significantly more than border prices. But when border prices are calculated taking the real appreciations into account, the actual increase in incentives was only 9 percent. For export crops, incentives nominally increased by about 2 percent. However, they actually declined sharply—by 27 percent. Compared with the situation in 1969–71, by 1981–83 real incentives to export crops declined in all the countries shown in the table. This illustrates that agri-

Table 4.3 Index of nominal and real protection coefficients for cereals and export crops in selected African countries, 1972–83
(1969–71 = 100)

| | Cereals | | | | Export crops | | | |
| | 1972–83 | | 1981–83 | | 1972–83 | | 1981–83 | |
Country	Nominal index	Real index	Nominal index	Real index	Nominal index	Real index	Nominal index	Real index
Cameroon	129	90	140	108	83	61	95	75
Côte d'Ivoire	140	98	119	87	92	66	99	71
Ethiopia	73	55	73	49	88	71	101	66
Kenya	115	94	115	98	101	83	98	84
Malawi	85	79	106	100	102	94	106	97
Mali	128	79	177	122	101	83	98	70
Niger	170	119	225	166	82	59	113	84
Nigeria	126	66	160	66	108	60	149	63
Senegal	109	79	104	89	83	60	75	64
Sierra Leone	104	95	184	143	101	93	92	68
Sudan	174	119	229	164	90	63	105	75
Tanzania	127	88	188	95	86	62	103	52
Zambia	107	93	146	125	97	84	93	80
All sub-Saharan Africa	122	89	151	109	93	71	102	73

Note: The nominal index measures the change in the nominal protection coefficient with border prices converted into local currency at official exchange rates. The real index measures the change in the nominal protection coefficient with border prices converted into local currency at real exchange rates. Data for Ghana are not available.
Source: Kerr (background paper).

cultural reforms need to go hand in hand with general economic reforms.

Counting the costs

There are many indications that the costs of discriminating against agriculture—either implicitly through macroeconomic policies or explicitly through sectoral policies—have been large. An important reason why this is so is that, contrary to a long-held belief, farmers in developing countries—as in industrial countries—respond strongly to prices. The crops they grow, the amounts they produce, and the technologies they adopt depend greatly on the policy environment.

There is a large body of evidence that indicates that the supply response in developing countries is not low. A sample of the numerous estimates made by researchers of supply responses for individual crops is shown in Table 4.4. The lower end of the range shows short-term supply responses, the upper end long-term responses. Even in the short term, the supply responses are significant, considering the high level of taxation to which farmers have often been subjected. Supply responses are widely believed to be especially low in Africa. In fact, however, many studies suggest that they can be as high as they are elsewhere. The high supply

response of African farmers, who have to make do with a poor infrastructure and imperfect markets, is evident in Niger (see Box 4.2).

Empirical work has indicated that the supply response for all crops taken together is lower than the responses for individual crops. This is partly to be expected: If a government taxes only one crop, resources need not be withdrawn from farming altogether. They can be shifted to other crops so that total farm output does not fall by as much as the

Table 4.4 Summary of output responses to price changes

| | Percentage change in output with a 10 percent increase in price | |
Crop	Africa	Other developing countries
Wheat	3.1–6.5	1.0–10.0
Maize	2.3–24.3	1.0–3.0
Sorghum	1.0–7.0	1.0–3.6
Groundnuts	2.4–16.2	1.0–40.5
Cotton	2.3–6.7	1.0–16.2
Tobacco	4.8–8.2	0.5–10.0
Cocoa	1.5–18.0	1.2–9.5
Coffee	1.4–15.5	0.8–10.0
Rubber	1.4–9.4	0.4–4.0
Palm oil	2.0–8.1	..

Source: Askari and Cummings 1976; Scandizzo and Bruce 1980.

Box 4.2 Flexible markets in Niger

Farmers in low-income economies are commonly assumed to be inflexible, slow to respond to prices, and sluggish in adapting to changing circumstances. This assumption is wrong or greatly exaggerated. Recent developments in the agricultural sector in Niger tell a story, not of passivity and slow response to change, but, rather, of quick adaptation and adjustment to new economic realities.

Niger is one of the poorest countries in the world. In the 1970s, farmers relied primarily on groundnuts for cash income; cotton and livestock were secondary sources of income. In recent years, farm households have begun to diversify their sources of income. Studies indicate that nonfarm earnings now account for more than 20 percent of total household income. Sales of animals, traditionally the most important source of noncrop income, account for an additional 30 percent. So, half of all agricultural income now comes from sources other than crop production. A census in 1980 revealed that approximately 6 percent of rural Nigerien men are wage earners. An additional 12 percent have some occupation outside agriculture; for men between the ages of thirty-five and forty-five, the figure is 20 percent. Ninety percent of villages send migrants to work in Nigeria or other countries farther south during the dry season.

In addition to diversifying out of crop agriculture, Niger's farmers have changed their farming patterns. In the 1970s, prices of millet, sorghum, and cowpeas rose faster than those of groundnuts. At the same time, groundnut yields were declining, and, after the 1973 drought, farmers wanted to rebuild their food stocks. All this encouraged farmers to sow more land to food crops, especially sorghum and cowpeas. The most dramatic result was that cowpeas overtook groundnuts as the country's main agricultural export. Production of cowpeas grew by more than 250 percent during the 1970s, while the area planted expanded by almost 70 percent. Earnings from cowpeas have begun to account for a measurable part of farm revenues—4 percent in all, but, according to some surveys, as much as 12 percent for smaller farmers in main producing areas. Meanwhile, groundnut sales have shrunk to almost nothing.

Cowpeas have a number of advantages over groundnuts. They can be grown in a variety of soils and allow farmers to adopt flexible cropping patterns. They are more resistant to drought. A large and accessible market exists in Nigeria, whereas groundnut's export markets are mainly in Europe. Cowpeas are traded almost exclusively on parallel markets, where prices have frequently been twice as high as the official prices paid by SONARA, the state marketing agency. It is hard to know the volume of ''unofficial'' cowpea exports to Nigeria, but annual production is believed to be 250,000–300,000 tons, while legal exports have never amounted to more than 30,000–40,000 tons.

Important points are illustrated by the example of Niger. It shows how buoyant open markets can be, even in unlikely places. The growth of cowpeas took place almost entirely through parallel markets and in the face of public policies that were not encouraging. The official price and marketing structure was bypassed. And it shows that change can be extraordinarily rapid. In a decade or less, one main cash crop disappeared and was replaced by another. All of this happened primarily in response to market signals, despite poor infrastructure, embryonic market information, and generally imperfect market conditions.

---

output of the crop taxed. But estimates of aggregate farm output responses have typically been of a short-term nature and have failed to reflect the fact that changes in prices have a long-term effect on the intersectoral flow of resources. When such effects are taken into account, the aggregate supply becomes price responsive as well.

Discrimination against agriculture on a sustained basis not only reallocates resources within agriculture but also draws them out of it. As labor and capital move out and technical progress slows, the long-term losses can be large:

• The International Food Policy Research Institute (IFPRI) studied the evolution of the Argentine and Chilean economies and the effects of pricing and exchange rate policies on agriculture. The study showed that, if agricultural prices in Argentina between 1950 and 1972 had been 10 percent higher than they in fact were (when the government was taxing farmers heavily), total agricultural output would have gradually increased to a level approximately 9 percent higher, on an annual basis, than it actually was over the period. The increase in production would have been achieved largely because more capital would have been attracted into agriculture and technical improvements would have been made. Box 4.3 on Argentina discusses how inappropriate macroeconomic and sectoral policies led to a large reduction in agricultural output. A similar simulation for the Chilean economy during the period 1960–82 indicated an even greater supply response: the level of output would have eventually become 20 percent higher each year than otherwise in response to a 10 percent sustained increase in agricultural prices. Sustained taxation of farming can thus lower the returns to investment, discourage technical progress, and encourage farmers to leave the land.

• Evidence about the long-term effects of price changes on farming can also be obtained by exam-

---

Box 4.3 Trade policies and agricultural performance: the case of Argentina

Argentina has ideal farming conditions and is one of the largest grain exporters in the world. It has had a long history of agricultural growth. Between 1965 and 1983, however, agricultural growth averaged only 0.8 percent a year, compared with 1.9 percent a year during 1950–64 and about 2.6 percent before World War II. Agriculture's recent poor performance reflected poor incentives. The internal terms of trade were deliberately turned against the agricultural sector through a combination of export taxes, tariffs, restrictions on imports of industrial goods, and exchange controls which led to an overvalued currency. Argentina's policies grew out of a perception that its exports, which were primarily agricultural, were facing declining real prices on world markets and therefore Argentina needed to diversify its economy by encouraging industry.

Moreover, in the 1950s and 1960s, the notion that agricultural output did not respond significantly to price changes was an essential part of the debate on growth, inflation, and distribution in the Argentine economy. Policymakers argued that taxing agriculture to support industries that made import substitutes would not result in big losses in farm output; similarly, they thought that increasing agricultural prices by reducing export taxes or by devaluing the currency would increase the budget deficit, accelerate inflation, and penalize poor consumers without significantly affecting agricultural supply. Indeed, inflation itself was considered to be structural, that is, a reflection of the food or foreign exchange shortages that resulted when industrialization pushed up income and increased domestic demand for food. These views have been changing since the 1960s, and, by now, agricultural supply responses have been shown to be strong in Argentina.

A recent study of the Argentine economy examined the combined impact of exchange rate, fiscal, and commercial policies on the agricultural sector. Besides estimating the level of taxation on agriculture created by the above policies, it also provided insights into the interrelationships among various macroeconomic policies. For example, it showed that, since physical controls on imports were the primary instruments used to protect industry, fiscal policy strongly influenced the degree to which Argentina's trade policy adversely affected agriculture. While the restrictions remained for the most part constant between 1960 and 1983, domestic prices for protected imports deviated widely from world prices when macroeconomic policies changed.

During periods of high government spending, demand for imports rose and domestic prices for protected imports jumped sharply, turning the internal terms of trade against agriculture (see Box figure 4.3).

By simulating what would have happened in the absence of these policies, the study indicated that:

• Real prices of all agricultural products would have been higher by about 38 percent a year on average during 1960–83. These prices were depressed not only because of import control and public spending policies, as described above, but also because of heavy taxation of agricultural exports. These exports, which are an important component of the sector, were taxed at an average annual rate of about 44 percent during the period.

• The annual value of agricultural output would have become 33 percent higher by 1983 had the agricultural prices not been depressed by 38 percent as a result of the sectoral and macroeconomic policies.

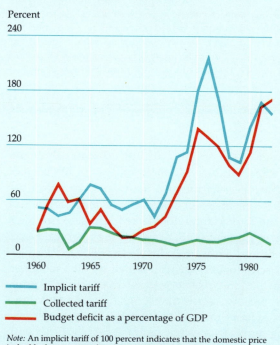

Box figure 4.3 Implicit and collected tariff rates and budget deficits in Argentina, 1960–82

Percent

— Implicit tariff
— Collected tariff
— Budget deficit as a percentage of GDP

Note: An implicit tariff of 100 percent indicates that the domestic price is double the corresponding international price.
Source: Cavallo (background paper).

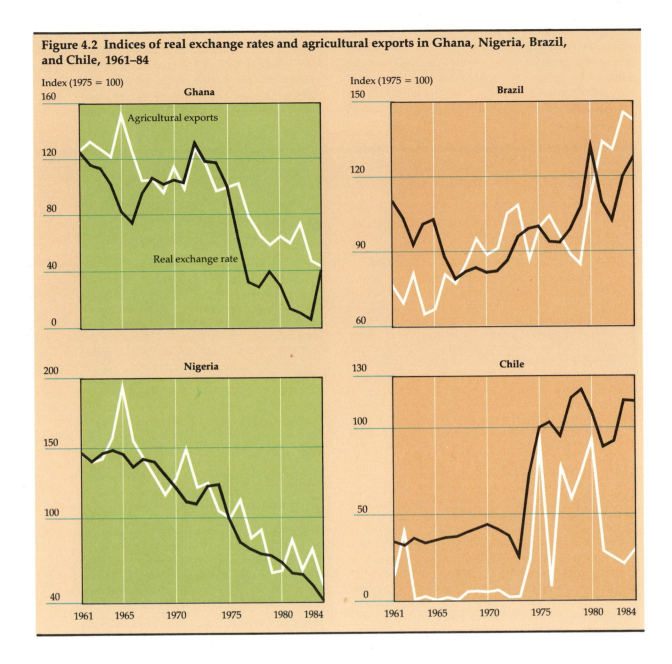

Figure 4.2 **Indices of real exchange rates and agricultural exports in Ghana, Nigeria, Brazil, and Chile, 1961–84**

ining what happened when the real exchange rate changed sharply and affected the real prices of farm goods received by producers. Two countries whose real exchange rates appreciated sharply—Ghana and Nigeria—can be compared with two countries whose real exchange rates depreciated—Brazil and Chile. Figure 4.2 shows a close connection between changes in the real exchange rates in these countries and the level of their agricultural exports. Detailed econometric studies show this is true more widely. On average, a percentage point fall in the real exchange rate reduces agricultural exports by 0.6–0.8 percentage point in

all developing countries and by more than one percentage point in sub-Saharan Africa. The results for Africa not only confirm the fact that supply responses are high in that region, but also show that exports are sensitive to exchange rate changes when there is the chance to sell on parallel markets. Correlations between real exchange rate movements and agricultural output have also been similarly close in many cases. The effects of real exchange rate movements on agriculture in Nigeria and Indonesia are discussed in Box 4.4, which compares the countries' different reactions to the oil booms of the 1970s.

• The emergence of parallel markets, most significantly in Africa, indicates that the taxes which marketing agencies have tried to impose and the large exchange rate overvaluations have gone well beyond what is enforceable. The main loser is the government itself. It loses tax revenues when farmers sell export crops unofficially, and it may end up worse off than it would have been had taxes been lower and the real exchange rate appropriate. Sierra Leone suffered large foreign exchange losses because exports of coffee, cocoa, palm kernels, and rice were smuggled out through

Box 4.4   Oil and agriculture: Nigeria and Indonesia

The oil boom of the 1970s and early 1980s proved a blessing and a curse for many oil-exporting countries. Oil revenues raised the standard of living, widened job opportunities, and increased the policy options available to governments. But they also altered the structure of incentives in the economy, raised expectations, and produced rapid and often destabilizing changes. Agriculture, especially, was affected by these changes.

Oil-exporting countries commonly experienced declines in the rate of growth of their agricultural sectors. Higher incomes led to an increase in the price of nontradable goods at the expense of tradable goods such as crops. Farmers abandoned the land for more lucrative employment in the booming construction industry. The ability to pay for larger imports of food and other agricultural products, which were then sold at subsidized prices, lowered the relative profitability of agriculture. The force of these changing incentives has been strongly influenced by government policies and the structure of the economy. Indonesia and Nigeria, two middle-income economies that had more than 40 percent of GDP originating in agriculture before the oil price increase of 1973, provide a revealing contrast.

In Nigeria, the oil boom led to a severe disruption of the agricultural economy and a large exodus to the cities. Between 1970 and 1982, annual production of Nigeria's principal cash crops fell sharply: cocoa by 43 percent, rubber by 29 percent, cotton by 65 percent, and groundnuts by 64 percent. The share of agricultural imports in total imports increased from about 3 percent in the late 1960s to about 7 percent in the early 1980s. Indonesia, all but unique among the oil-exporting developing countries with large populations, succeeded in avoiding serious disruption to its agriculture. Though agricultural growth slowed in the mid-1970s, by the late 1970s it had recovered to previous levels (see Box table 4.4).   Rice production grew by 4.2 percent a year from 1968 to 1978 and by 6.7 percent from 1978 to 1984, largely because of rapid increases in rice yields. The share of agricultural imports in total imports remained unchanged at about 1.0 percent. Indonesia increased its agricultural exports both as a proportion of developing countries' agricultural exports and as a proportion of world agricultural exports. The rates of increase were 2.0 percent a year and 0.5 percent a year, respectively, between 1965 and 1983. Nigeria's corresponding export market shares

declined at the rate of 5.7 percent a year and 7.1 percent a year, respectively.

Several policy differences between Nigeria and Indonesia explain these divergent results. The real exchange rate appreciated in both Nigeria and Indonesia by about 30 percent between 1970-72 and 1974-78. Thereafter, Indonesia kept its real exchange rate steady. It tightened its monetary and fiscal policies and between November 1978 and March 1983 devalued the rupiah by more than 50 percent against the dollar. In contrast, Nigeria resisted any devaluation of the naira, despite rapid appreciation of the real exchange rate. Nigeria also borrowed heavily on the basis of future oil earnings. By 1982 the real exchange rate was more than double its value in 1970-72.

The two countries also differed in their public spending on agriculture. The bulk of Nigeria's increased public expenditure was allocated to primary education, transport, and construction. Indonesia distributed spending more equally among physical infrastructure, education, capital-intensive industry, and agricultural development, especially in rice.

In recent years, Nigeria has made efforts to increase incentives and boost investment in agricultural infrastructure and extension services. Yet output has continued to stagnate. Reversing agriculture's long decline will require a sustained improvement in real farm prices and better exchange rates as well as continued and improved agricultural support programs.

Box table 4.4 Real exchange rate and agricultural performance in Nigeria and Indonesia, selected years, 1965–83

A. Index of real exchange rate

Year	Nigeria	Indonesia
1970–72	100.0	100.0
1974–78	76.3	74.7
1982–83	47.8	71.3

B. Growth of agriculture
(average annual percentage change)

	Agricultural output		Agricultural exports	
Year	Nigeria	Indonesia	Nigeria	Indonesia
1965–73	2.8	4.8	−4.0	1.9
1974–78	−2.5	2.8	−4.2	5.3
1973–83	−1.9	3.7	−7.9	3.1

Source: Pinto (background paper).

neighboring Liberia. The experience with parallel markets also reflects the changes that farmers make to their pattern of production when crops are discriminated against on official markets. In Tanzania, higher food prices on the parallel market resulted in a decline in the production of export crops (such as cotton, tobacco, and pyrethrum) when farmers switched to growing maize instead. The losses in foreign exchange contributed to further overvaluation of the currency, which depressed export production still more (see Box 4.5).

THE COSTS OF MISJUDGING MONOPOLY POWER AND COMPARATIVE ADVANTAGE. Perhaps the most striking evidence of the cost of export taxation can be found in the reduced shares of many developing countries in international trade. Many developing countries tax exports of raw materials and beverages in the hope of benefiting from their perceived monopoly power in trade. The less responsive the world demand is to prices and the higher a country's share in world markets, the greater the country's monopoly power. Quite a few developing countries have had large enough market shares to exercise some monopoly power. In the early 1960s, Burma and Thailand each accounted for about one-fifth of world exports in rice; India and Sri Lanka each accounted for about one-third of world tea exports; Nigeria and Zaire each accounted for about one-quarter of world exports of palm oil; Ghana accounted for two-fifths of world cocoa exports; Bangladesh had about four-fifths of world

exports of jute; and Indonesia and Malaysia accounted for 30 and 40 percent of world exports of rubber, respectively. All these countries, as well as Brazil (coffee) and Egypt (long-staple cotton), have tried to keep world prices high by restricting supply.

But the gains from exploiting monopoly power have usually been limited because foreign consumers have found alternative supplies or substitutes and because domestic producers have had lower incentives to invest in new technologies. Countries that instituted heavy export taxes have seen their market shares usurped by others with more favorable policies toward producers. Ghana and Nigeria have lost world market shares in cocoa (see Table 4.5). In the early 1960s, Nigeria and Zaire exported more palm oil than the main Asian producers; by the early 1980s the Asian exporters had captured more than 90 percent of the world market. Egypt's share of the world cotton market in the early 1960s had been cut in half by the early 1980s. Sri Lanka has seen its share of the world tea market fall from one-third in the early 1960s to one-fifth in the early 1980s. In contrast, Kenya, which encouraged tea producers, has seen its share increase from less than 3 percent to more than 9 percent during the same period. Box 4.6 discusses these trends.

Because prices of food and raw materials tend to decline in real terms over the very long term, many believe that investment in agriculture—especially in primary products—is a losing proposition and

Table 4.5 Growth in output and exports, and the export market shares of cocoa and palm oil in selected developing countries, 1961–84

Commodity and country	Average annual percentage change in output, 1961–84	Average annual percentage change in exports, 1961–84	Export market shares 1961–63	Export market shares 1982–84
Cocoa				
Africa	0.1	−0.6	80.0	64.1
Cameroon	1.5	0.5	6.8	6.9
Côte d'Ivoire	7.3	6.0	9.3	26.3
Ghana	−3.7	−4.2	40.1	14.4
Nigeria	−2.0	−1.9	18.0	11.2
Latin America	3.2	0.9	16.7	18.5
Brazil	4.5	2.7	7.3	10.9
Ecuador	2.5	2.2	3.2	2.6
Palm oil				
Africa	1.8	−6.4	55.8	1.9
Nigeria	1.4	−23.6	23.3	0.2
Zaire	−1.8	−15.5	25.1	0.1
Asia	15.0	14.8	41.8	95.0
Indonesia	9.7	6.2	18.4	8.2
Malaysia	19.0	18.0	17.9	70.6

Box 4.5 Agricultural prices and marketing in Tanzania

In Tanzania, the government controls most aspects of agricultural marketing. Marketing cooperatives responsible to national crop marketing boards began to take over from private traders during the 1960s. Between 1973 and 1976, ten state agencies were put in charge of buying, processing, and marketing twenty-seven widely grown crops and fifteen minor ones. The marketed surplus of most of these crops could be sold through state channels only. The government fixed the producer prices before the start of each season. Prices did not take into account differences in transport and were often the same throughout the country.

Some of the effects can be seen in Box figure 4.5A. Real prices for farmers fluctuated as fixed nominal prices were adjusted in unpredictable jumps every few years; thus, not even the aim of stabilizing prices was achieved. But, worse for farmers, average real producer prices declined steeply between 1970 and 1975, recovered somewhat in 1975–78, and have continued to fall ever since. By 1984 the weighted average of official producer prices was 46 percent below its 1970 level

Box figure 4.5B Ratios of producer prices to border prices in Tanzania, 1970–84

Percent

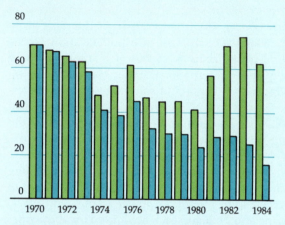

□ Ratio calculated using official exchange rates
■ The same ratio adjusted for overvaluation of the currency relative to the official exchange rate in 1970

Note: Prices are a weighted average of ten export crops.
Source: Ellis (background paper).

Box figure 4.5A Agricultural prices in Tanzania, 1970–84

Index (1970 = 100)

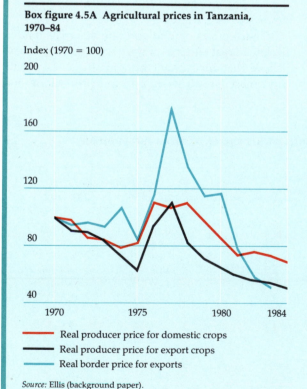

—— Real producer price for domestic crops
—— Real producer price for export crops
—— Real border price for exports

Source: Ellis (background paper).

in real terms; prices for export crops were almost half their 1970 levels, even though the weighted average of world prices for Tanzania's crops at official exchange rates was 17 percent higher in real terms in 1980 than it had been in 1970.

Rising export taxes and increased marketing costs reduced the farmers' share of the final sales value of export crops from 70 percent to 41 percent in 1980, although it has since recovered (see Box figure 4.5B). But the bias against export crops has been much more severe than is indicated when measured at official exchange rates. Correcting for the overvaluation of the currency during this period, the bias was much stronger, as is also shown in Box figure 4.5B. In reality, the bias against exports was even greater, because producers of food crops could sell their output on parallel markets, where prices were higher than official levels, but producers of export crops could sell only to the government.

The output of some export crops, notably cashews, cotton, and pyrethrum, fell drastically in the 1970s. Ambitious development programs for tea and tobacco failed to reach their targets. Coffee production also stagnated, because farmers had little incentive to replace old trees. By 1984 the tonnage of export crops marketed by the marketing boards was 30 percent less than it had been in 1970.

At first sight, it seems the boards had more success with domestic staples. In 1978–79, the marketing channels sold more than twice as much staple grains (particularly maize) as they had in 1970 (see Box figure 4.5C). This reflected the good harvests that followed droughts in 1974–75 and an increase in real producer prices as world market prices rose (though the absolute level of the producer price for maize was still less than one-third of the import price). Official marketing of drought-resistant crops (cassava, sorghum, and millet) in 1979 was more than eight times the 1970 level, and for oilseeds (groundnuts, sesame, sunflower, and castor) the level in 1980 was some 30 percent greater than in 1970. But problems emerged. As real producer prices for domestic crops declined sharply, the official marketing boards became increasingly dependent on imports; farmers shifted to parallel markets, where prices, though unstable, were many times higher than

Box table 4.5 Official and unofficial prices for selected crops in thirteen villages in Tanzania, 1979–81

(Tanzanian shillings per kilogram)

Crop	Official price		Parallel price	
	1979–80	1980–81	1979–80	1980–81
Maize	1.00	1.00	3.08	4.98
Paddy rice	1.50	1.75	2.31	4.23
Cassava	0.65	0.65	1.99	2.90
Sorghum	1.00	1.00	2.96	4.68
Millet	2.00	1.50	4.73	6.95

Source: Raswant (background paper).

official prices (see Box table 4.5). By 1984 the amount of maize marketed through official channels was less than one-third of its 1979 peak; official channels in 1984 handled less than one-third of the average annual amount of rice they had sold in the 1970s. Considerable diversion to parallel markets has also occurred with the drought-resistant and oilseed crops. Only in the one major crop in Tanzania where the producer price has generally been maintained above the import price—wheat—has state marketing been more stable.

In recent years Tanzania has tried to reform its system by relying more on village cooperatives. People may now transport up to 500 kilograms (rather than 30 kilograms) of grain without a permit; anyone with foreign exchange can use it to import goods; above all, the state marketing boards will control the prices of only eighteen main crops, not the forty or more regulated a few years ago. Controls on the retail price of maize flour, the main food staple, were lifted in 1984.

Relaxing controls on grain marketing may have been the single most important factor contributing to the recent increases in grain supplies and to the 50 percent real fall in food prices in 1985, but the success of Tanzania's reforms is far from ensured. Much will depend on whether the cooperatives can be set up quickly and whether they will be allowed to respond to farmers' demands. Few improvements in agricultural production are likely if the cooperatives turn out to be merely another form of monopoly. Much depends, too, on the flexibility of marketing arrangements for major export crops; on whether the official prices are recognized for what they tend to be in practice—minimum floor prices rather than fixed procurement prices; on whether the high costs of public sector marketing can be reduced; and, finally, on whether the government can reverse the substantial appreciation of the currency that occurred between 1979 and 1984.

Box figure 4.5C Marketed output of commodity groups in Tanzania, 1970–84

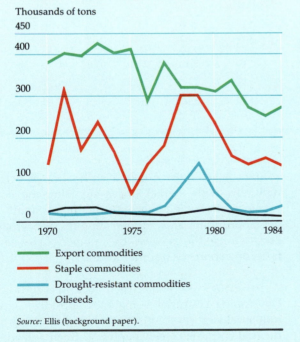

Thousands of tons

- ——— Export commodities
- ——— Staple commodities
- ——— Drought-resistant commodities
- ——— Oilseeds

Source: Ellis (background paper).

Box 4.6 Export taxation and monopoly power

Countries with a significant share of an export market can affect world prices, at least for a short period of time. But attempts to tax foreigners may easily turn into excessive taxation of domestic farmers. The result is often stagnation or decline in export crops.

Cocoa in Ghana

Cocoa pricing policies in Ghana provide one example. Since 1950, the Cocoa Marketing Board has had a monopoly on buying, transporting, and exporting cocoa. The board used its monopoly power to raise significant tax revenue from export sales. At the same time, the government kept the value of the currency high: in 1979 the real exchange rate was estimated to have been 347 percent higher than it had been in 1972. The combined effect was to raise the effective export duty from

Box table 4.6A Relative price incentives for cocoa farmers in Ghana, Togo, and Côte d'Ivoire, 1965–82

Year	Ratio of Ghana price to Togo price	Ratio of Ghana price to Côte d'Ivoire price
1965	0.97	0.97
1970	0.56	0.60
1975	0.74	0.48
1980	0.23	0.18
1981	0.36	0.26
1982	0.40	0.30

a high 54.3 percent in the last half of the 1960s to 88.9 percent in the last half of the 1970s. Producer prices in Ghana were far below levels in competing West African countries (see Box table 4.6A). Ghana's share of export markets slumped from 40 percent in 1961–63 to 18 percent in 1980–82; Togo's market share grew slightly; that of Côte d'Ivoire rose from 9 percent in 1961–63 to 29 percent in 1980–82. This was greater than the increase in its exportable surplus: the higher prices

in Côte d'Ivoire led to extensive smuggling of Ghanaian cocoa.

Tea in Sri Lanka

Sri Lanka had considerable scope for influencing world prices for tea in the early 1960s. In 1961–63 it accounted for 33 percent of world tea exports, and Sri Lankan tea had a long-established niche in the market. Kenya then accounted for only 2.6 percent of world exports. While other factors have also been important, the two countries followed very divergent pricing policies. In Sri Lanka, average tax rates exceeded 50 percent in the late 1970s; they have averaged 35 percent over the past decade. In Kenya, taxation was much more moderate. Box table 4.6B compares tax rates in 1985 at a range of world prices. Sri Lanka's tax captures most of the surplus above an estimated cost of production. In contrast, most of the returns remain with the producer in Kenya. When tea costs $2.40 a kilogram, tax rates in Sri Lanka are ten times higher than in Kenya. At $3.60 a kilogram, they are still more than three times as high. By 1980–82, Sri Lanka's share of world markets had fallen to 19 percent while Kenya's share had more than tripled to 9 percent.

Box table 4.6B Tax rates on tea in Kenya and Sri Lanka, 1985
(percent)

F.o.b. price (dollars per kilogram)	Kenya Average tax rate	Kenya Marginal tax rate	Sri Lanka Average tax rate	Sri Lanka Marginal tax rate
1.20	0.00	0	22.4	0
1.80	2.83	10	14.9	0
2.40	2.59	15	27.7	50
3.00	8.17	20	32.2	50
3.60	10.66	25	35.2	50
4.20	13.10	30	37.3	50
4.80	14.92	25	38.9	50

that planners should shift their attention elsewhere. This view is misleading for several reasons. First, long-term declines in real commodity prices have coexisted with, indeed have been partially caused by, technical progress in developing countries. Countries that have promoted technical progress—for example, Thailand in rubber and Malaysia in palm oil—continue to find specialization in primary commodity exports profitable. Second, if despite technical progress, economic rates of return to investments in agricultural commodities gradually fall to unacceptable levels, the economies concerned should at that time shift resources elsewhere. Such a shift should occur naturally, with market prices signaling the economic merits or demerits of further investments. It is inappropriate and self-defeating for policymakers to force the process by imposing excessive taxes on exports or by other means.

THE COSTS OF PROMOTING AGRO-INDUSTRIES. Developing countries sometimes subsidize agroindustrial exports to offset escalating tariffs in industrial countries (see Chapter 6). Such subsidies may be given directly, in the form of subsidized credit to processors, or indirectly, by restraining domestic raw material costs through export quotas or taxes. Systematic taxation of raw materials to ensure the financial viability of processing industries has been common in many countries, including Ghana and Tanzania. Although the taxation of raw material exports may reduce the financial costs of processing, the true costs of subsidies are borne by the developing countries themselves.

The growth of the soybean processing industry in Brazil illustrates how subsidies for agro-industries can become counterproductive. The expansion of soybean output in Brazil is a remarkable story: starting from a very small base in the late 1960s, soybean production expanded so rapidly that by the early 1980s Brazil was producing nearly 19 percent of world output. The expansion of soybean processing was even more rapid. Prior to the 1970s, soybean processing was composed of many small and medium-size plants; the total processing capacity was 800,000 tons. By 1980, processing capacity had increased to 20 million tons, or about 160 percent of domestic soybean production. Brazil began importing soybeans to process at home. In 1984, more than 63 percent of soybean production was exported, of which only 6 percent was in raw form.

This growth in processing capacity was induced by a policy, initiated in the early 1970s, of providing large credit subsidies, imposing controls and taxes on raw soybean exports, prohibiting imports of soybean oil and meal, and giving export subsidies to processors. During the period 1976 to 1984, the margins between the border prices of oil and meal and raw soybeans were insufficient to cover processing costs. If raw soybean inputs are valued at what they could have earned in the world market, processing actually resulted in foreign exchange losses. As a result of the encouragement given by the government to the processing industry, the economy lost about $1.7 billion between 1976 and 1984. Without the direct and indirect subsidies, the growth of processing capacity would have been smaller, because the true costs of processing and the risks of adverse world price movements would have been perceived by the private sector.

THE COSTS OF SELF-SUFFICIENCY. Developing countries proclaim self-sufficiency in food as a crucial national objective. Various means can be used to attain it—for example, import barriers, public investments to support food production, and taxation of crops that compete with food production. All of these means have been used, although, as

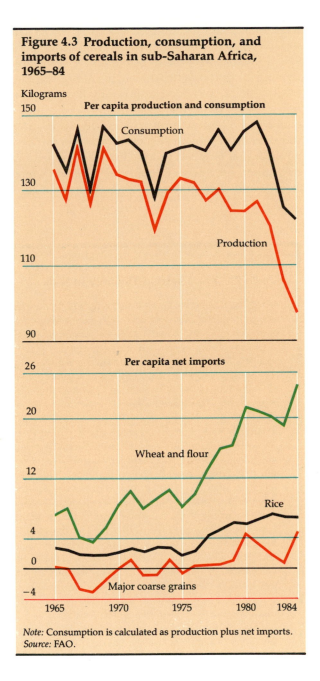

Figure 4.3 Production, consumption, and imports of cereals in sub-Saharan Africa, 1965–84

Note: Consumption is calculated as production plus net imports.
Source: FAO.

mentioned earlier, systematic protection of import substitutes has not been common. What has been much more common is discrimination against domestic producers through low procurement prices and through macroeconomic policies. The strong bias against agriculture has increased sub-Saharan Africa's dependence on imports of food, particularly wheat and rice (Figure 4.3).

Paradoxically, Africa's food problems are often ascribed to an overemphasis on nonfood crops. But data for the periods 1960–70 and 1970–82 paint a different picture. Countries that experienced satisfactory growth of one type of crop also experienced satisfactory growth of the other. In twenty-five out of thirty-eight African countries, the rate of growth of both food and nonfood production fell in 1970–82 compared with the 1960s. In six countries both growth rates increased; in only five did the rate of growth of food production increase while that of nonfood production fell. And in only two other countries—Kenya and Malawi, which are self-sufficient in food—did the growth of food production slow down while the rate of growth of nonfood production accelerated.

Export and food crops complement each other even more as farmers shift from traditional to modern practices. Modern agriculture requires more tradable inputs. In most of Africa, as well as in many developing countries elsewhere, these inputs must be imported. One obvious way of earning the foreign exchange needed is to expand agricultural exports.

It is likely that, had they followed the right type

Box 4.7 Food self-sufficiency in Asia

Most Asian countries cite self-sufficiency in food as an important policy aim, and many have achieved or are approaching it. India had a large surplus of wheat in 1985. Indonesia achieved self-sufficiency in rice in 1984 and 1985. Bangladesh greatly reduced cereal imports in the 1980s. China shifted from being a major importer of food grains in the 1970s to being a surplus producer in the 1980s. These achievements reflect the efficient adoption of new crop varieties and techniques by Asian farmers and improved policies for agriculture.

More than 22 million hectares were brought under irrigation in South and Southeast Asia between 1966 and 1982, which raised the proportion of total irrigated agricultural land from about 20 percent to more than 28 percent. By the late 1970s, modern rice varieties covered 80 percent of the cultivated area in China, more than 70 percent of the cultivated land in the Philippines and Sri Lanka, and more than 50 percent of such land in Indonesia and Pakistan. Modern varieties of wheat expanded to cover two-thirds of the total wheat area in India. Between 1966 and 1982, total fertilizer consumption increased more than sixfold in Southeast Asia and more than fourfold in South Asia.

But such successes do not necessarily mean that self-sufficiency is a desirable policy. Substantial gains from trade can be forgone in its pursuit. Such losses were evident in China when each province aimed to become self-sufficient in food grains. The same losses can occur if a country restricts trade in world markets. Take the case of Sri Lanka, where research spending, pricing policies, input subsidies, and investment in irrigation have all been geared to achieving self-sufficiency in rice. Many components of the effort were appropriate, but, from an economic point of view, the policies may have been pushed too far. The government's support price for producers of paddy, which is set to provide farmers with a reasonable rate of return, was Rs65 a bushel in 1983. This price is far below the economic cost of producing rice in some areas, because of input subsidies. Adjusting only for the subsidies provided

on fertilizers, the economic cost would be about Rs79 a bushel. The largest subsidy, however, is on irrigation water. In the areas of the Mahaweli irrigation system where costs are highest, development costs are almost Rs400,000 an acre (about $17,000). The costs are about half in the median-cost areas. Assuming yields of 160 bushels per double-cropped acre and an opportunity cost of 10 percent, the economic cost of rice would be about Rs250 a bushel in the high-cost areas and about Rs165 a bushel in the median areas. In Burma, by comparison, farmers supply a higher grade of paddy at Rs25 a bushel. Even if the significant subsidies on fertilizers in Burma are taken into account and a part of the costs of the Mahaweli scheme is allocated to activities other than rice growing, there remains a very large gap between marginal costs of production in Sri Lanka and those in Burma.

Countries often fail to capture the potential gains from trade for a complex array of reasons. First, countries may not be able to import at prices which reflect marginal economic costs of production in low-cost exporting countries. Exports in Burma, for instance, are a state monopoly, and the export price is well above the economic costs of production, processing, and marketing. Thailand has often raised its export tax on rice in periods of high world prices, such as 1973–75. Such policies have encouraged import substitution in countries with trade deficits. Second, and conversely, import restrictions in importing countries discourage investments in rice by exporters. Subsidies on rice exports by industrial countries also discourage higher production in low-cost countries. Third, the high cost of self-sufficiency has often been underwritten by grants or concessionary loans from donors. Taken in isolation, many components of each country's policies may have been logical. Taken together, however, they add up to a bias against a well-integrated world agriculture capable of capturing the full benefits from trade.

of pricing policies, many developing countries would have progressed further toward self-sufficiency than they in fact have. The key issue, however, is not self-sufficiency, but comparative advantage. If a country can use its resources better on exports—whether agricultural or not—there is little reason for wasting resources to pursue self-sufficiency in food. In Chile, for example, both agricultural exports and imports increased dramatically following the realignment of prices in the early 1970s (see Chapter 5). But, as discussed in Box 4.7, self-sufficiency remains a popular noneconomic objective, and some countries have been willing to incur large costs to attain it.

THE COSTS TO THE ENVIRONMENT. Protection of the environment is a task that has recently attracted much attention, especially because of the erosion of arable land in sub-Saharan Africa. Although it is not often realized, the pricing policies that developing countries follow can be important from this point of view also. When farming becomes unprofitable, farmers lose the incentive to care for their land. Equally important, different crops have different effects on soil conservation, and pricing policies may exacerbate soil erosion by inducing farmers to choose the wrong crops. In Haiti, for example, coffee and other tree crops bind the soil on hillsides better than field crops do. The taxation of coffee relative to field crops has had the unfortunate side effect of increasing soil erosion. This is discussed in Box 4.8.

INTERSECTORAL LINKAGES. These illustrations of the bias against agriculture and its costs have focused mainly on agriculture. But the question may be raised as to whether the sacrifices in agricultural output are offset by growth elsewhere. The effects of wrong policies in one sector are never confined to that sector alone. The experience of decades suggests that a healthy agricultural sector is critical to national growth. Taxing agriculture to force resources to industry will retard agricultural growth, lower domestic food and raw material supplies to industry, and reduce demand for industrial products. This will harm agricultural and industrial prospects in the long run. With some exceptions, such as the oil and mineral exporters, countries with low agricultural growth have low industrial growth and countries with high agricultural growth have high industrial growth (see Figure 4.4). Agriculture's intimate connections with growth and the wider economy mean that the costs of discrimination against agriculture are not borne by farming alone.

The role of agricultural growth in industrialization is well documented in England, where the Industrial Revolution began: the story was the same in Japan between the Meiji Restoration in 1868 and World War I. Substantial transfers of capital and labor from agriculture to the rest of the economy contributed much to Japan's industrial development, but those transfers came about as agricultural productivity increased. The Japanese experience has special relevance to the developing countries because it was achieved by farmers with only small plots of land and did not involve manipulation of the terms of trade against agriculture (see Box 4.9).

The industrialization of the fast-growing East Asian economies follows to a large extent the Japanese pattern of rapid agricultural growth supporting the drive toward industrial growth. The fact that agricultural and industrial growth complement each other is also evident from recent studies on developing countries. In India, a 1.0 percentage point increase in the agricultural growth rate is correlated with an increase in industrial growth of 0.5 percentage point and in national income of around 0.7 percentage point. Agriculture is linked to industry through rural expenditure on manufactures. Increases in agricultural output raise household and government incomes and the demand for consumer goods. Although per capita incomes in India are higher in towns than in the countryside, the absolute size of the market for manufactured goods is larger in rural areas. Moreover, villagers spend so much of any extra income on manufactures that an increase in agricultural income generates substantial demand for industrial goods. Studies in other countries confirm how important this connection is. In Nueva Ciga province in the Philippines, a 1 percent increase in agricultural income generates a 1 to 2 percent increase in value added in most sectors of the local nonfarm economy. In the Muda district of Malaysia, every $1.00 increase in agricultural output indirectly adds $0.80 in value added to the rest of the village economy.

The role of agriculture envisaged in the strategy of industrialization behind high protective barriers ignores the lessons of history. While it is true that the share of agriculture in national income declines in the long run, transfers of resources from agriculture should come about naturally through growth in its productivity rather than through highly discriminatory policies against agriculture.

Agriculture as a source of tax revenues

In many developing countries the agricultural sector is the largest tax base, and some taxation is unavoidable for financing public expenditures in

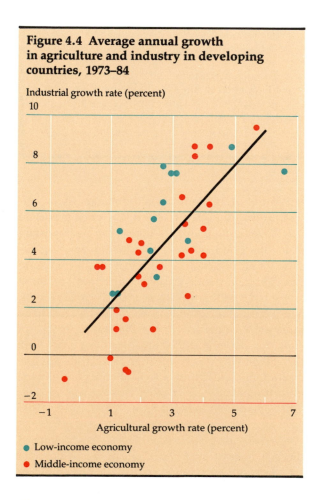

Figure 4.4 Average annual growth in agriculture and industry in developing countries, 1973–84

Industrial growth rate (percent)

Agricultural growth rate (percent)

● Low-income economy
● Middle-income economy

Box 4.9 Agricultural taxation in Japan

The contribution of agriculture to the Japanese economic miracle is a test case for the role of agriculture in development. On the face of it, agriculture in Japan displayed many of the characteristics shown in today's developing countries. For most of the past century, its growth rate was less than 2 percent a year, except after World War II, when it became heavily protected. Capital outflows from agriculture were substantial, transferring resources to other sectors of the economy. The agricultural tax system is thought to have played an important role, but, in fact, the lessons from Japan are more complicated.

The net capital flows out of agriculture were especially important in the first quarter century of Japan's development (see Box table 4.9A). They accounted for 27 percent of nonagricultural gross capital formation between 1888 and 1902 and 23 percent between 1903 and 1922. The public sector accounted for about two-thirds of the transfer in the earlier period, but only one-quarter in the later period. Tax transfers, therefore, do not seem to have been a dominant cause of the reallocation of capital for very long, but agricultural taxation was clearly important in the early years of development.

These public sector transfers, however, are only part of the picture. The movement of labor out of agriculture needs to be taken into account. Between 1888 and 1900 (see Box table 4.9B), two-thirds of the increase in nonagricultural labor was due to the migration of farmers and their families; this contribution increased to four-fifths in the next two decades. Econometric models that simulate what would have happened without the transfers of either capital or labor indicate which of the two played the more important role in the development process. The studies concern the periods 1907–37 and 1955–68. Their results suggest that labor migration—and not, as is commonly thought, the flow of savings—had the bigger impact. Given that private capital flows dominated public sector flows throughout both periods, it would appear that neither capital flows nor the tax system has contributed greatly to Japan's success story. This, however, may not have been true during the first quarter century of Japanese development, when tax transfers were largest. The public sector may have played an important role before the private sector was able to allocate private savings among different sectors of the economy.

The nature of the tax mechanism used in Japan was also of great importance. In sharp contrast to the case in many of today's developing countries, taxes were levied by a direct land tax. This did not undermine agricultural incentives by lowering producer prices. On the contrary, agriculture's terms of trade generally improved from 1888 until the 1930s, when the terms of trade turned moderately against it under the influence of increased agricultural supplies from Japan's colonies. Furthermore, the level of agricultural taxation was low in comparison with the tax burdens common in developing countries today. As shown in Box table 4.9C, the tax burden was less than 7 percent of gross output and less than 9 percent of value added; it was falling throughout the period.

Box table 4.9B Intersectoral movements of labor in the Japanese economy, 1888–1940

Period	Outflow of agricultural labor force (millions)	Increase in nonagricultural labor force (millions)	Agricultural contribution (percent)
1888–1900	1.5	2.3	67
1900–1920	3.7	4.7	79
1920–1940	3.7	7.3	51

Source: Ueno (background paper).

Box table 4.9C Tax burden as a share of output and value added in agriculture in Japan, 1888–1937

Period	Direct tax as a percentage of gross output	Direct tax as a percentage of value added
1888–1902	6.8	8.6
1903–1922	5.8	7.2
1923–1937	5.1	6.4

Note: Value added is gross output minus current input.
Source: Ueno (background paper).

Box table 4.9A Capital flows from agriculture to nonagriculture by source of flow, 1888–1937

Period	Net public sector		Net private sector	
	Flows (millions of yen)	Percentage of nonagricultural investment	Flows (millions of yen)	Percentage of nonagricultural investment
1888–1902	36	18	19	9
1903–1922	65	6	198	17
1923–1937	−37	−2	−30	−1

Source: Ueno (background paper).

agriculture and elsewhere. The key issue is not whether agriculture should be taxed, but how developing countries can avoid the excessive costs of taxing agriculture.

Whether revenues accrue to the central government, to a state government, or to a parastatal, all too often revenue requirements are taken as fixed before taxation policies are designed. The most common error is to assume that a certain amount of revenue has to be raised. Public expenditure policies and taxation policies need to be examined together. There are often great wastes in public expenditures—for example, in the financing of inefficient and highly capital-intensive industrial projects that are entailed in forced industrialization strategies. And, as the next chapter will show, there are reasons to doubt the efficacy of spending on programs that bear more immediately on the agricultural sector. Apart from exploring the scope for reducing the total revenue raised from agriculture, governments should also be concerned with the form of taxation.

The previous sections have given some indication of the high costs of agricultural taxation. There are two reasons they are so high. First, countries have relied heavily on export taxes or on the pricing policies of export marketing boards because of the perceived difficulties of administering direct taxes in rural areas. Second, the rates of taxation on specific exports have often been high. As shown in Box 4.10, the losses in real national in-

come due to export taxes increase more than in proportion to increases in the tax rate. These losses are referred to by economists as efficiency costs, or efficiency losses.

The remedies for the high cost of taxation lie in the use of other tax instruments or, to the extent that countries are obliged to use export taxes, in lower rates. Searching for efficient ways to tax agriculture is clearly a matter of high priority in developing countries, although taxation should not be so great as to produce the sort of discrimination against agriculture described earlier in this chapter. With commodity taxes, the preferred approach is to focus on consumption rather than production. Commodity-specific excise taxes and broadly based value added taxes that bear on commodities purchased for consumption offer a convenient means of raising substantial amounts of revenue without impairing the efficiency of production. Although their imposition at the retail level may be beyond the administrative capabilities of most developing countries, taxes on consumer goods are regularly applied at the point of import or at the factory gate. To the extent that more of these goods are consumed by the relatively rich, this option also contributes to the overall progressivity of the tax system. As a source of revenue, greater use of economy-wide taxes on consumption offers an important alternative to the excessive taxation of agricultural production.

Direct taxes offer another alternative to export or

Box 4.10 The efficiency cost of export taxes

The loss in real national income caused by a tax is referred to as its efficiency cost. The efficiency cost of a tax is additional to the administrative and collection costs and summarizes the net impact of that tax on producers, consumers, and the government's budget.

In the case of an export product, for example, the tax will lower the price to producers and consumers and generate revenues for the government. The losses of the producers will have to be offset against the gains to consumers and the government. The efficiency cost per unit of revenue raised is a useful indicator in practice. At the margin, the cost per unit of revenue increases more than proportionately to the tax rate.

To illustrate this, assume that the exports of a commodity rise in proportion to its price—that is, if the border price increases by 10 percent, the export volume also increases by 10 percent. On that assumption,

the efficiency loss for the last unit of revenue raised from an export tax (t) is $t/(1-2t)$.

Thus, if the export tax is 5 percent, getting the last dollar of tax revenue will cost only 5.6¢. If, however, the tax rate is 40 percent, the last dollar of revenue will cost two dollars. Indeed, beyond 50 percent, total revenues will decrease when the tax rate is increased, so that it would be pointless to increase the tax further. This result is important for two reasons. First, the export supply response assumed above may well be conservative. This is quite likely because as the price increases, producers produce more and consumers consume less—the exportable surplus increases for both reasons. Second, as noted in the text, export taxes have often been very high, especially when excessive parastatal margins are taken into account.

output taxes. The taxation of land is an approach that has been used successfully in the past. Since land taxes are paid regardless of how the land is used, they discourage increases in productivity less than does taxation through depressed prices. The Japanese experience with an agricultural land tax is an object lesson in reducing the distortions caused by taxation (see Box 4.9). In this case, the rate of taxation was also moderate—it captured less than 7 percent of agricultural value added in a sector that was benefiting from rising relative prices. And Japan's land tax was not unique in the late nineteenth and early twentieth century. The agricultural tax system in Thailand, for instance, was also based on a land tax. Since there was an open land frontier in Thailand and since there was concern that a land tax would discourage settlement of new land, the tax was not applied to newly cultivated land. Different tax rates were applied to different kinds of land according to their fertility. As in Japan, rates were kept low (between 5 and 10 percent of agricultural output). Rights to land were linked to a household's ability to settle, cultivate, and meet the tax obligations on the land. The tax system and land settlement policy established a system of independent smallholders that is still evident in a low rate of landlessness and Thailand's particular tenancy arrangements.

Despite its attractions, land taxation, once a significant means of raising revenue, is now rarely used. Its demise cannot be explained by high administrative and collection costs alone. A land tax register can be much less detailed and accurate than the registers needed to establish ownership rights. Recent developments in satellite imagery and readily available information on access to water and proximity to markets can be used to set up a workable land classification. Given the attractiveness of land taxation, expenditures involved in generating such information are likely to be worthwhile. Market prices for land can also provide estimates of the quality of different types of land.

But broadly based land taxes are not the only alternative to commodity taxes. Other alternatives exist in most countries. For example, where the taxpaying unit can be easily identified and the potential revenue per taxpayer is large, the application of standard income taxes is both equitable and cost-effective. This is an easy option in countries where significant production takes place in private or public estates. Tea and tobacco estates in Malawi, for example, have long been subject to personal income tax—collected on a pay-as-you-earn basis—and to company income tax. In contrast, with one minor exception in fiscal 1985, estates have not been subject to export taxes. In this way, substantial amounts of revenue have been generated without depressing producer incentives. This approach could be replicated in other countries where land ownership is highly concentrated. In Latin America, for example, about 1 percent of the population controls more than 50 percent of the land and accounts for almost one-third of agricultural output and more than one-sixth of total GNP. The application of an income tax in such circumstances may be a more effective means of taxation than efforts to introduce a more broadly based but imperfectly implemented land tax.

This approach parallels procedures in other sectors of the economy where income taxes are usually confined to large-scale enterprises. Development of the tax system then involves expanding the tax base by gradually incorporating smaller and smaller units. In agriculture, this process can be accelerated by using export taxes as presumptive income taxes—that is, export taxes or other output taxes can be viewed as a prior collection of income tax. Large estates and other entities paying income tax on a regular basis would credit payments of export taxes against their income tax liabilities. Smaller concerns which may not have paid income tax in the past would have the option of submitting a return should their payment of export taxes seem excessive. Given that agricultural incomes are usually much lower than those in urban areas and may often be below the standard exemption for income tax, this procedure implies rates of effective export tax that are substantially lower than those prevailing in many countries.

Yet another option is the use of multitiered price systems whereby the tax falls on the intramarginal quota rather than at the margin. The agricultural pricing system prevailing in China before 1985 provides an example. To maintain incentives for increased output at the margin, farmers were paid a higher "above quota" price (or an even higher negotiated price) on supplies in excess of their quota deliveries. This approximated a land tax: the farmers were obliged to pay a fixed tax (equivalent to the difference between the quota price and the higher price on residual sales multiplied by the quota deliveries) and were free to sell all residual output at a free market price. However, the approximation was not exact. Quota deliveries were restricted to basic food grains and a few other commodities that enter the subsidized food distribution system. Thus, there was an incentive to evade the burdens and a need to restrict the freedom of choosing which crops to grow. Quotas were set at different levels in different regions, depending on the state's need for particular commodities, so that the farmer's ability to exceed "quota" deliveries, and therefore to gain access to high marginal prices, varied a great deal. Despite the disadvantages of such a multitiered system, it should still be an improvement over the high marginal tax rates imposed by marketing parastatals in many countries.

It is also important to examine direct taxation options for cost recovery in various projects financed by the government. Public sector projects in agriculture raise land values and thus create a potentially useful tax base. Even if land taxes are not possible in all areas of the country, betterment levies in project areas generally are. This issue is explored further in the next chapter in the context of irrigation projects.

This review of agricultural policies in developing countries has not focused on the assistance that governments have sought to provide through price stabilization and farm input subsidy measures, nor has it reviewed the efficacy of consumer subsidy programs in alleviating poverty and malnutrition. Do such programs reduce the bias against agriculture, or do they exacerbate it? That is the central question addressed in the next chapter.

5

Agricultural policies in developing countries
Marketing and stabilization, subsidies, and policy reform

Governments throughout the developing world want to provide the poor with an adequate diet and to promote a more productive and efficient agricultural sector. But, as Chapter 4 has shown, their general economic policies, as well as taxes on farm outputs, tend to create a bias against agriculture. A reexamination of development strategies and of the excessive taxation of farm outputs should be high on the agenda for policy reform.

At the same time, it is important to review the price stabilization, consumer subsidy, and input subsidy programs through which governments try to offset the bias against agricultural producers and to assist low-income groups. Because the net benefits of these types of programs are low in practice—as will be brought out in this chapter—they need to be redesigned or reduced considerably in size. The resources thus saved can be used for more productive purposes, including the many useful services that governments provide in agriculture. World Bank experience indicates that agricultural investment, when carefully designed and implemented, is no less productive than investment in other sectors. The rate of return can be, and has been, very high. The benefits from agricultural investments are sensitive, however, to the policy environment within which private markets operate. The types of reform discussed in Chapter 4 and in this chapter are important in improving that environment. Many countries have recognized the interdependence between projects and policies and have undertaken significant reforms. The trend toward policy reform in developing countries is reviewed at the end of this chapter.

Marketing and stabilization

Governments seeking ways to influence producer and consumer prices often establish public sector marketing agencies. Usually, the intent is to assist agricultural producers by preventing "monopolistic" private traders from exploiting them. But, in practice, marketing is an intrinsically difficult task for public agencies to perform well. This section looks at the performance of these agencies.

Public sector marketing

The form, legal status, and range of functions carried out by public agencies vary from country to country. In India, public corporations at both the national and state levels buy and distribute food. In Mexico, a large state monopoly controls imports, domestic procurement, and the distribution of a wide range of agricultural goods. In contrast to those organizations dealing in a variety of commodities, many marketing agencies—with or without monopoly positions—handle only one commodity. Statutory monopolies, or marketing boards, are commonly used to control the purchase and export of individual crops, both in Africa and elsewhere.

Governments often justify their involvement in marketing with the argument that the private sector is inefficient and can be monopolized by a small number of traders. There is little evidence that this is generally true. Various studies have compared the efficiency of private and public sector marketing. In Kenya, the public sector charged 15 to 20 percent more for marketing maize and beans than did the private sector. Other studies have compared seasonal price changes in private markets with the cost of storage, and price differences between regions with the cost of transport. Data from Ghana and Nigeria, for instance, revealed seasonal price rises that appeared to be close to the cost of storage, which suggests that private traders were not able to develop monopoly powers. Price movements for goods traded in free markets in West African countries also support the proposition that efficient marketing channels help bind markets together.

In contrast, numerous studies have indicated that public sector marketing agencies can be relatively inefficient. Staffing is one problem. Key managers are often chosen for political reasons. Even if the top management is competent, it is often pressured into expanding staff for political reasons. Flexibility in staffing is often lacking. Competence and morale often deteriorate. Financial problems also are common. Funds may be inadequate or released at the wrong time. Public agencies also often have unrealistic and inconsistent mandates to generate government revenue, provide cheap food, and create employment.

Perhaps more important, public marketing agencies find it hard to handle the sheer complexity of markets, especially in areas dominated by smallholders. The agencies have to buy small amounts of food from tens of thousands, even millions, of widely dispersed farmers in places where communications are poor and where existing local markets vary from place to place and change quickly. Whereas farmers want to sell a bewildering variety of maize or millet of different origins, freshness, or fine shadings of taste and quality, each at a different price, state-organized systems usually offer only one or two prices for each grain. Some offer only one purchase price throughout the year and for all locations.

As complex centrally controlled systems are open to corruption, it is difficult for public agencies to adopt the differentiated pricing policies which are needed to promote efficient trade. But the costs of not doing so can be great. For example, when an agency offers a single price for all grades of a crop, farmers want to sell to it only their lowest quality grade. When the agency is in charge of exporting the crop, as in the case of the rice marketing board in Guyana, the low quality of its supplies discourages foreign buyers.

In most of sub-Saharan Africa, public sector marketing agencies have a legal monopoly over trade for a wide range of commodities, although the growth of parallel markets has limited their influence. Even when there is no legal monopoly, inadequately differentiated and inflexible prices undermine private sector trading; so do unrealistic trading margins. Private traders have been crowded out in many countries, from Colombia and Peru to Kenya and the Philippines.

Marketing problems are less severe when public

Table 5.1 Price instability indices, 1964–84

Commodity	International price	
	1964–84	1974–84
Sugar	90.8	51.5
Cocoa	37.3	34.1
Rice	33.0	21.9
Coffee	32.0	37.7
Palm kernels	27.5	32.5
Wheat	24.3	16.9
Tea	21.7	23.6
Jute	21.2	26.8
Soybeans	20.8	9.9
Beef	16.7	11.3
Corn	16.6	15.6
Rubber	16.1	14.0
Sorghum	15.6	13.6
Cotton	14.3	10.7

Note: Index =

$$\sqrt{\frac{1}{N}\Sigma\left(\frac{P_t - \bar{P}_t}{\bar{P}_t}\right)^2}$$

where P_t and $\bar{P}_t$ are actual and exponential trend values, respectively, and N is the length of the period. Prices are mainly from the London and New York markets, and they are deflated by the manufacturing unit value (MUV) index (1984 = 100).
Source: MacBean and Nguyen, ''Commodity Price Instability'' (background paper).

marketing agencies are not subsidized or protected by legal monopolies. The government of Indonesia, for instance, encourages public estates to buy smallholder crops in order to guarantee farmers a ''fair'' price. In some cases the public estates coexist with private markets and influence their prices through competition. In many other countries (such as Sri Lanka in the case of rice) the public sector has been able to coexist and compete with the private sector. In both Indonesia and Sri Lanka, the private sector has proved more efficient and has increased its share of the market despite the subsidies that the public sector entities directly or indirectly receive.

Although they are often inefficient and costly, public marketing agencies nonetheless can provide useful services. Some export marketing boards have helped increase exports by exercising quality control, arranging shipping, and providing producers with technical advice and information. It is necessary to note, however, that these services do not require monopoly trading powers. Private exporters' or producers' associations could perform the same functions more efficiently.

Governments have an important role to play in encouraging efficient markets. They can assist competition, but creating public monopolies to offset the threat of private ones does not do this. The record of public marketing agencies suggests that physical trading in agriculture is a task better performed by competitive private markets. When public marketing is unavoidable, it is important to institute policies that do not discourage private sector participation.

Stabilization

Prices of agricultural commodities are expected to vary more than the prices of industrial products for three reasons: agricultural markets are vulnerable to climatic changes; the short-run responsiveness of supply and demand to changes in prices is usually less in the case of agricultural products than it is in industrial markets; and the output of most crops is necessarily seasonal. As shown in Table 5.1, world market prices of the major agricultural products have indeed fluctuated. The indices shown measure the average deviation from the price trend in any particular year. Thus, the 1974–

84 index for cocoa means that one can expect the price in a typical year to be 34 percent above or below the trend value for that year. The indices in the table were compared with those for a large number of manufactured products for the same periods: in the majority of cases the indices for manufactured products were lower than 10, and they seldom came close to 20.

The variability of agricultural commodity prices explains why governments in developing countries often try price stabilization schemes to protect farmers from large price falls and consumers from large price increases. When greater price stability leads to greater income stability, farmers benefit from reduced risks. These benefits, however, are extremely hard to estimate in practice, even though it is generally accepted that farmers are at least moderately "risk averse"—that is, they are willing to accept a somewhat lower average income stream for the sake of greater stability (see Box 5.1). Consumers and industrial users of agri-

---

Box 5.1 Risk aversion in agriculture

Farming is risky in that returns in any given year can be much above or below the average levels. Farmers are said to be risk averse if they prefer a stable income stream to an unstable one even if their average incomes are somewhat lower with the stable stream. Measures that stabilize farm incomes without lowering the average incomes should, then, benefit farmers and possibly encourage them to produce more.

The importance of income-stabilizing policies depends on how strongly risk averse the farmers are and on the nature of the risks they face. Economists have attempted to estimate the extent and importance of farmers' risk aversion in several developing and industrial countries. The investigations have relied on two general approaches: (a) statistical examinations of farmers' input and output decisions in the face of variable prices or returns and (b) interviews and experiments with controlled gambles intended to identify individual attitudes toward risk.

One statistical study, which investigated the effects of revenue variability on the acreages planted with grains in the San Joaquin Valley in California, found that increased price fluctuations around a given average price had a small but negative effect on acreages. Another study compared the actual use of fertilizers by farmers in Puebla, Mexico, with an estimate of the profit-maximizing use. While different farmers displayed different degrees of risk aversion, on average they would have required 11.2 percent more income in order to accept a 10 percent increase in the variability

of their incomes. With respect to controlled experiments and interviews, a notable set of experiments with games of chance was carried out on rural households in Maharashtra and Andhra Pradesh, India. Unlike many such experiments, the controlled gambles involved payoffs of the same order of magnitude as those at risk in households' economic decisions in farming. Attitudes toward risk varied widely among individuals when the stakes were low, but at payoff levels in the neighborhood of monthly labor incomes risk aversion was widespread.

Estimates of risk aversion vary widely, and no quantitative guidelines are available. All that can be said is that moderate risk aversion is widespread among farmers and therefore farmers will benefit if price stabilization schemes actually lead to stable income streams without much of a drop in average income levels. Nonetheless, such benefits—even if they could be quantified in particular cases—will tend to overstate gains to farmers, since what matters is their total income and its variability rather than the income from a particular crop. Farmers typically adopt risk-reducing strategies in planning their cropping and nonfarm activities, and they can also use formal or informal capital markets to smooth out income variations. The true gains from income stabilization schemes are therefore extremely difficult to measure and can easily be overstated. One should thus be wary of price stabilization schemes promoted on the grounds of farmers' risk aversion.

cultural raw materials can also be similarly risk averse.

But it is possible to overstate the benefits of stabilization. Farmers, for example, can lose rather than gain if incomes fluctuate because of variations in crop yields and outputs—stable prices can then destabilize incomes. It is also possible that, on average, the unit costs of raw materials for an agro-industry will be less if prices fluctuate than if they are stable. Moreover, farmers, consumers, traders, and industrial users can reduce the risks they face by diversifying their activities, by using capital markets, by storing products, and by sharing risks through purchase and sales contracts.

Stabilization is a particularly complex task for any government to undertake, and its costs can be very high. The mechanisms and costs of price stabilization depend on whether the commodity is internationally traded. The discussion below is confined to traded goods.

FOOD CROPS. Stabilization of the prices of staples—such as wheat, rice, and maize—is a major concern in many developing countries, where the poor spend a large proportion of their income on these foods. In many cases these staples are imported. What will happen if unrestricted private foreign trade is permitted without any border measures, and how can stabilization measures be introduced?

In the absence of trade duties and quotas, domestic prices are determined by world prices at the country border, the exchange rate, and domestic marketing margins. Private traders can and do import and store. Private markets can also manage risks in other ways:

• Farmers can adapt their cropping patterns, crop choices, and input uses to reduce the risks of income fluctuations; consumers can adapt their consumption patterns by substituting different items of food; agro-industries can smooth out cost fluctuations by using the capital market and by storing their inputs.

• International futures markets can be used to hedge risks, and options markets can be used to provide insurance. These special types of markets—explained in Box 7.2 in Chapter 7—are limited at present, but their growth would be promoted if developing countries were willing to use them.

An unregulated system can, of course, cause fluctuations in the availability of foreign exchange, and the need to make large outlays for imports in periods of high world prices cannot be ruled out.

Governments can reduce such risks by holding greater amounts of foreign exchange reserves, by using international capital markets, or by using the Compensatory Financing Facility (CFF) of the International Monetary Fund (see Chapter 7).

The use of these mechanisms will not, of course, make domestic prices more stable than international prices. If greater stability is sought, trade interventions become necessary. Thus, import tariffs can be used to keep domestic prices higher in periods of low prices, and import subsidies or rebates can be used to keep domestic prices lower when world prices are high. Such a scheme is all that would be necessary for a traded good; no public buffer stocks would be required. It is important to note that while these schemes might be simpler and less costly to operate than buffer stocks, they are not without cost. As seen in Chapter 4, trade interventions involve efficiency losses which can become large as tariffs and rebates are increased.

In the case of food, however, developing countries typically do not follow schemes of this sort. Instead of using import tariffs or rebates, governments establish trade monopolies; instead of relying on private storage, they run public buffer stocks. In some countries (Brazil, for example) specialized agencies operate buffer stocks, while in others (Mexico and India, for example) the stabilization function is combined with other functions—in particular, the provision of consumer subsidies in urban areas.

Practices vary in other ways too. In many South Asian and Latin American countries, imports are used sparingly to add to stocks, while more liberal policies are followed elsewhere, as in Indonesia. For any given size of buffer stock, the choice between domestic procurement and imports is critically important in controlling costs. For example, in the case of India, great savings might be possible by increasing the use of trade, as discussed in Box 5.2.

The chief costs involved in a buffer stock operation are the costs of storage facilities and interest charges. Because of inefficiencies in public operations, the multiplicity of objectives that public agencies may be required to pursue, and the fact that governments often seek degrees of stabilization that necessarily entail losses, public agencies often need subsidies—both direct cash subsidies and indirect subsidies in the form of low interest rates on loans (see Box 5.2).

Subsidization of public buffer stock operations crowds out private storage activities and leads to much larger public stocks—and higher costs—than

Box 5.2   Food-grain buffer stocks and price stabilization in India

The last two decades have witnessed a marked turn-around in India's food-grain sector. In the mid-1960s India's food-grain economy was in severe crisis, and the country was heavily dependent on imports of wheat, which were financed primarily through the P.L. 480 food assistance program. Since then the situation has gradually improved, and impressive increases in food output have been brought about by a combination of large investments in irrigation, introduction of high-yielding grain varieties, and increases in farm prices. In addition to its efforts to increase food-grain output, the government has tried to ensure the availability of food grains to low-income consumers at stable subsidized prices.

To do this the Indian government, through the Food Corporation of India (FCI) and other state agencies, runs one of the largest food distribution systems in the world. Typically, the government purchases a part of the domestic marketed surplus of grain, monopolizes external trade, adds to or depletes existing buffer stocks, and sells the resulting supply through special ''fair price shops.'' In a normal year the government sells about 10 percent of the total grain consumption; the figure rises to about 15 percent in a drought year. The system has succeeded in providing greater price stability for consumers than would have existed otherwise.

Despite the benefits to producers and to those consumers who have access to fair price shops, the costs of running the system have been a source of continual concern. In the 1960s and early 1970s, when India was a substantial grain importer, the food distribution system operated with relatively low buffer stocks in order to moderate import needs. In recent years the size and

therefore the costs of holding buffer stocks have increased dramatically. India is currently reported to be holding more than 30 million tons of grain as buffer stocks, equal to more than two years of sales from the fair price shop system. The large buffer stocks have accumulated not necessarily because of a conscious decision to hold stocks at this level, but as an unintended effect of other factors. The growth in food-grain output has outstripped growth in demand because the government has repeatedly raised the procurement price.

A study conducted by the Birla Institute of Scientific Research in India as early as 1977–78, when the buffer stock was about 12 million tons, showed that the total subsidy to the FCI was Rs6.75 billion (about 44 percent of total sales). Of this, Rs5.66 billion represented direct cash subsidies, about 60 percent of which was intended to cover the costs of buffer stock operations. Owing to the increase in the size of the buffer stock, the direct cash subsidies grew to about Rs11 billion in 1984–85.

The rising costs of buffer stock operations have led to a search for measures to improve the cost effectiveness of the system. A study by the International Food Policy Research Institute, reviewing the options prior to 1983, suggested that the same objectives of the wheat program could be met at about a third of the actual costs by increasing the reliance on international trade. A more liberal import policy would have allowed drastic reductions in the size of the buffer stock needed to meet the same stabilization objectives. While factors other than storage costs are relevant in deciding on the size of the buffer stock, this study indicates the importance of examining the increased use of international trade as an alternative to large domestic buffer stocks.

---

otherwise would occur. Especially when the agency is also responsible for subsidized food distribution in urban areas, the subsidies can be very large. They can also vary with fluctuations in domestic harvests and in international prices. This is one reason why public agencies can be forced to procure food at less than market prices; this naturally leads to restrictions on private internal trade. These policies defeat the objective of assisting domestic farmers. Restrictions on internal trade—which have been practiced not only in Africa but also in China and India—lead, like restrictions on international trade, to higher instability in prices. Three additional problems that tend to arise frequently are:

• As distinct from pure price stabilization, governments also try to guarantee a floor price for

farmers. It is extremely difficult to judge how floor prices are to be set. Usually, references are made to the cost of production, but this varies at the margin with the production level; the question becomes how much domestic production is desirable. Mistakes occur frequently. By setting procurement prices too high, the public agency may end up buying massive stocks, as happened recently in India (with wheat) and Brazil (with maize).

• Since public agencies can receive subsidies, considerations of profitability do not determine the difference between floor and ceiling prices. Floor and ceiling prices—and a public agency's ability to implement them—vary in practice from season to season because of conflicting pressures from different interest groups, fluctuations in the budgetary subsidies available, and changes in the trade and exchange rate policies of the country. The net result can be greater instability in domestic prices. A comparison of annual domestic and world price movements for the 1967–81 period for grain in thirty-seven developing countries indicated that domestic prices were not significantly more stable than world prices in many cases.

• With sufficient subsidization, complete price stability is feasible, and it is not uncommon for governments to maintain the same consumer price throughout the year. This can be enormously expensive, not only in terms of budgetary costs but also in terms of the distortions introduced in production and consumption patterns.

The objectives of stabilizing food prices and providing farmers with floor price guarantees present hard choices for any developing country. When guaranteed prices are set too high and stabilization is carried too far, governments in developing countries are likely to end up imposing higher costs on the economy than world price instability in itself would. Inefficient implementation of policies aggravates the problem. Greater priority should be given to moderating stabilization and producer support objectives, to bringing about stability and predictability of the public policy regime, and to encouraging private sector operations.

EXPORT CROPS. Prices of exportable raw materials and beverages can, in principle, be stabilized by variable export taxes and subsidies. Export subsidies are generally not used explicitly, but occur implicitly through changes in the profit margins of marketing boards. Sometimes the only measure used is a variable export tax that is waived when world prices become too low. But public buffer stocks and floor price policies are also used in connection with export crops and lead to the same types of problems discussed earlier.

Simplicity is as much a virtue in this case as in the case of basic staples. Papua New Guinea's buffer fund provides a good example (see Box 5.3). The desirability of promoting private sector stabilization and risk management functions deserves special emphasis in the case of export crops because farmers and traders in these sectors are often more commercialized and better organized than those in traditional crop sectors. However, the history of marketing board operations in Africa and elsewhere suggests that the stabilization objective can gradually give way to the objective of raising revenues at the expense of the producers. It also suggests that the marketing boards inhibit the emergence of efficient private markets.

Consumer subsidies

Governments in many developing countries try to provide essential foods to the poor at low and stable prices. Stable food prices help overcome so-called transitory food insecurity—the fact that the poor may not have enough to eat if the cost of food suddenly rises or their incomes suddenly fall. But stable food prices may not be enough to guarantee adequate food supplies for the poorest of the poor. Consumer subsidies on basic foods have, therefore, been used to overcome chronic food insecurity—the long-term inadequacy of the poorest people's diet. Such investment in improved nutrition is an investment in a country's most important asset—its human capital. This section explores the paradox that, while governments may be right to make these investments, they may go about it in the wrong way.

While food subsidy programs are common in the developing countries, they differ widely in the foods they cover and the people they aim to benefit. The way they are funded varies too, but in most countries the costs have been shifted back to farmers in the form of low farm prices. This has been accomplished through export taxes in food-exporting countries, through legal marketing mo-

Figure 5.1 Food subsidies as a percentage of total government expenditure in selected developing countries, 1973–83

Percent

Egypt

Sri Lanka

Bangladesh

Pakistan

India

1973   1976   1979   1983

nopolies which pay low prices for domestically produced food crops, and through sales at low prices of imported food.

As seen in Chapter 4, these measures depress food production and can be very costly if maintained over long periods. An alternative is to shift the burden of food subsidies to the general taxpayer. Governments can then raise farm prices and use budget revenues to subsidize consumer prices. However, when the difference between the high producer price and the low consumer price becomes sufficiently large, it is difficult to prevent the subsidized commodity from being sold back to the government at the higher producer price. In this case, subsidies may be needed on processed commodities. This is not always feasible. Even when it is, efficiency losses will still be implicit in consumer subsidy programs. While these losses may be more widely dispersed throughout the economy, they do not disappear—especially when, as shown in Figure 5.1, consumer subsidy programs account for large shares of government expenditures.

Food subsidy programs have other costs. Official pricing systems usually respond slowly, if at all, to changing market conditions. Price changes, which happen continuously in free markets, usually require complicated bureaucratic procedures and consultations. Sudden changes in market conditions can result in rapid increases in budgetary costs. The high world prices of 1972–74 had a dramatic impact upon the food subsidy budgets of Bangladesh, Korea, Morocco, Pakistan, Sri Lanka, and Tanzania. The stability of official prices was achieved at the cost of instability elsewhere: in the fiscal deficit or in the balance of payments as the subsidy burdens shifted to other activities competing for foreign exchange.

Some of the costs of food subsidy programs become readily apparent when an overvalued exchange rate or consumer subsidies increase consumption of imported foods at the expense of goods that are produced locally. Per capita consumption of wheat products and rice in West Africa grew at an average annual rate of 8.5 and 2.8 percent, respectively, between 1966–70 and 1976–80. Consumption of traditional foods has either barely grown (by 0.27 percent for maize) or declined (by 1.5 percent for millet and 1.69 percent for sorghum). Such changes in diet were partly connected with increasing incomes and urbanization. But the main reason was that urban consumption was implicitly subsidized by overvalued exchange rates which made imports appear cheap in comparison with domestically produced coarse grains. While the international price of rice was three times that of sorghum, in West Africa it was rarely more than twice as much and sometimes only the same. The price of wheat flour in Côte d'Ivoire and Nigeria was about the same as that of maize, while in developing countries with free trade policies wheat flour often cost more than twice as much as maize. The strong correlation between wheat imports and real bread prices in Table 5.2 shows the effects of exchange rate overvaluations and consumer pricing policies.

The benefits of food subsidy programs are harder to estimate than the costs because it is difficult to measure social gains objectively. Granted this, however, the programs may not benefit recipients in the way intended. Consider attempts to help unskilled workers in towns by providing cheap food. This may pull in more unskilled workers from the countryside and eventually reduce urban wages to parity with the level of rural ones. If part of the burden of these programs is shifted back to agriculture by depressing farm prices, rural wages will be reduced, which will harm unskilled workers in both rural and urban areas. This is what happened in Thailand, where rice prices were depressed for the benefit of urban consumers.

The rural poor (small farmers, small traders, and unskilled workers) tend to be dispersed, unorganized, and politically inarticulate. Urban elites (organized labor, the middle class, the military, and public sector employees) are typically organized and powerful. When governments intervene to set the price of a commodity, political decisionmaking tends to take over, so that prices are determined by the relative power of the interested parties. Budgetary limits often mean that only a part of total supplies will be available at the subsidized official price. If so, the more powerful urban groups tend

Table 5.2 **Trends in bread prices and consumption and imports of wheat, selected years, 1969–81**
(average annual percentage change)

| | | Wheat, 1969–71 to 1979–81 | |
Country group	Real bread price, 1970–80	Per capita consumption	Per capita imports
Algeria, Bolivia, Egypt, Ethiopia, Guatemala, Iran, Iraq, Mexico, Zaire	Less than −5.0	3.5	11.7
Brazil, Dominican Republic, El Salvador, Gambia, Ghana, Kenya, Paraguay, Tanzania	−3.0 to −5.0	3.2	4.9
Burundi, Cameroon, Ecuador, India, Kuwait, Libya, Malawi, Pakistan, Panama, Saudi Arabia, Somalia, Sudan	0.0 to −3.0	2.1	−1.9
Burkina Faso, Côte d'Ivoire, Hong Kong, Korea, Mauritius, Singapore, Turkey, Uruguay, Zambia	0.0 to 3.0	0.7	−3.7
Colombia, Costa Rica, Thailand, Venezuela	3.0 to 5.0	0.1	−4.4
Argentina, Bangladesh, Burma, Indonesia, Malaysia, Peru, Philippines, Senegal	More than 5.0	0.1	−11.5

Source: CIMMYT 1983.

Sri Lanka has a long history of food subsidy programs. Food rationing was instituted in 1943, and food subsidies for the whole population were continuously in effect for the following three decades. Governments of differing political persuasions continued to support the subsidies in order to encourage political stability and social equity.

For the most part, the programs provided cheap rice, with occasional subsidies on wheat flour, sugar, and powdered milk. The original rice ration of four pounds per person was distributed universally at between 40 and 70 percent of the market price. In the mid-1970s one pound was provided free, and two were available at about a 30 percent subsidy. Rationed rice was typically providing about 20 percent of total caloric intake. But in 1969–70, for each additional calorie consumed by those who did not have a nutritionally adequate diet, thirteen went to people with enough to eat or substituted for commercial purchases. More than half the benefits went to middle- and upper-income families.

In the late 1970s, as economic growth slowed partly because of high welfare expenditures at the expense of investment, the cost of the programs became too great. As the government tried to hold down the cost of providing the ration, the procurement price from domestic producers was kept low, which discouraged local rice production. As a result, the burden on the balance of payments increased as more than 30 percent of the supplies were imported in the late 1970s. In 1977 the new government undertook a comprehensive program of economic reform which included a significant realignment of the exchange rate, the decontrol of prices, and the opening of rice marketing to private traders. This provided a great boost to production, but the government also took measures to assist poor consumers during the transitional period. Initially, the government limited eligibility for food subsidies to lower-income groups only. In 1979, food rations were replaced with food stamps, and the programs were restricted to households with annual incomes below Rs3,600 ($240). While a household survey conducted in 1978–79 indicated that only 7.1 percent of the population lived in such households, it appears that almost one-half of the population managed to get food stamps. Nonetheless, the beneficiaries were generally from the bottom half of the population in terms of income.

By holding the nominal value of the subsidies constant, the government ensured that the real cost of the food subsidies would gradually decline without causing abrupt losses of benefits. Government spending was shifted from welfare programs toward investment. By 1984, food subsidies accounted for only 4 percent of government expenditures, compared with 19 percent in 1978 and 23 percent in 1970.

The process has not been without its reversals and problems. But the government has been sufficiently encouraged to consider a new round of reforms to improve the targeting of the food stamps and raise their value.

to get the cheap food first, and the others end up buying more expensive food on parallel markets.

Reforming consumer subsidy programs, though desirable, is not easy. Such reform often raises food prices for the urban poor, who in some cases depend on subsidized food. Without some means of dealing with this problem, needed reforms may not be implemented or, if implemented, may not stick. Box 5.4 discusses one case in which food subsidy programs were reformed: that of Sri Lanka. It successfully avoided the problems that arise with too abrupt a change in policies.

Groups suffering from chronic malnutrition deserve support, and the least-cost way of supporting them through government programs is to institute much better targeting. For example, programs that restrict subsidies to the poorest region, or to the poorest neighborhoods in poor regions, can be cost-effective and well targeted. Subsidies can also be cost-effective when they are concentrated on food that is eaten mainly by the poor. A high proportion of subsidized grain in Bangladesh goes to urban areas. In 1973–74, the poorest rural households consumed 167 pounds of grain a year, per capita, 14 percent of which was provided as food-grain rations. Comparable income groups in urban areas consumed 263 pounds each, 90 percent of which was from food rations. The inequality of the distribution system, although less than in 1973–74, is still evident from the results of household surveys in 1982–83, with urban households receiving about twice the amount of subsidized grain received by rural households. As a possible means of targeting food rations more effectively, experimental subsidies for sorghum, a grain less preferred in urban areas than rice and wheat, were introduced in one urban and two rural districts. As expected, less than 5 percent of the urban households purchased the subsidized sorghum, but in rural areas more than two-thirds of the poorest families and more than half of the lower-middle-income households bought it.

In Brazil, subsidies on cassava are likely to be more effective in helping the poor than subsidies on rice, bread, or maize. One study shows that a dollar of subsidy for cassava would generate 60¢ in benefits to low-income groups compared with 40¢ for maize, 23¢ for rice, and 18¢ for bread. While subsidies for sorghum or cassava may be a cost-effective way of helping the poor, they raise some potential problems. Many of the poorest people's foods are also used for animal feed. Subsidies intended to lower food costs for the poor may also lower production costs for livestock, and this, in effect, subsidizes the rich. Diversion of low-cost food to livestock feed has been a problem in both Egypt and Zimbabwe. Even if it happens on a small scale only, it is hard to generate net benefits from broadly based food subsidies once the administrative and distortionary costs of raising the necessary revenue are fully accounted for.

Many of these problems do not arise if subsidies are narrowly targeted to support nutritionally vulnerable groups, such as pregnant and nursing women, the very young, the sick, the very old, or the handicapped. Many governments have provided incentives for such schemes by offering tax advantages to nongovernment organizations. Direct government spending on well-defined target groups is also justified. The World Bank is supporting one such effort in Tamil Nadu, India, and the results look promising (see Box 5.5).

Producer support programs

Much of the growth in agricultural production in many developing countries is attributable to the expansion in irrigation (see Chapter 1). Between 1950 and 1983 the area under irrigation in developing countries more than doubled. Even though the rate of growth has slowed, about 3.2 million hectares are still being brought under irrigation each year, with Asia accounting for more than 40 percent of the growth. In parallel with this growth in irrigation, but not solely due to it, the use of such modern inputs as chemical fertilizers and machinery has also grown rapidly.

To bring about increased use of these inputs and of credit, governments in developing countries have generally followed a policy of subsidizing farm inputs. Increasing production has not been the only objective—improving the distribution of income in rural areas has also been important. But input and credit subsidy programs have run into

Box 5.5 Targeting economic assistance in Tamil Nadu, India

A successful project for helping nutritionally vulnerable children and mothers is now under way in Tamil Nadu in South India. A survey carried out by the state government in the early 1970s showed that half of rural families consumed less than 80 percent of their daily caloric needs. Approximately 50 percent of children between one and four years of age were classified as malnourished; 45–50 percent of child deaths were a direct consequence of malnutrition. The cost of treating nutrition-related diseases was around $5.5 million a year, or nearly one-third of the annual state expenditure for medical services. The government set out to improve this situation, especially for children under three years old. By 1980, twenty-five nutrition and feeding programs were operating at a total cost of $8.8 million. But their impact was less than it could have been, because they were not sufficiently targeted and were not monitored properly.

In 1980 the government initiated a five-year project to combat and prevent malnutrition and to promote health. It provides nutrition and health care for children six to thirty-six months of age and for pregnant and lactating women. A special team of local community nutrition workers was trained to take the program into their villages, and they are supported in their work by women's working groups, averaging twenty-five women in each village. Children are weighed every month to determine how fast they are gaining weight. Those who are gaining weight too slowly are enrolled in a special ninety-day program in which they are fed daily in community centers. Their mothers are counseled on how to recognize early signs of malnutrition and what to do about it. Severely malnourished children receive double rations. Complementary health services are also provided. Prenatal health care is routinely available to pregnant women; mothers in special need get extra food to take home. Nutrition and health education are a crucial part of the project. This approach, by employing a sensitive but practical growth surveillance system to identify children who are nutritionally at risk, allows supplementary feeding to be highly selective and short-term—two features that enhance cost effectiveness and avoid long-term dependence on food assistance.

The project is now working in 9,000 villages of Tamil Nadu, benefiting around one million children and

many problems, including the large cost to the budget. This raises the question of whether it would not be better to eliminate or greatly moderate subsidies and use the resources thus saved for other purposes, such as reducing taxes on farm outputs. The main problems and issues that tend to arise in practice with input and credit subsidies are reviewed below.

Fertilizer subsidies

In many countries subsidies cover the whole range of inputs—from plows to pesticides. But fertilizer subsidies are very common. Rates of subsidy for fertilizers in the early 1980s were rarely below 30 percent of delivered cost and were in some cases 80 to 90 percent (in Nigeria, for example). Rates of 50 to 70 percent are common. In Saudi Arabia and Venezuela, farmers pay half the ex-factory or landed cost; urea is sold at 56 percent below cost in Sri Lanka and at 60 percent below cost in Gambia.

There has always been some skepticism about the usefulness of subsidies on fertilizers (or other inputs). Until about the mid-1970s, it was commonly thought that, while there might be some justification for *temporary* subsidies, longer-term subsidies would result in nonoptimal input use

and output mixes. Recent analyses take fuller account of market imperfections and the existence of public objectives other than income maximization. This has led to a long list of arguments in favor of subsidies on fertilizers: to encourage learning by doing, to overcome risk aversion and credit constraints, to help poor farmers, to maintain soil fertility, to offset disincentives caused by taxing or pricing policies, or simply to increase output of priority crops. Taken together, this panoply of pro-subsidy economic arguments seems to present a formidable case for fertilizer subsidization. In fact, however, most of these arguments justify only temporary or small subsidies. And all of them ignore the negative institutional effects that almost always accompany fertilizer subsidization. For example:

• The learning by doing rationale is at best a reason for temporary subsidies, and it is probably not applicable in many places. Even in the least dynamic agricultural systems (for example, those in semiarid West Africa), fertilizers have been in use for at least a generation. Where there are functioning extension services, the fertilizer message enters general circulation after a few years. Even where services are poor, farmers have usually heard about what fertilizers can do or have ob-

more than 300,000 pregnant and lactating women. Participation rates in the project are unusually high; 80–95 percent of eligible children have taken part. About a quarter of them needed extra food at any one time, and 95 percent of those eligible took the supplements. Of those who received supplements, 65 percent showed adequate growth velocity within 90 days and a further 15 percent within 120 days; only 20 percent required extended supplementation.

The impact of the project has been monitored by comparing two blocks of villages, each with a population of 100,000. One block, the pilot block, benefited from the project; the other, the control block, was outside the project. After three years, this comparison revealed the following impact on nutritional status and on illness and mortality:

• Severe malnutrition decreased by 32 percent in the pilot block, but by only 12 percent in the control block.

• Moderate malnutrition decreased by 9 percent in the pilot block, but increased by 19 percent in the control block.

• The category of ''normal status or mild malnutrition'' increased by 20 percent in the pilot block and

decreased by 5 percent in the control block.

• The average weight of children increased in the pilot block and decreased in the other. Nutritional advantages derived from the project were shown to persist through five years of age. At that age, children who had been in the project were heavier by 1.75 kilograms than children in other areas. The disease and mortality rates of children in the project also appeared to be falling.

Preliminary estimates suggest that the nutrition and communications components cost approximately Rs72 ($6.50) per child per year, or Rs0.20 ($0.02) per child per day. Expanded statewide, the total cost would be less than 1 percent of the state revenue budget. This compares favorably with the estimated costs of similar programs elsewhere in India. By targeting feeding to those at risk—when they need it—the food cost is significantly below that of most feeding programs aimed at children of preschool age. The project appears to offer a model for a cost-effective way of protecting the nutrition and health of the most vulnerable part of the population.

served their effects on nearby farms.

• Risk aversion, which leads farmers to use less than profit-maximizing levels of fertilizers, may justify a little subsidization in some regions but not much. Moreover, fertilizer use need not involve substantial increases in risk; for example, farmers apply top dressings of urea only after they are sure the crop is established. The impact of risk aversion, judged by the difference between how much fertilizer should be used and actual levels of use, is small. A World Bank study suggests that even when farmers are strongly risk averse, their fertilizer use will be at most 15 percent less than it would be if they were trying to maximize profits.

• Credit constraints arise out of capital market imperfections such as inadequate information flows, high transaction costs, and requirements for collateral. As a general rule it is better to eliminate the source of a problem than to compensate for it. The long-term solution for imperfection in rural credit markets lies in improving the operation of credit markets, not in subsidizing other inputs.

• The income distribution argument involves many empirical questions concerning the nature of demand for fertilizers across households classified by income level and the adequacy and equity of the rationing systems that often accompany subsidized input distribution. A study of fertilizer use in Senegal revealed that the benefits of subsidization went mostly to better-off farmers—those in better-watered areas. This is true more generally: those farmers benefiting most from irrigation also benefit most from fertilizer subsidies, and they often tend to be better-off farmers.

• The soil-enrichment and conservation arguments in favor of fertilizer subsidies do not stand up under close analysis. There may be a case for a temporary subsidy where population growth has accelerated and farmers may not learn about fertilizers fast enough to prevent severe damage to soil quality. But in the most vulnerable areas—the semiarid tropics—what is most often needed is the adoption of less expensive and better adapted organic fertilizers and the use of moisture-retaining methods, such as ridging to prevent rainfall run-off. Neither of these is encouraged by the existence of fertilizer subsidies, and such subsidies actually discourage the use of organic fertilizers. Moreover, there is some evidence that sustained use of chemical fertilizers can actually reduce fertility. In Burkina Faso, for example, sorghum yields declined after seven years of chemical fertilization, as a result of soil acidification, potassium deficiencies, and aluminum toxicity. Only by combining large applications of animal manure with chemical fertilizers was soil fertility maintained or improved.

Apart from the foregoing considerations, special arguments are often put forward to encourage fertilizer subsidy policies. It is often thought that fertilizer subsidies are needed as a part of a fiscal package to minimize the efficiency cost of raising a given amount of revenue from farmers. If a government wants to tax smallholders and the only feasible method is a tax on their marketed surplus, the best way to raise a given amount of revenue may sometimes involve subsidizing fertilizers to boost production and the volume of marketed surplus. Such an argument needs to be treated with caution. First, the revenue targets should be examined carefully rather than taken for granted. Second, the subsidy and tax rates may change radically over time, so that rapid policy changes will be required. Third, it assumes that subsidizing fertilizers can offset the negative production response to low producer prices—an assumption that is questionable at best. Even when a subsidy can be justified in special cases, the large and indiscriminate subsidies often seen in practice are not warranted.

Fertilizer subsidies are typically provided through public distribution systems. Apart from the inefficiencies that may be entailed in these systems, the distribution policies discourage potential private suppliers, such as traders, shopkeepers, transporters, local artisans, and large farmers. The most significant long-term cost of subsidy programs may indeed lie in the obstacles they put in the way of private suppliers, whose services are essential to transforming backward farm economies. Some of the problems that arise with public monopolies of fertilizer distribution are:

• Fertilizers marketed by the public sector often arrive too late to be used to maximum effect. The reasons for late delivery vary from country to country, but some are often inherent in public sector marketing itself. The agency involved may not know what its budget is until relatively late in the crop cycle. Where there is a central tendering agency for all government purchases, the process is time-consuming. Distributing fertilizer in small quantities to widely dispersed farmers can be extremely demanding. Where the public sector dominates the transport system, the task often strains its capacity.

• Government suppliers offer few varieties of fertilizer, although particular crops or soils need particular kinds of nutrient. Governments often charge all users the same price, whatever their locations. They offer very few alternatives in nutrient mix. In Cameroon, for example, only three types of fertilizer were imported in the early 1980s: ammonium sulfate, NPK 20–10–10, and urea. But specific crops and specific regions (soils) have more finely defined needs. The ''shotgun-type'' approach nonetheless provides NPK 20–10–10, say, for both coffee and maize, in humid forest zones and semiarid regions. In much of the Sahel, the fertilizer mix most commonly recommended for millet and sorghum is based on the available cotton complex fertilizer. Some indication of the level of waste involved in these unrefined approaches is found in a study in Senegal that compared optimal nutrient requirements with the standard compound fertilizer. The study indicated that about 20 percent of the cost of fertilizer could have been saved with no negative effects on physical productivity. And this does not take account of the full gains possible from the use of more varied combinations of nutrients.

• In many cases all of farmers' demand cannot be met at subsidized prices. This leads to rationing. Who gets how much fertilizer then depends on the rationing process. Typically, the allocation process favors the bigger farmers and thus negates whatever equity benefits might otherwise have accrued.

• The rationing process also leads to erratic fluctuations in the actual cost of obtaining fertilizers, and this hinders the learning process. Even when farmers do learn the best uses of fertilizers, the feedback to public agencies is often slow and imperfect. For example, in Burkina Faso the extension services continue to recommend that compound fertilizers devised for cotton also be used for millet and sorghum, despite evidence that the long-term effects on yield are likely to be negative.

The difficulties discussed above also arise in the case of pesticides. Subsidies on pesticides can radically change the relative profitability of chemical-intensive as opposed to labor-intensive control programs for pests. For example, it has been shown that pests in cotton fields in Egypt can be controlled by (a) choosing planting times that avoid peak pest seasons, (b) adding fuel oil to the irrigation water on the preceding crop, (c) hand-picking egg masses from cotton plants, (d) carefully monitoring insect infestations to guide the timing and extent of chemical spraying, and (e) burning infested bolls at the end of the season. Rice farmers in South China have also reduced their use of pesticides by adopting pest-resistant varieties, raising insect-eating ducks in paddy

fields, releasing predatory insects and bacterial pathogens, and carefully monitoring pest populations. These techniques substitute labor and other inputs for chemical inputs. Heavy subsidies on pesticides geared to encouraging pest control can have costly and unanticipated impacts on the choice of techniques used to accomplish this goal. Especially in labor-abundant countries, it may be a waste of resources to encourage the substitution of chemical pesticides for human labor.

Mechanization subsidies

Many developing countries promote agricultural mechanization. Very large implicit subsidies arise when overvalued foreign exchange rates are combined with preferential allocation of rationed foreign exchange for mechanical inputs, a policy pursued at one time or another by countries as diverse as Colombia, Egypt, India, and Pakistan. Often, farm machinery receives preferential tariff treatment compared with what a uniform revenue tariff on all agricultural and industrial inputs would warrant. In Colombia in the early 1960s, for example, the 2 percent import duty and the 3 percent sales tax on imported tractors were small in relation to the degree of overvaluation of the currency, while in Peru the import duty on tractors, at 20 percent, was still lower than the average tariff on imports and far below the percentage by which the currency was realigned in 1967. In some cases agricultural income tax provisions provide another subsidy by allowing farm machinery to be used as a tax shelter. This is most often done via accelerated depreciation provisions. An extreme example of such a tax shelter is found in the income tax code of Brazil: it allows for a deduction from farm incomes of six times the value of the machine in the first year, thus generating tax losses whenever large machinery purchases are made. Other farm investments such as livestock are treated less favorably, and, of course, labor costs enjoy no preferential tax treatment at all.

The benefits of subsidies are typically confined to large farms and to regions with favorable climates and good infrastructure. The subsidies provide the wealthy rural population with a competitive advantage at the expense of poorer groups. For example, in Brazil, as industrialization took place in the state of São Paulo, labor was drained from rural areas to meet the growing demand for urban labor. In the face of rural labor scarcities, the degree of mechanization would have been limited by migration of labor from the northeast. However, the government provided large subsidies in an effort to build a farm machinery industry and eliminated payments in kind to labor; this deterred the use of labor and enabled the southern region to compete in the production of sugarcane by neutralizing the northeast's advantage of lower labor costs. While sugarcane became profitable in the south, resources were diverted from other crops that had a higher international value.

There is typically no economic justification for machinery subsidies. This is not to say that mechanization cannot be profitable—it can be when wages are high or when the nature of the operation makes it especially advantageous (for example, irrigation pumps). When it is profitable, farmers can afford it—even small farmers can benefit by using machinery rental markets.

Credit subsidies

In almost all developing countries, governments have special programs for providing credit to farmers, generally at low interest rates. Subsidized credit programs usually have harmful side effects on financial institutions, rural financial markets, and the wider economy.

Many of the problems encountered in practice result from the pursuit of two inconsistent objectives: promotion of efficient production and the provision of income transfers to the poor. As will be seen below, credit is an ineffective instrument for bringing about income transfers to the poor. As for the production objective, credit does not by itself promote productivity increases—all it does is provide opportunities that farmers can take advantage of. If less productive opportunities are exploited by farmers before more productive ones, something else is wrong—which is where attention should focus. Credit policy should not be seen as an instrument for offsetting distortions elsewhere which cause resource misallocations.

Credit policy is often motivated by the belief that small farmers are unable to obtain loans because of inadequate collateral despite their ability to repay: that is, private credit institutions overestimate the risks of lending to small farmers. If this were so, it would be quite inappropriate to force lenders to make such loans at highly subsidized rates. A better policy would be to subsidize credit institutions, rather than farmers, to induce them to take the higher risks of lending to small farmers. This would provide an incentive to collect information about the previously ignored borrowers and their investment opportunities.

Box 5.6   Credit subsidies in Brazil

Credit subsidies and controls have had a great impact on rural financial markets in Brazil. During the 1970s the level of credit subsidies increased rapidly. This was partly unintentional, as credit contracts were set in nominal terms and actual inflation exceeded projected rates.

Between 1969 and 1976 the annual value of rural credit disbursed increased by four and one-half times in real terms, while value added in agriculture roughly doubled. It is not clear that this credit was always used for the intended purposes. In fact, since agricultural credit in 1975–78 reached levels equal to total value added in agriculture, substantial amounts must have been diverted to other purposes. The diversion of credit is also indicated by many instances in which the total area for which farmers got subsidized credit for a particular crop was larger than the area actually harvested for that crop. This is all the more remarkable since only a minority of farmers received any subsidized credit at all. The 1975 census indicated that there were approximately 5 million farms, while in 1976 there were only 1.8 million credit contracts, and most farmers using credit take more than one contract. The Association of Development Banks estimated that 23 percent of agricultural credit was diverted to other purposes.

There are doubts about whether any significant net benefits were obtained from the credit subsidies, even within the small part of agriculture covered by these

---

INCOME DISTRIBUTION AND CREDIT. Rich farmers have few problems in gaining access to credit. It is the poor farmers who face credit constraints, especially if they do not have well-established claims to their land. Even if credit is available to them, it often seems excessively costly.

It is difficult to channel low-interest credit to low-income groups. Low interest rates stimulate heavy demand for loans when resources are limited. Excess demand for credit is therefore common (Box 5.6 provides an illustration from Brazil). Some form of rationing has to be introduced, implying an increase in the effective cost of credit above that suggested by the subsidized interest rate. The increase in effective rates can take several forms. It can be shifted from the lender to the borrower by requiring more documentation, extra trips to town, or more queuing. Or it can be reflected by requiring borrowers to hold compensating balances or to provide extra collateral. Low-income farmers tend to be excluded by the

programs. Since land provides a basis for access to credit subsidies, land values increased rapidly. Elaborate regulations were instituted to limit the diversion of subsidized credit. The tying up of entrepreneurial and professional time and talent in working through the credit maze may have been one of the most important costs of these policies.

The problem of credit diversion means that it is exceedingly difficult to assess the impact of credit, positive or negative, on farm activities. There is some evidence that excessive mechanization and fertilizer use were encouraged by the credit subsidies, but there is no clear empirical evidence to suggest that credit subsidies have increased production or yields. It is also doubtful that the subsidy programs have benefited low-income farmers, despite an intended bias in favor of the low-income northeast and smallholders. The higher administrative costs of lending to large numbers of small farmers were a disincentive to the banks.

Credit subsidies contributed to inflation and helped destabilize the overall economy. The growth in the volume of credit, together with the widening gap between low interest rates and the cost of funds, led to subsidies that at one point in the late 1970s exceeded 5 percent of GDP. By the end of the 1970s this had become unsustainable. Since 1980 the subsidies have been gradually cut back by reducing the volume of real credit. Since 1983 the value of the loans has been indexed. The decline in credit for investment was partic-

ularly sharp (see Box table 5.6). As the volume of credit from the federal and state banks fell more rapidly, commercial banks were forced to carry an increasing share of the burden of making unprofitable loans. They in turn transferred the costs to nonsubsidized loans—which in turn contributed to real interest rates of more than 25 percent for unsubsidized borrowers. This experience illustrates how the objective of sustaining the growth of agricultural credit in real terms can be defeated by excessive subsidies and the rigidity of nominal interest rate policies.

Box table 5.6 Indices of the real value of rural credit in Brazil for all banks, 1975–84
(1979 = 100)

Year	Total credit	Short-term credit	Investment credit
1975	86	79	108
1976	88	80	115
1977	79	80	76
1978	80	80	80
1979	100	100	100
1980	96	104	71
1981	83	93	51
1982	80	93	42
1983	61	67	41
1984	37	43	18

rationing process. Because transactions costs are frequently fixed according to the size of the loan, smaller amounts tend to be rationed out first. As studies from countries as diverse as Bangladesh, Bolivia, Brazil, and Honduras have shown, these costs can make the apparently low interest rate nearly as expensive, in real terms, as the much higher rates charged by moneylenders in informal markets.

Cheap loans are therefore unsuccessful in redistributing income toward the rural poor. The value of the subsidy is proportional to the size of the loan, and small farmers tend to receive small loans. Studies have revealed that the typical pattern is for large amounts of low-interest agricultural credit to be concentrated in the hands of relatively few borrowers, who are generally better-off and politically influential (see Box 5.6).

Governments can help low-income borrowers to get credit by removing obstacles that limit their access to commercial credit. Studies in a number of

countries, including Thailand and Kenya, show that access to credit depends partly on the nature of land titles, since land is one of the few assets farmers can use as collateral. The governments in both countries are now trying to improve the quality of land titles. By removing restrictions on interest rates, governments can make it profitable for financial institutions to develop their rural lending activities. Indonesia has gone some way toward encouraging this, as discussed in Box 5.7.

CREDIT PROGRAMS AND PRIORITY CROPS. Many rural credit programs use interest rate subsidies to encourage farmers to use particular inputs or to grow specific crops. But subsidized credit is widely diverted to other uses. Close supervision can limit the diversion, but it is costly and difficult because farmers can reallocate other funds. Credit diversion indicates that farmers' own judgments on the best investments do not coincide with the priorities set in credit programs.

Even if the diversion of credit could be controlled, credit subsidies may not be efficient ways to promote particular crops or techniques. Many of the benefits are offset by poor service and delays or wide swings in the availability of credit. By tying credit to particular inputs or crops, the programs can distort farmers' business decisions. If credit is subsidized to fund the purchase of tractors, premature mechanization can be encouraged.

When the policy environment is congenial and the technologies profitable, the private sector performs well in providing inputs and credit. As modern technology spread through the Philippines, sales of farm inputs became more lucrative and

---

Box 5.7 Improving rural financial markets in Indonesia

In the early 1970s the government of Indonesia began a credit program to promote rice production. Credit was provided at low interest rates (12 percent, which was negative in real terms during most years of the program), mainly for buying fertilizer. Fertilizer prices were subsidized, and the government raised the price of rice to about 30 percent above import prices and provided agricultural extension services. The subsidized credit was administered by the Bank Rakyat Indonesia (BRI), a government-owned, largely rural bank, through a series of village branches set up in irrigated areas where the potential for increasing rice production was highest.

Rice production duly expanded, greatly facilitated, it was thought, by subsidized credit. After the mid-1970s, however, although the amount of credit disbursed under the program declined sharply, rice production continued to increase; this suggested that subsidized credit was not as important as other elements, such as better extension services and higher farm prices for rice. And why had the amount of credit disbursed declined? This was partly because credit under the programs was not as cheap as the subsidized 12 percent interest rate might suggest. The actual costs of obtaining credit were higher, particularly because of attempts to tie the use of credit to a particular package of inputs. Disbursements also declined because many borrowers failed to repay their loans and thus became ineligible for further credit under the program. These repayment problems necessitated larger government subsidies and cast further doubt on the virtues of providing cheap credit.

The village branches set up by the BRI became involved in two other government programs that began in the mid-1970s. The first aimed to encourage saving by paying small depositors 15 percent a year on their minimum monthly balance. Since this interest rate was higher than the bank could charge on loans, a government subsidy was necessary. The second offered small loans at subsidized interest rates of 12 percent a year funded by grants from the Ministry of Finance for diversification in rural areas.

By the early 1980s, as the price of oil began to fall, it became clear that the government could no longer afford to support the program of subsidized credit for rice production. It also became clear that other BRI activities (such as small saver and small loan programs) would have to be scaled down or abolished. Since the government had covered the operating losses of the village branches as well as shared the risk for bad debts, it appeared that the BRI would be left with more than 3,000 branches—more than 14,000 employees—and no obvious way of supporting them.

When reform finally came, in mid-1983, it was sweeping: direct controls on interest rates and the volume of credit were eliminated. The BRI decided not to close its village branches (and thereby lose a substantial investment in trained employees) but, rather, to reorganize them. Interest rates on most loans were raised to more than 20 percent a year, and loans could be used for almost anything. This was wholly unlike the original credit program. The village branches continued to pay 15 percent a year on deposits (which was higher than the rate of inflation). They also had an incentive to attract savings, because they made a profit on lending, and the more deposits they had, the more they could lend. They also needed savings to offset the reduced financing from the central bank.

The end of the subsidies benefited even those whom the subsidies were designed to help. Between mid-1983 and mid-1985 deposits at the village branches almost doubled. This made more money available for lending, and the amount lent under the new small loan program reached more than $300 million. In addition, the village branches of the BRI had begun, overall, to break even. Far more borrowers repaid their loans: only 1 or 2 percent of total loans outstanding had payments overdue in mid-1985—far less than the default rates under the old program.

Because the loans did not have to be spent on rice, or on anything to do with farming in general, it may seem as if the loans were an opportunity to move resources out of farming altogether. Of the 900,000 borrowers, almost 750,000 said that they were borrowing for trading: 75 percent of these "traders," a recent survey found, were also farmers. Although other credit programs continue to carry heavy subsidies, the reform of the village credit operations has been an important step toward sustainable rural financial markets and higher rural savings.

attracted new entrants into the farm implement business. This was not hampered by credit constraints. Most of the new entrants were farmers, and they used credit to attract customers. They competed profitably with formal credit schemes by offering quick decisions and agreements adapted to local circumstances. Some of these farmers even allowed repayment in kind. In addition to tailoring repayment terms to customer needs, they minimized the risk of default by taking the advice of local farmers in assessing credit risks, by taking strict measures against defaulters, and by offering customers a reliable and mutually profitable business association that was likely to yield additional benefits in the future. Repayment rates to village bankers were much higher than to official lending institutions, even though the same groups of farmers borrowed from both sources of credit.

EFFECTS ON FINANCIAL MARKETS. Subsidized credit affects both rural financial markets and the fiscal system. Where financial institutions are required to allocate a fixed share of their lending funds to certain priority borrowers or sectors, the cost of the implicit subsidy must be recovered by increasing the margins between the institution's cost of funds and its lending rates elsewhere. Borrowers who do not have priority will receive less credit and pay more for it, and depositors will get lower interest rates.

Fixing nominal interest rates for long periods of time—the custom in most countries—means that the real interest rate varies with inflation. As the real interest rate falls (or rises), rationing and collateral adjustments vary in ways that make it difficult to judge how the effective cost of obtaining credit varies to match supply and demand. Thus, governments lose control of the very instrument that they seek to use in meeting their credit policy objectives. Furthermore, depending on the method of financing used, attempts to increase the volume of rural credit in real terms in periods of inflation can add substantially to the rate of inflation or lead to very high real interest rates in other markets. Rural credit reforms should be combined with general financial sector reforms, and much greater emphasis should be given to flexible and market-related interest rates.

Subsidized credit operations also make it difficult to encourage rural savings by increasing deposit rates. Higher deposit rates increase the budget costs of the subsidy program. Also, a borrower taking out a low-interest rate loan can simply deposit the proceeds to earn a profit. Thus, credit subsidies often go hand in hand with lower deposit rates. The effects on rural savings can be very important. If interest rates are below the rate of inflation, savings rates are affected negatively. Some have argued that a negative interest rate does not deter rural savings because they believe that these savings do not respond sharply to higher interest rates. But in India, where rural branches were opened primarily to disburse agricultural loans, deposits were so substantial owing to the availability of generally positive interest rates that some authorities were concerned about the drain of funds from rural areas. The response in India has also been repeated in many other countries which have improved incentives to rural savings. In Japan, deposits taken since the early 1920s by agricultural cooperatives have been greater than the agricultural loans financed by the cooperatives and have contributed to the private capital flows discussed in Box 4.9 in Chapter 4. Savings in rural households rose rapidly in postwar Japan as rural incomes increased. Similarly, in Korea, interest rates on loans and deposits almost doubled after 1965, resulting in real rates of more than 8 percent. Average savings in farm households rose rapidly by the mid-1970s. Sharply responsive savings have been features of the reformed village credit units established in Indonesia (see Box 5.7) and savings and loan programs developed by coffee cooperatives in Kenya.

Program-specific incentive systems

Subsidies and taxes of various types often form a part of the packages of measures that governments take to promote the development of particular areas and crops. Typically, these incentive systems are designed to help achieve the immediate objectives of development programs: for example, to attract farmer participation and to induce farmers to choose inputs, crops, and other practices which are judged necessary for their success.

A crucial aspect of the success of a promotional program is its continued financial and economic viability after the initial period of years so that public assistance can be withdrawn or substantially reduced. This requires not only that the farmers, traders, and others involved with program activities start off with the right practices, but also that they have the incentive to revise their decisions as circumstances change. And for long-term viability, the special incentives initially introduced need to be gradually withdrawn. If a government agency remains involved for a long period of time, it must emphasize flexibility in decisionmaking and take account of the broader ramifications of the various measures taken to assist program participants.

TREE CROP DEVELOPMENT. Development programs for tree crops illustrate some of the problems that arise with heavily subsidized programs. Many governments encourage farmers to adopt new tree crop varieties and modern technology by establishing special agencies which set targets for the amount of land to be replanted or newly planted with the crops. The agencies sometimes demonstrate the new varieties or techniques for limited areas and time. Where they do so, they do not disrupt markets, especially if beneficiaries repay the input costs. These projects can demonstrate the high returns of recommended activities to both farmers and potential suppliers of inputs and credit. They stimulate, rather than crowd out, the private sector.

But agencies can also intervene for the worse, especially if crop development activities are not limited in time or coverage. Incentive systems introduced through the programs can have perverse effects both within program areas and outside, and

decisions on such key matters as the choice of crop and technique of production can become inflexible and hard to change.

The types of issues that need to be considered in designing program-specific incentive systems for tree crops can be quite subtle. Box 5.8 provides an illustration with reference to the rubber replanting programs in Thailand.

IRRIGATION AND COST RECOVERY. While expansions in public irrigation have been a major achievement in developing countries during the past few decades, the benefits from irrigation have often been less than they might have been because of poor maintenance and operations. In some countries—such as Egypt and Pakistan—rehabilitation projects have become a higher priority than expansions into new areas. Excessive use of water has in some cases contributed to waterlogging and salinization. In Peru, for example, 25 percent of the 800,000 hectares developed for irrigation in the Costa area have salinity problems.

Charging farmers for the water they use can increase the benefits of irrigation. If they have to pay for the actual amounts they use, they would use

---

Box 5.8   Rubber replanting programs in Thailand

For twenty-five years the government of Thailand has supported schemes to encourage farmers to replant rubber trees. The main elements of this policy have been grants to farmers to cover about half the costs of replanting with high-yielding clonal varieties, a cess (tax) collected on exports of rubber to finance the replanting program, and a separate export tax to raise revenue for the government budget. Replanting grants are disbursed over a six-year period under the supervision of a replanting agency to make sure farmers follow recommended practices.

The replanting program in Thailand has two aims: to replant large areas of low-yielding rubber with modern high-yielding varieties and to make farmers aware of improved technology. After a slow and somewhat shaky start in the 1960s, about a half million hectares—about 50 percent of the total rubber area—had been replanted by the early 1980s. The substantial replanting assistance encourages farmers to enter the program despite the cess and the export tax. The replanting agency has successfully overcome many of the problems of implementation that have plagued efforts in other countries. Appraisals show satisfactory economic rates of return. The program, which is being supported by the World Bank, can be counted as an

example of successful public sector intervention.

Programs of this type can, however, have adverse side effects unless carefully designed. The efficiency of rubber farming is determined not just by the varieties of trees but also by the quality of the tapping. Low-intensity, good-quality tapping and costly maintenance are required to extend the productive life of the trees and to increase the total output before replanting becomes necessary. However, cost recovery measures and pricing policies affect the choice of technique: the cess and the export tax tend to discourage output, while substantial replanting grants may induce farmers to adopt high-intensity tapping and poor maintenance practices. If so, advantages of the techniques that the government wants to promote would be reduced, yields would be lower, and productive lives would be shorter than anticipated.

The scheme may also discourage putting new land under rubber cultivation. Farmers who plant new land are not eligible for grants, although they still bear the burden of the cess and export tax. New planting was the primary factor behind the growth in rubber output until recent years, when the accelerated replanting program became more significant. The decline in the rate of new planting may have been related to an earwater sparingly, and crop selection would reflect the cost of water and other inputs. The revenue generated would make it easier to fund maintenance and further expansions of irrigation. The ability of farmers to pay is unlikely to be an issue in well-maintained systems, especially if fertilizers and seeds are readily available in local markets. Their net incomes can be several times higher, and also more secure and stable, than those of farmers in nonirrigated areas.

Unfortunately, there are few countries where the controls on water use allow volumetric water charges. In pressurized distribution systems, such as those in Cyprus, France, and the United States, water use can be monitored through meters in much the same way as other public utilities. Volumetric charges are also feasible in surface irrigation schemes if calibrated sluice gates are used—as in Jordan, Morocco, and Tunisia. These charges are also being used in the public tube-well schemes in India's Uttar Pradesh. Even when water use cannot be monitored directly—as in most surface systems in developing countries—annual levies on irrigated hectares permit some linkages with water use if they are differentiated by the water-depth requirements of the crops grown.

When charges based on actual water use are not feasible, there is a strong case for introducing betterment levies or access fees. Such fees can be flat—so many dollars a hectare—or they can be broadly differentiated by income levels. The logic is simple. Governments in many countries spend large amounts of resources on irrigation—frequently half of the total investment budget in agriculture. As discussed in Chapter 4, raising a dollar's worth of public resources can often cost much more than a dollar because of the inefficiencies involved in taxation—in particular, the efficiency costs of taxes on farm outputs. In contrast, the efficiency costs involved in a per hectare betterment levy would be minimal. Unless the levy is very large, the only costs would be those to administer and collect it.

Like the land taxes discussed in Chapter 4, betterment levies are far better instruments for raising revenue than commodity taxes. Thus, the large expenditures on irrigation create not only benefits for farmers but also the potential for raising resources much more efficiently than through general taxation. In addition, betterment levies are equitable—using them is much like using urban property taxes to finance urban improvements.

Why is it, then, that the revenue generated from water charges and betterment levies in irrigated areas is typically not even adequate to pay for maintenance and operation costs in developing countries? Part of the reason is the persistent notion in some countries that water is a free good of nature and should not be charged for. More important, the ability to impose betterment levies depends on the actual betterment realized. This in turn depends on the reliability of timely water supplies to farmers, on the prices of outputs and of complementary inputs, and on the quality of extension services. The poor record of cost recoveries in developing countries suggests that the full benefits of irrigation investments are far from being realized.

In the case of irrigation—so critical to continued success in agriculture—the challenge is to design systems and policies which permit better realization of irrigation benefits and better cost recoveries. In view of the high cost of public finance, a scheme that permits higher cost recoveries is preferable to one that leads to low cost recoveries, other things being equal. It may well be justified in some cases to choose irrigation systems with higher capital costs if they ensure good cost recoveries.

lier increase in export taxation and the replanting effort itself, which focused public sector support on replanting.

Finally, the program may discourage diversification into alternative and possibly more profitable crops. Diversification into other crops could undermine financing of the replanting agency and its program, which depend on the rubber cess. Officials of the rubber replanting agency are most familiar with that crop and therefore tend to encourage replanting rubber with rubber. Moreover, replanting grants for other crops have been lower than for rubber and depend on meeting exacting conditions. These reasons may have contributed to the fact that, despite a wide variety of crops for which grants have been given, the areas replanted with a crop other than rubber have been insignificant.

These types of concerns have been kept in view in developing successive stages of Thailand's rubber replanting program. Despite the potential for such adverse effects, the program has continued to be economically viable. This case also illustrates that developing countries can successfully specialize in primary commodities for exports by promoting technical change, despite long-run declines in real world market prices.

Policy reforms

This chapter and Chapter 4 have highlighted many of the difficulties that inappropriate pricing, trade, and macroeconomic policies create for agriculture. Some of the important lessons are:

• Macroeconomic policies can introduce a severe bias against agriculture. Exchange rates and the general pattern of prices and taxes need to treat the different sectors of the economy in an even-handed manner.

• Consumer price subsidy policies are expensive and often do not benefit low-income groups as much as intended, whereas they benefit middle- and upper-income groups to a considerable degree. Consumer subsidies can be effective only if they are restricted to the lowest-income groups and if their costs are controlled at levels that most developing countries can afford without having to resort to highly distortionary or inflationary means of financing them.

• Input subsidies are not an effective method for offsetting the adverse effects of low output prices, nor are they appropriate instruments for redistributing income, since most of the subsidies accrue to the larger and better-off farmers.

• While governments have played an important role in agriculture through expenditures on activities which the private sector does not have the incentive to provide, their role in providing a sound environment for private markets should not be underestimated. Although significant progress has been made in a few countries, other governments could do more by eliminating parastatal monopolies and by improving the legal and institutional framework required for the functioning of competitive private markets.

The above list is not new: many governments in developing countries recognize the need for reform, and several have begun to implement reform programs. The experience of the past decade has begun to dispel the pessimistic notion that positive reform is impossible because of political constraints. There have been striking—one might say revolutionary—reforms, and there have been others of a less sweeping nature that have had significant positive effects nonetheless.

Policy reform in China

The most far-reaching agricultural reforms of the past decade have been undertaken in the People's Republic of China. Because of the scope of the reforms, which touch all aspects of the organization of agricultural production, pricing and marketing of farm products, and allocation of labor between farm and nonfarm activities, it is appropriate to consider the reforms and their effects in some detail.

Before 1955, farming in China was carried out on some 100 million family farms averaging slightly less than one hectare each. Between 1955 and 1958, the agricultural organization was transformed first into cooperatives and then into some 55,000 communes, and direct planning and procurement controls were introduced. Sown area, output, and procurement targets became the main instruments of policy. There were some successes: the development and diffusion of modern seed varieties (especially high-yielding dwarf rice, hybrid maize, and hybrid sorghum); a two-thirds increase in irrigated land and an even greater increase in the share of land irrigated with water supplied from pumps; and the development of a modern and large chemical fertilizer industry.

Nonetheless, agriculture contributed only modestly to the growth of the economy during 1958–77, which itself was modest. The main reasons were the haste with which the commune system was created, the emphasis on egalitarianism in the distribution of rewards within accounting units, the prohibition of private grain sales, the restrictions on internal trade, and the promotion of self-sufficiency in staple foods at the provincial level.

In the mid-1970s, per capita output of grain was no greater than two decades earlier. The production of soybeans in 1975–77 was 30 percent below the 1965–66 output, and per capita cotton production was a quarter lower than in 1965–66. The slow growth of farm output, combined with the strict controls over the nonfarm activities of farm people, led to near stagnation in farm incomes. By 1977–78, the average rural real income was, at best, only slightly above the level of 1955–57. By 1978, China was no longer self-sufficient in grain and had to import grain to supply about 40 percent of its urban population.

The reforms which began in 1979 were designed to improve incentives for farm people and to reduce the intervention of the planning officials. Some elements of reform were instituted from the grass-roots level rather than from the top-level government. The first major step was to increase farm prices by between 25 and 40 percent in 1979, the first significant adjustment in farm prices in twelve years. The multitiered price system that was set up provided better prices, increased production, and boosted marketing through state channels, as mentioned in Chapter 4. At the same time, relative prices of various agricultural commodities were altered and the state eased long-standing prohibitions against grain sales in rural markets. The aim was to encourage different regions to specialize in the crops they could grow most efficiently. In a few cases the state guaranteed supplies of grain to encourage specialized production of nongrain crops. Restrictions on trade between regions were relaxed. The government also allowed experiments with disbanding the collectives in the poorest regions of the country. These reforms proved popular and successful, and by the end of 1983 about 95 percent of farm households were managing their own plots under contracts from collectives. To provide greater security and more incentives to invest in improving the land, many households have been guaranteed the right to manage their farms for at least fifteen years. There is now some scope for subletting land, and in some provinces new laws allow parents to hand down farms to their children. Collective agriculture, by the mid-1980s, has given way to individual household management, if not formal ownership.

The pace of agricultural growth since the reforms began has been unprecedented (see Table 5.3). Grain output grew from 305 million tons in 1978 to 407 million in 1984, an average annual rate of almost 5 percent. Grain production per capita has exceeded both the government's benchmark level of 302 kilograms per capita in 1957 and the level of per capita output achieved in the early 1930s—the last normal years before World War II. Performance has been even more impressive in the nongrain crops. After two decades of sluggish growth, output has soared since 1978. In the case of cotton, traditionally China's second most important crop

Table 5.3 Growth in production of selected commodities in China, 1957–84

(average annual percentage change)

Commodity	1957–78	1978–84
Grain	2.1	4.9
Soybeans	−1.1	4.2
Cotton	1.3	18.7
Oil-bearing crops	1.0	14.6
Sugarcane	3.4	11.1
Sugar beets	2.8	20.5
Tea	4.2	7.4
Tobacco	7.0	15.2
Meat	3.7	10.1
Fish	1.9	4.6

Source: Lardy (background paper).

Table 5.4 Growth in yields of selected commodities in China, 1957–83

(average annual percentage change)

Commodity	1957–78	1978–83
Grain	2.6	6.1
Cotton	2.1	11.5
Peanuts	1.4	6.0
Rapeseed	3.1	10.2
Sugarcane	0.0	4.3

Source: Lardy (background paper).

(after cereals), harvests almost tripled between 1978 and 1984. The output of oilseed crops more than doubled. Production of pork, beef, and mutton exceeded 15 million tons in 1984, up about 80 percent since 1978. With the exception of aquatic products, the levels of agricultural output achieved by the end of 1984 far surpassed the target levels for 1985 that were established by the Central Committee when it approved the first steps in agricultural reform in December 1978. China has also reversed its growing dependence on imported grains and has become a net exporter of coarse grains (particularly maize), soybeans, and raw cotton—all products that China had to buy on international markets only a few years ago. In 1984, China registered its largest agricultural trade surplus in thirty-five years.

The remarkable growth in Chinese agriculture since 1978 was achieved without sharp increases in total farm inputs: only the use of chemical fertilizers increased. The amount of land under cultivation declined by about 4 percent between 1978 and 1983; so did the use of other inputs, such as water and pesticides. The area of farmland under irrigation, the quantity of irrigated land served by mechanized pumping, and the use of tractors for land preparation all fell in absolute terms between 1979 and 1983. Given increased employment opportunities in rural small-scale enterprises, the number of rural workers engaged in farming has probably declined as well. Average per capita farm income in current prices increased from 134 yuan in 1978 to 355 yuan in 1984. Even after allowing for price increases, there is little doubt that the real income gains in rural areas during the past seven years have been very substantial and probably exceed those achieved in the previous three decades.

With the possible exception of cotton, there is no evidence of a breakthrough in farm technology that could account for the growth in yields indicated in Table 5.4. It is true that there have been increases in the number of small tractors, in the number of trucks used for rural transportation, and in the use of chemical fertilizers. Yet most of the increase in productivity that lies behind China's remarkable success story is the result of using existing resources more efficiently.

The reforms had numerous components in addition to those mentioned. In particular, families were permitted to engage in nonfarm activities that had been forbidden on most communes. Rural fairs or markets that were circumscribed during the Cultural Revolution were encouraged again, and there are now more than 43,000 such markets in rural areas and 4,500 in cities. Direct sales to urban consumers by farmers were prohibited prior to 1979. Township enterprises employed 60 million surplus farmhands by the end of 1980. At least 20 million farm families have been permitted to become specialized households and are no longer required to produce grain or other specific crops.

Nor have the reforms come to an end. In 1984

and 1985 the required deliveries to the state were eliminated for most farm products, including both cotton and grain. The two-tier price system has been replaced by a single price and by procurement agency contracts with farmers.

Other reforms

Far-reaching changes in agricultural policies have also occurred elsewhere—for example, in Chile and Turkey. The policy changes in agriculture that accompanied the general economic liberalization in Chile after 1973 led to spectacular growth in the volume of agricultural trade. Agricultural exports grew from $18 million in 1972 to $375 million in 1984, partly the result of the more than tenfold increase in the volume of exports of fruits and vegetables. Exports of wood products, pulp, and timber rose from $26 million in 1972 to $376 million in 1984. While the agricultural trade balance greatly

---

Box 5.9 Agricultural policy improvements in Bangladesh

Bangladesh shows how the types of policy reforms discussed in Chapters 4 and 5 can bear fruit on a large scale in even the poorest countries. Bangladesh is one of the most densely populated countries in the world, and its 100 million people had an average per capita income of only $130 in 1983. It has fertile soils and a relatively abundant supply of water, but few other natural resources. Situated in the world's largest active delta, the country is prone to floods and cyclones during the monsoon and droughts during the dry season. Agriculture is the heart of the Bangladesh economy, generating about 50 percent of GDP and accounting for about three-quarters of employment and exports.

The government's policy reforms began in the late 1970s under exceptionally difficult circumstances. After the war for independence, agricultural production declined, domestic food prices rose well above world market prices, and rural wages fell in real terms between 1971 and 1975. There was a famine in 1974, and Bangladesh became heavily dependent on food aid. Although growth in annual agricultural production picked up to 3 percent in the late 1970s, output increased only slightly faster than population, which was growing at the rate of 2.6 percent a year. Another famine occurred in 1979, after a serious drought.

The government responded to these difficulties by expanding public investment in agriculture, concentrating on small irrigation projects with low costs and quick returns, increasing the role of the private sector, and improving the effectiveness of public agencies.

The allocation to agriculture in the development budget, excluding the fertilizer subsidy, was restored to 28 percent on average between 1978–79 and 1984–85. It had fallen from 34 percent in 1973–74 to only 19 percent in 1977–78. The acreage covered by modern irrigation facilities doubled, at a rate of expansion about three times faster than during the previous five years.

The increase in public investment in agriculture would have been impossible without a sharp reduction in subsidies, particularly the fertilizer subsidy. Between 1978–79 and 1984–85, the fertilizer subsidy was reduced from about 10 percent of the development budget to 2.4 percent. The unit subsidy fell from 50 percent of cost to 17 percent. Yet, despite this, fertilizer sales have continued to grow by more than 10 percent a year. One reason is that retail distribution of fertilizer was transferred to the private sector, which found it profitable to distribute fertilizer throughout the country at the right time—a marked contrast to the frequent shortages of the 1970s, which often meant that fertilizers could be had only at prices far higher than the official prices. Similarly, the entry of the private sector into the distribution of minor irrigation equipment has been an important reason for the rapid growth in farm mechanization over the past few years.

Similar successes have been achieved in the distribution of food grains. The government suspended antihoarding laws, abolished the accreditation system whereby grain dealers were designated to procure grains on behalf of the government, and lifted restric-

improved, imports of food—especially wheat, rice, and maize—also increased during the 1970s. However, as a result of better exchange rate policies, the domestic production of cereals grew by about 48 percent between 1982 and 1984 and imports declined significantly.

The reforms in Turkey are much more recent. As part of the general reforms adopted by the government in 1980, input subsidies and production price supports were reduced and credit subsidies curtailed. The real exchange rate was significantly increased, with assurance that the new level would be maintained. Exports were encouraged. While the growth of agricultural GDP was low in 1981, due in part to oil shortages and poor weather, it soon recovered to an annual rate of about 3.0 percent in 1982 and 1983 and 3.7 percent in 1984. Agricultural exports, by contrast, responded immediately, growing at an annual rate of 17.7 percent in 1980 and 1981. The annual rate of growth of the

value of exports dropped sharply thereafter, owing to the fall in world commodity prices, but the increase in agro-industrial exports partially compensated for this decline. Broader reforms within agriculture, which began in 1984, have already led to more liberal policies for the parastatals.

Substantial policy reforms have also been undertaken in Bangladesh, as discussed in Box 5.9. The main elements in the policy shift were a sharp reduction in the subsidies on fertilizers (which accounted for as much as 10 percent of the development budget in 1979); an increase in, and redirection of, spending on the infrastructure to emphasize small-scale irrigation, drainage, and flood control facilities; the liberalization of marketing (with retail distribution of fertilizer privatized); the elimination or reduction of export taxes on many agricultural products; and the adoption of a more realistic exchange rate policy.

Serious reform efforts can also be seen through-

tions that prevented the private sector from importing food grains. The private sector now handles about 85 percent of the internal marketing of grains. Aided by the construction of adequate storage facilities, the private sector has been particularly effective in limiting temporary increases in food-grain prices between harvests. The reduction of subsidies to urban consumers enabled the government to expand rural investment and relief programs rapidly, providing food-for-work and nutrition schemes for the poor. The investments have provided rural jobs equivalent to the full-time employment of close to 1 million landless laborers and have been used to maintain roads, canals, and embankments, which are essential to agricultural growth.

The government combined its reduction of subsidies and expansion of rural assistance schemes with more appropriate exchange rate policies and the provision of export incentives. It reduced or abolished export taxes on jute, tea, shrimp, and other agricultural exports, which helped to sustain growth in agricultural exports. As a result:

• Agricultural production has grown at about 3.5 percent a year.

• Agriculture has directly or indirectly generated most of the growth in employment, and rural wages have risen about 15 percent more than food-grain prices.

• The adoption of high-yielding varieties has increased, fertilizer consumption has grown by more than 10 percent a year, and irrigation, drainage, and

flood control facilities now cover nearly one-quarter of the cultivated area, as compared with less than 10 percent in the early 1970s.

• Agriculture has become more resilient to natural disasters. In four of the past five years, the grain crop has set new records, despite bad monsoons, floods, and drought.

• Food-grain imports, though still high, have fallen as a proportion of total consumption, and Bangladesh is now less dependent on food aid. A large and growing proportion of such aid, currently about 50 percent, goes to finance programs specially aimed at helping the rural poor.

• Farmers have diversified away from rice to wheat. Wheat is grown during the dry season between rice crops, when fields would otherwise lie fallow; it is less expensive to produce and is better nutritionally. Over the past decade production of wheat has risen from almost nothing to nearly 10 percent of total food-grain production. Consumption has increased from about 10 percent to nearly 20 percent of total grain consumption.

• Exports have increased and become more diverse. Jute exporters have won a higher world market share, despite slumping prices and declining demand. Exports of other agricultural commodities, such as shrimp, tea, and leather, have grown by more than 10 percent a year and now account for 30 percent of total exports, compared with about 15 percent in the early 1970s.

Box 5.10 Cotton sector reform in Sudan

Cotton is Sudan's main cash crop. It accounted for 56 percent of the country's export earnings in 1980–81. Public irrigation is the heart of cotton farming. The first large irrigation project was started in 1925 in the Gezira, which is now the world's largest irrigation scheme under single management; in all, more than 4 million acres are under irrigation using Nile waters, with more than a quarter of the area under cotton. There are six large schemes operated by agricultural parastatals, each divided into 200,000 tenancies of uniform size. The parastatals provide most inputs and machinery, the Ministry of Irrigation (MOI) supplies the water, and the tenants supply the labor, tend the crop, sprinkle the water, pick the cotton, and transport it to the ginnery. The ginned cotton is then handed over to the Cotton Public Corporation for export.

Cotton production fell sharply in the 1970s, dropping from 659,000 tons in 1974–75 to 259,000 tons in 1980–81. Both the area under cotton and the yield fell. The main reasons for the decline were:

• Low and declining producer prices. Some of the problems were common to other developing countries: an overvalued exchange rate, export duties on cotton, high parastatal profit margins, and delays in payment to tenants, sometimes as long as two years. Others were peculiar to Sudan: a sixty-year-old revenue-sharing formula between government, the parastatal, and the tenant (known as the Joint Account) under which the government siphoned off 36 percent of total revenue and distributed the rest in a way which taxed the more productive tenant; and the practice of offsetting the input costs of other crops (groundnuts, wheat, and sorghum) marketed by parastatals with earnings from cotton. This was administratively simple but made the inputs of other crops seem free, while cotton was made even less attractive.

• Shortage of the foreign exchange and local currency needed to maintain the irrigation works and the marketing operations. Low cotton prices meant the parastatals could not to cover their costs, which led to foreign exchange shortages. Government money was spent on new investments rather than maintenance. External development agencies neglected the maintenance and rehabilitation of existing schemes and invested in new projects instead.

• Poor performance of parastatals. Senior and skilled personnel migrated to oil-producing countries, where job opportunities were more attractive. Remaining managers were handicapped by red tape and weak accounting systems. The agriculturalists running the parastatal and the irrigation engineers running the Ministry of Irrigation failed to coordinate water supplies. In the end agricultural services were not provided and known technologies were not adopted. The cotton became severely infested by pests, which proved difficult to control with the available technology.

By late 1979, the country's balance of payments was in crisis. The current account deficit reached 11 percent of GDP, external debt rose to five times the value of annual exports, and the debt service ratio exceeded 40 percent. This triggered bold reforms for financial stabilization and promotion of exports.

The government abolished the export tax on cotton, lowered the exchange rate applicable to cotton exports, set the domestic price near the export price, announced the price before harvest, and paid it as soon as tenants delivered their cotton. As a result, for the first time in more than half a century, the tenants were able to estimate incomes from cotton reliably and could lobby for, and negotiate, a remunerative price for cotton. Simultaneously, several measures were taken to improve parastatal performance. These ranged from new statutes and better training to more concentration on research, extension, and marketing.

Helped by good weather and new supplies of equipment, spare parts, and other inputs, cotton production had a spectacular revival (see Box table 5.10).

The success of Sudan's cotton farmers survived even the severe problems which beset the country in 1984: the abrupt introduction of Islamic law, the escalation of civil war in the south, and the unprecedented drought in the west. The country's creditworthiness declined, and capital fled from the country. But because domestic cotton prices remained high enough to offset the effects of an overvalued exchange rate, cotton output continued to rise. Special arrangements were made to guarantee the foreign exchange (mainly from donors) required to finance the needs of cotton production. While the government's budget deficit widened, the parastatals' finances improved because of higher yields, better uses of inputs, and higher output prices.

Box table 5.10 Production and yield of seed cotton in Sudan, 1980–85

Item	1980–81	1981–82	1982–83	1983–84	1984–85
Production (thousands of tons)	306	461	573	586	625
Yield (tons per hectare)	0.82	1.39	1.57	1.54	1.69

out sub-Saharan Africa. The reform of the cotton sector in Sudan illustrates how much can be gained by taking small steps despite unfavorable trends in the overall economy. Sudan's irrigated farming sector has been revitalized through changes in the relationship between farmers and management in irrigation schemes such as the Gezira. This has involved abolishing the export tax on cotton (the major crop in the Gezira scheme), lowering the nominal exchange rate applied to cotton exports, and announcing producer prices before the harvest and paying farmers promptly for their cotton. Cotton production doubled between 1980–81 and 1984–85 (see Box 5.10).

In many other African countries producer prices for food have been increased in real terms, and it has now become more profitable to grow staples to substitute efficently for imports. Real producer prices of traditional export crops have also risen. Unskilled workers can earn higher incomes in farming than in wage employment—a radical shift from a decade ago. Consumer food price policies are also changing in Africa, where urban consumption has been heavily subsidized for many decades. In countries from Madagascar to Mauritania and Zambia to Mali, sharp increases in prices have reversed long-standing subsidy policies.

More competitive marketing arrangements are emerging. In some West African countries, export marketing parastatals have either disappeared (for instance, for groundnuts in Mali) or have been exposed to competition. In Somalia the monopoly of parastatals in maize, sorghum, and imported foods has been eliminated. Madagascar has liberalized domestic rice marketing, and Zaire has eliminated its food marketing parastatals. The tendency is not universal, and there are cases where marketing controls have been made more, rather than less, extensive in recent years. But the trend is toward more open marketing arrangements and price policies that are more favorable for agricultural growth.

Policy reforms in the pricing of fertilizers are also noteworthy. Following the early years of the Green Revolution, few notions took root as deeply as the notion that fertilizers need to be subsidized to encourage rapid technological change. Yet, recently many of the East Asian countries have abandoned fertilizer subsidies; such subsidies are declining in Bangladesh and Pakistan. They have been cut back sharply in Benin, Burkina Faso, Mali, Niger, Senegal, and Togo. The subsidization of fertilizers and other inputs seems to be in clear retreat throughout the developing world.

These examples illustrate the numerous reforms that have been undertaken or are under consideration in developing countries. Whether sweeping in scope or restricted to particular aspects of sectoral policies, the reforms illustrate that political institutions can have the capacity and the commitment to devise and carry out significant policy changes. This was also evident in the case of Sri Lanka's reform of its long-entrenched consumer subsidy program for rice, as discussed in Box 5.4.

While this reformist trend also illustrates the scope there is in developing countries for doing better, one must not lose sight of the policies in industrial countries which greatly influence the external environment. Do policies in industrial countries ease or exacerbate the difficulties faced by developing countries? What domestic objectives are being pursued by industrial countries, and can they be met at lesser cost to themselves and to the developing world? These are the questions discussed in the next chapter.

6

Agricultural policies in industrial countries

In the United States, the government pays farmers not to grow grain; in the European Communities, farmers are paid high prices even if they produce excessive amounts. In Japan, rice farmers receive three times the world price for their crop; they grow so much that some of it has to be sold as animal feed—at half the world price. In 1985, farmers in the EC received 18¢ a pound for sugar that was then sold on the world markets for 5¢ a pound; at the same time, the EC imported sugar at 18¢ a pound. Milk prices are kept high in nearly every industrial country, and surpluses are the result: Canadian farmers will pay up to eight times the price of a cow for the right to sell that cow's milk at the government's support price. The United States subsidizes irrigation and land clearing projects and then pays farmers not to use the land for growing crops.

The main purpose of such policies is simple: to raise farmers' incomes from what they otherwise would be. But why do the policies produce such anomalous results? And what costs do they impose on the industrial countries that implement them and on the developing countries that are affected by them? This chapter addresses these questions in three sections:

• The first section explains the characteristics of agricultural policies in industrial countries. It shows that, although the objective of raising farm incomes is straightforward, the results have been complicated. As each policy runs into trouble, a new one is added. This increases administrative complexity, raises costs, and makes agriculture more and more subject to political rather than economic decisions.

• The second section counts the costs and benefits of these policies to industrial countries and concludes that, while they have surprisingly little

effect on farmers' incomes in the long run, they impose heavy costs on taxpayers and consumers. The net costs are large—more than \$40 billion a year in industrial countries.

• The final section examines the impact on developing countries of agricultural policies in industrial countries. Though some developing countries suffer less than others, farming is hurt in all of them. Prices for their products are depressed because industrial countries import less, and their subsidized exports even undercut developing countries' farmers in their own markets.

The characteristics of agricultural policies

The main objectives of agricultural policies in industrial countries are to stabilize and increase farmers' incomes and slow the migration of people out of the sector. Underlying these objectives are the social and political aims of stable food prices and self-sufficiency in production, particularly in countries that have experienced wartime food shortages. These aims go hand in hand with such other goals as preventing environmental damage to the countryside and preserving the traditional unit of farming. Support of farm incomes, however, has contributed to rapid technical change and higher production. The basic problem that many industrial countries now face is how to counteract excessive production while maintaining farm incomes at politically acceptable levels.

How policies evolve

Most industrial countries impose controls on agricultural prices, output, and acreage, as well as on international trade. Agricultural policies do not change predictably in response to each new economic shock or shift in priorities. They evolve unevenly, balancing changing economic circumstances and a variety of often conflicting interests: the legacy of past policies, the political influence of farm lobbies, and the constraints arising from public spending limits, administrative convenience, and international treaty obligations. And, while direct income supplements may be the most efficient way of raising farmers' incomes, governments almost invariably try to do so by means of agricultural price supports or cost-reducing subsidies. Within that broad approach, however, there are different policies for different circumstances:

• If a country has a large enough share of the world market to influence the price, net importers will favor policies that reduce world prices; net exporters will favor the opposite. The EC—a large importer of cereals when its common agricultural policy (CAP) was designed—protects grain producers with tariffs and import levies, which tend to depress world prices; the United States, currently the world's biggest grain exporter, imposes acreage controls that are intended to raise prices.

• If public spending limits are tight, governments will—other things being equal—favor import taxes over export subsidies. Both drive a wedge between domestic and world prices, but, while import taxes earn revenue for the government, export subsidies absorb it.

• Some markets are easier to support than others. Support is easiest and cheapest for crops and products in which supply and demand are inelastic, that is, quantities do not respond much to changing prices. As a rule of thumb, land-intensive products have lower short-run elasticities of supply than others. It is no coincidence that governments intervene more often in the market for cereals than in those for poultry and pork. Administrative convenience is also important. More complicated rules are needed if products are heterogeneous and markets are geographically dispersed. Governments can control the prices of fruits and vegetables, which are highly perishable, less easily than they can those of cereals, sugar, and milk. Because sugar and milk are marketed almost entirely through relatively centralized processing facilities, governments are able to monitor their output without much difficulty.

• Exchange rate and macroeconomic fluctuations since 1972 have at times dominated commodity policies. In the early 1970s the worldwide commodity boom and the weak U.S. dollar pushed world grain prices above the levels that had been established by U.S. price supports. In the early 1980s the strong dollar caused even nominally constant U.S. support prices to be very high from the point of view of grain importers and non-U.S. exporters. This led to drastic cuts in U.S. support prices in 1986.

• International commitments sometimes constrain domestic policies. Because of international ties dating back to colonial times, the EC still imports sugar even though it has become self-sufficient and even exports surplus sugar.

• The legacy of past policies weighs heavily upon current ones. Policymakers are averse to dismantling an administrative machinery that has been laboriously constructed. Farm interest groups are adept at defending gains from previous policies. It is difficult to change a policy even if its failure can be demonstrated. Instead, a new policy is introduced to offset its shortcomings. During the 1970s, improvements in milk yields reduced dairy costs below official milk support prices, which were actually raised. Governments found themselves flooded with milk surpluses, and spending soared, increasing sixfold in the EC and fivefold in the United States between 1974 and 1984. Instead of lowering prices and letting consumers benefit from the technical progress, however, governments have attempted to limit the amount of milk sold at guaranteed prices (see Box 6.1).

How much protection?

The first and most obvious effect of industrial countries' agricultural policies is to raise domestic prices. Estimates of nominal protection coefficients (NPCs)—domestic prices divided by border prices—for several industrial countries and areas are shown in Table 6.1.

These estimates need to be treated with caution. With variable world prices but relatively stable domestic ones, nominal protection coefficients vary widely over time. Table 6.1 shows values for 1980–82, but in 1985 protection was typically greater because world market prices were lower. Domestic prices can be measured at several stages: the farmgate, the intervention board, or the wholesale market. Different countries report prices at different stages, which makes comparison difficult. Qualities and varieties of commodities also vary; for example, many types of rice are consumed, and their importance varies from country to country. Because agricultural policies affect world prices, the estimates do not measure what would happen to world prices if the policies were abolished. Finally, nominal protection coefficients do not mea-

Box 6.1 Price support in the dairy industry

The world market for dairy products is a creature of protection. Nearly every industrial country isolates and protects its dairy farmers with import barriers and through domestic market intervention. Producer prices are determined by governments and are unrelated to the value of milk products in international trade. In the OECD countries, average domestic prices have been roughly double world prices for the past twenty years; however, because such large quantities of dairy products are dumped in international trade, the world market price is greatly depressed. Farmers have responded to the high internal prices in a rational manner: they have invested heavily in animals and equipment, they have adopted technical innovations to improve yields, and consequently they have increased output (see Box figure 6.1). Governments have therefore found themselves buying increasing amounts of milk and have accumulated huge stocks. These stocks usually have to be disposed of on depressed world markets or given away as food aid.

In some extreme cases, EC farmers paid more to import feedstuff for their cows than they could have received on world markets for the milk which the feed helped to produce. Not only was no surplus generated to cover the costs of domestic inputs—labor, transport, dairy equipment, processing, and so on—but the EC even lost foreign exchange. The European Communities would have been better off as a whole if some of the farmers had not worked at all—indeed, if they had been paid not to work.

The EC's budgetary rules compound the inefficiencies of its dairy support program. The financial burden of agricultural support is shared among the member countries roughly in proportion to their GNP, but receipts from price supports are proportional to milk output. So countries race to increase national milk output, for they receive the full intervention price from the CAP but have to contribute only a fraction of that price. In fact, they are even encouraged to subsidize their milk production, for they are reimbursed by the EC for part of their subsidy. The results have been dramatic. Subsidies from the individual countries amounted to almost 8 percent of the gross value of milk at domestic prices. CAP dairy expenditures have grown by more than 20 percent a year for a decade; transfers from consumers and taxpayers reached $6,200 per dairy farmer ($410 per cow) in 1982.

By April 1984, the burden of the EC's dairy policies had become unsupportable. Rather than reduce support prices, however, the EC imposed production quotas. These are fixed nationally and are generally distributed within each country to individual farmers. Quantities produced in excess of quotas receive the world price or less, so there is a strong incentive to restrain production. Indeed, production has fallen below quota levels because farmers have sought to avoid selling milk at merely its world price. But production remains far above consumption. Although consumption averages about 85 million tons a year, the quota is fixed at 99 million tons. Thus, the quota system penalizes consumers by keeping prices high, encourages an inefficient pattern of production, and institutionalizes the EC's current excessive output. In response to these problems the EC has decided to reduce dairy quotas by 3 percent starting in 1987–88.

The United States has had a similar experience. Support prices for milk were steadily increased during the 1970s in the face of low world market prices. Net spending on dairy support programs (valuing products given away at their cost to the government) grew from $150 million annually to $3 billion between the mid-1970s and 1983–84; transfers to producers were estimated to have reached $26,000 per farmer in 1982 ($835 per cow). The government cut the producer price of raw milk from 13.1¢ a pound in 1982–83 to 11.6¢ in mid-1985, but stocks continued to accumulate. In De-

Table 6.1 Nominal protection coefficients for producer and consumer prices of selected commodities in industrial countries, 1980–82

Country or region	Wheat		Coarse grains		Rice		Beef and lamb	
	Producer NPC	Consumer NPC	Producer NPC	Consumer NPC	Producer NPC	Consumer NPC	Producer NPC	Consumer NPC
Australia	1.04	1.08	1.00	1.00	1.15	1.75	1.00	1.00
Canada	1.15	1.12	1.00	1.00	1.00	1.00	1.00	1.00
EC[b]	1.25	1.30	1.40	1.40	1.40	1.40	1.90	1.90
Other Europe[c]	1.70	1.70	1.45	1.45	1.00	1.00	2.10	2.10
Japan	3.80	1.25	4.30	1.30	3.30	2.90	4.00	4.00
New Zealand	1.00	1.00	1.00	1.00	1.00	1.00	1.00	1.00
United States	1.15	1.00	1.00	1.00	1.30	1.00	1.00	1.00
Weighted average	1.19	1.20	1.11	1.16	2.49	2.42	1.47	1.51

a. Averages are weighted by the values of production and consumption at border prices.
b. Excludes Greece, Portugal, and Spain.

cember 1985, legislation was passed to allow the government to control milk production by buying and butchering up to 1 million cows, but it is unlikely that this will constitute a long-term solution to the problem.

Most surpluses end up in stockpiles, for under an agreement concluded in the GATT's Tokyo Round, butter cannot be exported at less than $1,200 a ton. Stockpiling dairy products is expensive, and quality is difficult to maintain. But patience can reap its own reward. In 1984 the EC claimed that its stored butter had so deteriorated that it had become a new, inferior product—butter oil. Since there is no international agreement on butter oil, the EC was able to sell some of its stock to the U.S.S.R. at $450 a ton—a mere 14 percent of the price paid to farmers.

Box figure 6.1 Milk production in the EC, 1974–84

Millions of tons of milk

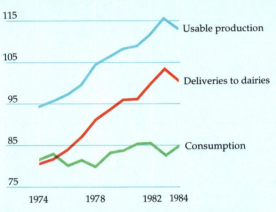

Note: Data include butter, cheese, and powdered milk, converted to fluid milk equivalents.
Source: Bureau of Agricultural Economics (Australia) 1985.

sure those internal policies that are not supported by border policies; in such cases domestic prices and world prices are equal. For example, U.S. acreage controls and deficiency payments affect internal and border prices of maize equally.

Nonetheless, certain conclusions can be drawn from the table. First, dairy farmers receive generous support nearly everywhere; so do rice and sugar producers. Second, Japanese and European farmers are more highly protected than farmers in countries that rely on agricultural exports. Third, the relative rate of protection between commodities varies from country to country, which implies that internal relative prices also vary. Thus, even within countries there are distortions, as farmers react to prices that have been set by policy rather than to indicators of scarcity and opportunity.

Trade measures

Behind these complexities lies a distinction between border measures, which act on imports and exports, and domestic measures, which directly affect internal supply and demand. Take border measures first. The simplest border measure for an importer is the tariff—that is, an import tax—and for an exporter, the export subsidy. Matters are rarely that simple. Variable import levies and variable subsidies—called export restitutions—are more common.

VARIABLE IMPORT LEVIES. Variable levies are the cornerstone of the EC's common agricultural policy. They are also used by other European countries, namely, Austria, Sweden, and Switzerland. They make up the difference between the price of imports delivered at the port and an officially fixed entry price at which foreign goods can be sold. The entry price—known in the EC as the threshold

Pork and poultry		Dairy products		Sugar		Weighted average[a]		
Producer NPC	Consumer NPC	Producer NPC	Consumer NPC	Producer NPC	Consumer NPC	Producer NPC	Consumer NPC	Country or region
1.00	1.00	1.30	1.40	1.00	1.40	1.04	1.09	Australia
1.10	1.10	1.95	1.95	1.30	1.30	1.17	1.16	Canada
1.25	1.25	1.75	1.80	1.50	1.70	1.54	1.56	EC[b]
1.35	1.35	2.40	2.40	1.80	1.80	1.84	1.81	Other Europe[c]
1.50	1.50	2.90	2.90	3.00	2.60	2.44	2.08	Japan
1.00	1.00	1.00	1.00	1.00	1.00	1.00	1.00	New Zealand
1.00	1.00	2.00	2.00	1.40	1.40	1.16	1.17	United States
1.17	1.17	1.88	1.93	1.49	1.68	1.40	1.43	Weighted average

c. Austria, Finland, Norway, Sweden, Switzerland.
Source: Tyers and Anderson (background paper).

Box 6.2   Protecting sugar producers

Sugar and its very close substitutes, glucose sugar and high fructose corn syrup (HFCS), are derived mainly from three sources: sugarcane, sugar beets, and high-starch products such as maize. Sugarcane was the earliest and cheapest source of sugar; use of the other two products expanded significantly only when supplies of sugarcane were curtailed. The possibility of obtaining sugar from beets was recognized in the late eighteenth century, but it took Britain's blockade of Continental Europe during the Napoleonic wars to make the process commercially viable. More than 300 sugar beet factories were established in France between 1811 and 1813. Peace and sugar imports brought about their demise, and it was only later in the nineteenth century that European beet production revived—once again behind protective barriers. Since then, sugar beet production has enjoyed high protection.

The level of protection proved costly to industrial countries, especially when, in the 1970s, the new sweetener HFCS became available. HFCS developed in the shelter of sugar protection as the internal prices for beet and cane sugar were driven further above world market prices than were those of its own raw material, maize.

The EC and the United States dealt with the impact of HFCS production differently, but the effects on world trade in sugar and on developing countries were similar. The EC, already a major sugar exporter at the beginning of the 1970s, included glucose sugar production in its quota system for sugar beets, thus generating even more subsidized export surpluses. The EC's share of world sugar exports rose from less than 9 percent in the 1960s to more than 20 percent in the 1980s, making the EC the world's largest exporter in 1982. In contrast, the United States allowed the HFCS industry to expand behind an import quota. As a result, the share of domestic sweetener consumption

accounted for by HFCS increased, with corn sweeteners surpassing sugar in consumption for the first time in 1984. The U.S. share of world raw sugar imports dropped from an average of 20 percent between 1960 and 1973 to around 10 percent in the early 1980s. Preferential deals continue to dominate international trade in sugar, the free market being of a residual nature.

The experience of the United States illustrates the practical difficulties of operating trade restrictions. Until 1983, imports of sugar mixed with as little as 6 percent of corn sweeteners were not restricted under the sugar import quotas. This, in effect, allowed consumers to buy sugar at world prices, but growing imports led local producers to complain until the "loophole" was plugged. However, with the domestic sugar price four to seven times the world price, it was worth it for firms to extract sugar from processed products such as cake mixes. In January 1985, emergency regulations imposed a quota on all imports of sweetened "edible preparations" for nine months. Unfortunately, edible preparations included chicken pie, pizza, and noodles (with a sugar content of 0.002 percent); within two months the nine-month quota had been exhausted and imports of an unintentionally wide range of goods ceased.

Neither the EC nor the United States has been able to adjust its sugar policies to the changing economic environment. Rather, they have accepted increased market distortions and growing economic costs. In addition, they have placed a great burden of adjustment on their trading partners, mainly developing countries. One study estimated that industrial countries' sugar policies cost developing countries about $7.4 billion in lost export revenues during 1983, reduced their real income by about $2.1 billion, and increased price instability in the residual world market for sugar by about 25 percent.

---

price—represents the minimum price of imports to domestic users. Domestic prices are fixed annually by the agriculture ministers of the member states. The cost of threshold pricing varies because world prices and exchange rates change but domestic prices remain fixed as long as imports continue and the domestic price is higher than the border price.

Variable levies can insulate farmers and consumers from world markets. But such insulation is costly. Consumers continue to buy goods whose world prices have risen sharply; producers continue to produce goods whose prices have fallen. Importers cannot, therefore, take advantage of

changing world prices; nor can exporters. Worse, by isolating a part of world consumption and production from world prices, variable levies reduce the efficiency and stability of world markets. Box 6.2 spells out these points with reference to sugar policy.

EXPORT RESTITUTIONS. Export restitutions are the exporter's equivalent of variable levies. They permit domestic prices to be independent of world prices and above them. The result is to depress and destabilize world prices. Although the effect is equivalent to that of an import levy, export restitutions are less widespread. Indeed, an export restitution most commonly originates as a prop to an overextended system of import levies: having introduced levies to protect local farmers from cheap imports, governments find themselves accumulating surpluses as the high level of support leads domestic production to outstrip demand. Unable to abandon price supports for political reasons, they resort to export restitutions to dispose of their surpluses abroad. The EC provides the best-known example of this phenomenon: a large-scale grain importer in the 1960s, it became a big exporter in the 1980s, and the switch was not the result of any comparative advantage in cereal production.

Export restitutions entail the same kind of losses to the economy that import levies do, but can be even more difficult to administer—especially when, as in the EC, the restitution varies according to the destination of the exports. Moreover, they are a drain on the public purse. This often leads governments to reduce the level of price supports as products switch from imports to exports. For example, the EC's support prices increased by an average 0.3 percent annually in real terms between 1973 and 1978, but fell by 1.1 percent a year between 1979 and 1986, when surpluses and the need for restitutions grew.

Variable levies and export restitutions can be high. Sweden's levies raise domestic beef prices to about 250 percent of world prices. Figure 6.1 shows the gap between threshold and border prices in the EC for grains since 1968. In 1982–83 the cereal regime is estimated to have transferred 7.9 billion European currency units (ECUs), or $8.9 billion, from consumers—and ECU 2.3 billion from taxpayers—to producers.

TARIFFS. Fixed tariffs are less common than variable levies in agricultural trade. They do not stabilize domestic prices and cannot guarantee farm incomes, even in the short term, because internal prices vary along with world prices. High tariffs tend to be limited to markets which either are too heterogeneous for variable levies or were not deemed important enough when the policies were introduced. Most industrial countries apply tariffs to fruits and vegetables; tariffs on meat products, oilseeds, and tobacco are also fairly common. Tariffs are relatively important in the protection of processed agricultural goods and tend to escalate with the degree of processing. This makes it difficult for developing countries to establish processing industries.

IMPORT QUOTAS. An import quota restricts imports of a product to a specified quantity or value (sometimes zero). Quotas are commonly imposed on dairy products, sugar, beef, vegetables, and fruits and are applied by a wide range of countries, including Canada, the EC, Japan, Switzerland, and the United States. Import quotas are sometimes dressed up as voluntary export restraint agreements between exporting and importing countries. Examples include Australia's dairy imports from New Zealand and U.S. imports of beef

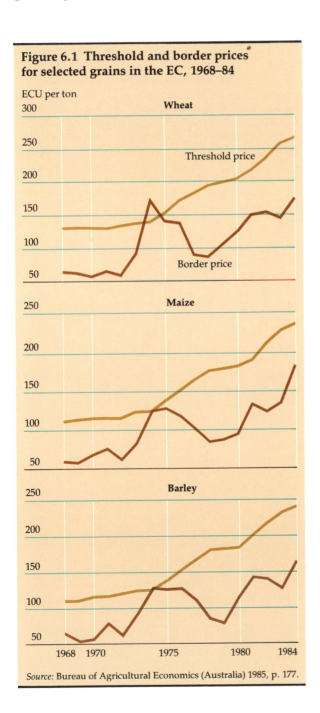

Figure 6.1 Threshold and border prices for selected grains in the EC, 1968–84

ECU per ton

Source: Bureau of Agricultural Economics (Australia) 1985, p. 177.

from Australia. Import restrictions are sometimes associated with special trade schemes in which both the price and quantity of imports are fixed. U.S. imports of sugar from the Caribbean and the EC's imports of beef and sugar from certain developing countries are examples.

Like variable import levies, quotas isolate a country from changes in the world markets and raise domestic prices. They can be even more costly to the country that imposes them. The difference between domestic and border prices may be captured by exporters rather than collected by the government as tariff revenue. And the imports may not come from the cheapest sources, because

---

Box 6.3 Land restrictions and part-time farming

Agricultural policy in Japan is based on two pieces of legislation passed in the 1940s. Aiming to combine self-sufficiency in rice with stable consumer prices, the Staple Food Control Act of 1942 divorced producer and consumer prices. It said that government purchase prices "are to be determined for the purpose of securing reproduction of rice by taking into consideration the cost of production, prices and other economic conditions." Consumer prices "are to be determined for the purpose of stabilizing the consumer's budget by taking into consideration the cost of living, prices and other economic conditions."

The second piece of legislation concerned land reform. Agricultural land reforms between 1945 and 1950 transferred the ownership of approximately one-third of all farmland to former tenants, imposed maximum sizes on farms, prohibited nonfarm residents from owning farmland, prohibited resident landowners from renting out more than one hectare, and effectively outlawed the sale of land between farmers. These measures reduced the proportion of farms operated by tenants from 46 percent in 1945 to 10 percent by 1950 and 5 percent by 1965. Some renting was permitted, but rent ceilings and the difficulties of reoccupying rented land made it unattractive. Even after later liberalization, only 4 percent of Japanese farmland was leased in 1978.

The land law inhibited the creation of bigger farms. The average Japanese farm expanded from 1.01 hectares in 1950 to 1.17 hectares in 1977, whereas farms in the United States grew by 50 percent on average. At the same time, the cultivated land area in Japan fell by about 8 percent and the amount of land that was double-cropped dropped from around one-third to almost zero; also, agricultural employment declined at about the same rate as in other countries.

Because the farms are small, total factor productivity—output divided by an index of all input quantities—has not risen as rapidly in Japan as elsewhere in the world. Farm size has been critical since 1960, when technology became more sophisticated and capital-intensive. In 1960 the costs of rice cultivation were 20 percent higher on farms of 0.3 to 0.5 hectare than on those larger than 3.0 hectares; by 1975 the differential was more than 60 percent.

In 1955 Japanese agriculture appeared to be reasonably competitive—certainly compared with that of Western Europe. The farm price of rice was only 13 percent above the import price, and Japan was close to self-sufficiency. Thereafter, however, rising labor costs—driven by Japan's industrial success—coupled with the cost of increasing capital intensity on such small farms, pushed up costs on farms faster than in the rest of the economy. Given the government's aims of promoting self-sufficiency and supporting the farm labor force, more protection from imports became necessary. Behind strict import restraints, the domestic price of rice rose from one and a half times the import price in 1961, to more than double it in 1970, to four times as much in 1979. Similar, though less extreme, relative price movements occurred for such products as wheat, beef, and dairy products.

Restrictions on ownership and leasing have encouraged farmers to subcontract certain tasks, such as weeding, soil preparation, and harvesting. More often, however, the restrictions have encouraged farmers to take part-time or full-time jobs outside agriculture. Only 20 percent of Japanese farm households contain one or more full-time farm workers; 70 percent obtain more than half their income from outside activities. Living standards in these latter households are around 25 percent higher than in full-time farm households.

The 20 percent of farms that have one full-time farm worker produce about 60 percent of total agricultural production on 48 percent of the land. In rice production, however—which lends itself well to part-time work—farming is dominated by part-timers. They produce about two-thirds of total output.

In 1980, new legislation permitted larger farms and encouraged part-time farmers to lease their land. Simultaneously, attempts were made to keep support prices below the average costs of very small farms. Although the domestic price fell back to only three times the import price during the 1980s, the structure of farming has not changed significantly. The principal beneficiaries of Japanese rice policy are still part-time farmers. Full-time farmers have been prevented from exploiting their efficiency by the legacy of restrictive land legislation.

quotas on exports from different countries almost inevitably fail to reflect differences in costs.

A prominent set of import quotas or quantity restrictions can be found in Japan. Behind very tight restrictions on rice and beef imports, the Japanese government has raised domestic producer prices to around three times world prices (see Box 6.3). These prices have generated large domestic rice surpluses, some of which have been sold as animal feed or as subsidized exports. The losses in this market alone totaled about $6 billion in 1980.

It is often alleged that countries use health and quality standards to restrict imports. No one doubts the need for such regulations, but their excessive or discriminatory use can be implicitly protectionist. Comparison of import restrictions in four countries for which comprehensive figures are available indicates that the percentage of food imports subject to health standards is 95 percent in Japan and 94 percent in Norway, but only 55 percent in Switzerland and 60 percent in Australia. These percentages do not tell the full story of protection, however, since they exclude the total prohibition of entry for certain products.

Table 6.2 summarizes data on border policies for agriculture pursued by industrial countries. It shows which imports in industrial countries are subject to nontariff barriers (NTBs). The figures do not indicate how much each import is affected, nor the value of imports affected, but merely the presence (or absence) of particular kinds of restriction in each trade category. The table shows that industrial countries' imports of raw materials are largely unimpeded by nontariff barriers; so are their im-

ports of tropical beverages. However, 70 percent of their sugar and confectionary imports and more than half of their meat and live animals and dairy imports face at least one barrier. Fruits and vegetables and beverages other than tea, coffee, and cocoa (mainly wine and fruit juice) are hardly affected by variable levies; they are restricted either quantitatively or by seasonal tariffs. Variable levies are important for sugar, dairy products, meat, and cereals.

Production quotas and input controls

Production quotas grant farmers the right to sell a specified quantity of a crop at a guaranteed price. If a farmer produces more, he must sell at lower prices. To implement the quotas, governments must monitor the output of individual farmers. So far, this approach has been found administratively feasible only for sugar, milk, peanuts, and tobacco.

Quotas are usually introduced when the budget cost of surpluses becomes intolerable. If, for political reasons, price levels cannot be reduced, quotas are the only way to stem the outflow of public funds. While production quotas have no direct budgetary costs, they have significant economic costs. They penalize consumers by raising prices, they frequently allocate production rights to inefficient farmers, and they can distort the markets for competing products. Import quotas on sugar in the United States have artificially stimulated the production of corn syrup. Similar consequences in the EC have been forestalled by domestic production quotas on corn-based substitutes.

Table 6.2 The frequency of application of various nontariff barriers in industrial countries, 1984
(percent)

Commodity	Tariff quotas and seasonal tariffs (1)	Quantitative restrictions (2)	Minimum price policies		Total[a] (5)
			All (3)	Variable levies (4)	
Meat and live animals	12.3	41.0	26.0	23.8	52.2
Dairy products	6.9	29.6	28.6	25.6	54.6
Fruits and vegetables	15.7	18.8	4.9	0.8	33.1
Sugar and confectionary	0.0	21.7	58.0	58.0	70.0
Cereals	1.7	10.9	21.7	21.7	29.0
Other food	0.8	16.3	13.5	13.2	27.0
Tea, coffee, cocoa	0.4	4.0	2.5	2.5	6.6
Other beverages	18.5	22.9	18.4	0.6	42.3
Raw materials	0.0	7.5	0.3	0.3	7.8
All agriculture	8.2	17.2	11.5	8.2	29.7
Manufactures	2.2	6.7	0.6	0.0	9.4

Note: Data are the number of import items subject to the nontariff barriers shown as a percentage of the total number of import items. The industrial-country markets considered are Australia, Austria, the EC, Finland, Japan, Norway, Switzerland, and the United States.
a. This column will be less than the sum of columns (1), (2), and (3) if some imports are subject to more than one barrier.

The U.S. tobacco program is the oldest system of production quotas still in effect today. According to a recent study, it cost consumers about $1 billion a year from 1980 to 1984. It did not even benefit all those who were growing tobacco. True, quota holders were better off by $800 million, but many of them had rented out their quotas. Producers without quotas were worse off by $200 million. The overall gain of $600 million to producers and quota owners, coupled with the $1 billion loss to consumers, implies a net loss to all concerned of $400 million.

Once granted, production quotas are difficult to remove because they become valuable property rights. In British Columbia, Canada, the right to sell the milk of a cow costs about eight times more than the cow itself. Such rents create substantial entry barriers to farming. They increase the amount of initial capital required, although they do not affect the long-term rate of return on investment in agriculture. Table 6.3 shows the prices that tradable quotas command and the capital outlay that they imply for family farms in Ontario, Canada.

Controls on inputs are more common than controls on output. Commonest of all are restrictions on land. The United States has the longest history of acreage controls. The first legislation, on grains and cotton, was passed in 1933; the most recent scheme, the payment-in-kind (PIK) program, was started in 1983 and is in use again in 1986. Japan has also used such measures, first to reduce rice acreage and then to reduce citrus fruit output. The government sometimes paid to uproot trees which had been planted on paddy fields that had been idled under a previous program.

In a large and open economy, voluntary acreage controls are easier to administer than production quotas. With quotas, all output has to be monitored, and surpluses may have to be destroyed. With acreage controls, only the land has to be monitored, and governments can induce farmers to join the system by paying them for each acre they do not plant or by offering them higher prices

for their output if they leave some acres fallow (the current practice in the United States).

The administrative costs of commodity programs are formidable. The U.S. Agricultural Stabilization and Conservation Service maintains a staff of about 2,600 full-time employees, several thousand more part-time employees, and some 3,000 county committees, each made up of three local citizens, usually farmers. In 1985 this cost $400 million. Countless decisions must be made: What is each farmer's program acreage (the land on which payments may be made) for each crop? What is the program yield—which determines how much the farmer gets per acre from the legislated payment per bushel? What can the farmer use his idled land for, if anything? Are his storage facilities adequate? Is he complying with the programs' provisions? Not surprisingly, it is too costly to monitor every requirement, and local administrators may be tempted to give farmers the benefit of the doubt.

Acreage controls are also wasteful because they distort farmers' input costs. They encourage farmers to farm their permitted acreage more intensively and at higher cost. Ironically, in order to benefit when their program acreage is updated, farmers may plow up land that might otherwise be left as pasture, woodland, or swamp. Acreage controls and input subsidies work at cross purposes; each increases the cost of the other.

In the PIK program of 1983, U.S. farmers agreed not to grow crops on a total of 77 million acres, 37 percent of the land sowed to grains, cotton, and rice in 1982. Drought scourged the Midwest farm states in 1983, and output in these crops fell by 41 percent. Prices rose by an average of 16 percent. Farmers also gained because in payment for idling their land they received up to 80 percent of the quantity they could normally have grown. These in-kind payments came from crops that had been stored by the government. The total transfer from consumers and taxpayers was worth about $20 billion. On top of this, the PIK program cost livestock farmers and farm input industries billions of dollars because increases in feed grain prices could

Table 6.3 The market value of quotas in Ontario, Canada, 1984

Product	Unit price	×	Size of family farm unit	=	Quota cost to acquire farm
Eggs	$23 a hen		25,000 birds		$580,000
Milk	$3,500 a cow		40 cows		$140,000
Tobacco	$1.50 a pound		40 acres		$310,000
Turkeys	54¢ a pound		25,000 birds a year		$270,000

Source: Johnson, ''Agricultural Protection'' (background paper).

not be fully passed on to consumers and because farmers cut down on their use of fertilizers, seeds, and other inputs.

Intervention and target prices

In nearly every industrial country, the government offers to buy produce at a fixed price. This intervention price represents the minimum return to farmers and, unless they are constrained by quota, determines their level of production. The government finds it expensive to hold the stock it buys and usually ends up selling it at less than cost, either at home or abroad.

In the United States the federal Commodity Credit Corporation (CCC) "lends" cash to participating farmers, using grain held in approved storage facilities as collateral. Farmers may repay the loans, retrieve their crops, and sell them. Or they may turn the crops over to the CCC as repayment. The loan rate—the price at which the CCC lends—defines farmers' minimum prices. Because the United States is the dominant grain exporter and has few border measures to insulate its domestic prices from world trading prices, the CCC loan rate establishes a floor price in the world grain markets. This means that when CCC stocks are large, as they have been in the 1980s, the world market price is fixed in dollar terms by the loan rate, and this rate together with the value of the dollar determines the border prices facing other countries. Consequently, problems were created for many grain-trading countries when, in 1986, the loan rates for wheat and feed grains were cut by 25 to 30 percent at the same time that the dollar was weakening substantially. The reduction in the support price for rice was even larger.

Since the mid-1970s, the United States has also set a target price that is higher than the loan rate. Deficiency payments make up the difference between market and target prices. In and of themselves, such payments would encourage production and hence drive down domestic and world prices. But this result is forestalled because farmers must participate in acreage reduction schemes in order to receive payments. Deficiency payments for corn came to 48¢ a bushel in 1985—more than 20 percent of the market price. The percentage is higher for wheat, rice, and cotton. These payments are almost certain to rise even further in the future as new U.S. legislation cuts loan rates and hence market prices. Deficiency payments are often defended on the grounds that they help farmers who are in financial trouble. But in the

United States two-thirds of the payments in 1985 were estimated by the U.S. Department of Agriculture to have gone to farmers who were wealthier than the average citizen.

Consumer subsidies

Subsidies to consumers also contribute to the cost of agricultural price supports. By making food comparatively cheap, subsidies raise demand for domestic output. Temporary or selective subsidies can help reduce government stocks of surplus commodities. European pensioners have periodically received slices of the EC's butter mountain. In the United States, the CCC donated $2.5 billion in stockpiled commodities for domestic and foreign distribution in 1985. Subsidies shield consumers from the high prices paid to producers and probably reduce the political costs of agricultural price support. In Japan, the official aim of supporting the price of rice is to ensure consumers adequate quantities of reasonably priced rice. Once the government decided on a policy of self-sufficiency in rice—because it feared the effects of external shocks—consumer subsidies became necessary. Japanese consumer food subsidies cost about $3.5 billion a year.

Other measures

Other policy instruments exist. Some countries have state monopolies on imports, exports, or domestic purchases, and their actions generate many of the effects of subsidies or border measures. State marketing boards have been important for certain commodities in Canada, Australia, and New Zealand. The range of subsidies is wide: transport (in Canada, see Box 6.4), insurance (in Canada and the United States), fertilizers (in Australia), water (in the United States), and income tax concessions (in France, Italy, the United Kingdom, and the United States). Tax breaks are estimated to have accounted for almost 20 percent of recent capital goods investment in U.S. agriculture.

The domestic gains and losses from agricultural policies

Agricultural policies in industrial countries transfer income from consumers and taxpayers to farmers and landowners. They also reduce national income in several ways. Subsidies cause farmers to use inputs inefficiently. Artificially high food prices mislead producers into using too many resources

Not all export subsidies draw directly on the public purse, and those that do not can be very long-lived. In 1897 the Canadian government subsidized the building of a railroad through the Crow's Nest Pass of the Rocky Mountains. In return, the railroads agreed to freeze their freight rates for transporting wheat and coarse grains from the Prairie provinces to the ports for export.

By 1981–82, it is estimated, farmers were paying only one-sixth of the cost of freight on grain exports. The railroad—or, rather, its other customers—contributed most of the remaining five-sixths. The subsidy amounted to about $30 a ton, or about 15 percent of the price of wheat and about 25 percent of the price of barley. The subsidy has raised grain and oilseed prices in the Prairie provinces, increased rents, and discouraged the development of alternative industries such as lumber and coal (which have to pay excess transport costs) and agroprocessing and livestock (which have to pay higher grain prices). As an implicit tax on the railroads, the subsidy has also led to substantial underinvestment in rail facilities, which hinders all economic activity in the Prairie provinces. Finally, it has caused additional distortions elsewhere in the economy. To compensate eastern livestock farmers for the effects of the Crow's Nest rates on domestic feed prices, further subsidies were introduced to encourage the shipment of feed grains from western Canada for domestic use in the east.

Recently, the government has begun to reform the Crow's Nest system. It now pays the railroads $659 million a year plus a declining share of any increases in freight rates. It is estimated that by 1990 farmers will be paying about half of the freight costs themselves.

for producing food—resources which could be better used to produce something else. They also induce consumers to purchase less food than they would otherwise. While accurate estimates of these effects are difficult to obtain, economists have amassed a body of evidence that presents a strong case against such policies. This section reviews that evidence.

Net losses

Table 6.4 summarizes some estimates of the domestic real national income losses to industrial countries. The estimates differ in coverage, method, and time, but they all show that agricultural protection is expensive. Rice protection alone is estimated to have cost Japanese society $2.9 billion in 1980; in 1976 it cost about $3.9 billion—0.6 percent of Japan's GNP. The costs of the CAP to the EC were $15.4 billion in 1980, or 0.6 percent of GDP. Even traditional agricultural producers were not immune. Canada lost $400 million protecting its dairy industry between 1976 and 1979, and the United States lost almost $4 billion in total agricultural support in 1984–85.

These efficiency, or real income, losses are underestimates because they omit administrative expenses and ignore the distortions that high agricultural prices cause in the long term—such as the diversion of fixed investment and research from industry to agriculture. The underestimation can be substantial because agriculture changes so quickly. One indication of how much it can change is the way nine EC countries converted themselves from net importers of 20 million tons of wheat a year to net exporters of 10 million tons between 1965 and 1983. Another is the development of sugar substitutes in the United States; the substitutes reduced sugar imports from 5 million tons (half of U.S. consumption) in 1981, to 3 million tons in 1982, to possibly 1½ million tons in 1986.

Much larger than the net costs of agricultural support are the costs borne by consumers and taxpayers. Table 6.5 shows estimates of the components of the costs as well as the benefits that are reaped by producers. The figures are necessarily imprecise, but they give an indication of the massive volume of transfers involved. In every case, producers gain less than consumers and taxpayers lose. The ratio of domestic losses to gains is expressed as the transfer ratio—the average loss to consumers and taxpayers per dollar transferred to producers.

The high transfer ratio for Japan reflects high levels of protection. Taxpayer costs, however, are lower for Japan. The United States and the EC spend billions on payments to farmers and on export and domestic consumption subsidies, whereas Japan's import restrictions actually provide revenue through tariff collections. The U.S. policies cost less per dollar transferred because the relative price distortions are smaller. Also, since

U.S. output affects world market prices, part of the cost of the acreage controls is borne by foreign consumers.

The figures in Table 6.5 suggest that agricultural protection is an expensive way of transferring income between various sections of society. In Japan, consumers and taxpayers lost $2.58 for every $1.00 transferred to producers, not including the efficiency losses caused by taxes raised to pay farm subsidies. Furthermore, protection can transfer income from the poor to the rich. In most countries the main beneficiaries of price support are landowners and quota holders; the poor bear a disproportionate share of the cost because they spend a larger share of their income on food.

The figures in Tables 6.4 and 6.5 indicate the resource wastes that could be avoided if trade were liberalized. They show what countries would gain—after all the effects have worked through the economy—if they abolished their agricultural policies. In the short term, however, because land, capital, and labor would remain in farming, sup-

Table 6.4 The domestic efficiency loss from agricultural intervention in selected industrial countries

Country or region and source	Coverage	Year	Efficiency loss (billions of 1980 dollars)
Canada			
Josling 1981	Dairy products	1976–79	0.4
Barichello 1986	Wheat, barley, milk, poultry, eggs	1980	0.3
Harling 1983	Wheat, barley, oats, potatoes, beef, poultry, eggs	1976	0.1
Europe			
Bale and Lutz 1981[a]	Wheat, maize, sugar, barley, beef	1976	1.9
Buckwell and others 1982[b]	All CAP commodities	1980	15.4
Bureau of Agricultural Economics (Australia) 1985[b]	All CAP commodities	1978	9.4
Bureau of Agricultural Economics (Australia) 1985[c]	All CAP commodities	1983	6.7
Tyers and Anderson (background paper)[b]	Grains, meats, dairy products, sugar	1980–82	24.1
Japan			
Bale and Lutz 1981	Wheat, barley, sugar, beef, rice	1976	6.0
Otsuka and Hayami 1985	Rice	1980	2.9
Tyers and Anderson (background paper)	Grains, meats, dairy products, sugar	1980–82	27.4
United States			
Rosine and Helmberger 1974	All commodities	1970–71	5.5
Gardner, ''Economic Consequences'' (background paper)	Grains, dairy products, sugar, cotton, tobacco, peanuts	1984–85	3.9
Johnson, Womack, and others 1985	Grains, soybeans, cotton	1981–84	0.3

a. Data are for France, Germany, and the United Kingdom.   b. Data are for the EC, excluding Greece, Portugal, and Spain.
c. Data are for the EC, excluding Portugal and Spain.

Table 6.5 The annual domestic costs and benefits of agricultural protection to consumers, taxpayers, and producers in the EC, Japan, and the United States
(billions of dollars unless otherwise noted)

Country and year	Consumer costs	+ Taxpayer costs	− Producer benefits	= Total domestic costs	Transfer ratio
EC (1980)[a]	34.6	11.5	30.7	15.4	1.50
Japan (1976)	7.1	−0.4	2.6	4.1	2.58
United States (1985)	5.7	10.3	11.6	4.4	1.38

a. Excludes Greece, Portugal, and Spain.
Source: For the EC: Buckwell and others 1982; for Japan: Bale and Lutz 1981; for the United States: Gardner, ''Economic Consequences'' (background paper).

plies would be maintained even in the face of changing policies. As a result, prices would be depressed more in the short term than in the long term.

Long-term issues

One argument in favor of supporting agricultural prices is that it stimulates agricultural technology and boosts crop yields. Indeed, it does. But higher yields reflect gains which only partly offset the cost of inputs such as fertilizers, oil, and pesticides. Investment in agriculture draws skilled manpower and sophisticated equipment away from other sectors of the economy. These resources could be used more efficiently elsewhere. Investment that generates ever more output of a product that already costs more than it is worth is not progress.

Agricultural intervention also places heavy burdens on most countries' treasuries. Indeed, soaring budget costs in the mid-1980s provide the main impetus for agricultural reform. In the EC, agricultural spending accounts for around 70 percent of the total community budget. Of the ECU 18.6 billion ($23.5 billion) spent on price supports in 1984, about ECU 1.9 billion was raised from customs duties and levies on agricultural imports; the rest was met from general taxes. As recently as 1974, agricultural spending was only ECU 4.7 billion ($5.6 billion), of which ECU 3.0 billion was raised from agricultural levies. So the increase both in spending and in the burden placed on general taxation has been great.

Spending is also significant in the United States and Japan. The U.S. government's costs were $11.9 billion in 1984 (up from about $3.0 billion in 1980 and 1981). They are likely to rise to $20 billion a year in 1986–88 under the newly enacted Food Security Act of 1985. In Japan, the total agriculture, fisheries, and forestry budget was $14.7 billion in 1984, of which $3.4 billion was devoted to food subsidies. This, however, represents a fall from 1980.

The benefits from all this spending are questionable. The main aim is to raise farmers' incomes and keep them from fluctuating. Some stability has probably been achieved, but it is doubtful that high product prices have raised farm incomes in the long term, although the rental value and price of land have been supported.

There are problems in assessing the effect of agricultural policies on farmers' incomes. In many industrial countries, figures on farmers' incomes are unreliable or unavailable. Rising prices tend to raise incomes in the short term, so their long-term effects are obscured by the constant stream of new policies. Because the policies depend in part on farmers' incomes, it is difficult to distinguish between cause and effect.

The evidence available does not inspire confidence that commodity policies can solve farmers' economic problems. Price supports and payments have been ineffective in halting the rise in farm failures that has occurred since 1981 in the United States, and unprotected commodity producers have fared no worse than protected ones. The start

---

Box 6.5   Old wine in new bottles

The arguments in this chapter about the relation between commodity prices and returns to land are far from new. They date back to the English economist David Ricardo, who was one of the first to analyze formally the benefits of free trade. His arguments against the early-nineteenth-century form of agricultural protection, Britain's so-called Corn Laws, are as relevant today as they ever were:

• "[The price of] corn is not high because a rent is paid, but a rent is paid because corn is high" (Ricardo [1817] 1973, p. 38).

• "The sole effect of high duties on the importation, either of manufactures or of corn, or of a bounty on their exportation, is to divert a portion of capital to an employment which it would not naturally seek. It

causes a pernicious distribution of the general funds of the society—it bribes a manufacturer to commence or continue in a comparatively less profitable employment. It is the worst species of taxation, for it does not give to the foreign country all that it takes away from the home country, the balance of loss being made up by the less advantageous distribution of the general capital" (ibid., p. 210).

• "The market price of corn would, under an increased demand from the effects of [an export] bounty . . . be raised. By a continued bounty, therefore, on the exportation of corn, there would be created a tendency to a permanent rise in the price of corn, and this, as I have shown elsewhere, never fails to raise rent" (ibid., p. 209).

of the EC's cereal regime in 1967–68 cut average agricultural prices in Germany by 8 percent, but farm profits per family worker rose. So did the value added by each farm worker compared with the value added elsewhere in the economy. Figure 6.2 plots rates of protection against GDP per capita in agriculture in relation to other sectors. It shows an inverse relationship—the higher the protection, the lower the relative income. Because of differences in farm size, the extent of part-time farming, and other factors, the plotted relationship cannot demonstrate any causal connection. But it provides no support for the idea that it is better for a country's farmers to have highly protected commodity markets.

In general, there is no reason to expect higher protection to be associated with higher farm incomes—a point made effectively by David Ricardo many years ago (see Box 6.5). Box 6.6 illustrates how extra revenues from higher farm prices are lost to rising land prices and rents as farmers bid against one another to acquire the means to produce goods that can be sold at high prices. The price rises cause a windfall gain for those lucky enough to own land when the programs are introduced, but become a component of costs for those who enter farming later. In any case, agriculture accounts for only a small proportion of GDP in industrial countries, and thus, in the long run, rates of return in agriculture are largely set by other parts of the economy.

In the United States, net farm income as a proportion of farmers' total income fell from 58 percent in 1960 to 36 percent in 1982. In Japan, where small-scale farming is more important, farm households derived 75 percent of their income from nonfarm sources in 1980. Furthermore, the families of part-time farmers with permanent jobs outside farming were approximately 25 percent better off than families with one or more full-time farm workers.

Many countries say agricultural self-sufficiency is an aim—and an outcome—of their agricultural support programs. Self-sufficiency is supposed to contribute to food security, stabilize food prices, and, occasionally (and perversely), make prices reasonable. None of these arguments is sound.

Take price stability. There is no doubt that the variable levies in Europe and the fixed intervention prices in Japan do stabilize consumer and producer prices. But self-sufficiency is not necessary to achieve this. Variable levies and subsidies could achieve the same effect at lower average prices without boosting domestic production. Self-

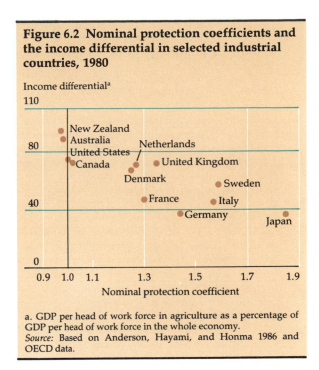

Figure 6.2 Nominal protection coefficients and the income differential in selected industrial countries, 1980

a. GDP per head of work force in agriculture as a percentage of GDP per head of work force in the whole economy.
Source: Based on Anderson, Hayami, and Honma 1986 and OECD data.

sufficiency contributes nothing to the quest for reasonable prices, for it increases the total cost of food.

The argument that self-sufficiency contributes to food security sounds simple, but it is not. Industrial countries need never go short of food because of crop failure, since they can always afford to buy enough on world markets. The argument for economic security hinges on cost—and it seems likely that it would be cheaper in the long run to pay high scarcity prices even as often as one year in five than to pay relatively high prices every year. As shown in Chapter 1, the long-term trend of real world market prices is downward, not upward.

What about so-called strategic security—the ability to produce food in times of political turmoil? It would take a worldwide crisis to make food unobtainable from any source. After all, the U.S.S.R. managed to purchase a record quantity of imports despite the U.S. grain embargo in 1980. Such a crisis would also stop the inputs—oil, fertilizers, pesticides—on which the present high levels of output in Europe and Japan depend. The goal of strategic security is illusory.

International consequences

Industrial countries' agricultural policies may be aimed at solving domestic problems, but their effects spill over onto the rest of the world. By ex-

Box 6.6 Commodity prices, rent, and rates of return

When the price of an agricultural commodity rises, the immediate result is an increase in the rate of return to farmers. If they expect the price to remain high in the future, they will grow more. Ordinarily, this would tend to drive the price down. But if the price rise is the result of government policy and can be maintained by subsidies or government purchases, the price may stay high for a long time. Then, as farmers attempt to increase their output, they compete for resources with businessmen elsewhere in the economy. As long as they are prepared to pay slightly more for labor and capital, farmers can attract these resources into agriculture. Prices of labor and capital in agriculture are therefore determined by the returns earned elsewhere and remain independent of agricultural prices and policy. In the long term, this is true even of the incomes of farmers. If their profits fall low enough, farmers will leave farming more rapidly.

For land, the situation is different. The stock of cultivable land in industrial countries is more or less fixed, so excess demand resulting from high farm prices and incomes will tend to bid up land rents. This will continue until the excess demand disappears—that is, un-

neither suppliers of capital nor land buyers gain from higher agricultural prices. Only landowners gain, because they can rent or sell land at higher prices.

Box figure 6.6A plots the rate of return to owning land against land prices in the United Kingdom. The rate of return is measured as the annual rental value of land divided by the price of land. Sharp increases in farm incomes during the 1960s and in 1973, when Britain joined the EC, are reflected in land prices but not in the rate of return, which has been declining for most of the period since 1955.

Box figure 6.6B Real land prices and the rate of return to land in the United States, 1950–83

Land price index (1977 = 100)   Rate of return (percent)

Source: Phipps 1985.

Box figure 6.6A Real land prices and the rate of return to land in the United Kingdom, 1950–84

Land price index (1977 = 100)   Rate of return (percent)

Source: Traill 1980.

til farmers who rent land earn only average profits. For this to happen, all the extra revenue generated by higher prices must be absorbed into rental values. Of course, if rents rise, so will the price of land, for people will try to buy land until the rate of return equals that available elsewhere in the economy. In the long run

Box figure 6.6B shows similar data for the United States, except here the returns include appreciation in the price of land as well as current income generated. A study of these data indicated that payments to farmers and acreage diversions were effective in raising the rental returns to land. Each $1 billion permanent rise in government payments generated a $0.96 increase in returns per acre and a $15.21 rise in the price of an acre of land. There was no effect on the rate of return to investment in farming. U.S. policies were more unstable than those of the United Kingdom, and commodity prices varied more. Large short-term price fluctuations occurred, especially during the commodity price boom of the 1970s and the price collapse of the 1980s. But, overall, the rate of return in agriculture tended to follow the general rate of return in the economy and was not affected by agricultural policies.

panding output and depressing domestic demand, their policies reduce world prices and distort the relative prices of agricultural and manufactured goods. By granting special trading privileges to remedy some of the harm, industrial countries can make matters worse. And by destabilizing international markets, their farm policies can amplify rather than dampen commodity price fluctuations. This section quantifies these effects using the results of recent studies that look at what would happen to trade if the policies were liberalized.

Supply and price effects

How much agricultural policies in industrial countries depress world prices depends on four things: the level of protection, the extent to which domestic surpluses lead to reduced imports or subsidized exports, the share of world output and consumption accounted for by the industrial countries, and the responsiveness of supply and demand to price changes in the world markets.

Agricultural prices and costs are the key to the profitability of investment in agriculture. In industrial countries, resources are diverted from other sectors to agriculture. In developing countries, which face low world prices for agricultural products but nonetheless tax domestic production, resources are diverted from agriculture to industry. As a result, agricultural production is favored in industrial countries, even though in some of them the costs of production are higher than in many developing countries. This makes developing countries export less and import more, even though they could become—if they are not already—efficient producers by making investments to acquire the necessary technology. The longer agricultural protection is maintained in industrial countries, the more damaging it will be to the world economy.

The impact of agricultural protection differs from one developing country to another. It depends on whether the country is a net importer or exporter of each product. Exporters of commodities that are in surplus in the industrial countries are most vulnerable. Thailand, which is heavily dependent on exports of rice, has been severely threatened by the recent cut in the U.S. export price of rice. To reduce its surpluses, the United States slashed the price almost in half—from $8.00 a hundredweight in 1985 to about $4.20 as of mid-April 1986. In contrast, net food importers benefit from the low world prices caused by current policies, and at first sight it may appear that they would lose from lib-

eralization. But this need not be so if they liberalize their domestic policies and allow domestic production to substitute for imports. Moreover, some developing countries would be able to increase their exports or become exporters for the first time.

The rate of protection varies among agricultural products. So protection not only depresses the overall level of world prices, but also distorts relative prices among agricultural products. Prices for the most highly protected products—dairy products, beef, and sugar—are depressed more than prices of other agricultural products. These distorted prices make the use of resources in world agriculture even less efficient. If Japan were to reduce its protection of rice of the varieties in which other Asian countries have a comparative advantage, they could produce more. Until recently, farmers in the Netherlands produced vegetables in greenhouses because energy costs were subsidized. This discouraged Mediterranean countries from exploiting their natural advantages in these products.

Differing rates of protection hit developing countries especially hard when the rate of protection is higher for processed agricultural products than for unprocessed ones. Tariffs in industrial countries are higher for wheat flour, pasta, cheese, and poultry than they are for wheat, milk, or feed grains (see Box 6.7). As a result, industrial countries export larger quantities, and import smaller quantities, of processed goods than of the related raw materials. The EC accounts for 11.4 percent of world wheat exports but 48.9 percent of wheat flour exports.

Subsidies and trade preferences

Some industrial countries have to give subsidies to sell crops on world markets. Developing countries' competitiveness, therefore, depends less on their own efficiency than on political decisions in industrial countries. And their ability to compete may be undermined at any time by increased export subsidies on industrial countries' exports. Even when industrial countries appear to provide developing ones with market opportunities, the gains may not last. High grain prices in the EC created new markets for feed grain substitutes such as cassava, corn gluten feed, and citrus pellets. But China, Indonesia, and Thailand, which produce cassava, had to sign "voluntary" export restraint agreements.

When a high-cost importing country becomes an exporter, potential gains from trade are wasted.

The losses are often made worse by the special trade preferences that industrial countries grant to developing ones in the hope of mitigating these distortions. In some cases, industrial countries which produce an exportable surplus of a crop have to import it under the trade preference scheme. The EC imports dairy products from New Zealand and beef from some African, Caribbean,

---

Box 6.7 Protection and agroprocessing

Most goods are not purchased in their raw form but go through several stages of processing. International trade can occur at any stage, so the location of particular activities is an important issue.

In some cases, transport costs and technology determine location. The dilution and bottling of concentrated soft drinks take place near the final point of sale to economize on transport costs. For the same reason, cassava is converted into pellets in its country of origin before export. In many cases, however, the best place to locate a processing industry depends on a wide range of production costs. For labor-intensive industries in particular, developing countries should be well represented among processing countries. Yet this is much less the case than might be expected.

An important reason is the pattern of industrial countries' protection. Industrial countries have escalating tariffs for most goods—that is, tariffs are higher on more highly processed forms of a good. For many agricultural goods, the higher tariffs are buttressed by a wide array of nontariff barriers. As goods become more highly processed—and embody more labor and capital services—developing countries face increasing barriers to sales in the world's major markets. Box table 6.7 illustrates tariff and nontariff barriers on a range of products imported by industrial countries.

Even apparently mild escalation can severely disadvantage developing countries that try to establish a processing industry. Suppose that 70 percent of the cost of processed leather is accounted for by the raw-hides and that all countries can purchase hides at the same price on world markets. A developing-country producer making leather worth $1.00 on the world market earns $0.30, out of which he must pay for labor and capital and retain profits. Now consider an industrial-country producer protected by a tariff barrier of 4 percent. The same leather worth $1.00 on world markets sells for $1.04 domestically. So he earns $0.34, or 13.3 percent more than the producer in the developing country. That is, the developing-country producer has to be 13.3 percent more efficient than the domestic producer if he is to sell in the industrial country. Economists refer to this 13.3 percent—the extent to which value added behind the tariff wall exceeds value added at world prices—as the effective rate of protection.

The degrees of escalation in the table often exceed 4 percent, so rates of effective protection can be very high. In an extreme case, that of Sweden in 1969–70, effective rates of protection have been as high as 1,480 percent (soybean oil), 1,050 percent (coconut oil), 165 percent (corn milling), and 102 percent (flour).

By blocking this first and most natural step toward industrialization, escalating protection on agroprocessing severely disrupts the process of development. Developing countries often respond by subsidizing local processing industries. Almost inevitably, this encourages inefficiency and compounds the direct harm arising from industrial countries' tariffs.

Box table 6.7 Tariffs and nontariff barriers in industrial countries

Product and stage of production	Average tariff rates[a] (percent)	Percentage of imports subject to NTBs[b]
Fish		
Stage 1: fresh	3.5	35
Stage 2: prepared	5.5	31
Vegetables		
Stage 1: fresh or dried	8.9	39
Stage 2: prepared	12.4	48
Fruit		
Stage 1: fresh	4.8	20
Stage 2: prepared	14.4	54
Coffee		
Stage 1: green, roasted	6.8	11
Stage 2: processed	9.4	17
Cocoa		
Stage 1: beans	2.6	0
Stage 2: processed	4.3	0
Stage 3: chocolate	11.8	14
Oils		
Stage 1: seeds	2.7	33
Stage 2: fixed vegetable oils	8.1	56
Tobacco		
Stage 1: unmanufactured	55.8	11
Stage 2: manufactured	81.8	22
Rubber		
Stage 1: natural	2.3	0
Stage 2: processed	2.9	6
Stage 3: rubber articles	6.7	14
Leather		
Stage 1: rawhide and skin	0.0	0
Stage 2: processed	4.2	13
Stage 3: leather articles and footwear	9.6	26

a. Data are for Australia, Austria, Canada, the EC (excluding Greece, Portugal, and Spain), Finland, Japan, New Zealand, Norway, Sweden, and Switzerland.
b. Data are for Australia, Austria, Canada, the EC (excluding Greece, Portugal, and Spain), Finland, Israel, Japan, New Zealand, Norway, Sweden, Switzerland, and the United States.
Source: Yeats 1981 and UNCTAD data.

and Pacific countries. These trade flows raise income in the exporting countries which are part of the preference scheme, but importers and potential exporters outside the scheme suffer greater losses. Increases in production costs and transport and other marketing costs account for the net worldwide loss.

Destabilization of world markets

Most industrial countries hold domestic consumer prices relatively constant when world market prices change. A shortfall in world output will not affect demand in a country which insulates its domestic markets. But someone's consumption must be reduced. And if some countries refuse to cut their consumption, others must reduce theirs disproportionately. To ration the world output, world prices have to rise by more. If meat consumption and demand for feed grains were allowed to change with world market prices, cereal prices would fluctuate less—thus reducing the risk of food shortages in developing countries. Figure 6.3 shows that among major industrial countries only the United States reduced per capita feed consumption significantly when prices soared in 1974–75. Consumption in the EC, in other industrial countries, and in the East European nonmarket economies hardly changed.

The price changes caused by sudden supply or demand shocks can be absorbed by commodity stockpiles. Chapter 7 looks at attempts to coordinate stockpiling policies internationally. But national stockpiles are no less influential. In theory, world prices could be stabilized even if most countries insulated their markets, as long as countries or private individuals that operated on the free market held big enough stocks. But the more countries insulate their economies, the greater the size of the stockpiles needed. One study of fourteen regions found that stocks had to be eight times larger if the regions completely insulated their economies than if they allowed free trade. The cost of the extra stocks indicates one source of gain from liberalization. For crops that can be grown under a wide variety of conditions at similar costs, important gains from trade arise from temporary trade flows as each country's yield varies from year to year. Policies that insulate domestic markets sacrifice these gains.

Decisions to build up or release stocks are often made not by private traders but by governments. As in developing countries (see Chapter 5), governments in industrial countries determine the size

Figure 6.3 Per capita feed utilization and maize prices in selected industrial regions, 1960–84

Feed utilization
(tons per capita)

Price of maize
(dollars per ton)

Source: USDA 1985d.

of public stockpiles according to how much money is available from the budget or in response to other political pressures rather than by the size of stockpile needed for stabilization purposes. In the mid-1970s some countries built up stocks when they should have been releasing them, and this made the world food crisis worse. In June 1973, after world wheat prices had almost doubled in twelve months, wheat stocks were estimated to have risen by 2.0 million tons in the U.S.S.R. and by 0.2 million tons in Japan. By the following June, when prices had increased by an additional 30 percent, stocks in the EC and the U.S.S.R. had increased by an additional 0.3 and 14.0 million tons, respectively. Even wheat exporters increased their stocks: Canada by 0.2 million tons and Australia by 1.4 million tons between 1972–73 and 1973–74.

Counting the costs of protection

Because of the distortions in every trading country, the whole world would be better off if industrial countries were to stop protecting their farmers

Table 6.6 Changes in export revenue, import costs, and efficiency gains for selected commodities of developing countries caused by a 50 percent decrease in OECD tariff rates, 1975–77
(millions of 1980 dollars)

	Absolute increase		
Commodity	All developing countries[a]	Low-income countries	Middle- and high-income countries
Change in export revenue			
Sugar	2,108	394	1,714
Beverages and tobacco	686	191	495
Meats	655	33	620
Coffee	540	123	417
Vegetable oils	400	60	339
Cocoa	287	21	265
Temperate-zone fruits and vegetables	197	60	137
Oilseeds and oil nuts	109	19	90
Other commodities	883	96	788
Total increase for all exports	5,866	998	4,867
Change in import costs			
Cereals	−876	−530	−345
Other commodities	−497	−152	−345
Total increase for all imports	−1,373	−683	−690
Memo item: efficiency gains	922	−4	926

Note: As explained in Chapter 4, efficiency gains are estimates of the increase in the net sum of producer and consumer gains and losses, adjusted for tax revenue changes; they are not measures of the difference between the increases in export revenues and import costs. Results of further work on a later period reported by Zietz and Valdes (1985) for sugar and beef indicate somewhat larger gains in export revenue than shown here.
a. Includes developing countries with populations of more than 4 million in mid-1985.
Source: Valdes and Zietz 1980, pp. 31, 47.

and liberalize agricultural trade. But by how much? Recent studies have made some progress in quantifying the gains from liberalization.

The effects of trade and policy liberalization can be observed when trade or domestic policies are liberalized. Unfortunately, liberalization experiments are rare. Estimates of multilateral or global liberalization can be made only with the aid of simulation models.

Table 6.6 shows the results of a study by Valdes and Zietz. They asked what would have happened to developing countries if the OECD countries had cut their tariffs on ninety-nine commodities by 50 percent. The study is based on figures for 1975–77. According to Valdes and Zietz, developing countries' income would have increased by $922 million in 1977 and their export revenues by almost $6 billion. Total export revenue would have risen by 11.0 percent; exports of low-income countries would have risen by 8.5 percent. Because protection in the OECD countries has increased since 1977, the benefits of liberalization would be substantially greater in 1985.

Developing countries' gains would have arisen mainly from increases in the prices of tropical exports. The price of roasted coffee would have been 10.8 percent higher, that of coffee extracts 6.4 per-

cent higher, cocoa paste cake 11 percent, and cocoa butter oil 9 percent. Losses would have occurred from higher prices of imported temperate-zone crops, especially cereals. But increases in export revenue would have more than compensated for such losses. Valdes and Zietz estimated that prices of most tropical products would have gone up more than the price of wheat, the most important agricultural import of developing countries. These estimates ignore certain nontariff barriers to trade. They also omit other important long-term effects. Liberalizing agricultural policies of industrial countries would encourage outward-oriented policies in developing countries, stimulate investment and research in agriculture, and increase the export potential of tropical products by more than the figures in Table 6.6 suggest. It is also likely that, because of cost advantages, some developing countries would become exporters of commodities that they import under current policies of the industrial countries. The estimates, therefore, probably represent the minimum benefits of liberalization.

Because policies interact, it is difficult to judge what would happen across the world as a result of liberalization by groups of countries. European and Japanese policies tend to reduce world prices of wheat and rice; the acreage control policies of the United States have tended to increase them. It is possible that the policies could offset one another so that industrial countries would lose while the trade of developing countries remained relatively unaffected. But if the policies of industrial countries reinforced one another (as in sugar and dairy products), the consequences for developing countries would be more dramatic.

Interactions between commodities are also important. Industrial countries do not, on the whole, intervene in markets for vegetable oils (such as palm oil or coconut oil). But these may still be depressed by industrial countries' policies in other markets. The EC's feed grain policies increase demand for feed grain substitutes, such as soybean meal. This helps oilseed exporters such as Argentina, Brazil, and the United States. But because meal and soybean oil are joint products, these policies also affect the oil markets. Similarly, U.S. grain price supports and acreage controls encourage production of soybeans, which is not controlled. Thus, as a by-product of industrial countries' policies, soybean production is encouraged, which depresses the world price of vegetable oils, which harms export earnings of developing countries from palm oil and coconut oil.

Estimates of liberalization can reflect the complexities of world markets by focusing on the connections between commodity markets. That is what a study by Tyers and Anderson does (see Box 6.8). They simulated the effects of unilateral trade liberalization by individual countries or groups of countries as well as of simultaneous liberalization

by both industrial and developing countries. Although Tyers and Anderson cover only the main temperate-zone commodities—and thus omit the most important sources of gains to developing countries—they nevertheless throw light on important aspects of trade and policy liberalization. Qualitatively similar results were also obtained in a study of free trade in agriculture carried out at the International Institute for Applied Systems Analysis.

Table 6.7 shows what Tyers and Anderson estimate would happen to world prices and trade under several scenarios: unilateral liberalization by the EC, Japan, and the United States; multilateral liberalization by all industrial countries and by all developing countries; and global liberalization. All the simulations indicate that the volume of world trade in the group of commodities studied would rise, although cross-price effects would entail small reductions for a few individual commodities. Unilateral liberalization by the EC would reduce world trade in sugar because both its subsidized exports and its preferential imports would end.

Most of the projections indicate that world prices would rise. There are two exceptions: U.S. liberalization, which would reduce world prices slightly because ending acreage controls would increase output of grains and rice; and developing-country liberalization of rice and some livestock products, which would reduce world prices by ending the taxation of domestic producers that currently holds down production.

Developing countries face higher import prices when industrial countries liberalize. As a result,

Table 6.7 International price and trade effects of liberalization of selected commodity markets, 1985

Country or country group in which liberalization takes place	Wheat	Coarse grains	Rice	Beef and lamb	Pork and poultry	Dairy products	Sugar
Percentage change in international price level following liberalization							
EC	1	3	1	10	2	12	3
Japan	0	0	4	4	1	3	1
United States	1	−3	0	0	−1	5	1
OECD	2	1	5	16	2	27	5
Developing countries	7	3	−12	0	−4	36	3
All market economies	9	4	−8	16	−2	67	8
Percentage change in world trade volume following liberalization							
EC	0	4	0	107	3	34	−5
Japan	0	3	30	57	−8	28	1
United States	0	14	−2	14	7	50	3
OECD	−1	19	32	195	18	95	2
Developing countries	7	12	75	68	260	330	60
All market economies	6	30	97	235	295	190	60

Note: Data are based on the removal of the rates of protection in effect in 1980–82. Data for the EC exclude Greece, Portugal, and Spain.
Source: Tyers and Anderson (background paper).

Box 6.8 Simulation of liberalized agricultural policies

A study by Tyers and Anderson constructs a model for simulating the effects of lowering trade barriers. It represents the world agricultural economy as a system of supply and demand equations for seven commodity groups in thirty countries or groups of countries. The commodities are wheat, coarse grains, rice, beef and lamb, pork and poultry, dairy products, and sugar. The effects of tariff and nontariff barriers are represented by nominal protection coefficients for each commodity, measured over the period 1980–82 (see Table 6.1).

To solve the model, a computer finds a set of international prices at which world supply and demand for each commodity balance and a set of domestic prices at which each country's own markets clear. The effects of liberalization can be worked out by solving the model twice: first by assuming current agricultural policies and then by assuming that the trade barriers and domestic interventions have been removed. The differences in prices represent the effects of liberalization. Once the prices are known, trade flows and transfers of income can be calculated for each country and commodity.

The Tyers and Anderson model can allow for random shocks to represent such factors as weather and disease. Under both assumptions—actual trade policy and liberalization—the model is solved 100 times using a specified series of shocks. These experiments suggest how different policy regimes cope with an uncertain world.

Results of this model are reported in Tables 6.7 and 6.8 in the text. Their relevance to the assessment of the long-term effects of liberalization in 1986 depends on a number of factors:

• The accuracy of the estimates of protection and the responses of supply and demand to changes in prices. While these can never be known with certainty, the estimates used here are based on the most recent data available and the most thorough analysis possible.

• Changes in protection since the model's 1980–82 base.

• The differences between behavior in the long run—when investment and research effort can be redirected and technology changed—and the medium-term estimates of behavior in the model.

• The importance of the fact that the model's coverage is limited, since it ignores tropical agriculture and all nonagricultural activities and income.

• The accuracy of the model's assumptions about how countries whose liberalization is not being considered would react to their neighbors' liberalization.

This list suggests that the model's results will be very imprecise. It does not, however, undermine the basic messages of the text. Indeed, the quoted figures will almost certainly be underestimates of the benefits of trade liberalization to developing countries for the following reasons:

• Current protection coefficients in industrial countries exceed those of 1980–82.

• In the long run, higher prices will stimulate investment and research in developing countries' agriculture.

• Unshackling agriculture will stimulate savings, growth, and efficiency throughout agriculturally dependent economies.

• If developing countries' export goods were liberalized as well as their (temperate-zone) import goods, trade expansion would occur.

• If developing countries exploit the opportunities that industrial-country liberalization would grant them, by deregulating their own agriculture, significant supply expansion would be feasible.

Overall, therefore, while the computer model is no substitute for economic analysis of observed policy experiments, its estimates of the benefits of trade liberalization indicate the strong advantages of such a policy.

---

they import less and export more. Because imports exceed exports, the simulated higher prices yield a net loss (estimated at $11.8 billion in Table 6.8) to consumers and producers. The implication that developing countries lose is misleading for three reasons. First, the study looks at temperate-zone crops, of which developing countries are the main importers. If tropical products were to be included, we would expect to see a substantially different story, as Valdes and Zietz did. Second, under free trade some developing countries might, in the long run, become exporters of these products. Third, even Tyers and Anderson's study shows that developing countries could gain $18.3 billion if

they liberalized their own agricultural policies along with the industrial countries.

In the Tyers and Anderson study, liberalization by developing countries means the removal of distortions in border prices by sixteen individual and four regional groups of developing countries and no overvaluations of the exchange rates. The results (see Table 6.7) are that the world price of rice would fall 12 percent, while prices of grain, sugar, and dairy products would rise. The grain and dairy prices would rise because the main developing countries in the study were importers of these products and they maintained internal prices above world prices. Ending this protection would

Table 6.8 Efficiency gains caused by liberalization of selected commodities, by country group, 1985
(billions of 1980 dollars)

Country group	Industrial-country liberalization	Developing-country liberalization	Industrial- and developing-country liberalization
Developing countries	−11.8	28.2	18.3
Industrial market economies	48.5	−10.2	45.9
East European nonmarket economies	−11.1	−13.1	−23.1
Worldwide	25.6	4.9	41.1

Note: Data are based on the removal of the rates of protection in effect in 1980–82.
Source: Tyers and Anderson (background paper).

increase imports and hence prices. Liberalizing the grain policies of developing countries would have a bigger impact on prices than liberalization by the OECD countries because the OECD countries' grain policies tended to offset one another in the period studied.

The projections show that the main beneficiaries of unilateral liberalization are the liberalizers themselves (see Table 6.8). Industrial countries would gain $48.5 billion if they liberalized unilaterally; developing countries would gain $28.2 billion if they did the same. But each imposes losses on the other. If both groups liberalized, neither would gain quite as much individually, but the world would be even better off.

So why do countries not tear down their agricultural policies? The reason, of course, is that the interest groups whose support the policies aim to capture would lose. With OECD liberalization, the overall gain to the industrial countries would be $48.5 billion. But this figure comprises a net gain of $104.1 billion to OECD consumers and taxpayers and a $55.6 billion loss to producers.

It is interesting to note that the OECD countries spent $27 billion annually during 1980–84 on official development assistance. With global liberalization, the industrial and developing countries would together gain about $64 billion annually—

more than double the level of official development assistance from OECD countries.

Losses to farmers would tend to be smaller if countries liberalized together rather than on their own. The reason is that the declines in producer prices would be less. Consider dairy products, one of the most protected products in industrial countries. Unilateral liberalization of the U.S. dairy policy would push up world prices by 5 percent (see Table 6.7). This would imply a cut in U.S. producer prices of as much as 46 percent. But if all industrial countries were to liberalize simultaneously, world dairy prices would rise 27 percent, and the U.S. producer price would have to fall only 24 percent. Indeed, if developing countries liberalized as well, the world price would rise above the former protected price.

The biggest gains from current policies accrue mainly to the East European nonmarket economies. They would be worse off by $11 billion if industrial countries liberalized, by $13 billion if developing countries liberalized, and by $23 billion with global liberalization. They would not reduce their imports as much as the developing countries, and they would have less scope for exporting those goods whose prices would rise.

Would prices become more volatile if agricultural policies and trade were liberalized? Two recent

Table 6.9 Effects of liberalization on price instability, 1985

Commodity	Coefficient of variation[a]			
	Without liberalization	With industrial-country liberalization	With developing-country liberalization	With global market liberalization
Wheat	0.45	0.30	0.23	0.10
Coarse grains	0.19	0.17	0.14	0.08
Rice	0.31	0.25	0.14	0.08
Beef and lamb	0.06	0.04	0.05	0.03
Pork and poultry	0.09	0.07	0.06	0.04
Dairy products	0.16	0.07	0.07	0.04
Sugar	0.20	0.17	0.07	0.04

a. The expected deviation from the long-term average price in any particular year as a percentage of the average price.
Source: Tyers and Anderson (background paper).

studies indicate that liberalization would make prices more stable. According to one estimate, by Schiff, the variability of world wheat prices could be reduced by 48 percent if all countries were to end their protective wheat policies. A second study found that liberalization by industrial countries would reduce the price variability of all the major temperate-zone commodities. The variability of wheat prices would fall by 33 percent and that of sugar by 15 percent (see Table 6.9). Liberalization by developing countries might stabilize prices even more, because these countries insulate their domestic markets to a greater extent than do some industrial ones; they also have a larger share of world consumption. This second study needs to be interpreted with more caution than usual: among other things, it assumes that internal prices in China and India would move in line with world prices. This seems unlikely, so consumption would not adjust fully to scarcity or abundance in world markets. Nonetheless, the findings of the two studies, even if they exaggerate the impact of developing countries, confirm that liberalized trade is more effective at price stabilization than even the most elaborate international commodity-stockpiling schemes. It is to those efforts that we turn in Chapter 7.

7

International initiatives in agricultural trade

International cooperation in agricultural trade has long been accepted as an effective means of fostering economic growth in developing countries. Enthusiasm for cooperation has been dented, however, by the continued failure to liberalize agricultural trade and by the declining and volatile agricultural terms of trade faced by some developing countries. These factors have prompted a search for means other than unregulated commercial trade to serve the interests of developing countries.

This chapter describes how these initiatives have affected the international trading system and assesses their record. The first section examines the economics of commodity agreements and concludes that they have not lived up to expectations. The next section deals with schemes to compensate commodity producers for shortfalls in their export earnings. It concludes that such schemes involve certain practical difficulties but are more efficient than commodity agreements. The chapter then looks at attempts to improve developing countries' access to the markets of industrial countries. These efforts have often taken the form of preferential treatment being granted to particular groups of developing countries—an approach of limited value because it can create additional distortions of world trade and thus hurt other developing countries. The final section of the chapter considers food aid. In emergencies, famine relief has an obvious humanitarian role, and longer-term food aid can also be useful in special circumstances. However, since it can easily discourage local production of food, it needs to be offered only with careful consideration of the market consequences.

International commodity agreements

An international commodity agreement (ICA) is a formal arrangement between the countries producing and consuming a commodity to control the market for it in some respect. Some forty ICAs covering thirteen commodities have been concluded since 1931. Although the details of their objectives have varied, virtually all have sought to stabilize as well as increase the price of the commodity concerned. Most have run into severe difficulties. At the end of 1985 only four agreements capable of influencing prices were still in operation, and only one of these was actively doing so. It is questionable whether any of them are effectively stabilizing prices in 1986.

Objectives and instruments

The precise purposes of ICAs differ from case to case, but two overriding objectives are evident. First, to stabilize commodity prices. Second, to ensure "fair," "remunerative," or "equitable" prices—that is, generally to raise them. While the two aims are frequently combined, they are logically quite separate and even potentially contradictory. They have different distributional implications and require different tools of policy. The two main instruments of ICAs have been buffer stocks and controls on production or exports.

BUFFER STOCKS. The problems with international buffer stocks are similar to the problems of running national buffer stocks discussed in Chapter 5. The basic questions to ask are, why they are desirable and how they can work? By buying a commodity when its price is low and selling it when the price is high, a buffer stock manager behaves just like a profit-seeking speculator. In that case, why should stabilization not be left to private speculators? Why do governments need to undertake transactions that do not look attractive to private dealers? Three possible sets of reasons exist. First, speculation might not always be stabilizing: by action or merely the threat of it, a buffer stock manager may be able to offset or discourage destabilizing speculation. Second, the buffer stock manager might have better information than private speculators and thus be able to push the market toward the long-run price more directly than they. The manager could have access to confidential material concerning plans for trading by centrally planned countries, for example. Third, the buffer stock manager may have access to more or cheaper capital than private traders. These advantages would allow him to trade more, or on finer margins, and hence increase his power to stabilize prices. These arguments are largely hypothetical. Empirical studies have not found private speculation to be destabilizing. Nor does it appear that inside information or access to capital provides substantial advantage to public stabilization authorities in practice.

Even if greater price stability than would result from unregulated markets is deemed desirable, an international buffer stock would be a cost-effective means of achieving this only if it overcame several serious difficulties in the following tasks:

• *Fixing the target range for prices.* The narrower the range, the greater the chance that it will be breached. This possibility actually may precipitate fluctuations that would not occur in the absence of the buffer stock; the mere existence of a narrow range for target prices can encourage speculation against the ceiling and floor, as well as reduce the level of private stocks that might be used to moderate price changes outside the declared range.

• *Choosing the reference price on which the target range is centered.* Over the long run, buffer stocks should stay the same size, and so their price range must include the long-run market-clearing price. However, this price tends to change over time, which makes it hard for the buffer stock manager to know whether his current range will eventually exhaust his physical stocks on the one hand or his cash resources on the other.

• *Defining the price range with respect to both the location and grade of the commodity and the currency of denomination.* Even if the buffer stock stabilizes its chosen price perfectly, producers interested in other grades and other currencies will still face uncertainty.

• *Deciding the size of a buffer stock.* It is impossible to guarantee that a buffer stock will never exhaust its stocks or its cash: there can always be runs of good (or bad) years. For the ICA to be credible, however, the probability of exhaustion must be small. The optimum size of a stockpile depends on the tradeoff between the costs of holding it and the benefits of improved credibility.

• *Taking account of the deterrent effect that buffer stocks have on private holders of stocks.* It has been estimated that for every ton added to the United States' stockpile of wheat between 1977 and 1982, between half and three-quarters of a ton was withdrawn from private stocks. Such withdrawals obviously offset much of the buffer stock's stabilizing influence and add considerably to the strain on its resources.

These difficulties do not rule out a buffer stock operation, but they do reduce its chances for success. Against the possibility of success must be set the known costs of running a buffer stock. These include the administrative expenses of the organizational units that negotiate and monitor the ICA, interest forgone on the value of physical stocks, storage costs, physical wastage, and the interest differential between the returns to long-term productive investment and the short-term interest that the buffer stock manager can earn on his unused liquid reserves. He can, of course, make money by buying cheap and selling dear, but only if the buffer stock is able to achieve its goals. Since excess stocks have to be sold, potential profits often turn out to be actual losses.

A basic problem with the buffer stock approach is that it aims at stabilization of prices rather than of export earnings. If a country can offset fluctuations in earnings by borrowing or by using reserves, price instability in itself probably does little harm. Furthermore, stabilizing prices may not stabilize export earnings. This is easily seen by considering the case of weather-induced output variation in which market forces lead the price of the commodity to rise in the same proportion as quantity falls. The value of trade will then remain constant if prices are allowed to vary freely, whereas price stabilization would destabilize earnings.

PRODUCTION AND EXPORT CONTROLS. The second objective of ICAs—to raise commodity prices—can ultimately be achieved only with controls on production. ICAs that adopt such controls basically act as producer cartels and face the well-known problems that plague all cartels. An ICA will be ineffective if any significant suppliers remain outside it. It will fail to raise producers' earnings (as opposed to prices) if the good can easily be replaced by other commodities, which would make the demand for it price responsive. And if it is to succeed, it will have to allocate quotas among producers and police its restrictions. Even in the case of oil, which was thought to be the most promising candidate for cartelization, these problems have not been overcome.

Few ICAs for agricultural products have tried to control output with internationally negotiated production quotas: the early agreements on coffee (1962) and cocoa (1972 and 1975) are perhaps the most prominent examples. It has been more common for producers to impose production quotas nationally so as to fulfill internationally agreed restrictions on exports. Examples of these include Brazilian coffee and set-asides for wheat in the United States. Recently, however, export controls have been supported more by national stockpiles than by production limits. Thus, their overall effect is similar to that of buffer stocks, for the ICA arrangements typically state that whenever the world price rises above some limit, export quotas may be increased and national stocks run down. Unlike production quotas, therefore, export controls principally stabilize prices rather than raise them.

Export controls are subject to the practical problems already mentioned, as well as some more of their own. First, quotas tend to ossify the pattern of supply. Even if they are initially allocated to low-cost producers, thereby minimizing the worldwide costs of supplying a certain volume of a commodity, they rarely continue to perform this function as economic conditions change. Potential newcomers are prevented from entering markets even if they have a comparative advantage. Second, the decentralized administration of quotas tends to produce "lumpy" stock movements. Once the market price rises to a point where countries are allowed to increase exports, there is a strong incentive to expand them rapidly before controls are reimposed. Third, policing the agreements can be very difficult.

Assessment

For all the reasons discussed in this section, ICAs have not been a success in practice. In recent years there have been four of them in agriculture—coffee, cocoa, rubber, and sugar—and one other in tin. The main features of the agricultural ICAs are summarized in Table 7.1 and their performance in Figure 7.1. Box 7.1 discusses their recent experience in some detail. All of them except coffee face uncertain futures. Negotiations on cocoa and sugar have collapsed. Negotiations on rubber continue, but their future is uncertain.

The prospects for ICAs are therefore bleak. Not only are specific agreements proving hard to operate and renegotiate, but much grander plans

Table 7.1 Current international commodity agreements in agriculture

Item	Cocoa	Coffee	Rubber	Sugar
Date of first agreement	1972	1962	1980	1954
Date of current agreement	1981[a]	1983	1980	1978[b]
Duration (number of years)	3	6	5	5
Extensions (number of years)	2	. .[c]	2	2
World trade (billions of dollars in 1984)	2.6	11.0	3.6	10.1
Percentage from developing countries	79	76	93	75
Percentage from low-income countries	14	16	6	2
Dependency[d]	6	21	3	9
Principal instrument	buffer stock	export quota	buffer stock	export quota
Permitted price range (percent)	±18	±15	±20	±13
Buffer stock as a percentage of 1980–83 average consumption	16	. .	15	. .

a. Expires September 1986; negotiations on renewal were abandoned in spring 1986.
b. Economic provisions expired December 1984.
c. Extended for an indefinite period.
d. Number of countries, based on a sample of eighty-eight, in which the commodity accounted for more than 10 percent of exports in 1980.
Source: Gilbert 1984, tables 7.1(A) to (E).

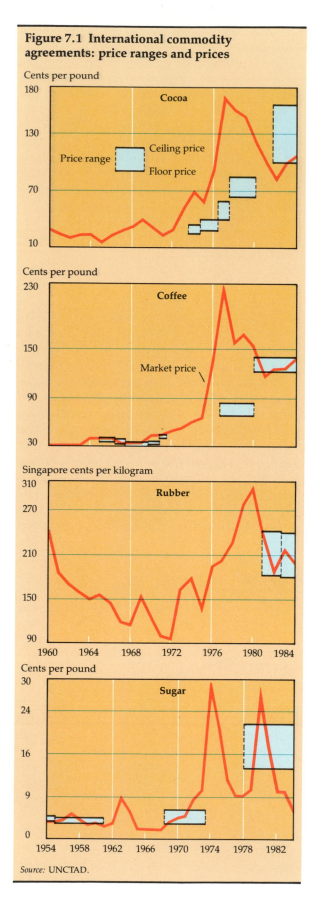

Figure 7.1 International commodity agreements: price ranges and prices

Cents per pound

Cocoa

Price range — Ceiling price — Floor price

Cents per pound

Coffee

Market price

Singapore cents per kilogram

Rubber

Cents per pound

Sugar

Source: UNCTAD.

Box 7.1 Recent commodity agreements in agriculture

The longest-lived agricultural ICA is the International Coffee Agreement. Based on export controls, it has probably raised coffee prices slightly above what they would have been otherwise. Although in recent years coffee prices have been kept mostly within the specified ranges, the agreement has had little success in stabilizing them over the long term. The agreement has been in operation for more than twenty years (with a five-year hiatus in the mid-1970s). An important factor in the ICA's longevity has been the support offered to it by the main coffee-consuming countries—largely for reasons of foreign policy. Periodic supply crises—most of them caused by adverse weather conditions in Brazil, such as the drought in 1985—have also contributed to its longevity, by permitting the release of stocks.

Two serious problems have recently confronted the coffee agreement and are likely to recur when the current supply crisis ends. First, the United States, the largest consumer, has been reassessing its commitment to the agreement. Second, increasing amounts of coffee have been traded outside the agreement's export restrictions. The agreement permits nonquota sales—small volumes of exports allowed in addition to normal export quota limits for the purpose of opening up new markets. Recently, however, the volume of nonquota sales has been growing, and some of it has

for strengthening market interventions have not been realized. The most prominent example was UNCTAD's proposal in 1976 for a common fund within the Integrated Program for Commodities (IPC). This would have established common financing for agreements in ten leading commodities. The plan led to the ICAs on cocoa and rubber, but that was all.

The argument for ICAs is that price fluctuations and uncertainty are harmful. Rather than try (and almost certainly fail) to eradicate price movements, it may be more useful to find ways of alleviating their effects. One obvious remedy is to encourage traders to use forward, futures, and options markets. Though their details vary, in general each allows a trader to negotiate the terms on which he will trade in the future, and thus transfer the risks of price fluctuations to speculators in these markets. This reduces uncertainty and achieves basically the same result as a successful attempt to stabilize prices. In addition, each market participant can choose how much stability he wants (at the

been reexported from new markets to traditional quota-bound ones. Although this may be efficient in the sense that it suits all the trading parties, it is not as efficient as free trade in coffee would be, because it increases transaction and transport costs and introduces unnecessary uncertainty.

The international cocoa agreements have been almost wholly unsuccessful. The first cocoa agreement, signed in 1972, was designed mainly to defend a floor price. Its advent coincided with a surge in prices that resulted from declining output and booming demand. Thus, market prices exceeded target prices throughout the 1970s. Since the agreements had no accumulated stocks, they were powerless to hold down prices.

Negotiations for the third cocoa agreement began in 1981 and proved protracted and difficult. Neither the principal consumer (the United States) nor the principal supplier (Côte d'Ivoire) took part. The United States felt the target price range was too high; Côte d'Ivoire thought it was too low. Subsequent events bore out the U.S. view. Cocoa prices have fallen substantially since 1981 as new production, stimulated by previous high prices, has become available. During the third cocoa agreement, therefore, the market price has almost always been below the target range. The agreement's executive arm intervened to support the price, but, lacking the support of the United States and Côte d'Ivoire, was ineffective. In the negotiations which be-

gan in 1985 for a fourth cocoa agreement, old disagreements resurfaced between producers, who want to charge $1.10 a kilogram, and consumers, who want to pay only $0.85 a kilogram. A plan to buttress the buffer stock with export controls was proposed, which opened new areas of disagreement. The negotiations have since been abandoned, at least temporarily.

The International Natural Rubber Agreement, having successfully defended a floor price for several years after it was set up in 1980, has been unable to divest itself of its large stocks, despite cuts in its target prices. The agreement was extended until 1987, although the decision to do so was made at the last minute, and it is unclear whether producers and consumers will be able to agree to a further renewal.

Recent international sugar agreements have had no material influence on the world sugar price. The free market accounts for only about 15 percent of world sugar trade; the rest is shipped under long-term or preferential agreements. The result is that the free market price of sugar is the most volatile of all agricultural commodity prices. The sugar agreement has had to cope with the EC's shift from being a major importer to a major exporter: the EC refused to sign the 1977 sugar agreement because it said its export quota was too low. Market support operations were abandoned in 1984, and the sugar agreement now merely collects data and fosters discussions.

going price) rather than having to accept the choice of a buffer stock manager. The markets are not at present suited to the needs of small commodity producers, but they could be adapted and developed (see Box 7.2).

Compensatory finance

The main argument for stabilizing commodity prices is that it stabilizes the export earnings of commodity producers and hence minimizes disruptive fluctuations in their imports, investment, and fiscal balances. The previous section showed that buffer stock policies could not be relied on to stabilize prices over the medium term, and that even if they could, they are expensive to operate and do not necessarily stabilize export earnings. This section examines an alternative approach—borrowing to stabilize a country's financial situation when its export earnings are fluctuating. Compensatory borrowing offers a cheaper route to stability because money is cheaper to store and

administer than commodities. It can also be easily extended to cover temporary rises in import prices, for example, or even increases in import requirements when crops fail.

Individual countries have two potential sources of compensatory financing. First, they can accumulate international reserves in good years and use them in bad ones. However, they thereby lose the returns they would have had if they had undertaken productive investments instead of holding liquid assets. Second, they could borrow on private markets when their export earnings fall. The possible drawbacks of this approach are the costs and difficulties of private borrowing, especially for the poorest countries. Since both sources are particularly difficult for developing countries to use, this group benefits most from official schemes of compensatory lending.

The two schemes currently in existence represent different approaches to compensatory financing. The IMF's Compensatory Financing Facility (CFF), established in 1963, is designed to address

Box 7.2 Commodity futures and options

Futures markets allow commodities to be bought and sold today for delivery at a future date. Such markets exist in London, New York, Winnipeg, Sydney, and elsewhere, but the most widely used exchanges are in Chicago, where contracts for corn, soybeans, wheat, cattle, and hogs are bought and sold for delivery up to eighteen months from the trading date. Futures contracts can be used to speculate on price, but they also allow buyers and sellers to fix a price for goods that are to be purchased or sold later.   Thus, the contracts can be used to transfer the risks of price fluctuations from risk-averse farmers to risk-seeking speculators. A wheat farmer can sell wheat futures when he plants his wheat. Later, when the wheat is harvested, he can sell the wheat and simultaneously buy the futures back. The whole process, which is called hedging, is equivalent to a forward sale in that both determine the price that the farmer receives at the time the crop is planted. Similarly, by buying futures a processor of wheat can hedge anticipated purchases.

Hedging via futures reduces, but does not eliminate, risk. If a farmer sells forward 1,000 tons of wheat and then his crop fails, he may have to buy at high prices to meet the commitments of his futures contract. Futures purchases can backfire in similar ways. In developing countries serious problems can arise for farmers when the local price does not vary consistently with the Chicago price or the price in other futures markets because of such factors as exchange rate fluctuations and changes in government policies: the possibility of this happening is known as basis risk. A futures sale in Chicago will do a producer little good if the local price falls in comparison with the Chicago price. When this problem is serious, the development of a local futures market denominated in local currency is an alternative that should be considered.

Many buyers and sellers do not wish to lock in a fixed price, because that forecloses potential gains as well as losses. Instead, sellers would like to insure themselves against extremely low prices, and buyers against extremely high prices. Such insurance can be accomplished by trading in options on futures contracts. Options are traded on sugar and cotton in New York and on soybeans, corn, hogs, and cattle in Chicago. A farmer can insure against low prices by purchasing a "put" option to sell at a specified "strike" price. If the actual price falls below the strike price, he exercises the option; if the price rises above it, he loses what he paid for the option but sells his crop for a higher cash price. There are several strike prices below the futures price, providing a range of insured price levels. Similarly, a buyer insures against high prices by purchasing a "call" option to buy at a strike price of his choice. The market price of options determines the cost of the insurance.

The usefulness of international futures and options markets for developing countries is greatly reduced because of basis risk. The alternative of a local futures market may be viable, but it requires active speculators to whom hedgers may transfer risk. In addition, a stable financial and regulatory environment is needed if futures markets are to thrive. Although farmers, corporations, and parastatal agencies in developing countries have made little use of futures and options, the opportunities for their use have been expanding. They may become important, especially if liberalized agricultural trade ties the world's agricultural commodity markets even more closely together.

---

the adverse effects on a country's overall balance of payments of a shortfall in its total export earnings. The EC's export earnings stabilization scheme (STABEX) is a commodity-specific arrangement that provides compensation to individual countries associated with the EC for shortfalls in their export earnings from individual agricultural commodities. Whereas a basic requirement for use of the CFF is the existence of a balance of payments problem, there is no such requirement under STABEX.

The IMF's Compensatory Financing Facility

The purpose of the CFF is "to provide financial assistance to members experiencing balance of payments difficulties resulting from export short-falls that are temporary and due largely to factors beyond the member's control" (International Monetary Fund 1984b, p. 47). The facility is open to all IMF members, but since the conditions for its use are more frequently met by countries that depend heavily on trade in primary commodities, its use has, in practice, been largely confined to developing countries. Coverage of the facility was expanded in 1981 to include cereal imports, but in most instances the CFF has been used to make up for shortfalls in merchandise exports.

Eligibility to use the CFF is subject to certain criteria: (1) there must be a balance of payments need; (2) the export shortfall must be temporary and due to factors largely beyond the control of the member; and (3) the IMF must be convinced that the member will cooperate with it in efforts to find appropriate solutions for its balance of payments difficulties. In addition, for requests that have the effect of raising outstanding CFF drawings above 50 percent of quota (upper tranche), the IMF must be satisfied that the member has already been co-operating with the IMF to find appropriate solutions for its balance of payments difficulties. All of these judgments can be difficult in practice.

A special provision relating to agriculture allows countries to borrow when they face balance of payments problems caused by increases in the cost of their cereal imports owing to circumstances beyond their control—such as weather-induced declines in domestic food supplies. Under the cereal decision the amount of a drawing is determined as the sum of the export shortfall and the cereal import excess, subject to quota limits. Since January 1984, the quota limits on drawings under the cereal decision have been 83 percent of quota for cereal import excesses and 83 percent of quota for export shortfalls, subject to a joint limit of 105 percent of quota for both components.

Since May 1981, there have been thirteen drawings under the cereal decision amounting to SDR 1.1 billion, of which SDR 0.5 billion was attributable exclusively to excess cereal imports. The limited use of the cereal decision largely reflects a global food supply situation from 1981 to 1985 characterized by record world cereal production levels, large stocks, declining cereal prices, and a substantial volume of food aid. All thirteen drawings under the cereal decision were caused by the effects of adverse weather on domestic food supplies.

The CFF is not commodity-specific, and it finances shortfalls in agricultural exports only to the extent that these contribute to the shortfalls in total export earnings. However, since agricultural products are subject to greater instability than most other products and constitute a significant share of the total export earnings of developing countries, shortfalls in agricultural exports have contributed to a large number of drawings by the developing countries.

STABEX

The EC's STABEX compensatory finance scheme was established under the first Lomé Convention of 1975. It is restricted to the EC's African, Caribbean, and Pacific (ACP) states and aims to stabilize their export earnings. Exports of forty-eight agricultural products are covered, mineral exports being the subject of a separate scheme. A total of ECU 375 million ($460 million) was allocated for the duration of the first convention (1975–79), ECU 550 million for the second (1980–84), and ECU 925 million for the third (1985–89), with the funds in each case divided evenly among the years concerned.

Subject to the threshold limits discussed below, compensable export shortfalls are calculated for each commodity separately—thus excess exports of one commodity do not offset shortfalls in exports of another. The intention is that compensatory payments should be directed to producers of the shortfall commodities, and claimants of STABEX funds must declare beforehand how they intend to use the funds and afterward how they did so. Usually, only exports to the EC are covered, although in certain cases coverage has been extended to exports to other ACP states or the world as a whole.

To qualify for compensation under the third STABEX, in use since 1985, a commodity must generally account for 6.5 percent of the country's export earnings and be 6.5 percent below the reference level. (Both limits are set at 1.5 percent for some countries.) The reference level is calculated as the arithmetic mean value of exports in the preceding four years. Export shortfalls must not be due to national policy.

The repayment provisions are generous. The least developed countries repay nothing. All loans are interest free. In the period 1975–82, STABEX made 205 transfers to 44 ACP countries, amounting to about $800 million. STABEX transfers exceeded aid flows from the European Development Fund (EDF) in several cases and represented a significant portion (10–66 percent) of the aid flow from the EDF for just under half of the ACP countries. Payments have been unevenly spread over commodities, countries, and time. Thus, under STABEX I (1975–79) three beneficiaries—Mauritania, Senegal, and Sudan—accounted for 30 percent of payments, and four others for another 20 percent. Prominent among the commodities supported are cotton, sisal, coffee, cocoa, and groundnuts. The EC Commission estimates that 69 percent of the transfers were due to weakening economic conditions and 31 percent to local circumstances, such as drought, disease, and flood.

The EC rejects a significant number of claims as ineligible—28 percent during 1975–79 and 32 percent during 1980–82. In 1980 and 1981, STABEX exhausted its funds and was able to honor only 53 percent and 43 percent of eligible claims, respectively, although unused funds from subsequent years allowed the coverage of these claims to be restored to 65 percent for both years.

For the ACP countries the most attractive feature of STABEX is its high grant elements. For the least developed countries—which repay nothing—all transfers are grants; for the remainder, the zero rate of interest and the possible waiver if exports stay depressed for a long period implied grant elements of about 60 percent during the period 1975–83. However, the grants were very unevenly distributed, and there is no discernible relationship between grant components and indicators of poverty or the need for foreign assistance. The principal beneficiaries are listed in Table 7.2.

STABEX affects the allocation of economic resources both within and between countries. For example, by supporting particular sectors STABEX seems likely to encourage excessive production of covered commodities, especially those which have the greatest market risks. Internationally, non-ACP countries producing STABEX commodities are put at a disadvantage because they do not receive protection from risk, and they may have to switch to producing goods in which their comparative advantage is less. Also, the restriction of STABEX to exports to the EC market redirects and distorts international trade.

Table 7.3 summarizes the main features of the CFF and STABEX. While they differ in many practical aspects, they are addressed to similar problems. A full assessment of their value is difficult. Both have assisted a large number of countries.

Table 7.2 The principal beneficiaries of STABEX's grant elements, 1975–83

A. Absolute amounts

Country	Receipts (millions of 1983 dollars)	As a percentage of 1983 exports
Senegal	77	13.2
Sudan	61	9.8
Côte d'Ivoire	33	1.6
Mauritania	30	10.5
Tanzania	23	6.2

B. Per capita amounts

Country	Receipts (1983 dollars)	As a percentage of 1983 estimated GNP per capita
Dominica	62	6.6[a]
Kiribati	53	11.5
Tonga	43	5.8
Western Samoa	40	7.1
Vanuatu	38	6.5

a. GDP per capita.
Source: Koester and Herrmann (background paper).

Box 7.3 The Lomé Convention

The EC's arrangements with African, Caribbean, and Pacific states, which replaced former colonial preference schemes, were formalized under the first Yaoundé Convention of 1963 and are now enshrined in the Lomé Convention, the third of which was signed in 1984. The STABEX compensatory financing facility is a principal feature of the Lomé Convention. Other features are the free access for most ACP goods into the EC and the European Development Fund, which administers foreign aid to ACP countries.

The Lomé Convention covers most of the EC members' former colonies, with the exception of the industrial and Asian members of the British Commonwealth. They were denied membership in 1973 on the grounds that they were either much bigger or much richer than the original associated states. There are sixty-six developing-country members of Lomé at present, the majority of which are among the smallest and poorest nations.

The preferences granted to ACP states in agricultural trade fall into three groups. First, small preferences are granted on commodities covered by the CAP. Since such commodities are mostly temperate-zone crops,

however, this matters little to the ACP states, which are by and large tropical. Second, preferences are extended for tropical products that are supplied principally by the ACP states and that pose little threat to the EC's domestic producers. Such goods are typically granted unrestricted tariff-free access. However, since similar rights accrue to many other exporters through the EC's other preferential arrangements or because tariffs are zero anyway, the margins enjoyed by the ACP countries over other developing countries are limited. More than half of the ACP exports are covered by other EC preference schemes.

Third, there is a small class of goods for which special arrangements exist—rum, bananas, beef, rice, and sugar. ACP rum quotas remain unfilled, and the ACP countries have not been able to increase their shares of the export market for bananas. In contrast, the arrangements for sugar grant the ACP countries both the right and the duty to sell in the EC at a fixed price. In general, this price far exceeds the world price, and so the system transfers income to the ACP countries. In the cases of both sugar and beef, the system transfers income to ACP countries. In some years the transfers

But by their very nature they do not fully compensate for earnings shortfalls. The purpose of compensatory finance is to maintain spending in the face of a temporary fall in export receipts. To be successful, compensatory schemes must have clear objectives, permit quick identification of shortfalls, and provide prompt payments without complicated conditions. Neither the CFF nor STABEX has been ideal in these respects. While, on average, the compensation rate has been around 60 percent,

Table 7.3 Characteristics of the CFF and STABEX

Item	CFF	STABEX
Year of initiation	1963	1975
Eligibility	Members of the IMF (137)	Sixty-six ACP states
Drawings 1977–82		
Number of transactions	112	171
Amount	$7.3 billion	$0.8 billion
Shortfall	$11.9 billion	$1.3 billion
Compensation rate	62 percent	59 percent
Coverage	Total exports (may include services and exclude cereal imports)	Forty-eight commodities
Shortfall	Net	Gross (sum of individual shortfalls)
Reference level	Five-year moving average, centered on shortfall year	Four-year moving average, centered two and a half years previous to shortfall year
Limits	Country-specific quotas	Overall budget limit
Interest rate	IMF standard (7.8 percent currently)	None
Repayment schedule	Three to five years after loan	Two to seven years after loan
Repayment obligation	In full	None for low-income economies, conditional for other countries
Grant element	Around 20 percent	More than 80 percent

have been huge. In 1979 up to 7 percent of Botswana's GNP came from beef transfers, and 22 percent of Mauritius' GNP came from sugar transfers in 1975–76. But the arrangements for sugar cause economic inefficiencies because they encourage some ACP countries to expand their output unduly. They also generate excessive transport costs because the EC, which produces more sugar than it consumes, also exports sugar.

The Lomé Convention also grants ACP countries preferential access for manufactured and semimanufactured exports. However, since most manufactures face low general tariffs and are covered by the GSP, the preference is small. Only where the GSP limit on tariff-free access is tight have the ACP countries been able to exploit their preferences.

It has proved hard to measure the effects of the Lomé Convention on world trade, not least because the historical trading links that bind former colonies to Europe are weakening. Since 1965 most ACP states have diversified their exports away from Europe, although their share in EC imports has not changed dramatically. But do ACP countries continue to depend disproportionately upon the EC market? One study of the ACP states examines trade intensity indices—the ratio of an exporter's share of a particular market relative to its share of the world market. Trade intensity has always been high between "related" states—for example, between Britain and the Commonwealth. It is correspondingly low between less related parties. With the advent of the Lomé Convention, however, ACP trade intensities with non-EC markets declined while those with EC markets rose. This was especially noticeable in the case of ACP states' trade with the United States.

While these facts suggest that the Lomé Convention has altered the pattern of world trade, the change has not been large. Moreover, it is difficult to say whether the Lomé Convention has increased trade or merely redirected it. The ACP countries may merely have taken market share in the EC away from other developing countries by diverting exports away from other markets. To put the argument in an extreme form, it is possible that all the Lomé Convention has achieved is to change the direction of world trade, without increasing it, while adding to transport costs.

there has been considerable variation from country to country that is not clearly attributable to either need or the ability to repay. Delays have occurred that might have been avoidable. Still, both schemes have provided valuable assistance on some occasions.

Trade preferences

The industrial countries have introduced several schemes that give access to imports from developing countries at reduced or zero tariffs. In theory, such preferences should increase the exports of developing countries, largely at the expense of those countries excluded from the schemes. The idea is to improve the economic welfare of developing countries. The actual benefits, however, have been limited, partly because the terms of the preferences are restrictive. The schemes exclude, or place tight limits on, precisely those products in which developing countries could be most competitive. Among the least favored goods are many agricultural products. Overall, these arrangements have had little impact on agricultural trade.

Trade preferences have a long history. Although the General Agreement on Tariffs and Trade (GATT) embodies the principle of nondiscrimination, from the start it accepted the continuation of special schemes such as the British Commonwealth Preferences. Later, the EC countries established preferences for their former colonies, preferences which continue today in the Lomé Convention linking the EC to sixty-six ACP states. The principle of nondiscrimination further eroded in 1964, when the GATT allowed developing countries to receive preferential access to industrial markets. This section considers the Generalized System of Preferences (GSP), which is open to all developing countries, as well as restricted schemes such as the EC's Lomé agreement with the ACP states and the Caribbean Basin Initiative (CBI) of the United States.

The Generalized System of Preferences

Under the GSP, developing countries' exports to markets in industrial countries enjoy tariff reductions or exemptions. The scheme has had little effect on exports, however, partly because its product coverage is so limited. Imports from beneficiaries are only a fraction of the total imports of industrial countries. For many imports, regular tariffs are zero. Overall, about 2 percent of OECD imports qualify for preferences, equivalent to

about 7 percent of developing countries' total exports.

Many agricultural goods are excluded. For example, the United States excludes sugar and dairy products (both of which are subject to overall import quotas), peanuts, and long-staple cotton. It does so because increased imports would make it harder to run a system of price support for domestic farmers. For the same reason, the EC and Japan also exclude most agricultural products.

Box 7.4   The EC's Sugar Protocol

The Sugar Protocol of the Lomé Convention allows eighteen developing countries to export fixed amounts of sugar to EC members free from the usual import restrictions. In addition to the countries that are signatories to the Sugar Protocol, India benefits from similar provisions.

The benefits of these arrangements to the favored exporters depend on the sizes of their quotas, which are unevenly distributed. In 1981–82, five countries accounted for 77 percent of the total quota, with Mauritius alone receiving 38 percent. Four countries had quotas covering half or more of their domestic production (80 percent for Mauritius), while four had quotas below 10 percent of domestic output (see Box table 7.4).

One of the peculiarities of the Sugar Protocol is that even net importers of sugar export to the EC. Kenya, which produced less sugar than it consumed between 1976 and 1978, still exported to the EC. The peculiarities are compounded by the fact that the EC itself is a net exporter and thus reexports the sugar imported under the protocol. Since transport, insurance, handling, and waste account for up to 20 percent of the value of sugar trade, the losses involved are considerable—about $42 million in 1981–82.

By paying producers more than the world price for sugar, the Sugar Protocol transfers income from consumers in the EC to producers in developing countries. Since the world price of sugar fluctuates widely, the transfer varies from year to year, but it is nearly always positive. Negative transfers occur when the world price rises above the guaranteed price at which developing countries are obliged to supply sugar.

The estimates for income transfers quoted in the table are exaggerated to the extent that the Sugar Protocol reduces the world price. If exporters behaved in a profit-maximizing way, world prices would not be affected by the protocol. This is because the high guaranteed price is received on only a fixed quantity of sugar, so there is no virtue in producing more sugar for the

EC market than the quota allows. Also, an ACP country is free to choose the cheapest way of obtaining the sugar it supplies to the EC. If, in the absence of the protocol, it would have imported sugar because its own production costs exceeded the world price, then with the protocol it should just import sugar and reexport it to the EC.

But this practice is rare. More frequently, the countries covered by the protocol tend to pay domestic producers a price somewhere between the EC price and the price in the world market. The marketing board in Mauritius, for example, pays producers more for producing sugar in excess of the EC quota than they could get in the world market. Some of the transfers from the

EC are passed on to producers in this manner. The additional supplies due to this policy lower the world price of sugar.

Because quotas are determined largely by historical levels of sugar exports, the protocol tends to freeze world trade patterns. This puts new producers or countries which have improved their efficiency at a disadvantage.

Finally, as a part of the mechanism for fixing the EC's internal sugar price, the protocol helps to isolate the EC from the world market. It also tends to isolate ACP producers. This increases the burden of adjustment elsewhere and the instability of world market prices.

Box table 7.4 EC sugar quotas and transfers, 1981–82

| | Annual delivery quotas in 1981–82 | | Exports as a percentage of quota, 1981 | Quota as a percentage of production, 1981 | Maximum transfer, 1981–82[a] | | |
Preferred countries	Quantity (tons)	Percentage of total quota			Total ECU (million)	ECU per capita	As percentage of GDP or GNP
Barbados	49,300	3.8	100	51	7.5	28.8	0.8
Belize	39,400	3.1	111	38	6.0	40.0	4.1
Fiji	163,600	12.7	116	34	21.8	33.0	2.3
Guyana	157,700	12.2	127	49	23.9	26.5	4.7
India	25,000	1.9	0	0	3.4	0.0	0.0
Jamaica	118,300	9.2	105	58	17.9	7.9	0.6
Kenya	93	0.0	0	0	1.4	0.1	0.0
Madagascar	10,000	0.8	0	9	1.5	1.6	0.5
Malawi	20,000	1.6	105	11	3.0	0.5	0.2
Mauritius	487,200	37.8	94	80	75.8	79.8	6.4
St. Christopher and Nevis	14,800	1.1	107	45	2.2	36.6	4.3
Suriname	2,667	0.2	..	33	0.4	10.8	0.3
Swaziland	116,400	9.0	106	32	18.9	32.0	3.5
Tanzania	10,000	0.8	0	8	1.5	0.1	0.0
Trinidad and Tobago	69,000	5.4	98	74	10.5	8.7	0.2
Uganda	409[b]	0.0	..	..	..	..	..
Zaire	4,957	0.4	0	31	0.8	0.5	0.0
Total	1,288,826	100.0	100	14	196.5	0.2	..

a. Allowing for transport, insurance, and handling costs.
b. Quota abolished in 1981.

The Lomé Convention

The Lomé Convention, described in Box 7.3, is the best known of the other preferential schemes. While the effective preference margins under the convention are reduced by the preferences offered under the GSP, the margins are quite significant for some products, such as canned tuna, certain tropical fruit products, and tobacco. Among agricultural products, the impact of the convention on

sugar is significant. Eighteen ACP countries have quotas to export sugar to the EC. As Box 7.4 shows, these quotas insulate ACP producers and EC consumers from world prices and thereby destabilize the unrestricted world sugar market. They discourage efficiency among producers, prevent EC consumers from buying cheaply, increase transport and handling costs, discriminate against efficient sugar producers outside the arrangement, and encourage higher world output of sugar. They

In 1980, agricultural trade among developing countries was worth $21 billion; it accounted for 25 percent of developing countries' total agricultural exports. From 1970 to 1980, developing countries' agricultural exports to one another grew faster than their corresponding exports to industrial countries, but the former still grew more slowly than the developing countries' agricultural imports from industrial countries.

About two-thirds of farm trade among developing countries takes place between regions. Asia trades with other developing regions the most, Africa and the Middle East the least. A few commodities—mainly rice, sugar, raw cotton, and coffee—dominate the trade among developing countries.

There may be good reasons why this trade remains relatively small. The expansion of trade among developing countries should be pursued within the overall aims of economic development; it is not a goal in itself. But the low volume of farm trade among developing countries also reflects a variety of constraints:

• Tariffs in developing countries tend to be biased against the types of goods exported by other developing countries; nontariff barriers tend to restrict agricultural trade more than manufactured trade. Among the fifteen largest developing-country importers, quotas, conditional prohibitions, and licensing are applied to 31 percent of agricultural imports but only 23.5 percent of manufactured imports. Although tariffs on rice are low, half of world rice imports are subject to direct government control and a further 20 percent are regulated by licenses.

• Transport and communication between developing countries are often inadequate. It is easier, cheaper, and more profitable to seek out information on large markets; this means that the trading potential of other developing countries may not be fully exploited.

• Subsidized exports from industrial countries, often combined with overvalued currencies in developing countries, tend to reduce developing countries' competitiveness.

• Slow growth in the demand for imported food by industrial countries discourages developing countries from increasing production and reduces their access to the foreign exchange they need in order to import from other developing countries.

Several measures have been proposed to increase agricultural trade among developing countries, including a global system of trade preferences and an international information system on trade financing. Trade preferences—either general or regional—are not likely to be very effective. There are now eleven economic integration or clearing arrangements among developing countries. Most offer tariff preferences among members but little relaxation of nontariff barriers. These groups account for a significant fraction of total agricultural trade among developing countries but only rarely for more than 20 percent of their members' trade. Increased emphasis on market information and intelligence holds out a better hope for assisting developing countries to expand their agricultural exports. Such systems are not cheap to develop, and countries that export similar crops need similar information. So it may be most economical for regions or groups of countries to cooperate in setting up market information systems. This could be supported by technical cooperation, harmonization of standards, increased use of long-term contracts, and joint ventures.

do, however, transfer a large amount of income to those who hold quotas.

Although the economic effects of the Lomé Convention are hard to quantify, there are several reasons for thinking that they are relatively small: first, preference margins are slim; second, the main effect of most preferences seems to have been to divert trade rather than to boost it; third, market structures sometimes allow monopsonistic European importers to capture the tariff preferences; and fourth, the ACP countries have not always taken (or been able to take) full advantage of any increase in trade opportunities that has arisen. The last point applies particularly to the smallest and least developed countries. In return for these generally small and uncertain benefits, the ACP countries are bound into EC protectionism. Fear-

ing the erosion of their preferences, they tend to oppose more widespread trade liberalization.

The Caribbean Basin Initiative

The CBI of the United States, signed in August 1983, gave twenty-seven Caribbean states duty-free access for most of their exports to the United States. In return, the Caribbean states agreed to certain changes in taxation and economic policy. While all the parties enjoy several obvious benefits from the CBI, its trade provisions have had negligible effects so far. Textiles, clothing, footwear, canned tuna, and petroleum are among the items excluded from preferences; sugar and beef are subject to special treatment. Sugar quotas for CBI countries have been reduced from about 1.5 million tons in 1980 to 1.0 million tons in 1986. The U.S. Food Security Act of 1985 requires them to be reduced further if they conflict with the domestic sugar price support program. Beef quotas are also subject to U.S. domestic policy constraints.

Preference schemes among developing countries

Apart from schemes already described, there are several other preference arrangements that developing countries use for trade among themselves; these normally involve regional groups. To the extent that these arrangements create extra trade, they are beneficial; but like other preference schemes, they tend to divert at least as much as they create. And too great a concentration on regional markets tends to blind countries to the advantages of supplying the world market, which offers more scope for exploiting comparative advantage and greater security from regional economic shocks. Box 7.5 discusses agricultural trade among developing countries.

Food aid

During the 1960s and early 1970s, many governments and observers were concerned about widespread shortages of food. The Food and Agricul-

---

Box 7.6 Food aid institutions

Large-scale international food aid started with the passing of U.S. Public Law 480 in 1954. This legislated for the disposal of grain surpluses abroad

> to expand international trade among the United States and friendly nations . . . to make maximum efficient use of surplus agricultural commodities in furtherance of the foreign policy of the United States, and to stimulate and facilitate the expansion of foreign trade in agricultural commodities produced in the United States by providing a means whereby surplus agricultural commodities in excess of the usual marketings of such commodities may be sold through private trade channels (68 Stat. 457).

The United States and other donors have also adopted the FAO's Principles of Surplus Disposal to minimize the disincentive effect that food aid has on commercial markets. A consultative subcommittee was set up to monitor the distribution of food aid and ensure that the so-called usual marketing requirements were being met. These require recipient countries to maintain commercial imports at a specified level even though they are also receiving food aid. The rule is still insisted upon and monitored by the subcommittee, although its effectiveness is questionable.

The impact of dumping surplus food gave rise to considerable concern, and the hope of correcting it was one of the motives behind the creation of the World Food Program (WFP) in 1961. Established under the joint auspices of the United Nations and the FAO, the WFP was the first multilateral food aid agency. It aims to supply and coordinate food aid not only for relief and emergency purposes, but also for development projects. It is hampered, however, because its food donations may not be sold in the recipient countries' markets. Donated food can be used for projects only if it is distributed through cumbersome channels such as direct feeding or food-for-work programs. By 1983–84,

about 25 percent of all food aid shipments were handled by the WFP, compared with 5 percent in the late 1960s.

Food aid reached record levels—17 million tons—in 1965–66. Almost immediately, concern arose that adequate flows might not be maintained because the United States appeared to be stepping up its policy of restricting the area planted to grain. This concern was manifest in the Food Aid Convention of 1967, which was adopted as part of the International Wheat Agreement. Under the convention, member countries promised to provide 4.5 million tons of cereal food aid a year.

The so-called world food crisis of 1972–74 led to the convening of a World Food Conference in 1974. The conference set up a variety of institutions to promote food production, including the International Fund for Agricultural Development (IFAD) and the World Food Council. It also sought to increase food aid. In 1979 the conference recommended a target of 10 million tons of cereal food aid a year and the establishment of an international emergency reserve of 500,000 tons, to be replenished annually. The current Food Aid Convention, signed in 1980, guarantees minimum supplies of 7.6 million tons a year from twenty-two donor countries.

The world food crisis also provided an impetus for using food aid for development purposes as well as for emergency relief. In 1977 the United States amended Public Law 480, allowing conversion of food loans to grants under a new Title III—''Food for Development.'' Its aims are to help small farmers, sharecroppers, and landless laborers increase food production and to stimulate rural development in general. The EC also adopted new food aid guidelines in 1983 to integrate food aid better with the development strategies of recipient countries and to reduce the adverse effects of such aid on local production and consumption patterns.

Table 7.4 Food aid in cereals, 1971–83

Region	Percentage share		
	1971–72	1976–77	1982–83
Africa	8.3	28.4	50.4
Sub-Saharan Africa	2.5	10.4	26.9
Asia	52.7	59.7	32.3
Bangladesh	3.4	17.3	13.6
India	10.1	16.2	3.1
Indonesia	6.1	2.0	1.7
Latin America	3.9	7.7	13.7
Colombia	0.9	3.8	0.0
Honduras	0.0	0.2	1.0
Memo items			
Low-income countries	43.1	79.0	84.2
Least developed countries	1.3	26.7	32.3
World total (thousands of tons)	17,513	6,847	9,198

Source: FAO and World Bank data.

ture Organization (FAO) had long maintained that food supplies were chronically inadequate to meet the basic needs of many of the world's people and were also prone to periodic crises. As a result, various international and bilateral arrangements were made to cope with both chronic and temporary food shortages (see Box 7.6).

Although famine relief is the most visible form of food aid, it is much less common than project food aid (assistance to particular development projects given or lent in the form of food) and program food aid (food donated as balance of payments or budgetary support). In all its forms, food aid accounts for a relatively small share of foreign assistance to developing countries. With commodities valued at world prices, food aid in recent years has amounted to about $2.6 billion annually, about 10 percent of official development assistance. In 1984–85, twenty-five donor countries provided more than 100 developing countries with about 12 million tons of cereals, 430,000 tons of vegetable oil, 356,000 tons of skimmed milk powder, 98,000 tons of other dairy products, and 21,000 tons of meat and fish products. Of this, only about 660,000 tons, less than 5 percent of food assistance, was for emergency food aid. The United States is the largest donor (about 50 percent of food aid), followed by the EC (about 30 percent). Australia, Canada, and Japan contribute about 14 percent collectively.

The distribution, quantity, and nature of food aid sometimes bear little relation to dietary deficiency. For example, 20 percent of all cereal aid goes to Egypt, a middle-income country where the average calorie intake is about 28 percent more than needed for a healthy diet. By contrast, Togo—

a low-income and food-deficit country—receives only 6 percent per person of what Egypt does. Over the past decade, donor governments have tried to send more food aid to areas where dietary deficits are largest, and they have made some progress in this direction (see the bottom part of Table 7.4). Food aid is now generally directed toward poorer countries, but some countries that are not poor receive significant aid.

The quantity of food aid is more closely related to the needs of donors than to those of recipients. For example, U.S. legislation on food aid—Public Law 480—makes explicit mention of foreign policy considerations, surplus disposal, and the avoidance of conflict between commercial and concessional exports. Donors have found food aid a convenient way of disposing of surplus stocks, particularly of milk products. The level of food prices also affects the amount of food aid. In 1973–74, when food was in short supply and prices were high, wheat shipments were less than 4 million tons, compared with around 10 million tons a year in the late 1960s.

International food aid is only part of the answer to famine. To begin with, it does not solve the massive problems of internal food distribution. India's recent success in avoiding famine-related deaths has owed much to its ability to shift grains from regions with surplus food to those with deficits and to provide aid to the needy, either as food or in the form of an income supplement. By contrast, the recent relief operations in Ethiopia and Sudan have been dogged by transport and communications failures and other problems, which have hindered the flow of food to many of the worst affected areas. These and other problems of emergency food aid are discussed in Box 7.7.

Food aid is also provided to supplement domestic production in normal times. As a result, domestic prices may fall, discouraging local production and reducing farm profits. To minimize this effect, food aid can be directed to the very poor, who are less likely to use it as an alternative to local supplies. But, in practice, food aid has not been so directed in many cases. In 1982–83, for example,

Bangladesh received cereal food aid worth about $160 million at world prices. This was distributed through the general food subsidy scheme, which—like such schemes in many other countries—benefits both the poor and the relatively affluent groups.

Two ways exist by which food aid can in principle be prevented from deterring local production. First, countries could resell food on the world market and buy back only as much as is genuinely

---

Box 7.7 The challenges of emergency food aid

The distribution of free food would appear to be a straightforward solution to the immediate problem of starvation. But emergency food aid will be effective only if certain conditions are met.

The first requirement is information. Famines do not happen suddenly. Farmers in Africa, accustomed to erratic rainfall, have evolved traditional means of coping with food shortages, especially in the first year of drought. But in the second year, widespread shortages may become unmanageable, and international aid may become necessary. Given the long period between the first signs that the harvest may fail and the point at which a large number of people starve, the provision of information would not seem too difficult. In many instances, however, the governments of affected countries have been reluctant to release details of impending famine and have hindered international agencies (both official and private) that wanted to publicize the emergency. Logistical difficulties (for example, in Ethiopia in 1973–74 and 1983–84 and in Mozambique in 1983–84) and sometimes merely lack of attention (as in Mali and Chad in 1983–84) have made the collection of information difficult.

The second requirement is the prompt reaction of donor countries. In the Sahelian drought of the late 1960s and early 1970s, large-scale relief efforts did not start until 1973, five years after the drought and famine had begun. The FAO announced late in 1982 that Ethiopia would need large quantities of food aid the following year. However, large-scale relief efforts did not start until late 1984. One possible solution to such political difficulties is to grant multilateral agencies, especially the World Food Program, a more prominent role in emergency relief. Currently they handle only between 10 and 20 percent of total emergency aid.

It would be a mistake, however, to assume that a simple shipment of food would cure starvation. In many cases aid throws substantial burdens onto fragile storage and distribution systems. In Sudan only 64 percent of the food aid pledged was distributed in 1984–85, although 91 percent was delivered to the ports. In Ethiopia only three-quarters of the food delivered was actually distributed.

The problem of transport is especially serious for landlocked countries. Imports into Burkina Faso, Chad, Mali, Niger, Zambia, and Zimbabwe must be handled in the ports of neighboring countries. Reports of delays are numerous. Take the case of Mali, which can import food through Senegal, Côte d'Ivoire, or Togo. Transportation through Senegal is by rail, and capacity is limited. It is often difficult to obtain trucks for the trip through Côte d'Ivoire because Mali may not have a cargo to send back and because trucks are not always available, especially during the busy season from November to June when they are used to transport Côte d'Ivoire's export crops to the ports. The route from Togo passes through Niger, where, because of unpaved roads, the going is very slow, especially during the rainy season. Food could be transported through Nigeria, but Nigeria's ports are frequently congested.

Food can also be held up on the seas or at the dockside. Estimates of the damage caused by delays in shipping and off-loading in Somalia in 1985 vary from 10 to 30 percent of total food aid flows. If aid is delayed, it can actually hinder the recovery from famine. When food that had been promised in late 1984 arrived six months later in Sudan and Ethiopia, the rainy season had begun. Many of the roads were impassable, and so the food could not be distributed. But when the rain ended and the harvest was gathered, the food aid became not only less urgent but also potentially counterproductive, because it forced prices below even the seasonal low point. Kenya did not have enough storage capacity for its own record food crop of 1985, but food aid was still arriving in response to 1984's drought. As a result, the Kenyan Marketing Board (the monopoly maize buyer) may have to refuse to buy some maize, delay payments to farmers, and even export maize at a loss.

Early-warning systems, quicker donor response, and improved distribution systems are all needed to make emergency food aid more effective.

needed in extra demand. Second, they could reduce commercial imports by the amount of the food aid. Donors of aid typically set terms which prohibit both means, with the intent of ensuring that food aid does not reduce the commercial demand for their food. If this prohibition is effective, food supplies in the recipient country will rise proportionately more than incomes, making the disincentive effects particularly hard to avoid. However, these provisions are so little enforced that the disincentive effects may be slight in practice.

Since food aid cannot legally be converted into cash, much of it has to be distributed in kind. This saddles recipient governments with extra costs of administration, and often of transport as well. The food-for-work projects—by which food aid pays in kind for infrastructural development—are at times inefficient and poorly designed, and thus further reduce the real benefits of food aid. To promote net additions to demand for their surplus products, aid-granting exporters sometimes supply commodities that are not part of the recipients' normal diets. The resulting distortions of consumption patterns tend to increase the dependency of aid recipients on continued food aid. While such problems do not undermine the case for food aid, they do show how the limits on its use can sharply reduce its worth. There is growing awareness among donors about these limitations, as mentioned in Box 7.6.

8

National and international priorities in agriculture

The past several decades of development have demonstrated that growth in agricultural production and productivity in developing countries can match or surpass the growth in industrial countries. As discussed in Chapter 1, the record has shown that agriculture can be a dynamic sector in developing countries and contribute greatly to growth in real incomes, employment, and foreign exchange earnings and to the alleviation of poverty. Although there is still substantial room for improvement, the policies and investments increasingly being pursued by governments in many developing countries have given rise to guarded optimism about the long-term prospects of food production increasing faster than population. This optimism replaces the Malthusian pessimism that resurfaced in the wake of the unusual increases in food prices in the early 1970s. Given the sharp drop in commodity prices since then, there is now little basis for believing that a fundamental break has occurred in the long-term trend of declining real food prices.

Episodes of commodity booms and slumps are nothing new; nor are dearths and famines, which continue to occur periodically, albeit with much less frequency than in earlier times. Such episodes should not detract from the progress already made, nor should they prevent recognition of the fact that agricultural programs and policies in different parts of the world affect one another. The pricing and trade policies that industrial and developing countries follow will have a great effect on the pace of future growth in rural incomes and the alleviation of poverty and hunger. At stake is the well-being of the hundreds of millions of very poor people in the world who depend on agriculture for their livelihood.

This chapter begins with a review of the priori-

ties for developing countries with respect to pricing and trade policies. The recommended changes will benefit developing countries individually and collectively. But these gains—as well as the gains for industrial countries—will be much larger if significant progress is made in liberalizing trade. The liberalization option is reviewed in the final section.

Priorities in developing countries

Many developing countries have begun to reform their agricultural and trade policies. In some cases, particular programs, crops, or public institutions have been affected. In others, sweeping changes have been made in conjunction with broader reforms of the whole economy. No generalizations are possible about the specifics of desirable reforms since their nature, design, and timing are largely determined by country circumstances. At best, it is possible to indicate those areas that merit careful consideration as candidates for reform.

Reforms of specific sectoral policies in agriculture should not be divorced from reforms of economy-wide policies and development strategies that induce strong biases against agricultural production and exports. As was discussed in Chapter 4, many developing countries have discriminated against agriculture through high industrial protection and through inappropriate macroeconomic and exchange rate policies. The taxation of domestic producers that results implicitly from overvaluations of the exchange rate can easily dominate the effects of sector-specific taxes and subsidies. The linkage between sectoral and macroeconomic policies is usually so strong that it is best to carry out agricultural reforms in conjunction with reforms of general economic policies.

The most important priority in agriculture is to ensure that the profitability of farming is not artificially depressed because of either macroeconomic or sectoral policies. Yet, as seen in Chapter 4, both types of policies often create a strong bias against agriculture.

Export taxes and quotas—whether they are used to exploit monopoly powers in trade, to subsidize agroprocessing, to raise revenue, or to promote domestic production of competing crops—are commonplace and often excessive. They can greatly reduce the benefits that developing countries can attain through trade. In the case of imports, one would expect the goal of self-sufficiency to lead countries to support domestic producers. But state trading in domestic and foreign markets and the high costs of financing urban food subsidies can lead to domestic procurement prices that are lower than import prices—an indirect subsidy to imports that has been very high in some cases.

Some taxation of agriculture is, of course, unavoidable, if only because of the need for revenue. But there are many different forms of taxation. Taxation of export and import-competing crops is perhaps the worst of the available options in developing countries. The costs of such taxation—in terms of real national income forgone—have been extremely high. Greater reliance is desirable on land and income taxes or on sales and value added taxes that bear on consumption.

Apart from moderating the taxation of farm outputs, it is also important to examine the principal public spending programs that affect farm profitability. Many governments have introduced subsidies on modern inputs and credit because they are thought to provide compensation for the taxation of farm outputs. But, as Chapter 5 made clear, the benefits of such subsidies are typically confined to small and relatively wealthy sections of the rural population. Excess demand at subsidized prices leads to rationing, and the actual costs of inputs to farmers often exceed officially sanctioned prices. The main concern of farmers throughout the developing world is not so much the prices of these inputs but their easy and timely availability. Input subsidies, as well as inefficiencies in public distribution agencies, tend to restrict availability. Moreover, input subsidies encourage the wrong mix of inputs and misdirect technological change. Credit and machinery subsidies, for example, lower the demand for rural labor. Public spending can be significantly reduced by eliminating or curtailing input subsidy programs—and the savings can be used to lower the taxation of farm outputs.

Reforms of pricing and trade policies that affect farmers cannot be separated from institutional issues since, in practice, many of the problems arise from the widespread use of public sector marketing agencies, which charge excessive margins, implement their policies inefficiently, and often require large subsidies from the government. The objective of price stabilization that many agencies pursue typically leads to high costs, erratic policies, and the displacement of private operations in stabilization and risk management. This, again, is an area that requires a great deal of emphasis in policy reforms.

Maintaining low food prices for urban consumers is an important motivation for having pricing policies that discriminate against farmers. The benefits of urban food subsidy programs are generally distributed widely across income classes; they are usually inefficient instruments for helping the poorest people. Since they are often very costly and since the costs can suddenly increase because of world price movements, they almost always lead to suppression of producer prices, which reduces incomes in rural areas where most of the extreme poverty is often to be found.

Small and well-targeted food distribution programs are more effective in promoting specific nutritional objectives in especially disadvantaged groups. To mitigate the effects of higher food prices in general, it is clear that governments should pursue other policies that aim at increasing incomes and employment; only if incomes rise can chronic malnutrition be eliminated.

Governments provide many essential services and facilities that private markets cannot, such as irrigation, research, extension, rural roads, and education. These types of activities should account for the bulk of public spending on agriculture. At the same time, it must be emphasized that the rationalization of pricing and marketing policies along the lines described above is required if the full benefits of public spending are to be realized.

Balanced agricultural strategies in developing countries require not only public spending on essential agricultural services, but also a sound policy environment within which private markets can efficiently function. Providing both is the basic challenge that governments in developing countries face. Many of them have taken measures to improve the policy environment; others need to review their macroeconomic and sectoral policies to avoid intersectoral biases and expensive consumer and producer subsidy programs that serve neither growth nor other objectives. They should also examine their taxation systems in order to lower the economic cost of raising revenues. It is critically important for governments to reduce their role in marketing agricultural outputs and inputs and to eliminate monopoly privileges for marketing parastatals. This will allow a much greater role for the private sector and improve the efficiency of domestic and international marketing.

Trade liberalization

This Report has argued that the barriers to trade that complement domestic programs—especially in industrial countries—constitute a fundamental policy problem for the international community. This is not only because trade liberalization will help developing countries attain faster rates of economic growth, but also because the benefits to the industrial countries will be high as well.

No firm estimates are possible of the total gains in world income that would occur if trade in agricultural and agro-industrial products were liberalized. The estimates cited in Chapter 6 refer to selected sets of commodities only. They do not take into consideration the long-term gains for both industrial and developing countries that could be achieved by allocating investment funds and research activity in directions consistent with each country's comparative advantage; nor do they reflect the gains in manufacturing and agricultural trade that would result from faster growth of world income if trade were liberalized. The estimates are nonetheless significant because they suggest that the potential gains can be very large indeed and would, in the first instance, accrue mostly to countries with the highest levels of protection. While some developing countries may lose as a result of higher import bills for some commodities, the losses are likely to be more than offset by gains in exports of other commodities—especially if they and the industrial countries reform their domestic policies simultaneously.

Even though the estimates of the potential gains from free trade presented in Chapter 6 are conservative, the gains to industrial countries would be nearly double their official development assistance. The adage ''Trade is better than aid'' is clearly of great relevance to agriculture.

Less government intervention, especially by industrial countries, will also help to stabilize international prices and will assist both industrial and developing countries in attaining their common objective of stability in farm incomes and prices. International commodity agreements—discussed

in Chapter 7—are often costly and inefficient international responses to the problems caused by the variability of world prices. They frequently degenerate into efforts by producer groups to raise, rather than stabilize, prices. Compensatory arrangements such as the IMF's Compensatory Financing Facility are superior instruments for promoting stability in earnings or outlays. Chapter 7 also showed that protection in agriculture has not been mitigated by the Generalized System of Preferences or by regional schemes such as the EC's Lomé Convention and the U.S. Caribbean Basin Initiative. Examination of the expansion of trade that has resulted from such schemes indicates that the effects have been very limited, especially for the poorest countries. The preference schemes appear also to erode the interest of their beneficiaries in promoting general trade liberalization. A reduction in protection generally reduces the special benefits from preferences.

While full liberalization is unlikely, there is justification for moving forward now with partial and gradual liberalization. One approach to partial liberalization for agricultural products would be for each country to review how it could reduce protection of the most heavily protected products. A large part of the net losses caused by agricultural protection, as well as a large share of taxpayer and consumer costs, is concentrated upon a small number of products with substantially higher than average rates of protection. In the United States the farm products whose prices deviate most strikingly from what they ought to be are sugar, cotton, rice, wheat, and peanuts; in the EC the products are milk, beef, sugar, and cereals. Particular efforts should be made to lower the rates of protection for these products, and alternative means of providing income support to farmers should be used to ease the transition to lower levels of protection.

As is the case in developing countries, many governments in industrial countries are considering policy reforms. This is particularly so in Canada, the EC, Japan, and the United States, where farm programs currently involve very large costs for their citizens, both as consumers and as taxpayers. The United States has cut its milk support prices, and Japan has been gradually reducing its rice price support relative to its avowed objective, namely that of covering the full cost of production. Still, the U.S. Food Security Act of 1985, which keeps most producer price guarantees roughly at current levels through 1990, suggests that the necessary reforms have barely begun.

Without policy changes that reduce protection,

domestic costs will continue to rise in the years ahead, whatever means are chosen for handling growing excess supplies. There are three main problems:

• Adding to stocks, as the EC and the United States have done for cereals and dairy products, will become increasingly costly and eventually unsustainable as stocks grow larger in relation to annual domestic use or exhaust the available storage capacity.

• Restricting output through direct interventions, such as the milk quotas in the EC or acreage restriction programs in the United States, is unattractive, economically and politically. Compulsory measures are unpopular with producers. If the measures are voluntary, U.S. experience indicates that the budgetary and economic costs of obtaining even a modest reduction in output are great.

• Encouraging consumption domestically or abroad via subsidies will require even more budgetary outlays.

The main justification for agricultural protection is to improve the incomes of farm families, especially those under financial stress. But the benefits of protection go primarily to better-off farmers, while the burden of higher food prices is borne disproportionately by poorer consumers. Moreover, most of the benefits of the programs become capitalized into the price of the land at the time the programs are inaugurated. Farmers who buy land once the programs are in effect benefit little, if at all, from their continuation but, unfortunately, face substantial losses when agricultural protection is reduced or abandoned.

The GATT negotiations

Preparations are under way for negotiations on agricultural protection in a new round of GATT negotiations. There seems to be increasing recognition in Western Europe and North America that a continuation of recent trends in the growth of productive capacity and the very slow growth of domestic and international demand will inevitably lead to higher and higher costs of protection. Most OECD members will soon find it necessary to modify their domestic farm programs to reduce the costs that are incurred.

The analytical studies reviewed in this Report provide solid evidence about the costs of existing policies and the benefits that would be realized if the market interventions were reduced. The fact that the various studies come to similar conclusions should make it easier for governments to ac-

cept these results as an important component of the information base from which negotiations could start.

The forthcoming negotiations have to deal with extremely complex assessments of the effects of modifying domestic farm programs. Previous methods of estimating the reciprocal increases in exports and imports resulting from reductions in tariffs are quite inadequate to reflect the combined effects of modifications of domestic policies upon both imports into and exports from a given country. With the increased use of deficiency payments, direct export subsidies, and variable levies and other nontariff barriers, what becomes important is the effect of a change in programs on the net balance of trade. This can be difficult to gauge in light of the complexity and variety of interventions present. The participants in the GATT negotiations on agricultural products must be willing to negotiate about the various features of their domestic programs. This does not mean that any particular set of price and income support programs—such as the variable levies and export subsidies of the EC or the target prices and deficiency payment programs of the United States—have to be abandoned. What governments must be willing to negotiate about are the degrees of protection provided by their price and income support programs and the effects that the programs have upon production, consumption, exports and imports, and international market prices. In other words, there must be a willingness to negotiate about the effects particular domestic measures have upon the markets available to others.

The role of the World Bank

The development of food and agriculture has been an important objective of the World Bank since its inception. In the past decade, roughly 25 to 30 percent of the Bank's lending has been for agricultural and rural development. Irrigation, drainage, and water control projects have been the major focus, followed by area and rural development and credit (see Table 8.1). Because the Bank finances only a part of total project costs, the $33 billion lent by the Bank for agriculture since 1975 has helped finance total investments of about $87 billion.

The Bank's experience with agricultural lending has demonstrated that economic rates of return in the agricultural sector are comparable with those in other sectors. Agricultural credit, irrigation, research and extension, rural development, and many other projects have proved to be successful

Table 8.1 World Bank lending for agricultural and rural development, by purpose and period

Major purpose	1975–79 Amount (billions of dollars)	1975–79 Percent	1980–85 Amount (billions of dollars)	1980–85 Percent
Agricultural credit	1.64	14.2	3.71	17.5
Agricultural sector loan	0.17	1.4	1.32	6.2
Area development	2.92	25.2	4.34	20.4
Irrigation	3.72	32.1	6.49	30.6
Research and extension	0.59	5.1	0.92	4.3
Other (forestry)	2.54	21.9	4.44	20.9
Total agriculture	11.58	100.0	21.22	100.0
Total lending	38.02	—	81.17	—

means of raising agricultural productivity and the incomes of the rural poor. However, there also have been failures. Agricultural projects are vulnerable to many factors, one of the most important being the policy environment.

Traditionally, Bank-supported projects, besides financing investments, have addressed a range of policy issues that are specific to the performance of the project and the sector. These have included cost recovery, interest rates, reforms of institutions, and counterpart funding. It has become increasingly apparent, however, that broad issues of reform involving pricing and trade policies to facilitate structural change cannot be addressed or financed through project lending.

Since 1980 the Bank has been involved in developing and supporting programs of structural and sectoral adjustment. With structural adjustment loans (SALs), funds are disbursed in support of a program of broad policy reforms rather than for a specific investment. Agreement is reached between the borrowing government and the Bank on specific measures of reform, and progress is monitored to form the basis for the release of funds. Generally, SALs have supported changes in pricing, trade, and public sector policies, as well as changes in the extent of government controls on various productive activities. Because economic restructuring normally takes several years, SALs are designed to span five or more years and may involve up to five separate loans. Since 1980 the Bank has approved thirty-two SALs in eighteen countries, for a total of more than $4.6 billion.

Many of these SALs address agricultural issues through changes in macroeconomic policies and through agricultural trade, pricing, and institutional adjustments. In some countries, however, the Bank's support of government reforms has been sector-specific. Since 1979 there have been seventeen agricultural sector adjustment loans. The majority (thirteen) were approved after 1983. The size of the loans has ranged from $5 million for Malawi to $303 million for Brazil. Most of these sector adjustment loans have focused on prices paid and received by farmers, controls on financial markets, performance of parastatals, trade barriers, and the size and composition of public expenditures. In some instances—for example, in Ecuador, Turkey, and Yugoslavia—the agricultural sector adjustment loans have been coordinated with SALs or with adjustment loans in other sectors. Coordination is also maintained with other agricultural lending, since the success of such lending often depends on the existence of an appropriate policy framework.

SALs and sector adjustment lending have proved to be important instruments for supporting reform programs of an economy-wide and sectoral nature. Improving agricultural policies can be a prolonged process; typically, a sequence of loans is required, and in some cases both SALs and sector adjustment loans are involved. In countries where the adjustment process is well established, Bank assistance generally takes the form of sector adjustment loans that support in-depth restructuring of policies and programs.

Statistical appendix

The tables in this statistical appendix present data for a sample panel of developing countries, along with information available for industrial countries and high-income oil exporters. The tables show data on population, national accounts, trade, and external debt. Readers should refer to the technical notes to the World Development Indicators for definitions and concepts used in these tables.

Table A.1 Population growth, 1965–85 and projected to 2000

Country group	1985 population (millions)	Average annual growth (percent)				
		1965–73	1973–80	1980–85	1985–90	1990–2000
Developing countries	3,451	2.5	2.1	2.0	2.0	1.8
Low-income countries	2,305	2.6	2.0	1.9	1.8	1.7
Asia	2,071	2.5	1.9	1.8	1.7	1.5
India	765	2.3	2.3	2.2	2.0	1.7
China	1,041	2.7	1.5	1.2	1.3	1.2
Africa	234	2.8	2.9	3.0	3.2	3.1
Middle-income countries	1,146	2.5	2.4	2.3	2.3	2.0
Oil exporters	502	2.5	2.6	2.6	2.6	2.3
Oil importers	643	2.4	2.2	2.1	2.0	1.8
Major exporters of manufactures	420	2.4	2.1	1.9	1.8	1.6
High-income oil exporters	20	4.6	5.4	4.3	3.9	3.3
Industrial market economies	737	0.9	0.7	0.6	0.5	0.4
World, excluding nonmarket industrial economies	4,209	2.2	1.9	1.8	1.7	1.6
Nonmarket industrial economies	393	0.8	0.8	0.8	0.7	0.6

Table A.2 Population and GNP per capita, 1980, and growth rates, 1965–85

Country group	1980 GNP (billions of dollars)	1980 population (millions)	1980 GNP per capita (dollars)	Average annual growth of GNP per capita (percent)					
				1965–73	1973–80	1981	1982	1983	1984[a]	1985[b]
Developing countries	2,064	3,124	660	4.1	3.2	1.0	−0.7	0.0	3.3	2.4
Low-income countries	550	2,102	260	3.0	2.7	3.0	3.2	6.1	7.4	6.1
Asia	497	1,900	260	3.3	3.0	3.5	3.7	6.9	8.3	6.6
China	287	978	290	5.0	3.8	3.5	6.1	8.8	12.8	9.6
India	162	687	240	1.6	1.8	3.5	0.5	5.1	2.2	1.9
Africa	53	202	260	1.2	0.1	−1.3	−2.4	−2.7	−2.8	−0.4
Middle-income oil importers	963	580	1,660	4.6	3.1	−0.8	−2.0	−1.6	1.8	1.0
East Asia and Pacific	212	162	1,310	5.7	5.7	3.9	1.8	4.7	4.7	1.0
Middle East and North Africa	25	31	820	3.5	4.2	−1.9	4.4	0.3	−0.9	1.6
Sub-Saharan Africa[c]	26	33	780	2.0	0.5	3.8	−5.0	−5.5	−4.5	−0.6
Southern Europe	213	91	2,340	5.4	2.9	0.2	0.0	−0.9	0.9	1.1
Latin America and Caribbean	411	234	1,760	4.5	2.9	−4.2	−4.9	−4.5	1.2	2.1
Middle-income oil exporters	551	441	1,250	4.6	3.4	1.5	−2.8	−4.4	0.7	0.0
High-income oil exporters	226	17	13,290	4.1	5.9	0.7	−7.6	−15.7	−3.0	−8.5
Industrial market economies	7,540	716	10,530	3.7	2.1	1.1	−1.3	1.6	3.9	2.4

a. Estimated.   b. Projected on the basis of GDP.   c. Excludes South Africa.

Table A.3 GDP, 1980, and growth rates, 1965–85

Country group	1980 GDP (billions of dollars)	Average annual growth of GDP (percent)						
		1965–73	1973–80	1981	1982	1983	1984[a]	1985[b]
Developing countries	2,094	6.6	5.4	3.5	2.0	2.0	5.4	4.3
Low-income countries	549	5.6	4.7	5.0	5.3	7.8	9.4	7.8
Asia	495	5.9	5.0	5.4	5.7	8.6	10.2	8.3
China	287	7.8	5.8	4.9	7.7	9.6	14.0	10.6
India	162	4.0	4.1	5.8	2.8	7.7	4.5	4.0
Africa	53	3.9	2.7	1.6	0.8	0.3	0.7	2.1
Middle-income oil importers	979	7.0	5.5	2.1	0.8	0.8	4.1	3.0
East Asia and Pacific	214	8.6	8.1	6.5	3.9	6.4	6.4	2.7
Middle East and North Africa	24	5.6	7.1	1.0	7.8	2.9	1.9	4.1
Sub-Saharan Africa[c]	27	5.1	3.6	6.9	−1.0	−1.4	−1.1	2.9
Southern Europe	212	7.0	4.8	2.0	2.1	0.9	2.7	2.5
Latin America and Caribbean	422	7.1	5.4	−1.0	−1.5	−1.7	3.7	4.1
Middle-income oil exporters	566	7.1	5.8	4.4	1.0	−1.9	3.1	2.5
High-income oil exporters	225	9.2	7.7	1.6	−1.7	−7.1	1.3	−5.0
Industrial market economies	7,440	4.7	2.8	1.9	−0.6	2.3	4.6	2.8

a. Estimated.   b. Projected.   c. Excludes South Africa.

Table A.4 Population and composition of GDP, selected years, 1965–85

(billions of dollars, unless otherwise specified)

Country group and indicator	1965	1973	1980	1981	1982	1983	1984[a]	1985[b]
Developing countries								
GDP	327	740	2,094	2,216	2,141	2,048	2,089	2,219
Domestic absorption[c]	331	747	2,141	2,288	2,198	2,066	2,083	2,223
Net exports[d]	−4	−7	−47	−72	−57	−18	5	−4
Population (millions)	2,207	2,691	3,124	3,187	3,255	3,319	3,386	3,451
Low-income countries								
GDP	141	252	549	541	539	571	571	627
Domestic absorption[c]	143	253	569	557	551	584	584	654
Net exports[d]	−2	−1	−20	−16	−12	−13	−13	−27
Population (millions)	1,493	1,827	2,102	2,141	2,185	2,225	2,265	2,305
Middle-income oil importers								
GDP	128	333	978	1,034	1,027	942	946	993
Domestic absorption[c]	130	340	1,018	1,079	1,059	953	948	986
Net exports[d]	−2	−7	−40	−45	−32	−11	−2	8
Population (millions)	412	497	580	593	605	618	631	643
Middle-income oil exporters								
GDP	58	155	566	641	576	535	571	598
Domestic absorption[c]	58	153	553	652	587	528	551	583
Net exports[d]	0	2	13	−11	−11	7	20	15
Population (millions)	301	369	441	453	465	477	489	502
High-income oil exporters								
GDP	7	28	225	264	257	222	211	..
Domestic absorption[c]	5	16	144	171	191	..	..	..
Net exports[d]	2	12	81	93	66	..	..	..
Population (millions)	8	11	17	17	18	19	20	20
Industrial market economies								
GDP	1,369	3,240	7,502	7,600	7,505	7,760	8,099	8,475
Domestic absorption[c]	1,364	3,231	7,562	7,612	7,504	7,757	8,124	8,505
Net exports[d]	6	9	−60	−12	1	3	−25	−30
Population (millions)	632	681	716	721	725	730	734	737

a. Estimated.   b. Projected.   c. Private consumption plus government consumption plus gross domestic investment.
d. Includes goods and nonfactor services.

Table A.5 GDP structure of production, selected years, 1965–84
(percent of GDP)

Country group	1965 Agriculture	1965 Industry	1973 Agriculture	1973 Industry	1980 Agriculture	1980 Industry	1981 Agriculture	1981 Industry	1982 Agriculture	1982 Industry	1983 Agriculture	1983 Industry	1984 Agriculture	1984 Industry
Developing countries	31	29	26	33	20	38	19	37	19	36	20	36	21	37
Low-income countries	44	27	40	33	36	36	36	34	36	34	37	34	36	35
Asia	42	28	39	34	35	38	35	36	36	35	36	35	36	36
India	47	22	50	20	37	25	35	26	33	26	36	26	35	27
China	39	38	33	44	33	48	35	46	37	45	36	45	36	44
Africa	47	15	42	19	41	18	41	17	43	17	43	15	38	16
Middle-income countries	22	31	17	35	14	39	14	38	14	37	14	37	14	39
Oil exporters	22	26	18	33	14	42	13	40	14	40	15	40	15	39
Oil importers	21	33	17	35	14	37	14	36	13	36	13	36	14	37
Major exporters of manufactures	20	35	15	37	12	39	12	38	12	38	12	38	12	38
High-income oil exporters	5	65	2	72	1	77	1	76	1	74	2	64	2	62
Industrial market economies	5	40	5	39	4	38	3	37	3	36	3	35	3	37
World, excluding nonmarket industrial economies	10	38	9	38	7	39	7	38	7	37	7	36	10	38

Table A.6 Sector growth rates, 1965–84

Country group	Agriculture 1965–73	Agriculture 1973–80	Agriculture 1980–84	Industry 1965–73	Industry 1973–80	Industry 1980–84	Service 1965–73	Service 1973–80	Service 1980–84
Developing countries	3.2	2.7	3.9	8.5	6.0	2.2	7.4	6.4	2.9
Low-income countries	3.0	2.5	6.2	8.7	7.3	7.7	6.8	4.8	6.4
Asia	3.1	2.6	6.5	8.8	7.6	8.0	7.3	4.9	7.7
India	3.7	2.0	2.8	3.7	5.0	4.2	4.5	5.7	8.0
China	2.8	2.8	10.1	12.1	8.6	9.3	11.7	3.4	6.2
Africa	2.2	2.2	1.1	8.1	1.3	−1.2	4.3	4.0	1.4
Middle-income countries	3.4	2.9	1.7	8.4	5.6	0.3	7.5	6.6	2.4
Oil exporters	3.9	2.0	2.2	8.3	5.2	−2.3	7.4	7.9	4.9
Oil importers	3.1	3.3	1.4	8.5	5.9	1.8	7.5	6.0	1.6
Major exporters of manufactures	3.0	3.2	1.6	9.2	6.4	2.1	8.1	6.2	3.8
High-income oil exporters	..	..	2.0	..	2.9	−16.4	..	..	27.4
Industrial market economies	1.7	0.9	0.4	5.1	2.3	1.0	4.6	3.3	2.4

Table A.7 Consumption, savings, and investment indicators, selected years, 1965–84
(percent of GDP)

Country group and indicator	1965	1973	1980	1981	1982	1983	1984[a]
Developing countries							
Consumption	79.8	76.7	75.6	77.2	78.1	78.0	76.9
Investment	21.1	24.1	26.7	26.0	24.6	22.9	22.3
Savings	20.2	23.3	24.4	22.8	21.9	22.0	23.1
Low-income Asia							
Consumption	79.8	75.4	75.8	76.8	75.8	75.5	75.7
Investment	21.3	24.8	27.2	25.4	25.7	26.1	26.5
Savings	20.2	24.6	24.2	23.2	24.2	24.5	24.3
Low-income Africa							
Consumption	88.6	85.7	91.0	91.6	93.1	92.8	95.7
Investment	14.2	17.0	19.2	18.5	16.9	15.3	11.8
Savings	11.4	14.3	9.0	8.4	6.9	7.2	4.3
Middle-income oil importers							
Consumption	79.1	77.0	77.2	78.5	79.4	79.7	78.3
Investment	22.0	24.9	26.9	25.9	23.8	21.7	20.5
Savings	20.9	23.0	22.8	21.5	20.6	20.3	21.7
Middle-income oil exporters							
Consumption	79.9	76.8	71.0	74.0	76.4	76.0	75.3
Investment	19.8	22.3	26.7	27.6	25.4	22.8	21.6
Savings	20.1	23.2	29.0	26.0	23.6	24.0	24.7
Industrial market economies							
Consumption	76.7	75.0	78.4	78.4	80.1	80.3	81.1
Investment	22.9	24.7	22.5	21.9	20.1	19.6	19.6
Savings	23.3	25.0	21.6	21.6	19.9	19.7	18.9

a. Estimated.

Table A.8 Growth of exports, 1965–85

Country group and commodity	Average annual change in export volume (percent)						
	1965–73	*1973–80*	*1981*	*1982*	*1983*	*1984*[a]	*1985*[b]
Export volume, by commodity							
Developing countries							
Manufactures	11.6	13.8	8.6	0.1	10.0	16.6	3.3
Food	3.3	3.9	9.7	−2.3	−1.1	7.6	3.9
Nonfood	3.1	1.1	2.5	−1.6	1.5	1.0	4.5
Metals and minerals	4.8	7.0	−2.6	−2.8	0.5	3.4	4.8
Fuels	4.0	−0.8	−9.2	0.6	2.3	7.1	−1.4
World, excluding nonmarket							
industrial economies							
Manufactures	10.2	5.9	4.2	−2.4	4.8	11.1	4.2
Food	4.7	5.9	8.7	1.6	−0.1	7.8	−3.2
Nonfood	3.4	4.0	3.7	−2.0	−1.1	5.4	0.7
Metals and minerals	6.9	8.5	−14.0	−6.4	4.6	4.9	2.8
Fuels	9.1	−0.8	−12.1	−6.8	−2.4	2.1	0.6
Export volume, by country group							
Developing countries	5.0	4.6	2.1	−0.5	4.7	10.7	2.3
Manufactures	11.6	13.8	8.6	0.1	10.0	16.6	3.3
Primary goods	3.8	1.1	−2.0	−0.9	1.0	6.2	1.5
Low-income countries	1.9	5.4	5.9	3.1	5.8	6.3	3.5
Manufactures	2.3	8.3	11.0	2.8	10.7	9.2	2.7
Primary goods	1.6	3.6	2.4	3.3	2.1	4.0	4.1
Asia	0.6	6.8	9.1	6.3	7.2	6.6	3.8
Manufactures	2.0	8.7	12.6	3.1	11.0	9.4	2.6
Primary goods	−0.6	5.2	5.4	9.9	3.2	3.5	5.1
Africa	4.6	1.3	−4.5	−9.3	−0.2	4.9	2.0
Manufactures	5.4	2.0	−20.1	−5.4	2.8	3.1	6.7
Primary goods	4.5	1.2	−3.1	−9.6	−0.4	5.0	1.7
Middle-income oil importers	7.1	9.0	7.4	−0.4	5.0	12.8	3.7
Manufactures	15.5	15.3	7.9	−0.4	8.6	17.0	3.2
Primary goods	3.8	3.3	6.8	−0.4	−0.1	6.0	4.6
Major manufacturing exporters	9.2	10.6	8.1	−1.2	6.6	13.1	3.2
Manufactures	15.6	15.9	7.5	−1.3	8.9	16.4	2.7
Primary goods	5.5	3.8	9.5	−1.1	2.0	5.9	4.5
Other middle-income oil importers	2.4	3.5	4.3	3.7	−2.1	11.5	6.0
Manufactures	14.8	9.1	14.4	12.6	4.7	25.7	8.7
Primary goods	1.2	2.4	1.6	1.1	−4.4	6.3	4.8
Middle-income oil exporters	4.3	0.0	−7.2	−1.9	3.6	8.6	−0.8
Manufactures	10.7	8.0	13.7	1.9	27.2	25.2	5.1
Primary goods	4.2	−0.4	−8.6	−2.2	1.6	6.8	−1.5
High-income oil exporters	12.7	0.0	−10.6	−25.0	−16.6	−0.5	−4.3
Industrial market economies	9.2	5.5	2.4	−1.6	3.2	9.1	4.0
World, excluding nonmarket							
industrial economies	8.8	3.9	0.1	−3.0	2.6	8.6	2.5

a. Estimated.
b. Projected.

Table A.9 Change in export prices and in terms of trade, 1965–85

(average annual percentage change)

Country group	1965–73	1973–80	1981	1982	1983	1984[a]	1985[b]
Change in export prices							
Developing countries	6.3	14.2	0.6	−4.7	−3.7	−1.2	−2.2
Manufactures	7.2	8.1	0.2	−3.2	−2.5	−1.9	1.3
Food	5.0	9.6	−8.2	−8.8	5.6	2.0	−8.1
Nonfood	4.2	10.5	−14.4	−8.6	5.7	−2.0	−10.0
Metals and minerals	2.4	4.8	−7.6	−8.5	−0.1	−1.7	−4.9
Fuels	7.9	27.2	12.5	−3.2	−12.4	−2.1	−2.5
High-income oil exporters	7.7	25.9	14.0	−0.9	−14.2	−2.1	−4.5
Industrial countries							
Total	4.9	10.9	−4.0	−4.2	−3.3	−3.4	0.0
Manufactures	4.7	10.6	−6.0	−2.1	−4.3	−3.4	1.3
Change in terms of trade							
Developing countries	0.8	1.5	−1.0	−0.1	−1.3	0.4	−1.1
Low-income countries	2.3	−2.3	−1.7	1.2	0.0	2.1	−2.4
Asia	3.2	−2.4	1.1	1.2	−1.2	1.5	−1.9
Africa	0.1	−1.8	−11.8	−0.9	4.8	5.0	−5.6
Middle-income oil importers	0.0	−3.0	−4.4	−0.6	2.3	0.1	−0.1
Middle-income oil exporters	−0.4	8.5	5.4	0.2	−7.7	0.3	−2.9
High-income oil exporters	2.1	13.2	19.9	1.9	−11.0	0.7	−4.2
Industrial countries	0.3	−1.6	−1.0	2.0	1.0	−1.0	2.0

a. Estimated.   b. Projected.

Table A.10 Growth of long-term debt of developing countries, 1970–85

(average annual percentage change)

Country group	1970–73	1973–80	1981	1982	1983	1984[a]	1985[a,b]
Developing countries							
Debt outstanding and disbursed	18.4	21.0	14.1	12.2	14.0	7.0	5.6
Official	15.6	17.3	10.5	10.8	10.3	8.2	9.0
Private	20.9	23.6	16.2	12.9	16.0	6.4	3.8
Low-income countries							
Debt outstanding and disbursed	13.2	16.3	6.5	9.3	8.6	4.6	11.0
Official	12.8	14.5	8.2	10.7	10.1	4.4	8.1
Private	16.0	25.4	0.2	3.8	2.7	5.6	23.2
Asia							
Debt outstanding and disbursed	11.3	13.5	4.4	10.7	9.4	7.3	12.8
Official	11.8	11.4	6.2	10.3	8.0	5.0	11.1
Private	4.1	33.6	−4.5	13.0	16.4	18.0	19.8
Africa							
Debt outstanding and disbursed	20.0	23.2	10.2	6.9	7.2	−0.1	7.5
Official	17.8	24.9	12.5	11.7	14.1	3.4	2.4
Private	24.2	19.9	5.1	−4.9	−12.6	−13.0	30.2
Middle-income oil importers							
Debt outstanding and disbursed	19.5	21.0	15.6	12.9	11.4	7.5	7.4
Official	17.8	18.2	13.4	11.7	12.7	11.2	10.1
Private	20.5	22.3	16.6	13.4	10.9	6.0	6.2
Major exporters of manufactures							
Debt outstanding and disbursed	22.3	20.8	15.7	12.7	12.1	7.7	7.7
Official	21.0	18.1	12.3	9.9	11.3	13.4	9.8
Private	22.7	21.7	16.6	13.5	12.3	6.2	7.1
Other middle-income oil importers							
Debt outstanding and disbursed	13.5	21.4	15.5	13.3	9.9	7.1	6.5
Official	14.6	18.4	14.6	13.6	14.2	8.9	10.5
Private	12.1	25.0	16.4	13.0	6.0	5.3	2.4
Middle-income oil exporters							
Debt outstanding and disbursed	20.1	23.6	14.8	12.1	20.8	7.0	0.8
Official	16.2	19.6	8.1	9.5	6.2	6.9	7.9
Private	22.7	25.8	17.8	13.1	26.5	7.1	−1.5

a. The increase in debt outstanding and disbursed and the shift from private to official sources are due in part to the impact of rescheduling.
b. Estimated.

Table A.11 Savings, investment, and the current account balance, 1965–84
(percent)

Country	Gross domestic investment/GNP			Gross national savings/GNP			Current account balance/GNP[a]		
	1965–72	1973–78	1979–84	1965–72	1973–78	1979–84	1965–72	1973–78	1979–84
Latin America and Caribbean									
*Argentina	20.4	24.6	19.3	20.3	26.2	16.7	−0.1	1.6	−2.6
Bolivia	17.5	21.1	13.6	12.9	16.4	3.4	−4.6	−4.7	−10.2
*Brazil	25.8	28.1	21.1	24.0	24.0	16.9	−0.8	−4.1	−4.2
*Chile	15.3	15.3	16.9	13.0	11.9	6.7	−2.3	−3.4	−10.2
Colombia	19.0	18.8	20.0	15.4	19.1	15.3	−3.6	−0.3	−4.7
Costa Rica	21.2	24.5	25.3	11.9	13.7	10.6	−9.3	−10.8	−14.7
Ecuador	18.6	26.4	23.9	11.3	20.4	19.6	−7.3	−6.0	−4.3
Guatemala	13.2	19.3	14.6	10.2	14.8	9.8	−3.0	−4.5	−4.8
Jamaica	32.2	21.0	21.9	22.3	13.2	6.1	−9.9	−7.8	−15.8
*Mexico	21.3	23.4	25.9	19.2	20.2	24.0	−2.1	−3.2	−1.9
Peru	17.3	18.0	16.8	15.9	10.5	12.9	−1.4	−7.5	−3.9
Uruguay	11.9	14.4	15.0	11.8	10.6	10.1	−0.1	−3.8	−4.9
*Venezuela	29.3	35.4	22.4	29.8	36.1	26.4	0.5	0.7	4.0
Africa									
Cameroon	15.9	22.0	25.7	11.9	18.8	24.7	−4.0	−3.2	−1.0
Côte d'Ivoire	21.3	26.8	25.9	15.6	24.8	12.5	−5.7	−2.0	−13.4
Ethiopia	13.1	9.5	10.6	10.7	7.6	3.1	−2.4	−1.9	−7.5
Ghana	12.4	10.0	5.0	8.8	9.1	4.2	−4.3	−0.9	−0.8
Kenya	21.7	25.4	25.2	17.0	17.3	15.3	−4.7	−8.1	−9.9
Liberia	24.7	33.9	26.2	23.6	16.7	9.0	−1.1	−17.2	−17.2
Malawi	19.6	29.8	24.4	4.6	17.9	11.2	−15.0	−11.9	−13.2
Niger	15.9	29.3	29.5	6.5	12.3	13.0	−9.4	−17.1	−16.5
Nigeria	20.0	28.0	21.9	15.2	28.8	19.8	−4.8	0.8	−2.1
Senegal	13.7	18.6	17.1	6.8	7.4	−2.7	−6.9	−11.2	−19.8
Sierra Leone	14.0	13.2	12.3	8.0	3.1	0.0	−6.0	−10.1	−12.3
Sudan	11.9	17.3	15.7	11.0	9.1	0.4	−0.9	−8.2	−15.3
Tanzania	19.7	20.5	21.2	17.5	11.3	9.3	−2.2	−9.2	−11.9
Zaire	27.7	29.8	23.4	20.9	9.9	19.0	−6.8	−19.9	−4.4
Zambia	31.9	31.4	18.4	39.1	27.0	8.1	7.2	−4.4	−10.3
South Asia									
*India	18.3	21.7	24.6	13.4	19.2	21.6	4.9	2.5	−3.0
Pakistan	16.3	15.9	15.8	10.2	10.0	12.1	−6.1	−5.9	−3.7
Sri Lanka	16.1	16.2	29.2	11.3	11.9	12.5	−4.8	−4.3	−16.7
East Asia									
*Indonesia	12.6	20.6	22.8	6.9	18.8	34.2	−5.7	−1.8	11.4
*Korea	24.1	29.0	30.0	15.3	24.6	27.8	−8.8	−4.4	−2.2
Malaysia	19.8	25.3	33.6	20.8	26.7	26.8	1.0	1.5	−6.8
Papua New Guinea	31.0	20.1	29.0	1.8	16.7	10.2	−29.2	−3.4	−18.8
Philippines	20.7	28.0	28.0	18.5	23.5	21.9	−2.2	−4.5	−6.1
Thailand	23.8	25.4	24.9	21.1	21.3	18.3	−2.7	−4.1	−6.6
Europe and North Africa									
Algeria	30.2	48.3	39.7	25.8	39.0	38.0	−4.4	−9.3	−1.7
*Egypt	14.1	26.1	28.3	8.8	17.4	16.6	−5.3	−8.7	−11.7
Morocco	14.5	24.9	22.3	12.5	16.5	12.2	−2.0	−8.4	−10.1
Portugal	25.9	28.2	33.3	21.5	14.7	13.5	−4.4	−13.5	−19.8
Tunisia	23.7	28.8	30.7	16.1	21.5	22.7	−7.6	−7.3	−8.0
*Turkey	18.0	21.9	20.3	17.1	17.9	16.1	−0.9	−4.0	−4.2
*Yugoslavia	30.2	33.1	35.2	27.6	27.3	30.0	−2.6	−5.8	−5.2

Note: Asterisk indicates a major borrower.
a. Excluding net unrequited transfers.

Table A.12 Composition of debt outstanding, 1970–84
(percent of total debt)

Country	Debt from official sources			Debt from private sources			Debt at floating rates[a]		
	1970–72	1980–82	1984	1970–72	1980–82	1984	1973–75	1980–82	1984
Latin America and Caribbean									
*Argentina	12.6	8.8	9.2	87.4	91.2	90.8	13.9	53.7	37.5
Bolivia	58.7	52.6	65.3	41.3	47.4	34.7	7.5	35.7	29.0
*Brazil	29.7	11.8	13.8	70.3	88.2	86.2	43.5	66.0	79.1
*Chile	47.2	10.5	8.8	52.8	89.5	91.2	9.6	58.1	81.2
Colombia	68.0	45.3	43.1	32.0	54.7	56.9	6.2	39.4	42.7
Costa Rica	39.9	37.6	39.8	60.1	62.4	60.2	24.6	50.2	56.9
Ecuador	51.1	31.0	27.9	48.9	69.0	72.1	12.7	50.9	71.5
Guatemala	47.6	71.9	72.9	52.4	28.1	27.1	5.2	8.6	20.3
Jamaica	7.4	66.3	76.0	92.6	33.7	24.0	35.7	22.6	21.9
*Mexico	19.5	11.1	8.8	80.5	88.9	91.2	46.9	74.3	83.0
Peru	15.7	40.3	38.4	84.3	59.7	61.6	31.0	28.2	40.6
Uruguay	48.7	20.8	15.3	51.3	79.2	84.7	11.6	33.5	66.4
*Venezuela	28.5	2.4	0.7	71.5	97.6	99.3	20.6	81.4	93.8
Africa									
Cameroon	81.6	57.0	58.2	18.4	43.0	41.8	2.0	12.3	5.7
Côte d'Ivoire	51.3	23.3	32.1	48.7	76.7	67.9	20.5	43.5	51.3
Ethiopia	87.8	92.4	86.9	12.2	7.6	13.1	1.5	2.1	7.7
Ghana	57.3	82.5	88.7	42.7	17.5	11.3	0.0	0.0	0.0
Kenya	58.4	52.6	70.2	41.6	47.4	29.8	3.3	11.8	6.6
Liberia	80.3	74.7	78.7	19.7	25.3	21.3	0.0	15.9	16.7
Malawi	77.5	67.8	82.5	22.5	32.2	17.5	2.3	21.2	12.8
Niger	96.5	42.4	62.1	3.5	57.6	37.9	0.0	20.2	16.1
Nigeria	70.2	15.1	17.2	29.8	84.9	82.8	0.7	65.8	56.0
Senegal	59.0	70.7	86.8	41.0	29.3	13.2	26.0	8.8	7.4
Sierra Leone	61.0	70.3	73.9	39.0	29.7	26.1	3.8	0.1	0.6
Sudan	86.3	74.4	83.3	13.7	25.6	16.7	2.2	10.2	2.9
Tanzania	63.6	76.6	80.3	36.4	23.4	19.7	0.4	0.6	0.4
Zaire	24.5	65.7	82.4	75.5	34.3	17.6	32.8	11.8	8.8
Zambia	22.0	70.6	76.7	78.0	29.4	23.3	22.6	10.0	17.4
South Asia									
*India	95.2	91.5	79.6	4.8	8.5	20.4	0.0	3.1	7.9
Pakistan	90.9	92.4	90.7	9.1	7.6	9.3	0.0	3.1	6.8
Sri Lanka	81.8	79.6	72.8	18.2	20.4	27.2	0.0	11.9	14.7
East Asia									
*Indonesia	71.5	51.7	48.1	28.5	48.3	51.9	10.2	18.2	23.6
*Korea	37.8	35.3	32.3	62.2	64.7	67.7	15.6	35.2	46.8
Malaysia	49.1	21.6	16.4	50.9	78.4	83.6	23.0	47.3	61.6
Papua New Guinea	7.2	23.9	20.8	92.8	76.1	79.2	0.0	37.4	46.3
Philippines	21.4	32.4	37.8	78.6	67.6	62.2	18.8	39.5	41.0
Thailand	40.1	40.1	43.6	59.9	59.9	56.4	0.9	30.7	29.4
Europe and North Africa									
Algeria	45.0	16.7	21.2	55.0	83.3	78.8	34.0	24.2	26.4
*Egypt	66.0	82.2	80.8	34.0	17.8	19.2	3.1	3.2	1.7
Morocco	79.2	52.0	62.7	20.8	48.0	37.3	2.7	31.9	31.4
Portugal	39.1	25.7	24.6	60.9	74.3	75.4	0.0	23.5	31.5
Tunisia	72.4	62.4	69.2	27.6	37.6	30.8	0.0	14.1	15.5
*Turkey	92.1	65.7	68.0	7.9	34.3	32.0	0.8	22.7	28.5
*Yugoslavia	37.3	24.1	25.7	62.7	75.9	74.3	7.6	31.8	56.0

Note: Asterisk indicates a major borrower.
a. Percent of public debt.

Bibliographical note

This Report has drawn on a wide range of World Bank reports, as well as on numerous outside sources. World Bank sources include ongoing economic analysis and research, as well as project and sector work on individual countries. Outside sources include research publications and reports, published and unpublished, of other organizations working on global economic and development issues. The principal sources used in each chapter are briefly noted below. These and other sources are then listed alphabetically by author or organization in two groups: background papers and notes commissioned for this Report and a selected bibliography. The background papers, some of which will be made available through future publications, synthesize relevant literature and Bank work. The views they express are not necessarily those of the World Bank or this Report.

In addition to the sources listed, many persons in and outside the World Bank helped prepare this Report by writing informal notes or by providing extensive comments. Among these were Paul Armington (Box 3.4), Bela Balassa (Chapters 2–4), Elliot Berg (Chapters 4 and 5), Dipak Dasgupta (Box 5.9), Isabel Guerrero (Box 2.3), Ralph Hanan (Box 4.8), D. Gale Johnson (Chapters 1 and 4–8), John Joyce (Box 5.6), Ulrich Koester (Chapters 6 and 7), Ernesto May (Chapter 4), Yair Mundlak (Chapter 4), John Nash (Chapter 5), Shlomo Reutlinger (Chapter 5), Jayasankar Shivakumar (Box 5.10), G. Edward Schuh (Chapters 1–8), Lyn Squire (Chapter 4), and Vinod Thomas (Box 4.1). However, none of the above is responsible for the views expressed in the Report.

Chapter 1

Primary data sources for this chapter are FAO publications and World Bank files. Two key references on nominal protection coefficients are Scandizzo and Bruce 1980 and Binswanger and Scandizzo 1983. On the pattern of protection and the efficiency of world agriculture, a comparable thesis is in Johnson 1973. Box 1.2 is based on Smith 1776, Sen 1981, and Sen 1986. Box 1.3 is based on a contribution from Johnson; see also Anderson 1983, Anderson, Hayami, and Honma 1986, Johnson 1985a, and Johnson 1985b.

Chapters 2 and 3

Data used in these chapters were obtained from GATT, IMF, OECD, and UNCTAD publications as well as World Bank sources. The discussion of developing-country debt relies on published World Bank reports—in particular, World Bank 1986a and 1986c. The discussion of real exchange rates in Chapter 2 relies on the background papers by Cavallo, Cottani, and Khan; and Harberger. The discussion in Chapter 3 of macroeconomic policies for growth in developing countries is based on the background papers by Balassa and Buiter. Boxes 2.2, 2.4, and 3.2 draw on papers by Kalantzopoulos, Harberger, and Fleisig, respectively.

Chapters 4 and 5

These chapters draw heavily on the World Bank's operational experience, country and sector economic work, and various contributions from the Bank's operational staff. In Chapter 4, the principal sources for the discussion of exchange rates and agriculture were the background papers by Balassa, Cavallo, Harberger, and Kerr; on supply responses, the sources were the paper by Mundlak, Mundlak 1979, and Cavallo and Mundlak 1982; on the linkages between agriculture and industry, the sources were Hazell and Roell 1983 and Rangarajan 1982. The taxation analysis and Box 4.10 are partially based on the paper by Squire. For a discussion of how this analysis relates to public spending policies, see Ray 1984 (pp. 86, 92–99). Box 4.4 is based on the papers by Pinto and Pearson and Dorosch, Box 4.5 on the papers by Ellis and Raswant, and Box 4.9 on the paper by Ueno.

The section on marketing and price stabilization in Chapter 5 draws on the papers by Jones, Knudsen and Nash, and Lewis as well as on Bates 1981 and Bauer 1954. The section on producer support policies is primarily based on the background papers by Berg, Vogel, and Virmani as well as on Binswanger 1984, Hanson and Neal 1985, Virmani 1982, and Virmani 1985. The discussion of the reforms in China is based on the paper by Lardy. Box 5.2 draws on Krishna and Chhibber 1983, and Box 5.6 on Mathew 1984.

Chapters 6 and 7

The estimates of nominal rates of protection and nontariff barriers use World Bank data and the Tyers and Anderson background paper on distortions in world food markets. The discussion of policies in the OECD countries is based largely on background papers by Gardner, Johnson, and Koester and Tangermann and on the following publications: Bale and Lutz 1981, Barichello 1986, Buckwell and others 1982, Harling 1983, Hayami and Honma 1983, Josling 1980, and Schuh 1974. The simulation of the results of trade liberalization draws primarily on the background paper by Tyers and Anderson and on Valdes and Zietz 1980. The discussion of price stability under trade liberalization is based on Johnson and Sumner 1976 and Schiff 1983. Box 6.6 is based on Phipps 1985 and Traill 1980. In Chapter 7, the section on international commodity agreements and Box 7.1 are based on the background papers by Gardner and MacBean and Nguyen as well as on Gilbert 1984 and UNCTAD sources. The section on compensatory finance is based on material from the IMF and on the paper by Koester and Herrmann. The principal source for the discussion of the EC's trade preferences and for Boxes 7.3 and 7.4 is again the paper by Koester and Herrmann. The paper by Johnson covers other types of preference schemes.

Background papers

Anderson, Kym, and Rodney Tyers. "China's Economic Growth and Re-entry into World Markets: Implications for Agricultural Trade."

Balassa, Bela. "Economic Incentives and Agricultural Exports in Developing Countries."

———. "Incentive Policies and Agricultural Performance in Sub-Saharan Africa."

Berg, Elliot. "Economic Issues in Fertilizer Subsidies in Developing Countries."

Bertrand, Trent. "Agricultural Taxation and Subsidy Policies in the Agricultural Sector in Sri Lanka."

———. "Issues Concerning the Scope and Design of Public Sector Support Programs for Agriculture."

———. "Public Sector Support Programs for Agriculture: A Case Study of the Rubber Sector in Thailand."

Bucci, Gabriella. "The Effects of Abolishing Major Nontariff Barriers on Intra-OECD Trade."

Buiter, Willem H. "Macroeconomic Responses by Developing Countries to Changes in External Economic Conditions."

Cavallo, Domingo F. "Exchange Rate Overvaluation and Agriculture: The Case of Argentina."

Cavallo, Domingo F., Joaquin Cottani, and M. Shahbaz Khan. "Real Exchange Rate Behavior and Economic Performance in LDC's."

Chhibber, Ajay. "Trade and Exchange Rate Policies and Agricultural Performance in LDC's."

Ellis, Frank. "Agricultural Price Policy in Tanzania."

Fleisig, Heywood. "How a $10 per Barrel Oil Price Drop Would Affect the Developing Countries."

Gardner, Bruce. "Economic Consequences of U.S. Agricultural Policies."

———. "Estimating Effects of Commodity Policy and Trade Liberalization in Agriculture."

———. "International Commodity Agreements."

Harberger, Arnold C. "Reacting to a Debt Crisis."

———. "The Real Exchange Rate."

Johnson, D. Gale. "Agricultural Protection: Japan, Canada and Australia."

———. "Import Restrictions: Tariff and Non-Tariff Barriers."

———. "Notes on Agricultural Policy Trends and Priorities."

———. "Trade Preferences."

Jones, William O. "Agricultural Marketing Boards in Tropical Africa."

Kalantzopoulos, Orsalia. "The Costs of Voluntary Export Restraints for Selected Industries in the U.S. and EEC."

———. "The Effects on World Trade of a Decrease in Post–Tokyo Round Tariffs and Major Nontariff Barriers."

Kerr, T. C. "Trends in Agricultural Price Protection, 1967–83."

Knudsen, Odin, and John Nash. "Lessons from Price Stabilization Schemes in Developing Countries."

Koester, Ulrich, and Roland Herrmann. "The EEC-ACP Convention of Lomé."

Koester, Ulrich, and Stefan Tangermann. "European Agricultural Policies and International Agriculture."

Lardy, Nicholas. "Agricultural Reform in China."

Lewis, Clifford M. "Managing Agricultural Risks."

MacBean, Alasdair, and Duc Tin Nguyen. "Commodity Price Instability: Evidence."

———. "Compensatory Financing."

———. "Prospects for Processing Agricultural Products in Developing Countries."

———. "Terms of Trade: The Facts."

———. "The NIEO Proposals on Food and Trade in Agriculture."

Meyers, Kenneth. "Agricultural Performance and Policy in Kenya."

———. "Agricultural Performance and Policy in Tanzania."

Minford, Patrick. "Assessment of Policy Scenarios Using the Liverpool World Model."

Mundlak, Yair. "The Aggregate Agricultural Supply."

Pearson, Scott R., and Paul A. Dorosh. "Macroeconomic Policy and Agricultural Development in Indonesia: How an Oil-Exporting Country Achieved Food Self-Sufficiency."

Pinto, Brian. "Nigeria during and after the Oil Boom: A Policy Comparison with Indonesia."

Raswant, V. "The Impact of Parallel Markets on Agriculture."

Scobie, Grant M. "Food Consumption Policies."

Sherbourne, Lynn. "Macroeconomic Policies and Agricultural Performance: Ghana."

———. "Macroeconomic Policies and Agricultural Performance: Ivory Coast."

Squire, Lyn. "Agricultural Pricing in Malawi."

Stryker, J. Dirck, and Lewis E. Brandt. "Price Policy in Africa."

Subbarao, K. "India's Agricultural Performance and Policy: A Note."

Tyers, Rodney, and Kym Anderson. "Distortions in World Food Markets: A Quantitative Assessment."

Ueno, Hiroshi. "Intersectoral Factor Transfers: Case of Japan."

Vaubel, Roland. "Would the Developing Countries Benefit from a New International Monetary System?"

Virmani, Arvind. "Credit Markets and Credit Policy in Developing Countries: Myths and Reality."

Vogel, Robert. "Government Intervention in Rural Financial Markets."

Selected bibliography

Acharya, Shankar, and Bruce Johnston. 1978. *Two Studies of Development in Sub-Saharan Africa*. World Bank Staff Working Paper 300. Washington,D.C.

Agarwala, Ramgopal. 1983. *Price Distortions and Growth in Developing Countries*. World Bank Staff Working Paper 575. Washington, D.C.

Anderson, Kym. 1983. "Growth of Agricultural Protection in East Asia." *Food Policy* 8, 4 (Nov.): 327–36.

Anderson, Kym, Yujiro Hayami, and Masayoshi Honma. 1986. "Growth of Agricultural Protection." In Kym Anderson, Yujiro Hayami, and others. *Political Economy of Agricultural Protection: The Experience of East Asia*. Sydney, Australia: George Allen & Unwin.

Anderson, Kym, and Rodney Tyers. 1986. "International Effects of Domestic Agricultural Policies." In R. H. Snape, ed. *Issues in World Trade Policy: GATT at the Crossroads*. London: Macmillan.

Askari, Hossein, and J. T. Cummings. 1976. *Agricultural Supply Responses: A Survey of Econometric Evidence*. New York: Praeger.

Balassa, Bela. 1985. "Public Finance and Social Policy—Explanations of Trends and Developments: The Case of Developing Countries." In *Public Finance and Social Policy*. Detroit, Mich.: Wayne University Press.

———. 1986. "Policy Responses to Exogenous Shocks in Developing Countries." *American Economic Review* 76.

Balassa, Bela, and Carol Balassa. 1984. "Industrial Protection in the Developed Countries." *World Economy* 7:179–96.

Balassa, Bela, and Constantine Michalopoulos. 1985. *Liberal-*

izing World Trade. Development Policy Issues Series. Report VPERS4. Washington, D.C.: World Bank, Office of the Vice President.

Bale, Malcolm D., and B. L. Greenshields. 1978. "Japanese Agricultural Distortions and Their Welfare Value." *American Journal of Agricultural Economics* 60, 1:59–64.

Bale, Malcolm D., and Ernst Lutz. 1978. *Trade Restrictions and International Price Instability*. World Bank Staff Working Paper 303. Washington, D.C.

———. 1981. "Price Distortions in Agriculture and Their Effects: An International Comparison." *American Journal of Agricultural Economics* 63, 1:8–22.

Barichello, Richard. 1986. "Government Policies in Support of Canadian Agriculture: Their Costs." In T. Kelly White and C. Hanrahan, eds. *Consortium on Trade Research and Agriculture: A Comparative Look at U.S., Canadian, and EC Policies*. Report AGES850208. Washington, D.C.: U.S. Department of Agriculture, Economic Research Service.

Barker, Randolph, Robert W. Herdt, and Beth Rose. 1985. *The Rice Economy of Asia*. Washington, D.C.: Resources for the Future.

Bates, Robert H. 1981. *Markets and States in Tropical Africa: The Political Basis of Agricultural Politics*. Berkeley: University of California.

Bauer, P. T. 1954. *West African Trade*. London: Routledge & Kegan Paul.

Bautista, Romeo M. 1985. "Effects of Trade and Exchange Rate Policies on Export Production Incentives in Philippine Agriculture." Washington, D.C.: International Food Policy Research Institute. Processed.

Bertrand, Trent. 1980. *Thailand—Case Study of Agricultural Input and Output Pricing*. World Bank Staff Working Paper 385. Washington, D.C.

Binswanger, Hans. 1980. "Attitudes toward Risk: Experimental Measurement in Rural India." *American Journal of Agricultural Economics* (Aug.).

———. 1984. *Agricultural Mechanization: A Comparative Historical Perspective*. World Bank Staff Working Paper 673. Washington, D.C.

Binswanger, Hans, and P. L. Scandizzo. 1983. *Patterns of Agricultural Protection*. Report ARU15. Washington, D.C.: World Bank, Agriculture and Rural Development Department, Operations Policy Staff.

Buckwell, Allan E., D. R. Harvey, K. J. Thomson, and K. A. Parton. 1982. *The Costs of the Common Agricultural Policy*. London: Croom Helm.

Bureau of Agricultural Economics. Australia. 1985. *Agricultural Policies in the European Community: Their Origin, Nature and Effects on Production and Trade*. Policy Monograph 2. Canberra: Australian Government Publishing Service.

Cavallo, Domingo, and Yair Mundlak. 1982. *Agriculture and Economic Growth in an Open Economy: The Case of Argentina*. Research Report 36. Washington, D.C.: International Food Policy Research Institute.

Cheong, Kee-Cheok, and Emmanuel H. D'Silva. 1984. *Prices, Terms of Trade, and the Role of Government in Pakistan's Agriculture*. World Bank Staff Working Paper 643. Washington, D.C.

Chow, Gregory C. 1985. *The Chinese Economy*. New York: Harper and Row.

CIMMYT. The International Maize and Wheat Improvement Center. 1983. *World Wheat Facts and Trends*. Report 2: *An*

Analysis of Rapidly Rising Third World Consumption and Imports of Wheat. El Batan, Mexico.

Commission of the European Communities. 1984. *The Agricultural Situation in the Community: Report.* Brussels.

Cuddihy, William. 1980. *Agricultural Price Management in Egypt.* World Bank Staff Working Paper 388. Washington, D.C.

Dell, S. 1985. "The Fifth Credit Tranche." *World Development* 13:245–49.

FAO. Food and Agriculture Organization. 1983. *The State of Food and Agriculture, 1983.* FAO Agriculture Series 16. Rome.

————. 1984. *FAO Production Yearbook.* Vol. 37. Rome.

————. 1984. *FAO Trade Yearbook 1983.* Vol. 37. Rome.

————. 1984. *Statistics on Prices Received by Farmers.* Rome.

————. 1985. *Agricultural Price Policies.* Rome.

————. 1985. "The Contribution of Food Aid to Food Security." Committee on World Food Security. Rome. Processed.

————. 1985. *The Fifth World Food Survey.* Rome.

Finger, J. M., and D. DeRosa. 1977. "Commodity-Price Stabilization and the Rachet Effect." *World Economy* 1:195–204.

————. 1980. "The Compensatory Finance Facility and Export Instability." *Journal of World Trade Law* 14:14–22.

Garcia, Jorge G. 1981. *The Effects of Exchange Rates and Commercial Policy on Agricultural Incentives in Colombia: 1953–1978.* Research Report 24. Washington, D.C.: International Food Policy Research Institute.

Gardner, Bruce. 1979. "Robust Stabilization Policies for International Commodity Agreements." *American Economic Review* 69:169–72.

Gary, V. K. 1980. *State in Foodgrain Trade in India.* New Delhi: Vision Books.

Gemmill, G. 1985. "Forward Contracts or International Buffer Stocks? A Study of Their Relative Efficiencies in Stabilizing Commodity Export Earnings." *Economic Journal* 95:400–17.

Gilbert, Christopher L. 1984. "International Commodity Agreements: Design and Performance." Oxford: Institute of Economics and Statistics, Oxford University. Processed.

Gordon-Ashworth, Fiona. 1984. *International Commodity Control: A Contemporary History and Appraisal.* London: Croom Helm.

Gulhati, Ravi, Swadesh Bose, and Vimal Atukorala. 1985. *Exchange Rate Policies in Eastern and Southern Africa, 1965–83.* World Bank Staff Working Paper 720. Washington, D.C.

Hamilton, Carl. 1980. *Effects of Non-Tariff Barriers to Trade on Prices, Employment, and Imports: The Case of the Swedish Textile and Clothing Industry.* World Bank Staff Working Paper 429. Washington, D.C.

Hanson, James A., and Craig R. Neal. 1985. *Interest Rate Policies in Selected Developing Countries, 1970–82.* World Bank Staff Working Paper 753. Washington, D.C.

Harberger, Arnold C., ed. 1984. *World Economic Growth: Case Studies of Developed and Developing Nations.* San Francisco: Institute for Contemporary Studies.

————. 1985. "Tax Policy in a Small, Open Developing Economy." In Michael Connolly and John McDermott,

eds. *The Economics of the Caribbean Basin.* New York: Praeger.

Harling, K. 1983. "Agricultural Protectionism in Developed Countries: Analysis of Systems of Intervention." *European Review of Agricultural Economics* 10:223–47.

Hayami, Yujiro, and Masayoshi Honma. 1983. *Agricultural Protection Level of Japan* (in Japanese). Tokyo: Forum for Policy Innovation.

Hazell, Peter B. R., and Ailsa Roell. 1983. *Rural Growth Linkages: Household Expenditure Patterns in Malaysia and Nigeria.* Research Report 41. Washington, D.C.: International Food Policy Research Institute.

Hemmi, Kenzo. 1982. "Agriculture and Politics in Japan." In E. Castle and K. Hemmi, eds. *U.S.-Japanese Agricultural Trade Relations.* Washington, D.C.: Resources for the Future.

Hickok, Susan. 1985. "The Consumer Cost of U.S. Trade Restraints." Federal Reserve Bank of New York *Quarterly Review* (summer): 1–12.

Honma, Masayoshi, and Yujiro Hayami. Forthcoming. "The Structure of Agricultural Protection in Industrial Countries." *Journal of International Economics.*

Howarth, Richard W. 1971. *Agricultural Support in Western Europe.* London: Institute of Economic Affairs.

Idachaba, Francis S. 1980. *Agricultural Research Policy in Nigeria.* Research Report 17. Washington, D.C.: International Food Policy Research Institute.

International Agricultural Economics Association. Forthcoming. "Exchange Rates and Trade Policy: Help or Hindrance to Agricultural Growth?" Proceedings of the Nineteenth International Conference of Agricultural Economists, held in Malaga, Spain, Aug. 26–Sept. 4, 1985.

International Monetary Fund. 1984a. *Balance of Payments Statistics Yearbook.* Vol. 35, part 1. Washington, D.C.

————. 1984b. "The International Monetary Fund: Its Evolution, Organization, and Activities." Pamphlet 37. Washington, D.C.

————. 1985. *International Financial Statistics Yearbook.* Washington, D.C.

International Wheat Council. 1984. *World Wheat Statistics.* London.

Jaspersen, Frederick. 1981. *Adjustment Experience and Growth Prospects of the Semi-Industrial Countries.* World Bank Staff Working Paper 477. Washington, D.C.

Johnson, D. Gale. 1973. *World Agriculture in Disarray.* London: Macmillan.

————. 1982. *Progress of Economic Reform in the People's Republic of China.* Washington, D.C.: American Enterprise Institute.

————. 1985a. "Agriculture in the Overall Liberalization Process." Chicago: University of Chicago, Office of Agricultural Economics Research.

————. 1985b. *International Perspectives of Agricultural Development.* Paper 81:10. Chicago: University of Chicago, Office of Agricultural Economics Research.

Johnson, D. Gale, Kenzo Hemmi, and Pierre Lardinois. 1985. *Agricultural Policy and Trade.* New York: New York University Press.

Johnson, D. Gale, and Daniel Sumner. 1976. "An Optimization Approach to Grain Reserves for Developing Countries." In David J. Eaton and W. Scott Steele, eds. *Analyses* of Grain Reserves. Washington, D.C.: U.S. Department of Agriculture.

Johnson, Stanley R., A. W. Womack, W. H. Meyers, R. E. Young, and J. Brandt. 1985. "Options for the 1985 Farm Bill." In B. L. Gardner, ed. U.S. Agricultural Policy: The 1985 Farm Legislation. Washington, D.C.: American Enterprise Institute.

Jones, W. I. 1983–84. "Agriculture's Changing Role in International Trade and Aid: Tastes and Techniques." Annales d'Etudes Internationales 13:53–68.

Josling, Timothy. 1980. Developed-Country Agricultural Policies and Developing-Country Supplies: The Case of Wheat. Research Report 14. Washington, D.C.: International Food Policy Research Institute.

—————. 1981. Intervention and Regulation in Canadian Agriculture: A Comparison of Costs and Benefits between Sectors. Technical Report E-14. Ottawa: Economic Council of Canada.

Just, R. E. 1974. "The Importance of Risk in Farmers' Decisions." American Journal of Agricultural Economics (Feb.).

Kennedy, Eileen, and Odin K. Knudsen. 1985. "A Review of Supplementary Feeding Programmes and Recommendations on Their Design." In Margaret Biswas and Per Pinstrup-Andersen, eds. Nutrition and Development. Oxford: Oxford University Press.

Knudsen, Odin K. 1981. Economics of Supplemental Feeding of Malnourished Children: Leakages, Costs, and Benefits. World Bank Staff Working Paper 451. Washington, D.C.

Koester, Ulrich. 1985. "Agricultural Market Intervention and International Trade." European Review of Agricultural Economics 12:87–103.

Koester, Ulrich, and Malcolm D. Bale. 1984. The Common Agricultural Policy of the European Community: A Blessing or a Curse for the Developing Countries? World Bank Staff Working Paper 630. Washington, D.C.

Krishna, Raj. 1982. "Some Aspects of Agricultural Growth, Price Policy and Equity in Developing Countries." Food Research Institute Studies 18, 3:219–54.

Krishna, Raj, and Ajay Chhibber. 1983. Policy Modeling of a Dual Grain Market: The Case of Wheat in India. Research Report 38. Washington, D.C.: International Food Policy Research Institute.

Krishna, Raj, and G. S. Raychaudhuri. 1980. Some Aspects of Wheat and Rice Price Policy in India. World Bank Staff Working Paper 381. Washington, D.C.

Krueger, Anne O. 1982. "Analysing Disequilibrium Exchange-Rate Systems in Developing Countries." World Development 10, 12:1059–68.

—————. 1983. Exchange-Rate Determination. New York: Cambridge University Press.

Krumm, Kathie L. 1985. The External Debt of Sub-Saharan Africa: Origins, Magnitude, and Implications for Action. World Bank Staff Working Paper 741. Washington, D.C.

Lardy, Nicholas R. 1983. Agricultural Prices in China. World Bank Staff Working Paper 606. Washington, D.C.

—————. 1986. "Agricultural Reform." Journal of International Affairs 39, 2:91–104.

—————. 1986. "Prospects and Some Policy Problems of Agricultural Development in China." China in Transition, a special issue of American Journal of Agricultural Economics 68, 2 (May).

Liebenthal, Robert. 1981. Adjustment in Low-Income Africa.

World Bank Staff Working Paper 486. Washington, D.C.

Liepmann, H. 1938. Tariff Levels and Economic Unity of Europe. London: George Allen & Unwin.

MacBean, A. L. 1966. Export Instability and Economic Development. Cambridge, Mass.: Harvard University Press.

McCalla, A. F. 1969. "Protectionism in International Agricultural Trade, 1850–1968." Agricultural History 43, 3 (July): 329–44.

McCrone, Gavin. 1962. The Economics of Subsidizing Agriculture. London: George Allen & Unwin.

Mathew, Susan. 1984. Tamil Nadu Integrated Nutrition Project: A Presentation. Madras, India: Department of Social Welfare, Government of Tamil Nadu.

Meilke, Karl D., and T. K. Warley. 1986. "Agricultural Protectionism in the Developing World." Paper prepared for Resources for the Future, Washington, D.C.

Moscardi, E., and Alain de Janvry. 1977. "Attitudes toward Risk among Peasants." American Journal of Agricultural Economics (Nov.).

Mundlak, Yair. 1979. Intersectoral Factor Mobility and Agricultural Growth. Research Report 6. Washington, D.C.: International Food Policy Research Institute.

Newbery, David, and Joseph E. Stiglitz. 1981. The Theory of Commodity Price Stabilization. Oxford: Clarendon Press.

OECD. Organisation for Economic Co-operation and Development. 1983. The Generalized System of Preferences: Review of the First Decade. Paris.

—————. 1985a. Employment Growth and Structural Change. Paris.

—————. 1985b. Labour Force Statistics: 1963–1983. Paris.

—————. 1985c. OECD Economic Outlook 38 (December). Paris.

—————. 1985d. Quarterly Labour Force Statistics 2. Paris.

—————. 1985e. Quarterly National Accounts 1. Paris.

Otsuka, K., and Y. Hayami. 1985. "Goals and Consequences of Rice Policy in Japan, 1965–80." American Journal of Agricultural Economics 67, 3:529–38.

Parikh, Kirit S., and others. 1986. Towards Free Trade in Agriculture. Laxenburg, Austria: International Institute for Applied Systems Analysis.

Peterson, Arthur G. 1928. Historical Study of Prices Received by Producers of Farm Products in Virginia, 1801–1927. Richmond, Va.: Virginia Agricultural Experiment Station and the Bureau of Agricultural Economics of the U.S. Department of Agriculture.

Phipps, Tim. 1985. Farm Policies and the Rate of Return on Investment in Agriculture. Occasional paper. Washington, D.C.: American Enterprise Institute.

Pick's Currency Yearbook. 1976. New York: Pick.

Rangarajan, C. 1982. Agricultural Growth and Industrial Performance in India. Research Report 33. Washington, D.C.: International Food Policy Research Institute.

Ray, Anandarup. 1984. Cost-Benefit Analysis: Issues and Methodologies. Baltimore, Md.: Johns Hopkins University Press.

Reca, Lucio G. 1980. Argentina: Country Case Study of Agricultural Prices, Taxes, and Subsidies. World Bank Staff Working Paper 386. Washington, D.C.

Ricardo, David. [1817] 1973. The Principles of Political Economy and Taxation. New York: Dutton.

Roger, Neil. 1985. "Trade Policy Regimes in Developing Countries." Washington, D.C.: World Bank, Office of the

Vice President, Economic Research Staff. Processed.

Rosine, John, and Peter Helmberger. 1974. "A Neoclassical Analysis of the U.S. Farm Sector." *American Journal of Agricultural Economics* 56, 4 (Nov.): 717–30.

Salathe, Larry, M. Price, and D. Banker. 1984. "An Analysis of the Farmer-Owned Reserve Programs." *American Journal of Agricultural Economics* 66 (Feb.): 1–11.

Saxon, Eric, and Kym Anderson. 1982. *Japanese Agricultural Protection in Historical Perspective.* Pacific Economic Paper 92. Canberra: Australian National University.

Scandizzo, Pasquale L., and Colin Bruce. 1980. *Methodologies for Measuring Agricultural Price Intervention Effects.* World Bank Staff Working Paper 394. Washington, D.C.

Schiff, Maurice W. 1985. *An Econometric Analysis of the World Wheat Market and Simulation of Alternative Policies, 1960–80.* ERS Staff Report AGES850827. Washington, D.C.: U.S. Department of Agriculture, International Economics Division.

Schmitz, P. M. 1984. "European Community Trade Preferences for Sugar and Beef." In *Recent German Research in International Economics.* Bonn: Deutsche Forschungsgemeinsche.

Schuh, G. Edward. 1974. "The Exchange Rate and U.S. Agriculture." *American Journal of Agricultural Economics* (Feb.): 1–12.

Schuh, G. Edward, and Helio Tollini. 1979. *Costs and Benefits of Agricultural Research: The State of the Art.* World Bank Staff Working Paper 360. Washington, D.C.

Schultz, Theodore W., ed. 1978. *Distortions of Agricultural Incentives.* Bloomington, Ind.: Indiana University Press.

Scobie, Grant M. 1981. *Government Policy and Food Imports: The Case of Wheat in Egypt.* Research Report 29. Washington, D.C.: International Food Policy Research Institute.

Sen, Amartya. 1981. *Poverty and Famines: An Essay on Entitlement and Deprivation.* Oxford: Clarendon Press.

———. 1986. *Food, Economics, and Entitlements.* Helsinki: World Institute for Development Economics Research, United Nations University.

Singh, Inderjit, Lyn Squire, and James Kirchner. 1985. *Agricultural Pricing and Marketing Policies in an African Context: A Framework for Analysis.* World Bank Staff Working Paper 743. Washington, D.C.

Smith, Adam. [1776] 1976. *The Wealth of Nations.* 2 vols. in 1. Edited by Edwin Cannan. Chicago: University of Chicago Press.

Squire, Lyn. 1981. *Employment Policy in Developing Countries: A Survey of Issues and Evidence.* New York: Oxford University Press.

Strauss, Frederick, and Louis H. Bean. 1940. *Gross Farm Income and Indices of Farm Production and Prices in the United States, 1869–1937.* U.S. Department of Agriculture Technical Bulletin 703. Washington, D.C.: Government Printing Office.

Sumner, D. A., and J. M. Alston. 1984. *Effects of the Tobacco Program.* Occasional paper. Washington, D.C.: American Enterprise Institute.

Thomas, Vinod. 1985. *Linking Macroeconomic and Agricultural Policies for Adjustment with Growth.* Baltimore, Md.: Johns Hopkins University Press.

Tolley, George S., Vinod Thomas, and C. M. Wong. 1982. *Agricultural Price Policies and the Developing Countries.* Baltimore, Md.: Johns Hopkins University Press.

Tracy, M. 1982. *Agriculture in Western Europe—Challenge and Response, 1880–1980.* Second edition. London: Granada.

Traill, W. B. 1980. *Land Values and Rents: The Gains and Losses from Farm Price Support Programmes.* Department of Agricultural Economics Bulletin 175. Manchester, England: University of Manchester.

Tyers, Rodney. 1985. "Agricultural Protection and Market Insulation: Model Structure and Results for the European Community." *Journal of Policy Modeling* 7, 2:219–51.

UNCTAD. United Nations Conference on Trade and Development. 1983. *Review of the Operation of the Compensatory Financing Facility of the IMF.* Document TD/B/C.1/243. Geneva.

———. 1985. *Compensatory Financing of Export Earnings Shortfalls.* Document TD/B/1029/Rev. 1. Geneva.

———. 1985. *Review of the Implementation, Maintenance, Improvement and Utilization of the Generalized System of Preferences.* Ninth General Report, TD/B/C.5/96/Corr. 1. Geneva.

United Nations. 1984. *Handbook of International Trade and Development Statistics.* Supplement. New York.

U.S. Bureau of the Census. Department of Commerce. 1975. *Historical Statistics of the United States: Colonial Times to 1970.* Bicentennial edition. Washington, D.C.: Government Printing Office.

———. 1982, 1985. *Statistical Abstract of the United States.* Washington, D.C.: Government Printing Office.

USDA. U.S. Department of Agriculture. 1973, 1976, 1984, 1985. *Agricultural Statistics.* Washington, D.C.: Government Printing Office.

———. 1984. *Background for 1985 Legislation.* Agricultural Information Bulletins 467–78. Economic Research Service. Washington, D.C.

———. 1984. *Report of Financial Condition and Operations.* Commodity Credit Corporation. Washington, D.C.

———. 1985a. *Economic Indicators of the Farm Sector: Farm Sector Review.* Economic Research Service. Washington, D.C.

———. 1985b. *Feed Outlook and Situation Yearbook.* Washington, D.C.

———. 1985c. *Foreign Agricultural Trade of the U.S.* Fiscal 1985 supplement. Economic Research Service. Washington, D.C.

———. 1985d. *Foreign Agriculture Circular—Grains: World Grain Situation and Outlook* (September). Washington, D.C.

———. 1985e. *Rice Outlook and Situation Report.* Washington, D.C.

———. 1985f. *Sugar and Sweetener Outlook and Situation Report.* Washington, D.C.

———. 1985g. *Wheat Outlook and Situation Report.* Washington, D.C.

Valdes, Alberto. 1985. "Exchange Rates and Trade Policy: Help or Hindrance to Agricultural Growth?" Washington, D.C.: International Food Policy Research Institute. Processed.

Valdes, Alberto, ed. 1981. *Food Security in Developing Countries.* Boulder, Colo.: Westview.

Valdes, Alberto, and Suzanne Gnaegy. 1984. "Trends and Structure of Agricultural Trade among Developing Countries, 1962–1979." Paper prepared for the Food and Agriculture Organization. Rome.

Valdes, Alberto, and J. Zietz. 1980. *Agricultural Protection in OECD Countries: Its Cost to Less Developed Countries.* Research Report 21. Washington, D.C.: International Food Policy Research Institute.

Verreydt, E., and J. Waelbroeck. 1980. *European Community Protection against Manufactured Imports from Developing Countries: A Case Study in the Political Economy of Protection.* World Bank Staff Working Paper 432. Washington, D.C.

Virmani, Arvind. 1982. *The Nature of Credit Markets in Developing Countries: A Framework for Policy Analysis.* World Bank Staff Working Paper 524. Washington, D.C.

————. 1985. *Government Policy and the Development of Financial Markets: The Case of Korea.* World Bank Staff Working Paper 747. Washington, D.C.

Von Pischke, J. D., Dale Adams, and Gordon Donald. 1983. *Rural Financial Markets in Developing Countries.* Baltimore, Md.: Johns Hopkins University Press.

Wallich, Christine. 1981. *An Analysis of Developing Country Adjustment Experiences in the 1970s: Low-Income Asia.* World Bank Staff Working Paper 487. Washington, D.C.

Webb, A. J. 1984. *Protection in Agricultural Markets.* Economic Research Service Staff Report AGES840524. Washington, D.C.: U.S. Department of Agriculture.

World Bank. 1982. *World Development Report 1982.* New York: Oxford University Press.

————. 1983. *Accelerated Development in Sub-Saharan Africa: An Agenda for Action.* Washington, D.C.

————. 1984. *Toward Sustained Development in Sub-Saharan Africa: A Joint Program of Action.* Washington, D.C.

————. 1986a. *Financing Adjustment with Growth in Sub-Saharan Africa, 1986–90.* Washington, D.C.

————. 1986b. *Poverty and Hunger: Issues and Options for Food Security in Developing Countries.* Washington, D.C.

————. 1986c. *World Debt Tables.* 1985–86 edition. Washington, D.C.

World Currency Yearbook. 1985. Brooklyn, N.Y.: International Currency Analysis Inc.

Yagci, Fahrettin, Steve Kamin, and Vicki Rosenbaum. 1985. *Structural Adjustment Lending: An Evaluation of Program Design.* World Bank Staff Working Paper 735. Washington, D.C.

Yeats, Alexander. 1981. *Shipping and Development Policy: An Integrated Assessment.* New York: Praeger.

Zietz, Joachim, and Alberto Valdes. 1986. *The Costs of Protectionism to Developing Countries: An Analysis for Selected Agricultural Products.* World Bank Staff Working Paper 769. Washington, D.C.

Annex

World Development Indicators

Contents

Key

In each table, economies are listed in their group in ascending order of GNP per capita except for those for which no GNP per capita can be calculated. These are listed in alphabetical order, in italics, at the end of their group. The reference numbers below reflect the order in the tables.

Figures in the colored bands are summary measures for groups of economies. The letter *w* after a summary measure indicates that it is a weighted average; the letter *m*, that it is a median value; the letter *t*, that it is a total.

.. Not available.

(.) Less than half the unit shown.

All growth rates are in real terms.

Figures in italics are for years or periods other than those specified.

Afghanistan	30	Haiti	23	Panama	81
Albania	123	Honduras	48	Papua New Guinea	50
Algeria	88	Hong Kong	92	Paraguay	67
Angola	72	Hungary	121	Peru	59
Argentina	86	India	15	Philippines	46
Australia	115	Indonesia	42	Poland	122
Austria	108	*Iran, Islamic Republic of*	95	Portugal	79
Bangladesh	2	*Iraq*	96	*Romania*	127
Belgium	107	Ireland	103	Rwanda	19
Benin	18	Israel	91	Saudi Arabia	99
Bhutan	31	Italy	104	Senegal	29
Bolivia	41	Jamaica	63	Sierra Leone	22
Botswana	57	Japan	111	Singapore	94
Brazil	78	Jordan	70	Somalia	17
Bulgaria	124	*Kampuchea, Democratic*	33	South Africa	87
Burkina Faso	5	Kenya	21	Spain	102
Burma	7	*Korea, Democratic People's Republic of*	74	Sri Lanka	26
Burundi	11			Sudan	27
Cameroon	54	Korea, Republic of	84	Sweden	116
Canada	117	Kuwait	100	Switzerland	120
Central African Republic	14	*Lao People's Democratic Republic*	34	Syrian Arab Republic	71
Chad	32	*Lebanon*	75	Tanzania	10
Chile	77	Lesotho	40	Thailand	56
China	20	Liberia	38	Togo	13
Colombia	69	Libya	98	Trinidad and Tobago	93
Congo, People's Republic of the	61	Madagascar	16	Tunisia	68
Costa Rica	66	Malawi	8	Turkey	65
Cote d'Ivoire	45	Malaysia	80	Uganda	12
Cuba	73	Mali	3	*Union of Soviet Socialist Republics*	128
Czechoslovakia	125	Mauritania	37		
Denmark	114	Mauritius	60	United Arab Emirates	101
Dominican Republic	58	Mexico	83	United Kingdom	106
Ecuador	62	*Mongolia*	76	United States	119
Egypt, Arab Republic of	51	Morocco	47	Uruguay	82
El Salvador	49	*Mozambique*	35	Venezuela	89
Ethiopia	1	Nepal	6	*Viet Nam*	36
Finland	112	Netherlands	109	Yemen Arab Republic	43
France	110	New Zealand	105	Yemen, People's Democratic Republic of	44
German Democratic Republic	126	Nicaragua	55		
Germany, Federal Republic of	113	Niger	9	Yugoslavia	85
Ghana	25	Nigeria	52	Zaire	4
Greece	90	Norway	118	Zambia	39
Guatemala	64	Oman	97	Zimbabwe	53
Guinea	24	Pakistan	28		

Note: For U.N. and World Bank member countries with populations of less than 1 million, see Box A.1.

Introduction

The World Development Indicators provide information on the main features of social and economic development. Most of the data collected by the World Bank are on its developing member countries. Because comparable data for developed market economies are readily available, these are also included in the indicators. Data for economies that are not members of the World Bank are included if available in a comparable form.

Every effort has been made to standardize the data. However, full comparability cannot be ensured and care must be taken in interpreting the indicators. The statistics are drawn from sources thought to be most authoritative, but many of them are subject to considerable margins of error. Variations in national statistical practices also reduce the comparability of data which should thus be construed only as indicating trends and characterizing major differences among economies, rather than taken as precise quantitative indications of those differences.

The indicators in Table 1 give a summary profile of economies. Data in the other tables fall into the following broad areas: national accounts, agriculture, industry, energy, external trade, external debt, aid flows, other external transactions, central government finances and income distribution, and population, health, education, labor force, and urbanization indicators.

The national accounts data are obtained from member governments by Bank missions and are, in some instances, adjusted to conform with international definitions and concepts to ensure consistency. Data on external debt are reported to the Bank by member countries through the Debtor Reporting System. Other data sets are drawn from the International Monetary Fund, the United Nations and specialized agencies.

Three new tables have been added this year. Two, along with some additional indicators, offer a more complete picture of external indebtedness, while the third gives information on receipts of official development assistance.

For ease of reference, ratios and rates of growth are shown; absolute values are reported only in a few instances. Most growth rates are calculated for two periods: 1965–73 and 1973–84, or for 1973–83 if data for 1984 are not available. All growth rates related to national accounts are in constant prices and are computed, unless noted otherwise, by using the least-squares method. Because this method takes all observations in a period into account, the resulting growth rates reflect general trends that are not unduly influenced by exceptional values. Table entries in italics indicate that they are for years or periods other than those specified. All dollar figures are U.S. dollars. The various methods used for converting from national currency figures are described, where appropriate, in the technical notes.

Some of the differences between figures shown in this year's and those of last year's edition reflect not only updating but also revisions to historical series.

As in the *World Development Report* itself, the economies included in the World Development Indicators are grouped into several major categories. These groupings are analytically useful for distinguishing economies at different stages of development. Many of the economies included are further classified by dominant characteristics—to distinguish oil importers from exporters, for instance. The major groups used in the tables are 36 low-income developing economies with a per capita income of less than $400 in 1984, 60 middle-income developing economies with a per capita income of $400 or more, 5 high-income oil exporters, 19 industrial market economies, and 8 East European nonmarket economies. Two new countries, Botswana and Mauritius, whose populations now exceed 1 million, are included in this year's tables. Note that because of the paucity of data and differences in the method for computing national income, as well as difficulties of conversion, estimates of GNP per capita for nonmarket economies are not generally available.

The format of this edition follows that used in previous years. In each group, economies are listed in ascending order of income per capita except for those for which no GNP per capita figure can be calculated. These are listed in italics in alphabetical order at the end of each appropriate group. This order is used in all tables. The alphabetical list in the key shows the reference number for each economy; italics once again indicate those economies placed at the end of a group due to unavailability of GNP per capita figures. Economies with populations of less than a million are not reported in the main tables, but a separate table in Box A.1 shows some basic indicators for 34 small economies that are members of the United Nations, the World Bank, or both.

In the colored bands are *summary measures*—totals or weighted averages—that are calculated for the economy groups if data are adequate and thus meaningful statistics can be obtained. Because China and India heavily influence the overall summary measures for the low-income economies, summary measures are shown separately for several subgroups: China and India, sub-Saharan Africa, and other low-income economies. Note that sub-Saharan Africa includes all countries south of the Sahara—except South Africa. Because trade in oil affects the economic characteristics and performance of middle-income economies, summary measures are shown separately for oil importers and exporters and for sub-Saharan Africa. In addition, the group of middle-income economies is divided into lower and upper categories, which provides more meaningful summary measures.

The methodology used for computing the summary measures is described in the technical notes. The letter *w* after a summary measure indicates that it is a weighted average; the letter *m*, that it is a median value; and the letter *t*, that it is a total. Because the coverage of economies is not uniform for all indicators and because the variation from measures of central tendency can be large, readers

Groups of economies

The colors on the map show what group a country has been placed in on the basis of its GNP per capita and, in some instances, its distinguishing economic characteristics. For example, all low-income economies, those with a GNP per capita of less than $400 (in 1984), are colored yellow. The groups are the same as those used in the 31 tables that follow, and they include only the 128 countries with a population of more than 1 million.

Low-income economies
Middle-income oil importers
Middle-income oil exporters
High-income oil exporters
Industrial market economies
East European nonmarket economies

Not included in the Indicators

should exercise caution in comparing the summary measures for different indicators, groups, and years or periods.

In incorporating the three new tables, the opportunity has been taken to rearrange other tables into a more logical order, keeping the economic indicators together and running the social indicators last.

The technical notes should be referred to in any use of the data. These notes outline the methods, concepts, definitions, and data sources used in compiling the tables. The bibliography gives details of the data sources, which contain comprehensive definitions and descriptions of concepts used.

The report includes four world maps. The first map, below, shows country names and the groups in which economies have been placed. The maps

on the following pages show population, life expectancy at birth, and the share of agriculture in gross domestic product (GDP). The Eckert IV projection has been used for these maps because it maintains correct areas for all countries, though at the cost of some distortions in shape, distance, and direction. The maps have been prepared exclusively for the convenience of the readers of this report; the denominations used and the boundaries shown do not imply on the part of the World Bank and its affiliates any judgment on the legal status of any territory or any endorsement or acceptance of such boundaries.

The World Development Indicators are prepared under the supervision of Ramesh Chander, assisted by David Cieslikowski.

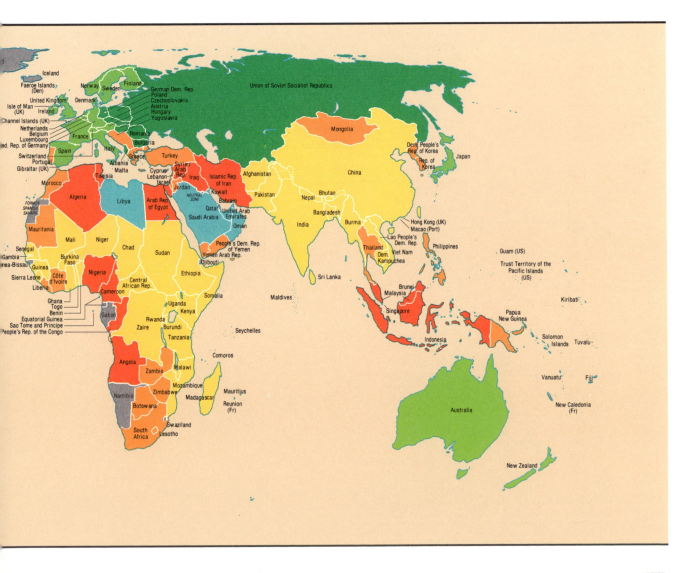

Population

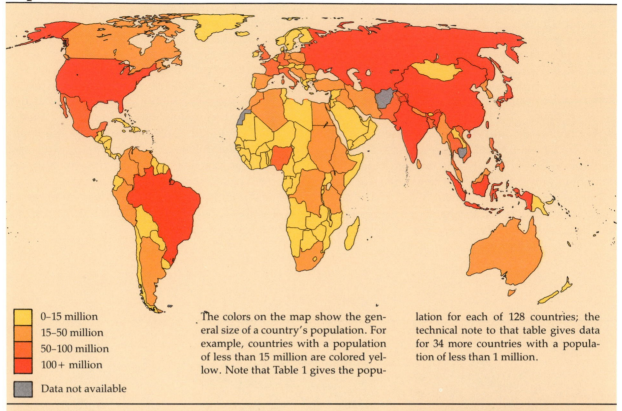

0–15 million
15–50 million
50–100 million
100+ million

Data not available

The colors on the map show the general size of a country's population. For example, countries with a population of less than 15 million are colored yellow. Note that Table 1 gives the population for each of 128 countries; the technical note to that table gives data for 34 more countries with a population of less than 1 million.

Population by country group, 1965, 1984, 2000

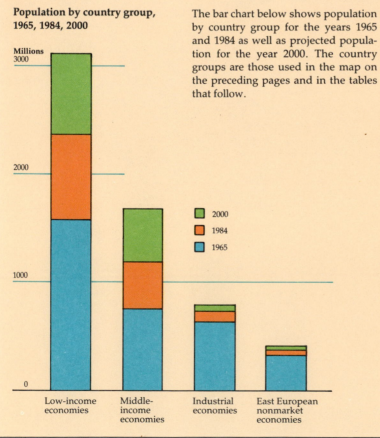

2000
1984
1965

The bar chart below shows population by country group for the years 1965 and 1984 as well as projected population for the year 2000. The country groups are those used in the map on the preceding pages and in the tables that follow.

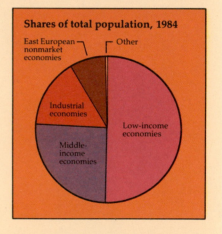

Shares of total population, 1984

The pie chart above shows the proportion of total population, excluding countries with populations of less than 1 million, accounted for by each country group. "Other" refers to high-income oil producers.

Life expectancy

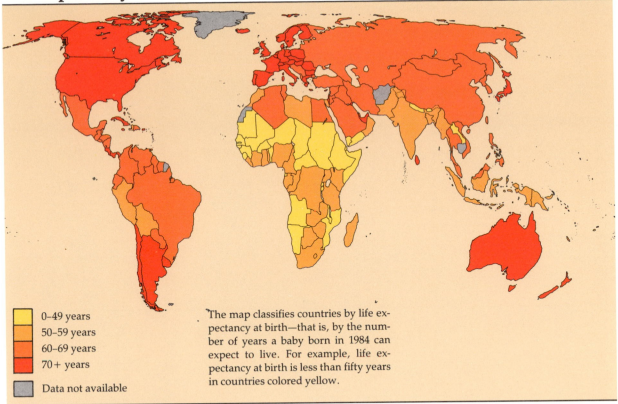

0–49 years

50–59 years

60–69 years

70+ years

Data not available

The map classifies countries by life expectancy at birth—that is, by the number of years a baby born in 1984 can expect to live. For example, life expectancy at birth is less than fifty years in countries colored yellow.

Share of agriculture in GDP

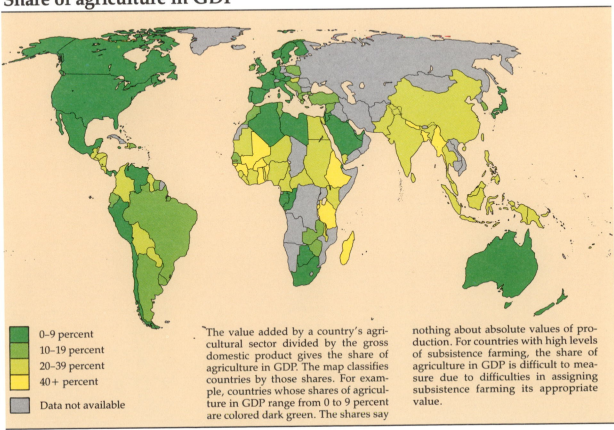

0–9 percent

10–19 percent

20–39 percent

40+ percent

Data not available

The value added by a country's agricultural sector divided by the gross domestic product gives the share of agriculture in GDP. The map classifies countries by those shares. For example, countries whose shares of agriculture in GDP range from 0 to 9 percent are colored dark green. The shares say nothing about absolute values of production. For countries with high levels of subsistence farming, the share of agriculture in GDP is difficult to measure due to difficulties in assigning subsistence farming its appropriate value.

Table 1. Basic indicators

	Population (millions) mid-1984	Area (thousands of square kilometers)	GNP per capita[a] Dollars 1984	GNP per capita[a] Average annual growth rate (percent) 1965–84[b]	Average annual rate of inflation[a] (percent) 1965–73	Average annual rate of inflation[a] (percent) 1973–84[c]	Life expectancy at birth (years) 1984
Low-income economies	2,389.5 t	31,795 t	260 w	2.8 w	1.6 w	5.9 w	60 w
China and India	1,778.3 t	12,849 t	290 w	3.3 w	1.0 w	4.0 w	63 w
Other low-income	611.2 t	18,946 t	190 w	0.9 w	4.6 w	14.9 w	52 w
Sub-Saharan Africa	257.7 t	15,646 t	210 w	−0.1 w	4.1 w	20.1 w	48 w
1 Ethiopia	42.2	1,222	110	0.4	1.8	4.4	44
2 Bangladesh	98.1	144	130	0.6	7.3	9.9	50
3 Mali	7.3	1,240	140	1.1	7.6	10.4	46
4 Zaire	29.7	2,345	140	−1.6	18.7	48.2	51
5 Burkina Faso	6.6	274	160	1.2	2.6	10.6	45
6 Nepal	16.1	141	160	0.2	5.8	8.1	47
7 Burma	36.1	677	180	2.3	2.8	6.0	58
8 Malawi	6.8	118	180	1.7	4.5	9.4	45
9 Niger	6.2	1,267	190	−1.3	4.0	11.5	43
10 Tanzania	21.5	945	210	0.6	3.2	11.5	52
11 Burundi	4.6	28	220	1.9	2.9	12.2	48
12 Uganda	15.0	236	230	2.9	5.6	64.5	51
13 Togo	2.9	57	250	0.5	3.1	8.2	51
14 Central African Rep.	2.5	623	260	−0.1	3.0	13.8	49
15 India	749.2	3,288	260	1.6	6.3	7.8	56
16 Madagascar	9.9	587	260	−1.6	4.1	14.4	52
17 Somalia	5.2	638	260	. .	3.8	20.2	46
18 Benin	3.9	113	270	1.0	3.6	10.8	49
19 Rwanda	5.8	26	280	2.3	7.7	10.5	47
20 China	1,029.2	9,561	310	4.5	−0.9	1.8	69
21 Kenya	19.6	583	310	2.1	2.3	10.8	54
22 Sierra Leone	3.7	72	310	0.6	1.9	15.4	38
23 Haiti	5.4	28	320	1.0	4.0	7.9	55
24 Guinea	5.9	246	330	1.1	3.0	4.5	38
25 Ghana	12.3	239	350	−1.9	8.1	52.2	53
26 Sri Lanka	15.9	66	360	2.9	5.1	14.9	70
27 Sudan	21.3	2,506	360	1.2	7.2	19.3	48
28 Pakistan	92.4	804	380	2.5	4.8	10.8	51
29 Senegal	6.4	196	380	−0.5	3.0	9.0	46
30 Afghanistan	. .	648	. .	. .	3.8	. .	. .
31 Bhutan	1.2	47	. .	. .	. .	. .	44
32 Chad	4.9	1,284	. .	. .	. .	. .	44
33 Kampuchea, Dem.		181	. .	. .	. .	. .	. .
34 Lao PDR	3.5	237	. .	. .	. .	. .	45
35 Mozambique	13.4	802	. .	. .	. .	. .	46
36 Viet Nam	60.1	330	. .	. .	. .	. .	65
Middle-income economies	1,187.6 t	40,927 t	1,250 w	3.1 w	5.5 w	38.0 w	61 w
Oil exporters	556.1 t	15,510 t	1,000 w	3.3 w	4.9 w	21.6 w	58 w
Oil importers	631.5 t	25,417 t	1,460 w	3.1 w	5.7 w	44.5 w	64 w
Sub-Saharan Africa	148.4 t	6,228 t	680 w	2.4 w	4.9 w	12.2 w	50 w
Lower middle-income	691.1 t	19,132	740 w	3.0 w	5.6 w	20.6 w	58 w
37 Mauritania	1.7	1,031	450	0.3	3.9	7.7	46
38 Liberia	2.1	111	470	0.5	1.5	6.7	50
39 Zambia	6.4	753	470	−1.3	5.8	10.4	52
40 Lesotho	1.5	30	530	5.9	4.4	11.9	54
41 Bolivia	6.2	1,099	540	0.2	7.5	54.5	53
42 Indonesia	158.9	1,919	540	4.9	63.0	17.4	55
43 Yemen Arab Rep.	7.8	195	550	5.9	. .	12.6	45
44 Yemen, PDR	2.0	333	550	. .	. .	. .	47
45 Cote d'Ivoire	9.9	322	610	0.2	4.1	11.7	52
46 Philippines	53.4	300	660	2.6	8.8	12.9	63
47 Morocco	21.4	447	670	2.8	2.0	8.3	59
48 Honduras	4.2	112	700	0.5	2.9	8.6	61
49 El Salvador	5.4	21	710	−0.6	1.6	11.3	65
50 Papua New Guinea	3.4	462	710	0.6	6.6	6.8	52
51 Egypt, Arab Rep.	45.9	1,001	720	4.3	2.6	13.1	60
52 Nigeria	96.5	924	730	2.8	10.3	13.0	50
53 Zimbabwe	8.1	391	760	1.5	1.1	11.4	57
54 Cameroon	9.9	475	800	2.9	5.8	12.8	54
55 Nicaragua	3.2	130	860	−1.5	3.4	17.2	60
56 Thailand	50.0	514	860	4.2	2.5	8.2	64
57 Botswana	1.0	600	960	8.4	4.4	9.8	58
58 Dominican Rep.	6.1	49	970	3.2	2.7	9.0	64
59 Peru	18.2	1,285	1,000	−0.1	10.1	56.7	59
60 Mauritius	1.0	2	1,090	2.7	5.6	12.7	66
61 Congo, People's Rep.	1.8	342	1,140	3.7	4.6	12.3	57
62 Ecuador	9.1	284	1,150	3.8	6.2	17.8	65
63 Jamaica	2.2	11	1,150	−0.4	5.9	16.6	73
64 Guatemala	7.7	109	1,160	2.0	1.9	9.4	60
65 Turkey	48.4	781	1,160	2.9	10.5	42.4	64

Note: For comparability and coverage, see the technical notes. For U.N. and World Bank member countries with populations of less than 1 million, see Box A.1.

	Population (millions) mid-1984	Area (thousands of square kilometers)	GNP per capita[a] Dollars 1984	GNP per capita[a] Average annual growth rate (percent) 1965–84[b]	Average annual rate of inflation[a] (percent) 1965–73	Average annual rate of inflation[a] (percent) 1973–84[c]	Life expectancy at birth (years) 1984
66 Costa Rica	2.5	51	1,190	1.6	4.7	24.1	73
67 Paraguay	3.3	407	1,240	4.4	4.3	12.9	66
68 Tunisia	7.0	164	1,270	4.4	3.3	9.9	62
69 Colombia	28.4	1,139	1,390	3.0	10.8	23.8	65
70 Jordan	3.4	98	1,570	4.8	. .	9.6	64
71 Syrian Arab Rep.	10.1	185	1,620	4.5	3.1	11.9	63
72 *Angola*	9.9	1,247	. .	. .	. .	. .	43
73 *Cuba*	9.9	115	. .	. .	. .	. .	75
74 *Korea, Dem. Rep.*	19.9	121	. .	. .	. .	. .	68
75 *Lebanon*	. .	10	. .	. .	2.5	. .	. .
76 *Mongolia*	1.9	1,565	. .	. .	. .	. .	63
Upper middle-income	**496.6 *t***	**21,795 *t***	**1,950 *w***	**3.3 *w***	**5.6 *w***	**44.0 *w***	**65 *w***
77 Chile	11.8	757	1,700	−0.1	50.3	75.4	70
78 Brazil	132.6	8,512	1,720	4.6	23.2	71.4	64
79 Portugal	10.2	92	1,970	3.5	4.9	20.5	74
80 Malaysia	15.3	330	1,980	4.5	1.2	6.2	69
81 Panama	2.1	77	1,980	2.6	2.4	6.7	71
82 Uruguay	3.0	176	1,980	1.8	51.7	50.0	73
83 Mexico	76.8	1,973	2,040	2.9	4.8	31.5	66
84 Korea, Rep. of	40.1	98	2,110	6.6	15.5	17.6	68
85 Yugoslavia	23.0	256	2,120	4.3	10.9	24.6	69
86 Argentina	30.1	2,767	2,230	0.3	24.1	180.8	70
87 South Africa	31.6	1,221	2,340	1.4	6.0	13.2	54
88 Algeria	21.2	2,382	2,410	3.6	3.8	12.2	60
89 Venezuela	16.8	912	3,410	0.9	3.3	11.7	69
90 Greece	9.9	132	3,770	3.8	4.4	17.3	75
91 Israel	4.2	21	5,060	2.7	8.2	84.4	75
92 Hong Kong	5.4	1	6,330	6.2	6.4	9.8	76
93 Trinidad and Tobago	1.2	5	7,150	2.6	5.7	*15.6*	69
94 Singapore	2.5	1	7,260	7.8	3.1	4.4	72
95 *Iran, Islamic Rep.*	43.8	1,648	. .	. . .	. . .	. . .	61
96 *Iraq*	15.1	435	. .	. .	3.2	. . .	60
High-income oil exporters	**18.6 *t***	**4,311 *t***	**11,250 *w***	**3.2 *w***	**6.1 *w***	**11.8 *w***	**62 *w***
97 Oman	1.1	300	6,490	6.1	7.1	16.4	53
98 Libya	3.5	1,760	8,520	−1.1	9.4	10.8	59
99 Saudi Arabia	11.1	2,150	10,530	5.9	5.1	14.1	62
100 Kuwait	1.7	18	16,720	−0.1	4.6	9.2	72
101 United Arab Emirates	1.3	84	21,920	. .	. .	8.7	72
Industrial market economies	**733.4 *t***	**30,935 *t***	**11,430 *w***	**2.4 *w***	**5.2 *w***	**7.9 *w***	**76 *w***
102 Spain	38.7	505	4,440	2.7	7.0	16.4	77
103 Ireland	3.5	70	4,970	2.4	8.5	14.4	73
104 Italy	57.0	301	6,420	2.7	5.1	17.2	77
105 New Zealand	3.2	269	7,730	1.4	7.2	13.6	74
106 United Kingdom	56.4	245	8,570	1.6	6.2	13.8	74
107 Belgium	9.9	31	8,610	3.0	4.4	6.4	75
108 Austria	7.6	84	9,140	3.6	4.5	5.3	73
109 Netherlands	14.4	41	9,520	2.1	6.4	5.9	77
110 France	54.9	547	9,760	3.0	5.3	10.7	77
111 Japan	120.0	372	10,630	4.7	6.0	4.5	77
112 Finland	4.9	337	10,770	3.3	7.2	10.7	75
113 Germany, Fed. Rep.	61.2	249	11,130	2.7	4.7	4.1	75
114 Denmark	5.1	43	11,170	1.8	7.6	9.4	75
115 Australia	15.5	7,687	11,740	1.7	5.7	10.4	76
116 Sweden	8.3	450	11,860	1.8	5.3	10.2	77
117 Canada	25.1	9,976	13,280	2.4	4.4	9.2	76
118 Norway	4.1	324	13,940	3.3	6.3	9.4	77
119 United States	237.0	9,363	15,390	1.7	4.7	7.4	76
120 Switzerland	6.4	41	16,330	1.4	5.5	3.9	77.
East European nonmarket economies	**389.3 *t***	**23,421 *t***	**. .**	**. .**	**. .**	**. .**	**68 *w***
121 Hungary	10.7	93	2,100	6.2	2.6	4.3	70
122 Poland	36.9	313	2,100	1.5	. .	19.4[b]	71
123 *Albania*	2.9	29	. .	. .	. .	. .	70
124 *Bulgaria*	9.0	111	. .	. .	. .	. .	71
125 *Czechoslovakia*	15.5	128	. .	. .	. .	. .	70
126 *German Dem. Rep.*	16.7	108	. .	. .	. .	. .	71
127 *Romania*	22.7	238	. .	. .	. .	. .	71
128 *USSR*	275.0	22,402	. .	. .	. .	. .	67

a. See the technical notes.   b. Because data for the entire period are not always available, figures in italics are for periods other than that specified.   c. Figures in italics are for 1973–83 not 1973–84.

Table 2. Growth of production

	GDP		Agriculture		Industry		(Manufacturing)[a]		Services	
Average annual growth rate (percent)	1965–73[b]	1973–84[c]	1965–73[b]	1973–84[c]	1965–73[b]	1973–84[c]	1965–73	1973–84[c]	1965–73[b]	1973–84[c]
Low-income economies	5.6 w	5.3 w	3.0 w	3.6 w	8.9 w	7.4 w	..	..	6.8 w	5.0 w
China and India	6.2 w	5.7 w	3.2 w	3.9 w	9.3 w	7.7 w	..	..	7.8 w	5.5 w
Other low-income	3.7 w	3.5 w	2.5 w	2.4 w	5.0 w	4.3 w	..	..	3.7 w	3.5 w
Sub-Saharan Africa	3.7 w	2.0 w	2.6 w	1.4 w	5.7 w	1.8 w	..	..	3.4 w	1.4 w
1 Ethiopia	4.1	2.3	2.1	1.2	6.1	2.6	8.8	3.5	6.7	3.6
2 Bangladesh	(.)	5.0	0.4	3.1	−6.1	7.6	..	..	1.5	7.1
3 Mali	3.1	4.1	0.9	5.0	5.1	0.6	..	..	4.7	4.5
4 Zaire	3.9	−1.0	..	1.4	..	−2.0	..	−5.0	..	−1.1
5 Burkina Faso	2.4	2.9	..	1.3	..	5.2	..	..	..	3.2
6 Nepal	1.7	3.1	..	..	..	..	..	..	..	..
7 Burma	2.9	6.0	2.8	6.6	3.6	7.7	3.2	6.1	2.8	5.1
8 Malawi	5.7	3.3	..	2.5	..	3.3	..	..	..	4.0
9 Niger	−0.8	5.2	−2.9	1.6	13.2	10.9	..	..	−1.5	5.9
10 Tanzania	5.0	2.6	3.1	..	6.9	..	8.7	..	6.2	..
11 Burundi	4.8	3.6	4.7	2.3	10.4	8.3	..	..	3.0	5.3
12 Uganda	3.6	−1.3	3.6	−0.7	3.0	−8.8	..	..	3.8	−0.4
13 Togo	5.3	2.3	2.6	1.1	6.2	2.6	..	..	7.3	3.0
14 Central African Rep.	2.7	0.7	2.1	1.1	7.1	1.2	..	..	1.6	(.)
15 India	3.9	4.1	3.7	2.3	3.7	4.4	4.0	5.9	4.2	6.1
16 Madagascar	3.5	(.)	..	0.3	..	−3.0	..	..	..	0.9
17 Somalia	..	..	..	..	..	..	..	..	..	..
18 Benin	2.2	4.6	..	2.7	..	7.9	..	..	..	5.1
19 Rwanda	6.3	5.4	..	..	..	..	..	..	..	..
20 China	7.8	6.6	2.8	4.9	12.1	8.7	..	..	11.7	5.0
21 Kenya	7.9	4.4	6.2	3.5	12.4	4.8	12.4	6.0	7.6	4.9
22 Sierra Leone	3.7	1.8	1.5	2.0	1.9	−2.5	3.3	1.8	7.1	3.7
23 Haiti	1.7	2.7	−0.3	0.5	4.8	4.5	3.0	5.4	2.5	3.7
24 Guinea	3.0	3.1	..	2.4	..	5.7	..	−2.0	..	2.3
25 Ghana	3.4	−0.9	4.5	0.2	4.3	−6.9	6.5	−6.9	1.1	0.4
26 Sri Lanka	4.2	5.2	2.7	4.1	7.3	4.8	5.5	3.6	3.8	6.0
27 Sudan	0.2	5.5	0.3	2.7	1.0	6.4	..	10.1	0.5	7.5
28 Pakistan	5.4	5.6	4.7	3.0	6.6	7.6	6.2	7.5	5.4	6.4
29 Senegal	1.5	2.6	0.2	−0.2	3.5	6.0	..	..	1.5	2.3
30 Afghanistan	1.0	..	−1.5	..	4.0	..	..	..	5.1	..
31 Bhutan	..	..	..	..	..	..	..	..	..	..
32 Chad	0.5	..	..	..	..	..	..	..	..	..
33 Kampuchea, Dem.	..	..	..	..	..	..	..	..	..	..
34 Lao PDR	..	..	..	..	..	..	..	..	..	..
35 Mozambique	..	..	..	..	..	..	..	..	..	..
36 Viet Nam	..	..	..	..	..	..	..	..	..	..
Middle-income economies	7.4 w	4.4 w	3.6 w	2.7 w	9.1 w	4.4 w	9.2 w	5.5 w	7.8 w	5.1 w
Oil exporters	7.8 w	4.6 w	4.0 w	2.4 w	9.6 w	4.5 w	8.8 w	7.0 w	7.9 w	5.3 w
Oil importers	7.1 w	4.3 w	3.2 w	2.9 w	8.4 w	4.4 w	9.4 w	7.8 w	7.8 w	5.0 w
Sub-Saharan Africa	8.5 w	1.6 w	3.0 w	0.1 w	16.8 w	0.5 w	..	6.4 w	7.7 w	3.4 w
Lower middle-income	6.8 w	4.2 w	3.6 w	2.4 w	10.4 w	4.2 w	8.5 w	5.9 w	6.9 w	5.1 w
37 Mauritania	2.6	2.3	−2.1	2.3	4.3	0.9	..	..	7.6	3.1
38 Liberia	5.5	0.2	6.5	2.0	6.2	−1.5	13.2	0.5	3.8	0.8
39 Zambia	2.4	0.4	2.0	1.0	2.7	−0.1	9.8	0.8	2.3	0.6
40 Lesotho	3.9	5.0	..	..	..	..	..	..	..	..
41 Bolivia	4.4	0.8	3.5	1.1	5.1	−1.7	4.2	0.2	4.3	1.9
42 Indonesia	8.1	6.8	4.8	3.7	13.4	8.3	9.0	14.9	9.6	8.6
43 Yemen Arab Rep.	..	8.1	..	1.8	..	13.8	..	14.2	..	9.6
44 Yemen, PDR	..	..	..	..	..	..	..	..	..	..
45 Cote d'Ivoire	7.1	3.7	3.7	3.3	8.8	6.6	8.9	5.0	8.5	2.9
46 Philippines	5.4	4.8	4.1	4.0	7.4	5.3	8.5	4.3	4.8	4.8
47 Morocco	5.7	4.5	4.8	0.6	5.4	3.7	6.1	5.8	6.1	5.8
48 Honduras	4.5	3.8	2.2	3.6	5.7	4.4	6.5	4.2	5.8	3.8
49 El Salvador	4.4	−0.3	3.6	0.4	5.2	−0.6	5.1	−1.5	4.4	−0.5
50 Papua New Guinea	6.7	1.0	..	2.6	..	3.7	..	..	..	−0.1
51 Egypt, Arab Rep.	3.8	8.5	2.6	2.5	3.8	10.3	..	..	4.7	10.6
52 Nigeria	9.7	0.7	2.8	−0.5	19.7	−1.0	15.0	8.5	8.8	3.2
53 Zimbabwe	9.4	1.7	..	1.1	..	0.4	..	2.3	..	3.0
54 Cameroon	4.2	7.1	4.7	1.6	4.7	15.0	7.5	13.5	3.6	7.1
55 Nicaragua	3.9	−1.1	2.8	1.4	5.5	−0.8	7.2	0.9	3.6	−2.4
56 Thailand	7.8	6.8	5.2	3.7	9.0	8.7	11.4	10.0	9.1	7.5
57 Botswana	14.8	10.7	6.4	−4.0	30.2	15.6	..	8.2	10.6	10.8
58 Dominican Rep.	8.5	3.3	5.9	0.7	14.4	3.7	12.0	3.9	6.9	4.0
59 Peru	3.5	1.5	2.0	1.2	4.1	1.1	4.4	−0.1	3.6	1.9
60 Mauritius	2.3	3.6	..	−3.1	..	4.4	..	4.3	..	6.5
61 Congo, People's Rep.	6.8	8.1	4.1	0.4	9.3	12.7	..	..	6.7	6.9
62 Ecuador	7.2	4.8	3.9	1.6	13.9	4.8	11.4	7.6	5.1	5.8
63 Jamaica	5.4	−1.4	0.6	0.2	4.5	−3.9	4.0	−3.3	6.8	−0.2
64 Guatemala	6.0	3.1	5.8	1.9	7.2	4.3	7.4	3.4	5.8	3.3
65 Turkey	6.5	4.1	2.5	3.3	7.9	4.2	9.5	4.0	8.4	4.3

Note: For data comparability and coverage, see the technical notes.

	Average annual growth rate (percent)									
	GDP		Agriculture		Industry		(Manufacturing)[a]		Services	
	1965–73[b]	1973–84[c]	1965–73[b]	1973–84[c]	1965–73[b]	1973–84[c]	1965–73	1973–84[c]	1965–73[b]	1973–84[c]
66 Costa Rica	7.1	2.8	7.0	1.9	9.3	3.3	..	..	6.1	2.9
67 Paraguay	5.1	7.5	2.7	5.7	6.8	9.5	6.1	6.7	6.0	7.7
68 Tunisia	6.9	5.5	6.6	1.9	8.6	6.8	10.4	10.2	6.0	5.9
69 Colombia	6.4	3.7	4.0	3.5	8.2	2.5	8.8	2.0	6.9	4.4
70 Jordan	..	9.6	..	5.4	..	13.6	..	12.9	..	8.5
71 Syrian Arab Rep.	6.2	7.0	−0.7	6.8	14.9	4.5	..	..	5.7	8.3
72 Angola	..	..	..	..	..	..	..	..	..	..
73 Cuba	..	..	..	..	..	..	..	..	..	..
74 Korea, Dem. Rep.	..	..	..	..	..	..	..	..	..	..
75 Lebanon	6.2	..	1.4	..	5.5	..	..	..	7.1	..
76 Mongolia	..	..	..	..	..	..	..	..	..	..
Upper middle-income	**7.7** w	**4.5** w	**3.5** w	**3.0** w	**8.6** w	**4.6** w	**9.5** w	**5.3** w	**8.2** w	**5.1** w
77 Chile	3.4	2.7	−1.1	3.4	3.0	1.9	4.1	0.7	4.4	3.2
78 Brazil	9.8	4.4	3.8	4.0	11.0	4.2	11.2	4.9	10.5	4.6
79 Portugal	7.0	..	..	..	..	..	..	..	..	..
80 Malaysia	6.7	7.3	..	4.2	..	8.7	..	8.7	..	8.1
81 Panama	7.4	5.0	3.4	2.1	9.3	3.0	8.0	2.1	7.8	6.1
82 Uruguay	1.2	2.0	0.4	1.5	1.4	1.5	..	..	1.3	2.3
83 Mexico	7.9	5.1	5.4	3.4	8.6	5.5	9.9	5.0	8.0	5.2
84 Korea, Rep. of	10.0	7.2	2.9	1.7	18.4	10.9	21.1	11.5	11.3	6.8
85 Yugoslavia	6.1	4.2	3.2	2.0	7.1	4.7	..	..	6.4	4.7
86 Argentina	4.3	0.4	−0.1	1.6	5.1	−0.7	4.6	−0.2	5.5	0.9
87 South Africa	5.1	2.7	..	..	..	..	..	..	..	..
88 Algeria	7.0	6.4	2.4	4.2	9.1	6.3	10.9	17.8	5.3	7.0
89 Venezuela	5.1	1.9	4.5	2.4	4.1	1.1	5.7	3.4	6.0	2.3
90 Greece	7.5	2.7	2.5	1.2	11.1	1.9	12.0	2.3	7.3	3.7
91 Israel	9.6	3.1	..	..	..	..	..	..	..	..
92 Hong Kong	7.9	9.1	−0.6	0.8	8.4	8.0	..	..	8.1	9.6
93 Trinidad and Tobago	3.5	5.2	1.6	..	2.3	..	..	..	4.5	..
94 Singapore	13.0	8.2	5.7	1.4	17.6	8.6	19.5	7.6	11.5	8.1
95 Iran, Islamic Rep.	10.4	..	5.2	..	10.5	..	13.7	..	12.7	..
96 Iraq	4.4	..	1.7	..	4.8	..	8.9	..	5.1	..
High-income oil exporters	**9.0** w	**4.5** w	..	**6.8** w	..	**−0.2** w	..	**7.6** w	..	**10.8** w
97 Oman	21.9	6.1	..	..	..	..	..	..	..	..
98 Libya	7.7	3.0	11.5	6.5	6.6	−4.3	12.4	11.4	13.4	14.7
99 Saudi Arabia	11.2	6.0	2.6	6.9	13.3	2.4	10.6	8.2	8.3	12.5
100 Kuwait	5.1	1.5	..	10.2	..	−4.5	..	..	..	8.1
101 United Arab Emirates	..	..	..	..	..	..	..	5.3	..	..
Industrial market economies	**4.7** w	**2.4** w	**1.8** w	**1.1** w	**5.1** w	**1.8** w	**5.3** w	**2.1** w	**4.8** w	**2.1** w
102 Spain	6.4	1.6	2.8	..	8.6	..	9.8	..	5.6	..
103 Ireland	5.0	3.9	..	..	..	..	..	..	..	..
104 Italy	5.2	2.1	0.5	1.7	6.2	1.8	..	..	5.2	2.5
105 New Zealand	3.7	1.4	..	..	..	..	..	..	..	..
106 United Kingdom	2.8	1.0	2.6	2.7	2.1	−0.3	2.6	−1.7	3.3	1.7
107 Belgium	5.2	1.7	2.2	2.1	6.4	1.0	7.4	1.3	4.4	2.2
108 Austria	5.5	2.5	1.7	0.5	6.4	2.1	6.9	2.5	5.2	3.3
109 Netherlands	5.5	1.6	5.0	4.8	6.5	(.)	..	..	5.0	2.2
110 France	5.5	2.3	1.7	1.6	6.7	1.4	7.7	1.7	5.2	2.9
111 Japan	9.8	4.3	2.1	−1.3	13.5	5.9	14.4	7.2	8.3	3.3
112 Finland	5.3	2.9	1.0	1.1	6.4	3.0	7.5	3.7	5.6	3.2
113 Germany, Fed. Rep.	4.6	2.0	2.5	2.1	4.9	1.7	5.3	1.9	4.4	2.3
114 Denmark	3.9	1.7	−1.5	3.7	4.0	0.8	4.7	2.4	4.3	1.9
115 Australia	5.6	2.4	1.6	2.4	5.7	1.4	4.9	1.0	5.4	3.5
116 Sweden	3.6	1.4	1.1	−0.1	3.9	0.2	4.1	−0.1	3.6	2.1
117 Canada	5.2	2.5	1.2	1.8	5.2	1.0	5.4	1.1	5.5	3.2
118 Norway	4.0	3.7	−0.5	1.0	4.8	4.2	4.6	(.)	4.0	3.7
119 United States	3.2	2.3	1.8	1.4	2.8	1.2	2.9	1.4	3.5	3.0
120 Switzerland	4.2	0.8	..	..	..	..	..	..	..	..
East European nonmarket economies	..	..	..	..	..	..	..	..	..	..
121 Hungary[d]	6.1	3.5	3.1	3.5	6.5	4.1	..	..	7.5	2.8
122 Poland	..	..	..	..	..	..	..	..	..	..
123 Albania	..	..	..	..	..	..	..	..	..	..
124 Bulgaria	..	..	..	..	..	..	..	..	..	..
125 Czechoslovakia	..	..	..	..	..	..	..	..	..	..
126 German Dem. Rep.	..	..	..	..	..	..	..	..	..	..
127 Romania	..	..	..	..	..	..	..	..	..	..
128 USSR	..	..	..	..	..	..	..	..	..	..

a. Because manufacturing is the most dynamic part of the industrial sector, its growth rate is shown separately.   b. Figures in italics are for 1966–73, not 1965–73.   c. Figures in italics are for 1973–83, not 1973–84.   d. Services include the unallocated share of GDP.

Table 3. Structure of production

		GDP[a] (millions of dollars)		Distribution of gross domestic product (percent)							
				Agriculture		Industry		(Manufacturing)[b]		Services	
		1965[c]	1984[d]	1965[c]	1984[d]	1965[c]	1984[d]	1965	1984[d]	1965[c]	1984[d]
	Low-income economies			42 w	36 w	28 w	35 w	14 w	15 w	30 w	29 w
	China and India			42 w	36 w	31 w	38 w	15 w	15 w	27 w	26 w
	Other low-income			43 w	36 w	16 w	20 w	11 w	15 w	41 w	44 w
	Sub-Saharan Africa			43 w	39 w	16 w	18 w	9 w	10 w	41 w	43 w
1	Ethiopia	1,180	4,270	58	48	14	16	7	11	28	36
2	Bangladesh	4,380	12,320	53	48	11	12	..	..	36	39
3	Mali	..	980	49	46	13	11	..	..	38	43
4	Zaire	1,640	4,700	22	..	27	..	17	..	51	..
5	Burkina Faso	250	820	52	43	15	20	..	..	32	38
6	Nepal	730	2,290	65	56	11	12	3	4	23	32
7	Burma	1,600	6,130	35	48	13	13	9	9	52	39
8	Malawi	220	1,090	50	37	13	18	..	..	37	45
9	Niger	370	1,340	63	33	9	31	..	..	28	37
10	Tanzania	790	4,410	46	..	14	..	8	..	40	..
11	Burundi	160	1,020	..	58	..	16	..	..	..	26
12	Uganda	1,180	4,710	52	..	13	..	8	..	35	..
13	Togo	190	720	45	22	21	28	10	6	34	50
14	Central African Rep.	140	560	46	39	16	20	4	8	38	40
15	India	46,260	162,280	47	35	22	27	15	15	31	38
16	Madagascar	730	2,380	31	42	16	16	..	..	53	42
17	Somalia	220	1,364	71	..	6	..	3	..	24	..
18	Benin	210	900	53	43	9	14	..	..	38	43
19	Rwanda	150	1,600	75	..	7	..	2	..	18	..
20	China	65,590	281,250	39	36	38	44	..	..	23	20
21	Kenya	920	5,140	35	31	18	21	11	12	47	48
22	Sierra Leone	320	900	34	35	28	25	6	6	38	40
23	Haiti	350	1,820	..	..	..	..	..	..	..	..
24	Guinea	520	2,100	..	41	..	21	..	2	..	38
25	Ghana	1,330	4,485	41	52	19	9	10	5	41	40
26	Sri Lanka	1,770	5,430	28	28	21	26	17	14	51	46
27	Sudan	1,330	6,730	54	33	9	16	4	..	37	51
28	Pakistan	5,450	27,730	40	24	20	29	14	20	40	47
29	Senegal	810	2,390	25	17	18	28	..	18	56	55
30	Afghanistan	620	..	..	..	..	..	..	..	..	..
31	Bhutan	..	..	..	..	..	..	..	..	..	..
32	Chad	240	..	47	..	12	..	..	..	41	..
33	Kampuchea, Dem.	..	..	..	..	..	..	..	..	..	..
34	Lao PDR	..	..	..	..	..	..	..	..	..	..
35	Mozambique	..	..	..	..	..	..	..	..	..	..
36	Viet Nam	..	..	..	..	..	..	..	..	..	..
	Middle-income economies			21 w	14 w	31 w	37 w	20 w	22 w	48 w	49 w
	Oil exporters			22 w	15 w	28 w	39 w	16 w	18 w	50 w	46 w
	Oil importers			21 w	13 w	33 w	35 w	22 w	25 w	46 w	52 w
	Sub-Saharan Africa			38 w	25 w	25 w	31 w	9 w	7 w	37 w	44 w
	Lower middle-income			31 w	22 w	25 w	33 w	15 w	17 w	44 w	45 w
37	Mauritania	160	660	32	30	36	27	4	..	32	42
38	Liberia	270	980	27	36	40	26	3	7	34	38
39	Zambia	1,060	2,640	14	15	54	39	6	21	32	46
40	Lesotho	50	360	65	..	5	..	1	..	30	..
41	Bolivia	920	3,610	21	25	30	33	16	20	49	40
42	Indonesia	3,630	80,590	59	26	12	40	8	..	29	34
43	Yemen Arab Rep.	..	2,940	..	24	..	21	..	9	..	56
44	Yemen, PDR	..	..	..	..	..	..	..	..	..	..
45	Cote d'Ivoire	960	6,690	36	28	17	26	10	17	47	46
46	Philippines	6,010	32,840	26	25	28	34	20	25	46	41
47	Morocco	2,950	13,300	23	17	28	32	16	17	49	51
48	Honduras	460	2,840	40	27	19	26	12	15	41	47
49	El Salvador	800	4,070	29	21	22	21	18	16	49	58
50	Papua New Guinea	340	2,360	42	34	18	9	..	..	41	58
51	Egypt, Arab Rep.	4,550	30,060	29	20	27	33	..	..	45	48
52	Nigeria	4,190	73,450	53	27	19	30	7	4	29	43
53	Zimbabwe	960	4,580	18	14	35	40	20	27	47	46
54	Cameroon	750	7,800	32	22	17	35	10	11	50	43
55	Nicaragua	710	2,830	25	24	24	30	18	25	51	45
56	Thailand	4,050	41,960	35	20	23	28	14	..	42	52
57	Botswana	50	990	34	6	19	45	12	7	47	48
58	Dominican Rep.	960	4,910	26	15	20	31	14	19	53	53
59	Peru	4,900	18,790	15	8	30	40	20	25	55	51
60	Mauritius	190	860	16	14	23	25	14	17	61	61
61	Congo, People's Rep	200	2,010	19	7	19	60	..	6	62	33
62	Ecuador	1,150	9,870	27	14	22	41	18	19	50	46
63	Jamaica	870	2,380	10	6	37	39	17	18	53	56
64	Guatemala	1,330	9,400	..	..	..	..	..	..	..	..
65	Turkey	7,660	47,460	34	19	25	33	16	24	41	47

Note: For data comparability and coverage, see the technical notes.

	GDPª (millions of dollars)		Distribution of gross domestic product (percent)							
			Agriculture		Industry		(Manufacturing)ᵇ		Services	
	1965ᶜ	1984ᵈ	1965ᶜ	1984ᵈ	1965ᶜ	1984ᵈ	1965	1984ᵈ	1965ᶜ	1984ᵈ
66 Costa Rica	590	3,560	24	21	23	30	..	..	53	49
67 Paraguay	550	3,870	37	26	19	26	16	17	45	48
68 Tunisia	880	6,940	22	15	24	35	9	14	54	50
69 Colombia	5,570	34,400	30	20	25	30	18	18	46	50
70 Jordan	..	3,430	..	8	..	30	..	15	..	62
71 Syrian Arab Rep.	1,470	15,930	29	20	22	24	..	..	49	57
72 Angola	..	..	..	..	..	..	..	..	..	..
73 Cuba	..	..	..	..	..	..	..	..	..	..
74 Korea, Dem. Rep.	..	..	..	..	..	..	..	..	..	..
75 Lebanon	1,150	..	12	..	21	..	..	..	67	..
76 Mongolia	..	..	..	..	..	..	..	..	..	..
Upper middle-income			17 w	10 w	35 w	39 w	22 w	25 w	48 w	51 w
77 Chile	5,940	19,760	9	6	40	39	24	21	52	56
78 Brazil	19,260	187,130	19	13	33	35	26	27	48	52
79 Portugal	3,740	19,060	..	9	..	40	..	..	..	50
80 Malaysia	3,000	29,280	30	21	24	35	10	19	45	44
81 Panama	660	4,540	18	9	19	19	12	9	63	72
82 Uruguay	930	4,580	15	14	32	29			53	57
83 Mexico	20,160	171,300	14	9	31	40	21	24	54	52
84 Korea, Rep. of	3,000	83,220	38	14	25	40	18	28	37	47
85 Yugoslavia	11,190	38,990	23	15	42	46	..	..	35	40
86 Argentina	14,330	76,210	17	12	42	39	33	30	42	50
87 South Africa	10,540	73,390	10	5	42	47	23	23	48	48
88 Algeria	3,170	50,690	15	6	34	53	11	..	51	41
89 Venezuela	8,290	47,500	7	7	23	43	..	18	71	50
90 Greece	5,270	29,550	24	18	26	29	16	18	49	53
91 Israel	3,590	22,350	8	5	37	27	..	..	55	68
92 Hong Kong	2,150	30,620	2	1	40	22	24	..	58	78
93 Trinidad and Tobago	660	8,620	5	..	38	..	19	..	57	..
94 Singapore	970	18,220	3	1	24	39	15	25	73	60
95 Iran, Islamic Rep.	6,170	157,630	26	..	36	..	12	..	38	..
96 Iraq	2,430	..	18	..	46	..	8	..	36	..
High-income oil exporters			5 w	2 w	65 w	61 w	5 w	7 w	30 w	37 w
97 Oman	60	7,680	61	..	23	..	..	..	16	..
98 Libya	1,500	30,570	5	2	63	64	3	4	33	34
99 Saudi Arabia	2,300	109,380	8	3	60	60	9	7	31	38
100 Kuwait	2,100	21,710	0	1	73	58	3	8	27	41
101 United Arab Emirates	..	28,840	..	1	..	67	..	9	..	32
Industrial market economies			5 w	3 w	39 w	35 w	29 w	25 w	56 w	62 w
102 Spain	23,320	160,930	15	..	36	..	25	..	49	..
103 Ireland	2,690	18,270	..	11	..	25	..	14	..	64
104 Italy	62,600	348,380	11	5	41	40	..	..	48	55
105 New Zealand	5,580	23,340	..	9	..	32	..	23	..	60
106 United Kingdom	99,530	425,370	3	2	41	36	30	22	56	62
107 Belgium	16,840	77,630	5	3	41	34	30	24	53	64
108 Austria	9,470	64,460	9	4	46	38	33	27	45	58
109 Netherlands	19,700	132,600	..	4	..	32	..	24	..	64
110 France	97,930	489,380	..	4	..	34	..	25	..	62
111 Japan	90,970	1,255,006	9	3	43	41	32	30	48	56
112 Finland	8,190	51,230	15	7	33	34	21	24	52	59
113 Germany, Fed. Rep.	114,830	613,160	..	2	..	46	..	36	..	52
114 Denmark	10,180	54,640	8	5	32	25	20	17	60	70
115 Australia	23,260	182,170	10	..	41	..	28	..	50	..
116 Sweden	21,670	91,880	6	3	40	31	28	22	53	66
117 Canada	51,840	334,110	5	3	34	24	23	..	61	72
118 Norway	7,080	54,720	8	4	33	43	21	14	59	54
119 United States	688,600	3,634,600	3	2	38	32	29	21	59	66
120 Switzerland	13,920	91,110	..	..	..	..	..	..	..	..
East European nonmarket economies			..	..	..	..	..	..	..	..
121 Hungaryᵉ	..	20,150	24	20	37	42	..	..	39	38
122 Poland	..	75,410	..	15	..	52	..	..	..	33
123 Albania	..	..	..	..	..	..	..	..	..	..
124 Bulgaria	..	..	..	..	..	..	..	..	..	..
125 Czechoslovakia	..	..	..	..	..	..	..	..	..	..
126 German Dem. Rep.	..	..	..	..	..	..	..	..	..	..
127 Romania	..	..	..	..	..	..	..	..	..	..
128 USSR	..	..	..	..	..	..	..	..	..	..

a. See the technical notes.   b. Because manufacturing is the most dynamic part of the industrial sector, its share of GDP is shown separately.   c. Figures in italics are for 1966 not 1965.   d. Figures in italics are for 1983, not 1984.   e. Based on constant price series; services include the unallocated share of GDP.

185

Table 4. Growth of consumption and investment

	General government consumption		Private consumption		Gross domestic investment	
Average annual growth rate (percent)						
	1965–73	1973–84a	1965–73	1973–84a	1965–73	1973–84a
Low-income economies	6.5 *w*	6.7 *w*	4.3 *w*	5.1 *w*	8.0 *w*	6.5 *w*
China and India	6.9 *w*	7.0 *w*	4.8 *w*	5.3 *w*	9.1 *w*	6.8 *w*
Other low-income	4.8 *w*	4.3 *w*	3.0 *w*	4.2 *w*	3.2 *w*	4.1 *w*
Sub-Saharan Africa	4.6 *w*	3.5 *w*	2.6 *w*	2.8 *w*	6.3 *w*	0.8 *w*
1 Ethiopia	3.7	7.1	4.2	2.6	1.5	2.6
2 Bangladesh	b	b	0.9	5.1	−6.4	4.7
3 Mali	2.3	5.8	3.4	3.1	1.0	4.2
4 Zaire	5.8	..	2.2	..	10.2	..
5 Burkina Faso	10.7	3.0	0.4	4.1	13.7	−3.3
6 Nepal	..	..	..	..	..	..
7 Burma	b	b	2.9	5.4	2.5	14.1
8 Malawi	3.0	6.7	4.1	3.0	16.0	−2.6
9 Niger	2.1	2.3	−3.3	6.6	4.6	3.5
10 Tanzania	b	..	5.0	..	9.6	..
11 Burundi	12.3	5.4	4.7	2.8	−1.4	15.7
12 Uganda	b	..	3.8	..	2.1	..
13 Togo	7.9	8.4	6.0	3.3	3.3	−0.2
14 Central African Rep.	1.7	−2.0	3.6	2.6	2.3	−4.7
15 India	6.8	8.8	3.2	4.1	3.9	4.2
16 Madagascar	3.3	3.3	4.0	−0.5	4.2	−1.8
17 Somalia	16.9	..	0.7	..	5.6	..
18 Benin	3.6	3.7	1.1	3.1	3.9	10.3
19 Rwanda	2.8	..	7.7	..	6.3	..
20 China	7.0	6.4	6.3	6.3	12.9	8.0
21 Kenya	13.1	5.2	5.1	2.9	15.9	1.2
22 Sierra Leone	5.3	..	3.8	..	−1.4	..
23 Haiti	3.1	5.1	0.8	2.4	14.4	7.6
24 Guinea	..	5.0	..	2.5	..	−1.5
25 Ghana	1.1	5.4	2.3	−1.3	−3.5	−5.4
26 Sri Lanka	2.3	1.7	3.5	4.7	7.9	13.8
27 Sudan	1.4	3.3	−1.7	6.8	0.2	3.2
28 Pakistan	6.2	6.0	5.9	5.9	0.4	5.4
29 Senegal	−1.2	6.2	0.1	3.1	8.1	−0.7
30 Afghanistan	b	..	1.1	..	−2.2	..
31 Bhutan	..	..	..	..	..	..
32 Chad	6.0	..	0.7	..	4.5	..
33 Kampuchea, Dem.	..	..	..	..	..	..
34 Lao PDR	..	..	..	..	..	..
35 Mozambique	..	..	..	..	..	..
36 Viet Nam	..	..	..	..	..	..
Middle-income economies	8.2 *w*	4.8 *w*	7.1 *w*	4.5 *w*	8.9 *w*	3.0 *w*
Oil exporters	10.7 *w*	6.2 *w*	6.9 *w*	5.6 *w*	9.5 *w*	4.1 *w*
Oil importers	6.7 *w*	3.9 *w*	7.2 *w*	3.9 *w*	8.5 *w*	2.3 *w*
Sub-Saharan Africa	13.4 *w*	4.1 *w*	6.1 *w*	3.7 *w*	12.2 *w*	−1.2 *w*
Lower middle-income	8.7 *w*	6.0 *w*	5.9 *w*	4.7 *w*	8.3 *w*	3.5 *w*
37 Mauritania	6.1	−0.6	2.7	3.3	12.5	4.8
38 Liberia	4.5	4.1	0.3	−0.1	5.6	1.5
39 Zambia	10.4	−1.0	−1.2	0.9	6.2	−13.7
40 Lesotho	5.4	..	5.9	..	11.0	..
41 Bolivia	8.4	1.5	3.1	2.0	6.9	−12.2
42 Indonesia	9.8	10.3	7.1	9.1	17.5	11.3
43 Yemen Arab Rep.	..	17.9	..	5.7	..	12.3
44 Yemen, PDR	..	..	..	..	..	..
45 Cote d'Ivoire	15.2	8.1	5.1	3.3	10.2	2.9
46 Philippines	8.4	3.0	4.0	4.3	4.4	4.3
47 Morocco	5.5	9.9	5.1	3.7	11.0	1.6
48 Honduras	7.0	5.6	3.8	3.4	4.3	2.4
49 El Salvador	7.6	3.5	3.9	−0.9	3.4	−4.4
50 Papua New Guinea	2.4	−2.2	5.2	3.1	10.9	4.2
51 Egypt, Arab Rep.	b	b	5.3	8.4	−1.5	10.3
52 Nigeria	16.1	3.8	7.3	3.5	15.2	−2.0
53 Zimbabwe	8.3	..	7.2	..	7.6	..
54 Cameroon	4.6	6.5	3.4	6.6	8.6	10.6
55 Nicaragua	3.2	13.8	2.7	−4.8	2.2	−1.0
56 Thailand	9.8	8.8	6.9	6.0	7.6	5.3
57 Botswana	5.5	12.8	7.4	8.6	48.1	1.4
58 Dominican Rep.	−3.6	6.8	8.6	3.5	19.2	2.0
59 Peru	5.4	2.4	5.6	1.6	−2.6	−2.7
60 Mauritius	2.3	5.7	−0.7	4.7	5.2	−3.7
61 Congo, People's Rep.	7.4	5.3	3.9	6.2	9.3	6.3
62 Ecuador	7.0	7.5	5.2	5.8	6.0	3.1
63 Jamaica	13.6	2.4	4.5	−2.6	7.5	−5.8
64 Guatemala	5.7	6.1	5.4	3.2	5.3	−0.1
65 Turkey	5.7	5.5	6.0	2.6	9.7	2.3

Note: For data comparability and coverage, see the technical notes.

	Average annual growth rate (percent)					
	General government consumption		Private consumption		Gross domestic investment	
	1965–73	1973–84[a]	1965–73	1973–84[a]	1965–73	1973–84[a]
66 Costa Rica	6.8	2.9	5.1	1.9	9.3	0.7
67 Paraguay	6.2	8.9	5.0	7.3	8.3	10.3
68 Tunisia	5.9	7.1	7.2	7.0	1.5	6.0
69 Colombia	8.8	6.0	6.5	4.5	6.7	5.5
70 Jordan	. .	. .	. .	. .	. .	. .
71 Syrian Arab Rep.	12.5	10.0	6.5	8.4	7.2	10.0
72 Angola	. .	. .	. .	. .	. .	. .
73 Cuba	. .	. .	. .	. .	. .	. .
74 Korea, Dem. Rep.	. .	. .	. .	. .	. .	. .
75 Lebanon	3.7	. .	5.4	. .	5.1	. .
76 Mongolia	. .	. .	. .	. .	. .	. .
Upper middle-income	**8.0** *w*	**4.2** *w*	**7.7** *w*	**4.4** *w*	**9.1** *w*	**2.8** *w*
77 Chile	6.3	0.4	4.8	2.3	(.)	1.0
78 Brazil	7.3	3.1	10.2	4.9	11.3	(.)
79 Portugal	7.1	6.2	8.4	1.5	8.0	2.4
80 Malaysia	6.9	10.0	4.6	6.9	9.1	11.4
81 Panama	9.7	5.1	5.2	4.8	15.4	−0.4
82 Uruguay	1.9	3.0	4.1	0.6	4.0	3.9
83 Mexico	8.7	6.8	7.7	4.7	8.4	3.3
84 Korea, Rep. of	7.3	5.4	8.7	5.9	19.7	8.8
85 Yugoslavia	2.2	2.8	9.7	3.3	4.8	3.9
86 Argentina	2.4	b	4.3	0.7	6.7	−3.4
87 South Africa	5.5	. .	5.5	. .	6.4	. .
88 Algeria	5.8	10.1	6.4	9.2	17.4	6.8
89 Venezuela	6.8	*4.5*	5.5	5.6	9.0	*−0.8*
90 Greece	5.7	*5.2*	6.9	*3.1*	11.1	*−1.4*
91 Israel	15.8	−1.0	6.9	5.0	13.3	−1.5
92 Hong Kong	6.9	9.2	9.5	9.9	3.7	9.7
93 Trinidad and Tobago	b	. .	4.9	. .	2.4	. .
94 Singapore	16.3	6.5	9.9	6.2	22.7	9.5
95 Iran, Islamic Rep.	17.3	. .	7.9	. .	11.2	. .
96 Iraq	b	. .	3.3	. .	7.2	. .
High-income oil exporters	. .	. .	**8.7** *w*	. .	**4.3** *w*	. .
97 Oman	. .	. .	. .	. .	. .	. .
98 Libya	19.8	7.3	22.1	*9.0*	2.7	*3.7*
99 Saudi Arabia	b	b	8.8	*21.2*	9.4	*27.1*
100 Kuwait	b	. .	4.3	. .	0.8	. .
101 United Arab Emirates	. .	. .	. .	. .	. .	. .
Industrial market economies	**3.2** *w*	**2.5** *w*	**4.9** *w*	**2.6** *w*	**5.4** *w*	**0.9** *w*
102 Spain	4.0	4.2	6.1	1.3	6.7	−2.3
103 Ireland	6.4	3.8	4.8	1.1	8.5	1.8
104 Italy	4.1	2.5	5.7	2.2	5.9	−0.5
105 New Zealand	2.9	1.6	3.2	1.1	2.6	−1.8
106 United Kingdom	2.1	1.4	2.9	1.4	3.1	−1.0
107 Belgium	4.9	2.7	5.0	2.1	4.1	−2.6
108 Austria	3.8	2.9	4.7	2.6	6.9	0.7
109 Netherlands	3.2	2.3	5.1	1.8	5.9	−2.0
110 France	3.9	2.7	5.3	3.0	6.9	0.4
111 Japan	5.3	3.9	8.4	3.3	14.1	3.0
112 Finland	5.5	4.4	4.8	2.4	4.9	−0.2
113 Germany, Fed. Rep.	4.0	2.2	4.9	1.8	4.4	1.3
114 Denmark	6.0	3.6	2.9	0.8	4.9	−2.4
115 Australia	4.8	4.3	4.9	3.0	3.7	0.7
116 Sweden	4.9	2.8	2.9	0.9	2.1	−1.5
117 Canada	6.2	1.4	5.3	2.6	3.8	0.1
118 Norway	5.6	3.7	3.7	4.5	4.5	−2.1
119 United States	1.8	2.5	4.0	3.0	2.7	1.5
120 Switzerland	3.9	1.6	4.5	1.1	5.3	1.2
East European nonmarket economies	. .	. .	. .	. .	. .	. .
121 Hungary	. .	*3.3*	. .	*3.0*	. .	*2.0*
122 Poland	. .	. .	. .	. .	. .	. .
123 Albania	. .	. .	. .	. .	. .	. .
124 Bulgaria	. .	. .	. .	. .	. .	. .
125 Czechoslovakia	. .	. .	. .	. .	. .	. .
126 German Dem. Rep.	. .	. .	. .	. .	. .	. .
127 Romania	. .	. .	. .	. .	. .	. .
128 USSR	. .	. .	. .	. .	. .	. .

a. Figures in italics are for 1973–83, not 1973–84.   b. General government consumption figures are not available separately; they are included in private consumption.

Table 5. Structure of demand

	Distribution of gross domestic product (percent)											
	General government consumption		Private consumption		Gross domestic investment		Gross domestic savings		Exports of goods and nonfactor services		Resource balance	
	1965	1984a	1965	1984a	1965	1984a	1965	1984a	1965	1984a	1965	1984a
Low-income economies	13 w	13 w	68 w	64 w	21 w	25 w	19 w	23 w	7 w	9 w	−2 w	2 w
China and India	13 w	14 w	66 w	60 w	22 w	28 w	21 w	26 w	4 w	8 w	−1 w	−2 w
Other low-income	12 w	12 w	77 w	81 w	15 w	16 w	12 w	7 w	19 w	14 w	−3 w	−9 w
Sub-Saharan Africa	14 w	14 w	73 w	82 w	15 w	13 w	13 w	6 w	25 w	16 w	−2 w	−7 w
1 Ethiopia	11	17	77	81	13	11	12	2	12	12	−1	−9
2 Bangladesh	9	9	83	87	11	16	8	4	10	8	−4	−12
3 Mali	17	27	72	75	23	17	11	−2	13	23	−11	−19
4 Zaire	18	..	44	..	28	..	38	..	70	..	10	..
5 Burkina Faso	7	15	91	98	10	14	2	−13	9	18	−8	−28
6 Nepal	b	b	100	90	6	19	(.)	10	8	11	−6	−9
7 Burma	b	14	87	69	19	22	13	17	14	8	−6	−5
8 Malawi	16	16	84	67	14	16	(.)	17	19	27	−14	(.)
9 Niger	8	10	84	79	15	25	9	11	12	22	−7	−14
10 Tanzania	10	..	74	..	15	..	16	..	26	..	1	..
11 Burundi	7	14	89	79	6	21	4	7	10	9	−2	−14
12 Uganda	10	b	78	94	11	8	12	6	19	11	1	−3
13 Togo	8	17	76	79	22	23	17	4	20	31	−6	−19
14 Central African Rep.	22	13	67	91	21	12	11	−4	27	25	−11	−16
15 India	10	11	74	67	18	24	16	22	4	6	−2	−3
16 Madagascar	23	14	74	78	10	14	4	9	16	16	−6	−5
17 Somalia	8	..	84	..	11	..	8	..	17	..	−3	..
18 Benin	14	10	83	93	12	7	3	−3	14	18	−9	−10
19 Rwanda	14	..	81	..	10	..	5	..	12	..	−5	..
20 China	15	15	59	55	25	30	25	30	4	10	1	(.)
21 Kenya	15	19	70	61	14	22	15	20	31	26	1	−2
22 Sierra Leone	8	7	83	86	12	9	9	6	30	17	−3	−2
23 Haiti	8	12	90	84	7	16	2	4	13	24	−5	−12
24 Guinea	..	14	..	73	..	10	..	13	..	25	..	3
25 Ghana	14	6	77	89	18	6	8	5	17	11	−10	−1
26 Sri Lanka	13	7	74	73	12	26	13	20	38	29	1	−6
27 Sudan	12	12	79	91	10	11	9	−3	15	10	−1	−13
28 Pakistan	11	12	76	82	21	17	13	6	8	11	−8	−12
29 Senegal	17	19	75	76	12	15	8	5	24	29	−4	−11
30 Afghanistan	b	..	99	..	11	..	1	..	11	..	−10	..
31 Bhutan	..	..	..	..	..	..	..	..	..	..	..	..
32 Chad	14	..	84	..	9	..	2	..	23	..	−7	..
33 Kampuchea, Dem.	16	..	71	..	13	..	12	..	12	..	−1	..
34 Lao PDR	..	..	..	..	..	..	..	..	..	..	..	..
35 Mozambique	..	..	..	..	..	..	..	..	..	..	..	..
36 Viet Nam	..	..	..	..	..	..	..	..	..	..	..	..
Middle-income economies	11 w	13 w	68 w	67 w	21 w	21 w	21 w	22 w	18 w	25 w	(.) w	1 w
Oil exporters	11 w	13 w	68 w	62 w	19 w	22 w	21 w	25 w	19 w	24 w	2 w	3 w
Oil importers	11 w	14 w	67 w	70 w	22 w	21 w	21 w	21 w	18 w	25 w	−1 w	(.) w
Sub-Saharan Africa	10 w	14 w	70 w	68 w	19 w	14 w	20 w	18 w	27 w	22 w	1 w	4 w
Lower middle-income	11 w	13 w	73 w	71 w	17 w	19 w	16 w	16 w	17 w	21 w	−1 w	−3 w
37 Mauritania	19	17	54	84	14	22	27	−1	42	48	13	−23
38 Liberia	12	23	61	62	17	20	27	14	50	40	10	−5
39 Zambia	15	23	45	62	25	14	40	15	49	37	15	1
40 Lesotho	18	..	109	..	11	..	−26	..	16	..	−38	..
41 Bolivia	10	11	80	63	16	18	11	26	17	17	−5	8
42 Indonesia	6	10	88	70	7	21	6	20	5	23	(.)	−1
43 Yemen Arab Rep.	..	40	..	83	..	21	..	−22	..	7	..	−43
44 Yemen, PDR	..	..	..	..	..	..	..	..	..	..	..	..
45 Cote d'Ivoire	11	16	69	56	19	13	20	28	35	46	1	15
46 Philippines	9	6	70	76	21	18	21	18	17	21	(.)	−1
47 Morocco	12	18	76	70	10	23	12	12	18	25	1	−11
48 Honduras	10	15	75	71	15	19	15	14	27	27	(.)	−5
49 El Salvador	9	14	79	82	15	12	12	4	27	21	−2	−8
50 Papua New Guinea	34	24	64	60	22	31	2	16	18	42	−20	−14
51 Egypt, Arab Rep.	19	23	67	65	18	25	14	12	18	28	−4	−13
52 Nigeria	7	14	76	71	19	12	17	15	18	16	−2	2
53 Zimbabwe	12	19	65	72	15	13	23	9	..	22	8	−3
54 Cameroon	14	10	73	58	13	26	13	33	25	32	−1	7
55 Nicaragua	8	35	74	55	21	18	18	10	29	18	−3	−7
56 Thailand	10	13	71	66	20	23	19	21	18	24	−1	−2
57 Botswana	24	26	89	54	6	21	−13	20	32	61	−19	−1
58 Dominican Rep.	18	8	75	76	9	21	7	17	15	27	−2	−5
59 Peru	12	12	69	70	21	14	19	18	16	20	−1	4
60 Mauritius	13	13	74	69	17	18	13	18	36	48	−4	(.)
61 Congo, People's Rep.	14	13	80	48	22	35	5	39	36	64	−17	4
62 Ecuador	9	12	80	66	14	20	11	22	16	27	−3	2
63 Jamaica	8	17	69	65	27	22	23	18	33	55	−4	−4
64 Guatemala	7	8	82	84	13	11	10	9	17	13	−3	−2
65 Turkey	12	10	74	79	15	20	13	11	6	12	−1	−9

Note: For data comparability and coverage, see the technical notes.

	Distribution of gross domestic product (percent)												
	General government consumption		Private consumption		Gross domestic investment		Gross domestic savings		Exports of goods and nonfactor services		Resource balance	
	1965	1984[a]	1965	1984[a]	1965	1984[a]	1965	1984[a]	1965	1984[a]	1965	1984[a]
66 Costa Rica	13	16	78	61	20	25	9	24	23	34	−10	−1
67 Paraguay	7	8	79	83	15	17	14	9	15	21	−1	−9
68 Tunisia	15	17	71	63	28	32	14	20	19	34	−13	−12
69 Colombia	8	11	75	73	16	19	17	16	11	12	1	−2
70 Jordan	..	24	..	92	..	32	..	−16	..	43	..	−48
71 Syrian Arab Rep.	14	23	76	65	10	24	10	12	17	13	(.)	−11
72 *Angola*	..	..	..	..	..	..	..	..	..	..	..	..
73 *Cuba*	..	..	..	..	..	..	..	..	..	..	..	..
74 *Korea, Dem. Rep.*	..	..	..	..	..	..	..	..	..	..	..	..
75 *Lebanon*	10	..	81	..	22	..	9	..	36	..	−13	..
76 *Mongolia*	..	..	..	..	..	..	..	..	..	..	..	..
Upper middle-income	**11** *w*	**14** *w*	**65** *w*	**65** *w*	**23** *w*	**22** *w*	**24** *w*	**26** *w*	**18** *w*	**26** *w*	**1** *w*	**4** *w*
77 Chile	11	14	73	73	15	14	16	13	14	23	1	−1
78 Brazil	11	b	62	79	25	16	27	21	8	14	2	6
79 Portugal	12	14	68	70	25	23	20	16	27	39	−5	−7
80 Malaysia	15	18	63	50	18	31	23	32	44	56	4	1
81 Panama	11	19	73	64	18	18	16	17	36	36	−2	−1
82 Uruguay	15	12	68	75	11	9	18	13	19	25	7	5
83 Mexico	7	10	72	61	22	22	21	30	9	18	−1	8
84 Korea, Rep. of	9	10	83	60	15	29	8	30	9	37	−7	(.)
85 Yugoslavia	18	16	52	54	30	29	30	30	22	31	(.)	1
86 Argentina	8	b	69	81	19	14	22	19	8	13	3	4
87 South Africa	11	16	62	55	28	25	27	29	26	26	(.)	4
88 Algeria	15	16	66	45	22	38	19	39	22	26	−3	1
89 Venezuela	12	13	54	58	24	16	34	29	31	32	10	13
90 Greece	12	19	73	70	26	21	15	11	9	19	−11	−10
91 Israel	20	33	65	59	29	19	15	8	19	40	−13	−11
92 Hong Kong	7	7	64	64	36	24	29	29	71	107	−7	5
93 Trinidad and Tobago	11	..	66	..	23	..	23	..	39	..	(.)	..
94 Singapore	10	11	80	46	22	47	10	43	123	..	−12	−4
95 *Iran, Islamic Rep.*	13	..	63	..	17	..	24	..	20	..	6	..
96 *Iraq*	20	..	50	..	16	..	31	..	38	..	15	..
High-income oil exporters	**15** *w*	**30** *w*	**32** *w*	**34** *w*	**19** *w*	**30** *w*	**53** *w*	**36** *w*	**61** *w*	**48** *w*	**34** *w*	**6** *w*
97 Oman	..	34	..	31	..	23	..	35	..	43	..	12
98 Libya	14	34	36	31	29	23	50	35	53	43	21	12
99 Saudi Arabia	18	31	34	36	14	35	48	32	60	44	34	−3
100 Kuwait	13	20	26	49	16	21	60	30	68	60	45	9
101 United Arab Emirates	..	27	..	17	..	27	..	56	..	61	..	29
Industrial market economies	**15** *w*	**17** *w*	**61** *w*	**62** *w*	**23** *w*	**21** *w*	**23** *w*	**21** *w*	**12** *w*	**18** *w*	**(.)** *w*	**(.)** *w*
102 Spain	7	12	71	67	25	18	21	21	11	24	−3	3
103 Ireland	14	19	72	58	24	22	15	23	35	61	−9	2
104 Italy	15	19	62	62	20	19	23	18	16	27	3	(.)
105 New Zealand	12	16	63	62	27	23	25	22	22	32	−2	−1
106 United Kingdom	17	22	64	61	20	17	19	17	20	29	−1	(.)
107 Belgium	13	17	64	66	23	15	23	17	36	77	(.)	2
108 Austria	13	18	59	57	28	25	27	25	26	37	−1	(.)
109 Netherlands	15	17	59	60	27	18	26	23	43	63	−1	5
110 France	13	16	61	64	25	19	26	19	14	25	1	(.)
111 Japan	8	10	58	59	32	28	33	31	11	15	1	3
112 Finland	14	19	60	54	28	24	26	26	21	31	−2	3
113 Germany, Fed. Rep.	15	20	56	57	28	21	29	23	18	31	(.)	2
114 Denmark	16	26	59	54	26	19	25	20	29	37	−2	1
115 Australia	11	17	63	64	28	21	26	19	15	15	−2	−2
116 Sweden	18	28	56	50	27	18	26	22	22	37	−1	4
117 Canada	15	21	60	57	26	19	25	22	19	29	(.)	4
118 Norway	15	19	56	47	30	25	29	35	41	48	−1	10
119 United States	17	19	62	65	20	19	21	16	5	8	1	−3
120 Switzerland	10	14	60	62	30	24	30	25	29	38	−1	(.)
East European nonmarket economies	**..**	**..**	**..**	**..**	**..**	**..**	**..**	**..**	**..**	**..**	**..**	**..**
121 Hungary	b	10	75	61	26	27	25	28	..	40	..	2
122 Poland	..	10	..	63	..	26	..	27	..	18	..	1
123 *Albania*	..	..	..	..	..	..	..	..	..	..	..	..
124 *Bulgaria*	..	..	..	..	..	..	..	..	..	..	..	..
125 *Czechoslovakia*	..	..	..	..	..	..	..	..	..	..	..	..
126 *German Dem. Rep.*	..	..	..	..	..	..	..	..	..	..	..	..
127 *Romania*	..	..	..	..	..	..	..	..	..	..	..	..
128 *USSR*	..	..	..	..	..	..	..	..	..	..	..	..

a. Figures in italics are for 1983, not 1984.   b. General government consumption figures are not available separately; they are included in private consumption.

Table 6. Agriculture and food

	Value added in agriculture (millions of 1980 dollars)		Cereal imports (thousands of metric tons)		Food aid in cereals (thousands of metric tons)		Fertilizer consumption (hundreds of grams of plant nutrient per hectare of arable land)		Average index of food production per capita (1974–76 = 100)
	1970	1984[a]	1974	1984	1974/75	1983/84	1970[b]	1983	1982–84
Low-income economies			24,017 t	26,430 t	5,651 t	4,878 t	178 w	661 w	116 w
China and India			15,101 t	17,355 t	1,582 t	580 t	230 w	923 w	121 w
Other low-income			8,916 t	9,075 t	4,069 t	4,298 t	78 w	195 w	102 w
Sub-Saharan Africa			2,560 t	5,195 t	796 t	2,087 t	23 w	49 w	92 w
1 Ethiopia	1,663	1,971	118	506	54	172	4	35	100
2 Bangladesh	5,427	6,703	1,866	2,136	2,076	1,163	142	596	99
3 Mali	403	606	281	367	107	111	29	75	101
4 Zaire	1,503	1,866	343	246	1	53	8	14	92
5 Burkina Faso	444	521	99	89	28	57	3	50	94
6 Nepal	1,102	1,364	18	27	0	30	30	137	91
7 Burma	1,705	3,403	26	7	9	6	34	158	124
8 Malawi	257	427	17	20	(.)	3	52	164	100
9 Niger	851	649	155	45	73	13	1	5	113
10 Tanzania	1,583	. .	431	364	148	136	30	42	100
11 Burundi	468	585	7	14	6	11	5	21	106
12 Uganda	2,388	2,682	37	20	0	10	13	. .	98
13 Togo	212	238	6	95	11	9	3	21	92
14 Central African Rep.	256	324	7	30	1	8	11	7	94
15 India	45,772	59,681	5,261	2,170	1,582	371	114	394	110
16 Madagascar	1,111	1,269	114	172	7	74	56	46	89
17 Somalia	434	. .	42	330	111	177	31	23	69
18 Benin	. .	463	8	65	9	6	33	30	97
19 Rwanda	. .	. .	3	20	19	25	3	3	112
20 China	69,147	134,877	9,840	15,185	0	209	418	1,806	128
21 Kenya	1,198	2,183	15	560	2	122	224	376	82
22 Sierra Leone	261	330	72	61	10	16	13	11	95
23 Haiti	. .	. .	83	205	25	72	4	36	90
24 Guinea	. .	794	63	186	49	43	18	6	93
25 Ghana	3,360	2,522	177	311	33	74	9	77	73
26 Sri Lanka	812	1,224	951	685	271	391	496	740	125
27 Sudan	1,610	2,203	125	530	46	450	31	67	93
28 Pakistan	5,007	6,581	1,274	291	584	395	168	586	104
29 Senegal	603	567	341	698	27	151	20	48	66
30 Afghanistan	. .	. .	5	20	10	100	24	63	102
31 Bhutan	. .	. .	3	11	0	7	(.)	10	104
32 Chad	339	. .	37	74	20	69	7	17	95
33 Kampuchea, Dem.	. .	. .	223	25	226	43	13	16	107
34 Lao PDR	. .	. .	53	37	8	2	4	6	129
35 Mozambique	. .	. .	62	392	34	297	27	77	73
36 Viet Nam	. .	. .	1,854	436	64	2	512	471	123
Middle-income economies			41,135 t	84,988 t	2,329 t	4,719 t	214 w	443 w	104 w
Oil exporters			18,022 t	45,487 t	1,135 t	2,712 t	140 w	466 w	102 w
Oil importers			23,113 t	39,501 t	1,194 t	2,007 t	258 w	431 w	105 w
Sub-Saharan Africa			1,361 t	4,849 t	114 t	503 t	46 w	109 w	92 w
Lower middle-income			17,128 t	32,838 t	1,624 t	4,685 t	76 w	431 w	104 w
37 Mauritania	200	215	115	277	48	129	6	. .	95
38 Liberia	235	334	42	109	3	47	55	75	91
39 Zambia	473	627	93	236	5	76	71	130	74
40 Lesotho	94	. .	49	141	14	50	17	151	78
41 Bolivia	541	723	209	320	22	284	13	18	84
42 Indonesia	12,097	21,229	1,919	1,926	301	466	119	745	120
43 Yemen Arab Rep.	. .	. .	158	612	33	5	1	57	84
44 Yemen, PDR	. .	. .	149	291	(.)	16	(.)	103	83
45 Cote d'Ivoire	1,733	2,542	172	545	4	0	71	107	110
46 Philippines	5,115	8,694	817	964	89	54	214	320	107
47 Morocco	2,784	2,905	891	2,610	75	448	130	293	91
48 Honduras	475	687	52	130	31	97	160	159	99
49 El Salvador	740	868	75	221	4	263	1,048	1,132	88
50 Papua New Guinea	655	926	71	174	. .	. .	76	182	95
51 Egypt, Arab Rep.	3,282	4,795	3,877	8,616	610	1,783	1,282	3,605	91
52 Nigeria	17,943	19,062	389	2,351	7	0	3	87	96
53 Zimbabwe	556	823	56	334	0	76	466	576	69
54 Cameroon	1,492	1,991	81	121	4	1	28	48	83
55 Nicaragua	410	606	44	135	3	56	184	483	78
56 Thailand	5,631	9,829	97	150	0	13	76	240	115
57 Botswana	20	74	21	59	5	32	14	10	61
58 Dominican Rep.	953	1,235	252	436	16	148	354	288	99
59 Peru	1,716	1,893	637	1,205	37	207	297	224	84
60 Mauritius	178	152	160	188	22	22	2,081	2,538	88
61 Congo, People's Rep.	147	178	34	113	2	1	112	24	96
62 Ecuador	1,054	1,413	152	369	13	14	123	283	89
63 Jamaica	205	235	340	432	1	54	886	628	89
64 Guatemala	. .	. .	138	142	9	19	224	474	101
65 Turkey	8,701	13,400	1,276	1,627	16	0	166	581	103

Note: For data comparability and coverage, see the technical notes.

	Value added in agriculture (millions of 1980 dollars)		Cereal imports (thousands of metric tons)		Food aid in cereals (thousands of metric tons)		Fertilizer consumption (hundreds of grams of plant nutrient per hectare of arable land)		Average index of food production per capita (1974-76=100)
	1970	1984[a]	1974	1984	1974/75	1983/84	1970[b]	1983	1982-84
66 Costa Rica	666	961	110	139	1	39	1,086	1,323	87
67 Paraguay	678	1,381	71	75	10	8	58	46	105
68 Tunisia	712	1,358	307	1,071	59	146	82	160	84
69 Colombia	4,247	6,918	503	789	28	3	310	563	104
70 Jordan	187	311	171	835	79	24	20	394	136
71 Syrian Arab Rep.	1,057	2,415	339	1,855	47	17	67	320	123
72 Angola	..	..	149	375	0	69	45	25	81
73 Cuba	..	..	1,622	2,105	..	0	1,539	1,699	129
74 Korea, Dem. Rep.	..	..	1,108	200	..	..	1,484	3,452	113
75 Lebanon	..	..	354	506	26	18	1,279	1,191	145
76 Mongolia	..	..	28	54	..	..	18	116	90
Upper middle-income			24,007 *t*	52,150 *t*	705 *t*	..	248 *w*	455 *w*	103 *w*
77 Chile	1,597	2,142	1,737	1,038	323	21	317	249	102
78 Brazil	18,425	34,503	2,485	5,336	31	3	169	307	115
79 Portugal	..	2,241	1,860	3,046	(.)	..	411	655	86
80 Malaysia	3,511	6,593	1,017	2,064	1	..	436	1,115	112
81 Panama	275	353	63	85	3	2	391	396	99
82 Uruguay	913	879	70	98	6	0	392	259	105
83 Mexico	11,125	17,286	2,881	8,484	..	1	246	612	104
84 Korea, Rep. of	8,176	12,234	2,679	6,334	234	0	2,466	3,311	109
85 Yugoslavia	5,433	8,259	992	34	..	..	766	1,178	109
86 Argentina	3,947	5,455	(.)	(.)	(.)	..	24	35	109
87 South Africa	3,571	..	127	3,240	..	..	425	649	83
88 Algeria	1,731	2,790	1,816	4,155	54	7	174	213	79
89 Venezuela	2,477	3,425	1,270	2,653	..	..	165	385	88
90 Greece	4,929	6,332	1,341	280	..	..	858	1,611	103
91 Israel	..	..	1,176	1,804	53	0	1,394	1,831	98
92 Hong Kong	321	251	657	833	(.)	..	..	..	99
93 Trinidad and Tobago	160	..	208	269	0	..	640	494	60
94 Singapore	118	149	682	2,537	(.)	..	2,667	7,833	68
95 Iran, Islamic Rep.	10,314	..	2,076	5,349	0	..	76	758	99
96 Iraq	..	..	870	4,511	(.)	0	35	165	85
High-income oil exporters			1,379 *t*	10,067 *t*			58 *w*	918 *w*	..
97 Oman	..	..	52	214			(.)	884	..
98 Libya	168	572	612	1,005			64	432	94
99 Saudi Arabia	833	1,917	482	7,643			44	1,777	98
100 Kuwait	42	108	101	770			(.)	4,200	..
101 United Arab Emirates	..	294	132	435			(.)	2,991	..
Industrial market economies			65,494 *t*	62,579 *t*			985 *w*	1,233 *w*	107 *w*
102 Spain	10,888	..	4,675	3,973			595	710	107
103 Ireland	..	..	631	524			3,573	6,973	101
104 Italy	22,099	25,478	8,100	7,097			962	1,689	111
105 New Zealand	..	..	92	136			8,875	11,468	108
106 United Kingdom	7,907	11,476	7,541	2,991			2,521	3,746	124
107 Belgium[c]	2,370	3,272	4,585	6,638			5,686	5,467	104
108 Austria	2,950	3,091	165	67			2,517	2,520	118
109 Netherlands	3,986	7,180	7,199	4,655			7,165	7,888	120
110 France	24,282	30,484	654	1,747			2,424	3,116	111
111 Japan	38,299	39,972	19,557	26,944			3,849	4,370	91
112 Finland	4,379	4,351	222	53			1,931	2,220	102
113 Germany, Fed. Rep.	15,442	20,589	7,164	4,444			4,208	4,211	116
114 Denmark	2,427	4,137	462	364			2,254	2,639	122
115 Australia	7,090	11,083	2	20			246	242	105
116 Sweden	3,983	4,252	301	118			1,639	1,603	112
117 Canada	8,501	10,634	1,513	627			192	487	118
118 Norway	2,035	2,481	713	330			2,471	2,970	117
119 United States	62,108	66,669	460	785			800	1,045	105
120 Switzerland	..	..	1,458	1,066			3,842	4,296	117
East European nonmarket economies			18,543 *t*	50,425 *t*			635 *w*	1,221 *w*	103 *w*
121 Hungary	2,782	4,677	408	74			1,485	2,998	126
122 Poland	..	9,751	4,185	2,718	..	42	1,715	2,314	94
123 Albania	..	..	48	4			745	1,446	107
124 Bulgaria	..	..	649	55			1,446	2,437	119
125 Czechoslovakia	..	..	1,296	697			2,402	3,435	118
126 German Dem. Rep.	..	..	2,821	3,153			3,202	2,901	107
127 Romania	..	..	1,381	510			559	1,577	119
128 USSR	..	..	7,755	43,214			437	987	101

a. Figures in italics are for 1983, not 1984.   b. Average for 1969–71.   c. Includes Luxembourg.

Table 7. Industry

	Food and agriculture		Textiles and clothing		Machinery and transport equipment		Chemicals		Other manufacturing		Value added in manufacturing (millions of 1980 dollars)	
	1970	1983[a]	1970	1983[a]	1970	1983[a]	1970	1983[a]	1970	1983[a]	1970	1983[a]
Low-income economies												
China and India												
Other low-income												
Sub-Saharan Africa												
1 Ethiopia	30	38	34	28	1	..	2	2	33	32	282	453
2 Bangladesh	18	18	51	40	3	6	13	22	15	14	437	860
3 Mali	22	25	54	57	5	6	2	2	17	10	59	82
4 Zaire	41	44	16	11	5	..	5	7	33	38	213	168
5 Burkina Faso	74	..	4	..	..	..	6	..	17	..	73	157
6 Nepal	..	69	..	13	..	..	..	2	..	17	..	..
7 Burma	30	37	6	12	2	2	4	6	57	44	373	687
8 Malawi	33	46	23	18	3	..	..	..	42	36	72	136
9 Niger	15	33	42	27	..	..	..	11	43	28	53	152
10 Tanzania	23	26	27	26	7	9	9	9	34	31	336	..
11 Burundi	..	78	..	..	..	..	..	5	..	17	52	91
12 Uganda	59	59	8	17	(.)	..	8	2	26	22	311	137
13 Togo	51	43	38	38	..	..	..	..	12	19	149	61
14 Central African Rep.	14	41	72	38	(.)	1	3	4	11	17	114	47
15 India	11	13	37	27	14	18	8	11	30	32	16,294	27,091
16 Madagascar	22	23	31	42	10	..	4	5	32	31	492	395
17 Somalia	69	..	4	..	(.)	(.)	1	..	27	..	..	..
18 Benin	..	..	..	..	..	..	..	..	..	..	..	117
19 Rwanda	75	72	..	..	..	..	2	3	23	25	..	..
20 China	..	..	..	..	..	..	..	..	..	..	54,806	152,731
21 Kenya	39	37	10	12	11	15	10	8	29	29	263	881
22 Sierra Leone	35	42	..	..	..	..	3	6	61	52	37	52
23 Haiti	19	..	42	..	15	..	2	..	22	..	..	..
24 Guinea	..	..	..	..	..	..	..	..	..	..	..	39
25 Ghana	14	27	42	19	3	1	5	5	36	49	409	211
26 Sri Lanka	45	44	8	15	7	4	6	7	34	31	548	742
27 Sudan	30	38	24	..	2	3	2	4	42	56	298	521
28 Pakistan	19	28	57	23	7	10	7	21	11	18	2,359	5,205
29 Senegal	55	54	23	20	..	4	6	4	16	17	366	640
30 *Afghanistan*	..	..	..	..	..	..	..	..	..	..	..	..
31 *Bhutan*	..	..	..	..	..	..	..	..	..	..	..	..
32 *Chad*	46	48	37	34	..	..	(.)	(.)	17	18	27	..
33 *Kampuchea, Dem.*	..	..	..	..	..	..	..	..	..	..	..	..
34 *Lao PDR*	..	..	..	..	..	..	..	..	..	..	..	..
35 *Mozambique*	40	..	16	..	5	..	5	..	33	..	..	..
36 *Viet Nam*	..	..	..	..	..	..	..	..	..	..	..	..
Middle-income economies												
Oil exporters												
Oil importers												
Sub-Saharan Africa												
Lower middle-income												
37 Mauritania	91	91	..	..	..	..	..	..	9	9	32	48
38 Liberia	16	24	..	..	..	..	..	..	84	75	46	69
39 Zambia	49	44	8	11	10	8	8	9	26	27	524	720
40 Lesotho	..	..	..	..	..	..	..	..	..	..	3	..
41 Bolivia	24	36	43	16	1	2	4	4	28	42	369	646
42 Indonesia	18	21	7	7	5	7	7	6	62	60	2,350	9,611
43 Yemen Arab Rep.	..	..	..	..	..	..	..	..	..	..	43	254
44 Yemen, PDR	..	..	..	..	..	..	..	..	..	..	..	..
45 Cote d'Ivoire	24	38	24	27	18	8	6	8	29	19	680	1,204
46 Philippines	42	44	11	14	9	8	6	7	32	28	4,383	9,308
47 Morocco	28	32	27	23	9	6	6	9	30	31	1,772	3,170
48 Honduras	43	50	13	11	(.)	1	2	5	41	33	196	309
49 El Salvador	46	40	24	22	4	6	3	10	24	21	401	448
50 Papua New Guinea	..	..	..	..	..	..	..	..	..	..	95	227
51 Egypt, Arab Rep.	22	20	35	26	5	13	7	9	32	32	3,095	8,950
52 Nigeria	32	30	11	9	10	20	9	14	39	27	1,425	4,252
53 Zimbabwe	21	26	19	17	10	9	8	10	42	38	798	1,326
54 Cameroon	37	41	..	..	4	2	5	5	54	52	278	715
55 Nicaragua	60	62	10	14	2	1	11	7	17	16	419	593
56 Thailand	32	23	21	..	6	12	6	8	36	56	2,526	7,837
57 Botswana	..	..	..	..	..	..	..	..	..	..	11	55
58 Dominican Rep.	83	69	5	5	(.)	(.)	3	5	8	20	527	1,115
59 Peru	29	26	17	13	11	12	5	11	38	38	3,903	4,435
60 Mauritius	61	..	5	..	7	..	4	..	23	..	81	170
61 Congo, People's Rep.	70	52	2	4	3	..	3	6	21	38	117	191
62 Ecuador	51	36	19	20	(.)	1	3	4	27	38	835	2,283
63 Jamaica	41	43	9	6	7	..	11	16	32	35	513	458
64 Guatemala	79	..	..	..	..	..	..	..	20	..	..	..
65 Turkey	16	21	27	16	12	16	8	11	38	37	6,975	14,263

Note: For data comparability and coverage, see the technical notes.

	Distribution of manufacturing value added (percent; 1980 prices)										Value added in manufacturing (millions of 1980 dollars)	
	Food and agriculture		Textiles and clothing		Machinery and transport equipment		Chemicals		Other manufacturing			
	1970	1983[a]	1970	1983[a]	1970	1983[a]	1970	1983[a]	1970	1983[a]	1970	1983[a]
66 Costa Rica	55	..	8	..	6	..	8	..	23	..	439	806
67 Paraguay	57	42	17	18	1	2	3	3	23	36	305	651
68 Tunisia	26	24	28	21	3	8	10	10	33	37	353	1,289
69 Colombia	37	42	18	14	5	8	6	6	34	31	3,297	5,545
70 Jordan	26	26	..	..	..	..	2	4	72	71	102	509
71 Syrian Arab Rep.	27	32	38	28	1	3	6	7	28	30	1,159	2,341
72 Angola	..	..	..	..	..	..	..	..	..	..	..	..
73 Cuba	73	53	6	6	2	10	5	6	15	25	..	..
74 Korea, Dem. Rep.	..	..	..	..	..	..	..	..	..	..	..	..
75 Lebanon	..	..	..	..	..	..	..	..	..	..	..	..
76 Mongolia	29	22	35	30	..	..	2	4	34	45	..	..
Upper middle-income												
77 Chile	23	26	17	9	6	3	7	8	47	54	5,275	4,940
78 Brazil	21	21	15	11	16	17	4	11	44	40	26,963	56,878
79 Portugal	16	17	32	27	12	12	5	7	35	37	..	7,897
80 Malaysia	26	22	4	7	15	24	5	5	49	43	1,773	6,080
81 Panama	30	43	10	10	1	1	4	8	55	38	249	345
82 Uruguay	30	31	17	22	9	6	9	9	35	31	1,667	1,670
83 Mexico	29	28	16	13	11	12	9	13	35	34	21,533	41,346
84 Korea, Rep. of	13	10	16	19	9	24	16	12	46	36	4,047	21,788
85 Yugoslavia	13	11	18	15	21	23	5	7	44	43	7,629	19,512
86 Argentina	22	22	13	10	19	16	7	9	40	42	12,615	12,682
87 South Africa	12	13	10	9	26	21	7	9	46	48	9,747	..
88 Algeria	33	18	29	26	5	7	4	3	29	47	1,578	6,061
89 Venezuela	22	26	10	5	6	6	8	7	55	56	5,790	9,528
90 Greece	21	21	21	22	14	12	6	8	39	38	3,852	6,512
91 Israel	10	13	12	11	20	25	7	8	51	43	..	..
92 Hong Kong	4	..	50	..	16	..	1	..	28	..	3,148	6,944
93 Trinidad and Tobago	15	26	5	6	5	15	5	8	69	44	711	..
94 Singapore	8	4	8	4	20	51	3	5	61	36	1,148	3,451
95 Iran, Islamic Rep.	25	12	18	21	8	15	7	4	42	48	4,711	11,596
96 Iraq	19	..	24	..	18	..	4	..	35	..	..	..
High-income oil exporters												
97 Oman	..	..	..	..	..	..	..	..	..	..	..	..
98 Libya	66	..	..	..	..	..	7	..	28	..	196	760
99 Saudi Arabia	7	10	..	..	..	..	..	..	93	90	2,987	7,230
100 Kuwait	3	8	..	..	..	..	3	7	94	85	696	1,790
101 United Arab Emirates	..	..	..	..	..	..	..	..	..	..		2,428
Industrial market economies												
102 Spain	8	13	22	15	24	21	8	7	39	44	29,582	..
103 Ireland	35	36	19	11	12	15	5	14	29	24	..	..
104 Italy	10	12	18	18	23	26	8	7	40	38	..	..
105 New Zealand	26	24	12	12	17	17	5	5	41	41	..	..
106 United Kingdom	11	14	8	6	34	33	7	10	39	36	130,154	120,228
107 Belgium	16	19	13	9	23	25	10	12	37	35	21,769	30,660
108 Austria	15	15	12	9	21	24	5	7	47	45	14,400	21,534
109 Netherlands	14	..	7	..	24	..	10	..	44	..	30,533	39,185
110 France	16	16	10	7	30	34	10	8	34	34	120,210	173,370
111 Japan	12	10	8	6	27	38	6	7	47	40	157,947	387,272
112 Finland	13	11	9	7	18	22	5	6	55	53	8,471	14,107
113 Germany, Fed. Rep.	10	10	8	5	37	41	8	9	38	34	240,808	310,384
114 Denmark	21	23	7	6	23	24	6	9	43	39	8,257	11,935
115 Australia	19	18	7	7	23	19	5	8	46	48	24,857	29,059
116 Sweden	9	9	6	3	28	32	5	7	52	50	23,781	27,151
117 Canada	15	14	8	7	19	22	6	7	52	49	34,285	46,210
118 Norway	15	12	6	3	27	28	5	8	47	49	7,521	8,628
119 United States	9	10	7	6	30	33	7	9	46	42	448,167	592,504
120 Switzerland	12	15	9	8	26	25	8	12	45	40	..	..
East European nonmarket economies												
121 Hungary	11	11	15	11	25	29	8	11	41	38	4,257	8,343
122 Poland	22	18	19	15	23	29	7	8	29	30	..	..
123 Albania	..	..	..	..	..	..	..	..	..	..	..	..
124 Bulgaria	30	20	17	14	11	20	6	7	36	39	..	..
125 Czechoslovakia	11	8	12	10	30	39	7	8	40	35	..	..
126 German Dem. Rep.	12	9	15	12	27	34	12	13	35	32	..	..
127 Romania	25	16	8	9	21	34	9	11	36	30	..	..
128 USSR	27	22	19	15	19	29	5	6	29	28	..	..

a. Figures in italics are for 1982, not 1983.

Table 8. Commercial energy

	Average annual energy growth rate (percent)				Energy consumption per capita (kilograms of oil equivalent)		Energy imports as a percentage of merchandise exports	
	Energy production		Energy consumption					
	1965–73[a]	1973–84	1965–73	1973–84	1965	1984	1965	1984[b]
Low-income economies	10.0 *w*	6.1 *w*	9.7 *w*	5.3 *w*	130 *w*	288 *w*	8 *w*	. .
China and India	10.1 *w*	6.0 *w*	10.2 *w*	5.5 *w*	147 *w*	360 *w*	. .	17 *w*
Other low-income	7.8 *w*	6.7 *w*	6.1 *w*	3.1 *w*	67 *w*	79 *w*	7 *w*	. .
Sub-Saharan Africa	10.4 *w*	6.5 *w*	9.3 *w*	0.9 *w*	46 *w*	56 *w*	8 *w*	. .
1 Ethiopia	11.1	6.0	11.4	3.4	10	17	8	48
2 Bangladesh	. .	13.0	. .	7.9	. .	40	. .	20
3 Mali	80.5	13.2	4.6	6.5	15	26	16	. .
4 Zaire	4.8	8.8	6.0	1.2	67	77	6	. .
5 Burkina Faso	. .	. .	8.0	9.5	8	21	11	86
6 Nepal	27.2	10.9	8.8	8.6	6	16	. .	49
7 Burma	9.6	6.9	6.5	4.8	39	71	4	. .
8 Malawi	31.1	8.0	8.3	3.6	25	43	7	. .
9 Niger	. .	. .	14.7	11.2	8	42	9	. .
10 Tanzania	6.8	6.2	10.5	−2.0	37	38	. .	. .
11 Burundi	. .	28.5	5.6	12.2	5	17	11	. .
12 Uganda	3.7	−3.1	8.4	−5.2	36	22	. .	. .
13 Togo	−6.1	31.6	12.9	10.0	25	109	6	. .
14 Central African Rep.	10.6	3.5	9.8	4.5	22	33	7	. .
15 India	3.7	7.9	5.1	6.5	100	187	8	59
16 Madagascar	8.6	3.4	13.6	0.5	33	45	8	32
17 Somalia	. .	. .	9.3	14.9	15	83	9	. .
18 Benin	. .	. .	19.7	1.8	21	43	14	53
19 Rwanda	15.7	−1.2	11.4	14.7	8	43	10	. .
20 China	11.8	5.6	11.9	5.3	178	485	. .	1
21 Kenya	9.9	14.1	7.1	1.0	114	111	. .	51
22 Sierra Leone	. .	. .	4.6	3.5	104	77	11	63
23 Haiti	. .	9.0	6.2	6.2	25	55	. .	. .
24 Guinea	17.1	1.8	2.3	1.3	56	52	. .	. .
25 Ghana	43.4	−1.9	15.0	−1.8	76	101	6	. .
26 Sri Lanka	12.0	6.7	5.2	3.3	107	143	6	33
27 Sudan	14.7	7.9	12.1	−3.0	67	62	5	. .
28 Pakistan	5.1	8.7	1.4	6.9	136	188	7	56
29 Senegal	. .	. .	6.0	4.0	79	118	8	. .
30 *Afghanistan*	46.7	0.1	7.1	1.6	30	48	8	. .
31 *Bhutan*	. .	. .	. .	. .	. .	. .	. .	. .
32 *Chad*	. .	. .	. .	. .	. .	. .	23	. .
33 *Kampuchea, Dem.*	. .	. .	19.8	0.9	19	58	7	. .
34 *Lao PDR*	. .	16.9	16.6	−0.9	22	35	. .	. .
35 *Mozambique*	4.6	11.9	9.3	0.9	81	93	13	. .
36 *Viet Nam*	−3.4	5.1	6.7	−1.5	106	88	. .	. .
Middle-income economies	8.5 *w*	0.3 *w*	7.9 *w*	5.1 *w*	384 *w*	743 *w*	8 *w*	21 *w*
Oil exporters	9.1 *w*	−1.2 *w*	6.9 *w*	6.9 *w*	300 *w*	615 *w*	5 *w*	9 *w*
Oil importers	6.0 *w*	5.5 *w*	8.4 *w*	4.2 *w*	453 *w*	856 *w*	10 *w*	27 *w*
Sub-Saharan Africa	30.5 *w*	−2.3 *w*	7.8 *w*	6.1 *w*	89 *w*	175 *w*	5 *w*	. .
Lower middle-income	16.2 *w*	2.5 *w*	7.6 *w*	5.6 *w*	200 *w*	399 *w*	9 *w*	. .
37 Mauritania	. .	. .	16.0	3.2	48	127	2	. .
38 Liberia	37.0	1.0	16.1	2.0	181	358	6	17
39 Zambia	18.6	5.7	−0.1	1.6	464	422	5	5
40 Lesotho	. .	. .	. .	. .	. .	. .	. .	. .
41 Bolivia	17.8	(.)	5.2	5.8	156	276	1	. .
42 Indonesia	12.7	3.3	6.6	8.0	91	205	3	20
43 Yemen Arab Rep.	. .	. .	16.5	21.7	7	117	. .	. .
44 Yemen, PDR	. .	. .	−10.7	7.0	982	682	63	. .
45 Cote d'Ivoire	0.5	44.3	10.9	4.1	109	161	5	16
46 Philippines	4.6	21.8	9.0	2.3	160	271	12	44
47 Morocco	2.6	−0.7	8.9	5.0	124	256	5	47
48 Honduras	15.6	9.9	10.4	3.5	111	205	5	28
49 El Salvador	2.1	13.3	5.7	2.9	140	188	5	57
50 Papua New Guinea	16.5	8.0	20.3	4.1	56	232	7	25
51 Egypt, Arab Rep.	10.0	15.6	−0.7	11.2	313	562	11	10
52 Nigeria	33.4	−4.5	7.1	12.2	34	129	7	3
53 Zimbabwe	1.1	−2.6	10.7	0.4	441	468	(.)	. .
54 Cameroon	1.2	44.1	6.5	8.3	67	138	6	3
55 Nicaragua	4.8	3.8	9.8	0.7	187	234	6	46
56 Thailand	11.0	17.4	14.7	5.9	80	320	11	33
57 Botswana	8.4	7.0	7.8	8.2	207	409	. .	. .
58 Dominican Rep.	4.9	34.8	18.6	2.4	130	386	7	71
59 Peru	2.0	10.2	5.2	3.6	403	575	3	3
60 Mauritius	3.1	0.8	11.9	−0.1	163	308	6	23
61 Congo, People's Rep.	39.5	11.3	10.9	5.9	90	233	8	. .
62 Ecuador	36.6	3.0	9.3	14.8	163	796	11	1
63 Jamaica	−1.8	2.7	10.2	−3.0	707	919	12	54
64 Guatemala	18.3	21.1	7.1	2.0	148	178	9	. .
65 Turkey	5.7	3.9	10.0	4.5	258	634	12	53

Note: For data comparability and coverage, see the technical notes.

| | | Average annual energy growth rate (percent) | | | | Energy consumption per capita (kilograms of oil equivalent) | | Energy imports as a percentage of merchandise exports | |
| | | Energy production | | Energy consumption | | | | | |
		1965–73[a]	1973–84	1965–73	1973–84	1965	1984	1965	1984[b]
66	Costa Rica	10.2	9.3	12.2	2.7	267	486	8	22
67	Paraguay		8.2	9.1	8.9	86	231	14	..
68	Tunisia	58.7	3.9	8.7	7.8	170	495	12	19
69	Colombia	2.2	3.9	6.6	5.3	413	758	1	14
70	Jordan	..	..	4.3	14.8	226	813	33	74
71	Syrian Arab Rep.	164.4	3.3	9.7	11.8	212	799	13	..
72	*Angola*	47.1	0.5	10.6	3.9	111	197	2	..
73	*Cuba*	7.2	12.9	5.6	3.5	604	1,083	12	..
74	*Korea, Dem. Rep.*	9.3	3.0	9.5	3.5	504	2,058	..	..
75	*Lebanon*	2.4	−0.7	6.1	−3.8	713	656	50	..
76	*Mongolia*	11.2	8.4	9.1	8.8	..	1,168	..	..
Upper middle-income		**6.6** *w*	**−0.6** *w*	**8.1** *w*	**4.9** *w*	**630** *w*	**1,221** *w*	**8** *w*	**19** *w*
77	Chile	4.1	2.0	7.2	0.8	657	796	5	..
78	Brazil	8.7	9.4	11.6	4.7	286	753	14	30
79	Portugal	3.8	0.3	8.7	3.7	506	1,215	13	44
80	Malaysia	60.8	16.7	8.5	7.0	312	716	10	12
81	Panama	2.7	15.2	8.2	−3.5	517	504	..	138
82	Uruguay	5.2	10.1	1.8	0.3	765	738	13	28
83	Mexico	4.5	15.9	7.2	7.9	622	1,308	4	1
84	Korea, Rep. of	2.9	5.0	15.3	8.4	237	1,171	18	25
85	Yugoslavia	3.5	3.8	6.8	3.5	898	1,845	7	34
86	Argentina	6.4	4.4	5.9	2.6	975	1,460	8	6
87	South Africa	3.5	7.7	5.2	4.1	1,776	2,237	10	(.)
88	Algeria	6.7	3.3	6.1	15.6	226	1,140	(.)	2
89	Venezuela	0.1	−3.3	4.3	4.5	2,269	2,509	(.)	..
90	Greece	12.2	9.3	11.6	3.7	615	1,858	29	54
91	Israel	53.4	−33.2	6.1	2.2	1,574	1,890	13	25
92	Hong Kong	..	..	9.7	7.4	424	1,162	4	6
93	Trinidad and Tobago	0.6	0.2	3.4	6.1	2,554	4,107	59	4
94	Singapore	..	..	20.5	4.4	670	2,520	17	33
95	*Iran, Islamic Rep.*	16.3	−11.6	13.3	1.4	537	1,044	(.)	..
96	*Iraq*	4.5	−7.1	6.2	6.4	399	692	(.)	..
High-income oil exporters		**11.7** *w*	**−3.7** *w*	**11.2** *w*	**8.8** *w*	**1,721** *w*	**3,593** *w*	**(.)** *w*	..
97	Oman	57.2	4.6	89.7	8.5	14	2,405	..	1
98	Libya	8.6	−4.8	14.8	18.3	222	3,107	2	..
99	Saudi Arabia	15.7	−3.0	12.4	7.4	1,759	3,602	(.)	(.)
100	Kuwait	4.3	−9.1	2.6	2.8	..	3,974	(.)	(.)
101	United Arab Emirates	24.1	−2.2	65.3	18.6	108	5,369	..	3
Industrial market economies		**3.3** *w*	**1.9** *w*	**5.2** *w*	**0.1** *w*	**3,745** *w*	**4,877** *w*	**11** *w*	**23** *w*
102	Spain	3.5	3.6	8.7	1.9	901	1,801	31	46
103	Ireland	−1.4	13.4	5.8	2.7	1,504	2,395	14	12
104	Italy	2.1	0.6	7.0	(.)	1,568	2,487	16	32
105	New Zealand	4.5	4.8	4.7	1.7	2,622	4,005	7	15
106	United Kingdom	−0.7	7.8	2.6	−1.3	3,481	3,441	13	15
107	Belgium	−9.0	4.6	6.0	−0.9	3,402	4,402	9	20
108	Austria	−0.2	0.1	6.6	0.4	2,060	3,345	10	19
109	Netherlands	25.7	−1.0	9.1	−0.9	3,134	4,744	12	22
110	France	−3.1	6.1	6.0	0.5	2,468	3,516	16	27
111	Japan	−2.0	4.1	12.2	0.4	1,474	3,135	19	35
112	Finland	0.3	13.0	8.4	2.3	2,233	4,944	11	23
113	Germany, Fed. Rep.	−0.1	0.2	4.9	−0.3	3,197	4,238	8	18
114	Denmark	−32.5	36.5	4.8	−1.0	2,911	3,495	13	19
115	Australia	16.0	4.3	6.4	1.8	3,287	4,763	10	9
116	Sweden	2.8	6.0	4.5	0.4	4,162	5,728	12	18
117	Canada	9.5	1.7	6.1	1.8	6,007	9,148	7	6
118	Norway	6.0	15.2	5.4	2.6	4,650	8,575	11	8
119	United States	3.0	0.7	4.0	−0.1	6,535	7,302	8	29
120	Switzerland	2.5	3.9	6.0	0.9	2,501	3,777	8	12
East European nonmarket economies		**4.3** *w*	**3.4** *w*	**4.6** *w*	**3.0** *w*	**2,523** *w*	**4,360** *w*	..	..
121	Hungary	0.4	1.5	3.3	2.7	1,825	2,986	12	21
122	Poland	4.5	1.0	4.8	2.2	2,027	3,197	..	21
123	*Albania*	14.2	7.0	7.2	7.5	415	1,062	..	..
124	*Bulgaria*	0.8	4.7	7.7	3.9	1,788	4,366	..	..
125	*Czechoslovakia*	1.1	0.8	3.6	1.2	3,374	4,489	..	30
126	*German Dem. Rep.*	0.6	2.0	2.5	1.3	3,762	5,225	..	..
127	*Romania*	5.6	2.0	7.8	3.4	1,536	3,346	..	..
128	*USSR*	4.7	3.8	4.7	3.3	2,603	4,627	..	..

a. Figures in italics are for 1966–73, not 1965–73. b. Figures in italics are for 1982 or 1983, not 1984.

Table 9. Growth of merchandise trade

		Merchandise trade (millions of dollars)		Average annual growth rate[a] (percent)				Terms of trade (1980=100)	
		Exports 1984	Imports 1984[b]	Exports 1965–73	Exports 1973–84[c]	Imports 1965–73	Imports 1973–84[c]	1982	1984
	Low-income economies	48,319 t	64,903 t	1.7 w	5.4 w	−1.2 w	5.0 w	89 m	100 m
	China and India	34,259 t	41,152 t	..	7.9 w	..	8.1 w	105 m	104 m
	Other low-income	14,060 t	23,751 t	1.5 w	1.4 w	1.3 w	1.3 w	88 m	99 m
	Sub-Saharan Africa	7,892 t	12,129 t	3.0 w	−0.8 w	4.4 w	−1.4 w	88 m	99 m
1	Ethiopia	417	826	2.9	0.4	−0.2	4.6	90	104
2	Bangladesh	934	2,042	−6.6	2.9	−8.3	4.2	105	106
3	Mali	167	344	13.1	4.7	8.5	3.2	105	116
4	Zaire	1,584	1,115	6.4	4.1	9.4	−4.5	79	84
5	Burkina Faso	91	255	−1.0	0.9	7.5	2.9	100	117
6	Nepal	111	437	..	..	..	..	..	..
7	Burma	378	239	−4.9	3.2	−6.7	−1.8	86	89
8	Malawi	309	268	3.8	2.4	6.4	−1.5	107	137
9	Niger	311	361	6.1	17.8	4.4	8.8	88	81
10	Tanzania	456	782	0.9	−4.7	7.1	−4.3	88	94
11	Burundi	98	186						
12	Uganda	399	392	0.2	−6.2	−2.5	2.2	75	98
13	Togo	240	271	4.1	5.2	6.6	4.7	84	88
14	Central African Rep.	115	178	−0.6	1.4	−0.3	2.6	94	99
15	India	9,437	15,002	2.4	3.3	−5.7	5.4	104	107
16	Madagascar	349	480	5.4	−4.6	1.5	−4.0	80	105
17	Somalia	61	413	5.7	−0.7	5.1	5.9	94	93
18	Benin	112	363	14.3	−1.9	12.1	1.8	77	116
19	Rwanda	83	290	6.5	2.5	4.6	11.6	64	71
20	China	24,822	26,150	..	10.1	..	10.2	106	101
21	Kenya	1,078	1,547	3.8	−2.3	5.9	−1.7	92	101
22	Sierra Leone	148	166	3.7	−5.5	1.0	−6.8	85	95
23	Haiti	207	338	..	..	..	..	..	..
24	Guinea	457	313	..	..	..	..	..	..
25	Ghana	571	591	3.5	−4.0	−3.3	−7.4	84	99
26	Sri Lanka	1,454	1,847	−4.7	3.5	−3.3	4.6	88	111
27	Sudan	732	1,417	3.8	−0.2	4.9	1.2	87	96
28	Pakistan	2,592	5,873	3.7	7.4	−2.9	7.5	93	88
29	Senegal	416	1,039	−1.3	−0.8	5.6	−1.2	91	98
30	Afghanistan	..	..	5.9	6.5	−0.7	4.4	99	114
31	Bhutan	..	..						
32	Chad	..	..	−2.4	−2.9	8.4	−7.7	101	108
33	Kampuchea, Dem.	..	..						
34	Lao PDR	11	48	..	..	..	..	..	..
35	Mozambique	185	532	3.6	−10.7	7.2	−4.7	84	104
36	Viet Nam	..	..	..	..	..	..	..	..
	Middle-income economies	355,439 t	346,948 t	6.3 w	0.8 w	8.4 w	4.4 w	94 m	95 m
	Oil exporters	149,298 t	121,676 t	6.2 w	−4.2 w	6.0 w	6.8 w	106 m	99 m
	Oil importers	205,793 t	225,272 t	6.7 w	7.3 w	9.4 w	3.2 w	89 m	94 m
	Sub-Saharan Africa	25,485 t	17,923 t	8.2 w	−5.0 w	6.8 w	4.9 w	94 m	101 m
	Lower middle-income	96,964 t	111,245 t	7.0 w	0.7 w	4.9 w	4.9 w	91 m	95 m
37	Mauritania	297	246	9.7	2.0	15.4	−0.7	101	95
38	Liberia	452	363	8.9	−2.3	3.7	−5.1	93	102
39	Zambia	824	690	−0.3	−2.4	3.0	−7.9	72	74
40	Lesotho[d]	..	..	..	..	..	..	..	..
41	Bolivia	773	631	5.2	−3.5	0.9	−1.8	94	91
42	Indonesia	21,888	13,882	11.1	1.4	14.0	10.5	105	101
43	Yemen Arab Rep.	9	1,401	..	..	..	..	..	..
44	Yemen, PDR	379	825	..	..	..	..	..	..
45	Cote d'Ivoire	2,703	1,507	6.9	−2.2	8.0	−1.7	91	101
46	Philippines	5,391	6,365	4.2	5.6	3.0	2.3	89	101
47	Morocco	2,172	3,907	6.0	3.6	6.2	2.1	89	85
48	Honduras	746	954	3.6	3.0	3.1	0.5	80	93
49	El Salvador	708	970	2.7	1.8	2.1	−2.0	70	72
50	Papua New Guinea	897	1,114	..	..	..	..	..	..
51	Egypt, Arab Rep.	5,286	14,596	3.8	6.2	−3.9	15.3	111	100
52	Nigeria	14,295	10,500	8.8	−6.5	8.7	10.1	111	101
53	Zimbabwe	1,167	1,144	..	..	..	..	..	..
54	Cameroon	2,080	1,239	4.2	2.3	6.3	3.9	73	85
55	Nicaragua	385	826	2.7	−0.6	2.0	−2.9	64	70
56	Thailand	7,413	10,518	6.9	10.4	4.4	5.9	77	81
57	Botswana[d]	..	..						
58	Dominican Rep.	868	1,257	10.9	1.6	13.3	−0.9	82	95
59	Peru	3,147	2,212	−2.1	9.3	−2.0	−0.1	85	84
60	Mauritius	373	472	4.2	4.8	4.5	−0.7	94	93
61	Congo, People's Rep.	1,265	759	−2.6	5.6	−0.1	11.9	113	104
62	Ecuador	2,581	1,716	3.4	−3.1	8.5	3.9	105	98
63	Jamaica	745	1,146	3.7	−3.0	6.6	−4.6	87	86
64	Guatemala	1,129	1,278	5.1	3.9	3.6	−0.5	71	80
65	Turkey	7,134	10,663	..	11.4	..	2.8	88	90

Note: For data comparability and coverage, see the technical notes.

	Merchandise trade (millions of dollars)		Average annual growth rate[a] (percent)				Terms of trade (1980=100)	
	Exports 1984	Imports 1984[b]	Exports 1965–73	Exports 1973–84[c]	Imports 1965–73	Imports 1973–84[c]	1982	1984
66 Costa Rica	978	1,085	10.3	2.3	8.6	−2.4	89	103
67 Paraguay	381	564	6.6	4.6	4.7	4.2	84	95
68 Tunisia	1,796	3,115	8.6	2.5	7.6	6.4	96	91
69 Colombia	3,483	4,492	5.4	2.8	5.4	9.1	95	97
70 Jordan	755	2,689	5.0	17.6	3.9	11.8	102	95
71 Syrian Arab Rep.	1,853	4,116	1.0	−3.1	8.9	8.0	110	105
72 Angola	2,029	1,003	12.6	−6.7	8.3	1.2	106	102
73 Cuba	. .	. .	1.3	3.3	3.6	−0.6	. .	. .
74 Korea, Dem. Rep.	. .	. .	. .	. .	. .	. .	. .	. .
75 Lebanon	582	3,000	14.3	−3.4	5.7	3.3	94	91
76 Mongolia	. .	. .	. .	. .	. .	. .	. .	. .
Upper middle-income	**258,475** t	**235,703** t	**6.1** w	**0.9** w	**10.0** w	**4.1** w	**96** m	**97** m
77 Chile	3,650	3,191	−1.4	8.8	2.2	3.0	79	80
78 Brazil	27,005	15,209	10.0	8.1	18.4	−3.4	95	103
79 Portugal	5,208	7,975	2.8	5.2	15.1	2.1	87	98
80 Malaysia	16,407	14,060	8.0	7.5	4.4	8.9	85	93
81 Panama	417	1,423	1.0	−7.1	6.5	−4.6	84	84
82 Uruguay	925	776	−3.0	8.0	2.9	0.6	85	85
83 Mexico	24,054	11,267	1.0	19.2	5.8	3.2	110	100
84 Korea, Rep. of	29,248	30,609	31.7	15.1	22.4	9.7	100	100
85 Yugoslavia	10,255	11,996	7.7	4.9	12.3	0.4	109	110
86 Argentina	8,017	4,585	2.3	5.7	5.4	−1.1	89	97
87 South Africa[d]	17,632	16,364	1.6	7.9	6.5	5.7	87	86
88 Algeria	12,622	10,286	2.9	−0.5	12.1	5.7	113	99
89 Venezuela	13,340	7,594	0.2	−6.1	4.8	2.9	114	99
90 Greece	4,864	9,616	13.4	2.1	9.6	0.7	95	97
91 Israel	5,804	8,289	12.1	7.9	13.0	1.4	93	84
92 Hong Kong	28,317	28,567	11.7	12.9	10.6	9.3	110	109
93 Trinidad and Tobago	2,194	2,101	−1.1	−8.0	2.0	−5.7	98	93
94 Singapore	24,055	28,565	11.0	7.1	9.8	7.1	100	101
95 Iran, Islamic Rep.	13,218	13,250	12.4	−15.9	12.6	3.5	100	93
96 Iraq	11,243	9,980	1.1	−8.3	4.8	15.9	121	107
High-income oil exporters	**88,380** t	**59,328** t	**10.9** w	**−7.8** w	**10.2** w	**16.3** w	**116** m	**106** m
97 Oman	4,413	2,745	. .	. .	. .	. .	108	97
98 Libya	11,136	8,161	10.1	−8.6	14.2	6.0	128	116
99 Saudi Arabia	46,845	33,696	15.0	−6.8	10.4	24.1	128	116
100 Kuwait	11,882	7,696	5.9	−11.3	6.4	11.7	118	107
101 United Arab Emirates	14,104	7,030	18.3	−2.6	9.1	11.8	115	105
Industrial market economies	**1,999,846** t	**1,292,192** t	**9.5** w	**4.2** w	**10.1** w	**3.2** w	**100** m	**101** m
102 Spain	23,283	28,607	15.8	. .	7.0	. .	. .	. .
103 Ireland	9,627	9,658	8.4	8.5	7.8	5.1	101	104
104 Italy	73,358	81,971	10.2	4.6	10.7	2.5	95	96
105 New Zealand	5,508	6,181	6.0	4.3	4.0	1.0	98	96
106 United Kingdom	94,306	105,688	5.0	4.2	6.5	3.6	100	99
107 Belgium[e]	51,416	54,746	10.3	3.1	10.9	2.3	95	94
108 Austria	15,712	19,573	11.2	6.1	10.6	4.6	100	101
109 Netherlands	65,874	62,136	12.7	2.9	10.3	1.9	102	102
110 France	93,164	103,613	11.4	4.4	11.8	4.3	97	100
111 Japan	170,038	134,257	14.7	7.5	14.9	1.6	103	109
112 Finland	13,498	12,435	7.6	5.1	7.6	1.6	101	102
113 Germany, Fed. Rep.	171,014	152,872	10.7	4.5	11.3	3.9	97	96
114 Denmark	15,486	16,536	6.6	4.8	7.1	1.1	98	99
115 Australia	22,720	22,659	9.3	3.0	6.8	3.4	98	95
116 Sweden	29,258	26,331	7.9	1.3	5.4	1.1	99	103
117 Canada	84,938	73,230	9.5	4.3	9.4	2.1	95	94
118 Norway	18,914	13,885	8.3	6.4	8.2	3.1	111	117
119 United States	216,008	338,189	6.8	2.3	9.4	3.8	106	112
120 Switzerland	25,724	29,625	6.7	3.4	11.8	4.3	111	106
East European nonmarket economies	**180,033** t	**161,826** t	**8.0** w	**4.9** w	**7.0** w	**4.4** w	. .	. .
121 Hungary	8,560	8,084	10.3	8.4	10.0	8.0	97	93
122 Poland	11,647	10,547	−0.3	2.6	−1.7	−1.0	97	. .
123 Albania	. .	. .	. .	. .	. .	. .	. .	. .
124 Bulgaria	12,850	12,715	11.3	11.5	9.3	5.6	. .	. .
125 Czechoslovakia	17,196	17,080	6.9	5.5	6.7	1.6	93	. .
126 German Dem. Rep.	24,890	22,940	9.6	6.5	10.1	3.7	. .	. .
127 Romania	13,241	9,836	. .	. .	. .	. .	. .	. .
128 USSR	91,649	80,624	9.8	4.1	9.6	6.7	. .	. .

a. See the technical notes. b. Figures in italics are for 1983, not 1984. c. Figures in italics are for 1973–83, not 1973–84. d. Figures are for the South African Customs Union comprising South Africa, Namibia, Lesotho, Botswana, and Swaziland. Trade between the component territories is excluded. e. Includes Luxembourg.

Table 10. Structure of merchandise exports

	Percentage share of merchandise exports									
	Fuels, minerals, and metals		Other primary commodities		Textiles and clothing		Machinery and transport equipment		Other manufactures	
	1965	1983[a]	1965	1983[a]	1965	1983[a]	1965	1983[a]	1965	1983[a]
Low-income economies	12 *w*	..	65 *w*	..	15 *w*	..	1 *w*	..	8 *w*	..
China and India	..	21 *w*	..	24 *w*	..	18 *w*	..	6 *w*	..	32 *w*
Other low-income	12 *w*	..	77 *w*	..	5 *w*	..	(.) *w*	..	5 *w*	..
Sub-Saharan Africa	19 *w*	..	73 *w*	..	(.) *w*	..	(.) *w*	..	7 *w*	..
1 Ethiopia	(.)	8	100	91	(.)	(.)	(.)	(.)	(.)	1
2 Bangladesh	..	4	..	35	..	48	..	2	..	12
3 Mali	1	..	96	..	1	..	1	..	1	..
4 Zaire	72	..	20	..	(.)	..	(.)	..	8	..
5 Burkina Faso	1	(.)	94	89	2	2	1	4	1	4
6 Nepal	..	5	..	43	..	28	..	1	..	23
7 Burma	5	..	94	..	(.)	..	(.)	..	(.)	..
8 Malawi	(.)	..	99	..	(.)	..	(.)	..	1	..
9 Niger	(.)	..	95	..	1	..	1	..	3	..
10 Tanzania	1	..	86	..	(.)	..	(.)	..	13	..
11 Burundi	(.)	..	94	..	(.)	..	(.)	..	5	..
12 Uganda	13	..	86	..	(.)	..	(.)	..	1	..
13 Togo	33	..	62	..	(.)	..	1	..	4	..
14 Central African Rep.	1	..	45	..	(.)	..	(.)	..	54	..
15 India	10	18	41	29	36	14	1	7	12	31
16 Madagascar	4	12	90	81	1	4	1	1	4	2
17 Somalia	(.)	..	86	..	(.)	..	4	..	10	..
18 Benin	1	..	94	..	(.)	..	2	..	3	..
19 Rwanda	40	..	60	..	(.)	..	(.)	..	1	..
20 China	..	22	..	21	..	19	..	6	..	32
21 Kenya	13	22	77	65	(.)	(.)	(.)	2	9	11
22 Sierra Leone	25	29	14	28	(.)	(.)	(.)	(.)	60	42
23 Haiti	..	..	..	..	..	..	..	..	..	..
24 Guinea	..	..	..	..	..	..	..	..	..	..
25 Ghana	13	..	85	..	(.)	..	1	..	2	..
26 Sri Lanka	2	10	97	60	(.)	19	(.)	1	1	9
27 Sudan	1	..	98	..	(.)	..	1	..	(.)	..
28 Pakistan	2	2	62	34	29	50	1	1	6	13
29 Senegal	9	..	88	..	1	..	1	..	2	..
30 *Afghanistan*	(.)	..	87	..	13	..	0	..	(.)	..
31 *Bhutan*	..	..	..	..	..	..	..	..	..	..
32 *Chad*	5	..	92	..	(.)	..	(.)	..	3	..
33 *Kampuchea, Dem.*	(.)	..	99	..	(.)	..	(.)	..	(.)	..
34 *Lao PDR*	62	..	32	..	(.)	..	(.)	..	6	..
35 *Mozambique*	14	..	84	..	1	..	(.)	..	1	..
36 *Viet Nam*	..	..	..	..	..	..	..	..	..	..
Middle-income economies	36 *w*	31 *w*	48 *w*	23 *w*	4 *w*	9 *w*	2 *w*	14 *w*	10 *w*	23 *w*
Oil exporters	60 *w*	68 *w*	34 *w*	16 *w*	2 *w*	2 *w*	1 *w*	7 *w*	4 *w*	7 *w*
Oil importers	19 *w*	12 *w*	57 *w*	26 *w*	6 *w*	13 *w*	4 *w*	17 *w*	14 *w*	32 *w*
Sub-Saharan Africa	44 *w*	..	50 *w*	..	1 *w*	..	1 *w*	..	5 *w*	..
Lower middle-income	27 *w*	46 *w*	66 *w*	33 *w*	2 *w*	7 *w*	1 *w*	2 *w*	5 *w*	12 *w*
37 Mauritania	94	..	5	..	(.)	..	1	..	(.)	..
38 Liberia	72	68	25	31	(.)	(.)	1	(.)	2	1
39 Zambia	97	..	3	..	(.)	..	(.)	..	(.)	..
40 Lesotho[b]	..	..	..	..	..	..	..	..	..	..
41 Bolivia	93	..	3	..	(.)	..	(.)	..	4	..
42 Indonesia	43	80	53	12	(.)	1	3	1	1	6
43 Yemen Arab Rep.	..	..	..	..	..	..	..	..	..	..
44 Yemen, PDR	79	..	15	..	2	..	2	..	2	..
45 Cote d'Ivoire	2	12	93	77	1	3	1	2	3	6
46 Philippines	11	13	84	36	1	7	(.)	5	5	38
47 Morocco	40	37	55	31	1	14	(.)	2	4	16
48 Honduras	6	7	90	84	1	1	(.)	(.)	3	7
49 El Salvador	2	5	81	55	6	15	1	3	10	22
50 Papua New Guinea	(.)	51	90	40	(.)	(.)	(.)	2	10	7
51 Egypt, Arab Rep.	8	70	71	22	15	4	(.)	(.)	5	5
52 Nigeria	32	..	65	..	(.)	..	0	..	2	..
53 Zimbabwe	45	..	40	..	6	..	1	..	8	..
54 Cameroon	17	68	77	27	(.)	1	3	1	2	3
55 Nicaragua	4	1	90	91	(.)	(.)	(.)	(.)	5	7
56 Thailand	11	6	84	62	(.)	11	(.)	6	4	15
57 Botswana[b]	..	..	..	..	..	..	..	..	..	..
58 Dominican Rep.	10	(.)	88	76	(.)	(.)	(.)	4	2	19
59 Peru	45	69	54	17	(.)	8	(.)	1	1	5
60 Mauritius	(.)	(.)	100	69	(.)	23	(.)	1	(.)	7
61 Congo, People's Rep.	4	..	45	..	(.)	..	2	..	49	..
62 Ecuador	2	64	96	33	1	(.)	(.)	1	2	2
63 Jamaica	28	22	41	18	4	3	(.)	4	27	54
64 Guatemala	(.)	..	86	..	4	..	1	..	9	..
65 Turkey	9	9	89	45	1	26	(.)	5	1	16

Note: For data comparability and coverage, see the technical notes.

		Percentage share of merchandise exports									
		Fuels, minerals, and metals		Other primary commodities		Textiles and clothing		Machinery and transport equipment		Other manufactures	
		1965	1983[a]	1965	1983[a]	1965	1983[a]	1965	1983[a]	1965	1983[a]
66	Costa Rica	(.)	1	84	71	2	3	1	4	13	21
67	Paraguay	(.)	..	92	..	(.)	..	(.)	..	8	..
68	Tunisia	31	48	51	8	2	20	(.)	4	16	20
69	Colombia	18	15	75	66	2	4	(.)	1	4	14
70	Jordan	27	26	54	26	1	3	11	14	6	32
71	Syrian Arab Rep.	1	..	89	..	7	..	1	..	2	..
72	Angola	6	..	76	..	(.)	..	1	..	17	..
73	Cuba	4	..	92	..	(.)	..	..	..	4	..
74	Korea, Dem. Rep.	..	..	..	..	..	..	..	..	..	..
75	Lebanon	14	..	52	..	2	..	14	..	18	..
76	Mongolia	..	..	..	..	..	..	..	..	..	..
Upper middle-income		**42** w	**26** w	**37** w	**19** w	**5** w	**10** w	**3** w	**18** w	**12** w	**27** w
77	Chile	89	..	7	..	(.)	..	1	..	4	..
78	Brazil	9	15	83	44	1	3	2	14	6	23
79	Portugal	4	6	34	18	24	28	3	15	34	32
80	Malaysia	35	35	59	43	(.)	2	2	14	4	6
81	Panama	..	23	..	64	..	6	..	(.)	..	7
82	Uruguay	(.)	(.)	95	70	2	13	(.)	1	3	15
83	Mexico	22	64	62	9	3	1	1	16	13	10
84	Korea, Rep. of	15	3	25	6	27	25	3	32	29	34
85	Yugoslavia	10	8	33	16	8	9	24	31	25	36
86	Argentina	1	6	93	78	(.)	1	1	3	4	12
87	South Africa[b]	24	14	44	12	1	1	3	3	28	70
88	Algeria	57	99	39	(.)	(.)	(.)	2	(.)	2	1
89	Venezuela	97	..	1	..	(.)	..	(.)	..	2	..
90	Greece	8	15	78	35	3	22	2	3	8	24
91	Israel	6	3	28	16	9	6	2	17	54	57
92	Hong Kong	2	2	11	6	43	33	6	22	37	36
93	Trinidad and Tobago	84	84	9	2	(.)	(.)	(.)	3	7	11
94	Singapore	21	31	44	13	6	4	10	31	18	22
95	Iran, Islamic Rep.	88	..	8	..	4	..	(.)	..	1	..
96	Iraq	95	..	4	..	(.)	..	(.)	..	1	..
High-income oil exporters		**98** w	**95** w	**1** w	**(.)** w	**(.)** w	**(.)** w	**1** w	**2** w	**(.)** w	**2** w
97	Oman	..	95	..	1	..	(.)	..	4	..	1
98	Libya	99	99	1	(.)	(.)	(.)	1	(.)	(.)	1
99	Saudi Arabia	98	99	1	(.)	(.)	(.)	1	1	1	(.)
100	Kuwait	98	76	1	2	(.)	1	1	6	(.)	15
101	United Arab Emirates	99	92	1	1	(.)	1	(.)	3	(.)	4
Industrial market economies		**9** w	**12** w	**21** w	**14** w	**7** w	**4** w	**31** w	**38** w	**32** w	**32** w
102	Spain	9	13	51	18	6	5	10	26	24	39
103	Ireland	3	3	63	30	7	6	5	27	22	34
104	Italy	8	7	14	8	15	12	30	32	33	41
105	New Zealand	1	6	94	72	(.)	3	(.)	4	5	15
106	United Kingdom	7	26	10	9	7	3	41	31	35	32
107	Belgium[c]	13	13	11	12	12	7	20	22	44	46
108	Austria	8	5	17	10	12	9	20	29	43	46
109	Netherlands	12	26	32	24	9	4	21	16	26	30
110	France	8	7	21	19	10	5	26	35	35	34
111	Japan	2	1	7	2	17	4	31	58	43	35
112	Finland	3	9	40	17	2	5	12	25	43	44
113	Germany, Fed. Rep.	7	6	5	7	5	5	46	46	37	36
114	Denmark	2	6	55	36	4	5	22	25	17	28
115	Australia	13	42	73	35	1	1	5	6	9	16
116	Sweden	9	10	23	12	2	2	35	41	30	34
117	Canada	28	23	35	22	1	1	15	35	21	20
118	Norway	21	62	28	9	2	1	17	14	32	15
119	United States	8	8	27	22	3	2	37	44	26	24
120	Switzerland	3	3	7	4	10	7	30	34	50	52
East European nonmarket economies		**..**	**..**	**..**	**..**	**..**	**..**	**..**	**..**	**..**	**..**
121	Hungary	5	12	25	25	9	6	32	30	28	26
122	Poland	..	26	..	10	..	4	..	41	..	19
123	Albania	..	..	..	..	..	..	..	..	..	..
124	Bulgaria	..	..	..	..	..	..	..	..	..	..
125	Czechoslovakia	..	5	..	6	..	6	..	52	..	31
126	German Dem. Rep.	..	..	..	..	..	..	..	..	..	..
127	Romania	..	..	..	..	..	..	..	..	..	..
128	USSR	..	..	..	..	..	..	..	..	..	..

a. Figures in italics are for 1982, not 1983.   b. Figures are for the South African Customs Union comprising South Africa, Namibia, Lesotho, Botswana, and Swaziland. Trade between the component territories is excluded.   c. Includes Luxembourg.

Table 11. Structure of merchandise imports

	Percentage share of merchandise imports									
	Food		Fuels		Other primary commodities		Machinery and transport equipment		Other manufactures	
	1965	1983[a]	1965	1983[a]	1965	1983[a]	1965	1983[a]	1965	1983[a]
Low-income economies	21 w	.. w	5 w	.. w	9 w	.. w	31 w	.. w	34 w	.. w
China and India	..	12 w	..	16 w	..	13 w	..	18 w	..	41 w
Other low-income	20 w	.. w	5 w	.. w	5 w	.. w	27 w	.. w	43 w	..
Sub-Saharan Africa	18 w	.. w	6 w	.. w	5 w	.. w	27 w	.. w	44 w	..
1 Ethiopia	6	9	6	25	6	4	37	31	44	31
2 Bangladesh	..	20	..	11	..	11	..	23	..	36
3 Mali	20	..	6	..	5	..	23	..	47	..
4 Zaire	18	..	7	..	5	..	33	..	37	..
5 Burkina Faso	23	23	4	17	14	6	19	24	40	30
6 Nepal	..	15	..	11	..	4	..	15	..	56
7 Burma	15	..	4	..	5	..	18	..	58	..
8 Malawi	15	..	5	..	3	..	21	..	57	..
9 Niger	12	..	6	..	6	..	21	..	55	..
10 Tanzania	..	..	..	..	..	..	..	..	..	..
11 Burundi	16	..	6	..	8	..	15	..	55	..
12 Uganda	..	5	..	23	..	1	..	42	..	29
13 Togo	14	..	4	..	5	..	32	..	45	..
14 Central African Rep.	13	..	7	..	2	..	29	..	49	..
15 India	22	7	5	37	14	6	37	17	22	32
16 Madagascar	19	16	5	24	2	3	25	30	48	27
17 Somalia	31	..	5	..	8	..	24	..	33	..
18 Benin	18	16	6	5	7	10	17	22	53	47
19 Rwanda	12	..	7	..	5	..	28	..	50	..
20 China	..	15	..	1	..	18	..	19	..	47
21 Kenya	..	9	..	36	..	4	..	23	..	28
22 Sierra Leone	17	27	9	35	3	2	29	15	41	21
23 Haiti	..	26	..	12	..	4	..	21	..	37
24 Guinea	..	..	..	..	..	..	..	..	..	..
25 Ghana	12	..	4	..	3	..	33	..	48	..
26 Sri Lanka	41	17	8	24	4	3	12	26	34	31
27 Sudan	23	..	5	..	4	..	21	..	47	..
28 Pakistan	20	14	3	28	5	6	38	26	34	25
29 Senegal	36	..	6	..	4	..	15	..	38	..
30 Afghanistan	17	..	4	..	1	..	8	..	69	..
31 Bhutan	..	..	..	..	..	..	..	..	..	..
32 Chad	13	..	20	..	4	..	21	..	42	..
33 Kampuchea, Dem.	6	..	7	..	2	..	26	..	58	..
34 Lao PDR	27	..	14	..	6	..	19	..	34	..
35 Mozambique	17	..	8	..	7	..	24	..	45	..
36 Viet Nam	..	..	..	..	..	..	..	..	..	..
Middle-income economies	16 w	11 w	8 w	20 w	10 w	7 w	29 w	30 w	38 w	32 w
Oil exporters	15 w	17 w	6 w	9 w	7 w	5 w	33 w	37 w	39 w	32 w
Oil importers	16 w	9 w	8 w	24 w	11 w	7 w	27 w	27 w	37 w	33 w
Sub-Saharan Africa	12 w	20 w	5 w	6 w	3 w	3 w	33 w	36 w	47 w	36 w
Lower middle-income	17 w	14 w	7 w	18 w	6 w	5 w	29 w	30 w	41 w	33 w
37 Mauritania	9	..	4	..	1	..	56	..	30	..
38 Liberia	17	25	8	17	3	3	33	26	39	28
39 Zambia	9	9	10	19	3	1	33	34	45	37
40 Lesotho[b]	..	..	..	..	..	..	..	..	..	..
41 Bolivia	19	12	1	2	3	1	34	45	42	40
42 Indonesia	6	8	3	25	2	5	39	35	50	28
43 Yemen Arab Rep.	..	..	..	..	..	..	..	..	..	..
44 Yemen, PDR	19	..	39	..	5	..	10	..	26	..
45 Cote d'Ivoire	18	20	6	19	3	3	28	25	46	34
46 Philippines	20	8	10	27	7	5	33	21	30	39
47 Morocco	36	15	5	24	10	8	18	26	31	27
48 Honduras	11	10	6	22	1	2	26	18	56	47
49 El Salvador	15	18	5	25	4	3	28	12	48	42
50 Papua New Guinea	23	19	4	19	3	2	25	30	45	30
51 Egypt, Arab Rep.	26	30	7	3	12	6	23	29	31	30
52 Nigeria	9	21	6	3	3	3	34	38	48	35
53 Zimbabwe	7	..	(.)	..	4	..	41	..	47	..
54 Cameroon	11	9	5	4	4	3	28	35	51	49
55 Nicaragua	12	12	5	23	2	1	30	23	51	40
56 Thailand	6	4	9	24	6	8	31	29	49	35
57 Botswana[b]	..	..	..	..	..	..	..	..	..	..
58 Dominican Rep.	24	14	10	36	4	3	23	17	40	29
59 Peru	17	18	3	2	5	3	41	45	34	32
60 Mauritius	35	25	5	19	3	5	15	12	42	39
61 Congo, People's Rep.	15	17	6	15	1	1	34	25	44	42
62 Ecuador	10	5	9	2	4	6	33	43	44	45
63 Jamaica	21	19	9	29	5	4	23	18	42	30
64 Guatemala	11	..	7	..	2	..	29	..	50	..
65 Turkey	6	2	10	44	10	8	37	21	37	26

Note: For data comparability and coverage, see the technical notes.

| | Percentage share of merchandise imports | | | | | | | | | |
| | Food | | Fuels | | Other primary commodities | | Machinery and transport equipment | | Other manufactures | |
	1965	1983[a]	1965	1983[a]	1965	1983[a]	1965	1983[a]	1965	1983[a]
66 Costa Rica	9	9	5	20	2	3	29	15	54	53
67 Paraguay	14	13	14	24	2	(.)	37	37	33	26
68 Tunisia	16	15	6	12	7	9	31	29	41	35
69 Colombia	8	10	1	13	10	6	45	39	35	32
70 Jordan	28	17	6	19	6	4	18	23	42	36
71 Syrian Arab Rep.	22	..	10	..	9	..	16	..	43	..
72 Angola	17	..	2	..	3	..	24	..	54	..
73 Cuba	29	..	10	..	3	..	15	..	43	..
74 Korea, Dem. Rep.	..	..	..	..	..	..	..	..	..	..
75 Lebanon	28	..	9	..	9	..	17	..	36	..
76 Mongolia	..	..	..	..	..	..	..	..	..	..
Upper middle-income	**15** w	**10** w	**8** w	**21** w	**12** w	**7** w	**29** w	**30** w	**36** w	**32** w
77 Chile	20	..	6	..	10	..	35	..	30	..
78 Brazil	20	8	21	56	9	4	22	16	28	16
79 Portugal	16	14	8	27	19	9	27	26	30	24
80 Malaysia	25	9	12	14	10	5	22	44	32	28
81 Panama	..	9	..	27	..	1	..	26	..	37
82 Uruguay	7	7	17	36	16	6	24	25	36	26
83 Mexico	5	17	2	3	10	6	50	45	33	29
84 Korea, Rep. of	15	8	7	27	26	14	13	29	38	22
85 Yugoslavia	16	6	6	27	19	12	28	24	32	30
86 Argentina	6	4	10	10	21	10	25	32	38	43
87 South Africa[b]	5	3	5	(.)	11	4	42	43	37	50
88 Algeria	27	21	(.)	2	6	6	15	35	52	37
89 Venezuela	12	..	1	..	5	..	44	..	39	..
90 Greece	15	13	8	27	11	7	35	25	30	28
91 Israel	16	10	6	18	12	5	28	32	38	36
92 Hong Kong	25	12	3	7	13	6	13	21	46	54
93 Trinidad and Tobago	12	17	49	3	2	5	16	37	21	38
94 Singapore	23	7	13	31	19	6	14	30	30	26
95 Iran, Islamic Rep.	16	..	(.)	..	6	..	36	..	42	..
96 Iraq	24	..	(.)	..	7	..	25	..	44	..
High-income oil exporters	**22** w	**12** w	**2** w	**1** w	**5** w	**3** w	**32** w	**43** w	**40** w	**41** w
97 Oman	..	14	..	2	..	3	..	46	..	36
98 Libya	13	..	4	..	3	..	36	..	43	..
99 Saudi Arabia	30	12	1	(.)	5	3	27	43	37	42
100 Kuwait	22	13	1	1	7	3	32	44	39	40
101 United Arab Emirates	..	9	..	6	..	3	..	41	..	42
Industrial market economies	**19** w	**10** w	**11** w	**23** w	**20** w	**9** w	**19** w	**26** w	**31** w	**32** w
102 Spain	19	12	10	40	16	10	27	18	28	19
103 Ireland	18	13	8	13	10	5	25	29	39	40
104 Italy	24	14	16	31	24	11	15	18	21	25
105 New Zealand	7	6	7	18	10	5	33	31	43	39
106 United Kingdom	30	12	11	11	25	10	11	30	23	37
107 Belgium[c]	14	12	9	18	21	10	24	23	32	38
108 Austria	14	6	7	14	13	8	31	30	35	41
109 Netherlands	15	15	10	25	13	7	25	21	37	33
110 France	19	11	15	24	18	8	20	24	27	33
111 Japan	22	13	20	47	38	17	9	8	11	16
112 Finland	10	6	10	27	12	8	35	29	34	31
113 Germany, Fed. Rep.	22	12	8	21	21	9	13	22	35	36
114 Denmark	14	12	11	20	11	7	25	22	39	39
115 Australia	5	5	8	11	10	4	37	38	41	41
116 Sweden	12	7	11	23	12	7	30	30	36	34
117 Canada	10	7	7	7	9	6	40	51	34	30
118 Norway	10	7	7	10	12	7	38	37	32	40
119 United States	19	8	10	22	20	7	14	32	36	31
120 Switzerland	16	8	6	11	11	7	24	27	43	47
East European nonmarket economies	..	..	..	..	..	..	..	..	..	..
121 Hungary	12	7	11	23	22	10	27	27	28	33
122 Poland	..	10	..	26	..	11	..	25	..	27
123 Albania	..	..	..	..	..	..	..	..	..	..
124 Bulgaria	..	..	..	..	..	..	..	..	..	..
125 Czechoslovakia	..	7	..	30	..	13	..	32	..	19
126 German Dem. Rep.	..	..	..	..	..	..	..	..	..	..
127 Romania	..	..	..	..	..	..	..	..	..	..
128 USSR	..	..	..	..	..	..	..	..	..	..

a. Figures in italics are for 1982, not 1983.   b. Figures are for the South African Customs Union comprising South Africa, Namibia, Lesotho, Botswana, and Swaziland. Trade between the component territories is excluded.   c. Includes Luxembourg.

Table 12. Origin and destination of merchandise exports

| | Destination of merchandise exports (percentage of total) | | | | | | | |
| | Industrial market economies | | East European nonmarket economies | | High-income oil exporters | | Developing economies | |
Origin	1965	1984[a]	1965	1984[a]	1965	1984[a]	1965	1984[a]
Low-income economies	56 *w*	50 *w*	10 *w*	7 *w*	2 *w*	4 *w*	32 *w*	40 *w*
China and India	51 *w*	46 *w*	14 *w*	8 *w*	2 *w*	3 *w*	33 *w*	44 *w*
Other low-income	62 *w*	60 *w*	5 *w*	4 *w*	2 *w*	6 *w*	31 *w*	30 *w*
Sub-Saharan Africa	72 *w*	68 *w*	4 *w*	3 *w*	1 *w*	3 *w*	22 *w*	25 *w*
1 Ethiopia	78	79	3	1	6	6	14	15
2 Bangladesh	. .	51	. .	6	. .	2	. .	41
3 Mali	7	. .	4	. .	0	. .	89	. .
4 Zaire	93	92	(.)	(.)	(.)	(.)	7	8
5 Burkina Faso	17	35	0	0	0	0	83	65
6 Nepal	. .	21	. .	(.)	. .	(.)	. .	79
7 Burma	29	30	8	3	1	3	62	64
8 Malawi	69	68	(.)	0	(.)	(.)	30	31
9 Niger	61	56	(.)	(.)	(.)	18	39	26
10 Tanzania	66	61	1	4	1	1	32	35
11 Burundi	24	78	0	4	0	0	76	19
12 Uganda	69	89	2	0	1	2	28	9
13 Togo	92	63	2	5	0	0	6	32
14 Central African Rep.	71	93	0	0	0	0	29	7
15 India	58	59	17	15	2	6	23	20
16 Madagascar	85	72	1	3	(.)	(.)	14	25
17 Somalia	40	10	(.)	0	3	64	57	26
18 Benin	88	80	(.)	0	0	0	12	20
19 Rwanda	96	81	0	0	0	(.)	4	19
20 China	47	41	12	5	2	1	40	52
21 Kenya	69	51	2	1	1	1	28	47
22 Sierra Leone	92	71	(.)	0	(.)	0	8	29
23 Haiti	97	96	(.)	(.)	0	0	3	4
24 Guinea	. .	89	. .	0	. .	(.)	. .	10
25 Ghana	74	57	18	25	(.)	(.)	9	17
26 Sri Lanka	56	45	9	6	3	6	33	43
27 Sudan	56	40	13	8	4	17	27	35
28 Pakistan	48	47	3	5	4	17	45	31
29 Senegal	92	53	(.)	(.)	0	(.)	7	47
30 *Afghanistan*	47	. .	27	. .	0	. .	25	. .
31 *Bhutan*	. .	. .	. .	. .	. .	. .	. .	. .
32 *Chad*	64	. .	0	. .	2	. .	34	. .
33 *Kampuchea, Dem.*	36	. .	6	. .	0	. .	58	. .
34 *Lao PDR*	9	. .	0	. .	0	. .	91	. .
35 *Mozambique*	24	. .	(.)	. .	(.)	. .	76	. .
36 *Viet Nam*	. .	. .	. .	. .	. .	. .	. .	. .
Middle-income economies	69 *w*	64 *w*	7 *w*	3 *w*	1 *w*	2 *w*	23 *w*	31 *w*
Oil exporters	70 *w*	71 *w*	5 *w*	(.) *w*	1 *w*	2 *w*	24 *w*	28 *w*
Oil importers	68 *w*	58 *w*	8 *w*	5 *w*	1 *w*	3 *w*	23 *w*	33 *w*
Sub-Saharan Africa	81 *w*	75 *w*	2 *w*	(.) *w*	(.) *w*	(.) *w*	17 *w*	24 *w*
Lower middle-income	69 *w*	69 *w*	9 *w*	2 *w*	1 *w*	2 *w*	20 *w*	27 *w*
37 Mauritania	96	96	(.)	(.)	0	(.)	4	4
38 Liberia	98	77	0	(.)	0	(.)	2	23
39 Zambia	87	68	2	2	0	(.)	11	30
40 Lesotho[b]	. .	. .	. .	. .	. .	. .	. .	. .
41 Bolivia	97	45	0	2	0	(.)	3	53
42 Indonesia	72	73	5	1	(.)	1	23	26
43 Yemen Arab Rep.	. .	34	. .	(.)	. .	15	. .	52
44 Yemen, PDR	38	51	(.)	(.)	1	1	61	48
45 Cote d'Ivoire	84	70	2	3	1	(.)	13	27
46 Philippines	95	78	0	2	(.)	1	5	18
47 Morocco	80	66	7	6	(.)	3	12	25
48 Honduras	80	81	0	2	0	2	20	15
49 El Salvador	73	. .	1	. .	0	. .	26	. .
50 Papua New Guinea	98	87	0	1	0	(.)	2	12
51 Egypt, Arab Rep.	28	78	44	4	1	3	27	15
52 Nigeria	91	73	3	(.)	(.)	(.)	6	27
53 Zimbabwe	50	. .	1	. .	(.)	. .	48	. .
54 Cameroon	93	78	(.)	(.)	(.)	(.)	7	22
55 Nicaragua	81	. .	(.)	. .	0	. .	19	. .
56 Thailand	44	56	1	1	2	5	53	38
57 Botswana[b]	. .	. .	. .	. .	. .	. .	. .	. .
58 Dominican Rep.	99	91	0	3	0	0	1	5
59 Peru	86	72	3	2	(.)	(.)	12	26
60 Mauritius	94	95	0	(.)	0	(.)	6	5
61 Congo, People's Rep.	86	96	1	(.)	0	(.)	13	3
62 Ecuador	89	67	(.)	(.)	0	(.)	11	33
63 Jamaica	93	81	1	1	(.)	0	6	18
64 Guatemala	75	59	0	2	(.)	1	25	38
65 Turkey	71	51	15	4	(.)	9	14	36

Note: For data comparability and coverage, see the technical notes.

	Destination of merchandise exports (percentage of total)							
	Industrial market economies		East European nonmarket economies		High-income oil exporters		Developing economies	
Origin	1965	1984[a]	1965	1984[a]	1965	1984[a]	1965	1984[a]
66 Costa Rica	79	71	(.)	3	0	1	20	25
67 Paraguay	58	47	0	0	0	0	42	53
68 Tunisia	61	81	5	1	3	4	31	15
69 Colombia	86	81	2	2	(.)	(.)	12	17
70 Jordan	20	12	4	6	22	22	54	60
71 Syrian Arab Rep.	26	41	24	13	8	3	42	42
72 Angola	55	..	1	..	(.)	..	45	..
73 Cuba	14	..	62	..	(.)	..	24	..
74 Korea, Dem. Rep.	..	..	..	..	..	..	..	..
75 Lebanon	43	..	4	..	35	..	18	..
76 Mongolia	..	..	..	..	..	..	..	..
Upper middle-income	**69** w	**62** w	**6** w	**4** w	**(.)** w	**2** w	**25** w	**32** w
77 Chile	90	75	(.)	1	0	2	10	22
78 Brazil	77	62	6	7	(.)	2	18	29
79 Portugal	65	83	1	2	(.)	1	34	15
80 Malaysia	56	52	7	0	(.)	1	36	47
81 Panama	..	69	..	(.)	..	(.)	..	31
82 Uruguay	76	34	5	8	0	3	19	55
83 Mexico	82	92	6	0	(.)	(.)	13	8
84 Korea, Rep. of	75	69	0	0	(.)	6	25	25
85 Yugoslavia	40	35	42	46	(.)	3	17	17
86 Argentina	67	39	8	22	(.)	1	26	38
87 South Africa[b]	96	43	0	(.)	(.)	(.)	4	57
88 Algeria	90	92	1	(.)	(.)	0	8	8
89 Venezuela	63	66	(.)	(.)	(.)	0	37	34
90 Greece	64	68	23	6	2	8	12	18
91 Israel	72	70	4	1	0	0	24	29
92 Hong Kong	67	60	(.)	(.)	1	2	32	38
93 Trinidad and Tobago	92	74	0	0	0	(.)	8	26
94 Singapore	28	45	6	2	2	6	64	48
95 Iran, Islamic Rep.	67	..	3	..	2	..	28	..
96 Iraq	83	..	1	..	(.)	..	16	..
High-income oil exporters	**70** w	**59** w	**(.)** w	**(.)** w	**3** w	**3** w	**27** w	**33** w
97 Oman	..	63	..	(.)	..	0	..	36
98 Libya	97	74	(.)	2	(.)	0	3	24
99 Saudi Arabia	71	59	0	0	8	3	21	37
100 Kuwait	56	40	(.)	1	1	6	44	53
101 United Arab Emirates	69	79	0	(.)	5	3	26	18
Industrial market economies	**71** w	**70** w	**3** w	**3** w	**1** w	**3** w	**26** w	**24** w
102 Spain	73	64	3	3	(.)	4	24	29
103 Ireland	91	89	1	1	(.)	2	8	9
104 Italy	71	68	5	3	2	7	23	21
105 New Zealand	88	64	1	2	(.)	2	11	32
106 United Kingdom	63	75	2	2	2	5	33	18
107 Belgium[c]	86	83	1	2	(.)	2	12	13
108 Austria	71	71	15	12	(.)	3	13	14
109 Netherlands	83	84	2	1	1	2	14	12
110 France	68	69	3	3	(.)	4	28	24
111 Japan	49	55	3	2	2	6	47	37
112 Finland	71	68	21	21	(.)	1	9	11
113 Germany, Fed. Rep.	77	76	3	4	1	3	19	17
114 Denmark	85	80	4	2	1	2	11	17
115 Australia	69	52	4	4	1	3	26	41
116 Sweden	85	82	4	3	(.)	2	11	13
117 Canada	87	88	3	2	(.)	1	10	10
118 Norway	82	90	4	1	(.)	(.)	13	9
119 United States	61	59	1	2	1	3	37	36
120 Switzerland	76	74	3	3	1	4	20	19
East European nonmarket economies	**..**	**32** w	**..**	**51** w	**..**	**3** w	**..**	**14** w
121 Hungary	22	28	66	48	(.)	2	12	21
122 Poland	..	34	..	48	..	2	..	16
123 Albania	..	..	..	..	..	..	..	..
124 Bulgaria	..	11	..	69	..	8	..	12
125 Czechoslovakia	18	15	72	68	1	2	9	15
126 German Dem. Rep.	..	..	..	..	..	..	..	..
127 Romania	..	25	..	45	..	2	..	29
128 USSR	..	39	..	46	..	3	..	12

a. Figures in italics are for 1983, not 1984.   b. Figures are for the South African Customs Union comprising South Africa, Namibia, Lesotho, Botswana, and Swaziland. Trade between the component territories is excluded.   c. Includes Luxembourg.

Table 13. Origin and destination of manufactured exports

	Destination of manufactured exports (percentage of total)								Manufactured exports (millions of dollars)	
	Industrial market economies		East European nonmarket economies		High-income oil exporters		Developing economies			
Origin	1965	1983[a]	1965	1983[a]	1965	1983[a]	1965	1983[a]	1965	1983[a]
Low-income economies	56 *w*	..	8 *w*	..	2 *w*	..	34 *w*	..		
China and India	..	..	..	..	..	..	..	..		
Other low-income	58 *w*	..	1 *w*	..	2 *w*	..	39 *w*	..		
Sub-Saharan Africa	77 *w*	..	1 *w*	..	(.) *w*	..	22 *w*	..		
1 Ethiopia	67	76	(.)	9	20	2	13	13	(.)	3
2 Bangladesh	..	48	..	6	..	1	..	45	..	485
3 Mali	14	..	8	..	0	..	78	..	(.)	..
4 Zaire	93	..	(.)	..	(.)	..	7	..	28	..
5 Burkina Faso	2	34	0	0	0	0	98	66	1	6
6 Nepal	..	36	..	3	..	(.)	..	61	..	45
7 Burma	73	..	1	..	(.)	..	26	..	1	..
8 Malawi	3	..	0	..	0	..	97	..	(.)	..
9 Niger	43	..	(.)	..	0	..	57	..	1	..
10 Tanzania	93	..	(.)	..	(.)	..	7	..	23	..
11 Burundi	(.)	..	0	..	0	..	100	..	1	..
12 Uganda	7	..	(.)	..	0	..	93	..	1	..
13 Togo	37	..	(.)	..	0	..	62	..	1	..
14 Central African Rep.	60	..	0	..	0	..	40	..	14	..
15 India	55	51	12	0	2	7	31	19	828	5,080
16 Madagascar	80	*80*	0	*(.)*	0	*(.)*	20	*20*	5	*24*
17 Somalia	21	..	(.)	..	2	..	77	..	4	..
18 Benin	15	*8*	0	*0*	0	*0*	85	*92*	1	*20*
19 Rwanda	95	..	0	..	0	..	5	..	(.)	..
20 China	..	..	..	..	..	..	..	..	..	12,579
21 Kenya	23	8	2	(.)	2	3	73	89	13	128
22 Sierra Leone	99	99	(.)	0	(.)	0	1	1	53	29
23 Haiti	..	..	..	..	..	..	..	..	..	..
24 Guinea	..	..	..	..	..	..	..	..	..	..
25 Ghana	60	..	10	..	(.)	..	29	..	7	..
26 Sri Lanka	59	87	7	(.)	(.)	1	34	13	5	314
27 Sudan	79	..	(.)	..	2	..	20	..	2	12
28 Pakistan	40	41	1	5	3	21	57	33	190	1,964
29 Senegal	48	..	1	..	0	..	52	..	4	..
30 *Afghanistan*	98	..	(.)	..	0	..	2	..	11	..
31 *Bhutan*	..	..	..	..	..	..	..	..	..	..
32 *Chad*	6	..	0	..	25	..	69	..	1	..
33 *Kampuchea, Dem.*	28	..	1	..	0	..	71	..	1	..
34 *Lao PDR*	13	..	0	..	0	..	87	..	(.)	..
35 *Mozambique*	27	..	(.)	..	(.)	..	73	..	3	..
36 *Viet Nam*	..	..	..	..	..	..	..	..	..	..
Middle-income economies	52 *w*	54 *w*	9 *w*	4 *w*	2 *w*	5 *w*	37 *w*	38 *w*		
Oil exporters	45 *w*	75 *w*	9 *w*	1 *w*	3 *w*	2 *w*	43 *w*	23 *w*		
Oil importers	54 *w*	51 *w*	9 *w*	4 *w*	1 *w*	5 *w*	36 *w*	40 *w*		
Sub-Saharan Africa	29 *w*	..	(.) *w*	..	(.) *w*	..	71 *w*	..		
Lower middle-income	37 *w*	56 *w*	10 *w*	1 *w*	4 *w*	5 *w*	49 *w*	37 *w*		
37 Mauritania	61	..	0	..	0	..	39	..	1	..
38 Liberia	77	*54*	0	*(.)*	0	*(.)*	23	46	4	6
39 Zambia	14	..	0	..	0	..	86	..	1	8
40 Lesotho	..	..	..	..	..	..	..	..	..	..
41 Bolivia	86	..	0	..	0	..	14	..	6	..
42 Indonesia	25	42	1	(.)	(.)	7	74	52	27	1,618
43 Yemen Arab Rep.	..	..	..	..	..	..	..	..	..	..
44 Yemen, PDR	32	..	(.)	..	6	..	62	..	11	..
45 Cote d'Ivoire	50	31	(.)	(.)	(.)	(.)	50	69	15	235
46 Philippines	93	77	0	(.)	(.)	2	7	21	43	2,534
47 Morocco	63	56	2	3	(.)	3	35	37	23	707
48 Honduras	2	28	0	0	0	0	98	72	6	58
49 El Salvador	1	*8*	0	*0*	0	*(.)*	99	*92*	32	162
50 Papua New Guinea	100	*85*	0	*0*	0	*0*	(.)	*15*	5	72
51 Egypt, Arab Rep.	20	38	46	40	4	8	30	14	126	256
52 Nigeria	85	..	(.)	..	(.)	..	15	..	17	..
53 Zimbabwe	12	..	(.)	..	(.)	..	88	..	116	..
54 Cameroon	46	*39*	0	*0*	(.)	*(.)*	54	*61*	6	*78*
55 Nicaragua	4	*3*	0	*(.)*	0	*0*	96	*97*	8	*30*
56 Thailand	39	60	(.)	(.)	(.)	9	61	31	30	2,058
57 Botswana	..	..	..	..	..	..	..	..	..	..
58 Dominican Rep.	95	87	0	0	0	(.)	5	13	3	155
59 Peru	51	..	(.)	..	0	..	49	..	5	..
60 Mauritius	16	89	0	(.)	0	(.)	84	10	(.)	115
61 Congo, People's Rep.	88	..	0	..	0	..	12	..	24	..
62 Ecuador	25	*7*	0	*(.)*	0	*0*	75	*93*	3	69
63 Jamaica	93	*74*	1	*2*	0	*0*	6	*24*	64	*444*
64 Guatemala	9	..	0	..	0	..	91	..	26	..
65 Turkey	83	50	8	1	(.)	8	9	41	11	2,643

Note: For data comparability and coverage, see the technical notes.

	Destination of manufactured exports (percentage of total)								Manufactured exports (millions of dollars)	
	Industrial market economies		East European nonmarket economies		High-income oil exporters		Developing economies			
Origin	1965	1983[a]	1965	1983[a]	1965	1983[a]	1965	1983[a]	1965	1983[a]
66 Costa Rica	6	15	(.)	(.)	0	(.)	94	85	18	248
67 Paraguay	93	..	0	..	0	..	7	..	5	..
68 Tunisia	19	74	3	1	5	4	73	21	23	816
69 Colombia	43	50	0	1	(.)	(.)	57	49	35	595
70 Jordan	49	17	(.)	1	23	28	28	53	5	267
71 Syrian Arab Rep.	5	..	21	..	25	..	50	..	16	..
72 Angola	3	..	1	..	(.)	..	96	..	36	..
73 Cuba	27	..	70	..	0	..	3	..	27	..
74 Korea, Dem. Rep.	..	..	..	..	..	..	..	..	..	..
75 Lebanon	19	..	1	..	61	..	19	..	29	..
76 Mongolia	..	..	..	..	..	..	..	..	..	..
Upper middle-income	**56** *w*	**53** *w*	**9** *w*	**4** *w*	**1** *w*	**5** *w*	**34** *w*	**38** *w*		
77 Chile	38	..	(.)	..	0	..	62	..	28	323
78 Brazil	40	52	1	1	(.)	3	59	43	134	9,098
79 Portugal	59	85	(.)	1	(.)	1	41	13	355	3,464
80 Malaysia	17	63	(.)	0	2	1	81	35	75	3,965
81 Panama	..	..	..	..	..	..	..	..	..	39
82 Uruguay	71	52	6	7	0	(.)	23	41	10	298
83 Mexico	71	90	(.)	0	(.)	(.)	29	9	165	4,022
84 Korea, Rep. of	68	66	0	0	(.)	10	32	24	104	22,240
85 Yugoslavia	24	26	52	50	1	4	24	20	617	7,541
86 Argentina	45	52	3	5	(.)	1	52	42	84	1,283
87 South Africa	94	0	0	0	(.)	0	6	100	443	13,081
88 Algeria	50	70	1	6	1	(.)	48	24	24	82
89 Venezuela	59	..	(.)	..	(.)	..	41	..	51	..
90 Greece	56	60	8	5	9	15	27	20	44	2,194
91 Israel	67	69	4	(.)	0	0	29	31	281	4,122
92 Hong Kong	71	64	(.)	(.)	1	4	28	32	995	20,089
93 Trinidad and Tobago	78	79	0	0	0	(.)	22	21	28	330
94 Singapore	9	48	(.)	1	3	6	88	44	338	12,388
95 Iran, Islamic Rep.	61	..	1	..	17	..	21	..	58	..
96 Iraq	24	..	1	..	16	..	60	..	8	..
High-income oil exporters	**30** *w*	**..**	**(.)** *w*	**..**	**21** *w*	**..**	**49** *w*	**..**		
97 Oman	..	..	..	..	..	..	..	..	..	..
98 Libya	57	..	(.)	..	(.)	..	43	..	7	..
99 Saudi Arabia	31	10	0	(.)	18	16	52	73	19	824
100 Kuwait	18	38	(.)	(.)	33	20	49	42	17	2,448
101 United Arab Emirates	..	..	0	..	..	..	..	..	..	..
Industrial market economies	**67** *w*	**66** *w*	**3** *w*	**3** *w*	**1** *w*	**5** *w*	**29** *w*	**26** *w*		
102 Spain	57	58	1	2	(.)	6	42	34	382	13,755
103 Ireland	82	92	(.)	(.)	(.)	1	17	7	203	5,737
104 Italy	68	66	5	4	2	9	25	22	5,587	61,998
105 New Zealand	90	71	(.)	(.)	(.)	2	10	28	53	1,153
106 United Kingdom	61	65	2	2	2	8	35	25	11,346	60,350
107 Belgium	86	82	1	2	1	2	13	13	4,823	38,676
108 Austria	67	70	18	12	(.)	3	15	15	1,204	13,070
109 Netherlands	81	82	2	2	1	3	16	13	3,586	32,645
110 France	64	65	3	3	1	4	33	28	7,139	67,189
111 Japan	47	51	2	2	2	8	49	39	7,704	142,050
112 Finland	63	56	26	33	(.)	2	11	9	815	9,334
113 Germany, Fed. Rep.	76	73	3	5	1	4	20	19	15,764	147,003
114 Denmark	79	75	4	2	(.)	3	16	19	967	8,922
115 Australia	57	40	(.)	1	(.)	1	43	58	432	4,605
116 Sweden	82	79	4	2	(.)	4	14	14	2,685	21,236
117 Canada	88	92	(.)	(.)	(.)	1	12	7	2,973	39,917
118 Norway	78	76	3	2	(.)	1	19	21	734	5,311
119 United States	58	58	(.)	1	1	6	40	36	17,833	140,035
120 Switzerland	75	71	3	3	1	5	21	21	2,646	23,358
East European nonmarket economies	**..**	**..**	**..**	**..**	**..**	**..**	**..**	**..**		
121 Hungary	11	21	74	56	(.)	2	15	21	1,053	5,440
122 Poland	..	16	..	51	..	2	..	31	..	7,472
123 Albania	..	..	..	..	..	..	..	..	..	..
124 Bulgaria	..	..	..	..	..	..	..	..	..	..
125 Czechoslovakia	..	12	..	71	..	2	..	15	..	14,641
126 German Dem. Rep.	..	..	..	..	..	..	..	..	..	..
127 Romania	..	..	..	..	..	..	..	..	..	..
128 USSR	..	..	..	..	..	..	..	..	..	..

a. Figures in italics are for 1983, not 1984.   b. Figures are for the South African Customs Union comprising South Africa, Namibia, Lesotho, Botswana, and Swaziland. Trade between the component territories is excluded.   c. Includes Luxembourg.

Table 14. Balance of payments and reserves

	Current account balance (millions of dollars)		Receipts of workers' remittances (millions of dollars)		Net direct private investment (millions of dollars)		Gross international reserves		
							Millions of dollars		In months of import coverage
	1970	1984a	1970	1984a	1970	1984a	1970	1984a	1984a
Low-income economies									5.8 *w*
China and India									7.9 *w*
Other low-income									2.1 *w*
Sub-Saharan Africa									1.9 *w*
1 Ethiopia	−32	−201	..	..	4	..	72	109	1.1
2 Bangladesh	..	−521	..	437	..	−1	..	406	1.7
3 Mali	−2	−125	6	32	..	4	1	32	0.9
4 Zaire	−64	−310	2	..	42	138	189	269	1.5
5 Burkina Faso	9	−67	18	..	(.)	..	36	110	..
6 Nepal	..	−102	..	..	..	..	94	129	2.9
7 Burma	−63	−237	..	..	..	..	98	140	2.2
8 Malawi	−35	−20	..	..	9	3	29	61	1.9
9 Niger	0	−47	..	..	1	..	19	92	..
10 Tanzania	−36	−354	..	..	..	..	65	27	0.3
11 Burundi	..	66	..	..	..	1	15	25	..
12 Uganda	20	..	..	..	4	..	57	..	..
13 Togo	3	16	..	6	1	0	35	178	4.4
14 Central African Rep.	−12	−31	..	..	1	5	1	56	2.8
15 India	−394	−2,429	113	2,659	6	..	1,023	8,536	5.6
16 Madagascar	10	−176	..	..	10	..	37	59	1.1
17 Somalia	−6	−146	..	22	5	−1	21	7	0.1
18 Benin	−1	−30	2	..	7	..	16	6	..
19 Rwanda	7	−42	1	1	(.)	15	8	107	3.9
20 China	..	2,509	..	317	..	1,124	..	21,281	9.6
21 Kenya	−49	−135	..	..	14	54	220	414	2.6
22 Sierra Leone	−16	−33	..	..	8	2	39	16	1.0
23 Haiti	2	−110	17	89	3	4	4	18	0.4
24 Guinea	..	−19	..	..	..	..	..	..	..
25 Ghana	−68	−61	..	5	68	2	43	437	6.4
26 Sri Lanka	−59	9	3	301	(.)	33	43	530	2.8
27 Sudan	−42	25	..	284	..	9	22	17	0.2
28 Pakistan	−667	−1,118	86	2,567	23	62	194	1,610	2.4
29 Senegal	−16	−274	3	..	5	..	22	13	..
30 *Afghanistan*	..	..	..	..	..	..	49	526	..
31 *Bhutan*	..	..	..	..	..	..	..	..	..
32 *Chad*	2	10	..	..	1	9	2	48	2.6
33 *Kampuchea, Dem.*	..	..	..	..	..	..	..	..	..
34 *Lao PDR*	..	..	..	..	..	..	6	..	..
35 *Mozambique*	..	..	..	..	..	..	..	..	..
36 *Viet Nam*	..	..	..	..	..	..	243	..	..
Middle-income economies									2.9 *w*
Oil exporters									3.4 *w*
Oil importes									2.7 *w*
Sub-Saharan Africa									1.4 *w*
Lower middle-income									2.2 *w*
37 Mauritania	−5	−196	1	1	1	1	3	110	2.1
38 Liberia	..	−75	..	..	..	39	..	3	0.1
39 Zambia	108	−138	..	..	−297	..	515	55	0.6
40 Lesotho	..	31	..	..	..	3	..	49	1.2
41 Bolivia	4	−178	..	1	−76	7	46	533	5.8
42 Indonesia	−310	−2,113	..	..	83	227	160	5,730	2.8
43 Yemen Arab Rep.	..	−305	..	1,012	..	7	..	321	2.3
44 Yemen, PDR	−4	−368	60	494	..	..	59	262	3.0
45 Cote d'Ivoire	−38	−190	..	..	31	..	119	19	0.1
46 Philippines	−48	−1,241	..	59	−29	−6	255	844	1.0
47 Morocco	−124	−986	63	872	20	47	141	266	0.6
48 Honduras	−64	−243	..	..	8	7	20	133	1.3
49 El Salvador	9	−65	..	48	4	28	64	339	3.3
50 Papua New Guinea	..	−325	..	..	..	114	..	443	3.5
51 Egypt, Arab Rep.	−148	−1,978	29	3,963	..	713	165	1,486	1.3
52 Nigeria	−368	346	..	..	205	189	223	1,674	1.7
53 Zimbabwe	..	−97	..	..	..	−2	59	260	2.0
54 Cameroon	−30	−292	..	26	16	207	81	63	0.3
55 Nicaragua	−40	−444	..	..	15	8	49	230	2.8
56 Thailand	−250	−2,105	..	..	43	409	912	2,688	2.5
57 Botswana	..	59	..	..	..	47	..	474	6.3
58 Dominican Rep.	−102	−421	25	195	72	48	32	201	1.3
59 Peru	202	−253	..	..	−70	−88	339	2,061	5.6
60 Mauritius	8	−54	..	..	2	5	46	35	0.7
61 Congo, People's Rep.	..	−400	..	..	..	56	9	12	0.1
62 Ecuador	−113	−248	..	..	89	50	76	739	2.7
63 Jamaica	−153	−309	29	..	161	..	139	97	0.6
64 Guatemala	−8	−382	..	..	29	38	79	435	3.1
65 Turkey	−44	−1,409	273	1,820	58	113	440	2,443	2.2

Note: For data comparability and coverage, see the technical notes.

	Current account balance (millions of dollars)		Receipts of workers' remittances (millions of dollars)		Net direct private investment (millions of dollars)		Gross international reserves		
							Millions of dollars		In months of import coverage[a]
	1970	1984[a]	1970	1984[a]	1970	1984[a]	1970	1984[a]	1984[a]
66 Costa Rica	−74	−216	..	..	26	54	16	412	3 0
67 Paraguay	−16	−313	..	(.)	4	5	18	677	6.6
68 Tunisia	−53	−734	29	317	16	115	60	464	1.4
69 Colombia	−293	−1,237	6	79	39	411	207	1,785	3.2
70 Jordan	−20	−269	..	1,236	..	71	258	842	2.6
71 Syrian Arab Rep.	−69	−852	7	327	..	..	57	257	0.6
72 Angola	..	..	..	..	..	..	..	..	..
73 Cuba	..	..	..	..	..	..	..	..	..
74 Korea, Dem. Rep.	..	..	..	..	..	..	..	..	..
75 Lebanon	..	..	..	..	..	..	405	3,515	..
76 Mongolia	..	..	..	..	..	..	..	..	..
Upper middle-income									**3.3** w
77 Chile	−91	−2,060	..	..	−79	67	392	2,774	4.8
78 Brazil	−837	53	..	4	407	1,555	1,190	11,961	4.7
79 Portugal	..	−502	..	2,157	..	186	1,565	6,774	8.3
80 Malaysia	8	−1,597	..	..	94	912	667	4,441	2.6
81 Panama	−64	−70	..	..	33	37	16	216	0.4
82 Uruguay	−45	−124	..	..	..	3	186	942	7.5
83 Mexico	−1,068	3,905	..	..	323	392	756	8,019	3.3
84 Korea, Rep. of	−623	−1,344	..	..	66	75	610	2,849	1.0
85 Yugoslavia	−372	656	441	3,427	..	..	143	1,732	1.2
86 Argentina	−163	−2,542	..	..	11	269	682	2,591	2.5
87 South Africa	−1,215	−1,098	..	..	318	15	1,057	2,511	1.4
88 Algeria	−125	75	211	329	45	−14	352	3,185	2.8
89 Venezuela	−104	5,298	..	..	−23	42	1,047	12,434	11.1
90 Greece	−422	−2,123	333	899	50	486	318	2,220	2.4
91 Israel	−562	−1,499	..	..	40	8	452	3,374	2.6
92 Hong Kong	..	..	3	1	..	..	..	..	..
93 Trinidad and Tobago	−109	−552	..	..	83	299	43	1,373	5.2
94 Singapore	−572	−1,000	..	..	93	1,458	1,012	10,416	3.8
95 Iran, Islamic Rep.	−507	..	..	..	25	..	217	..	..
96 Iraq	105	..	..	..	24	..	472	..	..
High-income oil exporters									**4.4** w
97 Oman	..	148	..	43	..	157	13	989	3.1
98 Libya	645	−1,803	..	..	139	−327	1,596	4,759	5.3
99 Saudi Arabia	71	−24,036	..	..	20	5,228	670	26,165	4.3
100 Kuwait	..	5,570	..	..	..	−125	209	5,373	5.4
101 United Arab Emirates	..	7,137	..	..	..	..	..	2,539	4.1
Industrial market economies									**3.1** w
102 Spain	79	2,323	469	844	179	1,524	1,851	16,465	5.5
103 Ireland	−198	−916	..	..	32	120	698	2,463	2.3
104 Italy	902	−2,902	446	1,116	498	−694	5,547	41,351	4.8
105 New Zealand	−232	−1,444	40	301	137	97	258	1,794	2.4
106 United Kingdom	1,910	1,417	..	..	−185	−5,507	2,919	15,307	1.0
107 Belgium	717	205	154	358	140	106	2,947	15,102	2.4
108 Austria	−75	−633	13	175	104	68	1,806	10,760	4.7
109 Netherlands	−483	4,879	..	..	−15	−2,096	3,362	22,784	3.5
110 France	−204	−820	130	342	248	275	5,199	46,174	3.8
111 Japan	1,980	35,148	..	..	−260	−5,955	4,877	33,899	2.3
112 Finland	−239	1	..	..	−41	−359	455	3,146	2.3
113 Germany, Fed. Rep.	850	6,130	..	..	−290	−1,907	13,879	69,486	4.3
114 Denmark	−544	−1,634	..	..	75	−86	488	3,511	1.7
115 Australia	−837	−8,302	..	..	785	−1,442	1,709	9,886	3.3
116 Sweden	−265	356	..	..	−104	−885	775	5,716	1.9
117 Canada	821	1,974	..	..	566	−1,334	4,733	8,700	1.0
118 Norway	−242	3,228	..	9	32	−702	813	9,730	4.8
119 United States	2,320	−107,780	..	..	−6,130	17,948	15,237	104,856	2.7
120 Switzerland	72	4,019	..	70	..	−362	5,317	40,971	9.9
East European nonmarket economies									..
121 Hungary	−25	290	..	..	..	..	..	2,745	3.2
122 Poland	..	..	..	..	..	..	..	..	..
123 Albania	..	..	..	..	..	..	..	..	..
124 Bulgaria	..	..	..	..	..	..	..	..	..
125 Czechoslovakia	..	..	..	..	..	..	..	..	..
126 German Dem. Rep.	..	..	..	..	..	..	..	..	..
127 Romania	..	1,719	..	..	..	..	..	1,859	1.9
128 USSR	..	..	..	..	..	..	..	..	..

a. Figures in italics are for 1983, not 1984.

Table 15. Gross external liabilities

| | Long-term debt (millions of dollars) | | | | Use of IMF credit (millions of dollars) | | Short-term debt (millions of dollars) | | Total gross external liabilities (millions of dollars) | |
| | Public and publicly guaranteed | | Private nonguaranteed | | | | | | | |
	1970	1984	1970	1984	1970	1984	1970	1984	1970	1984
Low-income economies										
China and India										
Other low-income										
Sub-Saharan Africa										
1 Ethiopia	169	1,384	0	0	0	75	..	67	..	1,526
2 Bangladesh	..	5,154	..	0	..	356	..	133	..	5,644
3 Mali	238	960	0	0	9	64	..	60	..	1,084
4 Zaire	311	4,084	..	..	0	579	..	244	..	..
5 Burkina Faso	21	407	0	0	0	0	..	26	..	433
6 Nepal	3	427	0	0	0	4	..	24	..	454
7 Burma	101	2,219	0	0	17	77	..	15	..	2,311
8 Malawi	122	731	0	0	0	113	..	42	..	885
9 Niger	32	678	..	162	0	44	..	61	..	945
10 Tanzania	250	2,594	15	61	0	24	..	554	..	3,232
11 Burundi	7	334	0	0	8	0	..	12	..	346
12 Uganda	138	675	0	0	0	315	..	26	..	1,016
13 Togo	40	659	0	0	0	49	..	63	..	772
14 Central African Rep.	24	224	0	0	0	24	..	12	..	260
15 India	7,940	22,403	100	2,611	10	3,921	..	1,743	..	30,678
16 Madagascar	93	1,636	0	0	0	148	..	83	..	1,867
17 Somalia	77	1,233	0	0	0	102	..	49	..	1,384
18 Benin	41	582	0	0	0	0	..	62	..	644
19 Rwanda	2	244	0	0	3	0	..	37	..	281
20 China	..	..	..	..	..	..	..	5,546	..	..
21 Kenya	319	2,633	88	428	0	380	..	369	..	3,811
22 Sierra Leone	59	342	0	0	0	74	..	30	..	446
23 Haiti	40	494	0	0	2	84	..	80	..	658
24 Guinea	312	1,168	0	0	4	11	..	54	..	1,234
25 Ghana	495	1,122	..	..	46	468	..	208	..	..
26 Sri Lanka	317	2,420	..	44	79	322	..	301	..	3,087
27 Sudan	307	5,659	0	0	31	598	..	404	..	6,661
28 Pakistan	3,060	9,953	5	26	45	1,241	..	436	..	11,656
29 Senegal	100	1,555	31	10	0	201	..	260	..	2,026
30 Afghanistan	..	..	..	..	..	..	..	7	..	..
31 Bhutan	..	..	..	..	..	..	..	2	..	..
32 Chad	32	109	0	0	3	4	..	1	..	114
33 Kampuchea, Dem.	..	..	..	..	..	..	..	..	..	..
34 Lao PDR	..	..	..	..	..	..	..	7	..	..
35 Mozambique	..	..	..	..	..	..	..	116	..	..
36 Viet Nam	..	..	..	..	..	..	..	97	..	..
Middle-income economies										
Oil exporters										
Oil importers										
Sub-Saharan Africa										
Lower middle-income										
37 Mauritania	27	1,171	0	0	0	30	..	83	..	1,283
38 Liberia	159	757	0	0	4	208	..	42	..	1,007
39 Zambia	623	2,779	30	23	0	698	..	388	..	3,888
40 Lesotho	8	134	0	0	0	0	..	4	..	138
41 Bolivia	481	3,204	11	340	6	64	..	306	..	3,913
42 Indonesia	2,443	22,883	461	3,800	139	413	..	5,384	..	32,480
43 Yemen Arab Rep.	..	1,688	0	0	0	10	..	259	..	1,957
44 Yemen, PDR	1	1,252	0	0	0	15	..	70	..	1,337
45 Cote d'Ivoire	256	4,835	11	1,350	0	591	..	630	..	7,406
46 Philippines	574	11,176	919	2,959	69	757	..	9,492	..	24,383
47 Morocco	711	10,169	..	..	28	991	..	1,185	..	..
48 Honduras	95	1,841	19	162	0	136	..	169	..	2,308
49 El Salvador	88	1,388	88	114	7	105	..	102	..	1,709
50 Papua New Guinea	36	925	173	890	0	16	..	145	..	1,977
51 Egypt, Arab Rep.	1,750	15,808	..	550	49	48	..	6,800	..	23,206
52 Nigeria	480	11,815	115	895	0	0	..	7,032	..	19,742
53 Zimbabwe	233	1,446	..	78	0	256	..	344	..	2,124
54 Cameroon	131	1,738	9	609	0	0	..	381	..	2,728
55 Nicaragua	147	3,835	0	0	8	9	..	856	..	4,700
56 Thailand	324	7,568	402	3,368	0	791	..	3,551	..	15,278
57 Botswana	15	276	0	0	0	0	..	5	..	281
58 Dominican Rep.	226	2,388	141	156	7	221	..	291	..	3,057
59 Peru	856	9,825	1,799	1,465	10	675	..	1,200	..	13,164
60 Mauritius	32	354	0	13	0	154	..	39	..	560
61 Congo, People's Rep.	144	1,396	0	0	0	0	..	177	..	1,573
62 Ecuador	193	6,630	49	177	14	238	..	1,283	..	8,329
63 Jamaica	160	2,175	822	80	0	629	..	224	..	3,107
64 Guatemala	106	1,514	14	105	0	150	..	191	..	1,960
65 Turkey	1,854	15,774	42	425	74	1,426	..	4,642	..	22,267

Note: For data comparability and coverage, see the technical notes.

| | | Long-term debt (millions of dollars) | | | | Use of IMF credit (millions of dollars) | | Short-term debt (millions of dollars) | | Total gross external liabilities (millions of dollars) | |
| | | Public and publicly guaranteed | | Private nonguaranteed | | | | | | | |
		1970	1984	1970	1984	1970	1984	1970	1984	1970	1984
66	Costa Rica	134	3,380	112	317	0	156	. .	269	. .	4,122
67	Paraguay	112	1,287	. .	110	0	0	. .	98	. .	1,495
68	Tunisia	541	3,707	. .	193	13	0	. .	401	. .	4,301
69	Colombia	1,299	7,980	283	1,437	55	0	. .	2,868	. .	12,285
70	Jordan	119	2,336	0	0	0	0	. .	860	. .	3,196
71	Syrian Arab Rep.	232	2,453	0	0	10	0	. .	622	. .	3,075
72	Angola	. .	. .	. .	. .	. .	. .	. .	173	. .	. .
73	Cuba	. .	. .	. .	. .	. .	. .	. .	607	. .	. .
74	Korea, Dem. Rep.	. .	. .	. .	. .	. .	. .	. .	167	. .	. .
75	Lebanon	64	179	0	0	0	0	. .	260	. .	439
76	Mongolia	. .	. .	. .	. .	. .	. .	. .	. .	. .	. .
Upper middle-income											
77	Chile	2,067	10,839	501	6,427	2	779	. .	1,914	. .	19,959
78	Brazil	3,234	66,502	1,706	20,511	0	4,185	. .	13,186	. .	104,384
79	Portugal	485	10,583	85	570	0	561	. .	3,299	. .	15,012
80	Malaysia	390	11,846	. .	. .	0	258	. .	. .	. .	. .
81	Panama	194	3,091	0	0	0	271	. .	912	. .	4,274
82	Uruguay	269	2,545	29	129	18	222	. .	392	. .	3,288
83	Mexico	3,196	69,007	2,770	18,500	0	2,360	. .	7,440	. .	97,307
84	Korea, Rep. of	1,797	24,642	175	5,348	0	1,567	. .	11,500	. .	43,057
85	Yugoslavia	1,199	8,690	854	8,370	0	1,947	. .	837	. .	19,844
86	Argentina	1,878	28,671	3,291	9,500	0	1,098	. .	6,570	. .	45,839
87	South Africa	. .	. .	. .	. .	. .	. .	. .	12,246	. .	. .
88	Algeria	937	12,052	0	0	0	0	. .	1,759	. .	13,811
89	Venezuela	728	17,247	236	6,500	0	0	. .	10,500	. .	34,247
90	Greece	905	9,456	388	1,647	0	0	. .	3,267	. .	14,369
91	Israel	2,274	15,415	361	4,453	13	0	. .	3,581	. .	23,449
92	Hong Kong	2	270	. .	. .	0	0	. .	860	. .	. .
93	Trinidad and Tobago	101	941	0	0	0	0	. .	159	. .	1,100
94	Singapore	152	1,911	. .	. .	0	0	. .	208	. .	. .
95	Iran, Islamic Rep.	. .	. .	. .	. .	. .	. .	. .	. .	. .	. .
96	Iraq	. .	. .	. .	. .	. .	. .	. .	1,858	. .	. .
High-income oil exporters											
97	Oman	. .	1,232	. .	0	. .	0	. .	293	. .	1,525
98	Libya										
99	Saudi Arabia										
100	Kuwait										
101	United Arab Emirates										
Industrial market economies											
102	Spain										
103	Ireland										
104	Italy										
105	New Zealand										
106	United Kingdom										
107	Belgium										
108	Austria										
109	Netherlands										
110	France										
111	Japan										
112	Finland										
113	Germany, Fed. Rep.										
114	Denmark										
115	Australia										
116	Sweden										
117	Canada										
118	Norway										
119	United States										
120	Switzerland										
East European nonmarket economies											
121	Hungary	. .	7,380	. .	0	. .	953	. .	1,943	. .	10,276
122	Poland										
123	Albania										
124	Bulgaria										
125	Czechoslovakia										
126	German Dem. Rep.										
127	Romania	. .	6,296	. .	0	. .	937	. .	566	. .	7,799
128	USSR										

Table 16. Flow of public and private external capital

	Gross inflow (millions of dollars)				Repayment of principal (millions of dollars)				Net inflow[a] (millions of dollars)			
	Public and publicly guaranteed		Private nonguaranteed		Public and publicly guaranteed		Private nonguaranteed		Public and publicly guaranteed		Private nonguaranteed	
	1970	1984	1970	1984	1970	1984	1970	1984	1970	1984	1970	1984
Low-income economies												
China and India												
Other low-income												
Sub-Saharan Africa												
1 Ethiopia	27	246	0	0	15	53	0	0	12	193	0	0
2 Bangladesh	..	537	..	0	..	97	..	0	..	439	..	0
3 Mali	21	114	0	0	(.)	10	0	0	21	104	0	0
4 Zaire	31	220	..	..	28	143	..	..	3	77	..	..
5 Burkina Faso	2	57	0	0	2	15	0	0	(.)	43	0	0
6 Nepal	1	79	0	0	2	5	0	0	−2	74	0	0
7 Burma	16	286	0	0	18	96	0	0	−2	189	0	0
8 Malawi	38	111	0	0	3	50	0	0	36	61	0	0
9 Niger	12	73	..	..	2	40	..	..	10	33	..	..
10 Tanzania	50	160	..	..	10	41	..	..	40	119	..	..
11 Burundi	1	80	0	0	(.)	9	0	0	1	71	0	0
12 Uganda	26	92	0	0	4	55	0	0	22	37	0	0
13 Togo	5	51	0	0	2	30	0	0	3	21	0	0
14 Central African Rep.	2	34	0	0	2	6	0	0	−1	27	0	0
15 India	890	2,874	25	835	307	827	25	305	583	2,048	0	530
16 Madagascar	10	161	0	0	5	85	0	0	5	76	0	0
17 Somalia	4	106	0	0	1	24	0	0	4	82	0	0
18 Benin	2	38	0	0	1	22	0	0	1	17	0	0
19 Rwanda	(.)	42	0	0	(.)	3	0	0	(.)	39	0	0
20 China	..	..			..	..			..	..		
21 Kenya	32	527	..	..	16	205	..	..	17	322	..	..
22 Sierra Leone	8	23	0	0	10	13	0	0	−2	10	0	0
23 Haiti	4	58	0	0	4	11	0	0	1	47	0	0
24 Guinea	90	79	0	0	11	84	0	0	79	−5	0	0
25 Ghana	42	102	..	..	12	55	..	..	30	46	..	..
26 Sri Lanka	61	410	..	6	28	99	..	2	34	311	..	3
27 Sudan	52	181	0	0	22	43	0	0	30	139	0	0
28 Pakistan	485	1,183	3	4	114	617	1	11	371	566	2	−7
29 Senegal	15	219	1	..	5	40	3	2	11	179	−2	..
30 Afghanistan	..	..	0	0	..	..	0	0	..	..	0	0
31 Bhutan	..	..	..	..	..	..	..	..	..	..	..	..
32 Chad	6	7	0	0	2	2	0	0	4	6	0	0
33 Kampuchea, Dem.	..	..	..	..	..	..	..	..	..	..	..	..
34 Lao PDR	..	..	..	..	..	..	..	..	..	..	..	..
35 Mozambique	..	..	..	..	..	..	..	..	..	..	..	..
36 Viet Nam	..	..	..	..	..	..	..	..	..	..	..	..
Middle-income economies												
Oil exporters												
Oil importers												
Sub-Saharan Africa												
Lower middle-income												
37 Mauritania	4	100	0	0	3	19	0	0	1	81	0	0
38 Liberia	7	95	0	0	12	22	0	0	−4	73	0	0
39 Zambia	351	250	..	..	33	50	..	..	318	200	..	..
40 Lesotho	(.)	28	0	0	(.)	17	0	0	(.)	11	0	0
41 Bolivia	55	180	..	..	17	119	..	..	38	61	..	..
42 Indonesia	441	3,846	195	1,080	59	1,628	61	680	382	2,219	134	400
43 Yemen Arab Rep.	..	204	0	0	..	51	0	0	..	153	0	0
44 Yemen, PDR	1	169	0	0	0	24	0	0	1	145	0	0
45 Cote d'Ivoire	77	417	..	..	27	237	..	..	50	180	..	..
46 Philippines	128	1,264	276	70	73	354	186	174	56	910	90	−104
47 Morocco	163	1,330	..	..	36	639	..	..	127	690	..	..
48 Honduras	30	300	10	4	3	55	3	36	26	245	7	−33
49 El Salvador	8	212	24	(.)	6	122	16	8	2	90	8	−7
50 Papua New Guinea	25	86	111	245	0	47	20	175	25	39	91	70
51 Egypt, Arab Rep.	394	2,704	..	55	297	1,709	..	105	97	995	..	−50
52 Nigeria	62	2,124	25	300	36	1,991	30	200	26	133	−5	100
53 Zimbabwe	..	220	..	..	5	157	..	..	..	63	..	..
54 Cameroon	28	182	11	218	4	115	2	83	24	67	9	134
55 Nicaragua	44	346	0	0	16	25	0	0	28	321	0	0
56 Thailand	51	1,492	169	1,417	23	689	107	704	27	804	62	713
57 Botswana	3	76	0	0	(.)	18	0	0	3	58	0	0
58 Dominican Rep.	45	278	22	5	7	39	20	30	38	239	2	−25
59 Peru	148	1,000	240	130	101	321	233	214	47	679	7	−84
60 Mauritius	2	92	..	4	1	50	..	4	1	42	..	(.)
61 Congo, People's Rep.	21	127	0	0	6	173	0	0	15	−47	0	0
62 Ecuador	41	390	..	..	16	202	..	..	25	188	..	..
63 Jamaica	15	384	..	..	6	194	..	..	9	190	..	..
64 Guatemala	37	235	6	3	20	112	2	52	17	123	4	−49
65 Turkey	328	2,424	1	81	128	1,178	3	55	200	1,246	−2	26

Note: For data comparability and coverage, see the technical notes.

	Gross inflow (millions of dollars)				Repayment of principal (millions of dollars)				Net inflow[a] (millions of dollars)			
	Public and publicly guaranteed		Private nonguaranteed		Public and publicly guaranteed		Private nonguaranteed		Public and publicly guaranteed		Private nonguaranteed	
	1970	1984	1970	1984	1970	1984	1970	1984	1970	1984	1970	1984
66 Costa Rica	30	205	30	..	21	114	20	12	9	91	10	..
67 Paraguay	15	240	..	(.)	7	60	..	20	8	181	..	−19
68 Tunisia	87	707	..	..	45	460	..	..	42	247	..	..
69 Colombia	254	1,753	..	299	78	548	59	142	176	1,205	..	157
70 Jordan	14	625	0	0	3	165	0	0	12	460	0	0
71 Syrian Arab Rep.	60	435	0	0	30	247	0	0	30	188	0	0
72 Angola	..	..	..	..	..	..	..	..	..	..	..	..
73 Cuba	..	..	..	..	..	..	..	..	..	..	..	..
74 Korea, Dem. Rep.	..	..	..	..	..	..	..	..	..	..	..	..
75 Lebanon	12	29	0	0	2	40	0	0	9	−11	0	0
76 Mongolia	..	..	..	..	..	..	..	..	..	..	..	..
Upper middle-income												
77 Chile	398	2,125	247	232	164	321	41	295	234	1,804	206	−63
78 Brazil	884	9,615	900	290	255	1,603	200	706	629	8,012	700	−416
79 Portugal	18	2,521	20	46	63	1,533	22	108	−45	988	−1	−62
80 Malaysia	44	1,951	..	..	45	514	..	..	−1	1,437	..	..
81 Panama	67	347	0	0	24	231	0	0	44	116	0	0
82 Uruguay	38	189	13	0	47	127	4	24	−10	62	9	−24
83 Mexico	772	4,819	603	2,144	475	3,663	542	1,760	297	1,156	61	384
84 Korea, Rep. of	441	5,487	32	1,102	198	2,488	7	295	242	2,999	25	807
85 Yugoslavia	180	542	465	878	168	257	204	1,294	12	286	261	−416
86 Argentina	487	520	..	..	342	486	..	..	146	34	..	..
87 South Africa	..	..	..	..	..	..	..	..	..	..	..	..
88 Algeria	292	3,014	0	0	33	3,269	0	0	259	−255	0	0
89 Venezuela	224	316	..	..	42	1,099	..	..	183	−784	..	..
90 Greece	164	2,318	144	255	61	602	37	208	102	1,717	107	47
91 Israel	410	1,875	..	..	25	890	..	..	385	985	..	..
92 Hong Kong	0	105	..	..	1	36	..	..	−1	69	..	..
93 Trinidad and Tobago	8	104	0	0	10	36	0	0	−2	68	0	0
94 Singapore	58	630	..	..	6	188	..	..	52	441	..	..
95 Iran, Islamic Rep.	..	..	..	..	..	..	..	..	..	..	..	..
96 Iraq	..	..	..	..	..	..	..	..	..	..	..	..
High-income oil exporters												
97 Oman	..	275	..	0	..	128	..	0	..	147	..	0
98 Libya												
99 Saudi Arabia												
100 Kuwait												
101 United Arab Emirates												
Industrial market economies												
102 Spain												
103 Ireland												
104 Italy												
105 New Zealand												
106 United Kingdom												
107 Belgium												
108 Austria												
109 Netherlands												
110 France												
111 Japan												
112 Finland												
113 Germany, Fed. Rep.												
114 Denmark												
115 Australia												
116 Sweden												
117 Canada												
118 Norway												
119 United States												
120 Switzerland												
East European nonmarket economies												
121 Hungary	..	2,856	..	0	..	1,842	..	0	..	1,014	..	0
122 Poland												
123 Albania												
124 Bulgaria												
125 Czechoslovakia												
126 German Dem. Rep.												
127 Romania	..	159	..	0	..	1,259	..	0	..	−1,100	..	0
128 USSR												

a. Gross inflow less repayment of principal may not equal net inflow because of rounding.

Table 17. Total external public and private debt and debt service ratios

		Total long-term debt disbursed and outstanding				Total interest payments on long-term debt (millions of dollars)		Total long-term debt service as percentage of:			
		Millions of dollars		As percentage of GNP				GNP		Exports of goods and services	
		1970	1984	1970	1984[a]	1970	1984	1970	1984	1970	1984[a]
Low-income economies											
China and India											
Other low-income											
Sub-Saharan Africa											
1	Ethiopia	169	1,384	9.5	29.5	6	31	1.2	1.8	11.4	13.8
2	Bangladesh	. .	5,154	. .	40.0	. .	75	. .	1.3	. .	14.2
3	Mali	238	960	88.1	95.9	(.)	7	0.3	1.7	1.4	8.0
4	Zaire	. .	. .	. .	. .	. .	. .	. .	. .	. .	. .
5	Burkina Faso	21	407	6.4	42.6	(.)	7	0.6	2.3	6.2	. .
6	Nepal	3	427	0.3	17.0	(.)	5	0.3	0.4	. .	3.4
7	Burma	101	2,219	4.7	34.9	3	62	1.0	2.5	15.9	36.9
8	Malawi	122	731	43.2	63.5	3	32	2.1	7.2	7.2	. .
9	Niger	. .	840	. .	76.7	. .	. .	. .	. .	. .	. .
10	Tanzania	265	2,654	20.7	69.6	. .	. .	. .	. .	. .	. .
11	Burundi	7	334	3.1	35.8	(.)	8	0.3	1.9	. .	. .
12	Uganda	138	675	7.3	20.5	4	32	0.4	1.7	2.7	. .
13	Togo	40	659	16.0	100.1	1	37	0.9	10.1	2.9	26.3
14	Central African Rep.	24	224	13.5	37.1	1	6	1.6	2.0	4.8	8.0
15	India	8,040	25,014	15.1	13.6	195	863	1.0	1.1	23.4	13.8
16	Madagascar	93	1,636	10.8	73.0	2	31	0.8	5.2	3.5	. .
17	Somalia	77	1,233	24.4	90.4	(.)	3	0.3	2.0	2.1	28.9
18	Benin	41	582	16.0	59.8	(.)	17	0.7	3.9	2.3	. .
19	Rwanda	2	244	0.9	15.1	(.)	3	0.1	0.4	1.2	3.3
20	China	. .	. .	. .	. .	. .	. .	. .	. .	. .	. .
21	Kenya	406	3,062	26.3	53.3	. .	. .	. .	. .	. .	. .
22	Sierra Leone	59	342	14.3	34.7	2	4	2.9	1.6	9.9	7.2
23	Haiti	40	494	10.3	27.3	(.)	6	1.0	1.0	7.7	5.6
24	Guinea	312	1,168	47.1	59.5	4	21	2.2	5.3	. .	. .
25	Ghana	. .	. .	. .	. .	. .	. .	. .	. .	. .	. .
26	Sri Lanka	. .	2,464	. .	41.9	. .	106	. .	3.5	. .	11.5
27	Sudan	307	5,659	15.2	77.2	13	65	1.7	. .	10.6	13.6
28	Pakistan	3,065	9,979	30.6	29.7	77	317	1.9	2.8	23.7	27.1
29	Senegal	131	1,565	15.5	69.4	2	53	1.1	4.2	3.8	. .
30	*Afghanistan*	. .	. .	. .	. .	. .	. .	. .	. .	. .	. .
31	*Bhutan*	. .	. .	. .	. .	. .	. .	. .	. .	. .	. .
32	*Chad*	32	109	11.9	. .	(.)	1	1.0	. .	3.9	1.7
33	*Kampuchea, Dem.*	. .	. .	. .	. .	. .	. .	. .	. .	. .	. .
34	*Lao PDR*	. .	. .	. .	. .	. .	. .	. .	. .	. .	. .
35	*Mozambique*	. .	. .	. .	. .	. .	. .	. .	. .	. .	. .
36	*Viet Nam*	. .	. .	. .	. .	. .	. .	. .	. .	. .	. .
Middle-income economies											
Oil exporters											
Oil importers											
Sub-Saharan Africa											
Lower middle-income											
37	Mauritania	27	1,171	13.9	171.2	(.)	23	1.7	6.2	3.1	*10.0*
38	Liberia	159	757	49.9	77.4	6	20	5.5	4.3	8.1	8.6
39	Zambia	653	2,802	37.5	115.4	. .	. .	. .	. .	. .	. .
40	Lesotho	8	134	7.7	24.3	(.)	4	0.5	3.8	4.1	5.1
41	Bolivia	492	3,544	36.1	108.7	. .	. .	. .	. .	. .	. .
42	Indonesia	2,904	26,683	32.2	35.2	45	1,900	1.8	5.5	13.8	19.0
43	Yemen Arab Rep.	. .	1,688	. .	44.4	. .	16	. .	1.8	. .	26.6
44	Yemen, PDR	1	1,252	. .	106.9	0	12	. .	3.0	0	22.0
45	Cote d'Ivoire	267	6,185	19.1	107.5	. .	. .	. .	. .	. .	. .
46	Philippines	1,494	14,135	21.1	43.9	. .	912	. .	4.5	. .	17.9
47	Morocco	. .	. .	. .	. .	. .	. .	. .	. .	. .	. .
48	Honduras	115	2,003	16.3	66.1	4	90	1.5	6.0	5.2	20.4
49	El Salvador	176	1,502	17.3	38.0	9	74	3.1	5.2	12.0	*19.5*
50	Papua New Guinea	209	1,815	33.4	78.1	9	148	4.7	15.9	24.1	35.9
51	Egypt, Arab Rep.	. .	16,358	. .	51.3	. .	698	. .	7.9	. .	34.1
52	Nigeria	595	12,710	5.9	17.0	28	1,282	0.9	4.6	7.0	27.9
53	Zimbabwe	. .	1,523	. .	29.9	. .	. .	. .	. .	. .	. .
54	Cameroon	140	2,347	13.0	31.3	5	164	1.0	4.8	3.9	14.5
55	Nicaragua	147	3,835	14.8	141.8	7	34	2.3	2.2	10.5	*17.5*
56	Thailand	726	10,936	11.1	26.3	33	843	2.5	5.4	14.0	21.5
57	Botswana	15	276	17.9	31.3	(.)	15	0.7	3.8	. .	3.8
58	Dominican Rep.	368	2,544	25.2	53.6	13	119	2.7	3.9	15.4	28.1
59	Peru	2,655	11,290	39.1	68.2	162	457	7.3	6.0	40.0	24.9
60	Mauritius	. .	367	. .	36.5	. .	26	. .	7.9	. .	15.6
61	Congo, People's Rep.	144	1,396	53.9	76.2	3	78	3.3	13.7	11.0	*20.5*
62	Ecuador	242	6,807	14.7	75.1	. .	. .	. .	. .	. .	. .
63	Jamaica	982	2,255	72.8	108.8	. .	. .	. .	. .	. .	. .
64	Guatemala	120	1,619	6.5	17.6	7	96	1.6	2.8	8.2	20.6
65	Turkey	1,896	16,199	14.8	32.3	45	1,093	1.4	4.6	22.7	23.8

Note: For data comparability and coverage, see the technical notes. Public and private debt includes public, publicly guaranteed, and private nonguaranteed debt; data are shown only when available for all three categories.

| | Total long-term debt disbursed and outstanding | | | | Total interest payments on long-term debt (millions of dollars) | | Total long-term debt service as percentage of: | | | |
| | Millions of dollars | | As percentage of GNP | | | | GNP | | Exports of goods and services | |
	1970	1984	1970	1984[a]	1970	1984	1970	1984	1970	1984[a]
66 Costa Rica	246	3,697	25.3	114.0	14	228	5.7	10.9	19.9	27.9
67 Paraguay	..	1,397	..	36.2	..	60	..	3.6	..	15.5
68 Tunisia	..	3,900	..	48.5	..	..	..	..	..	..
69 Colombia	1,582	9,417	22.5	25.7	59	622	2.8	3.6	19.3	24.7
70 Jordan	119	2,336	23.5	62.0	2	117	0.9	7.5	3.6	14.8
71 Syrian Arab Rep.	232	2,453	10.6	15.2	6	83	1.6	2.0	11.0	12.9
72 Angola	..	..	..	..	..	..	..	..	..	..
73 Cuba	..	..	..	..	..	..	..	..	..	..
74 Korea, Dem. Rep.	..	..	..	..	..	..	..	..	..	..
75 Lebanon	64	179	4.2	..	1	13	0.2	..	..	..
76 Mongolia	..	..	..	..	..	..	..	..	..	..
Upper middle-income										
77 Chile	2,568	17,266	32.1	100.2	104	2,011	3.9	15.2	24.2	54.6
78 Brazil	4,940	87,013	11.7	44.0	222	8,529	1.6	5.5	21.7	35.8
79 Portugal	570	11,153	9.2	61.7	34	1,057	1.9	14.9	..	37.8
80 Malaysia	..	..	..	..	..	..	..	..	..	..
81 Panama	194	3,091	19.5	73.3	7	288	3.1	12.3	7.7	7.9
82 Uruguay	298	2,674	12.5	54.5	17	295	2.9	9.1	23.5	32.4
83 Mexico	5,966	87,507	17.0	54.2	283	10,298	3.7	9.7	44.3	48.6
84 Korea, Rep. of	1,972	29,990	22.4	37.0	75	2,555	3.2	6.6	20.3	15.8
85 Yugoslavia	2,053	17,060	15.0	42.2	104	2,341	3.5	9.6	19.7	28.0
86 Argentina	5,169	38,171	23.6	46.8	..	..	..	..	..	..
87 South Africa	..	..	..	..	..	..	..	..	..	..
88 Algeria	937	12,052	19.3	24.3	10	1,291	0.9	9.2	3.8	33.6
89 Venezuela	964	23,747	8.7	52.7	..	..	..	..	..	..
90 Greece	1,293	11,102	12.7	33.2	63	873	1.6	5.0	14.6	22.9
91 Israel	2,635	19,868	47.9	99.5	..	..	..	..	..	..
92 Hong Kong	..	..	..	..	..	..	..	..	..	..
93 Trinidad and Tobago	101	941	12.2	10.5	6	31	1.9	0.7	4.4	2.4
94 Singapore	..	..	..	..	..	..	..	..	..	..
95 Iran, Islamic Rep.	..	..	..	..	..	..	..	..	..	..
96 Iraq	..	..	..	..	..	..	..	..	..	..
High-income oil exporters										
97 Oman	..	1,232	..	17.2	..	86	..	3.0	..	4.6
98 Libya										
99 Saudi Arabia										
100 Kuwait										
101 United Arab Emirates										
Industrial market economies										
102 Spain										
103 Ireland										
104 Italy										
105 New Zealand										
106 United Kingdom										
107 Belgium										
108 Austria										
109 Netherlands										
110 France										
111 Japan										
112 Finland										
113 Germany, Fed. Rep.										
114 Denmark										
115 Australia										
116 Sweden										
117 Canada										
118 Norway										
119 United States										
120 Switzerland										
East European nonmarket economies										
121 Hungary	..	7,380	..	37.5	..	693	..	12.9	..	24.2
122 Poland										
123 Albania										
124 Bulgaria										
125 Czechoslovakia										
126 German Dem. Rep.										
127 Romania	..	6,296	..	16.3	..	415	..	4.3	..	12.3
128 USSR										

a. Figures in italics are for 1983, not 1984.

Table 18. External public debt and debt service ratios

| | External public debt outstanding and disbursed | | | | Interest payments on external public debt (millions of dollars) | | Debt service as percentage of: | | | |
| | Millions of dollars | | As percentage of GNP | | | | GNP | | Exports of goods and services | |
	1970	1984	1970	1984ᵃ	1970	1984	1970	1984	1970	1984ᵃ
Low-income economies	**14,647** t	**72,108** t	**16.8** w	**23.8** w	**360** t	**1,992** t	**1.1** w	**1.6** w	**12.5** w	**13.5** w
China and India	**7,947** t	**22,403** t	..	..	**189** t	**635** t	..			
Other low-income	**6,707** t	**49,705** t	**19.9** w	**42.4** w	**171** t	**1,358** t	**1.4** w	**3.0** w	**8.6** w	**17.0** w
Sub-Saharan Africa	**3,187** t	**29,037** t	**17.4** w	**54.3** w	**80** t	**793** t	**1.3** w	**3.9** w	**5.2** w	**13.8** w
1 Ethiopia	169	1,384	9.5	29.5	6	31	1.2	1.8	11.4	13.8
2 Bangladesh	..	5,154	..	40.0	..	75	..	1.3		14.2
3 Mali	238	960	88.1	95.9	(.)	7	0.3	1.7	1.4	8.0
4 Zaire	311	4,084	17.6	132.0	9	210	2.1	11.4	4.4	7.7
5 Burkina Faso	21	407	6.4	42.6	(.)	7	0.6	2.3	6.2	..
6 Nepal	3	427	0.3	17.0	(.)	5	0.3	0.4		3.4
7 Burma	101	2,219	4.7	34.9	3	62	1.0	2.5	15.9	36.9
8 Malawi	122	731	43.2	63.5	3	32	2.1	7.2	7.2	..
9 Niger	32	678	8.7	61.9	1	27	0.6	6.1	3.8	..
10 Tanzania	250	2,594	19.5	68.0	6	30	1.2	1.9	4.9	..
11 Burundi	7	334	3.1	35.8	(.)	8	0.3	1.9	2.4	..
12 Uganda	138	675	7.3	13.5	4	32	0.4	1.7	2.7	..
13 Togo	40	659	16.0	100.1	1	37	0.9	10.1	2.9	26.3
14 Central African Rep.	24	224	13.5	37.1	1	6	1.6	2.0	4.8	8.0
15 India	7,940	22,403	14.9	12.2	189	635	0.9	0.8	22.0	10.1
16 Madagascar	93	1,636	10.8	73.0	2	31	0.8	5.2	3.5	..
17 Somalia	77	1,233	24.4	90.4	(.)	3	0.3	2.0	2.1	28.9
18 Benin	41	582	16.0	59.8	(.)	17	0.7	3.9	2.3	..
19 Rwanda	2	244	0.9	15.1	(.)	3	0.1	0.4	1.2	3.3
20 China	..	..	..	..	..	..	..	..	..	..
21 Kenya	319	2,633	20.6	45.8	12	144	1.8	6.1	5.4	21.5
22 Sierra Leone	59	342	14.3	34.7	2	4	2.9	1.6	9.9	7.2
23 Haiti	40	494	10.3	27.3	(.)	6	1.0	1.0	7.7	5.6
24 Guinea	312	1,168	47.1	59.5	4	21	2.2	5.3		..
25 Ghana	495	1,122	21.9	22.9	12	26	1.1	1.7	5.0	13.2
26 Sri Lanka	317	2,420	16.1	41.2	12	103	2.0	3.4	10.3	11.2
27 Sudan	307	5,659	15.2	77.2	13	65	1.7	..	10.6	13.6
28 Pakistan	3,060	9,953	30.5	29.6	76	314	1.9	2.8	23.6	26.7
29 Senegal	100	1,555	11.9	68.9	2	53	0.8	4.1	2.8	..
30 *Afghanistan*	..	..	..	..	..	..	0		..	..
31 *Bhutan*	..	..	..	..	..	..	..	..	..	..
32 *Chad*	32	109	11.9	..	(.)	1	1.0	..	3.9	1.7
33 *Kampuchea, Dem.*	..	..	..	..	..	..	..	..	..	..
34 *Lao PDR*	..	..	..	..	..	..	..	..	..	..
35 *Mozambique*	..	..	..	..	..	..	..	..	..	..
36 *Viet Nam*	..	..	..	..	..	..	..	..	..	..
Middle-income economies	**34,462** t	**461,722** t	**12.4** w	**35.2** w	**1,312** t	**37,419** t	**1.6** w	**5.1** w	**9.7** w	**17.2** w
Oil exporters	**12,122** t	**187,348** t	**12.7** w	**34.9** w	**472** t	**16,146** t	**1.7** w	**5.9** w	**11.1** w	**21.8** w
Oil importers	**22,340** t	**274,424** t	**12.3** w	**35.3** w	**840** t	**21,273** t	**1.5** w	**4.5** w	**9.0** w	**14.4** w
Sub-Saharan Africa	**2,107** t	**26,700** t	**12.5** w	**26.3** w	**78** t	**2,031** t	**1.2** w	**4.8** w	**4.9** w	**20.1** w
Lower middle-income	**14,655** t	**168,064** t	**15.2** w	**35.0** w	**433** t	**10,284** t	**1.6** w	**4.6** w	**9.5** w	**19.4** w
37 Mauritania	27	1,171	13.9	171.2	(.)	23	1.7	6.2	3.1	10.0
38 Liberia	159	757	49.9	77.4	6	20	5.5	4.3	8.1	8.6
39 Zambia	623	2,779	35.7	114.4	26	63	3.4	4.7	5.9	11.3
40 Lesotho	8	134	7.7	24.3	(.)	4	0.5	3.8	4.1	5.1
41 Bolivia	481	3,204	35.4	98.3	7	201	1.7	9.8	11.4	38.3
42 Indonesia	2,443	22,883	27.1	30.2	24	1,620	0.9	4.3	6.9	14.7
43 Yemen Arab Rep.	..	1,688	..	44.4	..	16	..	1.8	..	26.6
44 Yemen, PDR	1	1,252	..	106.7	0	12	..	3.0	0	22.0
45 Cote d'Ivoire	256	4,835	18.3	84.0	11	404	2.7	11.1	6.8	21.3
46 Philippines	574	11,176	8.1	34.7	24	780	1.4	3.5	7.3	14.1
47 Morocco	711	10,169	18.0	82.9	23	494	1.5	9.2	8.4	37.6
48 Honduras	95	1,841	13.6	60.8	3	80	0.9	4.4	3.1	15.2
49 El Salvador	88	1,388	8.6	35.1	4	72	0.9	4.9	3.6	17.2
50 Papua New Guinea	36	925	5.8	39.8	1	86	0.1	5.7	0.6	12.9
51 Egypt, Arab Rep.	1,750	15,808	23.2	49.6	54	643	4.6	7.4	36.4	31.9
52 Nigeria	480	11,815	4.8	15.8	20	1,172	0.6	4.2	4.2	25.4
53 Zimbabwe	233	1,446	15.7	28.4	5	119	0.6	5.4	2.3	20.0
54 Cameroon	131	1,738	12.1	23.2	4	107	0.8	3.0	3.1	8.9
55 Nicaragua	147	3,835	14.8	141.8	7	34	2.3	2.2	10.5	*17.5*
56 Thailand	324	7,568	4.9	18.2	16	560	0.6	3.0	3.4	12.0
57 Botswana	15	276	17.9	31.3	(.)	15	0.7	3.8	1.0	3.8
58 Dominican Rep.	226	2,388	15.5	50.3	5	108	0.8	3.1	4.6	*18.0*
59 Peru	856	9,825	12.6	59.4	44	286	2.1	3.7	11.6	15.3
60 Mauritius	32	354	14.3	35.3	2	25	1.3	7.5	3.0	14.8
61 Congo, People's Rep.	144	1,396	53.9	76.2	3	78	3.3	13.7	11.0	*20.5*
62 Ecuador	193	6,630	11.7	73.1	7	790	1.3	10.9	8.6	33.4
63 Jamaica	160	2,175	11.8	104.9	9	92	1.1	13.8	2.7	21.0
64 Guatemala	106	1,514	5.7	16.5	6	85	1.4	2.1	7.4	15.5
65 Turkey	1,854	15,774	14.4	31.5	42	1,048	1.3	4.4	22.0	22.8

Note: For data comparability and coverage, see the technical notes.

		External public debt outstanding and disbursed				Interest payments on external public debt (millions of dollars)		Debt service as percentage of:			
		Millions of dollars		As percentage of GNP				GNP		Exports of goods and services	
		1970	1984	1970	1984[a]	1970	1984	1970	1984	1970	1984[a]
66	Costa Rica	134	3,380	13.8	104.2	7	207	2.9	9.9	10.0	25.3
67	Paraguay	112	1,287	13.1	33.3	4	58	1.2	3.0	11.8	13.0
68	Tunisia	541	3,707	38.6	46.1	18	222	4.5	8.5	19.0	24.4
69	Colombia	1,299	7,980	18.5	21.8	44	547	1.7	3.0	12.0	20.6
70	Jordan	119	2,336	23.5	62.0	2	117	0.9	7.5	3.6	14.8
71	Syrian Arab Rep.	232	2,453	10.6	15.2	6	83	1.6	2.0	11.0	12.9
72	*Angola*	..	..	..	..	..	..	..	..	..	..
73	*Cuba*	..	..	..	..	..	..	..	..	..	..
74	*Korea, Dem. Rep.*	..	..	..	..	..	..	..	..	..	..
75	*Lebanon*	64	179	4.2	..	1	13	0.2	..	..	..
76	*Mongolia*	..	..	..	..	..	..	..	..	..	..
Upper middle-income		**19,807** *t*	**293,708** *t*	**11.0** *w*	**35.3** *w*	**880** *t*	**27,135** *t*	**1.6** *w*	**5.3** *w*	**9.8** *w*	**16.3** *w*
77	Chile	2,067	10,839	25.8	62.9	78	939	3.0	7.3	19.0	26.2
78	Brazil	3,234	66,502	7.7	33.6	133	6,433	0.9	4.1	12.5	26.6
79	Portugal	485	10,583	7.8	58.5	29	1,007	1.5	14.0	..	35.6
80	Malaysia	390	11,846	10.0	39.4	21	959	1.7	4.9	3.6	7.7
81	Panama	194	3,091	19.5	73.3	7	288	3.1	12.3	7.7	7.9
82	Uruguay	269	2,545	11.3	51.9	16	284	2.6	8.4	21.6	29.8
83	Mexico	3,196	69,007	9.1	42.8	216	7,428	2.0	6.9	23.6	34.3
84	Korea, Rep. of	1,797	24,642	20.4	30.4	70	2,070	3.0	5.6	19.4	13.5
85	Yugoslavia	1,199	8,690	8.8	21.5	72	687	1.8	2.3	9.9	6.8
86	Argentina	1,878	28,671	8.6	35.1	121	2,392	2.1	3.5	21.5	29.1
87	South Africa	..	..	..	..	..	..	..	..	..	..
88	Algeria	937	12,052	19.3	24.3	10	1,291	0.9	9.2	3.8	33.6
89	Venezuela	728	17,247	6.6	38.3	40	1,437	0.7	5.6	2.9	13.4
90	Greece	905	9,456	8.9	28.3	41	742	1.0	4.0	9.3	18.3
91	Israel	2,274	15,415	41.3	77.2	13	996	0.7	9.4	2.7	17.9
92	Hong Kong	2	270	0.1	0.8	0	17	0.0	0.2	0.0	0.2
93	Trinidad and Tobago	101	941	12.2	10.5	6	31	1.9	0.7	4.4	2.4
94	Singapore	152	1,911	7.9	10.6	7	134	0.6	1.8	0.6	1.0
95	*Iran, Islamic Rep.*	..	..	..	..	..	..	..	..	..	..
96	*Iraq*	..	..	..	..	..	..	..	..	..	..
High-income oil exporters											
97	Oman	..	1,232	..	17.2	..	86	..	3.0	..	4.6
98	Libya										
99	Saudi Arabia										
100	Kuwait										
101	United Arab Emirates										
Industrial market economies											
102	Spain										
103	Ireland										
104	Italy										
105	New Zealand										
106	United Kingdom										
107	Belgium										
108	Austria										
109	Netherlands										
110	France										
111	Japan										
112	Finland										
113	Germany, Fed. Rep.										
114	Denmark										
115	Australia										
116	Sweden										
117	Canada										
118	Norway										
119	United States										
120	Switzerland										
East European nonmarket economies											
121	Hungary	..	7,380	..	37.5	..	693	..	12.9	..	24.2
122	Poland										
123	*Albania*										
124	*Bulgaria*										
125	*Czechoslovakia*										
126	*German Dem. Rep.*										
127	*Romania*	..	6,296	..	16.3	..	415	..	4.3	..	12.3
128	*USSR*										

a. Figures in italics are for 1983, not for 1984.

Table 19. Terms of external public borrowing

	Commitments (millions of dollars)		Average interest rate (percent)		Average maturity (years)		Average grace period (years)		Public loans with variable interest rates, as percentage of public debt	
	1970	1984	1970	1984	1970	1984	1970	1984	1970	1984
Low-income economies	3,028 *t*	10,357 *t*	2.8 *w*	4.9 *w*	31 *w*	29 *w*	9 *w*	7 *w*	0.1 *w*	6.1 *w*
China and India	..	..					..			
Other low-income	2,095 *t*	6,514 *t*	3.0 *w*	3.8 *w*	29 *w*	30 *w*	9 *w*	7 *w*	0.2	5.2 *w*
Sub-Saharan Africa	995 *t*	3,414 *t*	3.1 *w*	4.0 *w*	27 *w*	29 *w*	8 *w*	7 *w*	0.3	5.3 *w*
1 Ethiopia	21	448	4.3	4.5	32	31	7	6	0.0	7.7
2 Bangladesh	..	862	..	1.4	..	38		9	..	0.1
3 Mali	30	122	0.3	1.0	27	39	11	9	0.0	0.3
4 Zaire	258	117	6.5	3.5	13	24	4	5	0.0	8.8
5 Burkina Faso	9	78	2.3	1.8	37	29	8	8	0.0	1.4
6 Nepal	17	155	2.8	0.8	27	42	6	9	0.0	0.0
7 Burma	57	290	4.3	2.9	16	30	4	8	0.0	1.1
8 Malawi	13	124	3.8	3.0	30	42	6	9	0.0	12.8
9 Niger	18	116	1.2	2.6	40	29	8	7	0.0	16.0
10 Tanzania	284	75	1.2	6.6	40	15	11	4	1.6	0.4
11 Burundi	1	87	2.9	2.2	5	33	2	8	0.0	1.9
12 Uganda	12	252	3.7	3.5	28	38	7	8.	0.0	1.5
13 Togo	3	55	4.5	4.4	17	34	4	9	0.0	9.1
14 Central African Rep.	7	13	2.0	3.4	36	28	8	7	0.0	0.0
15 India	933	3,843	2.4	6.7	35	28	8	7	0.0	7.9
16 Madagascar	23	190	2.3	4.1	40	33	9	8	0.0	14.6
17 Somalia	2	112	0.0	0.2	3	29	3	7	0.0	0.0
18 Benin	7	119	1.8	4.6	33	31	7	7	0.0	8.9
19 Rwanda	9	57	0.8	1.0	50	39	10	10	0.0	0.0
20 China	..	..	..	..	..	..	..	..	..	..
21 Kenya	49	669	2.6	6.6	37	19	8	4	0.1	6.6
22 Sierra Leone	24	54	3.5	1.6	27	32	6	8	10.6	0.6
23 Haiti	5	68	6.8	2.9	10	29	1	8	0.0	3.1
24 Guinea	66	167	2.9	3.6	13	29	5	6	0.0	0.9
25 Ghana	55	144	2.4	0.6	39	47	10	10	0.0	0.0
26 Sri Lanka	79	340	3.0	4.9	27	28	5	7	0.0	14.7
27 Sudan	95	92	1.8	3.1	17	20	9	7	0.0	2.9
28 Pakistan	942	1,384	2.7	5.2	32	28	12	7	0.0	6.8
29 Senegal	6	320	3.7	5.0	26	21	7	6	0.0	7.4
30 *Afghanistan*	..	..	..	..	..	..	..	..	..	..
31 *Bhutan*										
32 *Chad*	4	6	4.8	2.6	7	25	2	8	..	0.0
33 *Kampuchea, Dem.*	..	..	..	..	..	..	..	..	..	
34 *Lao PDR*	..	..	..	..	..	..	..	..	..	
35 *Mozambique*	..	..	..	..	..	..	..	..	..	
36 *Viet Nam*	..	..	..	..	..	..	..	..	..	
Middle-income economies	9,356 *t*	57,251 *t*	6.2 *w*	10.0 *w*	17 *w*	13 *w*	5 *w*	4 *w*	1.8 *w*	51.4 *w*
Oil exporters	2,862 *t*	21,724 *t*	6.3 *w*	9.5 *w*	18 *w*	13 *w*	4 *w*	5 *w*	2.0 *w*	56.8 *w*
Oil importers	6,494 *t*	35,526 *t*	6.1 *w*	10.2 *w*	17 *w*	13 *w*	5 *w*	4 *w*	1.8 *w*	47.7 *w*
Sub-Saharan Africa	832 *t*	2,421 *t*	4.3 *w*	8.6 *w*	25 *w*	16 *w*	8 *w*	4 *w*	2.0 *w*	40.4 *w*
Lower middle-income	3,858 *t*	24,726 *t*	4.9 *w*	8.8 *w*	23 *w*	15 *w*	6 *w*	4 *w*	0.6 *w*	29.6 *w*
37 Mauritania	7	90	6.6	3.7	11	21	3	6	0.0	1.9
38 Liberia	12	92	5.5	6.6	19	29	5	6	0.0	16.7
39 Zambia	555	267	4.2	7.8	27	21	9	5	0.0	17.4
40 Lesotho	(.)	63	5.5	2.9	25	41	2	9	0.0	5.4
41 Bolivia	24	258	3.7	8.1	26	16	6	3	0.0	29.0
42 Indonesia	519	4,731	2.7	9.1	35	16	9	5	0.0	23.6
43 Yemen Arab Rep.	..	88	..	2.0	..	29	..	6	..	0.0
44 Yemen, PDR	62	137	0.0	2.7	28	22	13	4	0.0	0.0
45 Cote d'Ivoire	71	129	5.8	8.1	19	21	5	5	10.5	51.3
46 Philippines	158	1,551	7.4	9.0	11	15	3	4	0.9	41.0
47 Morocco	182	1,125	4.6	8.3	20	15	4	3	0.0	31.4
48 Honduras	23	237	4.1	8.8	30	19	7	4	0.0	16.8
49 El Salvador	12	246	4.7	7.5	23	18	6	6	0.0	16.0
50 Papua New Guinea	58	158	6.0	6.3	24	24	8	6	0.0	46.3
51 Egypt, Arab Rep.	448	2,522	7.7	6.9	17	17	2	4	0.0	1.7
52 Nigeria	65	928	6.0	10.4	14	9	4	2	2.6	56.0
53 Zimbabwe	..	278	..	9.0	..	16	..	5	0.0	40.1
54 Cameroon	41	271	4.7	4.9	29	25	8	6	0.0	5.7
55 Nicaragua	23	12	7.1	1.4	18	45	4	9	0.0	4.3
56 Thailand	106	1,194	6.8	8.7	19	17	4	7	0.0	29.4
57 Botswana	36	51	0.7	9.3	39	15	10	4	0.0	11.9
58 Dominican Rep.	20	391	2.7	7.1	28	16	5	5	0.0	36.1
59 Peru	125	763	7.4	10.0	13	13	4	4	0.0	40.6
60 Mauritius	12	65	0.0	11.1	24	11	2	3	6.0	29.5
61 Congo, People's Rep.	33	189	2.6	10.0	18	8	7	2	0.0	16.4
62 Ecuador	78	427	6.1	9.2	20	15	4	3	0.0	71.5
63 Jamaica	24	629	6.0	8.1	16	17	3	5	0.0	21.9
64 Guatemala	50	282	5.4	9.3	26	14	6	4	10.3	20.3
65 Turkey	487	3,199	3.6	9.6	19	12	5	4	0.9	28.5

Note: For data comparability and coverage, see the technical notes.

	Commitments (millions of dollars)		Average interest rate (percent)		Average maturity (years)		Average grace period (years)		Public loans with variable interest rates, as percentage of public debt	
	1970	1984	1970	1984	1970	1984	1970	1984	1970	1984
66 Costa Rica	58	121	5.6	7.1	28	8	6	5	7.5	56.9
67 Paraguay	14	145	5.6	9.4	25	15	6	3	0.0	17.2
68 Tunisia	141	602	3.4	9.5	27	12	6	4	0.0	15.5
69 Colombia	362	2,785	5.9	10.4	21	14	5	4	0.0	42.7
70 Jordan	34	550	3.9	5.9	12	14	5	4	0.0	8.2
71 Syrian Arab Rep.	14	152	4.5	8.5	9	13	2	3	0.0	0.7
72 Angola	..	..	..	..	..	..	..	..	..	..
73 Cuba	..	..	..	..	..	..	..	..	..	..
74 Korea, Dem. Rep.	..	..	..	..	..	..	..	..	..	..
75 Lebanon	7	0	2.7	0.0	22	0	1	0	0.0	15.0
76 Mongolia	..	..	..	..	..	..	..	..	..	..
Upper middle-income	5,498 t	32,524 t	7.1 w	10.8 w	13 w	11 w	4 w	4 w	2.8 w	63.9 w
77 Chile	344	2,041	6.9	12.4	12	9	3	4	0.0	81.2
78 Brazil	1,400	7,483	7.1	12.2	14	9	3	3	7.0	79.1
79 Portugal	59	2,557	4.3	9.9	17	10	4	3	0.0	31.5
80 Malaysia	83	2,710	6.1	9.4	19	15	5	9	0.0	61.6
81 Panama	111	25	6.9	2.1	15	29	4	9	0.0	59.5
82 Uruguay	72	344	7.9	10.7	12	12	3	2	0.7	66.4
83 Mexico	826	5,290	8.0	11.0	12	11	3	5	5.7	83.0
84 Korea, Rep. of	677	4,642	6.0	9.7	19	12	6	4	1.3	46.8
85 Yugoslavia	198	35	7.1	8.0	17	6	6	3	3.4	56.0
86 Argentina	489	620	7.4	10.7	12	19	3	2	0.0	37.5
87 South Africa	..	..	..	..	..	..	..	..	..	..
88 Algeria	289	3,002	6.5	10.0	10	9	2	1	2.8	26.4
89 Venezuela	198	30	8.2	10.0	8	20	2	3	2.6	93.8
90 Greece	242	1,994	7.2	10.5	9	9	4	5	3.5	69.0
91 Israel	439	921	7.3	12.3	13	30	5	10	0.0	2.7
92 Hong Kong	0	109	0.0	12.5	0	4	0	1	0.0	37.0
93 Trinidad and Tobago	3	109	7.4	8.6	10	8	1	4	0.0	51.7
94 Singapore	69	614	6.8	9.8	17	10	4	2	0.0	36.7
95 Iran, Islamic Rep.	..	..	..	..	..	..	..	..	..	..
96 Iraq	..	..	..	..	..	..	..	..	..	..
High-income oil exporters										
97 Oman	..	434	..	9.0	..	11	..	3	..	24.0
98 Libya										
99 Saudi Arabia										
100 Kuwait										
101 United Arab Emirates										
Industrial market economies										
102 Spain										
103 Ireland										
104 Italy										
105 New Zealand										
106 United Kingdom										
107 Belgium										
108 Austria										
109 Netherlands										
110 France										
111 Japan										
112 Finland										
113 Germany, Fed. Rep.										
114 Denmark										
115 Australia										
116 Sweden										
117 Canada										
118 Norway										
119 United States										
120 Switzerland										
East European nonmarket economies										
121 Hungary[a]	..	3,104	..	10.0	..	7	..	3	..	36.0
122 Poland										
123 Albania										
124 Bulgaria										
125 Czechoslovakia										
126 German Dem. Rep.										
127 Romania	..	0	..	0	..	0	..	0	..	46.0
128 USSR										

a. Includes only debt in convertible currencies.

Table 20. Official development assistance from OECD & OPEC members

	1965	1970	1975	1979	1980	1981	1982	1983	1984	1985[a]
OECD					**Millions of US dollars**					
104 Italy	60	147	182	273	683	666	811	834	1,133	1,099
105 New Zealand	..	14	66	68	72	68	65	61	55	54
106 United Kingdom	472	500	904	2,156	1,854	2,192	1,800	1,610	1,430	1,490
107 Belgium	102	120	378	643	595	575	499	476	442	430
108 Austria	10	11	79	131	178	220	236	158	181	248
109 Netherlands	70	196	608	1,472	1,630	1,510	1,472	1,195	1,268	1,123
110 France	752	971	2,093	3,449	4,162	4,177	4,034	3,815	3,788	4,022
111 Japan	244	458	1,148	2,685	3,353	3,171	3,023	3,761	4,319	3,797
112 Finland	2	7	48	90	111	135	144	153	178	211
113 Germany, Fed. Rep.	456	599	1,689	3,393	3,567	3,181	3,152	3,176	2,782	2,967
114 Denmark	13	59	205	461	481	403	415	395	449	439
115 Australia	119	212	552	629	667	650	882	753	777	747
116 Sweden	38	117	566	988	962	919	987	754	741	841
117 Canada	96	337	880	1,056	1,075	1,189	1,197	1,429	1,625	1,638
118 Norway	11	37	184	429	486	467	559	584	543	555
119 United States	4,023	3,153	4,161	4,684	7,138	5,782	8,202	8,081	8,711	9,555
120 Switzerland	12	30	104	213	253	237	252	320	286	301
Total	6,480	6,968	13,847	22,820	27,267	25,542	27,730	27,555	28,707	29,518
OECD					**As percentage of donor GNP**					
104 Italy	.10	.16	.11	.08	.17	.19	.24	.24	.33	.31
105 New Zealand	..	.23	.52	.33	.33	.29	.28	.28	.25	.25
106 United Kingdom	.47	.41	.39	.52	.35	.43	.37	.35	.33	.33
107 Belgium	.60	.46	.59	.57	.50	.59	.59	.59	.57	.53
108 Austria	.11	.07	.21	.19	.23	.33	.35	.24	.28	.38
109 Netherlands	.36	.61	.75	.98	1.03	1.08	1.08	.91	1.02	.90
110 France	.76	.66	.62	.60	.64	.73	.75	.74	.77	.79
111 Japan	.27	.23	.23	.27	.32	.28	.28	.32	.35	.29
112 Finland	.02	.06	.18	.22	.22	.28	.30	.32	.36	.39
113 Germany, Fed. Rep.	.40	.32	.40	.45	.44	.47	.48	.48	.45	.48
114 Denmark	.13	.38	.58	.77	.74	.73	.76	.73	.85	.80
115 Australia	.53	.59	.65	.53	.48	.41	.57	.49	.45	.49
116 Sweden	.19	.38	.82	.97	.79	.83	1.02	.84	.80	.86
117 Canada	.19	.41	.54	.48	.43	.43	.41	.45	.50	.49
118 Norway	.16	.32	.66	.93	.85	.82	.99	1.10	1.03	1.00
119 United States	.58	.32	.27	.20	.27	.20	.27	.24	.24	.24
120 Switzerland	.09	.15	.19	.21	.24	.24	.25	.31	.30	.31
OECD					**National currencies**					
104 Italy (billions of lire)	38	92	119	227	585	757	1,097	1,267	1,991	2,099
105 New Zealand (millions of dollars)	..	13	54	66	74	78	86	91	95	109
106 United Kingdom (millions of pounds)	169	208	407	1,016	797	1,081	1,028	1,061	1,070	1,149
107 Belgium (millions of francs)	5,100	6,000	13,902	18,852	17,400	21,350	22,800	24,339	25,527	25,528
108 Austria (millions of schillings)	260	286	1,376	1,751	2,303	3,504	4,026	2,838	3,622	5,132
109 Netherlands (millions of guilders)	253	710	1,538	2,953	3,241	3,768	3,931	3,411	4,069	3,730
110 France (millions of francs)	3,713	5,393	8,971	14,674	17,589	22,700	26,513	29,075	33,107	36,142
111 Japan (billions of yen)	88	165	341	588	760	699	753	893	1,026	906
112 Finland (millions of markkaa)	6	29	177	351	414	583	694	852	1,070	1,308
113 Germany, Fed. Rep. (millions of deutsche marks)	1,824	2,192	4,155	6,219	6,484	7,189	7,649	8,109	7,917	8,736
114 Denmark (millions of kroner)	90	443	1,178	2,425	2,711	2,871	3,458	3,612	4,650	4,655
115 Australia (millions of dollars)	106	189	421	563	585	566	867	834	883	1,066
116 Sweden (millions of kronor)	197	605	2,350	4,236	4,069	4,653	6,201	5,781	6,129	7,233
117 Canada (millions of dollars)	104	353	895	1,237	1,257	1,425	1,477	1,761	2,105	2,237
118 Norway (millions of kroner)	79	264	962	2,172	2,400	2,680	3,608	4,261	4,432	4,771
119 United States (millions of dollars)	4,023	3,153	4,161	4,684	7,138	5,782	8,202	8,081	8,711	9,555
120 Switzerland (millions of francs)	52	131	268	354	424	466	512	672	672	738
OECD					**Summary**					
ODA (billions of U.S. dollars, nominal prices)	6.48	6.97	13.85	22.82	27.27	25.54	27.73	27.56	28.71	29.52
ODA as percentage of GNP	.48	.34	.35	.35	.37	.34	.38	.36	.36	.36
ODA (billions of U.S. dollars, constant 1980 prices)	20.41	18.21	21.73	24.89	27.27	25.63	27.94	27.56	28.87	29.15
GNP (trillions of U.S. dollars, nominal prices)	1.35	2.04	3.92	6.56	7.31	7.42	7.33	7.61	7.94	8.31
GDP deflator[b]	.31	.38	.63	.91	1.00	.99	.99	1.00	1.00	1.01

Note: For data comparability and coverage, see the technical notes.

		Amount								
	1975	1976	1977	1978	1979	1980	1981	1982	1983	1984[a]
OPEC	**Millions of US dollars**									
52 Nigeria	14	80	51	27	29	34	143	58	35	51
88 Algeria	31	13	43	42	281	82	55	131	61	46
89 Venezuela	31	113	24	98	110	124	66	125	141	90
95 Iran, Islamic Rep.	642	751	162	231	−20	−72	−141	−193	15	. .
96 Iraq	258	121	98	138	658	863	203	57	−37	−48
98 Libya	270	102	102	118	115	376	262	43	142	17
99 Saudi Arabia	2,665	2,916	2,909	5,215	3,971	5,775	5,575	3,910	3,661	3,315
100 Kuwait	956	731	1,302	993	970	1,140	1,154	1,168	1,006	1,018
101 United Arab Emirates	1,046	1,028	1,076	887	968	1,052	800	395	364	43
Qatar	317	180	170	95	282	286	248	139	11	13
Total OAPEC[c]	5,543	5,091	5,700	7,488	7,245	9,574	8,297	5,843	5,208	4,404
Total OPEC	6,230	6,035	5,937	7,844	7,364	9,660	8,365	5,833	5,399	4,545
OPEC	**As percentage of donor GNP**									
52 Nigeria	.04	.19	.11	.05	.04	.04	.19	.08	.05	.07
88 Algeria	.21	.08	.22	.17	.90	.20	.13	.31	.13	.09
89 Venezuela	.11	.36	.07	.25	.23	.21	.10	.19	.22	.12
95 Iran, Islamic Rep.	1.22	1.16	.21	.33	−.02	−.08	−.15	−.18	.01	−.14
96 Iraq	1.95	.76	.52	.61	1.97	2.35	.92	.19	−.11	. .
98 Libya	2.39	.69	.58	.67	.48	1.16	.93	.14	.49	.06
99 Saudi Arabia	7.50	6.22	4.94	8.00	5.20	4.95	3.49	2.54	3.29	3.29
100 Kuwait	7.26	5.00	8.19	5.48	3.52	3.52	3.63	4.60	3.86	3.81
101 United Arab Emirates	11.69	8.95	7.39	6.36	5.08	3.82	2.60	1.34	1.44	.17
Qatar	14.59	7.35	6.79	3.26	6.07	4.28	3.74	1.66	.13	.16
Total OAPEC	5.73	4.23	3.95	4.52	3.35	3.28	2.58	1.83	1.86	1.61
Total OPEC	2.92	2.32	1.96	2.39	1.76	1.81	1.47	.99	.95	1.16

			Net bilateral flows to low-income economies							
	1965	1970	1975	1978	1979	1980	1981	1982	1983	1984
OECD	**As percentage of donor GNP**									
104 Italy	.04	.06	.01	.01	.01	.01	.02	.04	.05	.09
105 New Zealand	. .	. .	.14	.01	.01	.01	.01	.00	.00	.00
106 United Kingdom	.23	.15	.11	.14	.16	.11	.13	.07	.10	.09
107 Belgium	.56	.30	.31	.23	.27	.24	.25	.21	.21	.20
108 Austria	.06	.05	.02	.01	.03	.03	.03	.01	.02	.01
109 Netherlands	.08	.24	.24	.28	.26	.30	.37	.31	.26	.29
110 France	.12	.09	.10	.07	.07	.08	.11	.10	.09	.14
111 Japan	.13	.11	.08	.05	.09	.08	.06	.11	.09	.07
112 Finland	. .	. .	.06	.04	.06	.08	.09	.09	.12	.13
113 Germany, Fed. Rep.	.14	.10	.12	.09	.10	.08	.11	.12	.13	.11
114 Denmark	.02	.10	.20	.29	.28	.28	.21	.26	.31	.28
115 Australia	.08	.09	.10	.04	.06	.04	.06	.07	.05	.06
116 Sweden	.07	.12	.41	.36	.41	.36	.32	.38	.33	.30
117 Canada	.10	.22	.24	.17	.13	.11	.13	.14	.13	.15
118 Norway	.04	.12	.25	.34	.37	.31	.28	.37	.39	.34
119 United States	.26	.14	.08	.03	.02	.03	.03	.02	.03	.03
120 Switzerland	.02	.05	.10	.07	.06	.08	.07	.09	.10	.12
Total	.20	.13	.11	.07	.08	.07	.08	.08	.08	.07

a. Preliminary estimates. b. See the technical notes. c. Organization of Arab Petroleum Exporting Countries.

Table 21. Official development assistance: receipts

Net disbursements of ODA from all sources

	(millions of dollars)							Per capita (dollars) 1984	As percentage of GNP 1984
	1978	1979	1980	1981	1982	1983	1984		
Low-income economies	7,661 *t*	9,370 *t*	11,415 *t*	11,071 *t*	11,066 *t*	10,881 *t*	11,012 *t*	4.6 *w*	1.7 *w*
China and India	..	1,367 *t*	2,212 *t*	2,388 *t*	2,069 *t*	2,395 *t*	2,345 *t*	1.3 *w*	0.5 *w*
Other low-income	6,372 *t*	8,003 *t*	9,202 *t*	8,684 *t*	8,998 *t*	8,486 *t*	8,667 *t*	14.2 *w*	6.6 *w*
Sub-Saharan Africa	3,432 *t*	4,626 *t*	5,284 *t*	5,434 *t*	5,501 *t*	5,436 *t*	5,508 *t*	21.4 *w*	9.0 *w*
1 Ethiopia	140	191	216	250	200	344	363	8.6	7.7
2 Bangladesh	988	1,166	1,283	1,093	1,346	1,071	1,202	12.3	9.3
3 Mali	163	193	267	230	210	215	320	43.6	32.0
4 Zaire	317	416	428	394	348	317	314	10.6	10.1
5 Burkina Faso	159	198	212	217	213	184	188	28.7	19.7
6 Nepal	77	137	163	181	201	201	198	12.3	7.9
7 Burma	274	364	309	283	319	302	275	7.6	4.3
8 Malawi	99	142	143	138	121	117	159	23.2	13.8
9 Niger	157	174	170	193	259	175	162	26.1	14.8
10 Tanzania	424	588	678	702	683	621	559	26.0	14.7
11 Burundi	75	95	117	122	127	142	141	30.7	15.0
12 Uganda	23	46	114	136	133	137	164	10.9	3.3
13 Togo	103	110	91	63	77	112	110	37.3	16.7
14 Central African Rep.	51	84	111	102	90	93	114	45.1	18.8
15 India	1,289	1,350	2,146	1,911	1,545	1,725	1,547	2.1	0.8
16 Madagascar	91	138	230	234	251	185	156	15.8	7.0
17 Somalia	212	179	433	374	462	327	363	69.4	
18 Benin	62	85	91	82	80	87	77	19.7	8.0
19 Rwanda	125	148	155	154	151	151	165	28.2	10.2
20 China	..	17	66	477	524	670	798	0.8	0.3
21 Kenya	248	351	397	449	485	402	431	22.1	7.5
22 Sierra Leone	40	54	93	61	82	66	61	16.5	6.2
23 Haiti	93	93	105	107	128	134	135	25.1	7.5
24 Guinea	60	56	90	107	90	68	123	20.8	6.3
25 Ghana	114	169	193	148	142	110	216	17.5	5.7
26 Sri Lanka	324	323	393	378	416	474	468	29.5	8.0
27 Sudan	318	671	588	681	740	957	616	28.9	
28 Pakistan	639	684	1,075	768	850	669	698	7.5	..
29 Senegal	223	307	262	397	285	322	333	52.2	2.1
30 *Afghanistan*	101	108	32	23	9	14	7	0.4	14.8
31 *Bhutan*	3	6	8	10	11	13	18	4.8	..
32 *Chad*	125	86	35	60	65	95	115	23.6	6.0
33 *Kampuchea, Dem.*	0	108	281	130	44	37	17	2.4	..
34 *Lao PDR*	72	54	41	35	38	30	34	9.6	..
35 *Mozambique*	105	146	169	144	208	211	259	19.3	..
36 *Viet Nam*	370	336	229	242	136	106	109	1.8	..
Middle-income economies	10,312 *t*	12,418 *t*	14,061 *t*	13,862 *t*	12,329 *t*	12,213 *t*	12,291 *t*	10.8 *w*	0.9 *w*
Oil exporters	4,970 *t*	5,224 *t*	5,417 *t*	5,124 *t*	4,567 *t*	4,625 *t*	4,901 *t*	8.8 *w*	0.9 *w*
Oil importers	5,341 *t*	7,194 *t*	8,645 *t*	8,738 *t*	7,762 *t*	7,589 *t*	7,390 *t*	12.7 *w*	0.9 *w*
Sub-Saharan Africa	1,123 *t*	1,331 *t*	1,642 *t*	1,544 *t*	1,605 *t*	1,482 *t*	1,613 *t*	10.9 *w*	1.5 *w*
Lower middle-income	8,562 *t*	10,426 *t*	12,293 *t*	11,892 *t*	10,642 *t*	10,042 *t*	10,049 *t*	15.0 *w*	2.0 *w*
37 Mauritania	238	167	176	231	193	172	168	101.5	24.6
38 Liberia	48	81	98	109	109	118	133	62.6	13.6
39 Zambia	185	277	318	231	309	216	238	37.1	9.8
40 Lesotho	50	64	91	101	90	104	97	65.8	17.6
41 Bolivia	156	161	170	169	147	173	172	27.7	5.5
42 Indonesia	635	721	950	975	906	751	673	4.2	0.9
43 Yemen Arab Rep.	277	268	472	411	412	330	314	40.4	8.2
44 Yemen, PDR	91	76	100	87	143	106	85	41.9	7.3
45 Cote d'Ivoire	131	162	210	124	137	157	128	13.0	2.2
46 Philippines	249	267	300	376	333	429	397	7.4	1.2
47 Morocco	428	473	896	1,034	771	397	286	13.4	2.3
48 Honduras	93	97	103	109	158	192	290	68.6	9.6
49 El Salvador	55	60	97	167	223	295	263	48.6	6.6
50 Papua New Guinea	296	284	326	336	311	333	322	94.0	13.8
51 Egypt, Arab Rep.	2,370	1,450	1,387	1,292	1,417	1,431	1,764	38.4	5.5
52 Nigeria	43	27	36	41	37	48	33	0.3	0.0
53 Zimbabwe	9	13	164	212	216	208	298	36.7	5.8
54 Cameroon	178	270	265	199	212	130	188	19.0	2.5
55 Nicaragua	42	115	221	145	121	120	114	36.0	4.2
56 Thailand	260	393	418	407	389	432	475	9.5	1.1
57 Botswana	69	100	106	97	102	104	103	99.2	11.6
58 Dominican Rep.	50	78	125	105	137	102	198	32.4	4.2
59 Peru	143	200	203	233	188	297	310	17.0	1.9
60 Mauritius	44	32	33	58	48	41	36	35.1	3.5
61 Congo, People's Rep.	81	91	92	81	93	109	98	53.9	5.3
62 Ecuador	45	70	46	59	53	64	136	14.9	1.5
63 Jamaica	122	123	126	155	180	181	170	77.6	8.2
64 Guatemala	72	67	73	75	64	76	65	8.4	0.7
65 Turkey	178	594	952	724	659	353	242	5.0	0.5

Note: For data comparability and coverage, see the technical notes.

		Net disbursements of ODA from all sources								
		(millions of dollars)							Per capita (dollars)	As percentage of GNP
		1978	1979	1980	1981	1982	1983	1984	1984	1984
66	Costa Rica	51	56	65	55	80	252	217	86.0	6.7
67	Paraguay	43	31	31	55	85	51	50	15.3	1.3
68	Tunisia	299	210	233	252	210	214	180	25.8	2.2
69	Colombia	71	54	90	102	97	86	88	3.1	0.2
70	Jordan	431	1,299	1,275	1,065	799	789	677	200.0	18.0
71	Syrian Arab Rep.	728	1,803	1,727	1,495	952	970	859	85.1	5.3
72	Angola	47	47	53	61	60	76	93	10.9.	..
73	Cuba	49	49	32	14	17	13	12	1.2	..
74	Korea, Dem. Rep.	..	..	..	..	..	..			..
75	Lebanon	206	101	237	451	187	123	77	28.3	..
76	Mongolia	..	..	..	..	..	..	(.)	0.1	..
Upper middle-income		**1,750 t**	**1,992 t**	**1,768 t**	**1,970 t**	**1,681 t**	**2,171 t**	**2,243 t**	**4.8 w**	**0.3 w**
77	Chile	8	−27	−10	−7	−9	(.)	2	0.2	(.)
78	Brazil	113	107	85	235	208	101	161	1.2	0.1
79	Portugal	68	136	113	82	49	45	98	9.6	0.5
80	Malaysia	80	125	135	143	135	177	327	21.4	1.1
81	Panama	29	35	46	39	41	47	72	33.8	1.7
82	Uruguay	11	14	10	8	4	3	4	1.3	0.1
83	Mexico	18	75	56	100	140	132	83	1.1	0.1
84	Korea, Rep. of	164	134	139	331	34	8	−37	−0.9	0.0
85	Yugoslavia	−45	−29	−17	−15	−8	3	3	0.1	0.0
86	Argentina	29	43	18	44	30	48	49	1.6	0.1
87	South Africa	..	..	..	..	..	..	..	..	..
88	Algeria	133	102	176	163	137	150	122	5.8	0.2
89	Venezuela	−15	7	15	14	12	10	14	0.8	0.0
90	Greece	62	41	40	14	12	13	13	1.3	0.0
91	Israel	900	1,185	892	772	857	1,345	1,256	298.4	6.3
92	Hong Kong	2	12	11	10	8	9	14	2.6	0.0
93	Trinidad and Tobago	5	4	5	−1	6	6	5	3.9	0.1
94	Singapore	7	6	14	22	21	15	41	16.2	0.2
95	Iran, Islamic Rep.	128	6	31	9	3	48	13	0.3	..
96	Iraq	53	18	8	9	6	13	4	0.3	..
High-income oil exporters		**74 t**	**191 t**	**221 t**	**281 t**	**213 t**	**130 t**	**121 t**	**6.5 w**	**0.1 w**
97	Oman	40	165	174	231	132	71	72	63.6	1.0
98	Libya	12	5	17	11	12	6	5	1.4	(.)
99	Saudi Arabia	15	11	16	30	57	44	36	3.2	(.)
100	Kuwait	3	2	10	9	6	5	5	2.7	(.)
101	United Arab Emirates	4	7	4	1	5	4	3	2.6	(.)
Industrial market economies										
102	Spain									
103	Ireland									
104	Italy									
105	New Zealand									
106	United Kingdom									
107	Belgium									
108	Austria									
109	Netherlands									
110	France									
111	Japan									
112	Finland									
113	Germany, Fed. Rep.									
114	Denmark									
115	Australia									
116	Sweden									
117	Canada									
118	Norway									
119	United States									
120	Switzerland									
East European nonmarket economies										
121	Hungary									
122	Poland									
123	Albania									
124	Bulgaria									
125	Czechoslovakia									
126	German Dem. Rep.									
127	Romania									
128	USSR									

Table 22. Central government expenditure

	Percentage of total expenditure												Total expenditure (percentage of GNP)		Overall surplus/deficit (percentage of GNP)	
	Defense		Education		Health		Housing; amenities; social security and welfare[a]		Economic services		Other[a]					
	1972[b]	1983[c]	1972[b]	1983[c]	1972[b]	1983[c]	1972[b]	1983[c]	1972[b]	1983[c]	1972[b]	1983[c]	1972[b]	1983[c]	1972[b]	1983[c]
Low-income economies	17.2 w	19.5 w	12.7 w	4.7 w	4.6 w	2.7 w	7.3 w	5.8 w	22.8 w	24.0 w	35.4 w	43.3 w	18.2 w	16.3 w	−4.3 w	−6.6 w
China and India	..	..	..	..	..	..	..	..	..	..	..	..	..	..	..	..
Other low-income	17.2 w	18.5 w	12.7 w	9.9 w	4.6 w	3.3 w	7.3 w	8.1 w	22.8 w	23.8 w	35.4 w	36.4 w	18.2 w	19.9 w	−4.3 w	−5.6 w
Sub-Saharan Africa	13.2 w	10.3 w	15.5 w	15.9 w	5.2 w	4.5 w	5.7 w	5.0 w	20.9 w	21.5 w	39.5 w	42.8 w	21.0 w	20.1 w	−3.9 w	−4.4 w
1 Ethiopia	14.3	..	14.4	..	5.7	..	4.4	..	22.9	..	38.3	..	13.7	..	−1.4	..
2 Bangladesh	5.1	..	14.9	..	5.0	..	9.8	..	39.3	..	25.9	..	9.3	..	−1.9	..
3 Mali	..	7.9	..	10.1	..	2.5	..	4.6	..	7.1	..	67.8	..	68.9	..	..
4 Zaire	11.1	7.9	15.2	16.3	2.3	3.2	2.0	0.4	13.3	16.8	56.1	55.4	38.6	27.5	−7.5	−18.4
5 Burkina Faso	11.5	20.7	20.6	19.6	8.2	6.8	6.6	8.0	15.5	16.3	37.6	28.6	10.9	13.6	0.3	−3.0
6 Nepal	7.2	5.4	7.2	9.9	4.7	4.5	0.7	4.3	57.2	53.1	23.0	22.7	8.5	17.2	−1.2	0.9
7 Burma	31.6	..	15.0	..	6.1	..	7.5	..	20.1	..	19.7	..	20.0	..	−7.3	−5.2
8 Malawi	3.1	6.2	15.8	13.4	5.5	6.8	5.8	1.3	33.1	35.2	36.7	37.1	22.1	32.0	−6.2	..
9 Niger	..	..	..	..	..	..	..	..	..	..	..	..	..	..	..	−7.7
10 Tanzania	11.9	..	17.3	..	7.2	..	2.1	..	39.0	..	22.6	..	19.7	..	−5.0	..
11 Burundi	10.3	..	23.4	..	6.0	..	2.7	..	33.9	..	23.8	..	19.9	..	..	..
12 Uganda	23.1	17.0	15.3	12.9	5.3	4.6	7.3	2.6	12.4	9.5	36.6	53.4	21.8	4.5	−8.1	−1.2
13 Togo	..	6.8	..	19.6	..	5.7	..	8.2	..	18.2	..	41.6	..	34.1	..	−2.1
14 Central African Rep.	..	..	..	..	..	..	..	..	..	..	..	..	..	..	..	..
15 India	..	20.0	..	1.9	..	2.4	..	4.6	..	24.1	..	47.0	..	14.9	..	−7.0
16 Madagascar	3.6	..	9.1	..	4.2	..	9.9	..	40.5	..	32.7	..	20.8	..	−2.5	..
17 Somalia	23.3	..	5.5	..	7.2	..	1.9	..	21.6	..	40.5	..	13.5	..	0.6	..
18 Benin	..	..	..	..	..	..	..	..	..	..	..	..	..	..	..	..
19 Rwanda	25.6	..	22.2	..	5.7	..	2.6	..	22.0	..	21.9	..	11.7	..	−2.5	..
20 China	..	..	..	..	..	..	..	..	..	..	..	..	..	..	..	..
21 Kenya	6.0	13.8	21.9	20.6	7.9	7.0	3.9	0.7	30.1	24.6	30.2	33.3	21.0	26.6	−3.9	−5.1
22 Sierra Leone	..	4.2	..	14.8	..	6.2	..	1.5	..	32.1	..	41.2	..	21.2	..	−13.8
23 Haiti	..	..	..	..	..	..	..	..	..	..	..	..	14.5	17.6	..	−3.2
24 Guinea	..	..	..	..	..	..	..	..	..	..	..	..	..	..	..	..
25 Ghana	7.9	6.2	20.1	18.7	6.3	5.8	4.1	6.8	15.1	19.2	46.6	43.3	19.5	7.8	−5.8	−2.6
26 Sri Lanka	3.1	2.4	13.0	7.1	6.4	5.1	19.5	11.4	20.2	13.1	37.7	60.8	25.4	33.6	−5.3	−11.0
27 Sudan	24.1	9.5	9.3	6.1	5.4	1.3	1.4	2.3	15.8	23.5	44.1	57.3	19.2	16.9	−0.8	−4.6
28 Pakistan	39.9	34.8	1.2	3.1	1.1	1.0	3.2	9.3	21.4	28.0	33.2	23.8	16.5	17.8	−6.8	−6.2
29 Senegal	..	9.7	..	17.6	..	4.7	..	8.6	..	19.2	..	40.3	17.4	26.8	−0.8	−6.0
30 Afghanistan	..	..	..	..	..	..	..	..	..	..	..	..	..	..	..	..
31 Bhutan	..	..	..	..	..	..	..	..	..	..	..	..	..	..	..	..
32 Chad	24.6	..	14.8	..	4.4	..	1.7	..	21.8	..	32.7	..	18.1	..	−3.2	..
33 Kampuchea, Dem.	..	..	..	..	..	..	..	..	..	..	..	..	..	..	..	..
34 Lao PDR	..	..	..	..	..	..	..	..	..	..	..	..	..	..	..	..
35 Mozambique	..	..	..	..	..	..	..	..	..	..	..	..	..	..	..	..
36 Viet Nam	..	..	..	..	..	..	..	..	..	..	..	..	..	..	..	..
Middle-income economies	15.1 w	11.4 w	12.8 w	12.1 w	6.3 w	4.5 w	20.0 w	17.0 w	24.3 w	21.9 w	21.5 w	33.1 w	20.0 w	26.2 w	−3.0 w	−5.8 w
Oil exporters	22.5 w	15.4 w	14.5 w	12.8 w	3.9 w	3.7 w	4.3 w	9.3 w	26.5 w	25.7 w	28.3 w	33.1 w	16.7 w	26.7 w	−2.4 w	−4.0 w
Oil importers	14.3 w	14.4 w	11.9 w	10.9 w	6.9 w	4.8 w	26.8 w	21.2 w	21.9 w	19.8 w	18.2 w	28.9 w	21.4 w	25.1 w	−3.2 w	−5.7 w
Sub-Saharan Africa	..	13.2 w	9.1 w	17.2 w	4.9 w	6.3 w	4.3 w	8.4 w	21.6 w	24.0 w	47.0 w	30.9 w	13.1 w	32.4 w	−2.5 w	−5.4 w
Lower middle-income	18.4 w	15.5 w	16.4 w	15.0 w	4.1 w	4.2 w	5.5 w	7.6 w	30.3 w	26.5 w	25.3 w	31.2 w	16.8 w	24.4 w	−2.4 w	−4.7 w
37 Mauritania	..	..	..	..	..	..	..	..	..	..	..	..	..	..	..	..
38 Liberia	..	7.9	..	15.8	..	7.3	..	2.7	..	28.6	..	37.7	..	34.9	..	−10.6
39 Zambia	..	..	19.0	15.2	7.4	8.4	1.3	1.8	26.7	23.9	45.7	50.7	34.0	41.5	−13.8	−19.8
40 Lesotho	..	..	19.5	17.4	8.0	7.2	6.5	1.3	24.5	29.4	41.5	44.1	16.6	27.6	−0.9	−2.8
41 Bolivia	16.2	10.8	30.6	26.9	8.6	3.1	2.9	18.0	12.4	12.9	29.3	28.3	9.2	11.3	−1.4	−6.8
42 Indonesia	18.5	11.7	7.5	9.4	1.3	2.2	0.9	1.4	30.4	37.8	41.4	37.4	16.2	24.0	−2.6	−2.8
43 Yemen Arab Rep.	..	36.7	..	16.6	..	4.9	..	..	..	8.7	..	33.1	..	43.2	..	−24.6
44 Yemen, PDR	..	..	..	..	..	..	..	..	..	..	..	..	..	..	..	..
45 Cote d'Ivoire	..	..	..	..	..	..	..	..	..	..	..	..	..	..	..	..
46 Philippines	10.9	13.6	16.3	25.6	3.2	6.8	4.3	4.9	17.6	44.6	47.7	4.5	13.4	11.8	−2.0	−2.0
47 Morocco	12.3	14.6	19.2	18.6	4.8	2.9	8.4	7.1	25.6	28.8	29.7	27.9	22.4	33.2	−3.8	−8.0
48 Honduras	12.4	..	22.3	..	10.2	..	8.7	..	28.3	..	18.1	..	15.3	..	−2.7	..
49 El Salvador	6.6	15.8	21.4	16.6	10.9	8.4	7.6	4.7	14.4	21.3	39.0	33.1	12.8	17.4	−1.0	−5.5
50 Papua New Guinea	..	4.2	..	20.9	..	9.3	..	1.8	..	19.6	..	44.2	..	36.2	..	−4.7
51 Egypt, Arab Rep.	..	15.7	..	10.7	..	2.8	..	14.9	..	8.6	..	47.3	..	39.0	..	−8.2
52 Nigeria	40.2	..	4.5	..	3.6	..	0.8	..	19.6	..	31.4	..	10.2	..	−0.9	..
53 Zimbabwe	..	18.3	..	21.5	..	6.1	..	7.8	..	20.9	..	25.4	..	36.3	..	−6.9
54 Cameroon	..	9.6	..	13.2	..	3.7	..	8.5	..	26.0	..	39.0	..	21.8	..	1.3
55 Nicaragua	12.3	..	16.6	..	4.0	..	16.4	..	27.1	..	23.6	..	15.5	49.2	−4.0	−26.8
56 Thailand	20.2	19.8	19.9	20.7	3.7	5.1	7.0	4.6	25.6	21.8	23.5	28.0	17.2	19.6	−4.3	−4.2
57 Botswana	..	7.0	10.0	19.4	6.0	5.6	21.7	9.1	28.0	27.4	34.5	31.5	33.7	44.7	−23.8	11.5
58 Dominican Rep.	8.5	8.7	14.2	15.3	11.7	10.5	11.8	14.7	35.4	29.7	18.4	21.0	18.5	15.6	−0.2	−2.8
59 Peru	14.8	27.6	22.7	18.5	6.2	6.2	2.9	0.8	30.3	..	23.1	46.9	17.1	18.6	−1.1	..
60 Mauritius	0.8	0.9	13.5	15.6	10.3	7.8	18.0	21.1	13.9	9.2	43.4	45.3	16.3	28.7	−1.2	−9.3
61 Congo, People's Rep.	..	..	..	..	..	..	..	..	..	..	..	..	..	43.9	..	−3.0
62 Ecuador	15.7	10.6	27.5	26.0	4.5	7.5	0.8	1.3	28.9	13.9	22.6	40.7	13.4	14.3	0.2	−2.7
63 Jamaica	..	..	..	..	..	..	..	..	..	..	..	..	..	..	..	..
64 Guatemala	11.0	..	19.4	..	9.5	..	10.4	..	23.8	..	25.8	..	9.9	13.1	−2.2	−3.6
65 Turkey	15.4	13.2	18.2	12.5	3.3	1.8	3.3	2.0	41.9	31.8	17.9	38.7	21.8	24.3	−2.1	−4.2

Note: For data comparability and coverage, see the technical notes.

		Percentage of total expenditure												Total expenditure (percentage of GNP)		Overall surplus/deficit (percentage of GNP)	
		Defense		Education		Health		Housing; amenities; social security and welfare[a]		Economic services		Other[a]					
		1972[b]	1983[c]	1972[b]	1983[c]	1972[b]	1983[c]	1972[b]	1983[c]	1972[b]	1983[c]	1972[b]	1983[c]	1972[b]	1983[c]	1972[b]	1983[c]
66	Costa Rica	2.8	3.0	28.3	19.4	3.8	22.5	26.7	17.1	21.8	20.2	16.7	17.8	18.9	26.4	−4.5	−2.2
67	Paraguay	13.8	*12.5*	12.1	*12.0*	3.5	3.7	18.3	32.2	19.6	*14.0*	32.7	25.7	13.1	*11.7*	−1.7	*0.4*
68	Tunisia	4.9	..	30.5	..	7.4	..	8.8	..	23.3	..	25.1	..	22.8	37.1	−0.9	−5.1
69	Colombia	..	..	..	..	..	..	..	..	..	..	..	..	13.0	..	−2.5	..
70	Jordan	..	25.6	..	11.5	..	3.6	..	13.7	..	33.2	..	12.3	..	46.3	..	−7.7
71	Syrian Arab Rep.	37.2	..	11.3	..	1.4	..	3.6	..	39.9	..	6.7	..	28.1	..	−3.4	..
72	*Angola*	..	..	..	..	..	..	..	..	..	..	..	..	..	..	..	..
73	*Cuba*	..	..	..	..	..	..	..	..	..	..	..	..	..	..	..	..
74	*Korea, Dem. Rep.*	..	..	..	..	..	..	..	..	..	..	..	..	..	..	..	..
75	*Lebanon*	..	..	..	..	..	..	..	..	..	..	..	..	..	..	..	..
76	*Mongolia*	..	..	..	..	..	..	..	..	..	..	..	..	..	..	..	..
	Upper middle-income	14.0 *w*	9.8 *w*	11.5 *w*	11.0 *w*	7.0 *w*	4.7 *w*	24.9 *w*	20.6 *w*	22.3 *w*	20.2 *w*	20.3 *w*	33.7 *w*	21.3 *w*	26.9 *w*	−3.3 *w*	−6.2 *w*
77	Chile	6.1	12.0	14.3	13.7	8.2	6.0	39.8	45.7	15.3	6.3	16.3	16.3	42.3	34.8	−13.0	−2.9
78	Brazil	8.3	4.1	6.8	3.7	6.4	7.3	36.0	35.1	24.6	23.8	17.9	25.9	17.8	21.4	−0.4	−3.6
79	Portugal	..	..	..	..	..	..	..	..	..	..	..	..	..	..	−9.8	..
80	Malaysia	18.5	..	23.4	..	6.8	..	4.4	10.5	14.2	..	32.7	..	27.7	40.4	−6.5	−12.1
81	Panama	..	*20.7*	..	*11.0*	15.1	*13.1*	10.8	12.2	24.2	*13.5*	29.1	*50.2*	27.6	40.4	−6.5	−12.1
82	Uruguay	5.6	12.7	9.5	6.5	1.6	3.4	52.3	52.1	9.8	8.7	21.2	16.5	25.0	25.9	−2.5	−4.1
83	Mexico	4.2	2.0	16.4	11.0	5.1	1.2	25.0	12.5	34.2	26.2	15.2	47.2	12.0	27.9	−3.0	−8.5
84	Korea, Rep. of	25.8	31.9	15.9	20.5	1.2	1.6	5.8	5.9	25.6	13.6	25.7	26.5	18.1	18.3	−3.9	−1.1
85	Yugoslavia	20.5	..	..	..	24.8	..	35.6	..	12.0	..	7.0	..	21.1	..	−0.4	..
86	Argentina	8.8	9.1	8.8	7.6	2.9	1.4	23.5	33.9	14.7	22.7	41.2	25.2	16.5	22.3	−3.4	−13.0
87	South Africa	..	..	..	..	..	..	..	..	..	..	..	..	21.8	28.0	−4.2	−4.1
88	Algeria	..	..	..	..	..	..	..	..	..	..	..	..	..	..	..	..
89	Venezuela	10.3	5.2	18.6	19.1	11.7	8.6	9.2	9.7	25.4	20.6	24.8	36.9	21.3	27.4	−0.3	−3.4
90	Greece	14.9	..	9.0	..	7.3	..	30.2	..	26.4	..	12.3	..	27.5	..	−1.7	..
91	Israel	39.8	29.0	9.0	8.4	3.5	4.3	7.8	21.5	16.3	6.4	23.5	*30.4*	44.0	48.8	−16.3	−18.6
92	Hong Kong	..	..	..	..	..	..	..	..	..	..	..	..	..	..	..	..
93	Trinidad and Tobago	..	..	..	..	..	..	..	..	..	..	..	..	..	..	..	..
94	Singapore	35.3	18.5	15.7	21.6	7.8	6.4	3.9	5.6	9.9	14.3	27.3	33.7	16.8	23.7	1.3	1.5
95	*Iran, Islamic Rep.*	24.1	8.7	10.4	13.9	3.6	5.7	6.1	13.3	30.6	23.0	25.2	35.4	30.8	28.1	−4.6	−6.1
96	*Iraq*	..	..	..	..	..	..	..	..	..	..	..	..	..	..	..	..
	High-income oil exporters	13.0 *w*	27.7 *w*	13.6 *w*	9.4 *w*	5.6 *w*	6.0 *w*	14.9 *w*	12.1 *w*	17.8 *w*	21.9 *w*	35.1 *w*	22.9 *w*	24.2 *w*	30.9 *w*	9.2 *w*	..
97	Oman	39.3	51.3	3.7	7.4	5.9	3.5	3.0	1.9	24.4	21.6	23.6	14.3	62.1	54.3	−15.3	−10.1
98	Libya	..	..	..	..	..	..	..	..	..	..	..	..	..	..	..	..
99	Saudi Arabia	..	..	..	..	..	..	..	..	..	..	..	..	..	..	..	..
100	Kuwait	8.4	13.3	15.0	10.1	5.5	6.2	14.2	15.5	16.6	28.7	40.1	26.2	34.4	39.2	17.4	6.2
101	United Arab Emirates	24.5	43.2	16.2	9.8	4.5	7.7	6.4	5.2	18.2	7.0	30.2	27.2	*4.3*	16.5	*0.3*	..
	Industrial market economies	20.8 *w*	14.3 *w*	5.4 *w*	4.7 *w*	10.0 *w*	11.2 *w*	37.2 *w*	41.1 *w*	12.0 *w*	9.2 *w*	14.6 *w*	19.5 *w*	22.9 *w*	30.0 *w*	−1.6 *w*	−5.8 *w*
102	Spain	6.5	4.4	8.3	6.0	0.9	0.6	49.8	64.2	17.5	10.1	17.0	14.8	19.8	31.5	−0.5	−6.3
103	Ireland	..	..	..	..	..	..	..	..	..	..	..	..	33.0	58.1	−5.5	−13.6
104	Italy	6.3	3.5	*16.1*	8.6	*13.5*	11.5	*44.8*	34.3	*18.4*	6.1	*0.9*	36.0	*31.8*	52.8	−9.4	−13.4
105	New Zealand	5.8	4.9	16.9	11.9	14.8	12.6	25.6	30.2	16.5	17.6	20.4	22.7	28.5	41.7	−3.8	−9.5
106	United Kingdom	16.7	..	2.6	..	12.2	..	26.5	..	11.1	..	30.8	..	32.7	41.4	−2.7	−5.0
107	Belgium	6.7	5.2	15.5	*13.9*	1.5	1.7	41.0	42.8	18.9	16.3	16.4	20.1	39.2	56.7	−4.3	−12.9
108	Austria	3.2	3.2	10.2	9.6	10.1	11.5	53.7	48.6	11.2	13.2	11.5	13.9	29.7	39.9	−0.1	−5.4
109	Netherlands	..	5.3	..	11.2	..	11.3	..	41.2	..	10.0	..	21.0	40.8	59.4	..	−7.7
110	France	..	7.3	..	8.2	..	14.6	..	47.6	..	6.9	..	15.4	32.5	44.8	0.7	−3.6
111	Japan	..	..	..	..	..	..	..	..	..	..	..	..	12.7	18.6	..	..
112	Finland	6.1	5.5	15.3	13.8	10.6	10.6	28.4	32.0	27.9	25.1	11.6	13.0	24.8	31.6	1.3	−3.0
113	Germany, Fed. Rep.	12.4	9.3	1.5	0.8	17.5	18.6	46.9	50.3	11.3	7.0	10.4	13.9	24.2	31.1	0.7	−2.0
114	Denmark	7.2	..	15.9	..	10.0	..	41.4	..	11.9	..	13.6	..	32.8	46.6	2.7	−7.5
115	Australia	14.1	9.7	4.4	7.9	8.2	7.1	21.0	30.0	13.1	8.4	39.2	37.0	19.8	26.7	−0.5	−2.5
116	Sweden	12.5	6.9	14.8	9.2	3.6	1.5	44.3	49.4	10.6	9.3	14.3	23.7	28.0	46.9	−1.2	−10.1
117	Canada	..	8.0	..	3.6	..	6.3	..	37.6	..	16.7	..	27.8	..	25.6	..	−6.5
118	Norway	9.7	8.6	9.9	8.8	12.3	10.6	39.9	36.2	20.2	20.5	8.0	15.3	35.0	39.7	−1.5	1.9
119	United States	32.2	23.7	3.2	1.9	8.6	10.7	35.3	36.3	10.6	8.8	10.1	18.6	19.4	25.3	−1.6	−6.1
120	Switzerland	15.1	10.4	4.2	3.1	10.0	13.4	39.5	49.7	18.4	12.6	12.8	10.8	13.3	19.4	0.9	−0.3
	East European nonmarket economies	..	..	..	..	..	..	..	..	..	..	..	..	..	..	..	..
121	Hungary	..	..	..	..	..	..	..	..	..	..	..	..	..	55.2	..	0.4
122	Poland	..	..	..	..	..	..	..	..	..	..	..	..	..	..	..	..
123	*Albania*	..	..	..	..	..	..	..	..	..	..	..	..	..	..	..	..
124	*Bulgaria*	..	..	..	..	..	..	..	..	..	..	..	..	..	..	..	..
125	*Czechoslovakia*	..	..	..	..	..	..	..	..	..	..	..	..	..	..	..	..
126	*German Dem. Rep.*	..	..	..	..	..	..	..	..	..	..	..	..	..	..	..	..
127	*Romania*	..	5.5	..	2.5	..	0.8	..	24.9	..	50.4	..	15.8	..	27.4	..	3.2
128	*USSR*	..	..	..	..	..	..	..	..	..	..	..	..	..	..	..	..

a. See the technical notes. b. Figures in italics are for 1973, not 1972. c. Figures in italics are for 1982, not 1983.

Table 23. Central government current revenue

	Percentage of total current revenue												Total current revenue (percentage of GNP)	
	Tax revenue													
	Taxes on income, profit, and capital gain		Social security contributions		Domestic taxes on goods and services		Taxes on international trade and transactions		Other taxes[a]		Current nontax revenue			
	1972[b]	1983[c]	1972[b]	1983[c]	1972[b]	1983[c]	1972[b]	1983[c]	1972[b]	1983[c]	1972[b]	1983[c]	1972[b]	1983[c]
Low-income economies	18.6 w	17.7 w	..	..	27.3 w	37.5 w	34.1 w	26.7 w	3.6 w	1.4 w	16.4 w	16.7 w	14.2 w	13.6 w
China and India														
Other low-income	18.6 w	18.7 w	..	..	27.3 w	29.7 w	34.1 w	32.6 w	3.6 w	3.1 w	16.4 w	15.9 w	14.2 w	14.7 w
Sub-Saharan Africa	21.5 w	22.8 w	..	..	24.4 w	25.2 w	38.3 w	32.8 w	4.6 w	5.1 w	11.2 w	14.1 w	16.6 w	14.6 w
1 Ethiopia	23.0	..	..	..	29.8	..	30.4	..	5.6	..	11.1	..	10.5	..
2 Bangladesh	3.7	..	..	..	22.4	..	18.0	..	3.8	..	52.2	..	8.5	..
3 Mali		15.5		5.4		35.2		21.2		11.7		11.0		29.0
4 Zaire	22.2	30.6	2.2	1.1	12.7	24.4	57.9	28.8	1.4	3.4	3.7	11.7	27.9	20.2
5 Burkina Faso	18.6	16.1	..	8.8	19.9	15.7	50.1	35.5	3.5	16.3	7.9	7.7	10.1	14.5
6 Nepal	4.1	7.2			26.5	38.5	36.7	31.3	19.0	7.1	13.7	15.9	5.2	8.7
7 Burma	28.7	3.2			34.2	39.5	13.4	19.2	(.)	(.)	23.8	38.2	12.4	16.2
8 Malawi	31.4	33.6			24.2	30.9	20.0	21.0	0.5	0.6	23.8	13.9	16.0	21.5
9 Niger														
10 Tanzania	29.9	..			29.1		21.7			0.5	18.8		15.8	
11 Burundi	18.1		1.2		19.8		38.7		15.6		6.5		11.5	
12 Uganda	22.1	4.1			32.8	26.5	36.3	67.1	0.3	(.)	8.5	2.3	13.7	3.2
13 Togo		34.0		5.4		14.7		28.2		1.3		16.4		29.5
14 Central African Rep.														
15 India		17.2				41.1		24.0		0.5		17.1		13.1
16 Madagascar	13.1	15.5	7.2	13.7	29.9	41.7	33.6	22.2	5.5	3.3	10.8	3.6	18.3	13.7
17 Somalia	10.7	..			24.7		45.3		5.2		14.0		13.7	
18 Benin														
19 Rwanda	17.9		4.4		14.1		41.7		13.8		8.1		9.2	
20 China														
21 Kenya	35.6	28.6			19.9	36.8	24.3	21.3	1.4	0.6	18.8	12.7	18.0	21.6
22 Sierra Leone		27.4				24.6		36.6		3.3		8.1		7.9
23 Haiti		17.9		0.3		19.1		26.2		27.8		8.7		13.9
24 Guinea		21.1		4.8		1.4		37.7		0.7		34.5		23.1
25 Ghana	18.4	17.0		..	29.4	17.0	40.6	49.0	0.2	0.1	11.5	16.9	15.1	5.4
26 Sri Lanka	19.1	14.0			34.7	40.1	35.4	31.5	2.1	1.7	8.7	12.7	20.1	20.2
27 Sudan	11.8	15.8			30.4	14.1	40.5	49.7	1.5	0.7	15.7	19.7	18.0	11.8
28 Pakistan	13.6	15.2			35.9	32.5	34.2	32.7	0.5	0.3	15.8	19.3	12.3	14.5
29 Senegal	17.6	19.0		3.5	24.5	29.1	30.9	34.7	23.8	5.9	3.2	7.8	16.8	19.6
30 Afghanistan														
31 Bhutan														
32 Chad	16.7				12.3		45.2		20.5		5.3		13.1	
33 Kampuchea, Dem.														
34 Lao PDR														
35 Mozambique														
36 Viet Nam														
Middle-income economies	25.5 w	27.4 w	..	..	26.5 w	26.5 w	13.5 w	10.4 w	18.3 w	12.2 w	17.2 w	23.5 w	17.9 w	23.1 w
Oil exporters	29.3 w	44.7 w	..	..	24.4 w	15.5 w	20.7 w	11.7 w	7.9 w	10.2 w	17.7 w	17.9 w	15.5 w	24.9 w
Oil importers	23.3 w	25.2 w	..	..	29.6 w	30.1 w	12.7 w	9.6 w	21.5 w	17.0 w	12.9 w	18.1 w	19.0 w	23.2 w
Sub-Saharan Africa	42.3 w	42.5 w	..	..	25.0 w	24.0 w	18.7 w	20.1 w	0.5 w	3.6 w	13.5 w	9.8 w	13.2 w	27.5 w
Lower middle-income	26.5 w	37.7 w	..	..	28.6 w	23.3 w	20.0 w	14.6 w	10.2 w	8.6 w	14.7 w	15.8 w	15.1 w	20.9 w
37 Mauritania														
38 Liberia		39.6				27.0		28.0		2.4		3.0		23.1
39 Zambia	49.7	32.9			20.2	48.3	14.3	8.8	0.1	3.2	15.6	6.6	23.2	24.6
40 Lesotho	14.3	10.1			2.0	10.1	62.9	69.0	9.5	1.1	11.3	9.7	11.7	23.7
41 Bolivia	14.5	13.3		28.2	28.4	25.4	46.0	16.1	5.3	4.8	5.7	12.2	7.8	4.4
42 Indonesia	45.5	73.6			22.7	10.3	17.5	4.3	3.6	1.3	10.6	10.5	14.4	22.7
43 Yemen Arab Rep.		11.2				6.5		50.2		15.2		16.9		22.5
44 Yemen, PDR														
45 Cote d'Ivoire														
46 Philippines	13.8	19.3			24.3	37.7	23.0	26.8	29.7	3.6	9.3	12.6	12.4	11.9
47 Morocco	16.4	17.7	5.9	4.8	45.7	36.8	13.2	18.4	6.1	7.2	12.6	15.1	18.1	25.1
48 Honduras	19.2		3.0		33.8		28.2		2.3		13.5		12.5	
49 El Salvador	15.2	19.9			25.6	40.3	36.1	23.0	17.2	5.8	6.0	10.9	11.6	12.3
50 Papua New Guinea		48.3				13.5		23.0		1.6		13.7		21.8
51 Egypt, Arab Rep.		17.8		11.1		12.5		16.2		6.3		36.1		36.9
52 Nigeria	43.0				26.3		17.5		0.2		13.0		11.6	
53 Zimbabwe		41.9				31.9		15.0		0.9		10.3		32.6
54 Cameroon		59.3		5.9		10.5		19.1		1.9		3.4		24.2
55 Nicaragua	9.6	11.3	14.0	10.2	37.4	41.1	24.3	16.1	8.9	13.4	5.8	7.8	12.6	34.0
56 Thailand	12.1	19.6			46.3	47.3	28.7	21.4	1.8	2.1	11.2	9.5	12.9	15.2
57 Botswana	19.9	27.1			2.4	2.0	47.2	31.1	0.4	0.1	30.0	39.7	30.7	56.4
58 Dominican Rep.	17.9	19.8	3.9	4.4	19.0	30.8	40.3	26.3	1.8	2.2	17.0	16.5	17.9	12.7
59 Peru	17.5	15.3			32.2	44.8	15.7	24.6	22.1	5.8	12.4	9.6	16.0	17.8
60 Mauritius	22.7	14.1			23.3	18.8	40.2	50.6	5.5	3.4	8.2	13.1	15.6	22.4
61 Congo, People's Rep.	19.3				40.3		26.5		6.4		7.4		18.4	
62 Ecuador	19.6	55.7			19.1	20.1	52.4	21.1	5.1	2.4	3.8	0.7	13.6	11.6
63 Jamaica														
64 Guatemala	12.7	11.8		11.7	36.1	3.1	26.2	15.0	15.6	13.7	9.4	14.8	8.9	10.2
65 Turkey	30.8	48.2			31.1	23.3	14.5	7.2	6.1	5.5	17.6	15.9	19.7	20.1

Note: For data comparability and coverage, see the technical notes.

	Tax revenue										Current nontax revenue		Total current revenue (percentage of GNP)	
	Taxes on income, profit, and capital gain		Social security contributions		Domestic taxes on goods and services		Taxes on international trade and transactions		Other taxes[a]					
	1972[b]	1983[c]	1972[b]	1983[c]	1972[b]	1983[c]	1972[b]	1983[c]	1972[b]	1983[c]	1972[b]	1983[c]	1972[b]	1983[c]
66 Costa Rica	17.7	16.9	13.4	25.2	38.1	31.0	18.0	22.4	1.6	-0.2	11.2	4.7	15.8	24.3
67 Paraguay	8.8	15.4	10.4	12.9	26.2	21.4	24.8	14.6	17.0	21.9	12.8	13.9	11.5	11.6
68 Tunisia	15.9	14.7	7.1	8.9	31.6	21.0	21.8	27.3	7.8	4.4	15.7	23.6	23.3	34.0
69 Colombia	37.2	..	13.9	..	16.0	..	20.3	..	7.2	..	5.5	..	10.6	..
70 Jordan	..	12.3	..	..	..	11.2	..	37.2	..	12.0	..	27.3	..	26.6
71 Syrian Arab Rep.	6.8	..	..	..	10.4	..	17.3	..	12.1	..	53.4	..	24.5	..
72 Angola	..	..	..	..	..	..	..	..	..	..	..	..	..	..
73 Cuba	..	..	..	..	..	..	..	..	..	..	..	..	..	..
74 Korea, Dem. Rep.	..	..	..	..	..	..	..	..	..	..	..	..	..	..
75 Lebanon	..	..	..	..	..	..	..	..	..	..	..	..	..	..
76 Mongolia	..	..	..	..	..	..	..	..	..	..	..	..	..	..
Upper middle-income	25.1 w	23.8 w	19.2 w	12.0 w	25.9 w	27.7 w	11.4 w	8.9 w	0.4 w	1.4 w	18.0 w	26.2 w	19.1 w	24.1 w
77 Chile	12.9	14.3	27.1	8.3	28.6	39.3	10.0	6.9	4.3	9.9	17.1	21.2	30.2	30.0
78 Brazil	18.3	15.1	27.4	24.6	37.6	25.3	7.0	4.1	3.7	4.2	6.0	26.8	19.0	26.6
79 Portugal	..	..	..	..	..	..	..	..	..	..	..	..	..	..
80 Malaysia	26.2	..	0.1	..	21.2	..	29.0	..	1.5	..	22.1	..	20.4	..
81 Panama	23.3	22.5	22.4	21.8	13.2	14.8	16.0	10.0	7.7	3.5	17.3	27.4	21.8	30.2
82 Uruguay	4.7	8.3	30.0	24.0	24.5	39.2	6.1	11.7	22.0	6.9	12.6	9.8	22.7	22.4
83 Mexico	36.4	22.2	19.4	11.0	32.1	63.2	13.2	6.9	-9.8	-17.6	8.6	14.3	10.4	20.2
84 Korea, Rep. of	29.2	22.9	0.8	1.2	41.7	45.7	10.7	15.8	5.2	3.9	12.3	10.6	13.2	19.5
85 Yugoslavia	..	..	52.3	..	24.5	..	19.5	..	..	..	3.7	..	20.7	..
86 Argentina	7.4	4.3	25.9	16.9	14.8	38.5	18.5	16.2	-3.7	11.5	37.0	12.6	13.1	15.2
87 South Africa	54.8	52.3	1.2	1.3	21.5	27.9	4.6	4.9	4.9	3.0	12.9	10.7	21.2	25.6
88 Algeria	..	..	..	..	..	..	..	..	..	..	..	..	..	..
89 Venezuela	54.2	56.1	6.0	3.8	6.7	6.0	6.1	18.0	1.1	0.9	25.9	15.3	21.8	27.0
90 Greece	12.2	..	24.5	..	35.5	..	6.7	..	12.0	..	9.2	..	25.4	..
91 Israel	36.2	41.5	..	9.5	23.0	28.1	21.6	5.6	6.8	5.5	12.4	9.9	31.8	30.0
92 Hong Kong	..	..	..	..	..	..	..	..	..	..	..	..	..	..
93 Trinidad and Tobago	..	..	..	..	..	..	..	..	..	..	..	..	..	..
94 Singapore	24.4	33.0	..	..	17.6	13.6	11.1	4.8	15.5	14.8	31.4	33.8	21.6	30.8
95 Iran, Islamic Rep.	7.9	7.8	2.7	7.5	6.4	4.2	14.6	11.4	4.9	3.9	63.6	65.2	26.2	21.8
96 Iraq	..	..	..	..	..	..	..	..	..	..	..	..	..	..
High-income oil exporters	..	..	..	..	..	..	..	..	..	..	..	..	33.6 w	..
97 Oman	71.1	26.5	..	..	..	0.6	3.0	2.0	2.3	0.4	23.6	70.5	47.4	44.5
98 Libya	..	..	..	..	..	..	..	..	..	..	..	..	..	..
99 Saudi Arabia	..	..	..	..	..	..	..	..	..	..	..	..	..	..
100 Kuwait	68.8	2.2	..	..	19.7	0.4	1.5	1.9	0.2	0.2	9.9	95.2	55.2	52.6
101 United Arab Emirates	..	..	..	..	..	..	..	..	..	..	..	..	0.2	..
Industrial market economies	38.9 w	36.3 w	29.3 w	34.1 w	21.4 w	18.1 w	1.7 w	1.2 w	2.3 w	0.9 w	6.4 w	9.4 w	23.5 w	27.0 w
102 Spain	15.9	21.7	38.9	46.2	23.4	15.4	10.0	4.2	0.7	3.1	11.1	9.5	20.0	26.4
103 Ireland	28.1	32.2	8.9	13.8	32.6	26.6	16.6	13.7	3.2	2.3	10.5	11.4	30.6	46.2
104 Italy	16.6	35.7	39.2	33.1	31.7	22.9	0.4	0.2	4.3	2.8	7.7	5.3	26.9	42.3
105 New Zealand	61.4	63.6	..	..	19.9	20.5	4.1	4.0	4.5	1.3	10.0	10.6	27.3	34.6
106 United Kingdom	39.4	38.7	15.1	17.7	27.1	28.6	1.7	(.)	5.5	3.0	11.2	12.0	33.5	37.6
107 Belgium	31.3	38.4	32.4	31.2	28.9	24.4	1.0	(.)	3.3	1.9	3.1	4.1	35.0	44.6
108 Austria	20.6	20.0	30.3	35.9	28.2	26.1	5.3	1.4	10.1	8.4	5.5	8.2	29.8	34.9
109 Netherlands	32.5	24.3	36.7	41.4	22.3	19.8	0.5	(.)	3.4	2.1	4.7	12.4	43.2	53.2
110 France	16.9	17.7	37.1	44.2	37.9	29.5	0.3	(.)	2.9	3.5	4.9	5.1	33.5	41.7
111 Japan	..	..	..	..	..	..	..	..	..	..	..	..	..	..
112 Finland	30.0	29.3	7.8	9.0	47.7	48.8	3.1	1.3	5.8	3.2	5.5	8.4	27.1	28.6
113 Germany, Fed. Rep.	19.7	17.0	46.6	55.1	28.1	22.0	0.8	(.)	0.8	0.1	4.0	5.8	25.2	29.3
114 Denmark	40.0	33.7	5.1	4.9	42.1	44.6	3.1	0.8	2.8	3.0	6.8	13.1	35.5	37.9
115 Australia	58.3	61.7	..	..	21.9	23.3	5.2	4.7	2.1	0.2	12.5	10.0	21.4	24.9
116 Sweden	27.0	14.5	21.6	34.1	34.0	29.0	1.5	0.6	4.7	5.7	11.3	16.1	32.5	39.6
117 Canada	..	48.3	..	14.1	..	19.2	..	4.8	..	-0.1	..	13.6	..	20.0
118 Norway	22.5	25.1	20.5	23.9	47.9	38.7	1.6	0.5	1.0	1.0	6.6	10.7	37.0	43.8
119 United States	59.4	49.9	23.6	31.3	7.1	5.4	1.6	1.3	2.5	0.9	5.7	11.1	18.0	19.7
120 Switzerland	13.9	14.2	37.3	49.3	21.5	19.4	16.7	8.3	2.6	3.1	8.0	5.7	14.5	19.1
East European nonmarket economies	..	..	..	..	..	..	..	..	..	..	..	..	..	..
121 Hungary	..	17.7	..	17.4	..	38.7	..	7.1	..	7.2	..	11.9	..	55.4
122 Poland	..	..	..	..	..	..	..	..	..	..	..	..	..	..
123 Albania	..	..	..	..	..	..	..	..	..	..	..	..	..	..
124 Bulgaria	..	..	..	..	..	..	..	..	..	..	..	..	..	..
125 Czechoslovakia	..	..	..	..	..	..	..	..	..	..	..	..	..	..
126 German Dem. Rep.	..	..	..	..	..	..	..	..	..	..	..	..	..	..
127 Romania	..	..	..	18.3	..	..	..	..	..	13.1	..	68.7	..	30.6
128 USSR	..	..	..	..	..	..	..	..	..	..	..	..	..	..

a. See the technical notes.   b. Figures in italics are for 1973, not 1972.   c. Figures in italics are for 1982, not 1983.

225

Table 24. Income distribution

		Percentage share of household income, by percentile groups of households[a]					
	Year	Lowest 20 percent	Second quintile	Third quintile	Fourth quintile	Highest 20 percent	Highest 10 percent
Low-income economies							
China and India							
Other low-income							
Sub-Saharan Africa							
1 Ethiopia		..	..	..	..	..	..
2 Bangladesh	1976–77	6.2	10.9	15.0	21.0	46.9	32.0
3 Mali		..	..	..	..	..	..
4 Zaire		..	..	..	..	..	..
5 Burkina Faso		..	..	..	..	..	..
6 Nepal		..	..	..	..	..	..
7 Burma		..	..	..	..	..	..
8 Malawi		..	..	..	..	..	..
9 Niger		..	..	..	..	..	..
10 Tanzania		..	..	..	..	..	..
11 Burundi		..	..	..	..	..	..
12 Uganda		..	..	..	..	..	..
13 Togo		..	..	..	..	..	..
14 Central African Rep.		..	..	..	..	..	..
15 India	1975–76	7.0	9.2	13.9	20.5	49.4	33.6
16 Madagascar		..	..	..	..	..	..
17 Somalia		..	..	..	..	..	..
18 Benin		..	..	..	..	..	..
19 Rwanda		..	..	..	..	..	..
20 China		..	..	..	..	..	..
21 Kenya	1976	2.6	6.3	11.5	19.2	60.4	45.8
22 Sierra Leone		..	..	..	..	..	..
23 Haiti		..	..	..	..	..	..
24 Guinea		..	..	..	..	..	..
25 Ghana		..	..	..	..	..	..
26 Sri Lanka	1969–70	7.5	11.7	15.7	21.7	43.4	28.2
27 Sudan		..	..	..	..	..	..
28 Pakistan		..	..	..	..	..	..
29 Senegal		..	..	..	..	..	..
30 Afghanistan		..	..	..	..	..	..
31 Bhutan		..	..	..	..	..	..
32 Chad		..	..	..	..	..	..
33 Kampuchea, Dem.		..	..	..	..	..	..
34 Lao PDR		..	..	..	..	..	..
35 Mozambique		..	..	..	..	..	..
36 Viet Nam		..	..	..	..	..	..
Middle-income economies							
Oil exporters							
Oil importers							
Sub-Saharan Africa							
Lower middle-income							
37 Mauritania		..	..	..	..	..	..
38 Liberia		..	..	..	..	..	..
39 Zambia	1976	3.4	7.4	11.2	16.9	61.1	46.3
40 Lesotho		..	..	..	..	..	..
41 Bolivia		..	..	..	..	..	..
42 Indonesia	1976	6.6	7.8	12.6	23.6	49.4	34.0
43 Yemen Arab Rep.		..	..	..	..	..	..
44 Yemen, PDR		..	..	..	..	..	..
45 Cote d'Ivoire		..	..	..	..	..	..
46 Philippines	1970–71	5.2	9.0	12.8	19.0	54.0	38.5
47 Morocco		..	..	..	..	..	..
48 Honduras		..	..	..	..	..	..
49 El Salvador	1976–77	5.5	10.0	14.8	22.4	47.3	29.5
50 Papua New Guinea		..	..	..	..	..	..
51 Egypt, Arab Rep.	1974	5.8	10.7	14.7	20.8	48.0	33.2
52 Nigeria		..	..	..	..	..	..
53 Zimbabwe		..	..	..	..	..	..
54 Cameroon		..	..	..	..	..	..
55 Nicaragua		..	..	..	..	..	..
56 Thailand	1975–76	5.6	9.6	13.9	21.1	49.8	34.1
57 Botswana		..	..	..	..	..	..
58 Dominican Rep.		..	..	..	..	..	..
59 Peru	1972	1.9	5.1	11.0	21.0	61.0	42.9
60 Mauritius	1980–81	4.0	7.5	11.0	17.0	60.5	46.7
61 Congo, People's Rep.		..	..	..	..	..	..
62 Ecuador		..	..	..	..	..	..
63 Jamaica		..	..	..	..	..	..
64 Guatemala		..	..	..	..	..	..
65 Turkey	1973	3.5	8.0	12.5	19.5	56.5	40.7

Note: For data comparability and coverage, see the technical notes.

		Percentage share of household income, by percentile groups of households[a]					
	Year	Lowest 20 percent	Second quintile	Third quintile	Fourth quintile	Highest 20 percent	Highest 10 percent
66 Costa Rica	1971	3.3	8.7	13.3	19.9	54.8	39.5
67 Paraguay		..	..	..	..	..	..
68 Tunisia		..	..	..	..	..	..
69 Colombia		..	..	..	..	..	..
70 Jordan		..	..	..	..	..	..
71 Syrian Arab Rep.		..	..	..	..	..	..
72 *Angola*		..	..	..	..	..	..
73 *Cuba*		..	..	..	..	..	..
74 *Korea, Dem. Rep.*		..	..	..	..	..	..
75 *Lebanon*		..	..	..	..	..	..
76 *Mongolia*		..	..	..	..	..	..
Upper middle-income							
77 Chile		..	..	..	..	..	..
78 Brazil	1972	2.0	5.0	9.4	17.0	66.6	50.6
79 Portugal	1973–74	5.2	10.0	14.4	21.3	49.1	33.4
80 Malaysia	1973	3.5	7.7	12.4	20.3	56.1	39.8
81 Panama	1970	2.0	5.2	11.0	20.0	61.8	44.2
82 Uruguay		..	..	..	..	..	..
83 Mexico	1977	2.9	7.0	12.0	20.4	57.7	40.6
84 Korea, Rep. of	1976	5.7	11.2	15.4	22.4	45.3	27.5
85 Yugoslavia	1978	6.6	12.1	18.7	23.9	38.7	22.9
86 Argentina	1970	4.4	9.7	14.1	21.5	50.3	35.2
87 South Africa		..	..	..	..	..	..
88 Algeria		..	..	..	..	..	..
89 Venezuela	1970	3.0	7.3	12.9	22.8	54.0	35.7
90 Greece		..	..	..	..	..	..
91 Israel	1979–80	6.0	12.0	17.7	24.4	39.9	22.6
92 Hong Kong	1980	5.4	10.8	15.2	21.6	47.0	31.3
93 Trinidad and Tobago	1975–76	4.2	9.1	13.9	22.8	50.0	31.8
94 Singapore		..	..	..	..	..	..
95 *Iran, Islamic Rep.*		..	..	..	..	..	..
96 *Iraq*		..	..	..	..	..	..
High-income oil exporters							
97 Oman		..	..	..	..	..	..
98 Libya		..	..	..	..	..	..
99 Saudi Arabia		..	..	..	..	..	..
100 Kuwait		..	..	..	..	..	..
101 United Arab Emirates		..	..	..	..	..	..
Industrial market economies							
102 Spain	1980–81	6.9	12.5	17.3	23.2	40.0	24.5
103 Ireland	1973	7.2	13.1	16.6	23.7	39.4	25.1
104 Italy	1977	6.2	11.3	15.9	22.7	43.9	28.1
105 New Zealand	1981–82	5.1	10.8	16.2	23.2	44.7	28.7
106 United Kingdom	1979	7.0	11.5	17.0	24.8	39.7	23.4
107 Belgium	1978–79	7.9	13.7	18.6	23.8	36.0	21.5
108 Austria		..	..	..	..	..	..
109 Netherlands	1981	8.3	14.1	18.2	23.2	36.2	21.5
110 France	1975	5.3	11.1	16.0	21.8	45.8	30.5
111 Japan	1979	8.7	13.2	17.5	23.1	37.5	22.4
112 Finland	1981	6.3	12.1	18.4	25.5	37.6	21.7
113 Germany, Fed. Rep.	1978	7.9	12.5	17.0	23.1	39.5	24.0
114 Denmark	1981	5.4	12.0	18.4	25.6	38.6	22.3
115 Australia	1975–76	5.4	10.0	15.0	22.5	47.1	30.5
116 Sweden	1981	7.4	13.1	16.8	21.0	41.7	28.1
117 Canada	1981	5.3	11.8	18.0	24.9	40.0	23.8
118 Norway	1982	6.0	12.9	18.3	24.6	38.2	22.8
119 United States	1980	5.3	11.9	17.9	25.0	39.9	23.3
120 Switzerland	1978	6.6	13.5	18.5	23.4	38.0	23.7
East European nonmarket economies							
121 Hungary	1982	6.9	13.6	19.2	24.5	35.8	20.5
122 Poland		..	..	..	..	..	..
123 *Albania*		..	..	..	..	..	..
124 *Bulgaria*		..	..	..	..	..	..
125 *Czechoslovakia*		..	..	..	..	..	..
126 *German Dem. Rep.*		..	..	..	..	..	..
127 *Romania*		..	..	..	..	..	..
128 *USSR*		..	..	..	..	..	..

a. These estimates should be treated with caution. See the technical notes.

Table 25. Population growth and projections

	Average annual growth of population (percent)			Population (millions)			Hypothetical size of stationary population (millions)	Assumed year of reaching net reproduction rate of 1	Population momentum 1985
	1965–73	1973–84	1980–2000	1984	1990ᵃ	2000ᵃ			
Low-income economies	2.6 w	2.0 w	1.8 w	2,364 t	2,641 t	3,132 t			
China and India	2.5 w	1.8 w	1.5 w	1,778 t	1,952 t	2,240 t			
Other low-income	2.7 w	2.6 w	2.6 w	586 t	689 t	892 t			
Sub-Saharan Africa	2.7 w	2.9 w	3.1 w	258 t	308 t	416 t			
1 Ethiopia	2.6	2.8	2.7	42	49	65	204	2040	1.9
2 Bangladesh	2.6	2.5	2.4	98	114	141	310	2030	1.9
3 Mali	2.6	2.6	2.6	7	9	11	36	2035	1.8
4 Zaire	2.4	3.0	3.2	30	36	47	130	2030	1.9
5 Burkina Faso	2.0	1.8	2.0	7	7	9	31	2040	1.8
6 Nepal	2.0	2.6	2.6	16	19	24	74	2040	1.8
7 Burma	2.3	2.0	2.1	36	41	49	87	2020	1.8
8 Malawi	2.8	3.1	3.2	7	8	11	38	2040	1.9
9 Niger	2.3	3.0	3.2	6	7	10	36	2040	1.9
10 Tanzania	3.2	3.4	3.5	21	27	37	123	2035	2.0
11 Burundi	1.4	2.2	3.0	5	5	7	24	2035	1.9
12 Uganda	3.6	3.2	3.3	15	18	26	84	2035	2.0
13 Togo	3.8	2.8	3.3	3	4	5	16	2035	2.0
14 Central African Rep.	1.6	2.3	2.8	3	3	4	12	2035	1.8
15 India	2.3	2.3	1.9	749	844	994	1,700	2010	1.7
16 Madagascar	2.4	2.8	3.1	10	12	16	48	2035	1.9
17 Somalia	3.5	2.8	3.0	5	6	8	30	2040	1.9
18 Benin	2.6	2.8	3.2	4	5	6	20	2035	2.0
19 Rwanda	3.1	3.3	3.6	6	7	10	40	2040	2.0
20 China	2.7	1.4	1.2	1,029	1,108	1,245	1,600	2000	1.6
21 Kenya	3.8	4.0	3.9	20	25	35	111	2030	2.1
22 Sierra Leone	1.7	2.1	2.4	4	4	5	17	2045	1.8
23 Haiti	1.5	1.7	1.8	5	6	7	14	2025	1.8
24 Guinea	1.8	2.0	2.1	6	7	8	24	2045	1.8
25 Ghana	2.2	2.6	3.5	12	15	20	54	2030	1.9
26 Sri Lanka	2.0	1.8	1.8	16	18	21	32	2005	1.7
27 Sudan	3.0	2.9	2.9	21	25	34	101	2035	1.9
28 Pakistan	3.1	2.9	2.6	92	108	138	353	2035	1.8
29 Senegal	2.4	2.8	2.9	6	8	10	30	2035	1.9
30 *Afghanistan*	2.3	..	..	..	..	..	..	..	..
31 *Bhutan*	1.3	1.9	2.3	1	1	2	4	2040	1.8
32 *Chad*	1.9	2.1	2.5	5	6	7	22	2040	1.8
33 *Kampuchea, Dem.*	1.8	..	..	..	..	..	..	..	..
34 *Lao PDR*	1.4	1.6	2.6	4	4	5	17	2040	1.8
35 *Mozambique*	2.3	2.6	3.0	13	16	21	67	2035	1.9
36 *Viet Nam*	3.1	2.6	2.5	60	70	88	167	2015	1.9
Middle-income economies	2.5 w	2.4 w	2.1 w	1,188 t	1,365 t	1,676 t			
Oil exporters	2.6 w	2.7 w	2.4 w	556 t	651 t	826 t			
Oil importers	2.4 w	2.2 w	1.8 w	632 t	712 t	850 t			
Sub-Saharan Africa	2.6 w	3.0 w	3.3 w	148 t	182 t	249 t			
Lower middle-income	2.5 w	2.5 w	2.3 w	688 t	796 t	994 t			
37 Mauritania	2.3	2.1	2.7	2	2	3	8	2035	1.8
38 Liberia	2.8	3.3	3.2	2	3	4	11	2035	1.9
39 Zambia	3.0	3.2	3.4	6	8	11	35	2035	1.9
40 Lesotho	2.1	2.4	2.6	1	2	2	6	2030	1.8
41 Bolivia	2.4	2.6	2.5	6	7	9	22	2030	1.9
42 Indonesia	2.1	2.3	1.9	159	179	212	361	2010	1.8
43 Yemen Arab Rep.	2.6	2.8	2.8	8	9	12	39	2040	1.9
44 Yemen, PDR	2.1	2.3	2.5	2	2	3	7	2035	1.9
45 Cote d'Ivoire	4.6	4.5	3.7	10	13	17	46	2035	2.1
46 Philippines	2.9	2.7	2.2	53	62	76	137	2015	1.8
47 Morocco	2.7	2.4	2.4	21	25	31	66	2025	1.9
48 Honduras	2.9	3.5	3.0	4	5	7	15	2020	2.0
49 El Salvador	3.4	3.0	2.7	5	6	8	16	2015	1.9
50 Papua New Guinea	2.3	2.6	2.1	3	4	5	11	2030	1.8
51 Egypt, Arab Rep.	2.2	2.6	2.2	46	53	65	126	2020	1.8
52 Nigeria	2.5	2.8	3.4	96	118	163	528	2035	2.0
53 Zimbabwe	3.4	3.2	3.4	8	10	13	33	2025	2.0
54 Cameroon	2.4	3.1	3.3	10	12	17	51	2030	1.9
55 Nicaragua	3.2	3.0	2.9	3	4	5	12	2025	2.0
56 Thailand	2.9	2.2	1.7	50	56	66	101	2005	1.8
57 Botswana	3.3	4.4	3.4	1	1	2	5	2025	2.0
58 Dominican Rep.	2.9	2.4	2.2	6	7	9	15	2010	1.9
59 Peru	2.8	2.4	2.2	18	21	26	46	2015	1.8
60 Mauritius	2.0	1.4	1.5	1	1	1	2	2010	1.7
61 Congo, People's Rep.	2.6	3.1	3.7	2	2	3	9	2025	1.9
62 Ecuador	3.2	2.9	2.3	9	11	13	26	2015	1.9
63 Jamaica	1.5	1.2	1.2	2	2	3	4	2005	1.7
64 Guatemala	2.8	2.8	2.6	8	9	12	27	2020	1.9
65 Turkey	2.5	2.2	2.0	48	55	65	109	2010	1.7

Note: For data comparability and coverage, see the technical notes.

	Average annual growth of population (percent)			Population (millions)			Hypothetical size of stationary population (millions)	Assumed year of reaching net reproduction rate of 1	Population momentum 1985
	1965–73	1973–84	1980–2000	1984	1990[a]	2000[a]			
66 Costa Rica	3.0	2.9	2.1	3	3	3	5	2005	1.8
67 Paraguay	2.7	2.5	2.3	3	4	5	8	2010	1.9
68 Tunisia	2.0	2.4	2.3	7	8	10	18	2015	1.8
69 Colombia	2.6	2.0	1.8	28	31	37	59	2010	1.8
70 Jordan	3.0	2.8	4.0	3	4	6	17	2020	1.9
71 Syrian Arab Rep.	3.4	3.4	3.4	10	12	17	39	2020	1.9
72 Angola	2.1	3.1	2.7	9	10	13	43	2040	1.9
73 Cuba	1.8	0.7	1.0	10	10	11	14	2010	1.4
74 Korea, Dem. Rep.	2.8	2.6	2.1	20	23	28	46	2010	1.8
75 Lebanon	2.6	. .	. .	. .	. .	. .	. .		. .
76 Mongolia	3.1	2.8	2.5	2	2	3	6	2020	1.9
Upper middle-income	**2.4** w	**2.3** w	**1.9** w	**497** t	**566** t	**679** t			
77 Chile	1.9	1.7	1.4	12	13	14	20	2000	1.6
78 Brazil	2.5	2.3	2.0	133	150	179	293	2010	1.8
79 Portugal	−0.2	1.0	0.6	10	11	11	13	2010	1.3
80 Malaysia	2.6	2.4	2.1	15	17	21	33	2005	1.8
81 Panama	2.8	2.3	1.6	2	2	3	4	2000	1.7
82 Uruguay	0.6	0.5	0.7	3	3	3	4	2000	1.3
83 Mexico	3.3	2.9	2.3	77	89	110	196	2010	1.9
84 Korea, Rep. of	2.2	1.5	1.4	40	44	49	66	2000	1.6
85 Yugoslavia	0.9	0.8	0.6	23	24	25	29	2010	1.3
86 Argentina	1.5	1.6	1.3	30	33	37	53	2020	1.5
87 South Africa	2.3	2.4	2.5	32	36	45	94	2025	1.8
88 Algeria	3.0	3.1	3.3	21	26	34	81	2025	1.9
89 Venezuela	3.5	3.3	2.6	17	20	24	39	2005	1.8
90 Greece	0.5	1.0	0.4	10	10	11	12	2000	1.2
91 Israel	3.1	2.2	1.7	4	5	5	8	2005	1.6
92 Hong Kong	2.0	2.4	1.2	5	6	6	7	2010	1.4
93 Trinidad and Tobago	1.3	1.5	1.6	1	1	1	2	2005	1.7
94 Singapore	1.8	1.3	1.0	3	3	3	3	2010	1.4
95 Iran, Islamic Rep.	3.3	3.1	3.1	44	53	71	162	2020	1.9
96 Iraq	3.3	3.6	3.5	15	19	26	71	2025	1.9
High-income oil exporters	**4.5** w	**5.1** w	**3.7** w	**19** t	**24** t	**33** t			
97 Oman	2.9	4.5	3.0	1	1	2	5	2030	1.9
98 Libya	4.1	4.1	4.0	3	4	6	17	2025	1.9
99 Saudi Arabia	4.0	4.9	3.7	11	14	20	61	2030	1.8
100 Kuwait	8.3	5.8	3.5	2	2	3	5	2010	1.8
101 United Arab Emirates	11.8	10.7	3.8	1	2	2	3	2010	1.4
Industrial market economies	**1.0** w	**0.7** w	**0.5** w	**733** t	**755** t	**789** t			
102 Spain	1.0	1.0	0.7	39	40	43	49	2010	1.3
103 Ireland	0.8	1.3	1.0	4	4	4	6	2005	1.4
104 Italy	0.6	0.3	0.2	57	57	59	57	2010	1.1
105 New Zealand	1.4	0.6	0.7	3	3	4	4	2000	1.3
106 United Kingdom	0.4	(.)	0.1	56	57	58	59	2010	1.1
107 Belgium	0.4	0.1	0.1	10	10	10	9	2010	1.1
108 Austria	0.4	0.0	0.1	8	8	8	7	2010	1.1
109 Netherlands	1.1	0.7	0.4	14	15	15	15	2010	1.2
110 France	0.8	0.5	0.5	55	57	59	64	2010	1.2
111 Japan	1.2	0.9	0.5	120	123	129	129	2010	1.1
112 Finland	0.2	0.4	0.3	5	5	5	5	2010	1.1
113 Germany, Fed. Rep.	0.7	−0.1	−0.1	61	61	60	52	2010	1.0
114 Denmark	0.7	0.2	0.0	5	5	5	5	2010	1.1
115 Australia	2.1	1.3	1.1	16	17	18	22	2010	1.4
116 Sweden	0.7	0.2	0.0	8	8	8	8	2010	1.1
117 Canada	1.4	1.2	0.9	25	27	29	31	2010	1.3
118 Norway	0.8	0.4	0.2	4	4	4	4	2010	1.1
119 United States	1.1	1.0	0.7	237	248	263	288	2010	1.3
120 Switzerland	1.2	0.1	0.1	6	6	7	6	2010	1.1
East European nonmarket economies	**0.8** w	**0.8** w	**0.6** w	**389** t	**406** t	**430** t			
121 Hungary	0.3	0.2	−0.1	11	11	11	11	2010	1.0
122 Poland	0.7	0.9	0.7	37	39	41	49	2000	1.3
123 Albania	2.6	2.0	1.8	3	3	4	6	2005	1.7
124 Bulgaria	0.6	0.3	0.2	9	9	9	10	2010	1.1
125 Czechoslovakia	0.3	0.5	0.3	15	16	16	19	2010	1.2
126 German Dem. Rep.	0.0	−0.1	0.0	17	17	17	17	2010	1.1
127 Romania	1.2	0.8	0.6	23	24	25	29	2000	1.3
128 USSR	0.9	0.9	0.7	275	289	307	375	2005	1.3
Total[b]									

a. For the assumptions used in the projections, see the technical notes.   b. Excludes countries with populations of less than 1 million.

Table 26. Demography and fertility

	Crude birth rate per thousand population		Crude death rate per thousand population		Percentage change in:		Total fertility rate		Percentage of married women of childbearing age using contraception[a]	
					Crude birth rate 1965–84	Crude death rate 1965–84				
	1965	1984	1965	1984			1984	2000	1970[b]	1983[b]
Low-income economies	43 *w*	29 *w*	17 *w*	11 *w*	−31.2 *w*	−39.3 *w*	3.9 *w*	3.0 *w*		
China and India	42 *w*	25 *w*	16 *w*	9 *w*	−40.0 *w*	44.7 *w*	3.2 *w*	2.5 *w*		
Other low-income	46 *w*	42 *w*	21 *w*	16 *w*	−8.7 *w*	−25.9 *w*	5.9 *w*	4.3 *w*		
Sub-Saharan Africa	47 *w*	47 *w*	23 *w*	18 *w*	−0.9 *w*	−19.7 *w*	6.6 *w*	5.5 *w*		
1 Ethiopia	44	41	19	24	−5.7	26.3	6.1	5.5	. .	2
2 Bangladesh	47	41	22	15	−14.0	−28.8	5.7	3.7	. .	25
3 Mali	50	48	27	20	−5.3	−26.7	6.5	5.9	. .	1
4 Zaire	48	45	21	15	−5.8	−28.3	6.1	4.9	. .	3
5 Burkina Faso	46	47	24	21	2.2	−14.6	6.5	6.0	. .	1
6 Nepal	46	43	24	18	−5.6	−25.4	6.3	5.3	. .	7
7 Burma	40	30	19	11	−24.2	−43.6	4.0	3.0	. .	5
8 Malawi	56	54	27	22	−4.3	−17.0	7.6	6.4	. .	1
9 Niger	48	51	29	22	6.1	−26.0	7.0	6.4	. .	1
10 Tanzania	49	50	22	16	2.6	−30.0	7.0	5.7	. .	1
11 Burundi	47	47	24	19	−0.4	−24.0	6.5	5.9	. .	1
12 Uganda	49	50	19	16	2.1	−18.6	6.9	5.7	. .	1
13 Togo	50	49	23	16	−2.0	−30.5	6.5	5.4	. .	. .
14 Central African Rep.	42	34	24	17	−23.8	−32.0	5.6	5.4	. .	. .
15 India	45	33	21	12	−27.1	−41.4	4.6	2.9	12	35
16 Madagascar	44	47	21	15	6.6	−29.2	6.5	5.0	. .	1
17 Somalia	50	49	26	20	−1.4	−23.7	6.8	6.2	. .	1
18 Benin	49	49	25	17	0.6	−29.3	6.5	5.4	. .	18
19 Rwanda	52	52	17	19	0.8	8.4	8.0	6.7	. .	1
20 China	39	19	13	7	−51.3	−50.4	2.3	2.1	. .	71
21 Kenya	51	53	21	13	4.3	−37.4	7.9	5.6	6	17
22 Sierra Leone	48	49	33	26	1.0	−20.3	6.5	6.0	. .	4
23 Haiti	38	32	18	12	−15.2	−31.3	4.5	3.3	. .	7
24 Guinea	46	47	30	26	1.3	−12.0	6.0	5.6	. .	1
25 Ghana	49	46	20	14	−3.1	−29.5	6.4	4.7	. .	10
26 Sri Lanka	33	26	8	6	−21.1	−25.6	3.2	2.3	6	55
27 Sudan	47	45	24	17	−3.6	−28.0	6.6	5.5	. .	5
28 Pakistan	48	42	21	15	−12.5	−28.9	6.0	4.4	6	11
29 Senegal	47	46	23	19	−2.0	−17.9	6.6	5.5	. .	4
30 *Afghanistan*	54	. .	29	. .	. .	. .	. .	. .	2	. .
31 *Bhutan*	43	43	32	21	−0.7	−34.6	6.2	5.2	. .	. .
32 *Chad*	40	43	26	21	6.7	−19.6	5.6	5.5	. .	1
33 *Kampuchea, Dem.*	44	. .	20	. .	. .	. .	. .	. .	. .	. .
34 *Lao PDR*	44	42	23	19	−6.6	−15.9	6.4	5.4	. .	. .
35 *Mozambique*	49	45	27	18	−7.8	−32.2	6.3	5.7	. .	1
36 *Viet Nam*	45	35	17	8	−22.2	−55.3	4.7	3.0	. .	21
Middle-income economies	42 *w*	33 *w*	15 *w*	10 *w*	−19.5 *w*	−35.3 *w*	4.4 *w*	3.3 *w*		
Oil exporters	46 *w*	38 *w*	18 *w*	11 *w*	−16.9 *w*	−38.8 *w*	5.1 *w*	3.8 *w*		
Oil importers	38 *w*	29 *w*	13 *w*	9 *w*	−22.8 *w*	−32.5 *w*	3.8 *w*	2.9 *w*		
Sub-Saharan Africa	50 *w*	48 *w*	22 *w*	16 *w*	−2.8 *w*	−28.7 *w*	6.7 *w*	5.5 *w*		
Lower middle-income	45 *w*	36 *w*	18 *w*	11 *w*	−19.1 *w*	−36.7 *w*	4.8 *w*	3.6 *w*		
37 Mauritania	44	45	25	19	1.5	−25.1	6.2	5.9	. .	1
38 Liberia	46	49	22	17	6.1	−25.2	6.9	5.7	. .	. .
39 Zambia	49	48	20	15	−2.1	−26.3	6.8	5.6	. .	. .
40 Lesotho	42	41	18	14	−4.5	−19.7	5.8	4.7	. .	5
41 Bolivia	46	43	21	15	−7.1	−29.4	6.0	4.1	. .	24
42 Indonesia	43	33	20	12	−23.7	−39.2	4.2	2.8	. .	50
43 Yemen Arab Rep.	49	48	27	21	−3.0	−23.6	6.8	5.7	. .	1
44 Yemen, PDR	50	46	27	18	−6.9	−32.3	6.1	4.4	. .	. .
45 Cote d'Ivoire	44	45	22	14	2.4	−37.3	6.5	4.8	. .	. .
46 Philippines	42	33	12	8	−21.0	−35.3	4.4	3.0	2	48
47 Morocco	49	36	19	11	−26.8	−41.1	4.9	3.5	1	26
48 Honduras	50	43	17	10	−15.8	−43.5	6.2	3.8	. .	27
49 El Salvador	46	39	14	7	−16.6	−50.2	5.3	3.2	. .	34
50 Papua New Guinea	43	38	20	13	−12.9	−35.1	5.4	3.9	. .	5
51 Egypt, Arab Rep.	44	36	19	10	−17.2	−45.6	4.8	3.3	10	30
52 Nigeria	51	50	23	16	−3.4	−28.1	6.9	5.7	. .	5
53 Zimbabwe	55	47	17	12	−14.2	−31.0	6.3	4.0	. .	27
54 Cameroon	40	47	20	14	18.5	−28.5	6.7	5.6	. .	3
55 Nicaragua	49	43	16	10	−13.3	−38.4	5.7	3.8	. .	9
56 Thailand	43	26	12	8	−38.8	−38.7	3.3	2.3	15	63
57 Botswana	53	46	19	12	−13.3	−36.3	6.7	4.7	. .	. .
58 Dominican Rep.	47	33	14	7	−29.6	−48.1	4.0	2.7	. .	32
59 Peru	45	33	17	10	−26.1	−37.3	4.3	3.0	. .	41
60 Mauritius	37	21	8	7	−43.5	−21.9	2.7	2.3	. .	51
61 Congo, People's Rep.	41	45	18	12	9.3	−31.4	6.2	5.6	. .	. .
62 Ecuador	45	36	15	7	−21.4	−50.5	4.8	3.1	. .	40
63 Jamaica	38	28	9	6	−28.5	−33.3	3.3	2.3	. .	51
64 Guatemala	46	41	16	10	−10.8	−40.6	5.8	3.6	. .	25
65 Turkey	41	30	14	9	−26.6	−41.0	3.9	2.6	32	38

Note: For data comparability and coverage, see the technical notes.

	Crude birth rate per thousand population		Crude death rate per thousand population		Percentage change in:		Total fertility rate		Percentage of married women of childbearing age using contraception[a]	
					Crude birth rate 1965–84	Crude death rate 1965–84				
	1965	1984	1965	1984			1984	2000	1970[b]	1983[b]
66 Costa Rica	45	29	8	4	−35.9	−47.4	3.3	2.3	..	65
67 Paraguay	41	31	11	7	−25.9	−38.0	4.0	2.6	..	35
68 Tunisia	44	32	18	9	−27.1	−48.4	4.6	3.0	10	41
69 Colombia	45	28	15	7	−39.0	−50.5	3.4	2.5	34	55
70 Jordan	48	46	18	8	−4.8	−56.0	7.4	5.2	22	26
71 Syrian Arab Rep.	48	45	16	8	−5.9	−49.2	6.8	4.0	..	23
72 Angola	49	47	29	22	−3.8	−25.9	6.4	5.9	..	..
73 Cuba	34	17	8	6	−50.9	−25.0	2.0	2.0	..	79
74 Korea, Dem. Rep.	39	30	12	6	−23.9	−49.6	3.8	2.6	..	..
75 Lebanon	41	..	13	..	..	..	..	..	53	..
76 Mongolia	42	35	12	8	−15.5	−35.0	4.9	3.3	..	..
Upper middle-income	**37** w	**30** w	**12** w	**8** w	**−20.5** w	**−32.5** w	**4.0** w	**2.9** w		
77 Chile	32	21	11	6	−34.4	−41.7	2.5	2.1	..	43
78 Brazil	39	30	11	8	−24.6	−30.6	3.6	2.6	..	50
79 Portugal	23	14	10	10	−37.4	−7.7	2.0	2.0	..	66
80 Malaysia	41	30	12	6	−26.1	−46.8	3.7	2.4	33	42
81 Panama	40	27	9	5	−33.5	−40.9	3.3	2.1	..	61
82 Uruguay	21	18	10	9	−15.5	−3.0	2.5	2.1	..	..
83 Mexico	45	33	11	7	−25.5	−38.8	4.4	2.7	..	48
84 Korea, Rep. of	36	20	11	6	−43.8	−46.7	2.5	2.1	25	58
85 Yugoslavia	21	16	9	9	−21.9	5.7	2.1	2.1	59	55
86 Argentina	22	24	9	9	8.8	0.0	3.3	2.5	..	..
87 South Africa	41	38	19	13	−9.2	−31.1	4.9	3.5	..	..
88 Algeria	50	42	18	11	−16.6	−42.9	6.4	4.1	..	7
89 Venezuela	43	32	9	5	−26.8	−43.5	3.9	2.4	..	49
90 Greece	18	13	8	9	−27.7	12.7	2.1	2.1	..	..
91 Israel	26	23	6	7	−12.7	7.9	3.0	2.2	..	..
92 Hong Kong	28	14	6	5	−49.1	−17.2	1.8	2.0	42	80
93 Trinidad and Tobago	33	26	7	7	−21.2	−2.8	2.8	2.2	44	52
94 Singapore	31	17	6	6	−43.6	0.0	1.7	1.9	60	71
95 Iran, Islamic Rep.	50	41	17	9	−19.2	−45.3	5.6	4.2	3	23
96 Iraq	49	45	18	10	−8.7	−42.3	6.7	5.1	14	..
High-income oil exporters	**49** w	**42** w	**19** w	**8** w	**−14.2** w	**−56.0** w	**6.9** w	**5.1** w		
97 Oman	50	45	24	14	−11.0	−43.0	6.8	4.5	..	..
98 Libya	49	46	18	11	−7.4	−40.2	7.2	5.4	..	..
99 Saudi Arabia	49	43	20	9	−12.4	−58.0	7.1	5.6	..	..
100 Kuwait	47	35	8	3	−25.2	−56.9	5.4	2.9	..	..
101 United Arab Emirates	41	30	15	3	−26.5	−79.1	5.9	3.6	..	..
Industrial market economies	**19** w	**14** w	**10** w	**9** w	**−28.6** w	**−7.3** w	**1.8** w	**2.0** w		
102 Spain	21	13	8	7	−36.5	−11.9	2.1	2.1	..	51
103 Ireland	22	19	12	9	−14.0	−19.1	2.7	2.2	..	..
104 Italy	19	10	10	9	−46.1	−7.0	1.6	1.9	..	78
105 New Zealand	23	18	9	8	−21.8	−6.9	2.2	2.1	..	..
106 United Kingdom	18	13	12	12	−28.8	0.0	1.8	2.0	69	77
107 Belgium	17	12	12	11	−29.1	−9.0	1.6	1.9	..	85
108 Austria	18	12	13	12	−34.6	−10.8	1.6	1.9	..	..
109 Netherlands	20	12	8	8	−39.2	3.8	1.5	1.8	..	75
110 France	18	14	11	10	−22.5	−12.5	1.9	2.0	64	79
111 Japan	19	13	7	7	−32.6	−2.8	1.8	2.0	56	56
112 Finland	17	13	10	9	−21.6	−5.2	1.7	1.9	77	80
113 Germany, Fed. Rep.	18	10	12	11	−46.3	−1.7	1.4	1.8	..	..
114 Denmark	18	10	10	11	−43.9	10.9	1.4	1.8	67	63
115 Australia	20	16	9	7	−20.9	−19.3	2.0	2.0	..	..
116 Sweden	16	11	10	11	−28.9	7.9	1.6	1.9	..	78
117 Canada	21	15	8	7	−29.6	−7.9	1.7	1.9	..	..
118 Norway	16	12	10	10	−25.5	7.4	1.7	1.9	..	71
119 United States	19	16	9	9	−19.1	−7.4	1.8	2.0	65	76
120 Switzerland	19	12	10	9	−39.8	−4.2	1.5	1.9	..	70
East European nonmarket economies	**18** w	**19** w	**8** w	**11** w	**−5.7** w	**32.9** w	**2.3** w	**2.1** w		
121 Hungary	13	12	11	14	−10.7	29.2	1.7	1.9	67	74
122 Poland	17	19	7	10	9.2	29.7	2.3	2.1	60	75
123 Albania	35	26	9	6	−31.6	−27.1	3.4	2.3	..	..
124 Bulgaria	15	14	8	11	−10.5	37.8	2.0	2.1	..	76
125 Czechoslovakia	16	15	10	12	−10.4	18.0	2.0	2.1	..	95
126 German Dem. Rep.	17	14	14	13	−17.0	−1.5	1.8	2.0	..	..
127 Romania	15	14	9	10	−4.7	20.9	2.2	2.1	..	58
128 USSR	18	20	7	11	8.9	47.9	2.3	2.1	..	..

a. Figures include women whose husbands practice contraception; see the technical notes.   b. Figures in italics are for years or periods other than those specified; see the technical notes.

231

Table 27. Life expectancy and related indicators

		Life expectancy at birth (years)				Infant mortality rate (aged under 1)		Child death rate (aged 1–4)	
		Male		Female					
		1965	1984	1965	1984	1965	1984	1965	1984
	Low-income economies	49 *w*	60 *w*	51 *w*	61 *w*	125 *w*	72 *w*	19 *w*	9 *w*
	China and India	51 *w*	63 *w*	53 *w*	64 *w*	115 *w*	59 *w*	16 *w*	6 *w*
	Other low-income	44 *w*	50 *w*	45 *w*	52 *w*	147 *w*	114 *w*	27 *w*	18 *w*
	Sub-Saharan Africa	41 *w*	47 *w*	43 *w*	50 *w*	155 *w*	129 *w*	36 *w*	26 *w*
1	Ethiopia	42	43	43	46	166	172	37	39
2	Bangladesh	45	50	44	51	153	124	24	18
3	Mali	37	44	39	48	207	176	47	44
4	Zaire	42	49	45	53	142	103	30	20
5	Burkina Faso	40	44	42	46	195	146	52	30
6	Nepal	40	47	39	46	184	135	30	20
7	Burma	46	57	49	60	125	67	21	7
8	Malawi	38	44	40	46	201	158	55	36
9	Niger	35	42	38	45	181	142	46	29
10	Tanzania	41	50	44	53	138	111	29	22
11	Burundi	42	46	45	49	143	120	38	24
12	Uganda	43	49	47	53	122	110	26	21
13	Togo	40	50	43	53	156	98	36	12
14	Central African Rep.	40	47	41	50	169	138	47	27
15	India	46	56	44	55	151	90	23	11
16	Madagascar	41	51	44	54	. .	110	. .	22
17	Somalia	36	44	40	47	166	153	37	33
18	Benin	41	47	43	51	168	116	52	19
19	Rwanda	47	46	51	49	141	128	35	26
20	China	55	68	59	70	90	36	11	2
21	Kenya	43	52	46	56	113	92	25	16
22	Sierra Leone	32	38	33	39	221	176	69	44
23	Haiti	46	53	47	57	138	124	37	22
24	Guinea	34	38	36	39	197	176	53	44
25	Ghana	45	51	49	55	123	95	25	11
26	Sri Lanka	63	68	64	72	63	37	6	2
27	Sudan	39	46	41	50	161	113	37	18
28	Pakistan	46	52	44	50	150	116	23	16
29	Senegal	40	45	42	48	172	138	42	27
30	*Afghanistan*	34	. .	35	. .	223	. .	39	. .
31	*Bhutan*	34	44	32	43	184	135	30	20
32	*Chad*	39	43	41	45	184	139	47	27
33	*Kampuchea, Dem.*	43	. .	45	. .	135	. .	19	. .
34	*Lao PDR*	39	43	42	46	196	153	34	24
35	*Mozambique*	36	45	39	48	172	125	31	22
36	*Viet Nam*	47	63	50	67	89	50	8	4
	Middle-income economies	51 *w*	59 *w*	54 *w*	63 *w*	115 *w*	72 *w*	18 *w*	8 *w*
	Oil exporters	47 *w*	56 *w*	50 *w*	60 *w*	138 *w*	89 *w*	22 *w*	12 *w*
	Oil importers	55 *w*	62 *w*	58 *w*	67 *w*	97 *w*	57 *w*	15 *w*	5 *w*
	Sub-Saharan Africa	41 *w*	49 *w*	44 *w*	52 *w*	168 *w*	107 *w*	33 *w*	19 *w*
	Lower middle-income	47 *w*	56 *w*	50 *w*	60 *w*	133 *w*	83 *w*	22 *w*	11 *w*
37	Mauritania	39	45	42	48	171	133	41	25
38	Liberia	40	48	44	52	172	128	32	23
39	Zambia	42	50	46	53	123	85	29	15
40	Lesotho	47	52	50	56	143	107	20	14
41	Bolivia	42	51	46	54	161	118	37	20
42	Indonesia	43	53	45	56	138	97	20	12
43	Yemen Arab Rep.	37	44	38	46	200	155	55	35
44	Yemen, PDR	37	46	39	48	194	146	52	31
45	Cote d'Ivoire	43	51	45	54	176	106	37	15
46	Philippines	54	61	57	65	73	49	11	4
47	Morocco	48	57	51	61	147	91	32	10
48	Honduras	48	59	51	63	131	77	24	7
49	El Salvador	52	63	56	68	120	66	20	5
50	Papua New Guinea	44	51	44	54	143	69	23	7
51	Egypt, Arab Rep	47	59	50	62	173	94	21	11
52	Nigeria	40	48	43	51	179	110	33	21
53	Zimbabwe	46	55	49	59	104	77	15	7
54	Cameroon	44	53	47	56	145	92	34	10
55	Nicaragua	49	58	51	62	123	70	24	6
56	Thailand	53	62	58	66	90	44	11	3
57	Botswana	46	55	49	61	108	72	21	11
58	Dominican Rep.	52	62	56	66	111	71	14	6
59	Peru	49	58	52	61	131	95	24	11
60	Mauritius	59	62	63	69	64	26	9	1
61	Congo, People's Rep.	48	55	51	59	121	78	19	7
62	Ecuador	54	63	57	67	113	67	22	5
63	Jamaica	63	71	67	76	51	20	4	1
64	Guatemala	48	58	50	62	114	66	16	5
65	Turkey	52	61	55	66	157	86	35	9

Note: For data comparability and coverage, see the technical notes.

	Life expectancy at birth (years)				Infant mortality rate (aged under 1)		Child death rate (aged 1–4)	
	Male		Female					
	1965	1984	1965	1984	1965	1984	1965	1984
66 Costa Rica	63	71	66	76	72	19	8	(.)
67 Paraguay	56	64	60	68	74	44	7	2
68 Tunisia	50	60	51	64	147	79	30	8
69 Colombia	53	63	59	67	99	48	8	3
70 Jordan	49	62	51	66	117	50	19	3
71 Syrian Arab Rep.	51	62	54	65	116	55	19	4
72 Angola	34	42	37	44	193	144	52	30
73 Cuba	65	73	69	77	38	16	4	(.)
74 Korea, Dem. Rep.	55	65	58	72	64	28	6	2
75 Lebanon	60	..	64	..	57	..	4	..
76 Mongolia	55	61	58	65	89	50	11	4
Upper middle-income	**56** w	**63** w	**60** w	**68** w	**91** w	**56** w	**13** w	**5** w
77 Chile	56	67	62	73	110	22	14	1
78 Brazil	55	62	59	67	104	68	14	6
79 Portugal	61	71	68	77	69	19	6	1
80 Malaysia	56	66	59	71	57	28	5	2
81 Panama	62	70	64	73	59	25	4	1
82 Uruguay	65	71	72	75	47	29	3	1
83 Mexico	58	64	61	69	84	51	9	3
84 Korea, Rep. of	55	65	58	72	64	28	6	2
85 Yugoslavia	64	66	68	73	72	28	7	2
86 Argentina	63	67	69	74	59	34	4	1
87 South Africa	45	52	48	56	124	79	22	7
88 Algeria	49	59	51	62	155	82	34	8
89 Venezuela	60	66	64	73	67	38	6	2
90 Greece	69	72	72	78	37	16	2	1
91 Israel	70	73	73	77	29	14	2	(.)
92 Hong Kong	64	73	71	79	28	10	2	(.)
93 Trinidad and Tobago	63	67	67	72	43	22	3	1
94 Singapore	63	70	68	75	28	10	1	(.)
95 Iran, Islamic Rep.	52	61	52	61	150	112	32	17
96 Iraq	50	58	53	62	121	74	21	7
High-income oil exporters	**47** w	**61** w	**50** w	**64** w	**141** w	**65** w	**34** w	**6** w
97 Oman	40	52	42	55	175	110	43	17
98 Libya	48	57	51	61	140	91	29	10
99 Saudi Arabia	47	60	49	64	148	61	38	4
100 Kuwait	61	69	64	74	43	22	5	1
101 United Arab Emirates	57	70	61	74	104	36	14	1
Industrial market economies	**68** w	**73** w	**74** w	**79** w	**24** w	**9** w	**1** w	**(.)** w
102 Spain	68	74	73	80	38	10	3	(.)
103 Ireland	69	71	73	76	27	10	1	(.)
104 Italy	68	74	73	79	38	12	3	(.)
105 New Zealand	68	71	74	77	20	12	1	(.)
106 United Kingdom	68	72	74	78	20	10	1	(.)
107 Belgium	68	72	74	78	24	11	1	(.)
108 Austria	66	70	73	77	30	11	2	(.)
109 Netherlands	71	73	76	80	14	8	1	(.)
110 France	68	74	75	80	22	9	1	(.)
111 Japan	68	75	73	80	21	6	1	(.)
112 Finland	66	72	73	79	17	6	1	(.)
113 Germany, Fed. Rep.	67	72	73	78	26	10	1	(.)
114 Denmark	71	72	75	78	19	8	1	(.)
115 Australia	68	73	74	79	19	9	1	(.)
116 Sweden	72	74	76	80	13	7	1	(.)
117 Canada	69	72	75	80	24	9	1	(.)
118 Norway	71	74	76	80	17	8	1	(.)
119 United States	67	72	74	80	25	11	1	(.)
120 Switzerland	69	73	75	80	18	8	1	(.)
East European nonmarket economies	**66** w	**66** w	**73** w	**71** w	**31** w	**19** w	**2** w	**(.)** w
121 Hungary	67	67	72	74	42	19	3	1
122 Poland	66	67	72	76	46	19	3	1
123 Albania	64	67	67	73	87	43	10	3
124 Bulgaria	66	68	72	74	35	17	2	1
125 Czechoslovakia	64	66	73	74	23	15	1	1
126 German Dem. Rep.	67	68	73	75	27	11	1	(.)
127 Romania	66	69	70	74	53	25	1	1
128 USSR	65	65	74	74	30	..	2	..

Table 28. Health-related indicators

	Population per:				Daily calorie supply per capita	
	Physician		Nursing person		Total 1983	As percentage of requirement 1983
	1965[a]	1981[a]	1965[a]	1981[a]		
Low-income economies	8,357 _w_	5,375 _w_	5,037 _w_	3,920 _w_	2,336 _w_	102 _w_
China and India	4,218 _w_	2,096 _w_	4,443 _w_	2,917 _w_	2,415 _w_	105 _w_
Other low-income	26,631 _w_	17,234 _w_	7,951 _w_	7,546 _w_	2,275 _w_	102 _w_
Sub-Saharan Africa	38,649 _w_	42,670 _w_	5,714 _w_	3,022 _w_	2,084 _w_	90 _w_
1 Ethiopia	70,190	88,120	5,970	5,000	2,162	93
2 Bangladesh	..	9,010	..	19,400	1,864	81
3 Mali	49,010	25,380	3,200	2,320	1,597	68
4 Zaire	39,050	..	..	..	2,136	96
5 Burkina Faso	74,110	49,280	4,170	3,070	2,014	85
6 Nepal	46,180	30,060	..	33,430	2,047	93
7 Burma	11,660	4,660	11,410	4,890	2,534	117
8 Malawi	46,900	52,960	49,240	2,980	2,200	95
9 Niger	71,440	..	6,210	..	2,271	97
10 Tanzania	21,840	..	2,100	..	2,271	98
11 Burundi	54,930	..	7,310	..	2,378	102
12 Uganda	11,080	22,180	3,130	2,000	2,351	101
13 Togo	24,980	18,550	4,990	1,640	2,156	94
14 Central African Rep.	44,490	23,090	3,000	2,120	2,048	91
15 India	4,860	2,610	6,500	4,670	2,115	96
16 Madagascar	9,900	9,940	3,620	1,090	2,543	112
17 Somalia	35,060	15,630	3,630	2,550	2,063	89
18 Benin	28,790	16,980	2,540	1,660	1,907	83
19 Rwanda	74,170	29,150	7,450	10,260	2,276	98
20 China	3,780	1,730	3,040	1,670	2,620	111
21 Kenya	13,450	7,540	1,860	990	1,919	83
22 Sierra Leone	17,690	17,670	4,700	2,110	2,082	91
23 Haiti	12,580	..	12,870	..	1,887	83
24 Guinea	54,610	..	4,750	..	1,939	84
25 Ghana	12,040	6,760	3,710	630	1,516	66
26 Sri Lanka	5,750	7,620	3,210	1,260	2,348	106
27 Sudan	23,500	9,070	3,360	1,440	2,122	90
28 Pakistan	3,160	3,320	9,900	5,870	2,205	95
29 Senegal	21,130	13,060	2,640	1,990	2,436	102
30 _Afghanistan_	15,770	..	24,450	..	..	..
31 _Bhutan_	..	18,160	..	7,960	..	..
32 _Chad_	73,040	..	13,620	..	1,620	68
33 _Kampuchea, Dem._	22,500	..	3,670	..	..	..
34 _Lao PDR_	26,510	..	5,320	..	1,992	90
35 _Mozambique_	21,560	33,340	5,370	5,610	1,668	71
36 _Viet Nam_	..	4,310	..	1,040	2,017	93
Middle-income economies	11,192 _w_	4,764 _w_	3,526 _w_	1,474 _w_	2,611 _w_	110 _w_
Oil exporters	20,085 _w_	6,587 _w_	5,454 _w_	1,684 _w_	2,512 _w_	109 _w_
Oil importers	3,943 _w_	2,902 _w_	1,876 _w_	1,273 _w_	2,692 _w_	111 _w_
Sub-Saharan Africa	35,741 _w_	8,445 _w_	4,876 _w_	2,208 _w_	2,066 _w_	89 _w_
Lower middle-income	18,215 _w_	8,235 _w_	4,783 _w_	1,783 _w_	2,448 _w_	106 _w_
37 Mauritania	36,580	..	..	..	2,252	97
38 Liberia	12,450	8,550	2,300	2,940	2,367	102
39 Zambia	11,390	7,110	5,820	1,660	1,929	84
40 Lesotho	22,930	..	4,700	..	2,376	104
41 Bolivia	3,310	1,950	3,990	..	1,954	82
42 Indonesia	31,820	11,320	9,500	..	2,380	110
43 Yemen Arab Rep.	58,240	7,070	..	3,440	2,226	92
44 Yemen, PDR	12,870	7,120	1,850	820	2,254	94
45 Cote d'Ivoire	20,690	..	1,850	..	2,576	112
46 Philippines	1,310	2,150	1,130	2,590	2,357	104
47 Morocco	12,120	17,230	2,290	900	2,544	105
48 Honduras	5,450	1,540	1,540	..	2,135	94
49 El Salvador	4,630	3,220	1,300	..	2,060	90
50 Papua New Guinea	12,520	16,070	620	960	2,109	79
51 Egypt, Arab Rep.	2,260	800	2,030	790	3,163	126
52 Nigeria	44,990	10,540	5,780	2,420	2,022	86
53 Zimbabwe	5,190	6,650	990	1,000	1,956	82
54 Cameroon	29,720	..	1,970	..	2,031	88
55 Nicaragua	2,490	2,290	1,390	590	2,268	101
56 Thailand	7,230	6,770	5,020	2,140	2,330	105
57 Botswana	22,090	9,250	16,210	700	2,152	93
58 Dominican Rep.	1,720	1,390	1,640	1,240	2,368	105
59 Peru	1,620	..	880	..	1,997	85
60 Mauritius	3,850	1,730	1,990	570	2,675	118
61 Congo, People's Rep.	14,210	..	950	..	2,425	109
62 Ecuador	3,020	..	2,320	..	2,043	89
63 Jamaica	1,930	..	340	..	2,493	111
64 Guatemala	3,830	..	8,250	1,360	2,071	95
65 Turkey	2,860	1,500	2,290	1,240	3,100	123

Note: For data comparability and coverage, see the technical notes.

	Population per:				Daily calorie supply per capita	
	Physician		Nursing person		Total 1983	As percentage of requirement 1983
	1965[a]	1981[a]	1965[a]	1981[a]		
66 Costa Rica	2,040	..	630	..	2,556	114
67 Paraguay	1,840	1,310	1,550	650	2,811	122
68 Tunisia	8,040	3,620	1,150	950	2,889	121
69 Colombia	2,530	..	890	..	2,546	110
70 Jordan	4,670	1,170	1,810	1,170	2,882	117
71 Syrian Arab Rep.	4,050	2,160	11,760	1,370	3,156	127
72 Angola	12,000	..	3,820	..	2,041	87
73 Cuba	1,150	600	820	..	2,914	126
74 Korea, Dem. Rep.	..	..	..	..	2,968	127
75 Lebanon	1,240	..	2,500	..	..	..
76 Mongolia	710	440	310	240	2,841	117
Upper middle-income	**2,473** w	**1,374** w	**1,914** w	**975** w	**2,830** w	**116** w
77 Chile	2,080	950	600	..	2,574	105
78 Brazil	2,180	1,200	1,550	1,140	2,533	106
79 Portugal	1,170	450	1,160	..	3,046	124
80 Malaysia	6,220	3,920	1,320	1,390	2,477	111
81 Panama	2,170	1,010	680	..	2,275	98
82 Uruguay	870	510	590	..	2,647	99
83 Mexico	2,060	1,140	950	..	2,934	126
84 Korea, Rep. of	2,740	1,440	2,990	350	2,765	118
85 Yugoslavia	1,190	670	850	300	3,575	141
86 Argentina	640	..	610	..	3,159	119
87 South Africa	2,050	..	500	..	2,897	118
88 Algeria	8,400	..	11,770	..	2,750	115
89 Venezuela	1,270	930	560	..	2,451	99
90 Greece	710	390	600	370	3,601	144
91 Israel	410	400	300	130	3,110	121
92 Hong Kong	2,400	1,260	1,220	800	2,787	122
93 Trinidad and Tobago	3,820	1,390	560	390	3,120	129
94 Singapore	1,910	1,100	600	340	2,636	115
95 Iran, Islamic Rep.	3,770	2,630	4,170	1,160	2,855	118
96 Iraq	4,970	1,790	2,910	2,250	2,840	118
High-income oil exporters	**8,836** w	**1,408** w	**4,626** w	**573** w	**3,345** w	**..**
97 Oman	23,790	1,680	6,380	440	..	..
98 Libya	3,970	660	850	360	3,651	155
99 Saudi Arabia	9,400	1,800	6,060	730	3,244	134
100 Kuwait	830	600	270	180	3,369	..
101 United Arab Emirates	..	720	..	390	3,407	..
Industrial market economies	**867** w	**554** w	**425** w	**177** w	**3,352** w	**130** w
102 Spain	810	360	1,220	280	3,237	132
103 Ireland	960	780	170	120	3,579	143
104 Italy	1,850	750	790	250	3,521	140
105 New Zealand	820	590	980	110	3,493	132
106 United Kingdom	860	680	200	120	3,226	128
107 Belgium	700	380	590	130	3,705	140
108 Austria	720	580	350	170	3,479	132
109 Netherlands	860	480	270	..	3,477	129
110 France	890	460	..	110	3,514	139
111 Japan	970	740	410	210	2,653	113
112 Finland	1,290	460	180	100	3,077	114
113 Germany, Fed. Rep.	680	420	500	170	3,475	130
114 Denmark	740	420	190	140	3,525	131
115 Australia	720	500	110	100	3,068	115
116 Sweden	910	410	310	100	3,115	116
117 Canada	770	510	190	120	3,459	130
118 Norway	800	460	340	70	3,088	115
119 United States	640	500	310	180	3,623	137
120 Switzerland	750	390	270	130	3,472	129
East European nonmarket economies	**564** w	**329** w	**300** w	**199** w	**3,409** w	**132** w
121 Hungary	630	320	240	140	3,563	135
122 Poland	800	550	410	..	3,336	127
123 Albania	2,100	..	550	..	2,907	121
124 Bulgaria	600	400	410	190	3,675	147
125 Czechoslovakia	540	350	200	130	3,555	144
126 German Dem. Rep.	870	490	..	..	3,718	142
127 Romania	740	650	400	280	3,341	126
128 USSR	480	260	280	..	3,381	132

a. Figures in italics are for years other than those specified; see the technical notes.

Table 29. Education

	Number enrolled in primary school as percentage of age group						Number enrolled in secondary school as percentage of age group		Number enrolled in higher education as percentage of population aged 20–24	
	Total		Male		Female					
	1965[a]	1983[a]	1965	1983[a]	1965	1983[a]	1965[a]	1983[a]	1965[a]	1983[a]
Low-income economies	80 w	91 w	76 w	101 w	46 w	76 w	23 w	31 w	2 w	4 w
China and India	83 w	96 w	..	109 w	..	83 w	..	35 w	2 w	4 w
Other low-income	44 w	74 w	57 w	76 w	31 w	56 w	9 w	20 w	1 w	2 w
Sub-Saharan Africa	37 w	76 w	48 w	69 w	27 w	51 w	4 w	13 w	(.) w	1 w
1 Ethiopia	11	46	16	58	6	34	2	13	(.)	1
2 Bangladesh	49	62	67	67	31	55	13	19	1	4
3 Mali	24	24	32	30	16	18	4	7	(.)	1
4 Zaire	70	..	95	..	45	..	5	..	(.)	1
5 Burkina Faso	12	27	16	34	8	20	1	4	(.)	1
6 Nepal	20	73	36	100	4	43	5	22	1	5
7 Burma	71	91	76	..	65	..	15	23	1	5
8 Malawi	44	63	55	73	32	52	2	5	(.)	(.)
9 Niger	11	27	15	34	7	19	1	6	..	1
10 Tanzania	32	87	40	91	25	84	2	3	(.)	(.)
11 Burundi	26	45	36	55	15	36	1	4	(.)	1
12 Uganda	67	57	83	65	50	49	4	8	(.)	1
13 Togo	55	102	78	124	32	80	5	24	(.)	2
14 Central African Rep.	56	77	84	98	28	51	2	16	..	1
15 India	74	85	89	100	57	68	27	34	5	9
16 Madagascar	65	..	70	..	59	..	8	..	1	1
17 Somalia	10	21	16	28	4	15	2	14	(.)	1
18 Benin	34	67	48	92	21	43	3	22	(.)	2
19 Rwanda	53	62	64	64	43	60	2	2	(.)	(.)
20 China	89	104	..	116	..	93	24	35	(.)	1
21 Kenya	54	100	69	104	40	97	4	19	(.)	1
22 Sierra Leone	29	45	37	..	21	..	5	14	(.)	1
23 Haiti	50	69	56	74	44	64	5	13	(.)	1
24 Guinea	31	36	44	49	19	23	5	15	(.)	3
25 Ghana	69	79	82	89	57	70	13	38	1	2
26 Sri Lanka	93	101	98	103	86	99	35	56	2	4
27 Sudan	29	50	37	59	21	42	4	18	1	2
28 Pakistan	40	49	59	63	20	33	12	16	2	2
29 Senegal	40	53	52	63	29	42	7	12	1	2
30 *Afghanistan*	16	..	26	..	5	..	2	..	(.)	..
31 *Bhutan*	7	25	13	32	1	17	1	4	..	(.)
32 *Chad*	34	38	56	55	13	21	1	6	..	(.)
33 *Kampuchea, Dem.*	77	..	98	..	56	..	9	..	1	..
34 *Lao PDR*	40	87	50	94	30	80	2	16	(.)	1
35 *Mozambique*	37	79	48	91	26	68	3	6	(.)	(.)
36 *Viet Nam*	..	113	..	120	..	105	..	48	..	2
Middle-income economies	84 w	105 w	90 w	108 w	77 w	100 w	20 w	47 w	4 w	12 w
Oil exporters	70 w	107 w	79 w	115 w	60 w	104 w	15 w	45 w	2 w	8 w
Oil importers	96 w	103 w	100 w	106 w	92 w	100 w	24 w	49 w	6 w	15 w
Sub-Saharan Africa	45 w	98 w	54 w	106 w	35 w	90 w	5 w	22 w	(.) w	2 w
Lower middle-income	72 w	101 w	83 w	111 w	66 w	100 w	16 w	40 w	4 w	12 w
37 Mauritania	13	37	19	45	6	29	1	12	..	..
38 Liberia	41	76	59	95	23	57	5	23	1	2
39 Zambia	53	94	59	100	46	89	7	17	..	2
40 Lesotho	94	110	74	94	114	126	4	19	(.)	2
41 Bolivia	73	87	86	94	60	81	18	35	5	16
42 Indonesia	72	115	79	118	65	112	12	37	1	4
43 Yemen Arab Rep.	9	65	16	107	1	21	1	9	..	1
44 Yemen, PDR	23	67	35	97	10	36	11	19	..	..
45 Cote d'Ivoire	60	79	80	93	41	64	6	19	(.)	3
46 Philippines	113	114	115	115	111	113	41	63	19	26
47 Morocco	57	79	78	97	35	61	11	29	1	6
48 Honduras	80	101	81	101	79	100	10	33	1	10
49 El Salvador	82	69	85	69	79	69	17	24	2	12
50 Papua New Guinea	44	61	53	68	35	55	4	11	..	2
51 Egypt, Arab Rep.	75	88	90	101	60	76	26	58	7	16
52 Nigeria	32	98	39	..	24	..	5	..	(.)	2
53 Zimbabwe	110	131	128	136	92	127	6	39	(.)	3
54 Cameroon	94	108	114	117	75	98	5	21	(.)	2
55 Nicaragua	69	100	68	97	69	103	14	43	2	13
56 Thailand	78	99	82	101	74	97	14	29	2	22
57 Botswana	65	96	59	89	71	102	3	21	..	2
58 Dominican Rep.	87	109	87	104	87	115	12	45	2	10
59 Peru	99	116	108	120	90	112	25	61	8	22
60 Mauritius	101	112	105	112	97	112	26	51	3	1
61 Congo, People's Rep.	114	..	134	..	94	..	10	..	1	6
62 Ecuador	91	115	94	117	88	114	17	53	3	35
63 Jamaica	109	107	112	106	106	107	51	58	3	6
64 Guatemala	50	73	55	78	45	67	8	16	2	7
65 Turkey	101	112	118	116	83	107	16	38	4	7

Note: For data comparability and coverage, see the technical notes.

| | Number enrolled in primary school as percentage of age group | | | | | | Number enrolled in secondary school as percentage of age group | | Number enrolled in higher education as percentage of population aged 20–24 | |
| | Total | | Male | | Female | | | | | |
	1965[a]	1983[a]	1965	1983[a]	1965	1983[a]	1965[a]	1983[a]	1965[a]	1983[a]
66 Costa Rica	106	102	107	103	105	100	24	44	6	26
67 Paraguay	102	103	109	107	96	99	13	36	4	..
68 Tunisia	91	113	116	125	65	102	16	33	2	5
69 Colombia	84	120	83	119	86	122	17	49	3	13
70 Jordan	95	100	105	101	83	98	38	78	2	33
71 Syrian Arab Rep.	78	105	103	114	52	96	28	56	8	16
72 Angola	39	..	53	..	26	..	5	12	(.)	2
73 Cuba	121	108	123	111	119	105	23	74	3	20
74 Korea, Dem. Rep.	..	..	..	..	..	..	..	..	..	..
75 Lebanon	106	..	118	..	93	..	26	..	14	..
76 Mongolia	98	106	98	105	97	107	66	86	8	25
Upper middle-income	**96** w	**99** w	**100** w	**109** w	**92** w	**102** w	**25** w	**55** w	**5** w	**14** w
77 Chile	124	111	125	112	122	110	34	65	6	11
78 Brazil	108	102	109	106	108	99	16	42	2	11
79 Portugal	84	122	84	122	83	123	42	43	5	11
80 Malaysia	90	99	96	100	84	98	28	49	2	4
81 Panama	102	104	104	106	99	101	34	59	7	22
82 Uruguay	106	109	106	110	106	107	44	67	8	21
83 Mexico	92	119	94	120	90	117	17	55	4	15
84 Korea, Rep. of	101	103	103	104	99	102	35	89	6	24
85 Yugoslavia	106	101	108	101	103	101	65	82	13	20
86 Argentina	101	107	101	107	102	107	28	60	14	25
87 South Africa	90	..	91	..	88	..	15	..	4	..
88 Algeria	68	94	81	106	53	82	7	43	1	5
89 Venezuela	94	105	93	106	94	104	27	43	7	22
90 Greece	110	105	111	105	109	105	49	82	10	17
91 Israel	95	96	95	95	95	97	48	78	20	34
92 Hong Kong	103	106	106	107	99	104	29	68	5	12
93 Trinidad and Tobago	93	107	97	107	90	108	36	70	2	5
94 Singapore	105	113	110	115	100	111	45	69	10	12
95 Iran, Islamic Rep.	63	101	85	113	40	88	18	40	2	4
96 Iraq	74	106	102	113	45	99	28	53	4	10
High-income oil exporters	**43** w	**75** w	**59** w	**85** w	**25** w	**65** w	**10** w	**42** w	**1** w	**10** w
97 Oman	..	83	..	94	..	72	..	28	..	..
98 Libya	78	..	111	..	44	..	14	..	1	11
99 Saudi Arabia	24	69	36	81	11	56	4	36	1	9
100 Kuwait	116	95	129	96	103	94	52	83	..	14
101 United Arab Emirates	..	95	..	94	..	95	22	54	(.)	6
Industrial market economies	**106** w	**102** w	**107** w	**102** w	**106** w	**101** w	**63** w	**85** w	**21** w	**37** w
102 Spain	115	111	117	112	114	110	38	90	6	24
103 Ireland	108	97	107	97	108	97	51	93	12	22
104 Italy	112	103	113	103	110	102	47	75	11	26
105 New Zealand	106	102	107	103	104	101	75	87	15	28
106 United Kingdom	92	101	92	100	92	101	66	85	12	20
107 Belgium	109	97	110	96	108	97	75	108	15	28
108 Austria	106	99	106	100	105	98	52	74	9	25
109 Netherlands	104	96	104	95	104	97	61	101	17	31
110 France	134	108	135	109	133	107	56	89	18	28
111 Japan	100	100	100	100	100	100	82	94	13	30
112 Finland	92	102	95	102	89	101	76	103	11	31
113 Germany, Fed. Rep.	..	100	..	100	..	100	..	50	9	30
114 Denmark	98	101	97	100	99	101	83	105	14	29
115 Australia	99	105	99	105	99	104	62	92	16	26
116 Sweden	95	98	94	98	96	99	62	85	13	39
117 Canada	105	103	106	105	104	102	56	101	26	42
118 Norway	97	98	97	98	98	99	64	96	11	28
119 United States	..	100	..	100	..	100	..	..	40	56
120 Switzerland	87	..	87	..	87	..	37	..	8	23
East European nonmarket economies	**103** w	**104** w	**103** w	**98** w	**103** w	**98** w	**65** w	**91** w	**26** w	**20** w
121 Hungary	101	101	102	101	100	101	63	74	13	15
122 Poland	104	101	106	101	102	100	58	75	18	16
123 Albania	92	101	97	104	87	97	33	67	8	7
124 Bulgaria	103	100	104	100	102	100	54	85	17	16
125 Czechoslovakia	99	88	100	88	97	89	29	45	14	16
126 German Dem. Rep.	109	95	107	94	111	96	60	88	19	30
127 Romania	101	99	102	100	100	99	39	63	10	12
128 USSR	103	106	103	..	103	..	72	99	30	21

a. Figures in italics are for years other than those specified; see the technical notes.

Table 30. Labor force

	Percentage of population of working age (15–64 years)		Percentage of labor force in: Agriculture		Industry		Services		Average annual growth of labor force (percent)		
	1965	1984	1965	1980	1965	1980	1965	1980	1965–73	1973–84	1980–2000
Low-income economies	53 w	59 w	78 w	70 w	9 w	15 w	13 w	15 w	2.3 w	2.2 w	2.0 w
China and India	55 w	61 w	..	70 w	..	17 w	..	14 w	2.3 w	1.8 w	2.0 w
Other low-income	47 w	53 w	78 w	71 w	8 w	10 w	14 w	19 w	2.0 w	3.8 w	2.6 w
Sub-Saharan Africa	53 w	50 w	86 w	79 w	5 w	8 w	9 w	13 w	2.2 w	2.2 w	2.8 w
1 Ethiopia	52	51	86	80	5	8	8	12	2.2	2.2	2.5
2 Bangladesh	51	53	84	75	5	6	11	19	2.3	2.6	2.4
3 Mali	53	50	90	86	1	2	8	13	2.2	1.9	2.4
4 Zaire	52	51	82	72	9	13	9	16	1.9	2.3	2.8
5 Burkina Faso	53	52	89	87	3	4	7	9	1.6	1.4	1.7
6 Nepal	56	54	94	93	2	1	4	6	1.6	2.3	2.6
7 Burma	57	55	64	53	13	19	23	28	1.3	1.3	2.0
8 Malawi	51	48	92	83	3	7	5	9	2.3	2.5	2.7
9 Niger	51	51	95	91	1	2	4	7	2.1	2.8	3.0
10 Tanzania	53	50	92	86	3	5	6	10	2.6	2.6	3.2
11 Burundi	53	52	94	93	2	2	4	5	1.2	1.7	2.5
12 Uganda	53	49	91	86	3	4	6	10	3.1	2.2	3.2
13 Togo	52	50	78	73	8	10	13	17	3.2	2.0	2.9
14 Central African Rep.	57	55	89	72	3	6	8	21	1.1	1.6	2.4
15 India	54	56	73	70	12	13	15	17	1.8	2.1	2.1
16 Madagascar	54	50	..	88	..	3	..	9	1.9	2.0	2.9
17 Somalia	49	52	81	76	6	8	13	16	3.8	2.6	2.6
18 Benin	52	50	83	70	5	7	12	23	2.1	2.0	2.6
19 Rwanda	51	51	94	93	2	3	3	4	2.7	2.8	3.1
20 China	55	64	..	69	..	19	..	12	2.6	1.6	2.0
21 Kenya	48	45	86	81	5	7	9	12	3.3	2.8	3.5
22 Sierra Leone	54	54	79	70	11	14	11	16	1.0	1.8	1.9
23 Haiti	54	55	77	70	7	8	16	22	0.7	1.6	2.0
24 Guinea	55	53	87	81	6	9	6	10	1.2	1.2	1.8
25 Ghana	52	48	61	56	15	18	24	26	1.4	1.5	3.5
26 Sri Lanka	54	60	56	53	14	14	30	33	2.0	2.1	2.2
27 Sudan	53	52	82	71	5	7	13	22	2.8	2.4	2.8
28 Pakistan	50	53	60	55	18	16	22	30	2.3	3.3	2.9
29 Senegal	53	52	83	81	5	6	11	13	1.7	2.2	2.4
30 *Afghanistan*	55	..	69	..	11	..	20	..	1.9	..	..
31 *Bhutan*	55	56	95	92	2	3	3	5	1.0	1.9	2.2
32 *Chad*	55	56	92	83	3	5	5	12	1.6	2.3	2.3
33 *Kampuchea, Dem.*	52	..	80	..	4	..	16	..	1.3	..	..
34 *Lao PDR*	56	52	81	76	5	7	14	17	0.6	0.5	2.6
35 *Mozambique*	55	51	87	85	5	7	7	8	1.8	1.6	2.4
36 *Viet Nam*	..	55	79	68	6	12	15	21	..	..	2.7
Middle-income economies	53 w	56 w	57 w	44 w	17 w	22 w	26 w	34 w	2.2 w	2.6 w	2.3 w
Oil exporters	52 w	53 w	61 w	49 w	14 w	19 w	24 w	32 w	2.2 w	2.6 w	2.7 w
Oil importers	54 w	58 w	53 w	40 w	19 w	23 w	28 w	36 w	2.1 w	2.6 w	2.0 w
Sub-Saharan Africa	52 w	50 w	75 w	69 w	9 w	11 w	16 w	20 w	2.0 w	2.3 w	2.8 w
Lower middle-income	52 w	55 w	66 w	56 w	12 w	16 w	22 w	29 w	2.1 w	2.5 w	2.4 w
37 Mauritania	52	53	90	69	3	9	7	22	1.9	2.3	2.1
38 Liberia	51	52	79	74	10	9	11	16	2.1	3.6	2.5
39 Zambia	51	49	79	73	8	10	13	17	2.3	2.1	3.1
40 Lesotho	56	53	92	86	3	4	6	10	1.7	1.8	2.3
41 Bolivia	53	53	54	46	20	20	26	34	1.8	2.5	2.9
42 Indonesia	53	56	71	57	9	13	20	30	1.9	2.3	2.1
43 Yemen Arab Rep.	54	51	79	69	7	9	14	22	1.0	2.1	3.2
44 Yemen, PDR	52	51	54	41	12	18	33	41	1.1	1.8	2.6
45 Cote d'Ivoire	54	53	81	65	5	8	14	27	4.2	3.9	3.3
46 Philippines	52	56	58	52	16	16	26	33	2.1	3.1	2.6
47 Morocco	50	52	62	46	15	25	24	29	1.8	2.6	3.1
48 Honduras	50	50	68	61	12	16	20	23	2.4	3.3	3.4
49 El Salvador	50	51	59	56	16	14	25	30	3.2	2.9	3.4
50 Papua New Guinea	55	54	87	76	6	10	7	14	1.9	2.0	2.1
51 Egypt, Arab Rep.	54	57	55	46	14	20	30	34	2.1	2.5	2.5
52 Nigeria	51	49	72	68	10	12	18	20	1.7	2.0	3.1
53 Zimbabwe	51	45	79	*53*	8	*13*	13	*34*	2.7	1.5	3.4
54 Cameroon	55	50	87	70	4	8	9	22	1.9	1.8	3.0
55 Nicaragua	48	50	57	47	16	16	27	38	3.0	3.2	3.7
56 Thailand	50	59	82	70	5	*10*	13	*20*	2.4	3.0	1.9
57 Botswana	50	48	89	70	4	13	7	17	2.2	4.2	2.9
58 Dominican Rep.	48	55	59	46	13	16	27	39	2.7	3.3	3.0
59 Peru	51	56	50	40	19	18	31	42	2.4	2.9	2.9
60 Mauritius	52	62	37	28	25	24	38	48	2.8	2.3	2.1
61 Congo, People's Rep.	55	51	66	62	11	12	23	26	1.9	1.9	3.7
62 Ecuador	50	53	55	39	19	20	26	42	3.1	2.9	3.0
63 Jamaica	51	56	37	33	20	*18*	43	*49*	0.7	2.3	2.5
64 Guatemala	50	53	64	57	15	17	21	26	2.7	2.8	2.9
65 Turkey	53	58	75	58	11	17	14	25	1.8	2.0	2.2

Note: For data comparability and coverage, see the technical notes.

		Percentage of population of working age (15–64 years)		Percentage of labor force in:						Average annual growth of labor force (percent)		
				Agriculture		Industry		Services				
		1965	1984	1965	1980	1965	1980	1965	1980	1965–73	1973–84	1980–2000
66	Costa Rica	49	59	47	31	19	23	34	46	3.7	3.8	2.8
67	Paraguay	50	55	55	49	20	21	26	31	2.5	3.3	3.0
68	Tunisia	50	56	49	35	21	36	29	29	1.3	2.9	2.9
69	Colombia	49	59	45	34	21	24	34	42	3.1	2.8	2.5
70	Jordan	51	48	36	10	26	26	37	64	2.6	1.6	4.7
71	Syrian Arab Rep.	46	49	52	32	20	32	28	36	3.1	3.4	3.9
72	*Angola*	54	52	79	74	8	10	13	17	1.5	2.6	2.7
73	*Cuba*	59	65	33	24	25	29	41	48	1.0	2.2	1.7
74	*Korea, Dem. Rep.*	52	57	57	43	23	30	20	27	2.6	3.0	2.7
75	*Lebanon*	51	..	28	..	25	..	47	..	2.5	..	..
76	*Mongolia*	54	55	55	40	20	21	25	39	2.2	2.6	3.0
Upper middle-income		**54** *w*	**58** *w*	**45** *w*	**29** *w*	**23** *w*	**29** *w*	**32** *w*	**42** *w*	**2.3** *w*	**2.6** *w*	**2.2** *w*
77	Chile	56	63	27	16	29	25	44	58	1.3	2.5	2.1
78	Brazil	53	58	48	31	20	27	31	42	2.5	3.0	2.3
79	Portugal	62	64	38	26	31	37	32	38	0.1	0.9	0.7
80	Malaysia	50	58	59	42	13	19	28	39	2.9	3.2	2.9
81	Panama	51	57	46	32	16	18	38	50	3.3	2.6	2.2
82	Uruguay	63	63	20	16	29	29	51	55	0.3	0.5	0.9
83	Mexico	49	53	50	37	22	29	29	34	3.1	3.2	3.2
84	Korea, Rep. of	53	64	56	36	14	27	30	37	2.9	2.7	1.9
85	Yugoslavia	63	67	57	32	26	33	17	34	0.7	0.5	0.6
86	Argentina	63	61	18	13	34	34	48	53	1.4	1.1	1.5
87	South Africa	54	56	32	17	30	35	38	49	2.7	3.0	2.3
88	Algeria	50	49	57	31	16	27	26	42	1.6	3.6	4.1
89	Venezuela	49	55	30	16	24	28	47	56	3.5	3.9	3.4
90	Greece	65	64	47	31	24	29	29	40	0.1	0.9	0.5
91	Israel	59	59	12	6	35	32	53	62	3.2	2.3	2.2
92	Hong Kong	56	68	6	2	53	51	41	47	3.5	3.7	1.1
93	Trinidad and Tobago	53	61	20	10	35	39	45	51	2.0	2.3	2.2
94	Singapore	53	67	5	2	27	38	68	61	3.4	2.2	1.1
95	*Iran, Islamic Rep.*	50	52	49	36	26	33	25	31	3.1	3.0	3.6
96	*Iraq*	51	50	50	31	20	22	30	48	2.9	3.1	3.8
High-income oil exporters		**52** *w*	**55** *w*	**56** *w*	**36** *w*	**15** *w*	**21** *w*	**28** *w*	**44** *w*	**4.0** *w*	**5.6** *w*	**3.4** *w*
97	Oman	53	53	62	50	15	22	23	28	0.0	0.0	0.0
98	Libya	53	52	40	18	21	30	39	53	3.6	4.1	4.1
99	Saudi Arabia	53	54	68	49	11	14	21	37	3.9	5.9	3.2
100	Kuwait	60	57	2	2	34	32	64	67	5.3	6.9	3.1
101	United Arab Emirates	..	67	20	5	32	38	47	57	..	..	..
Industrial market economies		**63** *w*	**67** *w*	**14** *w*	**7** *w*	**38** *w*	**35** *w*	**48** *w*	**58** *w*	**1.2** *w*	**1.2** *w*	**0.7** *w*
102	Spain	64	64	34	17	35	37	32	46	0.4	1.3	0.8
103	Ireland	57	59	31	19	28	34	41	48	0.5	1.4	1.5
104	Italy	66	67	24	12	42	41	34	48	0.0	0.7	0.3
105	New Zealand	59	65	13	11	36	33	51	56	2.0	1.3	1.1
106	United Kingdom	65	65	3	3	47	38	50	59	0.2	0.5	0.2
107	Belgium	63	67	6	3	46	36	48	61	0.5	0.7	0.2
108	Austria	63	66	19	9	45	41	36	50	−0.2	1.0	0.3
109	Netherlands	62	68	9	6	41	32	50	63	1.4	1.4	0.5
110	France	62	66	17	9	39	35	43	56	0.7	1.1	0.7
111	Japan	67	68	26	11	32	34	42	55	1.7	1.1	0.7
112	Finland	65	67	23	12	36	35	41	53	0.5	0.5	0.5
113	Germany, Fed. Rep.	65	69	10	6	48	44	42	50	0.3	0.8	−0.1
114	Denmark	65	66	14	7	37	32	49	61	0.8	0.6	0.3
115	Australia	62	66	10	7	38	32	52	61	2.5	1.7	1.3
116	Sweden	66	65	11	6	43	33	46	62	0.7	0.4	0.3
117	Canada	59	68	10	5	33	29	57	65	2.7	2.0	1.1
118	Norway	63	64	15	8	37	29	48	62	0.6	0.7	0.6
119	United States	60	66	5	4	35	31	60	66	1.9	1.6	0.9
120	Switzerland	65	67	9	6	50	39	41	55	1.5	0.4	0.2
East European nonmarket economies		**62** *w*	**65** *w*	**35** *w*	**21** *w*	**34** *w*	**40** *w*	**31** *w*	**39** *w*	**0.8** *w*	**1.0** *w*	**0.5** *w*
121	Hungary	66	65	31	18	40	44	29	38	0.5	0.0	0.0
122	Poland	62	65	43	29	32	39	25	33	1.7	1.2	0.8
123	*Albania*	52	59	69	56	19	26	12	18	2.4	2.4	2.3
124	*Bulgaria*	67	66	46	18	31	45	23	37	0.6	0.1	0.1
125	Czechoslovakia	65	64	21	13	48	49	31	37	0.8	0.5	0.6
126	*German Dem. Rep.*	61	66	15	11	49	50	36	39	0.4	0.7	0.1
127	*Romania*	65	65	57	29	26	44	18	27	0.8	0.5	0.6
128	*USSR*	62	66	33	20	33	39	33	41	*0.7*	*1.1*	0.5

a. Figures in italics are for years other than those specified.

Table 31. Urbanization

	Urban population				Percentage of urban population				Number of cities of over 500,000 persons	
	As percentage of total population		Average annual growth rate (percent)		In largest city		In cities of over 500,000 persons			
	1965[a]	1984[a]	1965–73	1973–84	1960	1980	1960	1980	1960	1980
Low-income economies	17 _w_	23 _w_	4.5 _w_	4.6 _w_	10 _w_	16 _w_	31 _w_	55 _w_	55 _t_	147 _t_
China and India	18 _w_	23 _w_	..	..	7 _w_	6 _w_	33 _w_	59 _w_	49 _t_	114 _t_
Other low-income	13 _w_	22 _w_	5.2 _w_	5.1 _w_	26 _w_	29 _w_	19 _w_	41 _w_	6 _t_	33 _t_
Sub-Saharan Africa	11 _w_	21 _w_	6.2 _w_	6.1 _w_	34 _w_	42 _w_	2 _w_	36 _w_	1 _t_	14 _t_
1 Ethiopia	8	15	7.4	6.1	30	37	0	37	0	1
2 Bangladesh	6	18	6.6	7.7	20	30	20	51	1	3
3 Mali	13	19	5.4	4.5	32	24	0	0	0	0
4 Zaire	19	39	5.9	7.1	14	28	14	38	1	2
5 Burkina Faso	6	11	6.5	4.8	..	41	0	0	0	0
6 Nepal	4	7	4.3	8.4	41	27	0	0	0	0
7 Burma	21	29	4.0	4.0	23	23	23	23	1	2
8 Malawi	5	12	8.2	7.3	..	19	0	0	0	0
9 Niger	7	14	7.0	7.1	..	31	0	0	0	0
10 Tanzania	6	14	8.1	8.6	34	50	0	50	0	1
11 Burundi	2	2	1.4	3.3	..	..	0	0	0	0
12 Uganda	6	7	8.3	−0.1	38	52	0	52	0	1
13 Togo	11	23	6.4	6.5	..	60	0	0	0	0
14 Central African Rep.	27	45	4.4	4.6	40	36	0	0	0	0
15 India	19	25	4.0	4.2	7	6	26	39	11	36
16 Madagascar	12	21	5.3	5.5	44	36	0	36	0	1
17 Somalia	20	33	6.4	5.4	..	34	0	0	0	0
18 Benin	11	15	4.5	5.0	..	63	0	63	0	1
19 Rwanda	3	5	6.0	6.6	..	0	0	0	0	0
20 China	18	22	3.0	2.9	6	6	42	45	38	78
21 Kenya	9	18	7.3	7.9	40	57	0	57	0	1
22 Sierra Leone	15	24	5.0	3.5	37	47	0	0	0	0
23 Haiti	18	27	3.8	4.2	42	56	0	56	0	1
24 Guinea	12	27	5.0	6.2	37	80	0	80	0	1
25 Ghana	26	39	4.5	5.3	25	35	0	48	0	2
26 Sri Lanka	20	21	3.4	3.5	28	16	0	16	0	1
27 Sudan	13	21	6.3	5.5	30	31	0	31	0	1
28 Pakistan	24	29	4.3	4.4	20	21	33	51	2	7
29 Senegal	27	35	4.2	3.8	53	65	0	65	0	1
30 _Afghanistan_	9	..	5.6	..	33	..	0	..	0	1
31 _Bhutan_	3	4	−2.1	4.6	0	0	0	0	0	0
32 _Chad_	9	21	6.9	6.5	..	39	0	0	0	0
33 _Kampuchea, Dem._	11		3.4		..	..	..	..	..	..
34 _Lao PDR_	8	15	4.6	5.7	69	48	0	0	0	0
35 _Mozambique_	5	16	8.2	10.2	75	83	0	83	0	1
36 _Viet Nam_	16	20	5.5	2.3	32	21	32	50	1	4
Middle-income	36 _w_	49 _w_	4.5 _w_	4.1 _w_	28 _w_	29 _w_	35 _w_	48 _w_	54 _t_	126 _t_
Oil exporters	29 _w_	42 _w_	4.4 _w_	4.4 _w_	27 _w_	30 _w_	32 _w_	48 _w_	15 _t_	42 _t_
Oil importers	40 _w_	55 _w_	4.5 _w_	3.6 _w_	28 _w_	28 _w_	36 _w_	48 _w_	39 _t_	85 _t_
Sub-Saharan Africa	16 _w_	28 _w_	6.4 _w_	5.9 _w_	18 _w_	24 _w_	15 _w_	50 _w_	2 _t_	14 _t_
Lower middle-income	26 _w_	37 _w_	5.1 _w_	4.2 _w_	27 _w_	31 _w_	28 _w_	46 _w_	23 _t_	59 _t_
37 Mauritania	7	26	16.0	5.1	..	39	0	0	0	0
38 Liberia	22	39	5.3	6.0	..	..	0	0	0	0
39 Zambia	24	48	7.6	6.4	..	35	0	35	0	1
40 Lesotho	2	13	7.8	20.1	..	..	0	0	0	0
41 Bolivia	40	43	8.9	3.6	47	44	0	44	0	1
42 Indonesia	16	25	4.1	4.5	20	23	34	50	3	9
43 Yemen Arab Rep.	5	19	9.7	8.8	..	25	0	0	0	0
44 Yemen, PDR	30	37	3.4	3.5	61	49	0	0	0	0
45 Cote d'Ivoire	23	46	8.2	8.3	27	34	0	34	0	1
46 Philippines	32	39	4.0	3.7	27	30	27	34	1	2
47 Morocco	32	43	4.0	4.2	16	26	16	50	1	4
48 Honduras	26	39	5.4	5.7	31	33	0	0	0	0
49 El Salvador	39	43	3.6	3.6	26	22	0	0	0	0
50 Papua New Guinea	5	14	14.3	6.1	..	25	0	0	0	0
51 Egypt, Arab Rep.	40	23	3.0	3.0	38	39	53	53	2	2
52 Nigeria	15	30	4.7	5.2	13	17	22	58	2	9
53 Zimbabwe	14	27	6.8	6.1	40	50	0	50	0	1
54 Cameroon	16	41	7.3	8.2	26	21	0	21	0	1
55 Nicaragua	43	56	4.4	5.2	41	47	0	47	0	1
56 Thailand	13	18	4.8	3.1	65	69	65	69	1	1
57 Botswana	4	20	19.0	11.3	..	..	..	..	..	..
58 Dominican Rep.	35	55	5.6	4.7	50	54	0	54	0	1
59 Peru	52	68	4.7	3.6	38	39	38	44	1	2
60 Mauritius	37	56	4.6	3.4	..	..	..	..	..	..
61 Congo, People's Rep.	35	56	4.4	5.4	77	56	0	0	0	0
62 Ecuador	37	47	3.9	3.9	31	29	0	51	0	2
63 Jamaica	38	53	4.3	2.7	77	66	0	66	0	1
64 Guatemala	34	41	3.8	4.1	41	36	41	36	1	1
65 Turkey	32	46	4.9	4.0	18	24	32	42	3	4

Note: For data comparability and coverage, see the technical notes.

	Urban population				Percentage of urban population				Number of cities of over 500,000 persons	
	As percentage of total population		Average annual growth rate (percent)		In largest city		In cities of over 500,000 persons			
	1965[a]	1984[a]	1965–73	1973–84	1960	1980	1960	1980	1960	1980
66 Costa Rica	38	45	3.8	3.3	67	64	0	64	0	1
67 Paraguay	36	41	3.2	3.4	44	44	0	44	0	1
68 Tunisia	40	54	4.1	3.8	40	30	40	30	1	1
69 Colombia	54	67	4.3	2.9	17	26	28	51	3	4
70 Jordan	47	72	4.7	4.7	31	37	0	37	0	1
71 Syrian Arab Rep.	40	49	4.8	4.3	35	33	35	55	1	2
72 Angola	13	24	5.9	6.0	44	64	0	64	0	1
73 Cuba	58	71	2.8	1.6	32	38	32	38	1	1
74 Korea, Dem. Rep.	45	63	4.9	4.1	15	12	15	19	1	2
75 Lebanon	49	. .	6.2	. .	64	. .	64	. .	1	1
76 Mongolia	42	55	4.6	4.1	53	52	0	0	0	0
Upper middle-income	49 w	65 w	3.9 w	4.1 w	28 w	29 w	40 w	51 w	31 t	67 t
77 Chile	72	83	2.8	2.4	38	44	38	44	1	1
78 Brazil	51	72	4.5	4.0	14	15	35	52	6	14
79 Portugal	24	31	1.2	2.5	47	44	47	44	1	1
80 Malaysia	26	31	3.3	3.6	19	27	0	27	0	1
81 Panama	44	50	4.1	3.1	61	66	0	66	0	1
82 Uruguay	81	85	0.8	0.8	56	52	56	52	1	1
83 Mexico	55	69	4.8	4.0	28	32	36	48	3	7
84 Korea, Rep. of	32	64	6.5	4.6	35	41	61	77	3	7
85 Yugoslavia	31	46	3.1	2.7	11	10	11	23	1	3
86 Argentina	76	84	2.1	2.1	46	45	54	60	3	5
87 South Africa	47	56	2.6	3.7	16	13	44	53	4	7
88 Algeria	32	47	2.5	5.4	27	12	27	12	1	1
89 Venezuela	72	85	4.8	4.3	26	26	26	44	1	4
90 Greece	48	65	2.5	2.5	51	57	51	70	1	2
91 Israel	81	90	3.8	2.7	46	35	46	35	1	1
92 Hong Kong	89	93	2.1	2.6	100	100	100	100	1	1
93 Trinidad and Tobago	22	22	0.6	1.2	. .	. .	0	0	0	0
94 Singapore	100	100	1.8	1.3	100	100	100	100	1	1
95 Iran, Islamic Rep.	37	54	5.4	5.0	26	28	26	47	1	6
96 Iraq	51	70	5.7	5.5	35	55	35	70	1	3
High-income oil exporters	36 w	70 w	9.2 w	7.7 w	29 w	28 w	0 w	34 w	0 t	3 t
97 Oman	4	27	10.8	17.6	. .	. .	. .	64	. .	1
98 Libya	29	63	8.9	7.9	57	64	0	64	0	1
99 Saudi Arabia	39	72	8.4	7.3	15	18	0	33	0	2
100 Kuwait	75	93	9.3	7.7	75	30	0	0	0	0
101 United Arab Emirates	56	79	16.7	10.4	. .	. .	. .	. .	. .	. .
Industrial market economies	72 w	77 w	1.8 w	1.2 w	18 w	18 w	48 w	55 w	104 t	152 t
102 Spain	61	77	2.5	2.0	13	17	37	44	5	6
103 Ireland	49	57	2.0	2.2	51	48	51	48	1	1
104 Italy	62	71	1.4	1.0	13	17	46	52	7	9
105 New Zealand	79	83	1.9	0.9	25	30	0	30	0	1
106 United Kingdom	87	92	0.7	0.2	24	20	61	55	15	17
107 Belgium	86	89	0.9	1.2	17	14	28	24	2	2
108 Austria	51	56	0.8	0.6	51	39	51	39	1	1
109 Netherlands	79	76	0.8	−1.0	9	9	27	24	3	3
110 France	67	81	2.0	1.2	25	23	34	34	4	6
111 Japan	67	76	2.4	1.4	18	22	35	42	5	9
112 Finland	44	60	2.8	1.9	28	27	0	27	0	1
113 Germany, Fed. Rep.	79	86	1.2	0.3	20	18	48	45	11	11
114 Denmark	77	86	1.3	0.6	40	32,	40	32	1	1
115 Australia	83	86	2.6	1.5	26	24	62	68	4	5
116 Sweden	77	86	1.6	0.7	15	15	15	35	1	3
117 Canada	73	75	1.9	1.2	14	18	31	62	2	9
118 Norway	37	77	3.4	2.7	50	32	50	32	1	1
119 United States	72	74	1.6	1.3	13	12	61	77	40	65
120 Switzerland	53	60	1.9	0.8	19	22	19	22	1	1
East European nonmarket economies	52 w	64 w	2.6 w	1.8 w	9 w	7 w	23 w	32 w	36 t	65 t
121 Hungary	43	55	2.2	1.4	45	37	45	37	1	1
122 Poland	50	60	1.5	1.8	17	15	41	47	5	8
123 Albania	32	39	3.5	3.2	27	25	0	0	0	0
124 Bulgaria	46	68	3.2	2.1	23	18	23	18	1	1
125 Czechoslovakia	51	66	1.8	1.7	17	12	17	12	1	1
126 German Dem. Rep.	73	76	0.2	0.2	9	9	14	17	2	3
127 Romania	34	52	4.2	3.0	22	17	22	17	1	1
128 USSR	52	66	5.9	−3.0	6	4	21	33	25	50

a. Figures in italics are for years other than those specified.

Technical notes

This ninth edition of the World Development Indicators provides economic and social indicators for periods or selected years in a form suitable for comparing economies and groups of economies. It contains three new tables, two covering private nonguaranteed debt and one showing receipts of official development assistance.

The statistics and measures have been carefully chosen to give an extensive picture of development. Considerable effort has been made to standardize the data; nevertheless, statistical methods, coverage, practices, and definitions differ widely. In addition, the statistical systems in many developing economies are still weak, and this affects the availability and reliability of the data. Readers are urged to take these limitations into account in interpreting the indicators, particularly when making comparisons across economies.

All growth rates shown are in constant prices and, unless otherwise noted, have been computed by using the least-squares method. The least-squares growth rate, r, is estimated by fitting a least-squares linear trend line to the logarithmic annual values of the variable in the relevant period. More specifically, the regression equation takes the form of $\log X_t = a + bt + e_t$, where this is equivalent to the logarithmic transformation of the compound growth rate equation, $X_t = X_o (1 + r)^t$. In these equations, X_t is the variable, t is time, and $a = \log X_o$ and $b = \log (1 + r)$ are the parameters to be estimated; e_t is the error term. If b^* is the least-squares estimate of b, then the annual average growth rate, r, is obtained as [antilog (b^*)] -1.

Table 1. Basic indicators

The estimates of *population* for mid-1984 are based on data from the U.N. Population Division or World Bank sources. In many cases the data take into account the results of recent population censuses. Note that refugees not permanently settled in the country of asylum are generally considered to be part of the population of their country of origin. The data on *area* are from the FAO *Production Yearbook, 1984*. The table in Box A.1 shows data—for population, area, and the other basic indicators—for U.N. and World Bank member countries with populations of less than 1 million.

Gross national product (GNP) measures the total domestic and foreign output claimed by residents, and is calculated without making deductions for depreciation. It comprises gross domestic product (see the note for Table 2) adjusted by net factor income from abroad. That income comprises the income residents receive from abroad for factor services (labor, investment, and interest) less similar payments made to nonresidents who contributed to the domestic economy.

The *GNP per capita* figures are calculated according to the *World Bank Atlas* method. The Bank recognizes that perfect cross-country comparability of GNP per capita estimates cannot be achieved. Beyond the classic, strictly intractable "index number problem," two obstacles stand in the way of adequate comparability. One concerns GNP numbers themselves. There are differences in the national accounting systems and in the coverage and reliability of underlying statistical information between various countries. The other relates to the conversion of GNP data, expressed in different national currencies, to a common numéraire—conventionally the U.S. dollar—to compare them across countries. The Bank's procedure for converting GNP to U.S. dollars generally uses a three-year average of the official exchange rate. For a few countries, however, the prevailing official exchange rate does not reflect the rate effectively applied to actual foreign exchange transactions and in these cases an alternative conversion factor is used.

Recognizing that these shortcomings affect the comparability of the GNP per capita estimates, the World Bank has introduced several improvements in the estimation procedures. Through its regular review of member countries' national accounts, the World Bank systematically evaluates the GNP

Box A.1 Basic indicators for U.N. and World Bank member countries with populations of less than 1 million

U.N./World Bank member	Population (thousands) mid-1984	Area (thousands of square kilometers)	GNP per capita[a] Dollars 1984	Average annual growth rate (percent) 1965–84[b]	Average annual rate of inflation (percent) 1965–73	Average annual rate of inflation (percent) 1973–84[c]	Life expectancy at birth (years) 1984
Guinea-Bissau	870	36	190	..	..	9.1	38
Gambia, The	718	11	260	1.0	3.0	10.4	42
Cape Verde	320	4	320	..	..	12.6	64
Sao Tome and Principe	105	1	330	−1.6	..	8.3	64
Guyana	785	215	590	0.5	4.3	7.8	65
Swaziland	731	17	790	4.1	4.3	14.0	54
St. Vincent and the Grenadines	117	(.)	840	1.9	6.1	10.9	69
Grenada	94	(.)	860	1.7	..	12.6	68
Dominica	77	1	1,010	0.3	6.1	13.2	75
Belize	156	23	1,110	2.5	..	7.6	66
St. Lucia	134	1	1,130	3.1	5.5	10.3	70
St. Christopher and Nevis	55	(.)	1,150	3.2	6.4	8.9	64
Fiji	686	18	1,810	3.1	5.6	9.0	65
Antigua and Barbuda	78	(.)	1,860	−0.1	6.6	8.6	73
Malta	360	(.)	3,360	8.4	2.4	5.5	72
Suriname	383	163	3,510	4.2	..	9.6	66
Cyprus	654	9	3,650	..	1.6	10.4	74
Gabon	812	268	4,100	5.9	5.8	15.5	50
Barbados	253	(.)	4,370	2.5	7.2	11.7	73
Bahamas	229	14	6,690	−1.6	..	..	69
Bahrain	407	1	10,470	..	..	..	69
Iceland	239	103	11,020	2.6	15.1	47.4	77
Luxembourg	366	3	13,160	3.9	5.0	7.3	73
Qatar	304	11	19,810	−7.7	..	..	72
Brunei	218	6	..	..	..	..	74
Comoros	382	2	..	..	..	..	55
Djibouti	..	22	..	..	..	..	48
Equatorial Guinea	366	28	..	..	3.6	..	44
Maldives	173	(.)	..	..	..	..	53
Seychelles	65	(.)	..	..	..	14.8	69
Solomon Islands	259	28	..	..	4.8	10.1	58
Tonga	106	1	..	..	..	*10.2*	64
Vanuatu	130	15	..	..	..	..	55
Western Samoa	161	3	..	..	..	..	65

Note: Countries with italicized names are those for which no GNP per capita can be calculated.
a. See the technical notes.   b. Because data for the entire period are not always available, figures in italics are for periods other than those specified.   c. Figures in italics are for 1973–83, not 1973–84.

estimates, focusing on the coverage and concepts employed and, where appropriate, making adjustments to improve comparability. The Bank also undertakes a systematic review to assess the appropriateness of the exchange rates as conversion factors. An alternative conversion factor is used when the official exchange rate is judged to diverge by an exceptionally large margin from the rate effectively applied to foreign transactions. This applies to only a small number of countries.

In an effort to achieve greater comparability, the U.N. International Comparison Project (ICP) has developed measures of GDP using purchasing-power parities rather than exchange rates. So far the project covers 60 countries for the year 1980, but some inherent methodological issues remain unresolved.

The estimates of 1984 GNP and 1984 per capita GNP are calculated on the basis of the 1982–84 base period. With this method, the first step is to calculate the conversion factor. This is done by taking the simple arithmetic average of the actual exchange rate for 1984 and of adjusted exchange rates for 1982 and 1983. To obtain the deflated exchange rate for 1982, the actual exchange rate for 1982 is multiplied by the relative rate of inflation for the country and for the United States between 1982 and 1984. For 1983, the actual exchange rate for 1983 is multiplied by the relative rate of inflation for the country and the United States between 1983 and 1984.

This average of the actual and the deflated exchange rates is intended to smooth the impact of fluctuations in prices and exchange rates. The second step is to convert the GNP at current purchaser values and in national currencies of the year 1984 by means of the conversion factor as derived above. Then the resulting GNP in U.S. dollars is divided by the midyear population to derive the 1984 per capita GNP. The preliminary estimates of GNP per capita for 1984 are shown in this table.

The following formulas describe the procedures for computing the conversion factor for year t:

$$(\overset{\bullet}{e}_{t-2,t}) = \frac{1}{3}\ [e_{t-2}\left(\frac{P_t}{P_{t-2}}\bigg|\frac{P_t^\$}{P_{t-2}^\$}\right) + e_{t-1}\left(\frac{P_t}{P_{t-1}}\bigg|\frac{P_t^\$}{P_{t-1}^\$}\right) + e_t]$$

and for calculating per capita GNP in U.S. dollars for year t:

$$(Y_t^\$) = Y_t\ /\ N_t \div \overset{\bullet}{e}_{t-2,t}$$

where,

Y_t = current GNP (local currency) for year t
P_t = GNP deflator for year t
e_t = annual average exchange rate (local currency/U.S. dollars) for year t
N_t = mid-year population for year t
$P_t^\$$ = U.S. GNP deflator for year t

Because of problems associated with the availability of data and the determination of exchange rates, information on GNP per capita is not shown for most East European nonmarket economies.

The *average annual rate of inflation* is the growth rate of the gross domestic product (GDP) implicit deflator, for each of the periods shown. The GDP deflator is first calculated by dividing, for each year of the period, the value of GDP at current purchaser values by the value of GDP at constant purchaser values, both in national currency. The least-squares method is then used to calculate the growth rate of the GDP deflator for the period. This measure of inflation, like any other, has limitations. For some purposes, however, it is used as an indicator of inflation because it is the most broadly based deflator, showing annual price movements for all goods and services produced in an economy.

Life expectancy at birth indicates the number of years a newborn infant would live if patterns of mortality prevailing for all people at the time of its birth were to stay the same throughout its life. Data are from the U.N. Population Division, supplemented by World Bank estimates.

The *summary measures* for GNP per capita and life expectancy in this table are weighted by population. Those for average annual rates of inflation are weighted by the share of country GDP valued in current U.S. dollars for the entire period in the particular income group.

Tables 2 and 3. Growth and structure of production

Most of the definitions used are those of the U.N. *System of National Accounts, series F, no. 2, revision 3.*

Gross domestic product (GDP) measures the total final output of goods and services produced by an economy—that is, by residents and nonresidents—regardless of the allocation to domestic and foreign claims. It is calculated without making deductions for depreciation. For most countries, GDP by industrial origin is measured at producer prices; for some countries, purchaser values series are used. GDP at producer prices is equal to GDP at purchaser values, less import duties. Note that in previous editions GDP at producer prices and GDP at purchaser values were referred to as GDP at factor cost and GDP at market prices, respectively. The figures for GDP are dollar values converted from domestic currency by using the single-year official exchange rates. For a few countries where the official exchange rate does not reflect the rate effectively applied to actual foreign exchange transactions, an alternative conversion factor is used. Note that this procedure does not use the three-year averaging computation used for calculating GNP per capita in Table 1.

The *agricultural sector* comprises agriculture, forestry, hunting, and fishing. In developing countries with high levels of subsistence farming, much of the agricultural production is either not exchanged or not exchanged for money. This increases the difficulties of measuring the contribution of agriculture to GDP. *Industry* comprises mining, *manufacturing*, construction, and electricity, water, and gas. All other branches of economic activity are categorized as *services*.

National accounts series in domestic currency units were used to compute the indicators in these tables. The growth rates in Table 2 were calculated from constant price series; the sectoral shares of GDP in Table 3, from current price series.

In calculating the *summary measures* for each indicator in Table 2, constant U.S. dollar values for each country are first calculated for each of the years of the periods covered, and the values are then aggregated for each year. The least-squares procedure is used to compute the summary measure. The average sectoral percentage shares in Table 3 are computed from group aggregates of sectoral GDP in current U.S. dollars.

Tables 4 and 5. Growth of consumption and investment; structure of demand

GDP is defined in the note for Table 2.

General government consumption includes all current expenditure for purchases of goods and services by all levels of government. Capital expenditure on national defense and security is regarded as consumption expenditure.

Private consumption is the market value of all goods and services purchased or received as income in kind by households and nonprofit institutions. It excludes purchases of dwellings but includes imputed rent for owner-occupied dwellings.

Gross domestic investment consists of the outlays for additions to the fixed assets of the economy, plus net changes in the value of inventories.

Gross domestic savings are calculated by deducting total consumption from gross domestic product.

Exports of goods and nonfactor services represent the value of all goods and nonfactor services sold to the rest of the world; they include merchandise, freight, insurance, travel, and other nonfactor services. The value of factor services, such as investment income, interest, and labor income, is excluded.

The *resource balance* is the difference between exports of goods and nonfactor services and imports of goods and nonfactor services.

National accounts series were used to compute the indicators in these tables. The growth rates in Table 4 were calculated from constant price series; the shares of GDP in Table 5, from current price series.

The *summary measures* are calculated by the method explained in the notes for Tables 2 and 3.

Table 6. Agriculture and food

The basic data for *value added in agriculture* are from the World Bank's national accounts series in national currencies. The 1980 value added in current prices in national currencies is converted to U.S. dollars by applying the single-year conversion pro-

cedure, as described in the technical notes for Tables 2 and 3. The growth rates of the constant price series in national currencies are applied to the 1980 value added in U.S. dollars to derive the values, in 1980 U.S. dollars, for 1970 and 1984.

The figures for the remainder of this table are from the Food and Agriculture Organization (FAO).

Cereal imports and *food aid in cereals* are measured in grain equivalents and defined as comprising all cereals under the Standard International Trade Classification (SITC), Revision 1, Groups 041–046. The figures are not directly comparable since cereal imports are based on calendar-year and recipient-country data, whereas food aid in cereals is based on data for crop years from donor countries. Where data are for 1974, they provide the earliest available information.

Fertilizer consumption is measured in relation to arable land, defined as comprising arable land and land under permanent crops. This includes land under temporary crops (double-cropped areas are counted once), temporary meadows for mowing or pastures, land under market or kitchen gardens, land temporarily fallow or lying idle, as well as land under permanent crops.

The *index of food production per capita* shows the average annual quantity of food produced per capita in 1982–84 in relation to that in 1974–76. The estimates are derived by dividing the quantity of food production by total population. For this index, food is defined as comprising cereals, starchy roots, sugar cane, sugar beet, pulses, edible oils, nuts, fruits, vegetables, livestock, and livestock products. Quantities of food production are measured net of animal feed, seeds for use in agriculture, and food lost in processsing and distribution.

The *summary measures* for fertilizer consumption are weighted by total arable land area. The *summary measures* for food production are weighted by population.

Table 7. Industry

The percentage *distribution of value added* among manufacturing industries was provided by the United Nations Industrial Development Organization (UNIDO). UNIDO industrial statistics have been used for calculating the shares with the base values expressed in 1980 dollars.

The classification of manufacturing industries is in accord with the U.N. *International Standard Industrial Classification of All Economic Activities* (ISIC). *Food and agriculture* comprise ISIC Major Groups

311, 313, and 314; *textiles and clothing* 321–24; *machinery and transport equipment* 382–84; and *chemicals* 351 and 352. *Other manufacturing* generally comprises ISIC Major Division 3, less all of the above; however, for some economies for which complete data are not available, other categories are included as well.

The basic data for *value added in manufacturing* are from the World Bank's national accounts series in national currencies. The 1980 value added in current prices in national currencies is converted to U.S. dollars by applying the conversion procedure described in technical notes for Tables 2 and 3. The growth rates of the constant price series in national currencies are applied to the 1980 value added in U.S. dollars to derive the values, in 1980 U.S. dollars, for 1970 and 1983.

Table 8. Commercial energy

The data on energy are from U.N. sources. They refer to commercial forms of primary energy: petroleum and natural gas liquids, natural gas, solid fuels (coal, lignite, and so on), and primary electricity (nuclear, geothermal, and hydroelectric power)—all converted into oil equivalents. Figures on liquid fuel consumption include petroleum derivatives that have been consumed in nonenergy uses. For converting primary electricity into oil equivalents, a notional thermal efficiency of 34 percent has been assumed. The use of firewood and other traditional fuels, though substantial in some developing countries, is not taken into account because reliable and comprehensive data are not available.

Energy imports refer to the dollar value of energy imports—Section 3 in the Standard International Trade Classification (SITC), Revision 1—and are expressed as a percentage of earnings from merchandise exports.

Because data on energy imports do not permit a distinction between petroleum imports for fuel and for use in the petrochemicals industry, these percentages may overestimate the dependence on imported energy.

The *summary measures* of *energy production* and *consumption* are computed by aggregating the respective volumes for each of the years covered by the time periods, and then applying the least-squares growth rate procedure. For *energy consumption per capita*, population weights are used to compute *summary measures* for the specified years.

The *summary measures* of *energy imports as a percentage of merchandise exports* are computed from group aggregates for energy imports and merchandise exports in current dollars.

Table 9. Growth of merchandise trade

The statistics on merchandise trade, Tables 9 through 13, are from U.N. publications and the U.N. trade data system, supplemented by statistics from the U.N. Conference on Trade and Development (UNCTAD), the International Monetary Fund (IMF), and, in a few cases, World Bank country documentation. Values in these tables are in current U.S. dollars.

Merchandise exports and imports, with some exceptions, cover international movements of goods across customs borders. Exports are valued f.o.b. (free on board), imports c.i.f. (cost, insurance, and freight), unless otherwise specified in the foregoing sources. These values are in current dollars; note that they do not include trade in services.

The *growth rates of merchandise exports and imports* are in real terms and calculated from quantum indices of exports and imports. Quantum indices are obtained from the export or import value index as deflated by the corresponding price index. These indices are obtained from different sources. For about 40 developing economies, mostly major exporters of manufactures, the indices are from the World Bank data file. To calculate these quantum indices, the World Bank has used its own price indices, which are based on international prices for primary commodities and unit value indices for manufactures. These price indices are both country-specific and disaggregated by commodity groups, which ensures consistency between data for a group of countries and those for individual countries. Such data consistency will increase as the World Bank improves its trade price indices for an increasing number of countries. For the remaining developing economies these indices are from UNCTAD. For industrial economies the indices are from the U.N. *Yearbook of International Trade Statistics* and *Monthly Bulletin of Statistics*, and the IMF *International Financial Statistics*.

The *terms of trade*, or the net barter terms of trade, measure the relative level of export prices compared to import prices. Calculated as the ratio of a country's index of average export price to the average import price index, this indicator shows changes over a base year in the level of export prices as a percentage of import prices. The terms-of-trade index numbers are shown for 1982 and 1984, with 1980 = 100. The price indices are from the sources cited above for the growth rates of exports and imports.

The *summary measures* are calculated by aggregating the 1980 constant U.S. dollar price series for each year, and then applying the least-squares growth rate procedure for the periods shown. Note again that these values do not include trade in services.

Tables 10 and 11. Structure of merchandise trade

The shares in these tables are derived from trade values in current dollars reported in the U.N. trade data system and the U.N. *Yearbook of International Trade Statistics*, supplemented by other regular statistical publications of the U.N. and the IMF.

Merchandise exports and imports are defined in the note for Table 9.

The categorization of exports and imports follows the Standard International Trade Classification (SITC), Revision 1.

In Table 10, *fuels, minerals, and metals* are the commodities in SITC Section 3 (mineral fuels and lubricants and related materials), Divisions 27 and 28 (minerals and crude fertilizers, and metalliferous ores) and Division 68 (nonferrous metals). *Other primary commodities* comprise SITC Sections 0, 1, 2, and 4 (food and live animals, beverages and tobacco, inedible crude materials, oils, fats, and waxes) less Divisions 27 and 28. *Textiles and clothing* represent SITC Divisions 65 and 84 (textiles, yarns, fabrics, and clothing). *Machinery and transport equipment* are the commodities in SITC Section 7. *Other manufactures*, calculated as the residual from the total value of manufactured exports, represent SITC Sections 5 through 9 less Section 7 and Divisions 65, 68, and 84.

In Table 11, *food* commodities are those in SITC Sections 0, 1, and 4 and Division 22 (food and live animals, beverages, oils and fats, and oilseeds and nuts), less Division 12 (tobacco). *Fuels* are the commodities in SITC Section 3 (mineral fuels and lubricants and related materials). *Other primary commodities* comprise SITC Section 2 (crude materials excluding fuels), less Division 22 (oilseeds and nuts) plus Division 12 (tobacco) and Division 68 (nonferrous metals). *Machinery and transport equipment* are the commodities in SITC Section 7. *Other manufactures*, calculated as the residual from the total value of manufactured imports, represent SITC Sections 5 through 9 less Section 7 and Division 68.

The *summary measures* in Table 10 are weighted by total merchandise exports of individual coun-

tries in current dollars; those in Table 11, by total merchandise imports of individual countries in current dollars. (See note to Table 9.)

Table 12. Origin and destination of merchandise exports

Merchandise exports are defined in the note for Table 9. Trade shares in this table are based on statistics on the value of trade in current dollars from the U.N. and the IMF. *Industrial market economies* also include Gibraltar, Iceland, and Luxembourg; *high-income oil exporters* also include Bahrain, Brunei, and Qatar.

The *summary measures* are weighted by the value of total merchandise exports of individual countries in current dollars.

Table 13. Origin and destination of manufactured exports

The data in this table are from the U.N. and are among those used to compute special Table B in the U.N. *Yearbook of International Trade Statistics. Manufactured goods* are the commodities in SITC, Revision 1, Sections 5 through 9 (chemicals and related products, basic manufactures, manufactured articles, machinery and transport equipment, and other manufactured articles and goods not elsewhere classified) excluding Division 68 (nonferrous metals).

The country groups are the same as those in Table 12. The *summary measures* are weighted by manufactured exports of individual countries in current dollars.

Table 14. Balance of payments and reserves

Values in this table are in current U.S. dollars.

The *current account balance* is the difference between (1) exports of goods and services plus inflows of unrequited official and private transfers and (2) imports of goods and services plus unrequited transfers to the rest of the world. The current account balance estimates are primarily from IMF data files and conform to the IMF *Balance of Payments Manual* definitions.

Workers' remittances cover remittances of income by migrants who are employed or expect to be employed for more than a year in their new economy, where they are considered residents. Those derived from shorter-term stays are included in private transfers.

Net direct private investment is the net amount invested or reinvested by nonresidents in enterprises in which they or other nonresidents exercise significant managerial control. Including equity capital, reinvested earnings, and other capital, these net figures also take into account the value of direct investment abroad by residents of the reporting country. These estimates were compiled primarily from IMF data files.

Gross international reserves comprise holdings of monetary gold, special drawing rights (SDRs), the reserve position of IMF members in the Fund, and holdings of foreign exchange under the control of monetary authorities. The data on holdings of international reserves are from IMF data files. The gold component of these reserves is valued throughout at year-end London prices: that is, $37.37 an ounce in 1970 and $308.30 an ounce in 1984. The reserve levels for 1970 and 1984 refer to the end of the year indicated and are in current dollars at prevailing exchange rates. Due to differences in the definition of international reserves, in the valuation of gold, and in reserve management practices, the levels of reserve holdings published in national sources do not have strictly comparable significance. Reserve holdings at the end of 1984 are also expressed in terms of the number of months of imports of goods and services they could pay for, with imports at the average level for 1983 or 1984.

The *summary measures* are computed from group aggregates for gross international reserves and total imports of goods and services in current dollars.

Table 15. Gross external liabilities

The data on debt in this and successive tables are from the World Bank Debtor Reporting System, supplemented by World Bank estimates. That system is concerned solely with developing economies and does not collect data on external debt for other groups of borrowers, nor from economies that are not members of the World Bank. The dollar figures on debt shown in Tables 15 through 19 are in U.S. dollars converted at official exchange rates. In previous reports, debt with an original or extended maturity of more than a year was referred to as "medium- and long-term." To conform to current usage, this debt is now denoted as "long-term."

In this edition, the data on debt cover for the first time private nonguaranteed debt reported by twenty developing countries, and complete or partial estimates (depending on the reliability of information) for an additional twenty-four countries.

External public debt outstanding and disbursed represents public and publicly guaranteed loans drawn at year-end, net of repayments of principal and write-offs at year-end. For estimating external public debt as a percentage of GNP, the debt figures are converted into U.S. dollars from currencies of repayment at end-of-year official exchange rates. GNP is converted from national currencies to U.S. dollars by applying the conversion procedure described in the technical notes for Tables 2 and 3.

In addition to public long-term debt and private nonguaranteed long-term debt (whether reported or estimated), this table includes information on the use of IMF credit and estimates of short-term debt.

Use of IMF credit denotes repurchase obligations to the IMF for all uses of IMF resources, excluding those resulting from drawings in the reserve tranche and on the IMF Trust Fund. It is shown for the end of the year specified. It comprises purchases outstanding under the credit tranches, including enlarged access resources, and all of the special facilities (the buffer stock, compensatory financing, extended Fund, and oil facilities). Trust Fund loans are included individually in the Debtor Reporting System, and thus shown within the total of public long-term debt. Use of IMF credit outstanding at year-end (a stock) is converted to U.S. dollars at the dollar/SDR exchange rate in effect at year-end.

Short-term external debt is debt having an original maturity of one year or less. Available data permit no distinctions between public and private nonguaranteed short-term debt.

Gross external liabilities are defined for the purpose of this report as the sum of public long-term debt, private nonguaranteed long-term debt, use of IMF credit, and short-term debt. This is a gross stock because external liabilities are not offset against associated external assets.

Table 16. Flow of public and private external capital

Data on the *gross inflow* (disbursements) and *repayment of principal* (amortization) are for public, publicly guaranteed, and private nonguaranteed long-term loans. The *net inflow* estimates are disbursements less the repayment of principal.

Public loans are external obligations of public debtors, including the national government, its agencies, and autonomous public bodies. *Publicly guaranteed loans* are external obligations of private

248

debtors that are guaranteed for repayment by a public entity. These two categories are aggregated in the tables. *Private nonguaranteed loans* are external obligations of private debtors that are not guaranteed for repayment by a public entity.

Table 17. Total external public and private debt and debt service ratios

Total long-term debt data in this table cover public and publicly guaranteed debt and private non-guaranteed debt. Procedures for estimating total long-term debt as a percentage of GNP, average ratios of debt service to GNP, and average ratios of debt service to exports of goods and services are the same as those described in the notes for Table 15.

Table 18. External public debt and debt-service ratios

Interest payments are actual payments made on the disbursed and outstanding public and publicly guaranteed debt in foreign currencies, goods, or services; they include commitment charges on undisbursed debt if information on those charges is available.

Debt service is the sum of actual repayments of principal (amortization) and actual payments of interest made in foreign currencies, goods, or services on external public and publicly guaranteed debt. The ratio of debt service to exports of goods and services is one of several conventional measures used to assess the ability to service debt. The average ratios of debt service to GNP for the economy groups are weighted by GNP in current dollars. The average ratios of debt service to exports of goods and services are weighted by exports of goods and services in current dollars.

The *summary measures* are computed from group aggregates of debt service and GNP in current dollars.

Table 19. Terms of external public borrowing

Commitments refer to the public and publicly guaranteed loans for which contracts were signed in the year specified. They are reported in currencies of repayment and converted into U.S. dollars at average annual official exchange rates.

Figures for *interest rates*, *maturities*, and *grace periods* are averages weighted by the amounts of the loans. Interest is the major charge levied on a loan and is usually computed on the amount of principal drawn and outstanding. The maturity of a loan is the interval between the agreement date, when a loan agreement is signed or bonds are issued, and the date of final repayment of principal. The grace period is the interval between the agreement date and the date of the first repayment of principal.

Public loans with variable interest rates, as a percentage of public debt, refer to interest rates that float with movements in a key market rate; for example, the London interbank offered rate (LIBOR) or the U.S. prime rate. This column shows the borrower's exposure to changes in international interest rates.

The *summary measures* in this table are weighted by the amounts of the loans.

Table 20. Official development assistance from OECD and OPEC members

Official development assistance (ODA) consists of net disbursements of loans and grants made on concessional financial terms by official agencies of the members of the Development Assistance Committee (DAC) of the Organisation for Economic Co-operation and Development (OECD) and members of the Organization of Petroleum Exporting Countries (OPEC), with the object of promoting economic development and welfare. It includes the value of technical cooperation and assistance. All data shown were supplied by the OECD, and all U.S. dollar values converted at official exchange rates.

Amounts shown are net disbursements to developing countries and multilateral institutions. The disbursements to multilateral institutions are now reported for all DAC members on the basis of the date of issue of notes; some DAC members previously reported on the basis of the date of encashment. *Net bilateral flows to low-income economies* exclude unallocated bilateral flows and all disbursements to multilateral institutions.

The nominal values shown in the summary for ODA from OECD countries were converted into 1980 prices using the dollar GNP deflator. This deflator is based on price increases in OECD countries (excluding Greece, Portugal, and Turkey) measured in dollars. It takes into account the parity changes between the dollar and national currencies. For example, when the dollar appreciates, price changes measured in national currencies have to be adjusted downward by the amount of the appreciation to obtain price changes in dollars.

The table, in addition to showing totals for OPEC, shows totals for the Organization of Arab

Petroleum Exporting Countries (OAPEC). The donor members of OAPEC are Algeria, Iraq, Kuwait, Libya, Qatar, Saudi Arabia, and United Arab Emirates. ODA data for OPEC and OAPEC were also obtained from the OECD.

Table 21. Official development assistance: receipts

Net disbursements of ODA from all sources consist of loans and grants made on concessional financial terms by all bilateral official agencies and multilateral sources, with the object of promoting economic development and welfare. The disbursements shown in this table are not strictly comparable with those shown in Table 20 since the receipts are from all sources; disbursements in Table 20 refer to those made by members of OECD and OPEC only. Net disbursements equal gross disbursements less payments to donors for amortization. Net disbursements of ODA are shown per capita and as a percentage of GNP.

The *summary measures* of per capita ODA are computed from group aggregates for population and for ODA. Summary measures for ODA as a percentage of GNP are computed from group totals for ODA and for GNP in current U.S. dollars.

Table 22. Central government expenditure

The data on central government finance in Tables 22 and 23 are from the IMF *Government Finance Statistics Yearbook,* 1986, IMF data files, and World Bank country documentation. The accounts of each country are reported using the system of common definitions and classifications found in the IMF *Manual on Government Finance Statistics.* Due to differences in coverage of available data, the individual components of central government expenditure and current revenue shown in these tables may not be strictly comparable across all economies. The shares of total expenditure and revenue by category are calculated from national currencies.

The inadequate statistical coverage of state, provincial, and local governments has dictated the use of central government data only. This may seriously understate or distort the statistical portrayal of the allocation of resources for various purposes, especially in large countries where lower levels of government have considerable autonomy and are responsible for many social services.

It must be emphasized that the data presented, especially those for education and health, are not comparable for a number of reasons. In many economies private health and education services are substantial; in others public services represent the major component of total expenditure but may be financed by lower levels of government. Great caution should therefore be exercised in using the data for cross-country comparisons.

Central government expenditure comprises the expenditure by all government offices, departments, establishments, and other bodies that are agencies or instruments of the central authority of a country. It includes both current and capital (development) expenditure.

Defense comprises all expenditure, whether by defense or other departments, on the maintenance of military forces; including the purchase of military supplies and equipment, construction, recruiting, and training. Also in this category is expenditure on strengthening public services to meet wartime emergencies, on training civil defense personnel, on supporting research and development, and on funding administration of military aid programs.

Education comprises expenditure on the provision, management, inspection, and support of pre-primary, primary, and secondary schools; of universities and colleges; and of vocational, technical, and other training institutions by central governments. Also included is expenditure on the general administration and regulation of the education system; on research into its objectives, organization, administration, and methods; and on such subsidiary services as transport, school meals, and medical and dental services in schools.

Health covers public expenditure on hospitals, medical and dental centers, and clinics with a major medical component; on national health and medical insurance schemes; and on family planning and preventive care. Also included is expenditure on the general administration and regulation of relevant government departments, hospitals and clinics, health and sanitation, and national health and medical insurance schemes; and on research and development.

Housing and community amenities and social security and welfare cover (1) public expenditure on housing, such as income-related schemes, on provision and support of housing and slum clearance activities, on community development, and on sanitary services; and (2) public expenditure on compensation to the sick and temporarily disabled for loss of income; on payments to the elderly, the permanently disabled, and the unemployed; and on family, maternity, and child allowances. The second category also includes the cost of welfare services such as care of the aged, the disabled, and children, as well as the cost of general administration, regulation, and research associated with social security and welfare services.

Economic services comprise public expenditure associated with the regulation, support, and more efficient operation of business, economic development, redress of regional imbalances, and creation of employment opportunities. Research, trade promotion, geological surveys, and inspection and regulation of particular industry groups are among the activities included. The five major categories of economic services are fuel and energy, agriculture, industry, transportation and communication, and other economic affairs and services.

Other covers expenditure on the general administration of government not included elsewhere; for a few economies it also includes amounts that could not be allocated to other components.

Overall surplus/deficit is defined as current and capital revenue and grants received, less total expenditure less lending minus repayments.

The *summary measures* for the components of central government expenditure are computed from group totals for expenditure components and central government expenditure in current dollars. Those for total expenditure as a percentage of GNP and for overall surplus/deficit as a percentage of GNP are computed from group totals for the above total expenditures and overall surplus/deficit in current dollars, and GNP in current dollars, respectively.

Table 23. Central government current revenue

Information on data sources and comparability is given in the note for Table 22. Current revenue by source is expressed as a percentage of total current revenue, which is the sum of tax revenue and current nontax revenue, and is calculated from national currencies.

Tax revenue is defined as all government revenue from compulsory, unrequited, nonrepayable receipts for public purposes, including interest collected on tax arrears and penalties collected on nonpayment or late payment of taxes. Tax revenue is shown net of refunds and other corrective transactions. *Taxes on income, profit, and capital gain* are taxes levied on the actual or presumptive net income of individuals, on the profits of enterprises, and on capital gains, whether realized on land sales, securities, or other assets. *Social Security contributions* include employers' and employees' so-

cial security contributions as well as those of self-employed and unemployed persons. *Domestic taxes on goods and services* include general sales, turnover, or value added taxes, selective excises on goods, selective taxes on services, taxes on the use of goods or property, and profits of fiscal monopolies. *Taxes on international trade and transactions* include import duties, export duties, profits of export or import marketing boards, transfers to government, exchange profits, and exchange taxes. *Other taxes* include employers' payroll or manpower taxes, taxes on property, and other taxes not allocable to other categories.

Current nontax revenue comprises all government revenue that is not a compulsory nonrepayable payment for public purposes. Proceeds of grants and borrowing, funds arising from the repayment of previous lending by governments, incurrence of liabilities, and proceeds from the sale of capital assets are not included.

The *summary measures* for the components of current revenue are computed from group totals for revenue components and total current revenue in current dollars; those for current revenue as a percentage of GNP are computed from group totals for total current revenue and GNP in current dollars.

Table 24. Income distribution

The data in this table refer to the distribution of total disposable household income accruing to percentile groups of households ranked by total household income. The distributions cover rural and urban areas and refer to different years between 1970 and 1982.

The data for income distribution are drawn from a variety of sources including the Economic Commission for Latin America and the Caribbean (ECLAC), Economic and Social Commission for Asia and the Pacific (ESCAP), International Labour Organisation (ILO), the Organisation for Economic Co-operation and Development (OECD), the U.N. *Survey of National Sources of Income Distribution Statistics*, 1981, and *National Account Statistics: Compendiums of Income Distribution Statistics*, 1985, more recent U.N. data, the World Bank, and national sources.

Because the collection of data on income distribution has not been systematically organized and integrated with the official statistical system in many countries, estimates are derived from surveys designed for other purposes, most often consumer expenditure surveys, which also collect some information on income. These surveys use a variety of income concepts and sample designs. Furthermore, the coverage of many of these surveys is too limited to provide reliable nationwide estimates of income distribution. Thus, although the estimates shown are considered the best available, they do not avoid all these problems and should be interpreted with extreme caution.

The scope of the indicator is similarly limited. Because households vary in size, a distribution in which households are ranked according to per capita household income, rather than according to total household income, is superior for many purposes. The distinction is important because households with low per capita incomes frequently are large households, whose total income may be high, and conversely many households with low household incomes may be small households with high per capita incomes. Information on the distribution of per capita household income exists for only a few countries. The World Bank's Living Standards Measurement Study is developing procedures and applications that can assist countries to improve their collection and analysis of data on income distribution.

Table 25. Population growth and projections

The *growth rates of population* are period averages calculated from midyear populations.

The estimates of *population* for mid-1984 are based on data from the U.N. Population Division and from World Bank sources. In many cases the data take into account the results of recent population censuses. Note again that refugees not permanently settled in the country of asylum are generally considered to be part of the population of their country of origin.

The *projections of population* for 1990 and 2000, and to the year in which it will eventually become stationary, are made for each economy separately. Starting with information on total population by age and sex, fertility rates, mortality rates, and international migration in the base year 1980, these parameters are projected at five-year intervals on the basis of generalized assumptions, until the population becomes stationary. The base-year estimates are from updated computer printouts of the U.N. *World Population Prospects as Assessed in 1982*, from the most recent issues of the U.N. *Population and Vital Statistics Report*, from World Bank country data, and from national censuses.

The *net reproduction rate* (NRR) indicates the number of daughters a newborn girl will bear dur-

ing her lifetime, assuming fixed age-specific fertility and mortality rates. The NRR thus measures the extent to which a cohort of newborn girls will reproduce themselves under given schedules of fertility and mortality. An NRR of 1 indicates that fertility is at replacement level: at this rate childbearing women, on average, bear only enough daughters to replace themselves in the population.

A *stationary population* is one in which age- and sex-specific mortality rates have not changed over a long period, while age-specific fertility rates have simultaneously remained at replacement level (NRR=1). In such a population, the birth rate is constant and equal to the death rate, the age structure is constant, and the growth rate is zero.

Population Momentum is the tendency for population growth to continue beyond the time that replacement-level fertility has been achieved; that is, even after NRR has reached 1. The momentum of a population in the year *t* is measured as a ratio of the ultimate stationary population in the year *t*, given the assumption that fertility remains at replacement level from the year *t* onward. For example, the 1985 population of India is estimated at 765 million. If NRR had reached 1 in 1985, the projected stationary population would be 1,349 million—reached in the middle of the 22nd century—and the population momentum would be 1.8.

A population tends to grow even after fertility has declined to replacement level because past high growth rates will have produced an age distribution with a relatively high proportion of women in, or still to enter, the reproductive ages. Consequently, the birth rate will remain higher than the death rate and the growth rate will remain positive for several decades. It takes at least 50–75 years, depending on the initial conditions, for a population's age distribution to adjust fully to changed fertility rates.

To make the projections, assumptions about future mortality rates are made in terms of female life expectancy at birth (that is, the number of years a newborn girl would live if subject to the mortality risks prevailing for the cross-section of population at the time of her birth). Economies are divided according to whether their primary-school enrollment ratio for females is above or below 70 percent. In each group a set of annual increments in female life expectancy is assumed, depending on the female life expectancy in 1980–85. For a given life expectancy at birth, the annual increments during the projection period are larger in economies with a higher primary-school enrollment ratio and a life expectancy of up to 62.5 years. At higher life expectancies, the increments are the same.

To project fertility rates, the year in which fertility will reach replacement level is estimated. These estimates are speculative and are based on information on trends in crude birth rates (defined in the note for Table 20), total fertility rates (also defined in the note for Table 20), female life expectancy at birth, and the performance of family planning programs. For most economies it is assumed that the total fertility rate will decline between 1980 and the year of reaching a net reproduction rate of 1, after which fertility will remain at replacement level. For most countries in sub-Saharan Africa, and for a few countries in Asia and the Middle East, total fertility rates are assumed to remain constant for some time and then to decline until replacement level is reached; for a few countries they are assumed to increase until 1990–95 and then to decline.

In some countries, fertility is already below replacement level or will decline to below replacement level during the next 5 to 10 years. Because a population will not remain stationary if its net reproduction rate is other than 1, it is assumed that fertility rates in these economies will regain replacement levels in order to make estimates of the stationary population for them. For the sake of consistency with the other estimates, the total fertility rates in the industrial economies are assumed to remain constant until 1985–90 and then to increase to replacement level by 2010.

International migration rates are based on past and present trends in migration flow. The estimates of future net migration are speculative. For most economies the net migration rates are assumed to be zero by 2000, but for a few they are assumed to be zero by 2025.

The estimates of the hypothetical size of the stationary population and the assumed year of reaching replacement-level fertility are speculative. *They should not be regarded as predictions.* They are included to show the long-run implications of recent fertility and mortality trends on the basis of highly stylized assumptions. A fuller description of the methods and assumptions used to calculate the estimates is available from the Bank publication: *World Population Projections 1985—Short- and Long-term Estimates by Age and Sex with Related Demographic Statistics.*

Table 26. Demography and fertility

The *crude birth and death rates* indicate the number of live births and deaths per thousand population in a year. They come from the sources mentioned in the note for Table 25. Percentage changes are computed from unrounded data.

The *total fertility rate* represents the number of children that would be born per woman, if she were to live to the end of her childbearing years and bear children at each age in accordance with prevailing age-specific fertility rates. The rates given are from the sources mentioned in the note for Table 25.

The *percentage of married women of childbearing age using contraception* refers to women who are practicing, or whose husbands are practicing, any form of contraception. These generally comprise female and male sterilization, injectable and oral contraceptives, intrauterine devices (IUD), diaphragms, spermicides, condoms, rhythm, withdrawal, and abstinence. *Women of childbearing age* are generally women aged 15–49, although for some countries contraceptive usage is measured for other age groups.

Data are mainly derived from the World Fertility Survey, the Contraceptive Prevalence Survey, World Bank country data, and the U.N. report: *Recent Levels and Trends of Contraceptive Use as Assessed in 1983.* For a few countries for which no survey data are available, program statistics are used; these include Bangladesh, India, Indonesia, and several African countries. Program statistics may understate contraceptive prevalence because they do not measure use of methods such as rhythm, withdrawal, or abstinence, or contraceptives not obtained through the official family planning program. The data refer to a variety of years, generally not more than two years distant from those specified.

All *summary measures* are country data weighted by each country's share in the aggregate population.

Table 27. Life expectancy and related indicators

Life expectancy at birth is defined in the note for Table 1.

The *infant mortality rate* is the number of infants who die before reaching one year of age, per thousand live births in a given year. The data are from a variety of U.N. sources—"Infant Mortality: World Estimates and Projections, 1950–2025" in *Population Bulletin of the United Nations* (1983) and recent issues of *Demographic Yearbook* and *Population and Vital Statistics Report*—and from the World Bank.

The *child death rate* is the number of deaths of

children aged 1–4 per thousand children in the same age group in a given year. Estimates are based on the data on infant mortality and on the relationship between the infant mortality rate and the child death rate implicit in the appropriate Coale-Demeny Model life tables; see Ansley J. Coale and Paul Demeny, *Regional Model Life Tables and Stable Populations* (Princeton, NJ: Princeton University Press, 1966).

The *summary measures* in this table are country figures weighted by each country's share in the aggregate population.

Table 28. Health-related indicators

The estimates of *population per physician and nursing person* are derived from World Health Organization (WHO) data. They also take into account revised estimates of population. Nursing persons include graduate, practical, assistant, and auxiliary nurses; the inclusion of auxiliary nurses allows for a better estimation of the availability of nursing care. Because definitions of nursing personnel vary—and because the data shown are for a variety of years, generally not more than two years distant from those specified—the data for these two indicators are not strictly comparable across countries.

The *daily calorie supply per capita* is calculated by dividing the calorie equivalent of the food supplies in an economy by the population. Food supplies comprise domestic production, imports less exports, and changes in stocks; they exclude animal feed, seeds for use in agriculture, and food lost in processing and distribution. The *daily calorie requirement per capita* refers to the calories needed to sustain a person at normal levels of activity and health, taking into account age and sex distributions, average body weights, and environmental temperatures. Because no later figures are available, 1977 calorie requirement data are used for these calculations. Both sets of estimates are from the Food and Agriculture Organization (FAO).

The *summary measures* in this table are country figures weighted by each country's share in the aggregate population.

Table 29. Education

The data in this table refer to a variety of years, generally not more than two years distant from those specified, and are mostly from Unesco.

The data on *number enrolled in primary school* refer to estimates of total, male, and female enrollment of students of all ages in primary school; they are expressed as percentages of the total, male, or female populations of the primary school age to give gross primary enrollment ratios. While many countries consider primary school age to be 6–11 years, others do not. The differences in country practices in the ages and duration of schooling are reflected in the ratios given. For some countries with universal primary education, the gross enrollment ratios may exceed or fall below 100 percent because some pupils are above or below the country's standard primary-school age.

The data on *number enrolled in secondary school* are calculated in the same manner, with secondary-school age considered to be 12–17 years.

The data on *number enrolled in higher education* are from Unesco.

The *summary measures* in this table are country enrollment rates weighted by each country's share in the aggregate population.

Table 30. Labor force

The *population of working age* refers to the population aged 15–64. The estimates are based on the population estimates of the World Bank for 1984 and previous years.

The *summary measures* are weighted by population.

The *labor force* comprises economically active persons aged 10 years and over, including the armed forces and the unemployed, but excluding housewives, students, and other economically inactive groups. *Agriculture, industry, and services* are defined in the same manner as in Table 2. The estimates of the sectoral distribution of the labor force are from the International Labour Organisation (ILO), *Labour Force Estimates and Projections, 1950–2000*, 3rd edition, and from the World Bank.

The *summary measures* are weighted by labor force.

The *labor force growth rates* are derived from the Bank's population projections and from ILO data on age-specific activity rates in the source cited above.

The application of ILO activity rates to the Bank's latest population estimates may be inappropriate for some economies in which there have been important changes in unemployment and underemployment, in international and internal migration, or in both. The labor force projections for 1980–2000 should thus be treated with caution.

The *summary measures* for 1965–73 and 1973–84 are country growth rates weighted by each country's share in the aggregate labor force in 1973;

those for 1980–2000, by each country's share in the aggregate labor force in 1980.

Table 31. Urbanization

The data on *urban population as a percentage of total population* are from the U.N. *Estimates and Projections of Urban, Rural and City Populations 1950–2025: The 1982 Assessment*, 1985, supplemented by data from various issues of the U.N. *Demographic Yearbook*, and from the World Bank.

The *growth rates of urban population* are calculated from the World Bank's population estimates; the estimates of urban population shares are calculated from the sources cited above. Data on urban agglomeration are from the U.N. *Patterns of Urban and Rural Population Growth, 1980*.

Because the estimates in this table are based on different national definitions of what is "urban," cross-country comparisons should be interpreted with caution.

The *summary measures* for urban population as a percentage of total population are calculated from country percentages weighted by each country's share in the aggregate population; the other *summary measures* in this table are weighted in the same fashion, using urban population.

Bibliography of data sources

National accounts and economic indicators	International Monetary Fund. 1985. *Government Finance Statistics Yearbook*. Vol. IX. Washington, D.C..
	Sawyer, Malcolm. 1976. *Income Distribution in OECD Countries*. OECD Occasional Studies. Paris.
	U.N. Department of International Economic and Social Affairs. Various years. *Statistical Yearbook*. New York.
	———. 1981. *A Survey of National Sources of Income Distribution Statistics*. Statistical Papers, series M, no. 72. New York.
	———. 1985. *National Accounts Statistics: Compendium of Income Distribution Statistics*. Statistical Papers, series M, no. 79. New York.
	FAO, IMF, and UNIDO data files.
	National sources. World Bank country documentation. World Bank data files.
Energy	U.N. Department of International Economic and Social Affairs. Various years. *World Energy Supplies*. Statistical Papers, Series J. New York.
	World Bank data files.
Trade	International Monetary Fund. Various years. *Direction of Trade Statistics*. Washington, D.C..
	———. Various years. *International Financial Statistics*. Washington, D.C..
	U.N. Conference on Trade and Development. Various years. *Handbook of International Trade and Development Statistics*. Geneva.
	U.N. Department of International Economic and Social Affairs. Various years. *Monthly Bulletin of Statistics*. New York.
	———. Various years. *Yearbook of International Trade Statistics*. New York.
	FAO, IMF, and World Bank data files.
	U.N. trade tapes. World Bank country documentation.
Balance of payments, capital flows, and debt	The Organisation for Economic Co-operation and Development. Various years. *Development Co-operation*. Paris.
	———. 1986. *Geographical Distribution of Financial Flows to Developing Countries*. Paris.
	IMF balance of payments data files. World Bank Debtor Reporting System.
Labor force	International Labour Office. Forthcoming. *Labour Force Estimates and Projections, 1950–2000*. 3rd ed. Geneva.
	International Labour Organisation tapes. World Bank data files.
Population	U.N. Department of International Economic and Social Affairs. Various years. *Demographic Yearbook*. New York.
	———. Various years. *Population and Vital Statistics Report*. New York.
	———. 1980. *Patterns of Urban and Rural Population Growth*. New York.
	———. 1982. "Infant Mortality: World Estimates and Projections, 1950–2025." *Population Bulletin of the United Nations*, no. 14. New York.
	———. Updated printouts. *World Population Prospects as Assessed in 1982*. New York.
	———. 1983. *World Population Trends and Policies: 1983 Monitoring Report*. New York.
	———. 1984. *Recent Levels and Trends of Contraceptive Use as Assessed in 1983*. New York.
	———. 1985. *Estimates and Projections of Urban, Rural and City Populations, 1950–2025; The 1982 Assessment*. New York.
	World Bank data files.
Social indicators	Food and Agriculture Organization. October 1985. *Food Aid Bulletin*. Rome.
	———. December 1983. *Food Aid in Figures*. Rome.
	———. 1984. *Fertilizer Yearbook*.
	———. 1984. *Production Yearbook*.
	———. 1984. *Trade Yearbook*. "Standard" Computer Tape.
	U.N. Department of International Economic and Social Affairs. Various years. *Demographic Yearbook*. New York.
	———. Various years. *Statistical Yearbook*. New York.
	U.N. Educational Scientific and Cultural Organization. Various years. *Statistical Yearbook*. Paris.
	World Health Organization. Various years. *World Health Statistics Annual*. Geneva.
	———. Various years. *World Health Statistics Report*, vol. 29, no. 10. Geneva.
	FAO and World Bank data files.